International Aviation Law

Attila Sipos

International Aviation Law

Regulations in Three Dimensions

Springer

Attila Sipos
Faculty of Law
ELTE University
Budapest, Hungary

ISBN 978-3-031-39065-4 ISBN 978-3-031-39066-1 (eBook)
https://doi.org/10.1007/978-3-031-39066-1

This Springer imprint is published by the registered company Springer Nature Switzerland AG
The registered company address is: Gewerbestrasse 11, 6330 Cham, Switzerland

Foreword to Part I

Part I of this book, 'International Aviation Law', covers the key topics within Public Aviation Law in four chapters. Public Aviation Law concerns the relations, on the one hand, between States and, on the other hand, between States and non-State actors in all aspects relating to civil aviation.

Public Aviation Law traces its origins to the Paris Peace Conference (1919–1920), where State representatives codified the first-ever international aviation convention, the Convention Relating to the Regulation of Aerial Navigation (Paris Convention) 1919. Chapter 1 of this book tells the story of its successor, the Convention on International Civil Aviation (Chicago Convention) 1944, with reference to State sovereignty, the concept of airspace, and the external aviation relations of States within the Chicago System—all while keeping a close eye on the key events and developments in aviation that have impacted industrial actors, as well as the few, but all the same important, amendments to the Convention.

The book moves in Chap. 2 to discuss the construction and activities of the United Nations specialised agency—and thus the forum for civil aviation—the International Civil Aviation Organization (ICAO), headquartered in Montreal, Canada. As safe and sustainable global civil aviation operations depend significantly on the harmonisation and unification of rules and procedures, Chap. 3 appropriately discusses the concept of international standards and recommended practices (SARPs), as set out in the 19 Annexes to the Chicago Convention, which are largely implemented by ICAO Member States. Chapter 4 traces the evolution of aviation security, as traditionally separate from though increasingly connected to aviation safety, and the relevant treaties and other legal authorities that make up Criminal Aviation Law.

Part I is a compact yet comprehensive review of Public Aviation Law and the workings of ICAO, all within the Chicago System. It is clearly written and contains references to a wide range of academic literature. It is also filled with helpful examples and useful pictures to assist the reader in grasping the subject matter.

I am proud of Dr. Sipos, an Air and Space Law alumnus of Leiden University, for taking on the challenge of writing 'International Aviation Law'. I hope that you will enjoy the journey as much as I have!

International Institute of Air and Space Law
Leiden University, Leiden
The Netherlands

Steven Truxal

Foreword to Part II

Part II of this book, 'International Aviation Law', deals with International Private Aviation Law—i.e., legal issues arising from relations between persons and other non-State entities that have an international element, particularly conflicts of law issues.

That such issues were likely to arise frequently in such an international activity as air transport was recognised at a very early stage in its development, and as a result, the Convention for the Unification of Certain Rules Relating to International Carriage by Air was signed at Warsaw on 12 October 1929. Subsequently, most States involved in aviation ratified or adhered to it, and for many years, the Convention (supplemented and modified by various further international treaties) provided a valuable set of common rules that helped clarify the liability position in international carriage by air and resolve difficult conflicts of law issues.

Over time, however, the financial limit that the Convention imposed on air carriers' as liability in respect of passenger death and injury became increasingly controversial and difficult to justify, and so in 1999, a further Convention for the Unification of Certain Rules for International Carriage by Air was adopted at Montreal modernising and consolidating the Convention and related instruments, in particular as regards the issue of limited liability.

This complex history is explained by way of introduction in Part II of the book, before the author then discusses each of the main substantive features of the Convention system – its scope, types of liability of the carrier, exoneration, limited liability, and compensation, with due attention to particular issues, such as passengers with special needs, infectious and disruptive passengers, bodily injury (accident), embarking/disembarking and exclusivity, and reference to the most important jurisprudence from a variety of courts worldwide. The author also discusses the issues of liability for surface damage and of those with interests in mobile equipment (such as aircraft), which are dealt with not by the Warsaw or Montreal Conventions but by other international treaties.

All this the author does in a very clear, concise (yet sufficiently comprehensive), and, most importantly, readable manner, drawing on his extensive practical and academic experience so as to provide an account that will engage the interest of and inform both students of aviation law and those who require knowledge of it for their work in or with the aviation industry.

Indeed, *ne frustra scripsisse videtur*!

Solicitor, Former Partner of Clyde & Co LLP
London, UK
John Balfour

Preface

By writing this book, my primary objectives were to familiarise the readers interested in aviation with one of the most recent areas of international law and, furthermore, to support the everyday work of specialists in the area of aviation, as well as to enrich the knowledge of candidates for a career in law and contribute to the broadening of their horizons. Simultaneously, the book is an homage to practical experts of transportation and aviation, who, owing to their persistence and devotional work by providing the utmost of their expertise and occasionally sacrificing their lives, have facilitated the conquest of the air.

In this work, I deal with the two most important conventions of international aviation law. With respect to the fact that the Chicago Convention (1944) and the Montreal Convention (1999) have barely been amended, the interrelations and legal solutions revealed in this book will foreseeably serve the reading public for a long time. With a view to completeness, I am going to deal with all significant international aviation law treaties.

My first aviation law book was published by the Wolters Kluwer Publisher in 2015, then after a revision, it was issued under the editorship of ELTE Eötvös Publisher in Hungarian language. Currently, the reader is holding in hand the first edition of the wholly revised book in English. The most important impetus for renascence of the book was the expedient feedback from university students since they have cast light on the defects, occasionally too complicated phrasing, which aggravated comprehension and thereby dimmed the value of the volume. I am confident that I have managed to incorporate their comments as well as to rewrite and extend the norm text by reworking through the linkages. The process of reworking was significantly influenced by the COVID-19 pandemic, which has reformulated our everyday life in its foundations. However, the guiding principle did not change; it remained the same: the extension of the reader's legal knowledge related to aviation and the enrichment thereof with universal values.

I owe thanks for the support of the Eötvös Loránd University (ELTE), Faculty of Law, Department of International Law. Most of all, I am greatly indebted to Prof. Gábor Kardos, who, as a reader of the book, presented a constant source of inspiration for my work, and to Ms. Georgina Borsody, for the excellent work of editing and proofreading, as a result of which an engaging and updated work is placed into the reader's hands. I am very grateful to Prof. Steven Truxal (Leiden) and John Balfour (London) for the forewords to the book and to Dr. P. Nikolai Ehlers (Munich) who also takes the credit for the publication of the book. Likewise, I am thankful to the ELTE Eötvös Publisher for providing me the copyright and also to Springer Nature Publisher for its continued support.

Professor Kardos, the reader of the book, has emphasised that international treaties are not only imprints of the times, documents reflecting the quality of international relations, but also, like drops in the ocean, faithful reflections of the problems of life in the international community and of international law as a whole, and this book is a good proof thereof. I hope he is right. The book encourages the reader to think through the dilemmas with the author and to formulate his or her own views, not only on the fundamental issues that always keep coming to light but also on practical problems, as he added.

While writing this book, I was motivated by the advice of my best friend Annamária, according to which 'in life we should not strive to be the last but the first of the Mohicans'.

Ne frustra vixisse videar!

Aviation is a lifestyle. For many of us, first it is a dream, then it is our love and life, and for some of us, it remains a memory. The moments of air transport testing decency, its busy everyday life, and its history fraught with sacrifices need to remind us: strenuous life cannot be futile.

Budapest, Hungary Attila Sipos
May 2024

Contents

1 **Introduction** 1
1.1 The Civil Aviation Industry 1
1.2 Aviation Law 7
1.2.1 The Legal Sources of International Aviation Law 9
1.2.2 The Development of International Aviation Law 11
1.2.3 The Chicago Conference 17
1.2.4 The Legal Sources of the Chicago System 19
References 21

Part I The Public Law of International Civil Aviation

2 **The Chicago Convention** 25
2.1 The Preamble of the Convention 25
2.2 The Territory of the Sovereign State 27
2.2.1 The National Airspace of the Sovereign State 29
2.2.2 The Horizontal Boundary of the National Airspace 30
2.2.3 The Vertical Boundary of the National Airspace 32
2.2.4 International Airspace 37
2.2.5 Outer Space 39
2.2.6 Controlled and Uncontrolled Airspace 42
2.2.7 Restriction of National Airspace 45
2.2.8 Extension of the National Airspace for Identification Reasons 53
2.3 Aircraft 58
2.3.1 Unmanned Aerial Vehicles 61
2.3.2 Civil and State Aircraft 63
2.3.3 The Use of Weapons Against Civil Aircraft 66
2.3.4 The Prohibition to Use Weapons Against Civil Aircraft 71
2.3.5 The Nationality of the Civil Aircraft 80

2.3.6 The Registration of the Civil Aircraft 81
2.3.7 Registration of the Civil Aircraft for Dry and Wet Leasing 86
2.3.8 Exemption from Seizure on Patent Claims of Civil Aircraft 88
2.3.9 Documents Carried on Board the Civil Aircraft 89
2.4 Non-Scheduled flights 92
2.4.1 Flight without Prior Permission 95
2.4.2 The Misuse of Civil Aviation 100
2.5 Scheduled Flights 102
2.5.1 Freedoms of the Air 103
2.5.2 Transit Rights (1–2) 105
2.5.3 Commercial Traffic Rights (3–9) 105
2.5.4 Cabotage 107
2.5.5 The International Air Services Transit Agreement 109
2.5.6 The International Air Transport Agreement 114
2.5.7 Air Services Agreements 115
2.6 General Rules 120
2.6.1 Facilitations 120
2.6.2 Using Airports and Air Navigation Facilities 123
2.6.3 Airport Slots 124
2.6.4 Customs and Immigration Rules 126
2.6.5 Prevention of the Spread of Infectious Diseases 127
2.6.6 The Search and Rescue of the Aircraft in Distress . . . 130
2.6.7 Investigation of Accidents 131
References 136

3 The International Civil Aviation Organization 139
3.1 Strategic Objectives and Mission 139
3.2 Legal Capacity 144
3.3 Participation 145
3.4 The Member States 148
3.5 The Headquarters 150
3.6 The Institutional System 154
3.7 The Assembly 157
3.7.1 The Powers and Duties of the Assembly 158
3.7.2 The Meeting of the Assembly 159
3.7.3 Voting in the Assembly 163
3.8 The Council 169
3.8.1 Functions of the Council 170
3.8.2 Functions Related to Air Navigation Facilities 173
3.8.3 Functions Related to Joint Operating Organisations . . 174
3.8.4 Settlement of Disputes 176
3.8.5 Election of the Council 182
3.8.6 The Composition of the Council 187
3.8.7 President of the Council 188

3.8.8 Voting by the Council 190
3.8.9 Official Presents to ICAO 190
3.9 The Air Navigation Commission 192
3.10 Committees 193
3.10.1 The Legal Committee 193
3.10.2 The Climate and Environment Committee 194
3.10.3 The Council Committees 195
3.11 The Secretariat 197
3.11.1 The Secretary General 199
3.11.2 Professional Staff 200
3.11.3 Regional Offices 200
References 202

4 ICAO Standards and Recommended Practices (SARPs) 203
4.1 The Evolution of the System of Rules 203
4.2 The Rules Established by ICAO 205
4.3 Standards and Recommended Practices 206
4.4 The Uniformity, Reliability and Admissibility of Standards . . . 207
4.5 The Binding Effect of the Standards 209
4.6 The Creation of SARPs Rules 210
4.6.1 Initial Phase: The SARPs Recommendation is Made 212
4.6.2 Elaboration Phase: Consultation of the SARPs Recommendation 213
4.6.3 Review Phase: The Finalisation of the SARPs Recommendation 214
4.6.4 Adoption Phase: Adoption of the SARPs Recommendation 214
4.7 Annexes to the Chicago Convention 217
4.8 Differences from the SARPs Rules 219
4.9 The Implementation of SARPs Rules 221
4.9.1 Compliance with Uniform Requirements 221
4.9.2 Oversight of the Implementation of SARPs Rules . . . 222
4.10 The Development of the System of Oversight 224
4.10.1 The Universal Safety Oversight Audit Programme (1999–2004) 225
4.10.2 The Comprehensive Approach Audit Programme (2005–2010) 226
4.10.3 The Continuous Monitoring Audit Programme (2010–) 228
References 231

5 Aviation Security 233
5.1 The Tokyo Convention (1963) 234
5.1.1 Jurisdiction 236
5.1.2 The Competence of the Aircraft Commander 239

5.2 The Hague (1970), Montreal (1971), New York (1979) and Montreal (1991) Conventions and the Montreal Protocol (1988) 241
5.3 The Modernisation of the International Aviation Security Treaties 246
5.3.1 The General Risks Convention (2009) 247
5.3.2 The Beijing Convention and Protocol (2010) 247
5.3.3 The Montreal Protocol (2014) 250
5.4 The Result of Modernisation 252
References 253

6 Closing Words for Public Aviation Law 255
References 260

Part II The Private Law of International Civil Aviation

7 Liability in Transportation 263
7.1 Dangerous Operation 263
7.2 Criminal Liability 265
7.3 Civil Liability 265
7.3.1 General Liability 265
7.3.2 Increased Liability 267
7.4 The Legal Sources of Private Aviation Law 268
References 269

8 The Air Carrier's Liability for Damages Caused to the Second Party 271
8.1 The Warsaw Convention (1929) 272
8.1.1 Limited Liability 274
8.1.2 The Signification of Documentation 276
8.2 The Modernisation of the Warsaw Convention 280
8.2.1 The Hague Protocol (1955) 282
8.2.2 The Guadalajara Convention (1961) 282
8.2.3 The Montreal Agreement (1966) 283
8.2.4 The Guatemala City Protocol (1971) 283
8.2.5 Montreal Additional Protocols Nos. 1, 2, and 3, and Montreal Protocol No. 4 (1975) 284
8.2.6 The Japanese Initiative (1992) 285
8.2.7 The IATA Intercarrier Agreements (1995–1996) 286
8.2.8 The Regulation of the Council of the European Union (1997) 286
8.3 The Warsaw System and the Montreal Convention 288
8.4 The Montreal Convention (1999) 290
8.4.1 The Objectives of the Convention 293
8.4.2 The Liability System of the Convention 294
References 296

9 The Scope of Application of the Montreal Convention 297
9.1 Examination of Documentation 297
9.1.1 Contractual Relationship 299
9.1.2 The General Conditions of Carriage 301
9.1.3 Passenger Documentation: Air Ticket and Baggage Identification Tag 302
9.1.4 Cargo Documentation: Air Waybill and Cargo Receipt 305
9.1.5 Documentation of Carriage Performed in Extraordinary Circumstances 308
9.2 Jurisdictions 308
9.2.1 Arbitration 314
9.2.2 States with Different Systems of Law 314
9.2.3 Parallel Jurisdictions: Forum Shopping 315
9.3 The Substantive Scope of the Convention 317
9.3.1 International Carriage 318
9.3.2 Reservations 322
9.4 Personal Scope of the Convention 324
9.4.1 Persons 324
9.4.2 Air Transport Undertaking 326
9.4.3 Air Carrier 327
9.4.4 Carriage Performed by Successive Carriers 327
9.4.5 Carriage Performed by the Contracting or Actual Carrier 328
9.4.6 Combined Carriage 331
9.5 The Limitation of Actions 334
References 336

10 Examination of the Liability of the Air Carrier 337
10.1 Liability for Damage Caused to Passenger 337
10.1.1 Conditions and Definition of Accident 338
10.1.2 Death and Bodily Injury of the Passenger 357
10.1.3 Location of the Accident (Embarkation or Disembarkation) 367
10.2 The Air Carrier's Liability for Damage Caused to the Baggage 373
10.2.1 Checked Baggage and Unchecked Baggage 374
10.2.2 Delivery of the Checked Baggage 374
10.2.3 Limited Liability 375
10.3 The Air Carrier's Liability for Damage Caused to Cargo 379
10.3.1 The Time Period of Air Carriage 380
10.3.2 Liability for Live Animals 383
10.3.3 The Delivery of Cargo 383
10.4 The Air Carrier's Liability for Damage Caused by Delay 384
References 391

11 Exoneration of the Air Carrier from Liability 393
11.1 Exoneration from Indemnity of Damage Caused to the Passenger 394
11.2 Exoneration from Indemnity of Damage Caused to the Baggage and Cargo 394
11.3 Exoneration from the Indemnification of Damage Caused by Delay 395
11.4 Exclusive Remedy 397
References 400

12 The Liability of the Air Carrier 401
12.1 Limited Liability 401
12.1.1 Limited Liability of the Servants and Agents 403
12.1.2 Breaking the Limited Liability 403
12.2 Unlimited Liability 404

13 Compensation 407
13.1 The Measure of Compensation 408
13.1.1 Advance Payments 411
13.1.2 The Cost of the Proceedings 412
13.1.3 The Conversion of Monetary Units 413
13.1.4 Review of Limits 414
13.2 Insurance 415
References 417

14 The Air Carrier's Liability for Damage Caused to Third Parties on the Surface 419
14.1 The Rome Convention (1952) 419
14.2 The General Risks Convention and the Unlawful Interference Compensation Convention (2009) 421
References 424

15 The Liability of Interests in Mobile Equipment 425
15.1 The Cape Town Convention and its Aircraft Equipment Protocol (2001) 425
15.1.1 The Remedies of the Creditor 427
15.1.2 Validation of the Remedies of the Creditor 430
15.1.3 The Effect of the Cape Town Convention 431
References 432

16 Closing Words for Private Aviation Law 433

Part III Book Summary

17 Book Summary 439

Bibliography 443
Documents 443
Legal Cases 447
Webpages 451
Regulatory Sources 452

About the Author

Attila Sipos, PhD. (ELTE), Adv. LL.M. (Leiden), has been an Honorary Professor at Eötvös Loránd University (ELTE), Faculty of Law since 2011 and has been teaching International Air and Space Law since 2008. He was a Faculty Member of the Master's Program in Air and Space Law at the University of Sharjah (UOS) in the United Arab Emirates (2021–2024). He worked for Malév Hungarian Airlines in various positions, such as flight operation and navigation officer, commercial and industry affairs advisor, chief advisor to the CEO, and legal director (1989–2004). Subsequently, he became the permanent representative of Hungary on the Council of ICAO (2004–2007) and the Vice-President of the Council of ICAO (2006–2007). He was employed by the Hungarian Air Navigation Service Provider (HungaroControl) as legal and alliance director, later as legal advisor to the CEO (2008–2014). He worked as a bar association adviser at the Aviation Division of the Ministry of Defence Electronics, Logistics and Property Management, HM EI Plc (2018–2021). Attila Sipos has been a committee member of the European Air Law Association (EALA) since 2004.

Abbreviations

ACAC	Arab Civil Aviation Commission
ACC	Area Control Centre
ACD	Airline Coding Directory
ACI	Airports Council International
ACMI	Aircraft, Crew, Maintenance, and Insurance
ADB	Bureau of Administration and Services (ICAO)
ADIZ	Air Defence Identification Zone
ADREP	Accident/Incident Data Reporting
AFCAC	African Civil Aviation Commission
AEA	Association of European Airlines
AED	Automate External Defibrillator
AIP	Aeronautical Information Publication
AHCCC	Ad-Hoc Cybersecurity Coordination Committee (ICAO)
ALADA	Asociación Latino Americana de Derecho Aeronáutico
ANSP	Air Navigation Service Provider
ANB	Air Navigation Bureau (ICAO)
ANC	Air Navigation Commission (ICAO)
AOC	Air Operator Certificate
APEC	Asia-Pacific Economic Cooperation
APU	Auxiliary Power Unit
ARSIWA	Responsibility of States for Internationally Wrongful Acts
ASA	Air Services Agreement
ASC	Aviation Security Committee (ICAO)
ATA	International Air Transport Agreement
ATB	Air Transport Bureau (ICAO)
ATC	Air Transport Committee (ICAO)
ATC	Air Traffic Control
ATS	Air Traffic Services
AVSECP	Aviation Security Panel
AWG	Aviation Working Group

BCN	Bacteriological, Chemical, and Nuclear
CAEP	Committee on Aviation Environmental Protection (ICAO)
CART	Council Aviation Recovery Task Force (ICAO)
CANSO	Civil Air Navigation Services Organization
CAPSCA	Cooperative Arrangement for the Prevention and Management of Public Health Events in Civil Aviation
CE	Critical Elements
CEC	Climate and Environment Committee (ICAO)
CERG	Central European Rotation Group
CIR	Commission Implementing Regulations
CITEJA	Comité International Technique d'Experts Juridiques Aériens
CJEU	Court of Justice of the European Union
CMA	Continuous Monitoring Approach
CMP	Continuous Monitoring Programme
CRCO	Central Route Charges Office
CSA	Comprehensive System Approach
COG	Committee on Governance (ICAO)
CVR	Cockpit Voice Recorder
CYSECP	Cybersecurity Panel (ICAO)
DGCA	Director General of Civil Aviation
DoT	Department of Transportation (USA)
DVT	Deep Vein Thrombosis
EALA	European Air Law Association
EASA	European Aviation Safety Agency
ECAC	European Civil Aviation Conference
EFOD	Electronic Filing of Differences
EI	Effective Implementation
ER	Extended Range
ERA	European Regions Airline Association
ETOPS	Extended-Range Twin-Engine Operational Performance Standards
EU	European Union
EUR	Euro
EUROCONTROL	European Organisation for the Safety of Air Navigation
EWAC	Edward Warner Award Committee (ICAO)
FAA	Federal Aviation Administration (USA)
FAI	Fédération Aéronautique Internationale
FAO	Food and Agriculture Organization
FDR	Flight Data Recorder
FIC	Finance Committee (ICAO)
FLP	Flight Plan
FO	First Officer
FOC	Flags of Convenience
FSIX	Flight Safety Information Exchange (ICAO)

FUA	Flexible Use of the Airspace
GAT	General Air Traffic
GMBM	Global Market-Based Measure
GMs	Guidance Materials
GPS	Global Positioning System
HRC	Human Resources Committee (ICAO)
IAMSAR	International Aeronautical and Maritime Search and Rescue Manual
IAOPA	International Council of Aircraft Owner and Pilot Associations
IASTA	International Air Services Transit Agreement
IATA	International Air Transport Association
IBAC	International Business Aviation Council
ICAO	International Civil Aviation Organization
ICCAIA	International Coordinating Council of Aerospace Industries Associations
ICERD	International Convention on the Elimination of All Forms of Racial Discrimination
ICJ	International Court of Justice
ICCPR	The International Covenant on Civil and Political Rights
IFALPA	International Federation of Air Line Pilots' Associations
IFATCA	International Federation of Air Traffic Controllers' Association
IFR	Instrument Flight Rules
IFSO	Inflight Security Officer
IGA	Intergovernmental Agreements
IGO	Intergovernmental Organization
IIA	Intercarrier Agreement on Passenger Liability
ILA	International Law Association
ILO	International Labour Organization
IMF	International Monetary Fund
IMO	International Maritime Organization
ISTA	Interline Staff Travel Agreement
ITU	International Telecommunication Union
IVP	International Visitor Program
JSC	Joint Support Committee (ICAO)
KLM	Koninklijke Luchtvaart Maatschappij
LACAC	Latin American Civil Aviation Commission
LAGs	Liquids, Aerosols, and Gels
LEB	Legal Affairs and External Relations Bureau (ICAO)
LC	Legal Committee (ICAO)
LLM	Master of Laws
MALÉV	Hungarian Airlines
MANPADS	Man Portable Air Defence Systems
MBM	Market-Based Measure

MDR-TB	Multidrug-resistant Tuberculosis
MEDIF	Medical Information Form
MEL	Minimum Equipment List
MHz	Megahertz
MIA	Agreement on Measures to Implement the IATA Intercarrier Agreement
MRO	Maintenance Repair and Overhaul
MRTD	Machine Readable Travel Documents
NASA	National Aeronautics and Space Administration (USA)
NATO	North Atlantic Treaty Organization
NGO	Non-governmental
NLD	The Netherlands
NOTAM	Notices to Airmen
NTSB	National Transportation Safety Board
OAT	Operational Air Traffic
OJ	Official Journal (EU)
OS	Open Skies
OSCE	Organization for Security and Co-operation in Europe
PANS	Procedures for Air Navigation Services (ICAO)
PFLP	Popular Front for the Liberation of Palestine
PICAO	Provisional International Civil Aviation Organization
PIC	Pilot-in-Command
PSCRM	Passenger Services Conference Resolutions Manual
PTSD	Post-traumatic Stress Disorder
RAF	Royal Air Force
REIOs	Regional Economic Integration Organizations
RHCC	Committee on Relations with the Host Country (ICAO)
RPAS	Remotely Piloted Aircraft Systems
RPKs	Revenue Passenger Kilometres
SARPs	Standards and Recommended Practices (ICAO)
SARS	Severe Acute Respiratory Syndrome
SC	Security Council (UN)
SDR (XDR)	Special Drawing Rights
SEAL	Sea, Air, and Land
SES	Single European Sky
SG	Secretary General
SITA	Société Internationale de Télécommunications Aéronautiques
SSC	Significant Safety Concern
SUPPs	Regional Supplementary Procedures (ICAO)
TCB	Technical Cooperation Bureau (ICAO)
TCC	Technical Cooperation and Implementation Support Committee (ICAO)
TSP	Trusted Systems Panel (ICAO)
UAV	Unmanned Aerial Vehicle

UAS	Unmanned Aircraft Systems
UIC	Committee on Unlawful Interference (ICAO)
UPU	Universal Postal Union
USA	United States of America
USAF	United States Air Force
USAP	Universal Security Audit Programme (ICAO)
USD	United States Dollar
USOAP	Universal Safety Oversight Audit Programme (ICAO)
UN	United Nations
UNCITRAL	United Nations Commission on International Trade Law
UNCLOS	United Nations Convention on the Law of the Sea
UNCOPUOS	The United Nations Committee on the Peaceful Uses of Outer Space
UNCTAD	United Nations Conference on Trade and Development
UNDP	United Nations Development Programme
UNESCO	United Nations Educational, Scientific and Cultural Organization
UNIDO	United Nations Industrial Development Organization
UNIDROIT	International Institute for the Unification of Private Law
VFR	Visual Flight Rules
VSM	Vertical Separation Minima
WASG	Worldwide Airport Slot Guidelines (IATA)
WHO	World Health Organization
WIPO	World Intellectual Property Organization

List of Figures

Fig. 1.1 Flown kilometres by revenue passengers in the international scheduled service ... 4
Fig. 1.2 The vertical exercise of ownership ... 12
Fig. 2.1 National and international airspace ... 29
Fig. 2.2 The jurisdictional boundary according to Kármán ... 36
Fig. 2.3 Horizontal and vertical range of the airspace ... 38
Fig. 2.4 Separation of air traffic in controlled airspace ... 44
Fig. 2.5 Special airspaces ... 46
Fig. 2.6 The interception of a civil aircraft ... 49
Fig. 2.7 The ADIZ zones of China, South-Korea and Japan ... 55
Fig. 2.8 The military incident near Hainan Island (2001) ... 56
Fig. 2.9 Systematisation of aircraft ... 59
Fig. 2.10 The directions of the flight of the helicopter ... 60
Fig. 2.11 The route of Korean Air Lines Flight 902 ... 74
Fig. 2.12 The route of Korean Air Lines Flight 007 ... 76
Fig. 2.13 Transit rights (1–2) and commercial traffic rights (3–5) ... 106
Fig. 2.14 Commercial traffic rights (6–9) ... 107
Fig. 3.1 The organisational structure of ICAO ... 154
Fig. 3.2 The logo of ICAO ... 156
Fig. 3.3 ICAO Council Chamber ... 170
Fig. 3.4 Opening of the Polar Routes ... 172
Fig. 3.5 Pakistan's transit dispute with India ... 177
Fig. 3.6 The statue titled Generations ... 191
Fig. 4.1 The making and amendment of Standards and Recommended Practices ... 211
Fig. 4.2 Annexes of the Chicago Convention ... 218
Fig. 4.3 Critical Elements of the ICAO oversight system ... 224
Fig. 9.1 International carriage ... 321
Fig. 9.2 Non-international carriage ... 322

Fig. 12.1 The upper limits of the liability of the air carrier for damages 402
Fig. 13.1 Compensation for loss of life in the United States 411
Fig. 13.2 Change of upper limits 414
Fig. 14.1 The upper limit of damage inflicted on third parties 423

Chapter 1
Introduction

1.1 The Civil Aviation Industry

Aviation is the youngest generation of the transport of humankind. It is a world driven by passion and thrill, via which humankind fulfilled its greatest dream and conquered the third dimension, that is, height. Although aviation does not in the least trace back traditions such as maritime or railway transportation, among the sub-branches of transport it is primarily aviation that is designed to carry passengers, cargo and mail quickly and safely to any point in the world, to span great distances, and thereby, considerably affect the economic, social, cultural and environmental development of continents, regions and countries.

Aviation has become a reality accessible for all at the expense of extremely large efforts and sacrifices. In this reality, aviation is no longer the privilege of a narrow stratum, but it is part and parcel of the lives and weekdays of all of us. Air transport functions as public transport! Worldwide, in 2019 more than 4.5 billion people chose air transport and cleaved the 'Aerial Ocean'. The transport of the large and increasing number of passengers was carried out by nearly 1500 airlines on 33,000 airplanes. The air carriers made use of one of the 162 air navigation service providers and 3780 international airports of the world to transport the passengers and cargo to their destinations. The key performers of the air transport industry produced 4.1% of the GDP of the world, which accounted for an estimated global economic impact of 3500 billion dollars annually. Thus, it was no longer disputable that the role of civil

A. Sipos, *International Aviation Law*, https://doi.org/10.1007/978-3-031-39066-1_1

aviation in the global world is of outstanding significance.[1] This unequalled development was stopped by the COVID-19 pandemic, which as early as in the first months of 2020 took its drastic effect, and consequently, the revenue of air transport fell by 90% worldwide. This situation is well-illustrated by the fact that the number of passengers decreased to 1.8 billion in 2020 in the largest crisis of the aviation industry since World War II.[2] Millions have lost their jobs. Aircraft manufacturers downsized their capacities in succession, airports and navigation service providers registered severe losses. The greatest losers of the pandemic on an industry level were the airlines themselves, which represent essentially the financial driving force of this commercial activity (aircraft are manufactured for them, they carry out the transport of persons and cargo, while the ground and aerial infrastructure depend on them intensively). The majority of airlines requested and received large amounts of State subsidies;[3] nevertheless, the recovery from the crisis may extend over years with regard to the losses of the industry.[4]

Accordingly, the States support civil aviation in manifold ways, thereby promoting not only the development of the national economy and the increase of national and regional productivity, but also the enhancement of international trade. In air transport the enforcement of political interests and the protection of the national economy have crucial roles. The protectionist endeavour of the States targeting the protection of their markets has been considerably curtailed—primarily due to the liberalising efforts of recent decades—in parallel with the reinforcement of the commercial and market opportunities of air transport. Nevertheless, this does not imply the complete secession of the State from the sector, since the States still strongly influence the processes of the industry via systems of regulations, competition and aviation authorities. Aviation has become a modern battlefield of power, on which the system of relations between commercial and political interests basically determines the future of air transport.

[1] In 2019, 4.5 billion people travelled by airplane, while in 2018 there had been more than 4 billion air passengers. Apart from the 3780 airports used for scheduled flights, further 41,764 airports are at the disposal of civil, military (state) and commercial transport. Aviation Benefits Beyond Borders. Executive Summary. *ATAG Report*, September 2020, pp. 10–11 (aviationbenefits.org).

[2] IATA Annual Review. 11. 2020, pp. 11, 18 (www.iata.org/iata-annual-review-2020).

[3] Several large air carriers received State subsidies, but not all, for example, Indian airlines did not receive any financial support from the Government of India. Sandeepa (2020).

[4] In 2014, the following was written as a consequence of the influenza pandemic: 'Another factor that would affect the global economy is the psychological factor. Regionally, a virulent global pandemic could have serious results on the confidence of Europe, North America and Asia which have built their economies on their growth potential. There will be a significant loss to business. A direct corollary to this trend would be the closure of many businesses, lowering future investment and employment'. Abeyratne (2014), p. 222.

Transport has a crucial role in the financial prosperity of a State or region. This is instantiated by the air transport industry, which has become one of the most important impetuses to and simultaneously a symbol of the development of world economy and international commerce in a very short period of time.

An excellent example for this is the cargo business. Of the total transport of cargo in world trade, the air transport sector ships nearly 61 million tons of products annually. By weight, this quantity of products accounts for barely 1% of the total shipment of cargo in the world. However, considering its financial value the quantity of products shipped by air accounts for 35% of the total value of goods shipped in the world. These figures suggest that goods of higher value, of smaller volume as well as time-critical goods are the most worthwhile shipping by air.[5] It is also worth mentioning that during the COVID-19 pandemic the air cargo business generated a healthy economic profit (4–9%) in the year 2020, which is also an evidence of the potential of this part of the industry. In fact, there were only five airlines that reaped profits in 2020—AirBridgeCargo, Atlas Air, Cargojet, Cargolux and Kalitta—and they were all cargo carriers.[6] Cargo shipment is performed not only by cargo operators (cargo airlines and freight forwarders) but also by traditional airlines (e.g., the Boeing 747 Jumbo aircraft has 170 cubic metres of cargo space in addition to four hundred seats on the main deck).

In the aviation industry, the labour and energy invested in the service of shipment are integrated into the price of the shipped products, therefore, the consumer price of each product includes the cost of shipment, which entails a financial surplus of 30–40% on average. In addition to the transport of goods, the role of civil aviation in tourism is equally prominent. More than half of the constantly increasing number of tourists in the world opt for air transport.[7] Tourism is a global business, which was one of the most severely stricken sectors of the coronavirus pandemic; nevertheless, it is one of the largest segments of international trade.

---

[5] *Aviation Benefits Beyond Borders. Executive Summary.* ATAG Report, September 2020, p. 12.

[6] Bouwer et al. (2022).

[7] This proportion in 2019 was 58%, which changed drastically as a consequence of the COVID-19 pandemics. IATA Annual Review. 2020, pp. 12, 34.

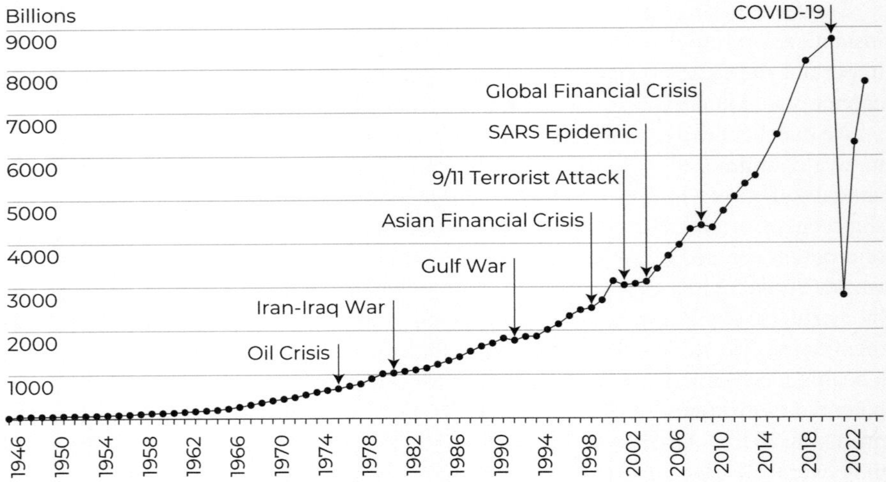

Fig. 1.1 Flown kilometres by revenue passengers in the international scheduled service
Source: From the data of the International Civil Aviation Organization and the International Air Transport Association (Facts and Figures)

The graph is vividly illustrative of the steady growth of the flown kilometres of revenue passengers (RPK)[8] in scheduled international civil aviation despite all international conflicts and world crises. However, the air transport industry has not recovered rapidly from the setback brought about by the COVID-19 pandemic, which will leave its everlasting mark. The driving force of escape from the recent situation has been the fact that, according to forecasts, the population of the Earth is going to grow from the current 8 billion people to approx. 9.7 billion by 2050,[9] which implies an increase in the number of potential passengers as well (Fig. 1.1).[10]

Via the production and utilisation of modern technology, aviation shapes the future, while via commercial and market expansion it conquers the whole world. Competition in the global world without the exploitation of the benefits and

[8]Revenue Passenger Kilometres (RPK) is the most accurate airline industry metric system that shows the number of kilometres travelled by paying passengers. It is calculated as the number of revenue passengers is multiplied by the total distance travelled. Since it measures the actual demand for air transport, it is often referred to as airline 'traffic'. For example, one air carrier operates an Airbus A321 aircraft with a capacity of 230 passengers between Abu Dhabi (AUH) and London (LHR). The revenue passengers for the route equal 230 passengers per leg. The distance between the two airports is 5470 km, which means that the RPK per leg flown is 230 (the passenger demand) multiplied by 5470 (the distance travelled by the passengers): 1,258,100 RPK/flight leg (on a fully booked flight).

[9]United Nations (2022).

[10]According to ATAG, the aviation industry will be able to meet the needs of over 10 billion passengers in 2050, connecting the world safely, securely and sustainably. ATAG Commitment to Fly Net Zero. 5 October 2021 (aviationbenefits.org/media/167501/atag-net-zero-2050-declaration.pdf).

opportunities of modern civil aviation is no longer practicable. The fact that air traffic is the fastest and safest form of transport in the world is prominent among the benefits. Undoubtedly, in the case of large distances aviation offers the shortest time of transport to any point of the Earth. That is why modern man takes advantage of the opportunity of air travel and does not any longer measure distance in kilometres or miles but in time.

In addition to velocity, a crucially important factor is the safety of air transport. Eventually, as pilots are instructed at the aviation academy: 'flying implies landing safely'.[11] Depending on the type of the aircraft, the features of the operating company and the preparedness of the pilots, the risk of flying does not exceed the elementary risk value of 10^{-6}. In practice, this means that the risk of a London-Warsaw flight is 20–40 times lower than driving from the city centre to the international airport depending on the traffic. In other words, a person would need to fly on a daily basis for 20 years to be exposed at all to a fatal flying accident to an extent of 1%. According to risk analyses, standing a fair chance of suffering a fatal accident would require travelling for 7 years by car and half a year by motorcycle. As early as at the end of the 1970s travelling by air was 25 times safer than in an automotive vehicle according to the Lloyd's insurance company based in London.[12] These days, the number of deaths in accidents involving international civil flights is well below 1000 persons annually. In one of the safest years of the history of international civil aviation, that is, in 2015, altogether 136 people lost their lives.[13] (In comparison, in the territory of the European Union more than 22,700 people died and 1.2 million people were injured in road accidents solely in 2019 despite the improving statistical data.)[14] In 2017, air transport reached a further milestone in the area of safety: 44 passengers and 35 people staying on the surface met with fatal accidents (a total of 79), which is a novel exceptional achievement considering the volume of traffic.[15]

Modern aviation is one of the most efficient users of infrastructure and resources; furthermore, it is an environmentally friendly form of transport. We should think about the little spatial demand of runways (in fact, one runway is actually two runways with two different directions) and the infrastructure including taxiways as

---

[11] Karlson (1938), p. 299.

[12] Varley (1978), p. 150.

[13] In these statistics, the International Air Transport Association (IATA) intentionally did not include the tragedy of Germanwings Flight 9525 (Airbus A320), when on 24 March 2015 the first officer of the airline crashed into a mountain with the intent of committing suicide, which caused the death of 150 people. Likewise, the IATA did not take into account the loss of the MetroJet Flight 9268 (Airbus A321) either, in which 224 persons died because the airplane was exploded by terrorists on 31 October 2015. *IATA Safety Report 2015*. 52nd edn., April 2016.

[14] In the European Union, 55,000 people died in road accidents in 2001, then in 2021 owing to the more rigorous rules 19,900 people lost their lives and more than 0.9 million people were injured. The European Commission has taken major steps to achieve close to zero fatalities and serious injuries on public roads by 2050. European Commission: *Road safety 2017*, p. 2.; European Commission: *European Road Safety Observatory, Annual statistical report on road safety in the EU 2022*. 13 March 2023, p. 1.

[15] Shepardson (2018).

opposed to the vast areas necessary for the construction of motorways and their expensive rearrangement, or about the fact that the price of a section of a motorway can cover the cost of building a new airport. This is true even if we consider that a smaller airport also needs basic infrastructure: buildings, facilities and special equipment.[16] Aviation is at the cutting-edge of the application of economical and environmentally friendly new technologies. In the forthcoming decade the engines of new airplanes will foreseeably consume 25% less fuel and operate perceptibly less noisily.

Since the 1960s–1970s civil aviation noise reduction of at least 75% has been accomplished thanks to engine manufacturers and the International Civil Aviation Organization (ICAO). This implies immense development, even if the residents living in the surroundings of airports do not perceive this sizeable change. Air transport currently contributes to the climate change of the Earth by merely 2% and foreseeably by 3% by 2050. (Since pollution by other sectors increases at a higher speed than that by air transport, it is not so noticeable that the pollution of 2% produced by aviation actually increases year by year.) The pre-eminent strategic objective of the aviation industry is to take a prominent part in the protection of the environment. The International Air Transport Association (IATA) and later ICAO raised the standard of the achievement of net-zero carbon emission by 2050 with respect to the release of the most harmful greenhouse gas, that is, carbon dioxide (CO2). Basically, 'zero pollution' is a vision which expresses the professional commitment of the aviation industry to the protection of the environment.[17]

Air transport is one of the most efficient value generating activities, since in proportion to the number of the employees of the industry, it produces at least three times more value than other sectors.[18] What underlie this value are especially the immense capital demand of the industry, the high-degree integration of expertise and the concentration of development bases equipped with cutting-edge technology materialised in developed countries. The creation and utilisation of modern technology simultaneously require extraordinary knowledge and organisation as well as complex international work-sharing by highly qualified specialists. We should bear in mind how much coordinated teamwork of a large number of experts (employees of authorities, technical staff, ground handlers, air navigation controllers, crew,

---

[16] For example: a passenger terminal, control tower, warehouse, hangars, radio locators, workshops, a fire station with equipment, devices required for ground services, runway maintenance machines, snow-ploughs.

[17] In fact, the IATA takes the carbon dioxide pollution of the year 2005 as a base value projected onto the period traffic and by 2050 half of that value needs to be achieved so that the growth of traffic to its multiple cannot be taken into account. Bisignani (2007).; The IATA 77th Annual General Meeting approved a resolution concerning the global air transport industry for the achievement of net-zero carbon emission by 2050. This commitment will align with the Paris Agreement (2016). The airlines support ICAO Carbon Offsetting and Reduction Scheme for International Aviation (CORSIA) as an effective measure to stabilise net emissions by international aviation at 2019 levels. IATA 77th Annual General Meeting. Boston, Press Release No. 66, 4 October 2021.

[18] ATAG Report. *Aviation Benefits Beyond Borders. Executive Summary.* September 2020 (www.aviationbenefits.org).

security staff, etc.) is required for the take-off and safe landing of a wide-body passenger plane. Air transport is unequivocally at the cutting-edge of state-of-the-art technology: it utilises the most modern systems and revolutionary new devices appear due to its operation. The way from the Wright brothers (1903) to the Concorde supersonic airplane (1969), and then to the SpaceShipOne private crewed space vehicle (2004) represents the result of incredible development.

Subsequently, what is going to materialise in this constantly renewing world? In a world in which the number of transistors produced (at a lower price) was higher than the number of the grains of rice grown in 2004,[19] and in which engineers are already designing the post-jet-propelled world and human civilisation will soon find its second 'home' in outer space? When the personal air transport system is realised, which is similar to intelligent motorways, will the easily and simply navigable flying devices take their passengers to their destinations at the push of a button? Before long, the revolutionary new technologies will fly passengers into outer space and the completion of the route between London and New York will not take more than half an hour. Whatever may happen in the future of civilisation and humankind, aviation will always have a principal role.

Air transport is one of the best and most rigorously regulated industries. The excellent figures of aviation safety in air transport may be attributed not only to the speedy development of technology but also to the extremely rigorous and comprehensive rules and their observance. This complex system of rules stipulates obligations for the key performers of the aviation industry basically determining their activity.

1.2 Aviation Law

Aviation law is a separate branch of law, an organic part of international law with a qualitatively detached, peculiar structure. This special field is continually developing and changing. The relation between international law and aviation law is determined by the ancient Roman maxim: a law governing a specific subject matter overrides a law that governs general matters *(lex specialis derogat legi generali)*. In such a case of general and particular rules the latter shall be applied first, since the particular annuls the general. All the principles and institutions of international law can be found in aviation law, in which State sovereignty, nationality, territorial and personal jurisdictions, State responsibility, cooperation among States and the settlement of conflicts among the subjects of international law (States and international organisations) figure in the focus of attention.

By drawing upon the time-honoured traditions and rules of maritime law, aviation law became one of the most recent and most modern branches of jurisprudence *(iurisprudentia)*. During this process the specialists of international law, in consideration of the special character of air transport, transplanted the rules applied in

[19] *FedEx Corporation Annual Report 2006*. Semiconductor Industry Association, 2007, p. 20.

maritime law with the appropriate amendments. (Then aviation law affected the law of outer space just as maritime law had influenced aviation law. Aviation law and the law of outer space as initially two autonomous branches of law have been developing interrelated and have become familiar as the interdisciplinary *aerospace law*.) As early as during World War I, acts regulating air transport were drawn up successively,[20] however, it ensued only in 1942 that by the adaptation of the Italian *Codice Della Navigazione*, which summarised the rules of maritime law and aviation law, the process of the detachment of aviation law could commence. The first international regulation of public aviation law was accomplished under the Paris Convention (1919), which later unfolded into the system of rules of the Chicago Convention (1944). Likewise, the first international regulation of private aviation law was completed under the Warsaw Convention (1929), which was later replaced by the Montreal Convention (1999). On a scientific level, international aviation law was first taught as early as in 1925 in the Institute of Air Law in Königsberg (currently Kaliningrad)[21] (which later moved to Leipzig, following that to Berlin), then in the forerunner of today's Institute of Air Law, Space Law and Cyber Law in Cologne, subsequently, the Air and Space Law Programme commenced at McGill University in Montreal in 1951, afterwards at the Leiden University in the Netherlands in 1985.

Aviation law is undoubtedly an enthusing interdisciplinary area of law, in which a multitude of norms of mainly administrative and civil law intertwine. The uniqueness of aviation law *(sui generis)* is substantiated by a system of extremely rigorous requirements concerning aviation safety and security. This justifies the appreciation and increased significance of aviation law within international law and in the area of avionics.

Aviation law consists of the totality of rules of conduct, which by the regulation of the legal relations of the users of the airspace and airports—in other words, of the performers of the aviation industry—due to the observance of the strict requirements of aviation safety and security based on cooperation, realises uniformity on an international level.

Thus, the strict system of the requirements and their observance have become the focus of the concept of aviation law since this is the basis of the highest predominance both of aviation safety and security and of the development of the industry. The most important performers of the civil aviation industry are the following: air carriers, airports and air navigation service providers (ANSPs), furthermore, the maintenance, repair and overhaul companies (MROs), the aircraft manufacturers, the ground handling service providers, the travel and transport service providers (agents), civil aviation authorities (CAAs), and last but not least, the passengers themselves. Insurance, telecommunication and aircraft financing companies also have an important role in attending to the activity of air transport besides the States.

[20] In Great Britain in 1911 and 1913, in the Austro-Hungarian Monarchy in 1912, in Germany in 1913 and in France in 1914.

[21] Hobe (2015), p. III.

1.2.1 The Legal Sources of International Aviation Law

The sources of international law establish rights and give rise to obligations for the States and international organisations.

The general sources of international law are as follows:

- International treaties (conventions, protocols, agreements, charters, covenants, pacts, etc.);
- Customary law (an unwritten legal rule as the earliest source of law);
- General principles;
- General legal principles of civilized nations;[22]
- Judicial rulings, decisions;
- Works and teachings of jurisprudents;
- Decisions of international organisations;
- Unilateral declarations of the States;
- Non-legally binding instruments: so-called 'soft legal' acts (declarations, recommendations).

The major sources of international aviation law and regulations:

- Universal and general rules of international law;
- International public and private treaties[23] concluded by the States;

Public international aviation law treaties:

  - Convention on International Civil Aviation [Chicago Convention (1944)];
  - International Air Services Transit Agreement (1944);
  - International Air Transport Agreement (1944);
  - Tokyo Convention (1963) and its amendment, the Montreal Protocol (2014);
  - The Hague Convention (1970) and its amendment, the Beijing Protocol (2010);
  - Montreal Convention (1971) and its amendment, the Montreal Protocol (1988);

[22] The Charter of the United Nations (26 June 1945) contains the major principles of international law. These include: Respect for State sovereignty and equality and for rights inherent in sovereignty; Refraining from the threat or use of force; Peaceful settlement of disputes; Cooperation among States; Fulfilment in good faith of obligations under international law, Equal rights as well as the Self-determination of peoples and nations. UN Charter. Chapter I, Articles 1–3, Purposes and Principles.

The Helsinki Accords of 1975 formulates further major principles: Invisibility of frontiers; Territorial integrity of the States; Non-intervention in internal affairs; Respect for human rights and fundamental freedoms, which encompass the freedom of thought, conscience, religion or belief. International legal principles originating in other legal sources embraced by the international community also prevail, such as Peaceful coexistence; Equal treatment; the Prohibition of discrimination and the principle of Mutuality. Organisation of Security and Cooperation in Europe (OSCE), Final Act, Declaration on Principles Guiding Relations between Participating States, 1975, 1 a) I–X.

[23] International Air Law (or Aviation Law) is divided into two broad categories, Public and Private. Dempsey (2015), p. 215.

- New York Convention (1979);
- Montreal Convention (1991);
- Beijing Convention (2010) superseding the Montreal Convention (1971) and its amendment, the Montreal Protocol (1988).

Private international aviation law treaties:

- Warsaw Convention (1929) and its amendments [The Hague Protocol (1955); Guadalajara Convention (1961); Montreal Agreement (1966); Guatemala City Protocol (1971); Montreal Additional Protocols Nos. 1, 2, 3 and Montreal Protocol No. 4. (1975)];
- Rome Convention (1933) and its amendment, the Brussels Protocol (1938);[24]
- Geneva Convention (1948);
- Rome Convention (1952)[25] and its amendment, the Montreal Protocol (1978);
- Montreal Convention (1999) superseding the Warsaw Convention (1929) and its amendments;
- Cape Town Convention (2001) and its Aircraft Equipment Protocol (2001)
- General Risks Convention (Montreal, 2009);
- Unlawful Interference Compensation Convention (Montreal, 2009).[26]

• Air Services Agreements (ASAs) concluded by the States on bilateral or multilateral level;
• Standards and Recommended Practices (SARPs) adopted by the Council of the International Civil Aviation Organization (ICAO) and designated as Annexes to the Convention.

The international rules of aviation law and the norms of public and private law under national law link up organically with one another, therefore, international sources of law only jointly with national regulations can have an impact on the development of the uniform system of the requirements of the industry.

---

[24] *Unification of Certain Rules Relating to the Precautionary Attachment of Aircraft* opened for signature at Rome on 29 May 1933. The *Cape Town Convention on International Interests in Mobile Equipment on Matters Specific to Aircraft Equipment* (2001) superseded the Rome Convention (1933), the Geneva Convention (1948) (not in all aspects), and the UNIDROIT Convention on *International Financial Leasing* (1988) as it relates to aircraft objects [see, Aircraft Equipment Protocol (2001), Articles XXIII, XXIV and XXV].

[25] The first third party liability treaty was the Rome Convention (1933), the *International Convention for the Unification of Certain Rules relating to Damage caused by Aircraft to Third Parties on the Surface*; and it was amended by the Brussels Protocol (1938), the *Additional Protocol to the Convention for the Unification of Certain Rules relating to Damage caused by Aircraft to Third Parties on the Surface*. The Rome Convention (1933) was replaced by the Rome Convention (1952), (Article 29).

[26] The two Montreal Conventions: (1) the General Risks Convention (2009) and (2) the Unlawful Interference Compensation Convention (2009) superseded ('prevail over') both the Rome Convention (1952) and its amendment, the Montreal Protocol (1978) (Article 25).

1.2.2 The Development of International Aviation Law

Jurisprudents seek answers to their questions first in the grandiose codified material of Roman law, a discipline with solid and eternal legal dogmatic foundations. For the contemporary lawyer, studying Roman law has direct significance and is expedient in practice as well. Roman law has a relatively simple and lucid structure; furthermore, it is not exposed to changes; in addition, a considerable part of modern legal regimes is founded on Roman law. In a certain sense, law itself is the 'invention' of the Romans. In many cases, the lawyer schooled in Roman law can judge specific modern legal problems more proficiently. The horizons of legal thought polished in Roman law are broader.[27] Thus, we need to reach back to Roman legal foundations, since the Romans sought legal solutions for all arising issues and found them for nearly all circumstances. Obviously, the Romans did not think about the legal destiny of the airspace in terms of flying but stipulated the vertical limitations of the exercise of the rights of ownership. For this purpose, ancient Roman jurisprudents divided the object of law into two parts: air and airspace.

- The air *(aer)* we breathe is not a negotiable object *(res extra commercium),* which in its entire volume cannot be subjugated to our power due to its naturalness, since it exists for the free use of all people *(res communis omnium).* Therefore, no one can acquire proprietary rights (private property) by entering into possession of the air.
- As opposed, the airspace above the estate *(coelum)* is not due to everyone freely, because it is negotiable *(res in commercio)* as it belongs to the soil *(solum),* to the estate, which the owner may possess.

The owner receives effective protection with respect to the airspace above their estate (the neighbour may not construct a building protruding into the airspace of the estate of the other owner). On the other hand, the owner during the exercise of their right of disposal may establish an easement, the entitled party of which (the neighbour) acquires the right to construct a building or an extension protruding into the airspace of the other estate.

Accursius (1182–1263), the famous glossator from Bologna in his gloss (interpretation of the law) drawing on the foundations of classical Roman law made the following conclusion significant from the viewpoint of aviation law: *Cuius est solum, eius est usque ad coelum et ad inferos*, which means: 'He who owns the soil owns everything above and below (up to the sky and down to the depths of the Earth)'.[28] The legal maxim *(axiom)* demonstrates the complete and exclusive power of the owner over the object of ownership in those times.

[27] Földi and Hamza (2022), p. viii.

[28] Yehuda (1962), p. 247.

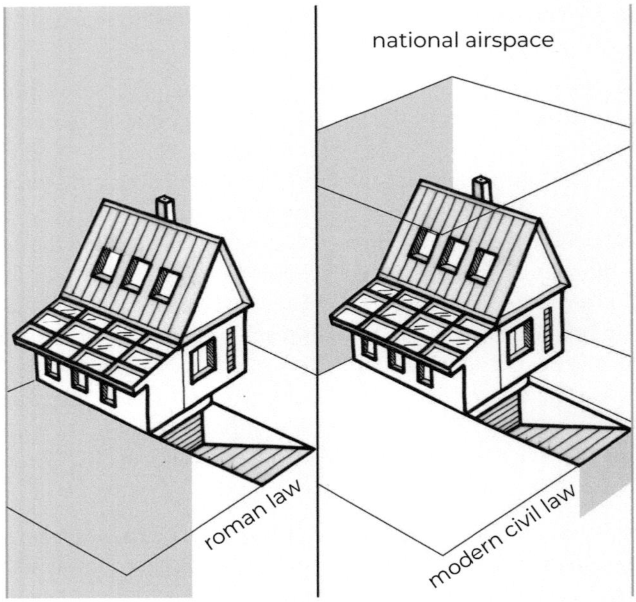

Fig. 1.2 The vertical exercise of ownership

In Roman law the owner who owns the soil (the estate) may rise into the skies, into 'heaven', or reach down to 'hell', into the depth of the Earth. The exclusive legal right has shrunk by our age and the owner is not more than a 'humble employee'.[29] In modern civil law, the power of the owner ranges to the boundary of the utilisation of the estate, i.e. to the point the building may extend: 'the top of the chimney' and 'the bottom of the cellar'. The airspace above the land and the earth below the surface, thus, the treasures of the bowels of the earth and its natural resources are the exclusive objects of State property (Fig. 1.2).

According to John Cobb Copper (1887–1967), the American aviation law specialist, the Romans and the legal system bequeathed by them grant exclusive power to the owner with respect to utilisation and ownership so that the owner of the estate in the airspace above their territory was protected without the limitations of height.[30] This approach had struck root not only in the Continental,[31] but also in the Anglo-Saxon (common law) legal system and it had prevailed until the end of the World War I.

In the development of aviation law, the doctoral dissertation of Johannes Stephanus Dancko (born in Zerbst—1730), titled 'The Jurisdiction of the Prince over the Air' written in October 1687, is noteworthy.[32] Chapter IV of the 38-page

[29] Menger (1906), pp. 100–101.

[30] Copper (1952a), pp. 23–65.

[31] Code Civil des Français 1804, Art. 552.; Bürgerliches Gesetzbuch (BGB), 1900, Article 905.

[32] Dancko (2002), pp. 1–94.

work is titled 'The Jurisdiction of the Prince over the Air which Applies to Expanding the Treasury'. The conception of the author is that the subject vests all their natural rights and freedoms apart from their life to the sovereign, the Prince, who is a legislator and from whom all powers are derived. Freedom abides in the terrain where law is silent. As a consequence, air is the terrain of freedom, since the Prince does not consider its regulation necessary (while his sovereign power encompasses the airspace above his empire). Essentially, the Prince merely takes care of the lands of the citizens, of the seas, rivers, but even of the air since these elements feed and preserve the community.[33]

The first notable flight took place in Bois de Boulogne in France on 21 November 1783. Pilatre de Rozier (1754–1785) and Marquis Francois Laurent d'Arlandes (1742–1809) ascended with the hot-air balloon named 'Globe Aérostatique' manufactured by the Montgolfier brothers. During their 25-min flight at a considerable altitude they were gliding over Paris. Before the 'pilots' a splendid world aloft and a breathtaking world beneath revealed itself. The structure was unsuitable for practical transport as it was not dirigible, but this achievement was a milestone in the universal history of aviation. From the viewpoint of aviation law, half a year after the event of universal significance the police in Paris adopted new rules concerning hot-air ballooning and attached such flights to individual permissions.[34] The regulation of aviation slowly gained ground and yielded an increasing number of remarkable steps.

The Institute of International Law (Institut de Droit International) dealt with the legal issues of air traffic in its first session assembling in Oxford in 1880. Subsequently, the first international aviation Congress was held in Paris in 1889. The participants of the Congress agreed that in the future the activity of civil aviation would be subject to the obtainment of permissions issued by State authorities.

As the scene of the first great epoch of flying was France, the first scholar and pioneer of aviation law was also a French professor living in Paris, Paul Fauchille (1858–1926), who put forward his study in aviation law published in 1901 titled 'Aerospace and the Legal Status of Airships' at the Congress of the Institute of International Law. The study was based on the principle of the *freedom of the seas*, which was formulated by Hugo Grotius (1583–1645), a Dutch lawyer, 'the father of the jurisprudence of modern international law' in his famous polemical treatise on 'The Freedom of the Seas' *(Mare Liberum)* in 1609.[35] Hugo Grotius in the battle fought with the 'glittering armoury' of jurisprudence[36] defeated the possibility of the

[33] Idem., pp. 53–67.

[34] Wissmann (1975), pp. 77, 79.

[35] The work of Hugo Grotius paved the way for the age of luminosity, although in the beginning his work was rejected, even provoked smiles. Later, more and more States adopted his views, since nautical nations as a matter of fact could not monopolise certain routes of world navigation. Thereby, the free navigation of the seas and straits became a pledge of the further development of world trade. Sándorfi Kamill (1924), pp. 6–8, 16.

[36] A decent lawyer 'brings the ballista of the law to work, and looks for weapons in the armoury of judicial contradictions, but he maintains his own convictions regarding the case, while he is doing his best to gain the day'. Balzac (1908), p. 195.

distribution of the seas by the nations among themselves and of the annexation of certain parts of the world seas to their homeland. Owing to the splendid work of Grotius, the freedom of the high seas was recognised by international law and has become a great tenet effective even today. Its significance is invaluable since it removed the obstacle in the way of maritime commerce: the legal possibility of acquiring property by the nations, thereby, the oceans and seas, according to the original purpose of Creation, became the peaceful connecting way of nations and continents in legal terms. The principle of the freedom of the high seas was applied by Paul Fauchille analogically to the Aerial Ocean, and thence, he elaborated the legal principle of *the freedom of the air (l'air est libre)*, according to which the airspace is open for all aircraft of all nations with the limitation that the States may take restrictive steps in the interest of the security of their territories. This theory had an extraordinarily large role in the initial elaboration of the system of aviation law.

The development of aviation law was expedited by the emergence of technical achievements, which was slightly impeded by the fact that for a long time the scholars' society refuted the possibility of the ascent of machinery heavier than air, similarly to the former view that a piece of iron could not float on water. 'It is impossible to ascend with a machine heavier than air', declared Lord Kelvin (1824–1907), a British physicist and mathematician, a privileged scholar of his age, the chairman of the Royal Society in 1895.[37] Although man lined up fire, learnt to speak, write and read in a relatively short time, travelled up and down the seas and the oceans, humankind could not break loose remarkably from its spatial and temporal limitations. Traffic in higher air remained strange and unfamiliar for thousands of years. The triumphant year of 1783 was noted as a milestone in the history of aviation, but vainly were (hot-air) balloons gliding over the heads of people, their navigability still remained doubtable. Let alone the chimerical phantasm of airplanes! The endeavours of 'winged' people were accompanied by mockery and lack of sympathy.

Notwithstanding, venturesome people kept turning up and they took great pains to make machinery that fundamentally changed the life of humankind, as they took delight in creating things which others had claimed to be impossible. To the greatest amazement of the contemporary society of scientists, at 10:35 a.m. on 17 December 1903, for the first time in history, Orwille Wright (1871–1948) with the help of his brother, Wilbur Wright (1867–1912) ascended on an airplane with a petrol engine heavier than air navigated by man. Thenceforth, the universal history of engine-driven aviation commenced. With the act of heroism of 'the birds of Dayton', humankind took a great step to become the ruler of the air, and indeed, conquer the apparently infinite realm of clouds. Some years later, on 25 July 1909 Louis Blériot (1872–1936), a reputed French pilot and engineer ascending from the Continent flew to England in 40 min. Crossing the La Manche Channel by air

[37] Although Sir Thomson, William, i.e., Lord Kelvin was erroneous in this issue, he still lived to hear the success of the Wright brothers in 1903. It is an interesting point that in Europe, before the first Paris Air Show of the Wright brothers (at Le Mans in 1908), nobody had really believed that the brothers would be capable of flying on an aircraft heavier than air. Anderson and Eberhardt (2010), p. 93.

implied an important historic deed, an 'incredible and unequalled' achievement, which in practice raised issues of aviation law, since the pilot of the airplane landed in the territory of another State without permissions and documents.[38]

The unflagging development of aviation created a new situation, which needed to be settled universally in the regulatory scope of international aviation law. At first, the regulation of aviation law drew upon the systems of norms and relations of maritime law shaped throughout centuries. In the course of this process international lawyers, in consideration of the special character of air transport, with due amendments, transplanted into aviation law the requirements of licensing and administration, the international rules of commerce and liability for damages applied in maritime law. Among the endeavours of international aviation law conferences,[39] the International Air Navigation Conference organised in France in 1910 predominates, the draft-law of which consists of 55 Articles, which was finally not signed by the States.[40] At the Paris Conference (1910), there were two main camps: the first advocated a general principle of 'freedom of the air', in parallel to that of the sea; the second argued that national (State) sovereignty extended into 'international airspace'.[41] At that time German Zeppelins would incessantly fly above French territories, therefore, the basic objective of the conference was the settlement of the right of flying over the territories and territorial waters of other countries. The principle of the freedom of the air became less tenable with the appearance of aerial warfare, which basically transformed the ideas of belligerent countries about the future of aviation. As a consequence of the rapid development of military aviation, the airspace of States and the defence of their territories gained principal significance. On the threshold of the belligerent collapse, the Aviation Law Conference held in Budapest (28–30 January 1918) could not make history, but it was here that the principle according to which 'the sovereignty of the State encompasses the airspace above its territory' was first declared. This tenet, still determining international civil aviation basically, was also established in the Paris Convention (1919) and then in the Chicago Convention (1944).

Thus, the regulation of aviation on an international level became indispensable, whereas, as a matter of course, the demand for the protection of national interests also strengthened. Subsequently to World War I, the Aeronautical Commission of the Peace Conference was set up with the participation of the Allies in Paris. The international treaty drafted by the Commission was signed by the contracting States on 13 October 1919. The Paris Convention Relating to the Regulation of Aerial Navigation was the first international aviation law treaty.[42] Article 1 of the

[38] Sipos (2023), p. 7.

[39] The venues of international aviation law meetings: Verona (1910); Vienna, Paris and Geneva (1912); Frankfurt and Madrid (1913); Santiago (1916); Stockholm, and Budapest (1918).

[40] Copper (1952b), pp. 127–128.

[41] Truxal (2016), p. 5.

[42] Convention Relating to the Regulation of Aerial Navigation, signed at Paris, 13 October 1919 (Paris Convention). *Journal of Air Law and Commerce* 94, 1930. 1., pp. 94–108 (www.scholar.smu.edu/jalc/vol1/iss1/6).

Convention stipulates: 'The High Contracting Parties recognize that every Power has *complete* and *exclusive sovereignty* over the airspace above its territory'. Thus, the principle of the freedom of the air remained effective related merely to aviation above the high seas. In the airspace above State territory, the supreme power of the State, its sovereignty prevails. The objective of the victorious Allied Powers was to secure an adequate monopoly for the acceding States to exploit the opportunities inherent in international civil aviation and to reserve the dominance of the air for themselves.

The Paris Convention, although it was epoch-making in its kind, since it declared sovereignty in the national airspace, permitted peaceful, *innocent passage* in the airspace above territorial seas,[43] distinguished civil aviation from State aviation, demanded the registration of aircraft, and established the international organisational background of aviation in its foundations, nevertheless, it was not universally embraced. It could not be, since it divided the world and restricted civil aviation in some States, moreover, it was not ratified by the two contemporary Great Powers, the United States[44] and the Soviet Union.[45]

At the same time, the United States and the Latin-American countries ratified the Habana Convention Regarding Commercial Aviation (1928), which was shaped in accordance with the interests of the air transport of the American Continent by the States Parties to the Convention. The Paris and Habana Conventions differed essentially from each other in their content as well. For example, the Habana (Pan-American) Convention did not have Annexes, therefore, all the rules and provisions were incorporated into the norm-text of the convention. Furthermore, it did not contain a provision requiring the establishment of an organisation with administrative tasks (Secretariat, Committees). These conventions had divided the world into two parts before the adoption of the Chicago Convention (1944).

Between the two World Wars, mainly with the use of military airplanes converted by civilians, air traffic was launched worldwide and aviation became increasingly international. On 20 May 1927, the American Charles Lindbergh (1902–1974) with his airplane, the *Spirit of St. Louis* landed successfully in Paris after departing from New York and flying over the Atlantic Ocean for 33 h. Lindbergh's courageous individual enterprise paved the way for aviation between continents. On 15 July 1931, George Endresz (1893–1932) pilot and Alexander Magyar (1898–1981) navigator on an airplane named *Justice for Hungary* of type Lockheed 8A Sirius achieved three world records when, after covering a distance of 5182 km, they landed in Hungary and proved the possibility of aerial connection between the American and the European continents.

---

[43] The contracting States secured this right under Article 2 besides the limitations under Articles 3 and 15. Correia, Vincent: The Legacy of the 1919 Paris Convention Relating to the Regulations of Aerial Navigation. *Behind and Beyond the Chicago Convention. The Evolution of Aerial Sovereignty* (Aerospace Law and Policy). Wolters Kluwer, 2019, pp. 14, 16–19.

[44] The United States did not sign the Paris Convention (1919).

[45] Sochor (1991), p. 2.

In the novel belligerent preparation, it became obvious for everyone that the acquisition of the domination of the air would be crucial for the achievement of the final victory. In World War II, the development of military planes progressed at an enormous pace. For the first time in history, the Germans successfully tested the gas turbine jet engine, and they were the first to construct the Messerschmitt Me–262, a mass-produced jet-propelled fighter plane. Later, the jet engine was transplanted from military aviation to civil aviation. Therefore, the so-called 'jet age', the jet powered aircraft era of modern civil aviation commenced and has been prevalent until this day. However, comprehensive international regulation and continual representation by an institution became vital. Thus, before the termination of World War II, the international community established the International Civil Aviation Organization (ICAO) in accordance with the purposes and interests of the Great Powers.

1.2.3 The Chicago Conference

In one of the gloomiest periods of human history, 6 months before the termination of World War II in Europe, following lengthy conciliations, upon the invitation of Franklin D. Roosevelt (1882–1945), the President of the United States, the diplomatic representatives of 52 States convened in the Stevens Hotel, the largest hotel in the period world in Chicago on 1 November 1944. Officially, 54 Allied and neutral States had been invited to the conference. However, Saudi Arabia did not accept the initiative. The Soviet Union welcomed the initiation positively, nevertheless, the Soviet delegation of six members arriving in Quebec in Canada was recalled with immediate effect by the leadership of the Communist Party, because (as they reasoned) countries with hostile politics figured among the States invited to the conference (Portugal, Spain and Switzerland), which was unacceptable for the Soviet Union. This step caused disappointment among the participants, because the country which was geographically the largest in extension in the world and had outstanding significance in international and domestic air transport was not represented at the conference designed to shape the post-war era of international civil aviation. In reality, the construction of the Iron Curtain commenced implicitly. As an element of this, the Soviets would have allowed transport in their national airspace exclusively for airplanes operated by Soviet staff and bearing Soviet markings. According to their conception, they wished to collect passengers and cargo at a selected airport abroad (e.g., in Cairo) and only afterwards could they have entered Soviet territory. This unique conception with its closed system was obviously not supported at the Chicago Conference. Therefore, it was not accidental that the Soviet Union had not become a party to the Chicago Convention until 1970.[46]

The objectives of the Chicago Conference included the discussion of international civil aviation, of technical and financial issues in the post-war era, furthermore, the

[46] Haanappel (2003), pp. 17–18.; Sipos (2023), pp. 13–14.

determination of the objectives and the designation of a new international aviation organisation. The contracting States adopted and signed the final version of the Chicago Convention on 7 December 1944; thereby, the International Civil Aviation Organization (ICAO) was established. The main purposes of the organisation were the development of the principles and technical standards of international aviation as well as the promotion of the planning and development of international air transport. Owing to the unique historical circumstances and the undeveloped market condition of the industry, the Member States did not pass essential rules in issues of commerce, but they supported the establishment of the International Air Transport Association (IATA) managed by the airlines.[47] (While ICAO is an intergovernmental organisation, its members may solely be the States, IATA is a non-governmental organisation as its active members have been those acceded airlines which operate international scheduled flights.)

On 7 December 1944, the contracting States signed the Chicago Convention and other treaties as well as the Provisional Agreement on International Civil Aviation, which took effect on 6 June 1945. Thus, the Provisional International Civil Aviation Organization (PICAO) was established, which possessed limited, essentially advisory rights and functioned under the leadership of the Provisional Assembly and the Temporary Council until entry into force of the Convention (4 April 1947).

7th December has been the World-Day for international civil aviation since 1994, which was determined at the 33rd General Assembly of ICAO (1992) by the Member States. During the discussion it was raised that the World-Day of aviation should be held on 4 April, on the day of taking effect of the Chicago Convention. This was modelled on the World-Day of the United Nations (UN), which is held on the day of taking effect of the Foundational Charter of the UN (24 October 1945). The selection of the date of 7 December did not win general approval, since this day coincided with 'the day of dishonour', the anniversary of the military air assault by the Japanese army against Pearl Harbour, the American naval base on the Hawaiian Islands (1941).[48]

[47] The IATA was set up for the second time in April 1945 during the International Air Transport Conference of international airlines held at Habana, Cuba. Initially, IATA operated a uniform system of charges. In our days, IATA deals with the standardisation of procedures and practices, the representation of member airlines and the uniformisation of tariffs and slot allocation. The headquarters of the organisation is in Montreal, whereas the top management has its sessions in Geneva. As of today, more than 300 airlines representing more than 83% of global air traffic are members of the IATA. Giemulla, Elmar Maria and Weber, Ludwig (editors): *International and EU Aviation Law: Selected Issues*. Weber (2011), pp. 112–128.; *IATA Annual Review*. 2022, pp. 4–5. (www.iata.org).

[48] Milde (2004), pp. 1–4.; ICAO Assembly Resolution A29–1, ICAO's 50th Anniversary Celebrations, 1994.; United Nations General Assembly Resolution 51/33, Proclamation of 7 December as the International Civil Aviation Day. 6 December 1996.

ICAO became a specialised agency of the UN among the first ones.[49] It is a matter of historical curiosity that ICAO just like the International Labour Organization (ILO), the Universal Postal Union (UPU) and the International Telecommunication Union (ITU) had been established before the foundation of the United Nations (UN). At the same time, the objectives of these organisations to serve the international community by relying on peaceful cooperation were in conformity with the basic values represented by the UN; therefore, in consideration of the common values, the UN concluded agreements with these organisations and ICAO itself, stipulating the rights and obligations of the specialised agencies therein.[50]

The Convention authorised ICAO that 'the Organization may, with respect to air matters within its competence directly affecting world security—by vote of the Assembly—enter into appropriate arrangements with any general organization set up by the nations of the world to preserve peace' (Article 64). For the entry into force of the arrangements, decisions of approval made by the General Assemblies of the UN and ICAO are necessary. In May 1947, the first Assembly of ICAO authorised the American Edward Warner (1894–1958), the first President of the ICAO Council to sign the arrangement solemnly, which ensued in New York on 3 October 1947. By doing so, ICAO became a part of the UN 'family'. In this 'family', ICAO promotes the conditions of friendship and peaceful alliance among the peoples and nations of the world by means of the instruments of aviation.

1.2.4 The Legal Sources of the Chicago System

The foundations of international aviation law are composed of the international treaties drafted at the Chicago Conference between 1 November and 7 December 1944, which are contained by the supplements to the Final Act summarising the achievements of the Conference. These multilateral treaties have constituted a uniform system and have determined international civil aviation in its foundations up to this day.

---

[49] The specialised agencies are international organisations with special competence, which were established via intergovernmental agreements. Their work supplements the general political and professional activities of the United Nations. The three general criteria of the specialised agencies include that (1) their foundational charters are framed under intergovernmental agreements, (2) they were established for definite special activities, (3) they are in contractual relation with the Economic and Social Council of the UN. Within the framework determined by their foundational charters, they are international legal entities, i.e., they may conclude international agreements and undertake international obligations. (www.un.org/en/about-us/specialized-agencies). UN Charter IX, X.

[50] ICAO Doc 7970 *Agreement between the UN and ICAO.* 13 May 1947, UNTS Vol. 8. (Revised in 2002).

The legal sources of the Chicago system adopted on 7 December 1944 are as follows:

- The Interim Agreement on International Civil Aviation;
- The Convention on International Civil Aviation (Chicago Convention);
- The International Air Services Transit Agreement (IASTA);
- The International Air Transport Agreement (ATA);
- 12 Annexes containing technical standards (at present, the Chicago Convention has 19 Annexes);
- 12 Recommendations of the Final Act.[51]

Each contracting State undertakes, immediately upon the coming into force of the Convention, *to give notice of denunciation* of the Convention,

- relating to the Regulation of Aerial Navigation signed at Paris in 13 October 1919; or
- on Commercial Aviation signed at Habana on 20 February 1928,[52]

if it is a party to either. As between contracting States, the Convention supersedes the Paris and Habana Conventions previously referred to (Article 80).

'The contracting States accept the Convention as abrogating all obligations and understandings between them which are inconsistent with its terms and undertake not to enter into any such obligations and understandings. A contracting State, which before becoming a member of the Organization has undertaken any obligations inconsistent with the terms of the Convention, shall take immediate steps to procure its release from the obligations. If an airline of any contracting State has entered into any such inconsistent obligations, the State of which it is a national shall use its best efforts to secure their termination forthwith and shall in any event cause them to be terminated' (Article 82). At the same time, 'any contracting State may make arrangements not inconsistent with the provisions of the Convention'. The Member States undertook the obligation that 'any such arrangement shall be forthwith registered with the ICAO Council, which shall make it public and accessible (for all Member States) as soon as possible' (Article 83). In a world of fragmented, diverse systems of regulation, the foundations of comprehensive uniformity in international civil aviation were established by the above-mentioned requirements formulated under the Chicago Convention, which became predominant as a foundational charter, 'the true Magna Charta' of air transport.[53]

---

[51] Among others for the demarcation of temporary air routes, the Standard Form of Bilateral Agreements for the Exchange of Routes and Services is recommended. Waldo (1946), pp. 609–610.; Sochor (1991), p. 13.

[52] Papers relating to the foreign relations of the United States, 1928, Volume I—Office of the Historian. Treaty Series No. 840 (www.history.state.gov/historicaldocuments/frus1928v01/d364).

[53] 'As an instrument of international aviation law, the Chicago Convention is remarkable like a true Magna Charta'. Kotaite (2013), p. 43.; Dempsey (2015), p. 215.

References

Abeyratne R (2014) Convention on International Civil Aviation: a Commentary. Springer, p 222

Anderson DF, Eberhardt S (2010) Understanding flight. 2nd edn., McGraw Hill, p 93

Balzac H (1908) Lost Illusions. The Gebbie Publishing Co. Ltd., Philadelphia, p 195

Bisignani G (2007) IATA Director General Statement. In: IATA Annual Conference, Vancouver, 3–5 June 2007

Bouwer J, Krishnan V, Saxon S, Tufft C (2022) Taking Stock of the Pandemic's Impact on Global Aviation. McKinsey's & Company. www.mckinsey.com/industries/travel-logistics-and-infrastructure/our-insights/taking-stock-of-the-pandemics-impact-on-global-aviation

Copper JC (1952a) Roman Law and the Maxim – Cuius Est Solum – in International Air Law. McGill Law J 1:23–65

Copper JC (1952b) The International Air Navigation Conference, Paris 1910. Journal of Air Law and Commerce, 19(2):127–128

Dancko JS (2002) De Iure Principis Aereo (The Jurisdiction of the Prince over the Air). In: Benkoe M, Schmidt-Tedd B (Eds), Heitz MH, Kertész P (Translators) Anhalt-Zerbst, 1867, Latin-English Synopsis. pp 1–94. www.researchgate.net/profile/Marietta-Benkoe/publication

Dempsey PS (2015) The Future of International Air Law in the 21st Century. ZLW Germ J Air and Space Law 64:215

Földi A, Hamza G (2022) A Római Jog Története és Institúciói (The History and Institutions of Roman Law). 26th edn., Novissima, Budapest, p viii

Haanappel PPC (2003) The Law and Policy of Airspace and Outer Space. Kluwer Law International, The Hague, pp 17–18

Hobe S (ed) (2015) Institute of Air and Space Law, University of Cologne (1925–2015). Cologne, Introduction. Wolters Kluwer, p III

Karlson P (1938) Der Mensch Fliegt. Ullstein, Berlin, p 299

Kotaite A (2013) My Memoirs: 50 years of International Diplomacy and Conciliation in Aviation. International Civil Aviation Organization, Montreal, p 43

Menger A (1906) Neue Staatslehre. G. Fischer, Jena, pp 100–101

Milde M (2004) Chicago Convention at Sixty: Stagnation or Renaissance? Annals of Air and Space Law, McGill Univ. 29:1–4

Sandeepa BB (2020) COVID-19 and Aviation Crisis in India. In: Latino Americana de Derecho Aeronáutico. Número 58 Cita, IJ–MIII–451, 21 December 2020

Sándorfi Kamill (1924) A légi közlekedés joga (The Law of Air Transport). Budapest, pp 6–8

Shepardson D (2018) 2017 Safest Year on Record for Commercial Passenger Air Travel: Groups. Reuters. www.reuters.com/article/us-aviation-safety

Sipos A (2023) Milde's International Air Law and ICAO. 4th edn., Eleven International Publishing, The Hague, pp 7, 13–14

Sochor E (1991) The Politics of International Aviation. MacMillan Press, pp 2, 13

Truxal S (2016) Economic and Environmental Regulation of International Aviation: from International to Global Governance. Routledge, p 5

Varley H (ed) (1978) The Air Traveller's Handbook: the Complete Guide to Air Travel, Airplanes, and Airports. Simon et Schuster, New York, p 150

Waldo RK (1946) Sequels to the Chicago Aviation Conference. Law and Contemporary Problems. Duke Law J 11(3):609–610

Weber L (2011) International and EU Aviation Law. Selected Issues. International Organizations, Chapter 3. Kluwer Law International B.V., pp 112–128

Wissmann G (1975) Geschichte der Luftfahrt von Ikarus bis zur Gegenwart. VEB Verlag Technik, pp 77–79

Yehuda A (1962) The Maxim: 'Cujus Est Solum Ejus Usque Ad Coelum' as Applied in Aviation. McGill Law J 8(4):247

Part I
The Public Law of International Civil Aviation

Chapter 2
The Chicago Convention

The Chicago Convention on International Civil Aviation (hereinafter: the Convention),[1] one of the masterpieces of international treaty-making consists of four major parts: Air Navigation, The International Civil Aviation Organization, International Air Transport and Final Provisions. The Convention contains 22 Chapters and 96 Articles. The Convention and its 19 Annexes exceed a total of 4000 pages.

In the first part of this volume on public aviation law, each provision of the Convention will be introduced in detail. The air carriers and airports will be designated with the codes determined by the organisation of the International Air Transport Association (IATA), not by ICAO. The reason for this is that in everyday life passengers encounter the two or three lettered IATA designator codes, therefore, they will be more familiar to the reader as well.[2]

2.1 The Preamble of the Convention

The Preamble *(preambulum)* does not bind legally; nevertheless, it is an essential and prominent part of international treaties, since it determines the objective of the regulation briefly and concisely. Furthermore, it contains the general principles of

---

[1] ICAO Doc 7300 *Chicago Convention on International Civil Aviation*. 9th edn., 2006.

[2] The codes determined by ICAO are less familiar for the travelling public. ICAO designates the airlines with three letters and the airports with four letters. These are used only for navigation and technical purposes. For example, the ICAO code of British Airways is BAW, while the ICAO code for London Heathrow Airport is EGLL, letter E denotes the northern part of Europe (Northern Europe), letter G means the country (Great Britain), while the letters LL refer to the city and its airport. The respective IATA airline and airport designator codes are shorter and well-known: BA and LHR. ICAO Annex 14 on Aerodromes; ICAO Doc 7910 *(Location Indicators)* and ICAO Doc 8585 *(Designators for Aircraft)*; IATA Resolution 763: *Airline Coding Directory* (ACD). 88th edn., June 2017.; Smith (2018), p. 77.

A. Sipos, *International Aviation Law*, https://doi.org/10.1007/978-3-031-39066-1_2

the relations to be regulated. The objectives and general principles formulated in the Preamble provide effective support for applier of the law to construe the rules. The most momentous word in the Preamble of the Convention is '*peace*'. In light of this, the contracting States declare uniformly that 'the future development of international civil aviation can help greatly to create and preserve friendship and understanding among the nations and peoples of the world'. Apart from friendship and understanding, it is prominently 'desirable to avoid friction and to promote the cooperation among nations and peoples upon which *the peace of the world* depends'.

Since the end of World War II, after humankind had become familiar with obliteration bombing and the incomprehensible horrors of nuclear strikes carried out with the involvement of airplanes,[3] every nation longed for peace and was striving for a world without terror. The Member States unanimously set the objective of the formation of peaceful and safe cooperation encompassing nations. Therefore, upon drafting the Convention political and nationalistic interests lost ground substantially owing to the intention to prevent that in the future some sovereign States based on their military and defence interests override the embraced peaceful objectives.

In the twentieth century, fraught with armed conflicts, the role of international law became paramount because the maintenance of international peace and security manifested itself as a universal value: in view of the past, the preservation of peace was rendered a higher stake. Therefore, the stabilising function of international law gained high significance. The concerned States need to settle international disputes with peaceful instruments so that humankind should not face the occurrence of the unprecedented largest disaster caused by weapons of mass destruction. Because of the above and other historical facts, the peaceful settlement of international disputes has become one of the most important general principles of international law.

The Convention contains the general basic principles of international law. These general principles permeate the complete norm-text of the Convention and determine its spirituality. Such universal basic requirements include the following:

- respect for State sovereignty (Article 1);
- equality of the States [Article 48 *b)*];
- the obligation of cooperation among States (Article 37);
- equal rights for peoples and nations [Article 44 *f)* and *g)*];
- the prohibition of discrimination (the principle of equal treatment) [Articles 4, 9, 11, 15];
- the principle of peaceful co-existence (Preamble); furthermore,
- the principle of the peaceful settlement of international disputes (Article 84).

Obviously, it is an excessive expectation to preserve world peace via the instruments of aviation, at the same time, it is a special challenge as well. In this process,

[3]The strategic bombing carried out by modern devices meant a gigantic menace for the civil population. While in World War I, all the air strikes targeting England had 1117 civilian victims, the air strike solely against Dresden in World War II demanded the lives of 35,000 civilians. It became one of the greatest challenges to humanity to demand the most far-reaching prohibition of the use of the most dangerous weapons of modern warfare, that is, the nuclear, biological and chemical weapons.

the Member States shape the development of international air transport by granting equal opportunities, they cooperate as equal parties by guaranteeing the prevalence of the principle of reciprocity, and they proceed in good faith *(bona fide)* under all circumstances.

2.2 The Territory of the Sovereign State

The definition of 'territory' is of extraordinary significance since the supreme power of the sovereign State is prevalent in the airspace above its territory. Sovereignty has a central role in air transport. Under the provision of the Convention 'the territory of a State shall be deemed to be the *land areas* and *territorial waters* adjacent thereto under the sovereignty, suzerainty, protection or mandate of such State' (Article 2).

The territory of the State encompasses the following:

- the mainland;
- the territorial waters (including the national rivers and lakes, the international rivers, in the case of seas: the coastal sea, furthermore, the archipelago and certain straits);
- the territory above the mainland and the territorial waters, the airspace itself; and
- the quasi territory of the State (from the viewpoint of jurisdiction): the embassy or consulate buildings, diplomatic cars, the board of a ship, an aircraft and a spacecraft or space station.

Of the surface of the Earth, 71% is covered by oceans and seas classified as the high seas (28% constitutes territorial waters and the remaining 43% is international waters). From the viewpoint of aviation law, we need to make clear distinction between territorial waters and the high seas, because

- the airspace above the *territorial sea* qualifies as *national*; thus, the coastal State has complete and exclusive sovereignty in the airspace above its territorial waters, whereas
- the airspace above *the high seas* qualifies as *international*; thus, above such territories no sovereign rights prevail.

In the lawsuit *Nicaragua versus the United States of America,*[4] the International Court of Justice (ICJ) condemned the United States because it breached international conventions, furthermore, it mined the ports of Nicaragua while it supported the anti-governmental forces. In the lawsuit the Court ruled: the

(continued)

[4]Case Concerning Military and Paramilitary Activities in and Against Nicaragua: *Nicaragua v. United States of America*—ICJ Summary of the Judgement, 5. State sovereignty, 27 June 1986, Paras. 212–214.

concept of sovereignty both in treaty-law and in customary international law extends to the internal waters, the *territorial sea* and to the airspace above the territory of the State.

Almost the entire mainland constituting 29% of the surface of the Earth is subject to State sovereignty. The sovereign State has complete and exclusive power in the national airspace above its territory to the boundary of outer space.

Sovereignty is a political, legal and historical concept. Sovereignty proceeds from the essence of the State; it is an exclusive attribute of the State. In other words, the State and solely the State is sovereign. All States are sovereign, and their sovereignties are equal. The 'State' is an entity which in international relations encompasses the community of people led by a government exercising actual power in a determined territory.

Sovereignty essentially consists of two inextricable concepts forming a unity:

1. the *territorial supreme power* implies the actual supreme power exercised by the State in its own territory, the exercise of exclusive control, the opportunity of drafting a constitution and other statutes and of the enforcement of these by the executive power. Only States are in possession of supreme power, i.e. the monopoly of recourse to legitimate violence (internal aspect); and
2. *international independence* which prevails between the given sovereign State and the international community, and in this system of equal international relations the independent State intervenes autonomously (external aspect).

The independence in international relations entails the exercise of actual territorial and personal jurisdiction in the internal life of the sovereign State. The two concepts supplement each other to form an entirety, since the State, in the absence of independence in international relations, in its internal life may neither exercise actual territorial and personal jurisdiction nor proceed autonomously in international relations.[5] Sovereign States are equal and according to the tenet of canon law: equals do not have authority over one another *(par in parem non habet imperium)*. A State may be obligated only owing to its consent, which may be granted under treaty-law or customary international law.

[5] International law takes only one circumstance into consideration, namely, whether a State proceeds autonomously in its international relations or it does not. No forum exists in the world which could examine whether a State is or is not actually sovereign. The United Nations may not play such a role either. Each State decides by itself whether it intends to enter into relations with a formation declaring itself a sovereign State. Valki (1999), pp. 1000–1007.

Fig. 2.1 National and international airspace

2.2.1 The National Airspace of the Sovereign State

The first and simultaneously one of the most important articles of the Convention provides that 'the contracting States recognise that every State has *complete* and *exclusive sovereignty* over the airspace above its territory' (Article 1). Since the airspace always shares the legal fate of the territory beneath, we need to distinguish between:

- *national airspace* above the territory of the State subject to the complete and exclusive sovereignty of the State; and
- *international airspace* not located above the territory of a State; thus, it is beyond the boundaries of State sovereignty (Fig. 2.1).

Completeness and exclusivity imply that the airspace of the sovereign State is, in legal terms *(de jure),* regarded as a detached territory, where the aircraft of other countries may not enter arbitrarily. The sovereign State may not be constrained from outside, nor may its territory be occupied. According to the reputed tenet pronounced in the *Island of Palmas* case (1928): 'Sovereignty in the relations among States denotes independence. Independence with respect to a part of the Globe is the right to exercise therein, with the exclusion of any other State, the functions of a State'.[6] However, the sovereign State proceeding as an autonomous and independent legal entity in international relations may not be considered absolute, since the States, by entering into international obligations, may be restricted in their rights. Thus, in the event of fulfilling the conditions and obligations assumed under international treaties, it is practicable for the States to *open* their national airspace above their territories and to permit the entrance of the aircraft of other States with the application of the general principles of mutuality and reciprocity.

In the first—a very important—provision of the Convention, the contracting States recognise the complete and exclusive sovereignty in their airspace of *all States*, not only of the contracting States.[7]

Nevertheless, it is possible to fly into the national airspace despite its closure and to land in the territory of the sovereign State. In that case, the aircraft of the other State needs to comply under all circumstances with the conditions assumed under the Convention for *non-scheduled flights*, while, in the case of (commercial) *scheduled flights,* besides compliance with the conditions under the Convention, the 'special permission or other authorisation' of the foreign State also needs to be obtained (Articles 5–6).

2.2.2 The Horizontal Boundary of the National Airspace

Since the legal status of the airspace above the territory of the State is determined by the legal status of the territory beneath, the airspace above the mainland of the State, or, in the case of coastal countries, the airspace above 'adjacent territorial waters' constitutes the territory of the State.[8] Horizontally, State sovereignty extends to the boundary of the mainland, but, if the country possesses seas, it extends to the boundary of territorial seas.

- *Territorial seas* and *internal waters* (national waters) constitute parts of the territory of the State. The water, depth (seabed) and airspace of these territories are subject to the sovereignty of the State, i.e. they qualify as State territories.

---

[6] *Island of Palmas case. Reports of International Arbitral Awards RSA*, Vol. II., 4 April 1928, p. 838.

[7] The difference between 'State' and 'contracting State' has faded by now, as almost all States are members of ICAO. In the beginning, however, the distinction had great significance. That is, in 1947, ICAO had merely 26 Member States; so currently, when the treaty-maker mentions the rights and obligations of the 'States', it has in mind every sovereign State all over the world (disregarding membership).

[8] The logic of aviation law considerably resembles that of maritime regulations. From the outset, we may assert that similarly to the principle of Roman law 'the thing built on the land goes with the land' *(aedificium solo cedit)*, therefore, the legal status of the airspace is determined by the status of the territory beneath.

Pursuant to the UN Convention on the Law of the Sea (UNCLOS),[9] territorial seas range to at most 12 nautical miles[10] from the coast. In the national airspace above territorial seas, aircraft are not authorised to fly into or over peacefully; that is, they may not fly freely in that airspace without special permission.

'Innocent (peaceful) passage' is a concept in maritime law, which is rightful for commercial ships and warships on territorial seas.[11]

The boundaries of jurisdictional waters of the State and of the airspace above can be demarcated by the precise determination of the baseline of the territorial sea. Due to the unique position of islands, the precise demarcation of 12 nautical miles is sometimes problematic in practice.[12] Aircraft pilots need to take the 12 nautical miles very seriously since the right of the States to defend their territory prevails entirely in this respect. As this part is the closest to the mainland, in the event of minor carelessness or a willful act, a controversial aviation incident or conflict related to the defence of the territory may develop.[13]

- The *high seas* (international waters) do not constitute part of the territory of the State. The high seas constitute areas *to be freely used by all* for peaceful purposes *(res communis omnium usus)*; they may not be appropriated or occupied; therefore, no State may extend its territorial jurisdiction thereto. The legal status of the high seas in the context of free use is identical to that of outer space. The high seas are open to all States, whether coastal or landlocked.

  This entails, inter alia, both for coastal States and landlocked States:

  (a) freedom of navigation;
  (b) freedom of fishing;
  (c) freedom to lay submarine cables and pipelines;

[9]The codification of the entirety of maritime law ensued in Geneva between 1958 and 1982 under the auspices of the United Nations (UN). The codification of maritime law encompassed its entirety; thus, the fate of the high seas was settled. In 1982, at the Conference of the UN on the Law of the Sea held in Montego Bay (Jamaica), the States adopted the Convention on the Law of the Sea, which contained the comprehensive regulations of maritime law and took effect on 16 November 1994.

[10]One nautical mile is 1852.2 m long, that is, 12 nautical miles equal 22.2 km.

[11]The passage of ships is considered to be peaceful as long as the security and the order of the coastal State are not disturbed, and it is in accordance with the general principles of international law. In contrast, for example, the passage is not peaceful, if during the passage, fighter planes take off from and land on an aircraft carrier. *The Law of the Sea Convention* (1982), Part II, Section 3, Subsection A, Article 19.

[12]Geneva Convention of 29 April 1958 on the Territorial Sea and the Contiguous Zone (1958)—Limits of the Territorial Sea. Articles 3–4, Section II.

[13]For example, a Soviet MIG-19 fighter plane unlawfully shot down an American reconnaissance aircraft, a Boeing RB-47H Stratojet completing a routine flight over international waters in international airspace at a distance of 50 miles from the Soviet coast on 1 July 1960, since they believed the reconnaissance plane 'was travelling close'. *National Museum of US Air Force: RB-47H Stratojet Shot Down* (posted 2006) (www.nationalmuseum.af.mil).

(d) freedom to construct artificial islands and other installations permitted under international law;
(e) freedom of scientific research;
(f) freedom of overflight above the high seas.[14]

Pursuant to the Convention on the Law of the Sea, the high seas include neither the *contiguous zone* measured from the end of the territorial sea with a width of 12 nautical miles, nor the *exclusive economic zone* of a range of 176 nautical miles.[15] These zones are not considered to be national territories, but the coastal States may exercise policing rights and pursue economic activities in these zones with boundaries. Consequently, the high seas stretch beyond 200 nautical miles measured from the coast. From the viewpoint of aviation law, however, beyond the national territory and the territorial sea, there is a non-State territory—which qualifies as high seas—since it is entirely free to fly and manoeuvre over the contiguous zone and the exclusive economic zone.

2.2.3 The Vertical Boundary of the National Airspace

Upon the launch of the first lunar satellites, the question logically emerged: where does the airspace end and where does outer space begin. The Soviet satellites orbited round the Earth at an altitude which exceeded the ceiling of traditional airplanes by far. Nevertheless, when they reached the point where they were close to the Earth (215 km) on their orbit, they may have sojourned within the airspace of the concerned States. Under the circumstances of the Cold War (1947–1991), the United States made attempts at shooting the Soviet Sputnik satellites. Its justification was that the space objects used the airspace of the United States and other countries several times during their orbit; therefore, they transgressed the territorial integrity of the concerned States in the absence of the theoretical and practical vertical delimitation of sovereignty. The launch of the Sputnik shook the United States in its foundations. They were deeply exasperated since they had lived in the belief that they were the pioneers in research and had more advanced technology than the Soviets.[16] This exasperation made history as the 'Sputnik-crisis'. At the same time, this meant the turning point of the Cold War, which culminated in the space competition.

[14] *The Law of the Sea Convention* (1982), Part VII, High Seas. Section I. Article 87.

[15] Idem. 'The coastal State shall make payments or contributions in kind in respect of the exploitation of the non-living resources of the continental shelf beyond 200 nautical miles from the baselines, from which the breadth of the territorial sea is measured' (Article 82).

[16] According to the PR manager of the President of the United States, Reedy, E. George (1917–1999): 'The simple fact is that we can no longer consider the Russians to be behind us in technology. It took them 4 years to catch up to our atomic bomb and 9 months to catch up to our hydrogen bomb. Now we are trying to catch up to their satellite'. Launius (2005).

Therefore, the 'theoretical' delimitation of the geographical boundary between the national airspace and outer space has significance. In legal terms this boundary demarcates the vertical range of the sovereign power of the State. Thus, the national airspace is not infinite; at the point where it ends, outer space begins. However, the legal fate of the two spaces differs. While national airspace is under the jurisdiction of the State, outer space can be freely utilised by all; here State sovereignty does not prevail. Consequently, each member of the international community may equally use outer space for peaceful purposes, whereas no State may demand the occupation or possession of such a territory or region. Therefore, from a legal point of view, it is essential where the *jurisdictional boundary* between the national airspace and outer space is demarcated.

The principle of *usque ad coelum* (who owns the soil, owns the estate up to the skies) of Roman law cannot be applied to solve the problem, because in property law it accepts vertical infinity without boundaries in altitude. By reason of the rotation of the Earth and its orbiting round the Sun, perpetually different sections of outer space would belong to the owners, let alone that on distant planets the exercise of property rights would make sense only as utopia. Nor is the delimitation viable according to scientific criteria. Notwithstanding, various theories have been coined,[17] but the parties could not, or were not willing to, agree on the issue.

The delimitation has special literature that could fill a library. Gyula Gál (1926–2012), an internationally acclaimed space lawyer, makes mention of 49 recommendations for delimitation in his book published in 1969,[18] some of which are noteworthy in this respect. According to the *theory of gravity*, the upper limit of the sovereign power of the State can be delineated at an altitude from where objects launched from the Earth still drop back. According to the *atmosphere theory,* outer space begins where the mass of air surrounding the Earth ends, whereas *the aerodynamic concept* claims that outer space begins where the machine's lift is not sufficient to hold the aircraft in the air. The *biological theory* holds that the airspace ranges to the point where man is capable of sojourning in the air without the help of technical devices, whereas the *rotational theory* maintains that the airspace ranges to the point where gravitation and centrifugal forces still counterbalance each other. According to the *theory of the security of the State,* the boundary needs to be established where the defence and security of the nation can still be guaranteed in the airspace by the State. It is likely, however, that the *functionalist theory* is the most welcomed, and practice is increasingly following this. The adherents of the functionalist delimitation do not accept that the State has the power to determine the upper limit of its airspace unilaterally, because they believe that

(continued)

[17] Goedhart (1996), p. 43.

[18] Gál (1969), pp. 59–116.

the boundary cannot be calculated in altitude, but the delimitation derives from the character of the activity; that is, outer space begins at the point where already orbiting movement takes place. Accordingly, aviation in the airspace becomes outer space activity when the objective is to place a given object (device) in orbit or its orbit injection beyond, when the object is in movement there or it is deorbited, furthermore, when the object lands or stays on celestial bodies or returns from there. [We refer to orbiting round the Earth, that is, orbiting movement when the object (satellite) travels round the Earth at least once.]

Drawing the jurisdictional boundary is necessitated by reasons which are far beyond the legal aspects. In the future commercial flights will be implemented via suborbital flights by specialised operators. During suborbital flights, prospective space travellers will intend to pay actually for staying in outer space and not for a trip in higher airspace. Suborbital flights are carried out by space objects not apt for orbiting round the Earth. This space object, which is neither a spaceship nor a space shuttle, has the capacity to rocket into outer space to an altitude of approximately 100 km. The passengers during suborbital flights, just like astronauts, will experience zero gravity for 8–10 min, but they will not be orbiting round the Earth during the trip.[19]

Andrew G. Haley (1904–1966), an American lawyer and outer space specialist, deserves credit for the most widespread theory on the vertical demarcation of the boundary between national airspace and outer space. It was him who delineated the *boundary of jurisdiction* at an altitude of 83 km (275,000 feet), which he designated 'the Kármán primary jurisdictional line'. Namely, Theodore von Kármán,[20] a scientist

[19]The first such space device was *SpaceShipOne* SS1 (2004), which was further developed under the name *SpaceShipTwo* SS2 (2010). In the near future, the space device carrying six passengers between London and Sydney will travel at a speed exceeding three times the sonic speed during the journey of 2.5 h while it will sojourn in outer space for 10 min. During the experimental flight above the Mojave-Desert (US) on 31 October 2014 an irregularity occurred, owing to which the space device crashed. Due to the accident the launch of space flights was cancelled. The first suborbital flight ensued on 11 July 2021 on board the space device named *Virgin Space Ship* (VSS) *Unity 22*. Pleasance, Chris: London to Sydney in TWO hours. *Daily Mail,* 19 October 2013; NTSB AAR-15/02, PB 2015–105454, Notation 8614, Adopted on 28 July 2015. p. 1.; Amos, Jonathan and Gill, Victoria: *Space tourism: Virgin space plane to fly above new base*. Science correspondents, BBC News, 12 December 2020.; Malik, Tariq: Virgin Galactic's SpaceShipTwo Unity 22 launch with Richard Branson, 12 July 2021 (www.space.com/virgin-galactic-richard-branson-unity-22-launch-explained).

[20]Theodore von Kármán (1881–1963) was a mechanical engineer, physicist and a scientist of applied mathematics. He was called the 'patron saint' of the US Air Force (USAF). He is the father of supersonic aviation and a pioneer of missile technology and hypersonic astronautics. Via the construction of wind-tunnels, he discovered the significance of streamlining and revealed the regularities of special forces, eddies and currents (see, Kármán's vortex), which affect airplanes and other aerial moving objects. Lee (1967).

of Hungarian descent, had calculated the altitude at which the aircraft needs to fly more speedily than the cosmic speed to be held at the given altitude by the aerodynamic lift.

According to the tenet of Daniel Bernoulli (1700–1782), the lift is based on the connection between speed and pressure. That was the outset for Theodore von Kármán, according to whom this boundary can actually be determined if we know the speed of the space vehicle and its altitude above the surface of the Earth. Let us consider, for instance, 'the record-breaking flight of Captain Ivan Carl Kincheloe Jr. (1928–1958) performed on board a Bell X–2 test rocket plane on 7 September 1956. Kincheloe was flying at a speed of 2000 miles per hour (3200 km/h) at an altitude of approx. 126,000 feet (38.5 km). At this altitude and speed, the aerodynamic lift still carries 98% of the weight of the plane, and only 2% is carried by the centrifugal force or Kepler force, as space scientists designate it. However, at 300,000 feet (91.4 km) or 57 miles up, this relationship is reversed because the air is too scarce to contribute to the lift: only the centrifugal force is prevalent at this altitude [note: the aircraft would be able to stay in the air if it moved with Cosmic Speed I (7.9 km/s) and its wings would also be unnecessary in such a case.] This is certainly a physical boundary where aerodynamics ends and astronautics begins: so why not could that also be a jurisdictional boundary?'.[21]

According to von Kármán, the jurisdictional boundary between aerodynamics, meteorology and astronautics stretches at an altitude between 80 and 100 km depending on the varying natural and atmospheric conditions; nevertheless, he wisely added: 'I am convinced that this tough legal issue will not be solved during my lifetime'. The problem of delimitation, still open today, needs to be resolved unambiguously sooner or later by humankind, while increasingly higher degrees of technical development are achieved.

[21] Idem., pp. 300–301.

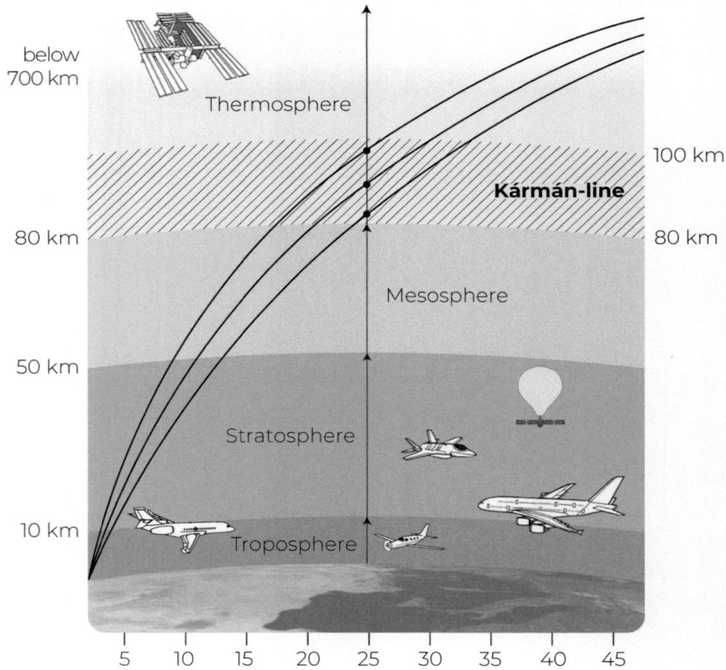

Fig. 2.2 The jurisdictional boundary according to Kármán

The spatial range of the Kármán-line is determined by the connection between altitude and speed. The higher the aircraft flies (feet × 10^3), the higher the speed needs to be to stay aloft (feet × 10^3/s), since the lift decreases because of the increasingly thinner air. At a certain physical point, at an altitude of approx. 92 km, but essentially anywhere in the range between 80 and 100 km, the lift is suddenly discontinued and the aircraft is no longer able to stay in the air. Obviously, this is merely a theoretical approach, since modern airplanes travelling at a cruising altitude of an average of 11 km are incapable of reaching this boundary or the necessary speed (Fig. 2.2).

Today some outer space powers generally and unilaterally demarcate the boundary between 100–110 km. On 14 April 1983, the Soviets recommended in a memorandum addressed to the UN establishing the boundary between the national airspace and outer space at an altitude not exceeding 110 km above sea level due to agreement among the States.[22] The Australian Government established this bound-

[22] *UN Chronicle,* 21 (4), 1984, p. 37.

ary at an altitude of 100 km above sea level under national law regulating outer space activity.[23] Although several developed States successfully pursuing outer space activity have national law pertinent to outer space research, it was only the Australians that declared how high their national airspace ranges vertically. At the same time, we need to note and emphasise that international treaties adopted by the international community do not contain universal rules or provisions to separate the national and international airspace from outer space vertically.[24]

2.2.4 International Airspace

In the international airspace, State sovereignty does not prevail; this airspace is not subject to State sovereignties. Above the high seas and the South Pole (the Antarctica),[25] where the right of sovereignty is not exercised by the States, international airspace stretches. Their legal status is similar to that of outer space, since above both territories, the airspace can be used by all; therefore, by staying in the international airspace above the high seas and the South Pole, 'we are in outer space', emphatically and solely with respect to their legal status and free use (Fig. 2.3).

---

[23] *Australian Space Activities Act* (1998), Sect. 8. [Amended by the Space (Launches and Returns) Act 2018].

[24] We need to mention the official standpoint of the International Aeronautic Federation (FAI) as an example. More than 100 Member States of the Federation have adopted the boundary of 100 km in the area of sports flights, but this in itself does not imply an internationally acknowledged prescription or obligation ('Space: for FAI purposes, more than 100 km above the Earth's surface'). *FAI Sporting Code. General Section. Classes and Definitions,* 2.7, 2022. p. 15.

[25] The South Pole (Antarctica) is a highly important area from strategic, economic and scientific points of view. The international legal relations of the one and only continent of the Earth, which is perpetually uninhabited and covered by ice, are regulated under the Antarctic Treaty (1959). Under the Treaty, which is essentially an international agreement establishing the status of the continent under public law, 7 States of the Parties to the Treaty renounced demands for national ownership only provisionally. The Parties to the Treaty, 12 industrially developed countries as founders, adopted the most important basic principles, which were later transplanted into the Outer Space Treaty (1967), then into the Moon Agreement (1979). The States Parties to the Antarctic Treaty guarantee peaceful utilisation and secure that any country may establish scientific research stations in the territory of the Antarctica. It is prohibited to store garbage, especially nuclear and radioactive waste on the continent and the Parties assumed the obligation not to deploy nuclear weapons or other weapons of mass destruction and not to pursue military activities (for instance, military exercises, arms tests) in the region. It is essential that the Parties maintain their territorial claims, at the same time, they agreed not to exploit any minerals on the snow-white continent. Secretariat of Antarctic Treaty (www.ats.aq/e/antarctictreaty.html).

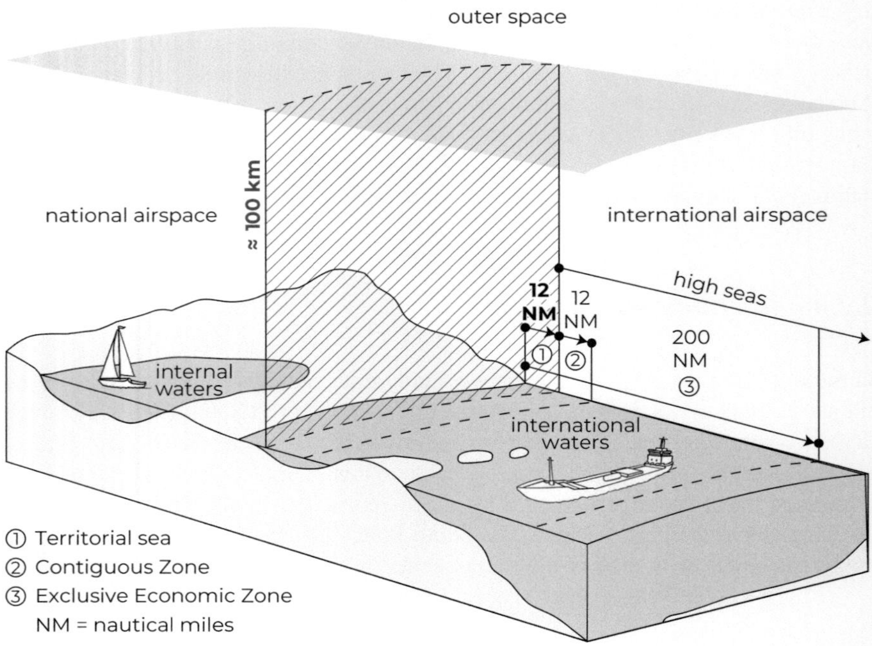

Fig. 2.3 Horizontal and vertical range of the airspace

Since the high seas are not subject to the territorial sovereignty of the States, and consequently, the airspace above them is international, the question arises as to who supervises order in the largest freely utilisable airspace in the world. In the international airspace above the high seas, the aviation rules formulated by ICAO have to be observed in accordance with the Convention and its Annexes,[26] since, 'over the high seas, the rules in force shall be those established (from time to time) under the Convention' (Article 12). During operation the old basic Roman principle should prevail: use your property in such manner that you do not damage other people's property *(sic utere tuo ut alienum non laedas)*.

At the same time, ICAO does not have authorisation for enforcement; therefore, the observance of aviation rules prescribed by ICAO on aircraft flying over the high seas shall be required by the country where the aircraft was registered. Air navigation services, as well as search and rescue, must be provided by the coastal States based on the mandate granted by the Council of ICAO. However, this does not mean that, in the air navigation zones above the high seas, the sovereignty of these States predominates. Over the high seas the rules of air traffic services, of safety, security, search and rescue are stipulated by international contracts concluded by the States.

[26] Annex 2 on Rules of the Air; Annex 6 on Operations of Aircraft; Annex 11 on Air Traffic Services and Annex 12 on Search and Rescue contain standards for flight above the high seas.

2.2.5 Outer Space

Similarly to international airspace, outer space also belongs to all and cannot be appropriated in any form *(res communis omnium usus)*. Outer space including the Moon and other celestial bodies *cannot be appropriated by any States* either owing to claims to sovereignty or via use or occupation. The Moon and other celestial bodies may be used exclusively for peaceful purposes. Therefore, nuclear weapons or other weapons of mass destruction may not be placed in orbit round the Earth or on celestial bodies. These general principles are laid down under the Outer Space Treaty[27] adopted in 1967 during the Cold War. The Outer Space Treaty constitutes the basic agreement on international outer space activity. It contains basic principles recognised by the international community, which determine the pursuit of activities related to outer space and its framework. The treaty-makers accomplished something exceptional. Their primary objective was to defend outer space in its foundations from the arms and acquisition of property races, thereby minimising the possibility of the contingent formation of a prospective armed conflict.

Pursuant to the Outer Space Treaty: 'Outer space, including the Moon and other celestial bodies, is not subject to national appropriation by claim of sovereignty, by means of use or occupation, or by any other means' (Article II). Thus, property may not be obtained in outer space either owing to the fact of first presence, nor to the placement of symbols of State power (e.g., national emblems, coats of arms, national flags). When the States framed the rules related to the regulation of outer space, they did not think of the future possibility of the emergence of private capital and private companies besides States in space research. Therefore, the express prohibition of ownership pertains only to nations. Some profiteers took advantage of this situation with the purpose of speculation, when they started selling 'parcelled' land (along with mining rights) on the Moon or other celestial bodies.[28] Thus, these sales contracts are null and void. However, plentiful people purchased the cheap Moon estates or the areas of other celestial bodies disregarding the general principle of Roman law and still effective civil law: '*nemo plus iuris transferre potest quam ipse habet*', which means that nobody can transfer more rights than his own, which means that ownership can be obtained only from an owner. In addition, it proceeds from the logic of the law that a private agreement may not annul public law, i.e. *privatorum conventio iuri publico non-derogate:* an agreement of private persons cannot derogate from public law. That is, the individual cannot have more rights than the nation itself, because the individual may not rise above the commu-

[27] Treaty on Principles Governing the Activities of States in the Exploration and Use of Outer Space, including the Moon and Other Celestial Bodies (1967), Article II.

[28] For example, Dennis M. Hope, an American businessman, who affirms to be a legitimate owner of the Moon, claims he has already provided service to more than six million customers (www.lunarembassy.com).

nity. Not talking of the fact that such sale targets an impossible object, which means the nullity of the contract, since the possession of the site, the harvest of its fruit or its visit is not possible for the individual.

We need to recognise that the significance of outer space is much larger than we can conceive. Outer space is not far away; where national or international airspace ends, outer space begins.

One of the most interesting eras of humankind, the 'Space Age' commenced on 4 October 1957 with the orbiting of the Sputnik-1 (*спутник* means fellow-traveller), the Soviet satellite round the Earth. The Sputnik was the first satellite of human civilisation, the first space object in outer space. On that day mankind opened the door into outer space, then on 12 April 1961, it orbited round the Earth and on 20 July 1969, humankind landed on the Moon.[29] We reached spiritual heights and humankind proclaimed in a resounding manner: 'we have conquered outer space'. Science as a collective enterprise encompassing human generations helped man reach outer space. Our astronauts arrived as the 'envoys of mankind'[30] and started to do research in outer space with peaceful purposes. It was the intellectual adventure that sent us over to outer space. Humankind could leave the gravity of the Earth behind and has reached several celestial bodies, while its telescopes span billions of light-years. However, despite these giant steps we need to acknowledge that outer space has become more distant than we would have expected: humankind has not conquered outer space.

Our rudimentary rocket technology and spaceships still do not facilitate reaching, for instance, Proxima Centauri, the star at a distance of 4.24 light-years, the closest one to our Sun (star) always shining at us (that is, by travelling at the speed of light and covering 300,000 km per second, the journey would take 4.24 years). By relying on contemporary technology, this interstellar journey would take approx. 18,000 years.[31] If, for example, we used the most modern technology applied in the driving device of space shuttles, we could reach this planet in approx. 900 years. To give an idea of that distance: merely in our galaxy, in the Milky Way System accommodating humankind, nearly 400 billion stars glow and at least 100 billion planets revolve, while it takes 100,000 light years to reach from one end to the other. When we search the depths of the Universe, we need to calculate with billions of galaxies like ours.[32]

---

[29] From the first ascent and flying a 37 m (120 feet) distance by the engine driven, heavier-than-air airplane on 17 December 1903, it took humankind only 54 years to reach outer space and 66 years for the 'envoys of mankind' to step on the Moon as a result of the development of aviation, rockets and computer technology.

[30] Outer Space Treaty (1967), Article V.

[31] Clery, May: US lawmaker orders NASA to plan for trip to Alpha Centauri by 100th anniversary of moon landing (in 2069), *Science*, 23 May 2016 (www.sciencemag.org/news).

[32] Baur (2014), pp. 6–7.

Therefore, the magnitude of outer space exceeds the boundaries of human thinking. The future of humankind, the comprehension of its existence also depends on our familiarity with the mysteries of the cosmos. In the cosmos, the same physical laws are prevalent.[33] In 1687, Sir Isaac Newton (1643–1727), a British physicist and astronomer, proved that the same laws of nature determine the movement of celestial bodies and objects on the Earth. The Sun also attracts its planets, nevertheless, as they move, revolve around it, they never crash down on it. Although we are reading this book motionless, the Earth rotates around its axis—at the Equator—at a speed of 1600 km/h, while the Earth revolves around the Sun at a speed of 30 km/s. We are constantly in motion. The Galaxy is adhered by gravitation and continual motion.

In its infinite conceitedness, humankind believed that the Earth was its empire. However, there are no miracles in the skies. Moreover, we do not even possess a prominent place in the universe, either. This fact was already familiar to Nicolaus Copernicus (1473–1543), the Polish scientist and monk.[34] The chance of human civilisation for survival decreased drastically by our days because of the existence of plentiful and various arsenals of weapons of mass destruction.[35] This risk is inconceivably enormous. By our days, it has become almost inevitable for humankind to expand into outer space.

Humankind, which has been building civilisation throughout over 40,000 generations,[36] has not confuted itself this time either: we have trashed even that place where we are heading. The 34,640 space objects weighing over 11,000 tons (exceeding the weight of the Eiffel-Tower) circling in outer space as space trash pose danger to human activities carried out in outer space.[37]

The finiteness of nutritive materials, clean fresh water and energy resources available on Earth necessary for the maintenance of the ecosystem has further reinforced the demand for the establishment of human bases on close celestial bodies and for the commencement of the exploitation of mineral resources found there. Consequently, we need a ‘second home’, which one day may be the Moon, the Mars, or Jupiter Europa, the fourth largest moon of Jupiter. Accordingly, the message of our first astronauts, setting foot on the Moon, left behind on the lunar module may assume more profound meaning: ‘We have arrived in peace on behalf of whole mankind’.[38]

The Outer Space Treaty settles the foundations of property relations, but it does not cover the exploitation and use of resources available in outer space. As a general principle, the exploration and use of outer space, including the Moon and other celestial bodies, shall be carried out for the benefit and in the interest of all countries,

[33] Tyson (2017), p. 45.

[34] Hawking (2005), pp. 4–5.

[35] Merely in our days altogether 13,082 nuclear weapons are registered officially in 9 States of the world. *World Nuclear Weapon Stockpile Report.* Ploughshares Fund, 31 August 2023.

[36] Sagan (1980), p. 365.

[37] ESA Space Debris Office: Space debris by the numbers (12 September 2023), (www.esa.int/Safety_Security/Space_Debris/Space_debris_by_the_numbers).

[38] Mailer (2010), pp. 266–267.

irrespective of their degree of economic or scientific development. Thus, all States without discrimination of any kind, on the basis of equality and in accordance with international law, may freely do research so that the work done there should be regarded as *the province of all mankind*.[39] However, in the course of exploration the interests of other States may not be violated, the work there may not be hindered, nor may experiments subverting the balance of nature be carried out.

The States advanced much further in the Moon Agreement (1979), namely, in addition to referring to the province of mankind, which favoured essentially the developed countries engaged actively in outer space exploration, they instituted a new legal formula advantageous for less developed countries as well: *the common heritage of mankind*.[40] Its scope includes the planets of the Solar System, except for the Earth, with all their treasures and the trajectories leading to and surrounding them. The objectives of the contracting Parties were to protect future generations and share the benefits obtained in outer space among all equally, that is, not to let natural resources be freely and selfishly exploited.[41]

The aviation industry has had a prominent role in the utilisation of the exceptional opportunities in outer space. The development of aviation and rocket technology has not only been the powerhouse of man in reaching outer space, but also its further guarantee. In the foreseeable future suborbital flights at higher altitudes and in outer space will open up new horizons before humankind.

2.2.6 Controlled and Uncontrolled Airspace

The airspace utilised for air traffic can be uniformly divided into *controlled* and *uncontrolled* airspaces. Uncontrolled airspace means basically any air traffic services airspace which is beyond controlled airspace. Wide-body and narrow-body aircraft[42]

---

[39] Outer Space Treaty (1963), Article I.

[40] *Agreement Governing the Activities of States on the Moon and Other Celestial Bodies,* UN RES 34/68, 1979. Article 11.

[41] As of today, merely 18 States have acceded to the Moon Agreement. What is the reason for underratification? It can be found in the legal institution of '*the common heritage of mankind*'. The legal institution may be magnanimous, but in fact it impedes future extracting and mining activities on the Moon or other celestial bodies, since it stipulates that the materials extracted on the Moon, the fructification of exploitation need to be shared under the guidance of an international organisation with other countries irrespective of their contribution to the success of the enterprise. This severely sets back the enterprising spirit, since the extractor is primarily interested in the profit. In addition, it may expect considerable expenditure by reason of adherence to the strict technical and safety regulations.

[42] According to ICAO, the following types are defined: (1) A *wide-body* aircraft is a large transport aircraft with internal cabin width sufficient for normal passenger seating to be divided into three axial groups by two aisles (in practice this means not less than 4.72 m); (2) A *narrow-body* aircraft is an aircraft having only one aisle in the cabin with passenger seating divided into two axial groups. ICAO Doc 9626 Manual on the Regulation of International Air Transport. Chap. 5.2, Aircraft, 3rd edn., 2018.

engaged in international commerce operate predominantly in controlled airspaces, if possible, whereas light or small air vehicles (we may think mainly of balloons, sailplanes and single- or two-engine aircraft) fly mostly in uncontrolled airspace. These types of airspaces are entirely dissimilar in their operation. In controlled airspace, air traffic control service is provided, which, by giving guidance clearances, and even instructions to the cockpit crew, guarantees the separation and safety of flights. For that purpose, the cockpit crew members [pilot-in-command (PIC) and first officer (FO)] are obliged to establish and maintain two-way radio communication and operate their on-board transponder equipment. However, in uncontrolled airspace, no air traffic control service, only flight information service is available in most cases. Consequently, the flight information service is not responsible for separation in the uncontrolled airspace, but by utilising its assistance and information, all pilots flying an aircraft bear responsibility for proper separation from the relevant traffic. In such airspaces, two-way radio communication and the use of transponder devices are not necessarily mandatory. Should an aircraft lack any of them, it can still comply with the rules, but these instruments contribute greatly to the safety of flight.

Controlled airspaces—where numerous air traffic control services carry out their duties[43] 24 h a day—are designated around busier airports and along air routes. In a controlled airspace, therefore, all air traffic falls under the supervision of an air navigation service provider, moreover, under the supervision of the air traffic control services. The safe flow of air traffic in controlled airspace is based on the rules of separation applied rigorously by the specialists of these services: the air traffic controllers. The purpose of separation is to prevent collision between aircraft, just as well as between taxiing aircraft and surface obstacles. We could also put it this way: the safety of aviation necessitates and is guaranteed by proper and constantly maintained spacing (separation based on distance or time) between two or more aircraft. The most important rule of the controllers' job is that they must always ensure a form of separation by the time the other one (any) is violated/lost.

Separation may be, on the one hand, *geographical* (two aircraft travel far from each other geographically, one, for example, in the airspace of Paris, the other one above Brussels), on the other hand, *vertical* or *horizontal* (Fig. 2.4).

Vertical separation is based on pre-determined distances between two aircraft, which are required to carry out flights safely. These values are pre-defined by vertical separation minima (VSM), which can be nominal 1000 feet (~300 m) below 8.8 km, and 2000 feet (~600 m) at and above a level of approx. 8.8 km in accordance with the principles of a reference system utilising calculations based on atmospheric pressure. The development of technical conditions (the intense improvement of the precision

[43] Commission Implementing Regulations (CIR) (EU) 2017/373, Part—Definitions 44, 'duty' means, any task that an air traffic controller is required to perform by the air traffic control service provider.

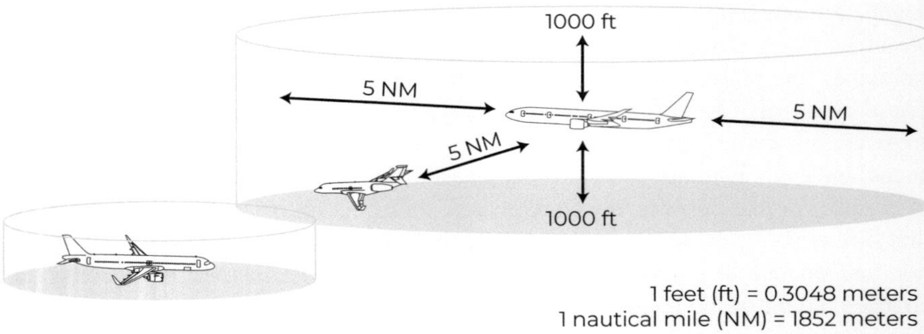

Fig. 2.4 Separation of air traffic in controlled airspace

of altitude measurement devices and their on-board application), as well as the rapid growth of the volume of air transport prompted the introduction of reduced vertical separation minima (RVSM), which further resulted in the designation of six new levels, hence an additional 20% increase in airspace capacity was achievable. Aircraft with suitable autopilot systems and altimeter as well as with appropriate authority certificates may travel in higher airspaces between FL290 (approx. 29,000 feet or 8.8 km) and FL410 (approx. 41,000 feet or 12.5 km) with a vertical separation of 1000 feet (approx. 300 m), which enhances the intensity of air traffic flow. The designated, obligatorily supervised flight levels available for aircraft are mandatory levels and the reference values provided to pilots have a certain degree of tolerance.[44]

Regarding *horizontal separation*, we differentiate three different categories, namely, lateral, longitudinal and radar separation. Air traffic controllers take care of maintaining these by carefully observing and calculating numerous factors such as time and distance. Turbulence separation represents a unique category among types of separation, when the minima are standardised/prescribed based on turbulence potentially rising.[45]

[44] In the case of VSM 300 feet (±91 m), while in the case of RVSM 200 feet (±61 m) diversion is permitted for aircraft as altitude tolerance limits.

[45] At the wings' outermost extremities, the higher-pressure air beneath is drawn toward the lower pressure air on top, resulting in a tight, circular flow that trails behind the aircraft like a pronged pair of sideways tornadoes. The vortices are most pronounced when a plane is slow and the wings are working hardest to produce lift. Thus, prime time for encountering them is during arrival or departure. As a rule, bigger planes brew up bigger, most virulent wakes, and smaller planes are more vulnerable. To avoid wake upsets, air traffic controllers are required to put extra spacing between large and small planes. Smith (2018), p. 38.

2.2.7 Restriction of National Airspace

Each contracting State may, for reasons of *military necessity* or public safety, *restrict* or *prohibit* uniformly the aircraft of other States from flying over certain areas of its territory provided that no distinction in this respect is made between the aircraft of the State whose territory is involved, engaged in international scheduled airline services and the aircraft of the other contracting States likewise engaged [Article 9 *a)*].

It is prerogative to the State to designate the airspace. National airspace means the airspace over the territory within the State borders. This is divided into airspace for air traffic and into special airspaces, which can be *restricted*, *temporary reserved*, *danger* and *prohibited areas*.

- Flights in a *restricted area* may enter only with the permission of the aviation authority, except for search and rescue, ambulance, air policing and air defence flights. Such restricted areas may also be designated for the purposes of environmental protection and nature conservation in the interest of protected species of birds or sensitive fauna.
- Flight in a *temporary reserved area* can be hazardous, where military (state) aircraft are engaged in activities which may pose a risk to aircraft not engaged in the activity. Therefore, during the announced operational hours, flight into such airspace is allowed only with the permission of the responsible services/units.
- Flights in *danger areas* (above artillery and infantry shooting ranges, parachute launch) imply great risk because activities posing actual threat to aircraft take place there. During the announced operational hours, flights engaged in the activity carried out in the danger area are admissible pursuant to the rules stipulated by law and with the permission of the service concerned. Within the timeframe, other flights may not enter the danger area (only with rare exceptions, in cases of emergency or urgent medical air transport/ambulance flight).
- In *prohibited areas*, air traffic is prohibited. These are generally designated above nuclear power plants, special objects, industrial facilities and research centres. Designations of 'such prohibited areas in the territory of a contracting State, as well as any subsequent alterations to them, shall be communicated as soon as possible to other contracting States and to the ICAO' [Article 9 *a)*] (Fig. 2.5).

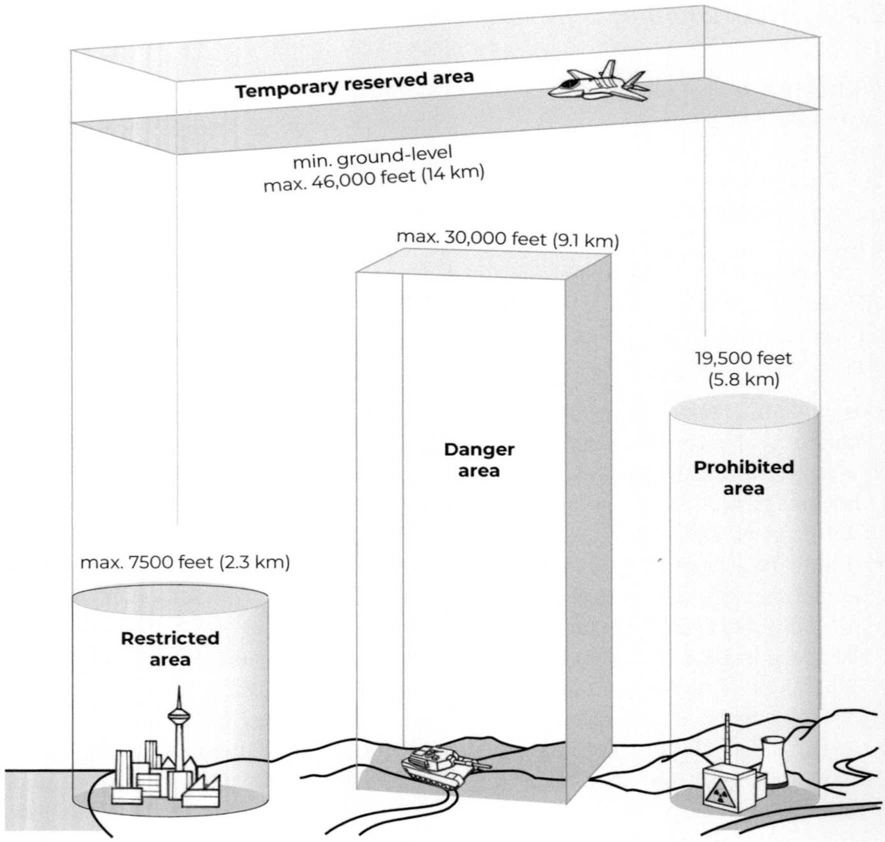

Fig. 2.5 Special airspaces

When we behold the skies, we do not think or even see that in fact we are looking at the secluded world of intersected, thematically delimited airspaces allocated into different provinces.

The restriction or prohibition in the national airspace affects all aircraft regardless of nationality. The restriction must not be discriminative against aircraft of another State; thus, parties should not make a distinction between their own registered aircraft or aircraft registered by other States performing international air services. (For example, they must not 'close down' part of the airspace for the sole purpose of making an aircraft spend a longer time in the airspace of the given State so that it should pay a higher route charge.[46] It is not admissible either that, in the airspace

[46] Air navigation charges must be paid by all the operators, who utilise the services of the air navigation service providers operating in the given airspace. The three groups of charges generated by air navigation services are (1) route, (2) terminal navigation and (3) communication charges. The

closed actually lawfully, the aircraft of the 'friendly' contracting State receives privileges, thus, in an unauthorised manner, although in possession of a permit, it can fly in a closed airspace, thereby, as opposed to the aircraft of other States, it travels on a shorter route more rapidly and economically.)

Each contracting State also reserves the right, in exceptional circumstances or during a period of emergency, or in the interest of public safety, and with immediate effect, to *restrict* or *prohibit* temporarily flying over the whole or any part of its territory (territorial waters) on condition that such a restriction or prohibition shall be applicable without distinction of nationality to aircraft of all other States [Article 9 *b)*].

A relevant example was the case of Eyjafjallajökull, an Icelandic volcano, which was an exceptional circumstance in civil aviation in April 2010. Due to the eruption, as the volcanic ash was spreading over the majority of Europe, most States in the region immediately prohibited air traffic in their national airspace in order to ensure the safety of aviation. The prohibition was quite reasonable because the volcanic ash composed vitreous volcanic particles, which rapidly erode and block the engines and other key instruments of the aircraft. During the 6 days of closure, at least ten million people were unable to travel and more than 100,000 flights were cancelled.[47]

In a temporarily reserved area, for instance, in order to isolate military training flights, the airspace is closed only up to a certain altitude, but above this airspace civil flights may travel freely. However, some airlines, in accordance with their internal operation manuals, do not fly above such airspaces; instead, they opt for longer routes, because they do not wish to expose their passengers to higher risk.

The Malaysian Airlines (MH) Flight 17 (registration number 9 M-RMD) on route from Amsterdam (AMS) to Kuala Lumpur (KUL) crashed due to a missile hit above Ukraine, 50 km from the Russian border on 17 July 2014, killing all persons on board. The perpetrators,[48] who used a Russian anti-aircraft missile system against a civil flight, violated the most fundamental principles of international law. The aircraft was flying over restricted airspace at an altitude of approx. 10 km (FL 330 that is 33,000 feet). In the spring of 2014, the ICAO, in a letter sent to the Member States and the United States

(continued)

route charge is calculated by the multiplication of three basic elements: the aircraft weight factor, the distance factor and the rate of the unit charge. Essentially, the longer the aircraft travels in the airspace, the heavier the body of the aircraft, multiplied by the unit charge, the more is paid for the service. EUROCONTROL Central Route Charges Office (CRCO) Customer Guide to Charges, February 2019, p. 8.

[47] Bisignani (2010).

[48] The Netherlands Public Prosecution Service initiated criminal procedures against the perpetrators. The Dutch Court found two Russians and one Ukrainian separatist guilty and sentenced them to life in prison on 17 November 2022. Dutch Safety Board: Crash of Malaysia Airlines (MH) Flight 17. The Hague, 13 October 2015, pp. 1–279; (www.prosecutionservice.nl/topics/mh17-plane-crash/prosecution-and-trial), (www.courtmh17.com/en).

Federal Aviation Administration (FAA), drew attention to the fact that an Eastern part of Ukrainian airspace, due to the escalating conflict, was not safe.[49] As a consequence, several countries' airlines avoided that airspace for safety reasons. However, not all airlines conformed, because they were willing to take advantage of the shorter route and the airspace at that altitude was still open. The representatives of Malaysia, Australia and the European countries at the 39th ICAO Assembly (2016), jointly initiated establishing a system supporting the avoidance of 'conflict zones', in which the operators and the air navigation service providers can share their experiences of concerned flights in due time with pilots and other participants travelling in the given region.[50]

'Each contracting State, under such regulations as it may prescribe, may require any aircraft entering the restricted or prohibited airspaces over its areas to effect a landing as soon as practicable thereafter at some designated airport within its territory' [Article 9 *c)*]. In the national airspace, the interest of public order (safety) and the defence of national security dictate that any aircraft may be intercepted—for the purpose of identification—and in certain, but lawful cases[51] might even be forced to land. After identification, the cockpit (flight deck) crew may continue their flight, otherwise they might either be diverted to leave the airspace or to land at a specified airport for further measures. The aircraft may be forced to land only in an exceptional case because it is a fundamental rule that civil aircraft may be intercepted only as a worst-case scenario. The intercepted aircraft must comply with the instructions or signal in all cases without delay. The cockpit crew has international responsibility and if they breach the rules, in a severe case, they may expect sanctions under criminal law. Nevertheless, the use of weapons must be avoided against in-flight civil aircraft disobeying the warning. Likewise, warning shots to call attention should also be avoided, since it may jeopardise the safety of the passengers, flight crew and the aircraft. The pilot-in-command of the intercepted civil aircraft must comply both with the instructions of the military unit and with the pilot of the interceptor aircraft regarding identification, diversion or landing. The pilot-in-command of the intercepted civil aircraft is obligated to follow the instructions of the proceeding military organisation and the pilot of the State aircraft related to identification, hold-on or landing. The

[49]FAA NOTAM—*Airspace Special Notice Ukraine,* FDC 4/7667 (A0012/14), 23 April 2014.

[50]Huyser (2016), pp. 5–7.; ICAO Assembly, 39th Session Working Paper, A39–WP/108TE/32, 19/8/2016.

[51]See, on 23 May 2021, Ryanair Flight 4978 en-route from Athens (ATH) to Vilnius (VNO) was diverted to Minsk Airport (MSQ) in Belarus while passing through the airspace of the Republic of Belarus. The official reason was a false bomb threat email, but after the forced landing one of the passengers was arrested for political reasons. Event Involving Ryanair Flight FR4978 in Belarus Airspace on 23 May 2021. Report of the ICAO Fact-Finding Investigation, July 2022, pp. 1–96 (www.icao.int/Security/Documents/Ryanair).

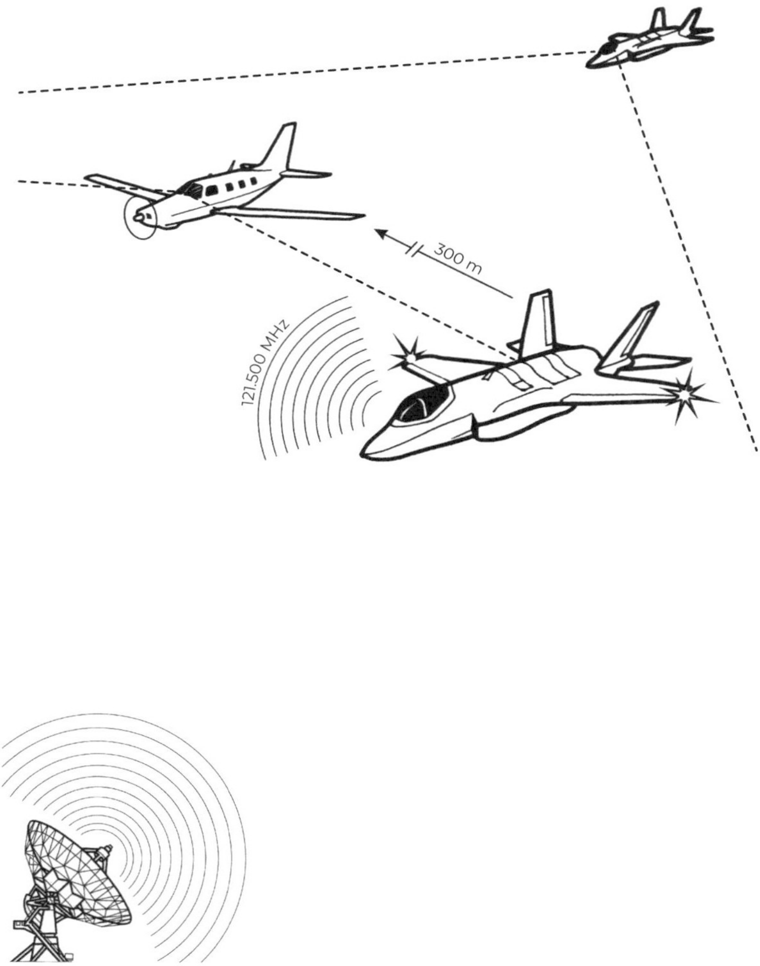

Fig. 2.6 The interception of a civil aircraft

instructions and measures for the civil aircraft must be issued primarily by the concerned air traffic services. Beyond this, the pilot-in-command of the intercepted civil aircraft is obligated to make an attempt at the establishment of two-way communication with the interceptor or with the intercepting control unit via general call on the emergency frequency at 121.500 MHz (Fig. 2.6).[52]

[52]The Commission Implementing Regulations (EU) No 923/2012—laying down the common rules of the air and operational provisions regarding services and procedures in air navigation. L 281/1, 13 October 2012.

If air traffic services notice that the aircraft is flying (in controlled airspace) by violating the rules, civil and military (air traffic) controllers intervene in cooperation (and enforce coercive measures). The air traffic service establishes connection at the available frequencies. The pilot of the interceptor communicates the instructions to the pilot of the intercepted aircraft. The additional fighter plane is positioned behind the intercepted aircraft since the pilot needs to react to any aggressive or non-compliant activity or escape manoeuvre of the intercepted plane immediately. To ensure the interception, the leading fighter plane performs the identification. The distance between the leading plane and the intercepted aircraft is approx. 300 m. In this first phase the leading fighter plane approaches the intercepted aircraft so that its pilot may clearly see the interceptor generally on the left, slightly above at a distance of 300 m.[53]

The interception of civil aircraft is governed by pertinent regulations and administrative directives issued by the contracting States in compliance with the Convention, particularly with Article 3 *d*), under which the contracting States undertake, when issuing regulations for their State aircraft, to have due regard for the safety of the navigation of civil aircraft.[54]

Due to the dangerous nature of interceptions, ICAO developed principles for the Member States to facilitate uniform and efficient national regulations and directives in this field:

(a) 'interception of civil aircraft will be undertaken only as a last resort;
(b) if undertaken, an interception will be limited to determining the identity of the aircraft, unless it is necessary to return the aircraft to its planned track, direct it beyond the boundaries of national airspace, guide it away from a prohibited, restricted or danger area or instruct it to effect a landing at a designated aerodrome;
(c) practice interception of civil aircraft will not be undertaken;
(d) navigational guidance and related information will be given to an intercepted aircraft by radiotelephony, whenever radio contact can be established; and,
(e) in the case where an intercepted civil aircraft is required to land in the territory overflown, the aerodrome designated for the landing is to be suitable for the safe landing of the aircraft type concerned'.[55]

All pilots are responsible for the rule: 'Aviate, Navigate, and Communicate' [see, Part I, Chap. 2. 4.1]. In international aviation during air navigation control verbal communication takes place 'in the world-language of aviation', that is, in English all over the world. When at the dawn of aviation, a choice needed to be made, English language dominated, since English-speakers were in majority [obviously it was impossible on a flight from Amsterdam (AMS) to Jakarta (CGK) to speak to every air traffic controller in their own language]. In the 1950s, English language became universally international although this practice has not been regulated officially under an international treaty until today. Moreover, the official languages of the United Nations and the ICAO itself as a specialised agency of the UN are English,

[53] ICAO Annex 2 on Rules of the Air. Chap. 3, 3.8, Appendix 2 and Attachment A.

[54] Idem., Chap. 3, 8.1.

[55] Idem., Appendix 2, 1.1.

French, Spanish, Russian, Arabic and Chinese.[56] This means that all of them are the official languages of civil aviation, but they were not adopted at the same time,[57] and, as safety is the utmost priority, the need for the communication of information in one language predominated, so the English language has become prevalent. English therefore became the 'lingua franca' of commercial aviation and professionals are required to speak it all over the world. Currently, thanks to local dialects, dozens of versions of English are differentiated, which involves further risks.[58] Therefore, all pilots and air traffic controllers need to have basic communication skills and need to be familiar with the professional vocabulary of aviation both in their own language and in English.[59]

The flight crew and the ground staff use the English 'phonetic alphabet', that is, the uniform English aviation language for communication during flight. The common language is vital in aviation. The introduction of phonetic alphabet was necessary because the standard expressions are short, which is crucial with respect to the increasing traffic. In addition, the well-formulated messages transmit the information more precisely by leaving no place for misunderstandings. Standard expressions reduce the risk of mixing up words with similar pronunciation. The English phony is a descriptive language containing special expressions and formulation rules. The requirements are strict, because a considerable part of accidents are a result of human errors.[60] Numerous incidents may be traced back obviously to incorrect English. Therefore, while speaking, if names, abbreviations or acronyms (registration mark, ICAO-codes of airports, waypoints, the navigation aids) with dubious spelling need to be spelled, communication has to take place in accordance with the ICAO 'phonetic alphabet'. It is very important to use the phony correctly, since the communicated information and instructions greatly affect safe operation and efficient control of air traffic.

---

[56] The text of the Chicago Convention was drafted in English. At the same time, the equally authentic versions in French and Spanish languages were opened for signature in Washington, D.C. Chicago Convention, Chap. XXII, Signature of Convention.

[57] ICAO Doc 8876 International Conference on the Authentic Trilingual Text of the Convention on International Civil Aviation (1944); Protocol on the Authentic Trilingual Text of the Convention on International Civil Aviation. Buenos Aires, September 1968; ICAO Doc 9208 Protocol Relating to an Amendment to the Convention on International Civil Aviation (Final Clause Russian Text); ICAO Doc 9664 Protocol Relating to an Amendment to the Convention on International Civil Aviation (Final Clause Arabic Text); ICAO Doc 9722 Protocol Relating to an Amendment to the Convention on International Civil Aviation (Final Clause Chinese Text).

[58] Boschen and Jones (2004), pp. 291–299.

[59] Jones (2003), pp. 233–248.

[60] According to the Federal Aviation Administration (FAA) Report, nearly 70% of the 'commercial' aviation accidents occurring between 1990 and 2002 were associated with some manners of cockpit crew or supervisory errors. However, the percentages differed slightly when air carrier (45%) and commuter (75%) aviation accidents were considered separately. The errors can be: decision errors, skill-based errors and perceptual errors. FAA Final Report: Human Error and Commercial Aviation Accidents: A Comprehensive, Fine-Grained Analysis Using HFACS. DOT/FAA/AM–06/18, Office of Aerospace Medicine, Washington, D. C. 20591. July 2006, pp. 2–3, 12 (www.faa.gov/data_research/research/med_humanfacs/oamtechreports/2000s/media/200618.pdf).

A—Alfa	N—November
B—Bravo	O—Oscar
C—Charlie	P—Papa
D—Delta	Q—Quebec
E—Echo	R—Romeo
F—Foxtrot	S—Sierra
G—Golf	T—Tango
H—Hotel	U—Uniform
I—India	V—Victor
J—Juliett	W—Whiskey
K—Kilo	X—X-ray
L—Lima	Y—Yankee
M—Mike	Z—Zulu

Interestingly, for the communication of letter F, the word Fox, while for letter Q, the word Queen were initially used. However, at the initiative of the British Government this rule was changed because upon the connection of F and Q, this expression was rightfully considered to be offensive for the British Queen.[61]

In case the intercepted civil aircraft must be forced to land, the designated airport needs to be suitable for the safe landing of the given type of aircraft. In order to eliminate or decrease the dangers of interception, close coordination between the interceptor cockpit crew and the control units is necessary; furthermore, during the proceedings while flying in close formation with the aircraft using the airspace unlawfully, the cooperation of civil navigation and military services needs to be established by all means.[62]

In 1961, the war of independence fought by Algeria was approaching its end. The French established a 60 km wide Air Defence Identification Zone (ADIZ) off the Algerian coast and unilaterally declared that flying in the determined airspace was prohibited. On 9 February 1961, the IL–18-type civil aircraft, on board with the President (Head of State) of the Soviet Union, on his way to Morocco flew into the airspace unilaterally prohibited by the French. Immediately three

(continued)

[61] Prof. Jean-Paul (Université de Montréal) worked on the problem (between 1948 and 1949) in collaboration with the ICAO Language Section. After those studies, consultations with communications experts and comments from all of ICAO's Member Governments, a new ICAO alphabet was adopted and incorporated in the Aeronautical Telecommunications Annex 10 for implementation as of 1 November 1951 in civil aviation. The new spelling alphabet was based on the following criteria: (1) A word could only be considered if it was a live word in each of the three working languages and had a similar spelling in English, French, and Spanish; (2) It had to be easily pronounced and recognised by airmen of all languages, clearly transmissible by radio and easy to read; (3) A chosen word could not have any negative meaning or association (www.applications.icao.int/postalhistory/annex_10_aeronautical_telecommunications.htm).

[62] In compliance with the international Standards determined under Annex 2 to the Chicago Convention on Rules of the Air, the Member States need to elaborate in detail and implement the proceedings in their national laws. Annex 2 contains only Standards!

Vautour-type fighter jets intercepted the airplane and established radio contact by two warning calls on the emergency frequency. In the meantime, one of the fighter jets shot a short series of tracer bullets in front of the civil airplane, thereby compelling it to leave the prohibited zone without delay.

In connection with the case, we may set forth as a fact that the Soviet airplane was flying above the high seas, where all States are allowed to fly over freely. This right may not be restricted by the States. The Convention stipulates that prohibited areas shall be of reasonable extent and location so as not to interfere unnecessarily with air navigation [Article 9 *a*)]. The French made a mistake not by driving out the airplane from the prohibited zone designated by them unilaterally over the high seas, because thereby they protected the airplane, but they violated the law by interpreting the rules of interception peculiarly. As the Soviet leadership in its protesting letter to the French Government formulated: 'How long has it been customary law that the identification of the aircraft is accompanied by opening with a broadside fire?'[63]

2.2.8 Extension of the National Airspace for Identification Reasons

One can reasonably ask then, how could coastal States lawfully defend themselves against attacks coming from the high seas? The latest versions of passenger or cargo airplanes with an average indicated airspeed of 900 km/h, fly over territorial waters with a range of 12 nautical miles in just 90 s. Obviously, in such cases there is insufficient time for actual and effective defence. With regard to air policing, in order to guarantee the highest level of defence achievable in national airspaces, coastal States exercise policing rights to flights in the international airspace.

After World War II, being the first as such in the world, the United States established its Air Defence Identification Zone (ADIZ) near the coasts of Alaska with an extension of 380 nautical miles for national security reasons citing the right of individual and collective self-defence.[64] The ADIZ is essentially a transitional zone, an extension of the boundary of the national airspace unilaterally by the State[65] to 200 nautical miles measured from the coast, which is an intermediary concept on the boundary of the international and national airspace not prohibited by international law. The ADIZ is demarcated primarily over territories, where an extended water surface stretches close to the coasts of the sovereign State. At the same time, it

[63] Plane Attack Shocks Moscow. *Miami News*, February 10, 1961. p. 1.; French Try to Shoot the Red Anger. *Miami News*, 11 February 1961, p. 1 (www.ipfs.io).

[64] United Nations Charter (1945), Article 51.

[65] In its general character, the unilateral legal act by the State is a declaration of intent, which aims to give rise to legal effect on an international basis. The legal binding force of the unilateral act is based on the principle of good faith and the according purpose of the State prescribing it, as long as it is issued clearly and intelligibly.

is necessary to emphasise that the State does not exercise in the airspace above the concerned high seas a claim for sovereignty; it merely asserts its demand for the right of surveillance and identification.[66] This means that a State cannot arrogate territorial sovereignty over the ADIZ to itself by any means, nor can it interfere with another State's exercise of legitimate rights to navigate over the high seas.[67] The exercise of the specific rights in the ADIZ, beyond the aspects of national defence, increases the safety of the airspace by decreasing the possibility of collision in the air. Furthermore, it may support search and rescue, while it renders air traffic in the airspace of the high seas more predictable and foreseeable strategically. No international convention has been drafted for the air defence identification zones. Thus, the applicable rules are unilaterally established by the States with adherence to the relevant national and international norms.

At the same time, the question arises: to what extent is the identification zone of national air defence established by the unilateral act of the nation compliant with international law and lawful with respect to freedom of aviation over the high seas? The international legal basis of the extension is that the State, on grounds of aviation security and self-defence, is authorised to prescribe obligations unilaterally concerning aircraft entering its national airspace. This requirement obliges the cockpit crew to identify the aircraft upon its entrance into the ADIZ. At the same time, the extension is not legally substantiated if the pilot does not intend to fly into the national airspace, to fly over the territory of the State or land thereon. In this case, the pilot is not obligated to follow the ADIZ requirements, since only those who intend to fly into the national airspace need to identify themselves.[68]

The legitimacy of ADIZ was particularly justified by the tragic terrorist attacks of 11 September 2001 committed by civil airplanes against the United States. The flights operated in domestic traffic in the national airspace, did not arrive from the high seas. Nevertheless, by reason of the method of commission the tragic event had direct effect on the process of the world-scale formation of ADIZ. Because of the terrorist attack committed in times of peace, causing the death of 2977 and later of even more innocent people, the United States prescribes far stricter identification rules than the above for all aircraft entering and flying in its ADIZ. In the zone of 200 miles measured from the coastline of the United States (which ranges to 400 miles off the coast of California) exclusively those civil aircraft may fly which have identified themselves according to the rule irrespective of whether their destination is in the territory of the United States or another country.

With different requirements, guided by national interests, an increasing number of countries have established their own air defence identification zones.[69]

---

[66] Butler, Richard J.: Sovereignty and Protective Zones in Space and Appropriate Command and Control of Assets. *Research Report*, AU/ACSC/034/04, 2001, p. 15.

[67] Abeyratne (2014), p. 39.

[68] Schmitt (2010), p. 307.

[69] ADIZ (Air Defence Identification Zone) zones have been demarcated among others by China, Taiwan, Russia, Canada, India, Pakistan, Japan, Vietnam, South-Korea, North-Korea, Sweden, Norway and Great-Britain.

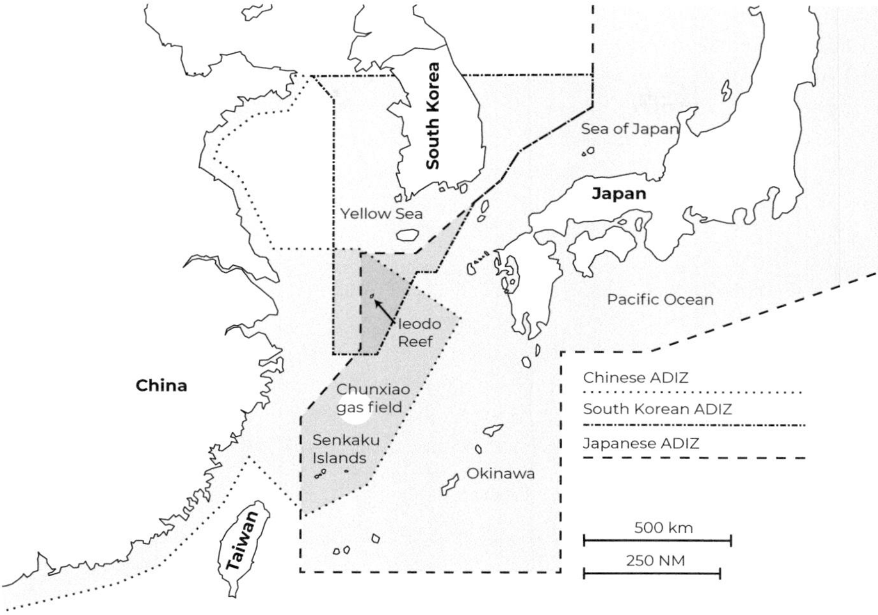

Fig. 2.7 The ADIZ zones of China, South-Korea and Japan

As the chart illustrates, the Chinese and Japanese ADIZ zones overlap above the Senkaku Islands and the Chunxiao Gas Field, which are supplemented by the ADIZ of South-Korea at the Ieodo bottom-rock. This division is the origin of the territorial conflicts between the countries in the region (Fig. 2.7).

It is the elementary interest of each State that international relations are secured above the high seas in the international airspace. During their flight, civil or State aircraft operating above the high seas may not violate the territorial sovereignty of other States by any chance. Namely, the countries with territorial seas are not deprived of their weapons—they are authorised to use them (Fig. 2.8).

On 1 April 2001, a Lockheed EP-3E (Aries II) reconnaissance plane of the American Navy collided with a Shenyang J-8II interceptor made in China, as a consequence of which the Chinese aircraft fell into the sea and the pilot lost his life. The grave accident could ensue because the Chinese pilot of the fighter jet approached the reconnaissance plane dangerously with a specifically construed interception, by 'chasing away' in a so-called 'Top Gun style' (within 3 m). The unarmed plane, which was hard to manoeuvre, became entangled with the fighter plane of the Chinese pilot, which crashed, while the four-engine American military airplane made an emergency landing on a military

(continued)

airfield on the Chinese Hainan Island. The case occurred to the south of Hainan Island, at a distance of 65 nautical miles from the coastline, in international airspace.[70]

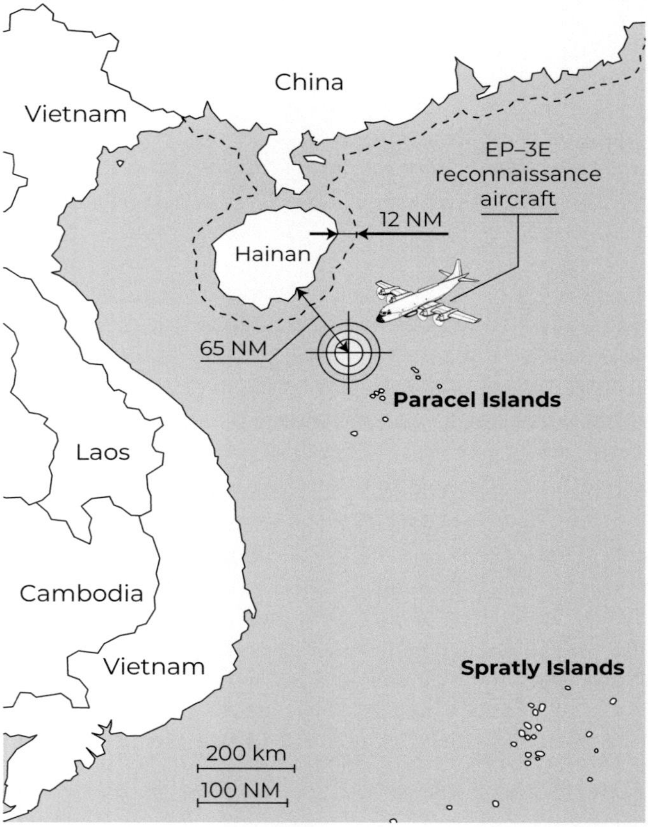

Fig. 2.8 The military incident near Hainan Island (2001)

[70] *CRS Report for Congress: China-US Aircraft Collision Incident of April 2001: Assessments and Policy Implications.* Order Code RL30946, 10 October 2001, pp. 1–21.

The Chinese Government in its diplomatic memorandum made immediate reference to an intrusion into the Chinese airspace without permission. It found two legal grounds for the allegation that the territorial sovereignty of China had been violated by the American military aircraft.

- In its justification, the Chinese Government stated that it recognises the Spratly and Paracel Islands in the South China Sea as its own territory; therefore, the boundary of 12 nautical miles away needs to be measured from these islands, thus, the American military plane had violated the Chinese national airspace.

However, the legal fate of the above-mentioned islands is dubious, since the right of control over the mostly uninhabited islands with exploitable mineral resources and an abundant stock of fish had been disputed for a long time by several States in the region (e.g., Taiwan, Vietnam, the Philippines and Malaysia). Therefore, China could not enforce its territorial sovereignty officially.[71]

- Furthermore, in its justification, the Chinese Government also highlighted that its right of control over its national airspace extends to the boundary of the exclusive economic zone ranging to 200 nautical miles measured from the mainland, which is recognised as maritime State territory under the UN Convention on the Law of the Sea (1982).[72]

However, the Chinese Government had not declared the unilateral establishment of its air defence identification zone before the incident; this had not ensued before 2013. Thus, in the absence of the Chinese ADIZ, the Convention on the Law of the Sea had to be observed, according to which, in the exclusive economic zone, the coastal State is authorised for the exploitation of the natural resources of the seabed and for fishing there, but not for the domination of the airspace. This zone, with a width of 200 nautical miles, consists of the territorial sea of 12 nautical miles qualifying as State territory and 188 nautical miles of sea not qualifying as State territory, over which, since its airspace is international, all parties can freely pass. It is notable that the United States, although it is one of the greatest maritime powers, is not a party to the Convention on the Law of the Sea. It merely assumed the obligation to observe its prescriptions while conforming to international customary law.[73]

---

[71] On 26 May 2015, the Chinese Government issued its strategic 'White Book', in which it stated that it prioritised defence on the high seas instead of on territorial seas. In this text, China emphasised that 'from the viewpoint of sovereignty, Chinese developments and constructions on its islands do not differ from the constructions in the domestic areas of the country'; furthermore, it pointed out that 'interference with affairs related to the southern seas by external parties qualifies as being provocative'. The fate of the islands is a source of grave tension in the region; in addition, China commenced large-scale construction and the establishment of a new airfield on the disputed Spratly Islands. In May 2015, the patrol flight of the American Navy with a CNN crew on board flew over the construction, while the Chinese party demanded several times that the airplane violating its airspace left. China's Military Strategy. Xinhua, 26 May 2015 (www.china.org.cn/china/2015-05/26/content.35661433).

[72] *Supra* note 9.

[73] Malone (1983), pp. 29–36.

After landing, the American airplane was 'tampered with' by the Chinese, to quote the words of President George W. Bush.[74] The Chinese did so despite the rule that they were not authorised to enter the American military aircraft without permission, because during peacetime its board is regarded as quasi State territory; hence, it is subject to United States jurisdiction. However, the general rules of international law do not always prevail. Therefore, probably relying on general experience, the 23 American flight crew members attempted to destroy or disable everything of military value during the landing, so that they should not fall into unauthorised hands. The aircraft was inspected with meticulous care by the Chinese, who later returned the military plane with some parts missing, thereby breaching international law. The detained flight crew in compliance with the prescriptions of international law was released.[75]

The Chinese Party suffering loss did not manage to justify its standpoint via the peculiar interpretation of the rules of the law of the sea. At the same time, it could not refer to the rules of the Chicago Convention either because the Convention is not applicable to State (military) aircraft.

2.3 Aircraft

In the provisions of the Convention, we cannot find the conceptual circumscription of aircraft. However, Annex 7 to the Convention on Aircraft Nationality and Registration Marks contains a punctual definition: 'an aircraft is any machine that can derive support in the atmosphere from the reactions of the air other than the reactions of the air against the earth's surface'.[76] This reaction:

- derives from the aerodynamic lift in the case of aircraft *heavier than air*, since these aircraft gain lift primarily from aerodynamic forces during flight;
- in the case of aircraft *lighter than air* derives from the difference in relative density since the lift of the air holds these aircraft in the air.

The concept of *aircraft* is broad, which besides the wide- and narrow-body passenger airplanes includes helicopters, balloons, airships, gliders and even paper kites. It follows from the former definition that all airplanes are aircraft, but not all aircraft are airplanes (Fig. 2.9).

In November 1967, the ICAO Council made a decision that aircraft do not include hovercraft planing boats; therefore, the rules on the law of the sea pertain to this vehicle (although not all Member States agreed with this decision).[77] The ekranoplan (ground-effect vehicle), which is a transition between hovercraft planing boats and

---

[74] Kukis and Arms (2001).

[75] Sipos (2018), pp. 141–172.

[76] ICAO Annex 7 on Aircraft Nationality and Registration Marks. 6th edn., July 2012.

[77] Cheng and Austin (1973), p. 183.

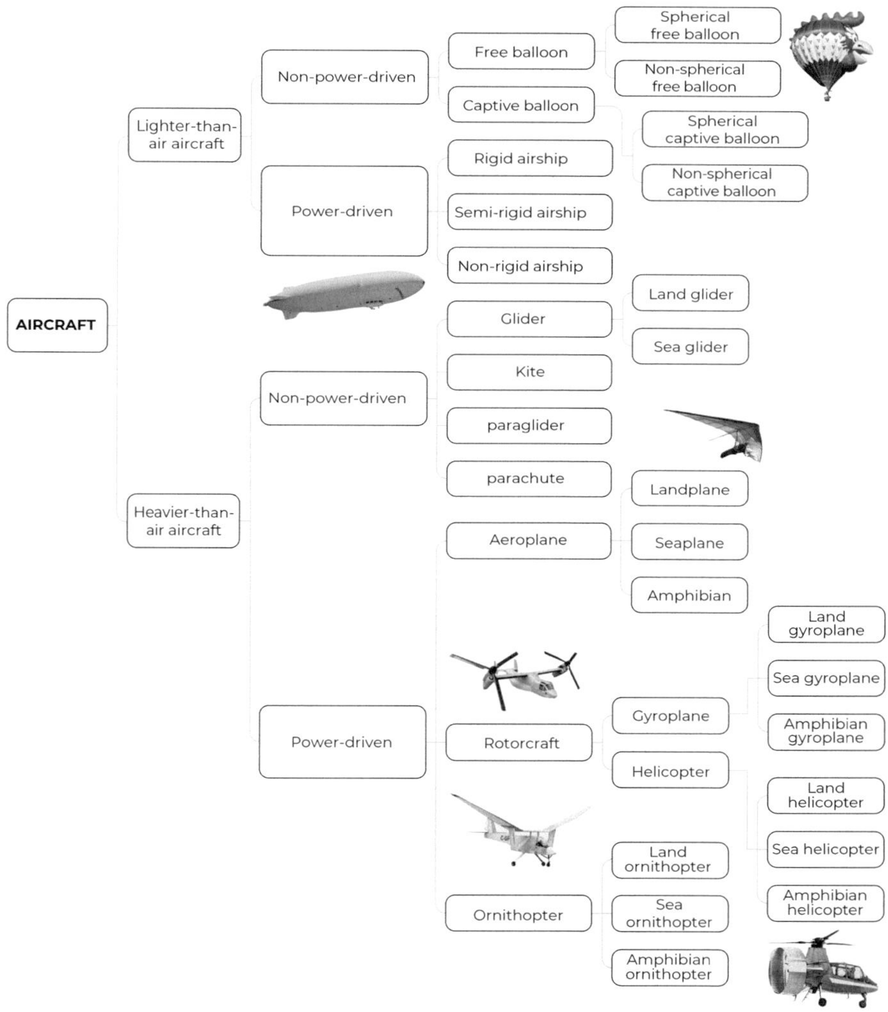

Fig. 2.9 Systematisation of aircraft

airplanes, also qualifies as ship according to the UN specialised agency, the International Maritime Organization (IMO). The space shuttle does not qualify as aircraft upon ascent either, since it travels with rocket propulsion when it leaves the surface of the Earth, but upon descent it behaves like an aircraft, since it touches down *in interaction with the air*.[78] Despite this, the States do not qualify the space shuttle returning from outer space as aircraft, since it is registered as a space object.

---

[78] Lachs (1964), p. 55.

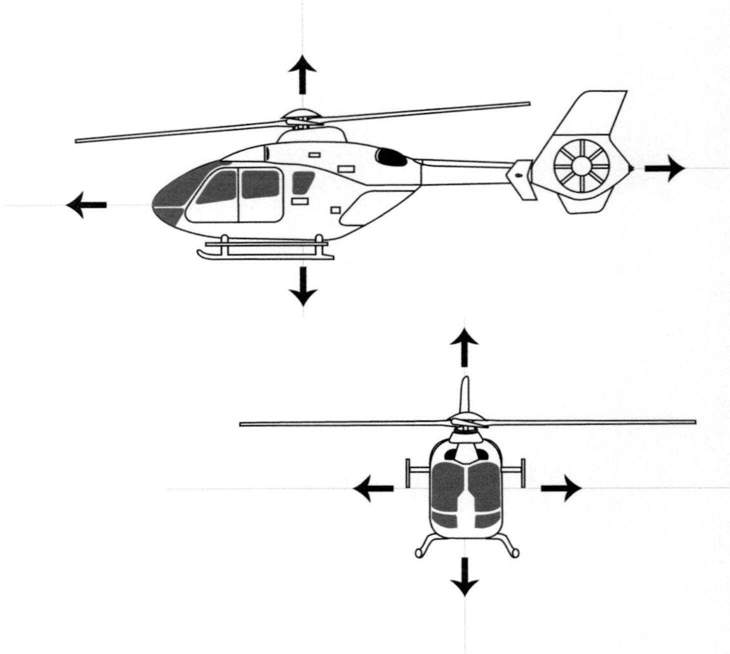

Fig. 2.10 The directions of the flight of the helicopter

Of the aircraft indicated in the figure primarily airplanes (with fixed wings) and helicopters (rotary-winged) have significance in international civil aviation (the transport of passengers and goods). While the *airplane* is a power-driven heavier-than-air aircraft deriving its lift in flight chiefly from aerodynamic reactions on surfaces which remain fixed under given conditions of flight,[79] the *helicopter* is a heavier-than-air aircraft supported in flight chiefly by the reactions of the air on one or more power-driven rotors fixed generally on the vertical axis. Helicopters increasingly tend to gain ground, namely in addition to the forms of flying considered traditional, helicopters are capable of autonomous vertical ascent and descent, hovering above one point, moving sideways in any direction and backwards owing to their rotary wings moved by the built-in power machine (Fig. 2.10). Helicopters can land almost anywhere if a relatively flat and obstacle-free field is available. A useful capacity of the helicopter to be highlighted is autorotation, which (in the case of ideal circumstances) facilitates injury-free landing if, for example, the engine is out-of-order.[80] Although the effective range of helicopters is heavily

[79] ICAO Annex 6 on Operation of *Aircraft. Part I-IV. 12th edn., 2022.*

[80] During the descent of helicopters, the streaming air provides the energy necessary for overcoming the aerodynamic resistance of the blades and rotating them. With the participation of the pilot, the helicopter loses altitude under controlled circumstances and the recovered energy is expended on the rotation of the blades, thereby, the aircraft remains controllable. Nagy (2017), p. 48.

limited due to their weight and weather circumstances, besides transportation they also have a significant role in search-rescue, fire extinction, and other operations which support special activities (e.g., oil rigs, medical air service, search and rescue, military missions, etc.).

The helicopter as an aircraft is increasingly widespread in modern air transport, which is due to its all-directional movement in three dimensions as opposed to aircraft with fixed wings.

Unmanned aircraft have not been listed in the chart separately because all the aircraft listed could well be unmanned.

2.3.1 Unmanned Aerial Vehicles

'No aircraft capable of being flown without a pilot shall be flown without a pilot over the territory of a contracting State *without special authorization by that State* and *in accordance with the terms of such authorization*' (Article 8). Already during World War II, several States utilised aircraft which could fly without flight deck crew. Thus, it is not inadvertent that the Convention addresses this issue. The development of unmanned flights is closely related to military applications, because it is generally true that wars and armed conflicts are the main driving force of research and development related to airplanes and other technical devices. As early as in the mid-eighteenth century, the military forces of the Habsburg Empire used balloons without crew for the bombardment of Venice. Their engine-driven successors, the unmanned airplanes appeared in World War I. One of the most familiar unmanned robot-airplanes of World War II was the aerial vehicle with rocket propulsion developed by the Germans, manufactured on a large scale and utilised in attacks with the name Vengeance Weapon (V-1). After the second cataclysm, the plans targeting the development of unmanned aircraft abated and the aerial robots were applied primarily in military exercises for the simulation of air targets. During the Cold War, they were used as reconnaissance and surveillance devices.

For example, in the nuclear experiments conducted at the Bikini Islands, unmanned surveillance airplanes equipped with registering devices and sensors were applied, which returned intactly from the area of the explosion with fatal radioactive radiation to the base at a distance of 350 km. The Bikini Atoll (a group of islands consisting of coral reefs) is an area of 8.8 sq.km at the Marshall Islands consisting of 23 islands, on which between 1946–1958 the United States exploded 23 nuclear and hydrogen bombs. The Bikini Islands were the scene of the first explosion of the hydrogen bomb, developed by Ede Teller (1908–2003) of Hungarian origin, which was released from an American military (State) aircraft in 1956.

The armed conflicts of the 1980s and 1990s triggered the truly speedy development of this device, and now it is curiosity if a type of unmanned aerial vehicle does not appear in the armed forces of a country.

The spectacular introduction of unmanned civil aircraft ensued with the first transatlantic *robot*-controlled *flight* on 22 September 1947. A converted four-engine Skymaster (DC-4) of the Douglas C-54 type passenger airplane, apart from the ascent and descent phases of the route, flew without direct human interference and interruption from the United States to England.[81] The technology became increasingly widespread, and unmanned aerial vehicles (UAVs), in need of aerodynamic forces for their flight, utilisable once or several times, have reached the level of development where they can carry out certain tasks more efficiently and safely than traditional airplanes. Aerial robots with remote control, programmed self-control or combined control have been transplanted from military application into civil use in manifold ways. Currently, they already control motorway traffic and monitor water levels and borders, but they also provide help in plant conservation and archaeological research. As a result of the remarkable spread of UAVs, detailed international and national regulation has become inevitable.[82]

'Each contracting State undertakes to ensure that the flight of such aircraft without a pilot in regions open to civil aircraft shall be so controlled as to obviate danger to civil aircraft' (Article 8). The objective of the contracting States was to secure the undisturbed international traffic of civil aircraft. Since the Convention is applicable to international civil flights, ICAO only provides for the operation of unmanned aerial vehicles with regulatory competence if they fly over the territory of another contracting State. However, the revolutionary spread of technology requires more detailed legal regulation on an international level. Therefore, ICAO needs to determine[83] the minimum operational conditions of unmanned aircraft systems (UAS), as they include the unmanned aerial vehicle as well as the environment

[81] The US Air Force C-54 aircraft was navigated by robot equipment with the help of radio remote control from Newfoundland to England [from Stephenville to Oxfordshire (2400 miles) with one stop in Prestwick]. 11 persons were flying on the plane for a case of emergency and control, but no physical intervention was necessary. However, there had been former experiments. From the mid-1930s several successful flights had taken place, one of the milestones of which had been the flight over the ocean. At that time, technological development had already facilitated the remote control of other flying airplanes from a closely flying airplane. Leviero, Anthony: Robot-Piloted Plane Makes Safe Crossing of Atlantic. *The New York Times*, 23 September 1947 (front page) (www.rarenewspapers.com/view/604613).

[82] Commission Implementing Regulation (EU) 2019/947 of 24 May 2019 on the rules and procedures for the operation of unmanned aircraft. C/2019/3824, OJ L 152, 11.6.2019, pp. 45–71.

[83] ICAO commenced the elaboration of the regulatory environment internationally and issued its circular note no. Cir 328–AN/190 on 11 March 2011. In February 2015, ICAO published its Manual on Remotely Piloted Aircraft Systems (RPAS), which prescribes the skeleton rules and procedural methods of further developed areas of the application of Unmanned Aerial Vehicles. At the 39th ICAO Assembly (2016), ICAO undertook the elaboration of a global regulation besides considering the regulations of the Member States.

ICAO Doc 10019 Manual on Remotely Piloted Aircraft Systems (RPAS), AN/507, 1st edn., 2015.

securing the operation of the technology: the ground control station, the communication channels, the technical preparatory and maintenance systems, the persons securing the launch and return as well as the commanding, controlling and servicing of the system itself. Within this, of remotely piloted aircraft systems (RPAS) widespread in civil use, their marking and registration, the licences necessary for their operation, the qualification of the operator, the sphere of application and the issue of aviation liability and insurance need to be regulated.[84]

2.3.2 Civil and State Aircraft

The contracting States formulate distinctly and definitively *(expressis verbis)* concerning the applicability of the Convention when they stipulate: 'The Convention *shall be applicable only to civil aircraft,* and *shall not be applicable to State aircraft*' (Article 3). Despite the importance of the distinction, the concept of civil aircraft is not defined clearly under the Convention. Instead, the Convention enumerates the examples for what qualifies as State aircraft during attendance to the functions of the State executive power *(acta iure imperii)*: 'Aircraft used in military, customs and police services shall be deemed to be State aircraft' [Article 3 *b)*]. As this enumeration is not exhaustive, the category of State aircraft also encompasses aircraft engaged in search-rescue, aerial rescue operations, humanitarian aid shipment, attendance to the national aerial survey-cartographic tasks and special tasks, for example, shipping prisoners, refugees and State leaders, as well as aircraft of the International Red Cross[85] and the Coast Guard.

The clear distinction between civil and State aircraft has significance. The most important difference is that State aircraft are governed by the internal rules of national law, not by the rules of the Convention. Another main aspect of the distinction is the difference proceeding from legal and administrative requirements, which manifests itself in different licensing processes and operational procedures.

State aircraft are registered by the military aviation authority, whereas civil aircraft are registered by the civilian aviation authority. It is essential to emphasise that the differentiation of State and civil airplanes itself is not reduced to the registration of aircraft (e.g., civil aircraft are obligated to carry registration marks,

[84] Palik (2012), p. 486.

[85] The medical aircraft of the International Red Cross generally operate under military use. In times of peace they carry out tasks of flying on the basis of military procedures and rules. However, there are civil Red Cross aircraft, to which the rules of the Convention are applicable, but in the case of war these aircraft are not under special protection. [Geneva Convention for the Amelioration of the Condition of the Wounded and Sick in Armed Forces in the Field (Geneva Convention I of 1949, Articles 36–37); Geneva Convention for the Amelioration of the Condition of Wounded and Sick and Shipwrecked Members of Armed Forces at Sea (Geneva Convention II of 1949, Articles 39–40); Geneva Convention Relative to the Protection of Civilian Persons in Time of War (Geneva Convention IV of 1949, Article 22).]

whereas military planes carry board identification signs), or to their property registry status or technical features, but their distinction is related to the objective of the given activity and its implementation. On the basis of functionality, the aircraft is categorised primarily according to the service it provides, to the task to be implemented. Therefore, several aspects need to be examined:

- what is the objective of the flight; what kind of flight crew (civilian or military) carries out the operation of the flight; on the basis of what flight plan and licences is the flight carried out and what kind of persons/objects are transported by the aircraft?

For example, if the pilot-in-command of the civil airplane carries *strictly classified* or *confidential* diplomatic baggage on behalf of the State, on the strength of this fact it will not be qualified as State aircraft. Diplomatic baggage is not qualified as checked-in baggage, and the inspection of such baggage is obligatory unless it is guaranteed preliminary exemption. For the forwarding of diplomatic baggage exclusively the diplomatic courier is responsible. In the absence of a diplomatic courier, the pilot-in-command is responsible for the baggage during the flight on the basis of authorisation specified under a statute. The pilot-in-command is provided with an official document indicating the number of parcels constituting the diplomatic baggage, but he is not considered to be a diplomatic courier.[86]

Real, exercising or demonstrative military flights, military secret missions, routine military operations and policing flights are unequivocally qualified as State flights. State flights also include the case when a military fighter plane or bomber with military crew using a civilian flight plan flies from one airport to the other. According to the conception of the so-called Flexible Use of Airspace (FUA), civilian and military cooperation distinguishes two types of flight:

- General Air Traffic (GAT), which means that a flight carried out in compliance with the rules of ICAO, specifically the provisions under Annex 2 to the Convention on the Rules of the Air; and
- Operational Air Traffic (OAT), which is neither commercial, nor directed at the pursuit of hobby or sports, but a flight carried out mainly by military aircraft implementing State (military) operations or manoeuvres in the public interest.

Likewise, if the State uses a civil aircraft for State or military purposes, it will be deemed to be a State aircraft—for example, for the delivery of State leaders or delegations, or when the civil aircraft in times of peace carry out special tasks such as military shipments for the fulfilment of specific demands and requirements of defence or alliance (for example, the shipment of soldiers, captives, relief experts or aid supplies to their destination), or for the implementation of search-rescue tasks.

[86] Vienna Convention on Diplomatic Relations (1961), [Article 27 (7)].

Civil Aircraft Interception

On 10 October 1985, the Boeing 737 of EgyptAir (MS) Flight 2843 operating a non-scheduled civil flight on route from Cairo (CAI) to Tunis (TUN) was delivering terrorist suspects on State order under armed military surveillance. The Americans with good reason formed the suspicion that several terrorists were on board who had participated in the capture of the cruiser Achille Lauro. The aircraft was intercepted over the high seas by the F-14 Tomcat fighter planes of the US Navy, which forced it to land on the Sicilian base of the North Atlantic Treaty Organization (NATO) in the territory of Italy.

On 7 October 1985, the Popular Front for the Liberation of Palestine (PFLP) terrorist organisation had captured the Achille Lauro luxury cruiser on its way from Alexandria to Port Said on Egyptian territorial waters in the Mediterranean. During the unlawful action an American citizen lost his life. The terrorists kept the murder in secret. They had not revealed their crime even to the wife of the victim, who all through believed that her husband had only been secluded. The Egyptian authorities negotiating for the safety of the passengers, consisting mostly of American retired people, not aware of the murder, with American authorisation granted free withdrawal to the terrorists, who were then fleeing on the airplane of *EgyptAir*. However, upon the receipt of Achille Lauro and its passengers by the authorities, the murder was revealed. Therefore, the special SEAL Team 6 formation of the American Air Force and Navy took action. This incident was the first known case of the history of aviation security where the fighter plane of a foreign air force intercepted a civil aircraft for such reason.[87]

In the former case no protest challenging the legality of the procedure was filed to the ICAO Council and it could not be filed, since due to the utilisation of the civil aircraft for State purposes it qualified as State aircraft.[88] Since exclusively civil aircraft are governed by the Convention, therefore, if air forwarding is carried out by a State aircraft, the national rules and procedures govern this flight. Pursuant to the Convention, the commander of the State aircraft has the opportunity to decide whether they wish to travel under the surveillance of military or civil air navigation control depending on the task and character of the flight. 'The contracting States undertake, when issuing regulations for their State aircraft, that they will have due regard for the safety of navigation of civil aircraft' [Article 3 *d)*]. Primarily because of safety, the relation between State and civil flights and their service providers has

[87] The Interception of EgyptAir 2843, Sierra Hotel Blog, 12 October 2020, (www.sierrahotel.net/blogs).

[88] ICAO Legal Committee/29 Session—WP/2–1, Attachment 1, 1994, pp. 11–12.

strategically prominent significance, which in practice implies extraordinarily close and efficient cooperation (mainly during the implementation of flights and the common use of the skies).[89]

Special rules and procedures are applicable to State aircraft; therefore, it is a highlighted task and simultaneously the responsibility of the national aviation authority that the principles of categorisation prevail completely and the differentiation in practice should be unambiguous. While upon the standard implementation of flights a civil aircraft has at its disposal relatively great freedom (especially in non-scheduled traffic), 'no State aircraft of a contracting State shall fly over the territory of another State or land thereon without authorization by special agreement or otherwise, and in accordance with the terms thereof' [Article 3 *c*)].

2.3.3 The Use of Weapons Against Civil Aircraft

International legal principles and the UN Charter prohibit carrying out military activities in general. The tasks of the United Nations are to maintain international peace and security, and 'to that end: to take effective collective measures for the prevention and removal of threats to the peace' [Article 1 (1)]. The fundamental pillars of the establishment of peace include respect for State sovereignty and equality, the prohibition of the use of force and intervention in internal affairs, the peaceful settlement of international disputes, the obligation of cooperation among the States, and the fulfilment in good faith of obligations assumed by the States.

The establishment of peace as the principal objective of international law was regarded as a highlighted aspect upon drafting the UN Charter, therefore, it requires that 'all Member States shall refrain in their international relations from the threat or use of force' [Article 2 (4)]. However, in the case of forbearance, there are two exceptions from the universal, objective and unconditionally applicable cogent prohibition. One of these is the natural right of the attacked State to self-defence, while the other one is the recourse to the application of armed force owing to the authorisation of the UN Security Council. Namely, forbearance does not imply that in compliance with the general principles of international law, the State could not take recourse to self-defence and could not defend itself with its arsenal of weapons vis-à-vis the armed attacker.

'Nothing in the UN Charter shall impair the inherent right of individual or collective self-defence if an armed attack occurs against a Member of the United Nations, until the Security Council has taken measures necessary to maintain international peace and security' (Article 51). The right of 'individual or collective self-defence' guaranteed by the UN Charter and customary law prevail in all cases; therefore, in case of an armed attack vis-à-vis a specific State or States, the attacked State is authorised to take military-defensive measures in response. The attacked and

[89] Abeyratne (2012), pp. 6–8.

violated State is authorised to do so, even if the prohibition of aggression is to be applied universally and unconditionally. This right, as it is provisional and ancillary, can be exercised exclusively according to rigorous criteria, thus, it is especially significant that the establishment by the State of the attack should be based on legal criteria.[90] Thus, the violation of the law cannot be presumed (*Omnia praesumuntur rite et solimniter esse acta*—all acts are presumed to have been done rightly and regularly).[91]

Of the set of conditions, the dimension of the armed attack (criterion of quantity), the conduct attributed to the aggressor and the circumstances related to the perpetrator (criterion of quality) need to be considered.[92] That is, each State targeted by armed attack may resort to the use of weapons besides the observance of the basic conditions of necessity and proportionality. Apart from the attacked State, the UN Security Council may also take concrete steps vis-à-vis the party manifesting unlawful conduct. Pursuant to the UN Charter, 'the Security Council shall determine the existence of any threat to the peace, breach of the peace, or act of aggression...' (Article 39). The Security Council may resort to action and if it proves to be inadequate, it may take such action by air, sea, or land forces as may be necessary to maintain or restore international peace and security. Considering all the circumstances of the case, the Security Council shall decide what measures are to be employed to give effect to its decisions (Articles 41–42).

It is a main rule that no weapons may be used vis-à-vis a civil aircraft in flight. The prohibition of the use of weapons is not a novel idea since Para. (4) of Article 2 of the UN Charter demands that 'all Members shall refrain in their international relations from the threat or use of force against (1) the territorial integrity, or (2) the political independence of any State, or (3) in any other manner inconsistent with the Purposes of the United Nations'.[93]

Despite the prohibition, the State may apply force exceptionally (to a proportional and limited extent and in manner, for a limited purpose and time) and only in the case if it resorts to self-defence as an attacked State for the purpose of the defence of its territory. An indispensable condition *(conditio sine qua non)* of the exercise of self-defence is armed attack. Its legal basis is Article 51 of the UN Charter, which guarantees the inherent right of *individual* or *collective self-defence* in case of an armed attack against any UN Member State. This general principle is a *jus cogens* rule; therefore, it is *imperative*, and it requires unconditional predominance.

---

[90] Kajtár (2018), p. 20.

[91] Case Concerning Certain German Interests in Polish Upper Silesia, Merits, PCIJ (1926) Series A. No. 7, 30.

[92] Kajtár (2022), pp. 283–301.

[93] According to the International Court of Justice (ICJ), this rule is one of the cornerstones of the UN Charter, which must be treated as a *jus cogens* norm. *Democratic Republic of Congo v. Uganda* case, ICJ Judgement, General List 116, 148, 19 December 2005, p. 59.

Pursuant to the Vienna Convention on the Law of Treaties (1969), *jus cogens* is a rule of general international law requiring unconditional application. 'A treaty is void if, at the time of its conclusion, it conflicts with a peremptory norm of general international law. . . .a peremptory norm of general international law is a norm accepted and recognised by the international community of States as a whole, a norm from which no derogation is permitted, and which can be modified only by a subsequent norm of general international law with the same character'.[94]

An armed attack does not simply consist of the application of force, but it is the most severe case of the latter. The right of armed intervention for the purpose of self-defence is due exclusively and legally to the State. Self-defence is lawful only if it is applied proportionately and its necessity can be established. During the exercise of this right in the interest of the defence of the nation, the use of weapons proportionate to the attack is admissible until the Security Council of the UN has instituted the measures necessary for the maintenance of international peace and security vis-à-vis the attacker.[95] Subsequently to 11 September 2001, in the case of the armed attack vis-à-vis the Afghan Taliban regime closely related to the Al-Kaida terrorist organisation launched by the United States and the United Kingdom, the Security Council did not prescribe armed sanction, whereas it recognised 'the right of individual and collective self-defence' in its resolution.[96] This may be construed in the given case that the Security Council did not intend to exercise its right guaranteed under the UN Charter pertaining to armed intervention against the attacker, but it gave free scope to the self-defence of the United States.

Thus, armed intervention against a civil aircraft is admissible only in exceptional cases when the civil aircraft is used in armed attacks or as a weapon. If the civil aircraft is used by one State for an armed attack against the other State (the delivery of military, partisan or mercenary troops qualifies as such),[97] consequently, the civil aircraft qualifies as State aircraft and it is no longer protected under the Convention.

The civil aircraft may be removed from the scope of the Convention in several cases, primarily, if it carries out a State task, if a state of war or emergency

---

[94] The jus cogens norms are not itemised, but according to the practice of the States, the national courts and the International Court of Justice, the following qualify as jus cogens: the prohibition of aggressive war, of genocide, of crimes against humanity, of trafficking, of slavery and piracy, of the application of apartheid, of torture and violence, furthermore, the principle of racial non-discrimination. *Vienna Convention on the Law of Treaties* (1969), Treaties conflicting with a peremptory norm of general international law (jus cogens). Part V. Section 2. Article 53.; Brownlie (1979), p. 513.

[95] Charter of the United Nations (1945), Chap. VII, Article 51; Action with respect to threats to the peace, breaches of the peace, and acts of aggression; See, the UN Security Council's Resolution no. 748, which the Council passed vis-à-vis the Libyan Government for the purpose of the protection of international peace and security. UN Security Council Resolution no. 748, 3063rd meeting, 31 March 1992.

[96] Kajtár (2017), p. 572.; UN Security Council Resolution 1368, 4370th meeting, 12 September 2001.

[97] *Nicaragua v. United States of America, Military and Paramilitary Activities in and against Nicaragua,* Merits, Judgement, ICJ Reports 14. 1986, Para. 195.

prevails, or if the incident occurs in domestic traffic. An example for the latter case is the terrorist attack of 11 September 2001 against the United States. The Chicago Convention could not be applied because the terrorist act did not take place during an international flight, but in a domestic aviation environment against domestic targets.[98] The terrorists committed their act with the use of the airplanes of the domestic airlines [United Airlines (UA), American Airlines (AA)] of the attacked State. Thus, in this case it is not obligatory to apply the prohibition under Article 3 *bis* and the related rules of the Convention. However, in practice it is important to highlight that since the United States is a Member of ICAO and from the outset proceeding from its membership (just like other Member States) it incorporated the rules on interception stipulated by ICAO into its national law and procedures and it assumed the obligation of their implementation on all flights above its territory.

'In case of war, the provisions of the Convention shall not affect the freedom of action of any of the contracting States affected, whether as belligerents or as neutrals. The same principle shall apply in the case of any contracting State which declares a State of national emergency[99] and notifies the fact to the Council' (Article 89). Thus, in the cases of war and a state of emergency, the concerned Member States may decide to disregard the Articles of the Convention as obligatory wholly or partially. In such cases, the rules of the Convention are not applicable. As the long-standing adage goes: 'During war laws keep silent' *(Inter arma enim silent leges)*.[100] Nevertheless, this does not imply that vis-a-vis the aircraft automatically force violating international rules, that is, intervention with weapons may be applied, since the proceeding parties are further on bound by customary law and the international rules of martial and humanitarian law.

---

[98] Even so these flights are subject to private international law since not all passengers were travelling to domestic destinations. The flight of the passengers in transit (who arrived from other States or would have been bound to fly to another State) can be qualified as international carriage, which implies that in their case the private international aviation law treaty, namely, the Warsaw Convention (1929) was applicable. As the terrorist attack was considered to be an accident by the court and although the affected airlines amended their general conditions of carriage, the limitation of liability was broken. S.1450—Air Transportation Safety and System Stabilization Act. 107th Congress (2001–2002) (www.congress.gov/bill/107th-congress/senate-bill/1450).

[99] Necessity: 1. Necessity may not be invoked by a State as a ground for precluding the wrongfulness of an act not in conformity with an international obligation of that State unless the act: (a) is the only way for the State to safeguard an essential interest against a grave and imminent peril; and (b) does not seriously impair an essential interest of the State or States towards which the obligation exists, or of the international community as a whole.

2. In any case, necessity may not be invoked by a State as a ground for precluding wrongfulness if: (a) the international obligation in question excludes the possibility of invoking necessity; or (b) the State has contributed to the situation of necessity.

Responsibility of States for Internationally Wrongful Acts (ARSIWA), United Nations, 2001, Article 25.

[100] Cicero, Marcus Tullius: From His Speech Pro Milone (IV. 10), 52 B.C.

As the International Court of Justice (ICJ) emphasised in the *Corfu Channel Case*,[101] martial rules are not valid in times of peace, and the preservation of humanity in peace is a much more required basic aspect than in war. All States have the right to defend their borders, their internal sovereignty and territory, but this right may be exercised exclusively in line with the consideration and predominance of the basic aspect of humanity. Nevertheless, if the civil aircraft is used by individuals for the commission of unlawful acts, these acts in themselves do not substantiate the qualification of the civil aircraft as State aircraft and its removal from the scope of the Convention. Since if no will, peculiar interest of the State or provable real relation underlies the commission of unlawful acts by individuals, the responsibility of the State does not arise. The primary objective and constitutional obligation of the States consist in the protection of the life, safety and property of the passengers, the crew members and of third parties on the surface; therefore, civil aircraft fall under the scope of the rules of the Convention.

An interesting situation may also emerge when owing to the special activity of a civil aircraft, for example, of a helicopter, the perpetrators attempt to help prisoners escape from prison. Within the purview of the rules of the Convention, even if the perpetrators obviously abuse civil aviation, the helicopter qualifies as civil aircraft. This entails that while the helicopter is on the ground, the escape may be impeded by weapon, legally thwarted via the application of force, but when the aircraft ascends, it travels as a *civil aircraft in flight*; that is, pursuant to the Convention the use of weapons needs to be avoided.[102]

If the civil aircraft is used as a weapon or it is exploded by terrorists, they become the enemies of humankind *(hostis humani generis)*;[103] therefore, they need to get their deserved punishment under all circumstances and may not be granted legal protection. The terrorist acts against the United States have re-founded the exercise of the right to self-defence and the general interpretation of the prohibition of the use of weapons. To a certain extent the new foundations burst open the normative framework related to the right to self-defence (for example, by disregarding the

[101] Albanian soldiers shelled British warships passing across the Corfu Channel combining two parts of the high seas. In the incident on the attacked British ships 44 soldiers lost their lives and further 42 soldiers were injured. Later, the British warships returned and two ships of the fleet struck mines. The explosions caused severe damage but there were no casualties. In its ruling, the International Court of Justice condemned the State of Albania, since the right of innocent (peaceful) passage across channels is also due to warships, which does not require the preliminary consent of the coastal State. *United Kingdom v. Albania (Corfu Channel Case),* ICJ 4 Reports 22, Judgement of 9 April 1949.

[102] Cheng (1985), p. 47.

[103] The perpetrators of torture, all pirates and human traffickers are *hostis humani generis,* i.e. the enemies of humankind. *Filártiga v. Pena-Irala,* 630 F.2d 876 US Court of Appeals, Second Circuit, No. 191, Docket 79–6090. 30 June 1980. p. 19.

conditions of necessity and proportionality), because owing to the new doctrine, all guaranteeing rules related to the right to self-defence may be radically extended and the application of force becomes increasingly admissible.[104] This much is certain: the new rules were framed not by lawyers but primarily by life itself. That is, the State attacked by a civil aircraft will undoubtedly exercise its natural right to self-defence. In such a situation after considering all the possible circumstances, military officials will make swift and legally defendable decisions. The missile armed for the purpose of defence will be launched for absolute necessity besides the calculation of the expectable trajectory of the wrecked aircraft, since the possibility of the lawful use of weapons still prevails in international law and national procedures.

2.3.4 The Prohibition to Use Weapons Against Civil Aircraft

At the Tenth UN General Assembly (1955), the Member States made a proposal for the regulation of emergencies deriving from the unintended, inadvertent or erroneous incursion into another State by civil aircraft.[105] The direct cause of the proposal for regulation was the incident on 27 July 1955, when the Lockheed Constellation airplane of the EL AL Israeli Airline on route from Tel-Aviv (TLV) to London (LHR) was shot without any advance warning by an MIG-15 fighter plane of the Bulgarian Air Force above the territory of Bulgaria.[106] The case was filed at the International Court of Justice (ICJ), but no meritorious judgement was passed since the mandatory jurisdiction of the court in the case was not established.[107] In the beginning the Bulgarian State blamed the other party, but eventually, it apologised (admitted that the application of force had been disproportionate) and paid compensation for the victims.

Unfortunately, the destruction of civil aircraft for military or other purposes and incidentally for error has ensued on several occasions in the history of aviation.[108] These fatal events and tragedies keep occurring even in the twenty-first century and create immense stir. Think of the Russian passenger plane annihilated by the

---

[104] Kajtár (2011), p. 2.

[105] UN General Assembly Resolution 927, *Question of the safety of commercial aircraft flying in the vicinity of, or inadvertently crossing, international frontiers.* UN General Assembly Official Records, tenth Sess. Supp. No. 19 on 14 December 1955.

[106] ICAO Circular 50–AN/45: Aircraft Accident Digest, No. 7, No. 35, pp. 146–159.

[107] *Israel v. Bulgaria,* Aerial incident of 27 July 1955. General List No. 35—Judgement 26 May 1959.; ICAO Council Working Paper/5764.

[108] For example, Cathay Pacific (CX) flight on route from Bangkok (DMK) to Hong Kong (HKG) was mistakenly shot down by the Chinese interceptors on 23 July 1954. The civil aircraft was Douglas DC-4 which is very similar to its military version C-54. The Chinese Government apologised and paid compensation for the families of the victims and the airline. Last Act in the Hainan Incident (HistoricWings.com), Parts 1–3, July 2012.

Ukrainian Air Defence (4 October 2001), the perfidious shot of the flight of the Malaysian airline over the territory of Ukraine (17 July 2014), or the airplane of the Ukrainian airline destroyed by the Iranian Air Defence erroneously on 8 January 2020.

Weapons Used Against Civil Aircraft

On 21 February 1973, the Boeing 727–224 airplane (with the marking 5A-DAH) of the Libyan Arab Airline (LAA) on route from Tripoli (TIP) to Cairo (CAI) was shot by the F-4E Phantom II fighter plane of the Israeli Air Force above the Sinai Peninsula. Owing to a navigational error the cockpit crew of the civil airplane deviated from the prescribed route and flew astray to Israeli territory. After recognising the trouble, they reversed with a tight turn, but in the meantime fighter planes intercepted them and forced them to land with side-slips and annunciating shots. The pilot-in-command of the civil airplane did not follow the instructions during the interception, as a result, it was shot unlawfully by an automatic machine-gun aboard, while already flying in the airspace above Egyptian territory. The Council of ICAO condemned the Israeli conduct infringing the general principles of the Chicago Convention.[109] The State of Israel admitted its responsibility related to the 'faulty decision' and compensated the families of the victims as reparation.

On 3 July 1988, the Airbus 300 civil aircraft (with the marking EP-IBU) of the Iranian Airline (IRA) on route from Bandar Abbas (BND) to Dubai (DXB) was shot after its erroneous identification as an F-14 fighter plane by the USS Vincennes CG-49 American cruise missile warship sojourning in the Strait of Hormuz, thereby causing the death of 290 passengers and the crew on board. At the initiative of Iran, the case was filed at the International Court of Justice on 17 May 1989. Eventually, the incident did not unfold into trial, since the parties reached a full scope out-of-court settlement. The United States admitted causing a 'horrible human tragedy' and on the basis of '*ex gratia*' paid the families 300,000 USD for each victim capable of earning a living, and 150,000 USD for victims unable to work.[110]

The essence of the payment based on *ex gratia* is that, despite the provision of material compensation, this act does not imply the admission of responsibility. For example, on the basis of *ex gratia* the Ukrainian government, sharing the mourning of families, paid 200,000 USD for the family of every passenger and the flight crew, after Ukrainian soldiers had shot the TU-154 aircraft, Flight 1812 of the Russian Siberia Airlines (S7) inadvertently above the Black Sea during military exercises on

[109] ICAO Council Working Paper/5764, Report concerning the Libyan Arab Boeing 727-224, 5A–DAH (Sinai, 21 February 1973), 1 May 1973.

[110] *Islamic Republic of Iran v. United States of America*—ICJ (Case Concerning the Aerial Incident of 3 July 1988), 2001.

4 October 2001, and as a consequence the airplane had been destroyed. (For example, under the pretext of *ex gratia* the Government of the Soviet Union after a lengthy dispute made a partial payment to Canada for the damage generated by the spread of radioactive debris owing to the crash of the reconnaissance satellite Cosmos-954 on Canadian territory.[111] However, on the basis of *ex gratia* the Soviet Union did not make a payment for the shot of KAL Flight 007 on 1 September 1983.)

On 20 April 1978, the Boeing 707-321B airplane of the South-Korean national airline (KAL) on route from Paris (CDG) to the Alaskan Anchorage airport (ANC) [the final destination of the KAL Flight 902 was Soul (GMP)] due to the defect of the navigation system was severely lost. The pilots navigated the aircraft in the opposite direction; consequently, they flew wrongly into the prohibited Soviet airspace above the Kola Peninsula (the area of Murmansk) (Fig. 2.11). The chief commander of the Soviet National Air Defence was aware that the airplane was a civil aircraft, nevertheless, as its cockpit crew did not react appropriately to the acts of interception, the commander issued the order to fire.[112] The pilot of the Sukhoi-15TM intercepting fighter plane shot two air-to-air missiles: one of them missed its target, the other one burst into the airplane, and as a result, two passengers lost their lives, but the hit could not do vaster damage to the body of the airplane, because the commander of the fighter plane had not activated the missile before firing. Thus, the pilot-in-command of the transgressing airplane could make a successful forced landing on the ice of a frozen lake in the north-western territory of the Soviet Union.

Merely 5 years passed since the incident of the KAL Flight 902, when history repeated itself. The Soviet Air Defence attacked another flight of the South-Korean national airline, which caused an even greater international uproar and serious diplomatic tension. The diplomatic relations of the Cold War parties had not touched such bedrock since the Cuban missile-crisis (1962) as on 1 September 1983, when the Boeing 747-200 airplane of KAL Airline, on route from New York (JFK) to Soul (GMP), after landing at the Alaskan Anchorage Airport (ANC) was shot by the Sukhoi-15TM intercepting fighter plane of the Soviet Air Force above the Sea of Okhotsk. All of the 269 people, among them 22 children on board the KAL Flight 007 plane, fell into the sea and lost their lives. The civil passenger airplane due to the fault of the pilots had diverged, then it had gradually drifted from the planned route. Consequently, the Korean airplane had flown into the Soviet airspace during the flight several times, and it had also flown over the Kamchatka Peninsula infested with strictly top-secret military facilities. The commander of the Soviet air defence in

[111] The power source providing the energy supply of the satellite was a nuclear reactor operating with the application of 20 kg uranium dressed with the uranium–235 isotope, from which 25% of the radionuclides fell on the surface of the Earth. Contrary to common belief, this was not the first such case. In 1964, upon the fall of an American naval satellite into the Indian Ocean, radioactive plutonium-238 was released. Haanappel (2003), p. 99.; Gorove (1978), pp. 137–146.

[112] Mullany (1989), p. 430.

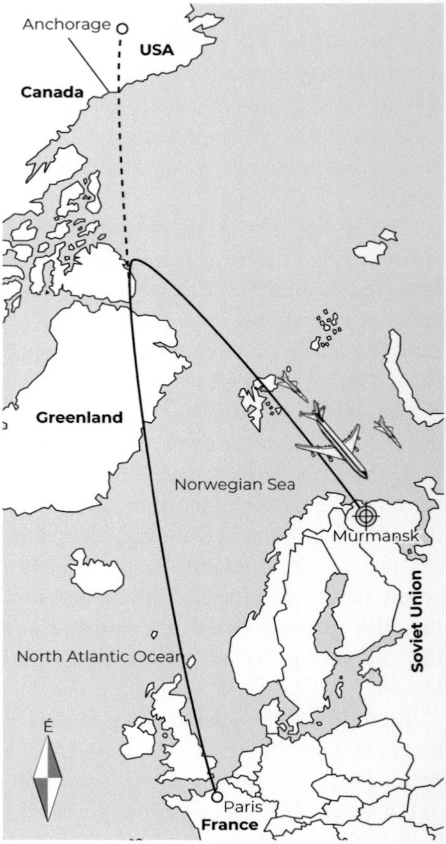

Fig. 2.11 The route of Korean Air Lines Flight 902

charge, although he was not convinced whether the transgressing plane was a civil or State aircraft, issued the order to fire.

Like so many times in the course of human history, devoid of all the facts, the concerned Great Powers in their own interests rendered an exaggerated and simplified description of the incident. Although questions have remained unanswered up to this day, after the international analysis of the data recorder (black box),[113] it is

[113] In our days two kinds of black boxes are simultaneously aboard. During the flight one of the black boxes (Cockpit Voice Recorder—CVR) records the voice of all the people and the noises in the cockpit, generally the last 120 min of the flying time, while the other one (Flight Data Recorder—FDR) is designed to record the condition and movement of the aircraft. It is only a legend that the 'black' box is black; in reality, it is painted orange or red. This is necessitated by the expectation to find the recording devices among the debris of the airplane or further away more easily. The plating of the black box needs to endure an acceleration of 3400 g (g-force), furthermore, it is acid-, water- and heat-proof up to 1000°C. All the devices are equipped with locator, which operates for a period of 30 days to 6000 m underwater.

increasingly manifest that because of the gross navigational error of the experienced pilots, the airplane had drifted away from the route authorised in the official flight plan, as a result of which and of several other unfortunate and interrelated circumstances, the tragedy could ensue.

The KAL Flight 007 violated the Soviet airspace unequivocally and was flying in the prohibited airspace over Kamchatka, thereby violating international law. At the same time, the Soviet Air Force omitted both the doubtless establishment of whether the plane was a civil or State aircraft and compliance with the rules prescribed by international and national law. The procedure to be applied in the case of the interception of an aircraft issued by the ministry for civil aviation made accessible for civil, military and foreign pilots prescribes the following steps: the establishment of communication and connection on radio (at any frequency including the emergency frequency at 121.500 MHz), giving light, visual (visible) signals, for example, side-slips. All these acts raising attention need to be continued, with respect to the possibilities, until they achieve their goal and the cockpit crew of the intercepted flight reacts.[114]

The reason for the omission of doubtless identification could be that the commandership of the Soviet Air Defence was pressed for time. That is, during the intercepting operations the transgressing airplane was bound to leave the national airspace, therefore, the time for the interception of the unidentified airplane above Soviet territory was running out. According to the ICAO Report,[115] the airplane at the moment of its interception was at a distance of 21 nautical miles from the nearest Soviet continental baseline, and it crashed at a distance of 30 miles measured from the coast of Sakhalin Island.[116] The lost civil airplane in trouble due to a navigational error was fatally hit above the Sea of Okhotsk in international airspace. The Sea of Okhotsk is surrounded from almost all directions by Russian territory, the continent, the Kamchatka Peninsula, Sakhalin Island and the Kuril Islands, but it is not qualified as territorial waters (closed sea), thus, Russian territory, because in the south it is adjacent to Hokkaido Island, the territory of Japan. Therefore, the armed attack was unlawful in that particular moment and the application of force was disproportionate; therefore, the general principles and rules of international law were severely injured.

After the tragedy, the families of the passengers lodged legal action against the company manufacturing the aeronautical maps (Jeppesen Sanderson Inc.), because the maps did not contain an express warning about the consequences of the violation of the Soviet airspace. In addition, the map indicated a restricted airspace instead of a dangerous airspace on the spot where the aircraft before its actual shot had travelled. The court dismissed the action of the plaintiffs because it did not establish a causal

[114]ICAO Report—Appendix H, Interception Procedures Issued by USSR. 1993.

[115]*Destruction of Korean Air Lines of Boeing 747–200 on 31 August 1983*. Report of the completion of the ICAO fact-finding investigation. June 1993.

[116]Degani (2004), p. 55.

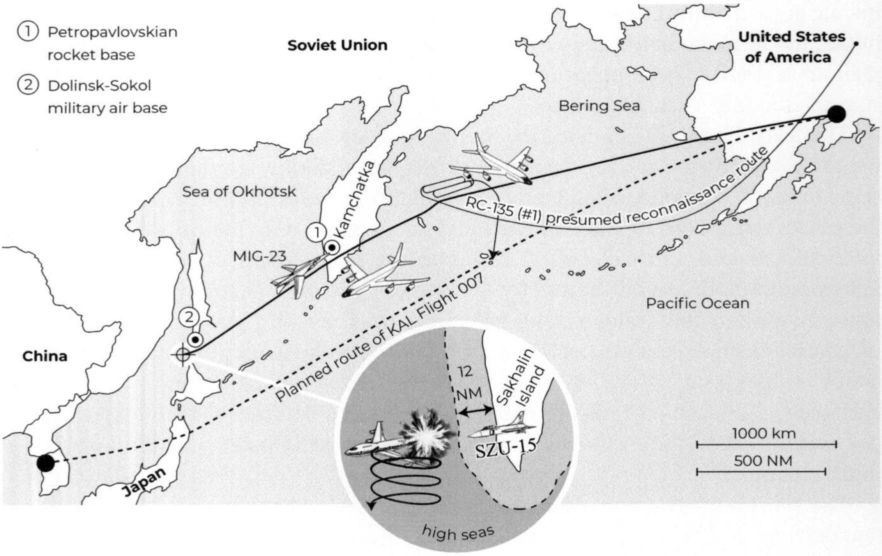

Fig. 2.12 The route of Korean Air Lines Flight 007

link between the event of the accident and the inappropriate text of the map.[117] The four-engine Boeing RC-135 American scouting airplanes developed on the base of the Boeing 707 civil airplanes had been flying regularly into the extraordinarily defended regions and would violate the Soviet jurisdiction, the national airspace, therefore, the Soviet Air Defence could rightly presume that the hostile forces were implementing a novel military scouting flight in the region (Fig. 2.12).

What can we do with the instruments of law? The legal personality of ICAO as an international organisation is partial and derivative. Thus, it does not have competence as an authority or supervisor, nor the legal capacity to apply direct coercive instruments or sanctions. Nevertheless, ICAO is the only organ that can react globally to issues related to aviation in the world by reason of its regulatory function. The ICAO Council has taken the necessary steps and reformed the international rules pertaining to the interception and identification of civil aircraft. ICAO has prescribed for the cockpit crew on routes over the oceans to continuously monitor the coastline for the purpose of checking their positioning via their meteorological radar. ICAO demanded the establishment of a hotline connection in the northern basin of the

[117] Aeronautical maps contain all relevant information for the precise and safe implementation of the flight. The standards included in Annex 4 to the Convention on Aeronautical Charts contain 17 requirements concerning aeronautical maps. On the maps issued by the national Air Navigation Service Provider (ANSP), the determined air routes with the prohibited airspaces, the airports and borders as well as the data about navigational and radio devices and the radio frequencies used in the district are indicated in detail. ICAO Annex 4 on Aeronautical Charts. *In Re Korean Air Lines Disaster of 1 September 1983.* 597 F. Supp. 619 (D.D.C. 1984), 26 June 1984.

Pacific Ocean among the American, Soviet and Japanese aviation authorities and made a recommendation for the global development of communication between civil and military aircraft and the air navigation control staff.[118]

ICAO would often be blamed that as a political plenary organisation considering the interests of the Member States would react slowly.[119] Of course, in the present case the international community urged meritorious, comprehensive and rapid measures. A written regulation was necessary, the international recognition of which by all the States could make the practice, not always prevailing in customary law, legitimate and legally binding besides following the general principles of international law. Subsequently to the tragedy, at the 25th Extraordinary Assembly of ICAO (1984), the Member States unanimously adopted Article 3 *bis* with its four paragraphs supplementing the Convention:

(a) The contracting States recognize that every State *must refrain from resorting to the use of weapons against civil aircraft in flight* and that, in case of interception, the lives of persons on board and the safety of aircraft must not be endangered.
(b) The contracting States recognize that every State, in the exercise of its sovereignty, is entitled *to require the landing* at some designated airport of a civil aircraft flying above its territory without authority or if there are reasonable grounds to conclude that *it is being used for any purpose inconsistent with the aims of the Convention*; it may also give such aircraft any other instructions to put an end to such violations.
(c) Each contracting State shall establish all necessary provisions in its national laws or regulations to make such compliance mandatory. Each contracting State shall make any violation of such applicable laws or regulations punishable by severe penalties and shall submit the case to its competent authorities in accordance with its laws or regulations.
(d) Each contracting State shall take appropriate measures to prohibit the deliberate use of any civil aircraft for any purpose inconsistent with the aims of the Convention.

The rule unambiguously prohibits the use of weapons, but it does not prohibit the use of force in the case of interception vis-à-vis the civil aircraft in flight. The interception of the civil aircraft by fighter planes is lawful as long as the intercepting fighter planes do not commit an act which endangers the intercepted aircraft. Such an act without the use of weapons may be a dangerous manoeuvre implemented with a

[118] Leich (1984).

[119] Two years had passed after the explosion of the Air India (AI) Flight 182—operating on the Montreal (YMX)-London (LHR)-Delhi (DEL)-Bombay (BOM) (today Mumbai) route on 23 June 1985 (a terrorist killed 329 persons on board)—before ICAO issued its new standards for the checking of passenger baggage. Because of the threat caused by radio bombs and plastic explosives known for a long time, ICAO took decisive measures only after the catastrophe of Pan Am (PA) Flight 103 (1988). *Report to the President of the United States titled 'The Safety of Air Traffic and Terrorism'.* Washington, D.C., 10 May 1995. p. 25.

view to reprimand or showing off force.[120] A basic requirement is that the intercepting forces guaranteeing the defence of the State need to proceed with consideration of proportionality, since force may be applied only to such an extent which is absolutely necessary for the aversion of danger.[121] Besides the application of force, the treaty-maker positions the most important basic objective, i.e., aviation safety above the interest of the defence of the contracting States. However, the flight crew is required to respect the rules of aviation of the State in the airspace of which it travels. If the crew members do not fulfil the concerned requirements, the territorial State is entitled to institute proceedings and take the appropriate measures vis-à-vis the persons infringing the rules in compliance with its national law. Such acts include the cases when an aircraft flies into the airspace of a State without authorisation or fails to identify itself. In such cases, pursuant to the detailed specification of Annex 2 to the Convention on Rules of the Air, the State is authorised to intercept, identify, and if necessary, coerce the aircraft to land. However, the interceptor may not apply violence vis-à-vis the aircraft breaching rules and may not attack it solely with reference to territorial sovereignty.

The amendments passed at the 25th Extraordinary Assembly of ICAO obligated the Member States to introduce new procedures. In the interest of the avoidance of the above-mentioned navigational errors, the President of the United States, Ronald Reagan (1911–2004), in his press release 2 weeks after the tragedy, informed the world that they would make the precise movement tracking device, the Global Positioning System (GPS), under confidential military development, available for civil air traffic instead of its exclusive strategical application.[122] The GPS technology developed by the Americans carries out three dimensional positioning, time and speed measurements on the surface, in water and in the air. Its precision is metric, but with differential measurement methods, it can be millimetric. Since its introduction, the GPS covering the whole world and tracking the precise movement of aircraft has guaranteed that similar tragedies do not occur again. The new rule was supported to the utmost and unanimously by the Member States and adopted on 10 May 1984, but its taking effect needed the fulfilment of a prospective condition, namely, the amendment of the Chicago Convention. Pursuant to the Convention all amendments must be approved by a two-thirds vote of the Assembly and shall then come into force in respect of States which have ratified such amendment [94 Article *a)*]. The Assembly determined the condition of coming into force as ratification by 102 contracting States; however, this act was awaited for an additional 14 years.

---

[120] Sulyok (2006), pp. 5–30.

[121] The International Court of Justice confirmed the principle of proportionality in the lawsuit *Nicaragua v. the United States* on 27 June 1986. ICJ—Summary of the Judgement, XI. 1. The prohibition of the use of force and the right of self-defence, Paras. 227–238.

[122] *The White House*: *Statement by the principal deputy press secretary to the President,* 16 September 1983.

Eventually, Article 3 *bis* took effect on 1 October 1998 owing to ratification by Guinea and Cuba. The bizarre turn of destiny was that preceding the ratification, Cuba had attacked three unarmed civil airplanes in international airspace at a distance of 20 nautical miles from the Cuban coastline on 24 February 1996. The main objective of the pilots of the small airplanes was the search and rescue of emigrants fleeing on the high seas, which the Cuban Government viewed disapprovingly. It was not inadvertent that the two Cessna 337 civil airplanes were shot by the MIG-29 fighter planes of the Cuban Air Force. This happened despite the fact that the pilots of the airplanes were in contact with the Cuban air navigation control, their on-board transponders were working, and because of observing the rules of aviation, they were flying in international airspace. This incident caused the death of four innocent civilians. The third airplane managed to escape thanks to the camouflaging effect of the clouds. The pilots of the eluded airplane informed the public of the tragic event, and the families took legal action.[123]

The Security Council (SC) of the UN made a decision concerning the case and emphasised that it 'condemns the use of weapons against civil aircraft in flight as being incompatible with elementary considerations of humanity, the rules of international customary law as codified in Article 3 *bis* of the Chicago Convention, and the Standards and Recommended Practices set out in the Annexes to the Convention'.[124] The decision makes it unequivocal that the cause of the protracted ratification process of the unanimously adopted Article 3 *bis* consists in the fact that the ICAO Assembly framed such a norm under an international rule that had already prevailed in customary law.

Eventually, the United States did not ratify the amendment, although it had been one of the main initiators, an active participant in the elaboration of the recommendation. The general justification up to this day has been that the authorities of the United States do not recognise the exclusive jurisdiction of the International Court of Justice (ICJ) in controversial issues. Namely, pursuant to the Convention if a disagreement cannot be settled by negotiation, the dispute shall be decided by the ICAO Council on the application of any of the States concerned. On such an occasion the contracting State may appeal from the decision of the Council to an *ad hoc* arbitral tribunal or to the International Court of Justice (Article 84).[125]

[123] *Armando Alejandre Jr. and Others v. Cuba,* 11.589, Report No. 86/99, OEA/Ser.L/V/II.106 Doc. 3 rev. at 586, 1999.

[124] UN Security Council Resolution 1067, 3683rd meeting, 26 July 1996.

[125] Chicago Convention, Article 84 of Chap. XVIII on the Settlement of Disputes.

2.3.5 The Nationality of the Civil Aircraft

The board of ships and aircraft registered by the State needs to be regarded as part of the territory of the State, on which pursuant to *the right of the flag (lex bandi),* the registering State has jurisdiction. 'Aircraft *have the nationality of the State* in which *they are registered* (Article 17)', irrespective of the ownership of the aircraft, the headquarters of the company, or the citizenship of the pilot-in-command. The State of registry is indicated by the nationality marking and the national flag.

The board of the aircraft qualifies as quasi-State territory; therefore, the registering State has jurisdiction in the 'mobile territory'. The right of the flag does not imply territorial sovereignty (in fact it is not the territory of the State), merely specific jurisdiction. Over the high seas (that is, in international airspace) the States may not exercise territorial sovereignty, since the high seas imply a territory to be utilised by all. Therefore, the board of the aircraft and the ship in this territory is to be regarded as the territory of the State where it was registered.[126] The extension of jurisdiction beyond the State border provides opportunity for the complete observance not only of the primarily applicable international rules, but also of the domestic statutes of the State registering the aircraft in the given legal relations. Aboard the civil airplane in flight, the legal consequences of private legal acts giving rise to citizenship or other legal relations (for example, giving birth, making a last will and testament, death, conclusion of a contract or wedding) are governed by the national law of the registering State. This establishes the connection between the private international legal facts of the case and the legal regime to be applied.

Principles Concerning Child Birth

For example, in the case of the person born aboard an aircraft if the national law of the parent follows the principle of *descent by blood (jus sanguinis),* the child by reason of the fact of birth and the force of law *(ex lege)* inherits the citizenship of the parent as a basic civil right irrespective of the place of birth.

If national law stipulates the principle of *descent by territory (jus soli),* according to the place of birth, the child obtains the citizenship of the State registering the aircraft, irrespective of the citizenship of the mother.

If the principles of *descent by blood* and *descent by territory* combine, interesting situations may arise:

[126] ICAO Doc 7364 Convention on Damage Caused by Foreign Aircraft to Third Parties on the Surface. Signed at Rome on 7 October 1952, Chap. V, Article 23 (2).

Combination of Principles in Child Birth
If childbirth takes place on the aircraft registered by a State siding with the *territorial principle* (e.g., the United States)[127] by a citizen of a State following the *principle of descent by blood* (e.g., Hungary),[128] the child shall be a dual citizen.[129] Sharpening the situation by inverting the preceding example: the child is born by an American parent during the flight on an aircraft registered in Hungary, the child shall be stateless until the completion of the naturalisation procedure. If the childbirth takes place on an aircraft registered in either of two States aligning with the territorial principle (e.g., the United States and Canada),[130] the born child *ipso iure* acquires the citizenship of the registering State (e.g., the child of the mother with United States citizenship giving birth on an airplane registered in Canada shall be Canadian straightaway).[131]

For reassurance, in practice the air carriers according to their General Conditions of Carriage facilitate the journey of expectant mothers exclusively under proper conditions, therefore, childbirth rarely takes place on board an aircraft [see, Part II, Chap. 9. 1.2].

The principle of territorial descent widespread in Anglo-Saxon law is increasingly driven to the background and becomes ancillary, whereas, lineal descent prevalent in continental law has become established primarily because of its practicality.

2.3.6 *The Registration of the Civil Aircraft*

Irrespective of its ownership, the aircraft *belongs to the State of registry*. Already the Paris (1919), Madrid (1926) and Habana (1928) Conventions regulated the institution transplanted from maritime law uniformly, according to which *the nationality of the aircraft is determined by the country of registration*.

In international commercial transportation the protection of the ship or the aircraft by the registering State has always had prominent significance. The board of the ship

---

[127] 8 U.S.C. §1401—U.S. Code—Unannotated Title 8. Aliens and Nationality § 1401. Nationals and citizens of United States at birth.

[128] 'By birth the child of a Hungarian citizen shall be a Hungarian citizen'. Hungary's Constitution of 2011. Foundations. Article G), Para. (1).

[129] The majority of the States do not recognise dual citizenship, therefore, in such a case the child is not bound to be entitled to dual citizenship (www.politikapedia.hu/kettos-allampolgarsag).

[130] Citizenship Act, R.S.C., 1985, c. C-29 (2) Part I, The Right to Citizenship.

[131] Dual citizenship is legally permitted if both parents are United States citizens and one of them was a resident in the United States before the birth of the child. 8 U.S.C. §1401—U.S. Code *c)*.

is governed by the national jurisdiction of the State under the flag of which the ship travels. The right of the flag has been a general principle established and applied in maritime navigation for centuries. In the case of registered watercraft, the law of the State of the flag is decisive; however, this rule does not pertain to objects which do not qualify as baggage or freight (cargo).

The following are deemed to be quasi *floating State territories*:

- the board of the *warship* always during the complete voyage and it maintains this special legal status in times of peace in foreign ports as well (obviously, mooring requires preliminary authorisation, but no foreigners may embark the board of a warship or enforce acts thereon);
- the board of *commercial ships* always on the high seas, on territorial seas as a main rule (with the exception if the coastal State exercises jurisdiction by reason of an act disturbing the peace of the coastal State or the order of the territorial sea), but in foreign ports the territorial sovereignty of the coastal State prevails, that is, the competent authority of the coastal State may examine the ship, may levy the cargo and sanction in the case of the violation of the law.

A genuine link must exist between the State and the ship.[132] In this case the rules of the State of the flag need to be applied *mutatis mutandis*. According to the viewpoint of the International Tribunal for the Law of the Sea manifest in the case of *Saint Vincent and Grenadines v. Guinea,*[133] the objective of the UN Convention on the Law of the Sea (1982) consists in the establishment of a unique relationship between the ship and the State of the flag, which promotes the more efficient fulfilment of the obligations of the State of the flag, but it does not establish a system of requirements which could substantiate the contingent attack of another State. At the same time, the Chicago Convention does not set forth that the *existence of a genuine link* between the State and the registered aircraft is required, because this follows from the spirit and the rules of the Convention.

However, there are States with flags which do not adhere to international rules or do not expect strict adherence and their authorities are lenient upon the exercise of the right of supervision. The lack of commitment of the registering State to such a degree has facilitated the use of the *Flags of Convenience* (FOC) and contributed to its practical spread in commerce.

The largest maritime fleets in the world remarkably belong not only to the historic nautical nations but to Liberia, Panama and the Marshall Islands. Approximately, 40% of the commercial fleets of the world is registered in

(continued)

[132] *UN Convention on the Law of the Sea, UNCLOS* (1982)—Nationality of the Ships, Part VII, Article 91 on High Seas, Para. 1.

[133] M/V ‘SAIGA’ case, *Saint Vincent and Grenadine v. Guinea,* ITLOS, No. 2, 1 July 1999, Paras. 62–66.

these countries.[134] The reason for the registration of ships usually in foreign ownership in another State is that the regulations of the registering State contain a minimal number of conditions pertaining to shipping, the taxes imposed on ships are low and the authorities of the State do not always exercise their rights proceeding from supervision, nor do they enforce the international rules consistently.

The popularity of the use of Flags of Convenience, of the so-called 'cheap flags' derives basically from economic benefits. Nevertheless, we cannot disregard the involved safety, security and policing risks. It is precisely for this reason that the convenience option has not spread in the world of air traffic (although we must allow for exceptions) because the prohibition of dual registration, the rigorous licensing procedures, and the domestic regulations based on international requirements and operation in sovereign airspaces in compliance with international standards do not facilitate following that practice. For example, the Member States of the European Union, in the interest of the complete enforcement of aviation safety and of the defence of their national airspace, inform air passengers (all European citizens must have access to this particular information) and do not let the registered airplanes of the Member States—not observing the stipulations of the Convention, with high deficiencies of aviation safety at international audits (aircraft subject to an operating ban[135] imposed by the EU Commission)—enter their territories. In case they admit them (for example, they do not appear on a blacklist), the authority of the recipient State may check observance of the safety prescriptions at the airport, which facilitates that the aircraft and its staff not observing or jeopardising the rules of aviation safety, should be subject to a take-off ban until they avert the threat.[136] The registering State is responsible for compliance with the Rules of the Air, but the Member State, which makes its sovereign national airspace available, is also responsible. As the Convention prescribes: 'Each contracting State undertakes to adopt measures to insure that every aircraft flying over or manoeuvring within its territory or every aircraft carrying its nationality mark, wherever such aircraft may be, shall comply with the national rules and regulations relating to the flight and manoeuvre

---

[134] United Nations Conference on Trade and Development (UNCTAD) (unctadstat.unctad.org/EN/Index.html).

[135] Decree No. 2111/2005 (EC) of 14 December 2005 of the European Parliament and of the Council on the adoption of a Community list of air carriers subject to an operating ban within the Community and on informing air passengers about the identity of the operator, and repealing Article 9 of Directive 2004/36/EC. HL L 344., 27 December 2005, p. 15.; Schnitker and Kaar (2013), pp. 83–86, 135–167.

[136] Regulation (EU) 1139/2018 of 4 July 2018 of the European Parliament and the Council on common rules in the field of civil aviation and the establishment of a European Union Aviation Safety Agency. HL L 212., 22. 08. 2018. Chap. IV, [Article 62 *d*)].

of aircraft there in force. Each contracting State undertakes to keep its own regulations in these respects uniform, to the greatest possible extent, with those established from time to time under this Convention' (Article 12).

Thus, the board of the aircraft is subject to the national jurisdiction of the State *where it is registered*. The following qualify as quasi *mobile State territory*:

- the board of a *State aircraft* always during the whole flight, and it preserves such special legal status during peace time at foreign airports;
- the board of the *civil aircraft* during flight from departure (closure of the door of the aircraft) to arrival (opening of the door) always over the high seas and in the airspace of a foreign State nearly always, with the exception if
  - a crime committed on board an airplane affects the territorial State or is directed at it;
  - an offence has been committed by or against a national or permanent resident of such State;
  - the offence consists of a breach of any rules or regulations, relating to the flight or manoeuvre of the aircraft, in force in such State; or
  - the exercise of jurisdiction is necessary to ensure the observance of any obligation of such State under a multilateral international agreement.[137]

At foreign airports the territorial sovereignty of the recipient State prevails; that is, the competent authority of the Member State may search the aircraft, examine the certificates and other documents and sanction in the case of the breach of law.

The irrevocable fact *(fait accompli)* of the registration, irrespective of the ownership of the aircraft, entails the legal consequence of belonging to the registering State. Registration is a legal act, the legal consequences of which include the jurisdiction of the registering State, the right of disposal over the aircraft and undertaking the related responsibility by the State. Several articles of the Convention[138] and almost all aviation law conventions attach legal consequences to the fact of registration. For example, the Tokyo Convention (1963)[139] stipulates that 'the State of registry of the aircraft is competent to exercise jurisdiction over offences and acts committed on board', whereas pursuant to the Rome Convention (1952),[140] 'a ship or aircraft on the high seas is regarded as part of the territory of the State in which it is registered'. 'The registration or transfer of the registration of the aircraft in any contracting State is made *in accordance with its laws* and *regulations*' (Article 19).

The detailed rules of registration must be elaborated by the Member State in accordance with Annex 7 to the Convention on Aircraft Nationality and Registration Marks. The registration marks must be displayed visibly on the aircraft, therefore,

[137] Convention on Offences and Certain Other Acts Committed on Board an Aircraft. Tokyo. 14 September 1963, Article 4 of Chap. II on Jurisdiction.; ICAO Doc 8364.

[138] Chicago Convention, Articles 12, 25, 26 and 31–33.

[139] Tokyo Convention, Article 3 of Chap. II on Jurisdiction.

[140] Rome Convention, Article 23 (2) of Chap. V on the Application of the Convention and General Provisions.

'every aircraft engaged in international air navigation must bear its appropriate *nationality* and *registration marks*' (Article 20). Civil aircraft bear the nationality mark manifesting belonging to the State and the registration mark consisting of numbers or letters (whereas military aircraft are identified by the nationality mark and the serial number).

The use of the nationality mark is uniform; this undoubtedly identifies the State of the registration of the aircraft. The nationality mark precedes the registration mark. The nationality mark consists of the colours of the national flag and the combination of one or two initials or numbers (for example, the nationality mark of Germany is D, of Canada it is C, of the Czech Republic it is OK, of Hungary it is HA, of the Netherlands it is PH, of Singapore it is PV, of the United Arab Emirates it is A6, of Israel it is 4X, of Indonesia it is PK, of the Russian Federation it is RA, and of the United States it is N, etc.). The nationality mark of the aircraft registered in the United Kingdom is the Union flag (a white-fimbriated symmetric red cross on a blue field with a white-fimbriated counter changed saltire of red and white) and it starts with the letter G in all cases followed by a hyphen and the registration mark of letters or numbers. For example: G-BOAC; G is the UK nationality mark, whereas BOAC is the registration mark of the aircraft.

The registration mark is attached to the specific airplane, since its main function is the identification of the aircraft beyond doubt within the State of registration.[141] The nationality marks are determined by ICAO with the consent of the International Telecommunication Union (ITU), a UN specialised agency and these are announced under Annex 7 to the Convention. The registration mark is assigned by the competent aviation authority of the State pursuant to the rules of the State of registry. If the Member States use letters (generally three or four letters) as registration marks, they cannot use letter combinations which can be confused with the general distress signal SOS, other similar emergency signals or international words. The letters must be Latin capital letters without ornament, and in the case of numbers, they must be Arabic numbers without ornament.

Nothing in the Convention prevents two or more contracting States from constituting joint air transport operating organisations or international operating agencies, which have a common registration mark.

In the case of multinational airlines, the States and their airlines participating in a joint venture [for example, the well-established SAS Airline operated jointly by Denmark, Norway and Sweden [see, Part I, Chap. 8. 3] settle in a separate agreement which contracting State undertakes the role of the State of registry of an aircraft. The aircraft receives a *common sign*, which ICAO issues for the registering authority. The common sign precedes the registration mark. The authority registering the common sign does not register the aircraft of the

(continued)

[141] ICAO Annex 7 on Aircraft Nationality and Registration Marks. 6th edn., 2012, Articles 3–8.

international operating agency on a *national basis*. Thus, all the aircraft of the international operating agency not registered on a national basis bear the same common sign.

Dual (multiple) registration is prohibited;[142] therefore, 'an aircraft *cannot be validly registered in more than one State*, but its registration may be changed from one State to another' (Article 18). 'Each contracting State undertakes to supply to any other contracting State or to ICAO, on demand, information concerning the registration and ownership of any particular aircraft registered in that State. In addition, each contracting State shall furnish reports to ICAO giving pertinent data that can be made available concerning the ownership and control of aircraft registered in that State and habitually engaged in international air navigation. The data thus obtained by ICAO shall be made available by it on request to the other contracting States' (Article 21).

Broadly construing the general rules above, the ICAO Council passed a special rule for the first time in its history. Pursuant to the rule the Council, instead of requesting, demanded the Member States to submit monthly updated data continually and regularly, which are publicised on the official website of ICAO.[143] This method guarantees to make the real relationship between the registering State and the aircraft more obvious and transparent, thereby reducing the possibility of the practical use of Flags of Convenience.

2.3.7 Registration of the Civil Aircraft for Dry and Wet Leasing

It is recognised in the practice of international air transport that the air carrier in the possession of flying authorisations does not carry out international commercial activity with its own aircraft, but it leases the aircraft. Two classic forms of leasing are well-established: *dry-leasing* and *wet-leasing*.

- *Dry-leasing* is the lease of the aircraft *without flight crew*, when the operation of the aircraft is carried out by the *lessee* based on its Air Operator Certificate (AOC). (In possession of the AOC the aircraft may carry out the specific commercial activity of air transport.)

[142] The Supreme Court of Hong Kong ruled that the simultaneous registration of 70 aircraft in China and the United States is unlawful under Article 18 of the Convention. *Civil Air Transport Incorporated v. Central Air Transport Corporation,* International Law Reports, 1952, p. 86.

[143] *Rules for the Provision of Pertinent Data Concerning Aircraft Registered in a State Pursuant to Article 21 of the Convention on International Civil Aviation*—C/1155 C-Min. 179/1–20; ICAO Council Working Paper/12697.

In this basic case the lessee leases the aircraft without flight crew and implements the activity of air forwarding due to its own right to commercial activity with the use of its own identification sign (flight number) and its right to traffic. At that time for the duration of the lease, the aircraft is transferred to the registration of the lessee's State and an authorisation by the authority is necessary for the operation of the aircraft. The AOC is issued by the aviation authority. At the request of the aeronautical enterprise, the aviation authority issues a certificate to justify that the enterprise is in possession of professional capacity, organisational and administrative background, owing to which in compliance with regulations it can secure (organise, manage and control) the safe implementation of the spheres of activity determined in the certificate.

- *Wet-leasing* implies letting the aircraft on lease *with the flight crew* or *part of the flight crew* when the operation of the aircraft is carried out by the *lessor* based on its own AOC.

In this case the lessor places the aircraft at the lessee's disposal along with the flight crew (and technical maintenance, insurance, operational support). The lessor carries out commercial air transport activity according to its own control with the use of its identification sign (flight number) and traffic rights. [This construction also applies to leasing with a part of the crew, that is, the so-called *damp leasing*. In this case the cockpit crew (pilots) are generally provided by the lessor, whereas, the cabin crew (flight-attendants) are secured by the lessee.] Furnishing *aircraft*, *crew*, *maintenance* and *insurance* (ACMI) is a form of wet-lease. The operator/lessor provides ACMI for the lessee, which is an arrangement most prevalent in the cargo market.

Leasing agreements may also facilitate that aircraft are transferred for continued use abroad via lease, charter or interchange so that the aircraft remains in the registry of the State of the lessor. In that case the aviation authorities of the two concerned States conclude a separate agreement, in which they stipulate that the aviation authority of the State of the lessee wholly or partly exercises the functions of the State of registry and carries out its duties. 'The State of registry shall be relieved of responsibility with respect to the functions and duties transferred' related to that aircraft [Article 83 *bis a)*].

In the case of the construction of *wet-leasing* (lease and operation with crew) an agreement between the two aviation authorities (registering and controlling the operator) may be concluded if the operation is maintained with the use of the signal, flight number and commercial rights of the lessee (the operator). Thus, the aircraft is in the registry of the lessor, whereas the operation is controlled by the aviation authority of the State of the lessee. The transfer is not implemented automatically because its conditions are the conclusion of a written agreement between the parties as well as the registration and publication of the agreement by the ICAO Council, or the direct notification of other countries' civil aviation authorities by the contracting States. Otherwise, the transfer of responsibility will have no legal force.[144] The contracting States have extended the application of the rule to the airlines of jointly operated organisations [Articles 77, 83 *bis c)*].

[144] Schnitker and Kaar (2013), pp. 92–94.

The first meritorious amendment of the Convention ensued under Article 83 *bis*,[145] which required professional preparation of nearly 20 years. Despite this, pursuant to the rule, which was accepted by the ICAO Assembly in 1980 and took effect 17 years later, an insignificant number of agreements between authorities have been made.[146]

2.3.8 Exemption from Seizure on Patent Claims of Civil Aircraft

The aircraft sales contract contains various essential elements to protect the parties from further debates.[147] One of the elements of aircraft financing contracts is patent indemnities. This means that the manufacturer will indemnify the buyer against liabilities, costs and expenses for any actual or alleged patent infringement via the buyer's use of the aircraft. The indemnity will normally be limited to States and the benefits mentioned below 'shall apply only to such States, parties to the Chicago Convention (1944), as they

1. are either parties to the International Convention for the Protection of Industrial Property (1883) and to any amendments thereof;[148] or
2. have enacted domestic patent laws which recognize and give adequate protection to inventions made by the nationals of other States parties to the Chicago Convention' [Article 27 *c)*].

---

[145] ICAO Doc 9318 Protocol Relating to an Amendment to the Convention on International Civil Aviation (Article 83 *bis*) signed at Montreal on 6 October 1980, 23rd Session of the Assembly.

[146] On the basis of Article 83 *bis* few agreements (altogether 174 before 2018) have been concluded. The construction has not become persuasive, although it has advantages, for example, financial ones. For aircraft manufactured and registered in the United States, financed by a US bank and let on lease to a foreign airline, the bank may reclaim the tax locally. *Legal Committee 37th Session, Safety aspect of economic liberalisation and Article 83 bis*, LC/37–WP/2–7, September 2018, p. 1.; Guidance on the Implementation of Article 83 *bis* of the Convention on International Civil Aviation. Cir 295 LE/2, February 2003.

[147] Such as in sales contract for new aircraft: (1) Warranties and Exclusions, (2) Patent Indemnities, (3) Assignability, (4) Excusable Delay, (4) Purchase Price, (5) Manufacturer Supports, (6) Service Life Policy, (7) Customer Support, (8) Buyer Furnished Equipment, (9) Performance Guarantees, (10) Delivery, Certification, Registration, (11) Governing Law, etc.

[148] The Paris Convention (1883) provides for the protection of industrial property, which was passed by the contracting States on 20 March 1883 and has been amended several times [Brussels (1900), Washington D.C. (1911), The Hague (1925), London (1934), Lisbon (1958) and Stockholm (1967)]. The Paris Convention applies to industrial property in the broadest sense, including patents, trademarks, industrial designs, utility models, service marks, trade names, geographical indications and the repression of unfair competition. The Paris Convention has 180 contracting States (www.wipo.int/treaties/en/ip/paris).

'While engaged in international air navigation, any authorised entry of aircraft of a contracting State into the territory of another contracting State or authorised transit across the territory of such State with or without landings *may not entail any seizure* or *detention* of the aircraft or any claim against the owner or operator thereof or any other interference therewith by or on behalf of such State or any person therein, on the ground that the construction, mechanism, parts, accessories or operation of the aircraft is an infringement of any *patent*, design, or *model* duly granted or registered in the State whose territory is entered by the aircraft'. This protection is affirmed by the contracting States via the stipulation that 'no deposit of security in connection with the foregoing exemption from seizure or detention of the aircraft may in any case be required' [Article 27 *a)*].

The provisions above shall also be applicable to the storage of spare parts and spare equipment for the aircraft and the right to *use* and *install* the same in the repair of an aircraft of a contracting State in the territory of any other contracting State, provided that any patented part or equipment so stored may not be sold or distributed internally in or exported commercially from the contracting State entered by the aircraft [Article 27 *b)*].

If a computer software is installed on the aircraft (the computer equipment and the engines are the most expensive parts of the aircraft), the manufacturer should also provide an indemnity in respect of any actual or alleged copyright infringement. The manufacturer will normally limit the indemnity to claims in States which are Members of the Berne Union and recognise computer software as 'work' under the Berne Convention for the Protection of Literary and Artistic Works (1886).[149]

2.3.9 Documents Carried on Board the Civil Aircraft

'The appropriate authorities of each of the contracting States shall have the right, without unreasonable delay, to *search* aircraft of other contracting States on landing or departure, and *to inspect the certificates* and *other documents prescribed by the Convention*' (Article 16). The treaty-maker does not prescribe the inspection of documents as an obligation, but it provides this opportunity of inspection for the authorities of the Member States. The question arises to what scope this authorisation ranges beyond the physical limitations of the avoidance of unreasonable delay.

In its resolution, the ICAO Council[150] construes the inspection in a broad scope and permits, beyond the checking of certificates and documents enumerated below, the inspection of all the documentation and procedures related to operation as well as

[149]The Berne Convention (1886) deals with the protection of works and the rights of their authors. It provides creators such as authors, musicians, poets, painters, etc., with the means to control how, by whom and under what terms their works are used. The Berne Convention has 181 contracting States (www.wipo.int/treaties/en/ip/berne).

[150]ICAO Council/1139 Attachment to Council Resolution of 13 June 2001, C–Min 163/8. p. 93.

of technical requirements and circumstances related to the aircraft, which is in conformity with the Convention and its Annexes, that is, reasonable from the viewpoint of aviation safety.

It is both the responsibility and obligation of the pilot-in-command of the aircraft to make sure before the departure of the flight that the documents are on board, and then in case of inspection, to show them to the experts of the competent authority.

Every aircraft of a contracting State engaged in international air navigation carries the following documents in conformity with the conditions prescribed in the Convention:

(a) *Certificate of registration*

Each aircraft has to dispose of such a certificate, which facilitates the precise identification of the aircraft within the State of registry.

(b) *Certificate of airworthiness*[151]

Each aircraft engaged in international navigation shall be provided with a certificate of airworthiness issued or rendered valid by the State in which it is registered (Article 31).

Without a certificate of airworthiness, no aircraft may be operated and may fly; otherwise, it qualifies as a sheer object or a simple movable device. The certificate of airworthiness in addition to the certificate of design adequacy of the aircraft certifies the adequacy of the aircraft for air navigation. The authority issues the certificate of airworthiness on the basis of preliminary inspection, the checking of good working order on the ground and in the air, if necessary, as well as on the basis of documents which manifest whether the aircraft fulfils the specifications of airworthiness and meets the requirements of aviation safety.

(c) *Appropriate certificates of competency and licences*[152] for each member of the flight crew.

ICAO attaches the obtainment of the appropriate certificates of competency and licences to the fulfilment of a strict system of conditions determined under Annex 1 to the Convention on Personnel Licensing. The Convention prescribes the obtainment of appropriate certificates of competency and licences for the pilots, the navigators, the engineers, the air traffic controllers, the flight operation and navigation officers, the ground handling and airport operators. 'The pilot of every aircraft and other members of the operating crew of every aircraft engaged in international navigation shall be provided with certificates of competency and licenses issued or rendered valid by the State in which the aircraft is registered. Each contracting State reserves the right to refuse to recognize, for the purpose of flight above its own territory, certificates of competency and licenses granted to any of its nationals by another contracting State' [Article 32 *a)–b)*].

---

[151] ICAO Annex 8 on Airworthiness of Aircraft, Chap. V, Article 31.; ICAO Doc 9760 Airworthiness Manual. 4th edn., 2020.

[152] ICAO Annex 1 on Personnel Licensing. 13th edn., July 2020.

(d) *Journey log book* (or board calendar), which contains data on the aircraft, crew members and flights.

For each aircraft engaged in international navigation a journey log book is kept, in which the 'particulars of the aircraft, its crew and of each journey' are entered in such form as may be prescribed from time to time pursuant to the Convention (Article 34).

(e) 'If it is equipped with a *radio apparatus, the aircraft radio station licence*' (Article 30).

'The aircraft of each contracting State may, in or over the territory of other contracting States, carry a radio transmitting apparatus only if a license to install and operate such apparatus has been issued by the appropriate authorities of the State in which the aircraft is registered. The use of the radio transmitting apparatus in the territory of the contracting State whose territory is flown over is in accordance with the regulations prescribed by that State' [Article 30 *a)*]. 'Radio transmitting apparatus may be used only by members of the flight crew who are provided with a special licence for the purpose issued by the appropriate authorities of the State in which the aircraft is registered' [Article 30 *b)*].

It proceeds from the latter rule that passengers may not use a mobile phone in the air, which, however, has been surpassed by technological development. At the 29th Assembly of ICAO (1992), the Member States decided that persons with no authorisation from an authority (passengers) may also use such devices for telephone conversations, if they observe the pertinent rules.[153]

(f) 'If it carries passengers, a *list of their names* and *places of embarkation and destination*'.
(g) 'If it carries cargo, a *manifest* and *detailed declaration of the cargo*' [Article 29 *f)–g)*].

After a time keeping further documents on board became reasonable, but the Member States did not deem the amendment of the Convention expedient, therefore, these requirements were set forth under the Annexes. In practice, it is necessary to keep on board the documents of the Air Operator Certificate (AOC), the Certificate of Aircraft Liability Insurance, the Noise Certificate, the declaration issued by the MRO technical organisation on the technical adequacy of the aircraft, the dispatch under the Minimum Equipment List (MEL) of the aircraft and the certification of the periodical destruction of rodents on board. At the time of epidemics, the World Health Organization (WHO) may require the disinfection of the aircraft and the production of certifying documents.

'Certificates of airworthiness and certificates of competency and licences issued or rendered valid by the contracting State in which the aircraft is registered are recognized as valid by the other contracting States, provided that the requirements under which

[153] ICAO Doc 9848 *Assembly Resolution* A29–19.

such certificates or licenses were issued or rendered valid are equal to or above the *minimum standards* which may be established from time to time' by ICAO (Article 33). So far as the conditions required by valid international standards do not comply with the content of the certificates of airworthiness or of competency and licences issued by the authority of the Member State, that is, the documents do not comply in every respect with the prescriptions of ICAO, these differences need to be indicated in a clause. In the case of the airworthiness certificate a complete enumeration of the details needs to be endorsed. In the case of competency and licences certificates the particulars of which do not satisfy the conditions in full shall be indicated on the licence or its attachment [Article 39 *a)–b)*]. 'No aircraft or personnel having certificates or licenses so endorsed may participate in international navigation, except with the permission of the State or States whose territory is entered' (Article 40).

However, the application of this regulation does not ensue in practice, since the sanctions in response to the differences elucidate several basic problems; namely, the situation proceeding from the differences of certificates cannot be treated efficiently and transparently bilaterally. Therefore, due to such presumed or real transitional exemptions, ICAO has not been interested in the halt of international air traffic between two Member States, but it may also frown upon the continuation of commercial air transport between two amicable States despite the persistent differences. The interest of ICAO is that these differences are corrected as a final solution in the system of checks and balances instead of being sanctioned. Pursuant to the Convention, there may be differences from the rules of ICAO as in the case above, but emphatically only if the difference is registered (announced) in the multilateral aviation safety and security system of ICAO, and it is corrected and implemented within a specific time.

2.4 Non-Scheduled flights

The international character of aviation proceeds from its nature of traversing borders. From the title of the Convention, that is, Convention on International Civil Aviation, we may basically infer *rubro ad nigrum*.[154] The title positively conveys to the applier of the law, even if it is explicitly not highlighted in the text, that the rules of the Convention are to be applied to international civil flights, not domestic civil flights. Pursuant to the Convention, the air service is *international* if the aircraft 'passes through the air space over the territory of more than one State' [Article 96 *b)*]. The separation of international and domestic flights does not have special significance from the viewpoint of performing the flights. Thus, ICAO Members' legal relations imply the obligation of the Member States to transplant the prescribed

[154] Rubro ad nigrum, that is, 'from the red to the black'; which implies that the meaning of the text of the law is elucidated and explicated by the title of a statute. In the Middle Ages, glossators wrote the titles of the chapters of statutes in red, while the content was in black. Bánk (1993), p. 10.

international Standards and Recommended Practices (SARPs) into their national rules. In these terms, the major performers of the industry (air carriers, airports, air traffic service providers, maintenance and ground handling companies, etc.) must apply the ICAO regulations upon carrying out domestic civil flights as well. The essence of the separation is that in the event of incidents, disputes or inspections related to domestic civil flights, the Convention does not have legal force and any reference thereto is inadmissible. At the same time, if international and domestic flights take place in the same airspace, there may be an incident when domestic and international flights are implicated in conflict. The examination must ensue within the purview of the Convention since one of the parties was engaged in international flight.

As a main rule, the Convention does allow flights carried out unilaterally between countries. Air traffic is always delimited by the sovereign airspace of the other country, that is, if an aircraft leaves the airspace of its homeland (A) and flies into the airspace of country (B), the aircraft will be governed by the sovereign power of country (B). If an air carrier flies into the national airspace of another State during a *non-scheduled flight*, it needs a flight plan and authorisation from the air traffic management (ATM) in all cases. If the air carrier intends to operate an international *scheduled air service* continually with regular traffic to another country for *commercial purposes*[155]—besides the flight plan and the ATM authorisation—further permissions and bilateral or multilateral Air Services Agreements (ASAs) between the concerned States are to be obtained mandatorily. Each aircraft, irrespective of the character of its operation (non-scheduled or scheduled flight), is obliged to observe consistently and implement the rules of the air in foreign airspaces.

'Each contracting State agrees that all aircraft of the other contracting States, being an aircraft *not engaged in scheduled* international air services shall have the right, *subject to the observance of the terms of the Convention,*

- to make flights into; or
- in transit non-stop above the territory; and
- to make stops for non-traffic purposes' in the contracting States.

The exercise of these rights does not necessitate '*obtaining prior permission*', but it is 'subject to the right of the State flown over *to require landing*' (Article 5).

Due to accession to the Convention, these rights of flying may be exercised by all aircraft not engaged in scheduled operations. The ICAO Council has not defined the concept of non-scheduled flight, thereby entrusting its definition to national law. In practice, non-scheduled aircraft generally operate for private, business, commercial (seasonal tourist flights) or other purposes (e.g., aid shipment). The rule of the Convention, according to which making 'stops for non-traffic purposes' in the contracting States is admissible, is to be interpreted broadly, because these flights may also be engaged in commercial activity, although not regularly, according to a

[155] 'Air service' means any scheduled air service performed by aircraft for the public transport of passengers, mail or cargo [Article 96 *a)*]. The air carrier operates for commercial purposes, if the flight is carried out for remuneration or hire for the public transport of passengers, cargo or mail.

schedule. The most established form of non-scheduled flights is the charter flight. The operator of charter flights travels without a preliminarily publicised schedule, not under the auspices of intergovernmental agreements and it determines the charges for its services freely. 'Such aircraft, if engaged in the carriage of passengers, cargo, or mail for remuneration or hire on other than scheduled international air services... shall also have the privilege of taking on or discharging passengers, cargo, or mail, subject to the right of any State where such embarkation or discharge takes place to impose such regulations, conditions or limitations as it may consider desirable' (Article 5).

While *non-scheduled* operation does not require air carriers to obtain State permission in advance, *scheduled* operators are obligated to obtain special permission or other authorisation granted under bilateral Air Services Agreements concluded between the parties concerned for commercial activity between two Member States (nota bene: more than two States can be involved). It follows that non-scheduled operators managed flexibly are in an advantageous situation to the detriment of scheduled operators; therefore, the treaty-maker restricted the sphere of action of non-scheduled operators. Any contracting State may request the cancellation of non-scheduled flights, if it deems that these affect detrimentally the scheduled flights operated in the territories where the Convention is applicable.

Undoubtedly, non-scheduled aircraft may operate more freely. However, this does not imply literally that they may fly in the sovereign airspace of a State in the absence of all permissions, without adherence to basic requirements:

1. Although non-scheduled flights are authorised to make flights into the territory of a contracting State; or to fly in transit non-stop over its territory; or to make stops for *non-traffic purposes* on route to their destination *without prior permission*, they may exercise these rights exclusively in compliance with the Rules of the Air (Annex 2) and with the observance of the conditions of the Convention (Article 5). Pursuant to the Convention, the activity of the carrier upon 'a stop for non-traffic purposes means a landing for any purpose other than taking on or discharging passengers, cargo or mail' [Article 96 *d)*].
2. The conditions in accordance with the international rules of ICAO are regulated on a national level by the State, which demands adherence to these rules and procedures by the user of its airspace. In practice, the pilot or the operator of the non-scheduled flight announces the fact of flying in advance and submits a flight plan with a view to its performance, in which the pilot informs the States over the territory of which the aircraft will traverse at a pre-determined speed.[156] Keeping to

---

[156]Speed at higher altitudes is indicated by the so-called 'Mach number'. Mach is the speed of sound, and the Mach number is a percentage of that speed. The number was designated in honour of Ernst Mach (1838–1916). Long-haul airplanes fly slightly faster than short-haul ones. The Boeing 747, Airbus A380, or Boeing 777 will fly between 0.84 and 0.88 Mach (84–88% of the speed of sound). For narrow-body jets like the B-737 or Airbus A320, this range is between 0.74 and 0.80 Mach. The optimum speed is different for every flight. If the aircraft needs to be on time, or if fuel burn is a decisive factor, the pilots will plan at what Mach the flight is the most fuel-efficient. The recommended Mach is provided to the cockpit crew as part of the flight plan. Smith (2018), p. 20.

the speed is one of the guarantees of safe separation from other aircraft on the same route and of the precise arrival of the cockpit crew at a busy destination according to the predetermined landing slot. If the aircraft does not possess a valid flight plan, it may not enter the airspace of the other country. Alternatively, if it does possess a flight plan, but the pilot of the airplane does not observe the rules of the air in the national airspace of the sovereign State, the State flown over may require landing and take measures vis-a-vis the pilot of the non-scheduled flight (Article 5).

3. The contracting States may not only coerce the airplane to land, but they may also 'reserve the right, for reasons of safety of flight, to *require aircraft* desiring to proceed over regions which are inaccessible or without adequate air navigation facilities *to follow prescribed routes*, or to *obtain special permission* for such flights' (Article 5). 'Each contracting State undertakes to adopt measures to ensure that every aircraft flying over or manoeuvring within its territory and that every aircraft carrying its nationality mark, wherever such registered aircraft may be, shall comply with the rules and regulations relating to the flight and manoeuvre of aircraft there in force.... Each contracting State *undertakes to insure the prosecution* of all persons violating the regulations applicable' (Article 12).

2.4.1 Flight without Prior Permission

Safeguarding, surveillance and active defence of their airspaces are primary tasks for all States, since the strike of a contingent enemy may most of all be expected through the airspace. The long-range radars and satellites monitoring all events to the most minute detail work in a concentrated system and they furnish data for the centre, on the basis of which the changes in the airspace can be tracked precisely and the necessary measures may be issued promptly for execution. The States defend their national airspaces 24 h a day. In the event of unauthorised access to the airspace, the air defence may detain (intercept) any aircraft for the purpose of identification and may demand landing in specific cases. If the aircraft does not obey the demand, coercive measures may be applied.

Violation in National Airspace

A strange incident occurred early in the morning on 28 May 1987. The 19-year-old Mathias Rust from West Germany managed to fly on his private airplane into the depth of one of the most defended Soviet airspaces and as the culmination of the journey he landed on the Red Square in Moscow. Although the air defence had been alerted twice, moreover, intercepting fighter planes

(continued)

had also ascended toward the conspicuous target, the Soviet air defence failed to apply tactical instruments due to its 'inadmissible carelessness and irresoluteness' as the report of the investigating committee claimed.[157]

Due to a lack of the complete cognizance of facts, the confidential diplomatic efforts of international power games and the connections of the case may only be adumbrated. Why does a fledgling pilot fly unlawfully into a foreign airspace defended by qualified soldiers? According to the management of the Cessna airplane manufacturing company, the action was devised for the purpose of advertising and marketing (promoting this theory, Franz Josef Strauss (1915–1988), the Bavarian Prime Minister arrived for negotiations in Moscow on a Cessna airplane piloted by himself). Mathias Rust himself alleged that he had intended to become a celebrity as a peace activist thanks to this adventurous and spectacular act. At the same time, it is also possible that a well-organised and well-timed political action was orchestrated, which could not be effectuated single-handed. In the tense international situation, these events coincided with the planned drafting of the Soviet-American agreement on the disarmament of European medium-range nuclear missiles and the underlying NATO-dispute. If the plane had been shot, which was highly likely, for the purpose of the enervation of the then increasing confidence in the Soviet Union, the opponents of the détente could have intervened with reference to provocation in the interest of the isolation of the Soviets and of the impediment of the disarmament talks in Geneva.[158] This much is certain and a fact that Mathias Rust, 'the dwarf with wishing cap' from tales, the 'Captain Köpenick' of the nuclear age carrying out

(continued)

[157] The Cessna-172P airplane with the registration mark D-ECJB is a single-engine aircraft originally with four seats, its engine is only 160 horsepower and its maximum speed is 220 km/h. The fuel tank of the airplane could hold fuel sufficient for a 6.5 h' flight. Rust needed a 5 h' flight and 750 km to reach his destination after departing from the Helsinki/Malmo airport (HEM) serving military purposes but also receiving private airplanes. Having flown extraordinarily low, provided with a pilot's licence valid for a couple of weeks and having had hardly 50 h' practice of flying, Rust landed in the heart of Moscow approaching it from the river at about 7:00 p.m. according to local time. On the Red Square, he distributed autographs and talked to people. The police believed that he was an actor from a film, who 'was starring' himself after shooting a film. Two hours later he was arrested. The charges were violation of the frontier, unlawful inflight, the violation of international navigation rules, and related to his acts on the Red Square, malicious hooliganism, mala fide ruffianism and the grave violation of public order. Rust was sentenced to 4 years' imprisonment by the Soviet Supreme Court. Sipos (1987).

[158] Here we may draw a historical parallel with period events such as the coming to light of the letter of Caspar W. Weinberger (1917–2006), the American Defence Minister written on 15 November 1985 about Soviet breaches of law, which stirred up an international scandal after being publicised just before the meeting of Ronald Reagan (1911–2004) and Mikhail Gorbachev (1931–2022) in Geneva. In this respect the case of Nicholas Daniloff, the reputed American journalist is relevant, who was arrested by the Committee of State Security (KGB) with the charge of spying in 1986 and released after 13 days' imprisonment preceding the Reykjavik Summit (11–12 October 1986).

the masterly stroke[159] (as he was called by contemporary journalists),[160] flew into the sovereign airspace of another State without permission, wilfully and systematically violating international law, and breaching navigational and aviation security prescriptions.

What matters beyond the law? History, social relations, and casual human relations imbued with the heavily determined pasts of the two powerful European countries, which permeate the memories of the two nations. With the help of diplomacy and international law, the parties gave an appropriate response to the political provocation, which entwined the relations of the two countries even closer in an approach to the end of the Cold War (1947–1991). The incredible action also entailed unforeseen, but extraordinary avails: the undiminishable damage and disgrace to the reputation of the Soviet Air Defence provided an opportunity for Mikhail Gorbachev (1931–2022), the Chief Secretary of the Central Committee of the Communist Party to remove the supreme chiefs of the military staff opposed to change. Thus, he paved the way for the adoption of comprehensive and renowned reforms familiar as perestroika (restructuring) and glasnost (openness).

At any rate, Mathias Rust would have had the right to fly into the territory of a contracting State if he had complied with the conditions of the Convention. However, he did not observe these conditions, because he did not have a flight plan for the controlled Soviet airspace, furthermore, he switched off his radio after take-off while the Finnish air traffic controller was trying to warn him at all available frequencies that he had committed a navigational error and was flying in the wrong direction. He had designated the Bromma Stockholm Airport (BMA) as a place of destination, whereas, he was not heading in that direction. He overreached all the possible rules. Moreover, when the Soviet fighter plane spotted his plane, he started flying in circles maliciously pretending that he had got lost.

---

[159] The German historical town of Köpenick is indebted for its worldwide fame to the great swindler, Friedrich Wilhelm Voigt (1849–1922), who spent almost his whole life, 40 years in prison for the commission of crimes against property. In 1906, shortly after his release from prison at the age of 56, he got hold of a Prussian Guard captain's uniform from shops and dressed in it, then he tested the effect of the uniform successfully. As a result, he summoned a sergeant and four grenadiers to follow him to the town of Köpenick. With his soldiers, he occupied the town hall and arrested the mayor and the treasurer with the charge of falsifying the cash book. He removed 4002 Marks 37 Pfennigs from the safe-deposit and made out an acknowledgement of the receipt with the signature of his former governor of the prison. From the town hall, he headed for the railway station and after putting on his civilian garment, he disappeared in the crowd. He was arrested ten days later. He was sentenced to 4 years' imprisonment for theft, forging documents, abuse of the identity of an official functionary as well as for the unlawful restraint of personal freedom. The 'blushing impudence' provoked smiles and having become a hero, 'the Captain of Köpenick' was granted a reprieve by William II (1859–1941) in August 1908. Földes, György: The Captain of Köpenick—a German hero's Luxembourg past. *Luxemburg Times*, 25 March 2017 (www.luxtimes.lu/en/luxembourg/the-captain-of-koepenick-a-german-hero-s-luxembourg-past).

[160] *BRD Zeitung* and *Lübecker Nachrichten*, June 1987.

The Chicago Convention formulates lucidly: 'Each contracting State agrees not to use civil aviation for any purpose inconsistent with the aims of the Convention' (Article 4). In addition to the continual observance of State sovereignty, the parties are obligated to cooperate. The Rules of the Air shall be applied to the aircraft engaged in international air navigation of all contracting States without distinction as to nationality. These rules shall be complied with by such aircraft upon entering or departing from or while within the territory of a contracting State (Article 11).

Beyond the regulatory framework, under Annex 2 to the Convention on the Rules of the Air (like the rules of the Highway Code related to traffic on public roads), ICAO defines the standard procedure of international civil aviation as mandatory. This implies that the States need to notify differences from any provision of the Annex as it is stipulated by the Convention (Article 38). Annex 2 contains the general requirements for Visual Flight Rules (VFR) and Instrument Flight Rules (IFR).[161] Each of these rules is a Standard, so their observance by the Member States is mandatory. On that basis, the cockpit crew (pilots) need to submit a flight plan before take-off to cross the State border and need to request prior permission actually to ascend. During the whole flight time, the pilots need to be in radio contact with the air navigation control service concerned, and as a main rule, the cockpit crew need to take off from and land at the airports requested and designated in advance. The pilots also need to be in possession of meteorological data and information to carry out the flight safely.

Preceding the flight, the pilots check whether the aircraft is capable of the safe implementation of the task (e.g., all required instruments and equipment are functioning properly; the gross weight of the aircraft[162] does not exceed the limitation;

---

[161] In visual flight, it is the responsibility of the pilot to separate from other aircraft since orientation is dependent on the visual skills of the pilot. During instrument flight, the pilot follows the designated route based on the navigation instruments of the aircraft: 99% of commercial civil flights are carried out according to the latter solution.

[162] There are weight limits for the different operational regimes, including limits for taxiing, taking off and landing. The maximum take-off weight of the Airbus A380 exceeds 453,000 kg. A Boeing 747's weight can be as high as 400,000 kg. For an Airbus A320 or Boeing 737, it is approx. 77,000 kg. A 50-passenger turboprop or regional jet will top out at around 27,215 kg. These are maximums. The actual, admissible take-off weight varies with weather, runway length and other factors. Passengers are calculated to weigh 86 kg per person (including carry-ons) and 13.6 kg per checked bag. The boarding tallies are added to Basic Operating Weight (BOW), another fixed value that accounts for the plane itself, replete with all furnishings, supplies, and crew. Once fuel and cargo are added in, the result is the total gross 'ramp' or taxi weight. Fuel used for taxiing is subtracted to reveal the take-off weight. In the case of a fully loaded Boeing 747, four hundred passengers and their suitcases—about 34,000 kg together—make up only around 10% of the total bulk. Fuel, rather than people or their belongings, is the greater factor, sometimes accounting for a third or more of a plane's sum heft. Because of this, pilots calculate their kerosene in kg, not litres. Everything from initial fuelling to enroute burn is added or subtracted by weight, not volume. Both weight and its distribution are important. A plane's centre of gravity, which shifts as fuel is consumed, is calculated prior to flight and must remain within limits for take-off and landing. Pilots are trained in the particulars of weight and balance, but the grunt work is taken care of by the load-planners and dispatchers. Smith (2018), p. 22.

the aircraft is correctly loaded for all stages of the flight; the fuel supplies are sufficient for a particular flight; the aircraft is safe for the flight in all respects; the crew members are in good physical condition to perform their duties; all relevant aeronautical maps, charts and other documentation are carried, etc.). Beyond this, the pilots need to familiarise themselves with all the information at their disposal concerning the planned flight, and they need to study the available meteorological reports and forecasts.[163] Furthermore, the pilot-in-command needs to devise an alternative plan for the case if the flight cannot be implemented according to the original plan.

The pilot-in-command is responsible for the following:

- the commencement, continuation, diversion and closure of a flight by the aircraft;
- safety and operation of the aircraft during flight time;
- safety of the persons and cargo carried on aircraft;
- safety and conduct of the crew members on the aircraft;
- compliance with any information, instructions or directions relating to the whole flight;
- the observance of the requirements of the operations manual provided by the operator of the aircraft.[164]

The pilot-in-command must fulfil the above-mentioned obligations before and during the flight. It is always the pilot-in-command who is responsible for operations according to the Rules of the Air, furthermore, he is obligated to make decisions on issues concerning the operation of the aircraft under his command. For flying in the *controlled airspace* subject to the surveillance of the air navigation control, the fulfilment of two basic requirements is necessary:

1. In the interest of aviation safety and crossing State borders, it is pre-eminently significant from the viewpoint of air traffic management that, at least 30 min before take-off, a *flight plan* (FLP) is submitted by the operator of the aircraft to the air navigation service provider (ANSP). The utilisation of the airspace for air traffic is based on a valid flight plan submitted to and acknowledged by the air navigation service provider, without which no flight is admissible. The flight plan contains all the data prescribed for air navigation control; it also contains data necessary for the search and rescue of the aircraft in trouble in a case of emergency, such as the brake release time, the time of arrival of the airplane,

[163] According to Annex 3 to the Convention on Meteorological Service for International Navigation, the meteorological service is obligated to provide meteorological data on the basis of the rules stipulated for international air navigation for crew members, the air traffic controller, the search-rescue unit, the airport control service and all parties concerned with operation. The service provides constant telecommunication connection, prepares reports and forecasts at determined periods, which, for example, help the pilots prepare for the journey. Thus, a forecast for the changing weather of the recipient airport determines the preparation of the flight plan and the designation of an alternate aerodrome. ICAO Annex 3 on Meteorological Service for International Navigation, 20th edn., July 2018.

[164] Bartsch (2018), p. 225.

the designated airport and the secondary (alternate) airport in the event of an unforeseen problem. The air traffic controller enters these data included in the flight plan into the system of air navigation control so that, at the time of take-off, the necessary information should be available for, or it may be issued (e.g., in the form of permission) to the cockpit crew of the aircraft. The movement of the aircraft is tracked on the secondary radar equipment.

2. The other basic requirement is the availability on board of an electronic unit, the *transponder*, which sends automatic responses to the secondary radar on the ground, which continuously relays questioning impulses. In this system, the radio signal relayed from the radar station on the ground initiates the radiation of the radio signal of the other station on board the aircraft, then it receives the arriving responses and forwards them to the processing unit. Due to its use, the data of the specific aircraft appear on the radar screen, so the air traffic control officers (ATCOs) can see the line signal of the aircraft, its exact position, speed, altitude and the tendencies in its movement (at many airports, the transponder-radar link is used to track planes along taxiways as well). The air traffic control (ATC) carries out its work on the basis of continuously updated databases and real-time positioning data. In addition, by comparing the routes and data of airplanes, conflict research can also be carried out.

Basically, from these two significant data stores and on the basis of the information yielded by them, air traffic controllers can safely control the flow of air traffic within their area of competence by giving permissions and concrete instructions.

2.4.2 The Misuse of Civil Aviation

Each contracting State agrees not to use civil aviation for any purpose inconsistent with the aims of the Convention (Article 4).

The contracting States refer to the use of civil aviation inconsistent with the aims of the Convention under Paras. *b)* and *d)* of Article 3 *bis*, which, however, does not enlarge upon its essential content. Perhaps it is because of the general formulation that the concrete enforcement of this rule has never ensued either by the ICAO Assembly or the Council in practice.[165] The Preamble of the Convention promotes the interpretation, since it states lucidly: the misuse of civil aviation can become a threat to the general security. Beyond peaceful cooperation and the enforcement of all other international basic principles, the Member States have assumed the obligation to carry out air carriage benevolently and to decrease the risk of the evolution of situations of danger proceeding from unlawful activities.

The categorisation of misuse is not a simple task, in addition, the treaty-maker entrusts the Member States with defining these activities. In a broad construction, all

[165] Milde (1986), pp. 105–130.

activities committed unlawfully and maliciously belong here. In a narrow construction, this rule is designed to promote the protection of universal objectives and values formulated under the Preamble of the Convention ('yet its abuse can become a threat to the general security'). We do not need vivid imagination to understand the following: abuse may include the wilful overreaching of rules, unlawful conduct, the support of the perpetrators of criminal acts, secret missions targeting other States (observation with detectors fitted on civil aircraft),[166] spying, the transport of soldiers disguised as passengers for deployment. Furthermore, the illegal carriage of drugs or dangerous products or smuggling persons on board a civil aircraft may also occur. In daily routine the carriage of illegal cargo causes trouble most of the time. It has also occurred that the cargo disguised as commercial products (e.g., bearings or heavy pétanque boules) actually consisted of strategic weapons or ammunition. If such products are placed in the storage space or on the board of the civil aircraft, they must be preliminarily declared since '*no munitions of war* or *implements of war may be carried* in or above the territory of a State in aircraft engaged in international navigation, except by *permission of such State*. Each State *shall determine by regulations* what constitutes munitions of war or implements of war for the purposes of this Article of the Convention' [Article 35 *a)*].

In cases when directly the State is the consignor behind the carriage of implements of war, the activity of the aircraft registered as civilian navigated by civilian crew (pilot-in-command and first officer/second officer) does not fall under the Convention, but it is deemed to be a flight carried out by a State aircraft. If this carriage remains camouflaged and the civilian character as a disguise is maintained, we still deem it to be the activity of a State aircraft. Of course, this is revealed only in case an accident or incident occurs, or, if the authority of the other Member State having jurisdiction inspects the cargo of the airplane or searches its board at the airport or gains cognizance about the case in any other way. That is, '*the appropriate authorities* of each of the contracting States *shall have the right, without unreasonable delay, to search the aircraft* of other contracting States on landing or departure or to inspect the certificates and other documents prescribed by the Convention' (Article 16). No grounded suspicion has to substantiate the search or inspection. In addition, no suspicion is necessary, and a random inspection is admissible in compliance with the rules of international law. From the point of view of jurisdiction, the board of the civil aircraft qualifies as quasi-State territory during flight and at the airport, which means that the jurisdiction of the registering State prevails. However, the authorities of the recipient State have the right to embark the board of the aircraft registered in another State and effect official acts there.

For the purpose of the prevention of misuse 'each contracting State reserves the right, for reasons of public order and safety, *to regulate or prohibit the carriage in or above its territory of articles* other than' munitions of war or implements of war [Article 35 *b)*]. Such objects, products include, for example, food forwarded by helicopter to hostile forces. Drugs distributed by aircraft may also belong here.

---

[166] Tuck (1986), p. 167.

Handbills and prints distributed from balloons capable of the disturbance of public order and causing a great deal of trouble for the reigning power are also regarded as such. ‘Each contracting State may prohibit or regulate the use of photographic apparatus in aircraft over its territory’ (Article 36). This stipulation outdated today has been overridden by the development of technology, whereas non-adherence to this rule in the Cold War (1947–1991) era may easily have compelled the curiously prying ‘perpetrator’ diligently using their cameras to give an explanation. Today, military and civil satellites can see everything that needs to be seen, not to mention the unmanned drones and balloons carrying out special missions.

Upon the misuse of civil aviation, it has no significance that on board what type of aircraft, of what registration the unlawful act endangers the objectives of the Convention and severely threatens the general safety of aviation. What matters essentially is that the authorities of the recipient Member State may avail themselves of the broad scope of competence guaranteed for them: they may demand landing (Article 5), restrict or prohibit flight above their territory (Article 9), search the aircraft and inspect the documents (Article 16), and regulate or prohibit the carriage of certain products above their territory [Article 35 *b)*].

2.5 Scheduled Flights

Upon the conclusion of the Chicago Convention, concerning the issues of aviation, the interests of the Great Powers differed according to their positions and losses sustained in World War II. With respect to the fact that, in the territory of the United States, no battles were fought in the physical sense, the approx. 20,000 military aircraft (mainly Dakota DC-3 and Skymaster DC-4 designed to carry troops, cargo and casualties) manufactured for the Allied Powers under relatively ‘peaceful’ circumstances, could be technically converted by the United States to line up for civil aviation. Thus, the United States advocated the freedom of the air and complete liberalisation. In contrast, Great Britain, having suffered huge losses and in possession of few usable airplanes, among them mainly bombers, urged the establishment of a system in which competition was heavily restricted. Accordingly, the Member States themselves as well as an international organisation congregating the airlines instead of the States would have made decisions on commercial issues (tariffs, frequencies and capacity) and on the allocation of air routes.

As a result of negotiations, the British principle professing the freedom of the States to make decisions gained the upper hand. This has determined the system of permissions and authorisations necessary for the operation of scheduled flights set forth under bilateral or multilateral Air Services Agreements up to this day. In this system, ‘no scheduled international air service may be operated over or into the territory of a contracting State, except with the *special permission* or *other authorization* of that State, and in accordance with the terms of such permission or authorization’ (Article 6). In other words, in the national airspaces of the Member

States, the scheduled airlines of other States may carry out air services with commercial purposes exclusively on the basis of bilateral and multilateral agreements concluded by the States.

The ICAO Council defined the concept of scheduled international air service at the request of the Member States. According to the ICAO, a scheduled international air service is a series of flights described by all the following characteristics:

- it passes through the airspace over the territories of more than one State; and
- it is performed by aircraft for the transport of passengers, mail or cargo for remuneration in such a manner that
  - each flight is open to be used by the members of the public, and
  - it is operated so as to serve traffic between the same two or more points, either according to a publicised timetable or with flights so regular or frequent that they constitute a recognisably systematic series.[167]

The rules of international law pertaining to aviation must be construed as a uniform system, which guarantees framework regulation. The Convention regulates the international dimension of civil aviation and establishes minimum requirements concerning aviation safety, security and technology in the relations between Member States. Simultaneously, it entrusts States to regulate further, mainly commercial issues under Air Services Agreements. The conclusion of Air Services Agreements between States became the prerequisite for the launch of air traffic carried out by scheduled commercial flights via registered and designated air carriers between the two States. Under these circumstances, a scheduled flight is subject to the same conditions as a non-scheduled flight, so both need to dispose of flight plans and transponders on board the aircraft, but the operation of scheduled flights, because of their commercial character, requires prior permission at governmental level. This permission is designated as an Air Services Agreement. The system of bilateral or multilateral Air Services Agreements is the outcome of a historical situation and a compromise,[168] which has basically determined the activity of air transport among countries, that is, international civil aviation up to this day.

2.5.1 Freedoms of the Air

The Freedoms of the Air are not part of the Convention as these are related to commercial activities. Therefore, in the Air Services Agreements, the parties designate the operating airlines and determine the destinations, the capacity and frequency of the flights, furthermore, they mutually guarantee the most important right of access to the market: traffic rights. Traffic rights are the privileges granted in

[167] ICAO Doc 7278—C/841 *Definition of Scheduled International Air Service* (1952).

[168] Cheng (1962), pp. 7–9.

scheduled international air transport, on the basis of which it is up to the decisions of Member States which *air carriers*, with what *route rights* and traffic rights (*Freedoms of the Air)* they permit to fly into their national airspace and to land at their airports[169] for the purpose of carrying out commercial activities (that is, the carriage of passengers, baggage, mail or cargo for remuneration).

- *Route rights* consist of the right of access to markets, in possession of which the operators of the aircraft may fly to endorsed geographical points. This right is manifest in the determined geographical specification of the route(s) or in the combination of geographical specifications, according to which the operators carry out activities of air services and land at designated points of the routes determined in the flight plan.
- *Traffic rights (Freedoms of the Air)* consist of the right of access to markets, according to which the parties to Air Services Agreements determine the traffic rights to be exercised by their airlines and registered aircraft during scheduled flights in and above their territories.

The two rights are to be construed as closely interwoven; one of them determines the routes, i.e., between which cities the traffic can be launched, while the other right determines the commercial content of the traffic (whether the flight may be continued, whether the aircraft may forward between two other countries or within the given country). The air carriers publicise the route rights they exercise in timetables, whereas traffic rights are contained under the Annexes to Air Services Agreements (ASAs).

As the Chicago Convention does not provide for the air freedoms of *scheduled flights*; these are contained by two supplementary agreements (1944), which qualify as sources of law of the Chicago system:

- the ‘Two Freedoms’ Agreement: the International Air Services Transit Agreement (IASTA);[170]
- the ‘Five Freedoms’ Agreement: the International Air Transport Agreement (ATA).[171]

[169] ICAO Doc 9626 *Manual on the Regulation of International Air Transport.* Part IV, Chap. 2, 2.2.1, 2018.

[170] ICAO Doc 7500 *International Air Services Transit Agreement (1944).*

[171] ICAO shall also carry out the functions placed upon it by the International Air Services Transit Agreement and by the International Air Transport Agreement drawn up at Chicago on December 7, 1944, in accordance with the terms and conditions set forth therein [Article 66 *a)*]. The International Air Services Transit Agreement has been ratified by 135 States. The International Air Transport Agreement has been ratified by only 11 States (www.icao.int/secretariat/legal/List).

2.5.2 *Transit Rights (1–2)*

Pursuant to the International Air Services Transit Agreement (1944), the contracting States guarantee for other Member States two *transit rights* with respect to *scheduled international flights*: [It is important to note here that the Chicago Convention guarantees these transit rights (also referred to as technical rights) for non-scheduled flights as well]:

1. Privilege for the air carrier of the home country [A] to fly into the airspace of another country [B], or fly over without landing;
2. Privilege for the air carrier of the home country [A] to land for non-traffic purposes, for technical or safety reasons (e.g., emergency, technical failure, bad weather conditions, fuel intake, unruly passenger, terrorist attack, etc.), while flying in the airspace of another country.

No prior authorisation for carrying out such a landing manoeuvre is necessary, since the Member States are obliged to manifest flexibility in such strained situations, to provide assistance for the landing aircraft and to give permission to interrupt the flight. If the scheduled flight engaged in commercial activity (e.g., carrying tourists) during its journey is obliged to land for problems endangering safety, it may not carry out commercial activity (may not take on passengers or baggage for remuneration) on the spot (other than the destination).

2.5.3 *Commercial Traffic Rights (3–9)*

Pursuant to the International Air Transport Agreement (1944), the Parties to the Convention guarantee traffic rights (3–4–5) beyond transit rights for other Member States with respect to *scheduled international flights*.

3. Privilege for the air carrier of the home country [A] to operate to the airport of the contracting partner State [B] for commercial purposes.

For example, Dubai [A]—New York [B].

4. Privilege for the air carrier of the home country [A] to operate from contracting partner State [B] to the airport of the home country [A] for commercial purposes.

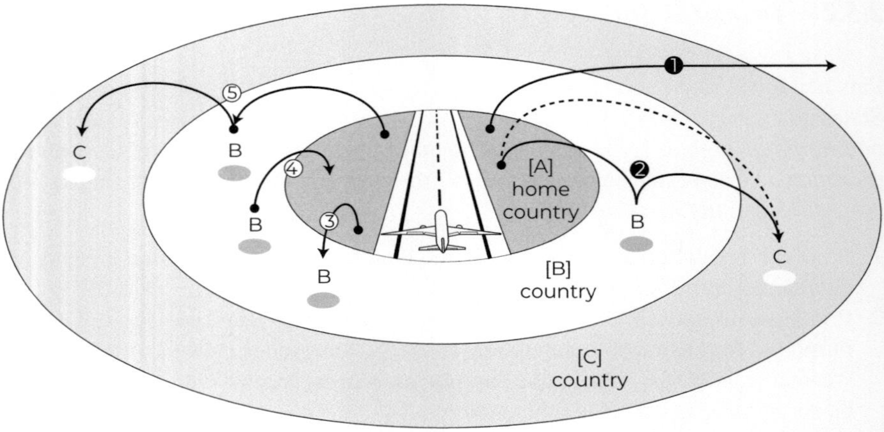

Fig. 2.13 Transit rights (1–2) and commercial traffic rights (3–5)

For example, New York [B]—Dubai [A].

5. Privilege for the air carrier of the home country [A] to operate for commercial purposes on the route between country [B] and a third country [C] so that both the place of departure and the place of destination[172] of the operation are the airport of the home country [A] (Fig. 2.13).

For example, Dubai [A]—New York [B]—Shanghai [C] (and back to Dubai [A]).

The right of the fifth freedom (just like the sixth and seventh) may be exercised with the approval of the third country. In Air Services Agreements, the contracting States made use of further combinations of the rights described above; thus, with respect to *scheduled international flights,* traffic rights 6 and 7 were established. These rights are not stipulated under agreements; they are not legally regulated but have evolved in commercial practice. Freedom 6 is in fact the combination of Freedoms 3 and 4. Cabotage rights (Freedoms 8-9) have evolved over several centuries of commercial practice (Fig. 2.14).

6. Privilege for the air carrier of the home country [A] to operate for commercial purposes in two phases between two other countries [B] and [C] and use the airport of the home country [A] as a point of transfer.

For example, New York [B]—Dubai [A]—Shanghai [C].

[172] *The place of departure*: the town or airport indicated in *the first place* in the air ticket (or the air waybill upon the consignment of cargo); and *the place of destination*: the town or airport indicated as *the last place* in the air ticket/air waybill. It is important to know, for example: on the Dubai (DXB)-New York (JFK) flight with one-way ticket, the place of departure is Dubai and the place of destination is New York, but on the Dubai-New York-Dubai flight with return ticket, the place of departure is Dubai and the place of destination is Dubai [see, Part II, Chap. 9. 3.1].

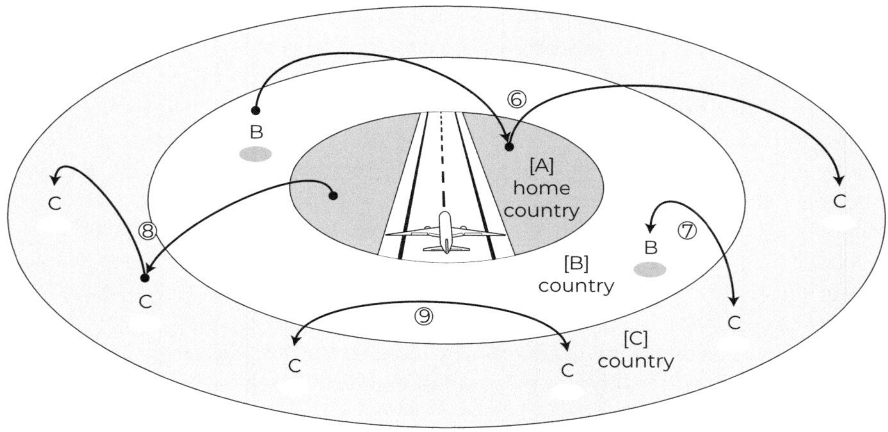

Fig. 2.14 Commercial traffic rights (6–9)

7. Privilege for the air carrier of the home country [A] to operate for commercial purposes between two other countries [B] and [C] without using the airport of the home country [A].

For example, New York [B]—Shanghai [C].

8. Privilege for the air carrier of the home country [A] to operate for commercial purposes between internal points of country [B] (or country [C]), so that both the places of departure and destination of the operation is the airport of the home country [A] (consecutive *cabotage*).

For example, Dubai [A]—New York [B]—Los Angeles [B]; or Dubai [A]—Shanghai [C]—Beijing [C] (and back to Dubai [A]).

9. Privilege for the airline of the home country [A] to operate for commercial purposes among the internal points of country [C] (or country [B]) without the use of the airport of the home country [A] carrying out full domestic air traffic (stand-alone *cabotage*).

For example, New York [B]—Los Angeles [B]; or Beijing [C]—Shanghai [C].[173]

2.5.4 *Cabotage*

The cabotage rights are maritime institutions and the freedoms derive from maritime law. Cabotage was permitted by a coastal State for another State to carry out

[173] Sipos (2018), pp. 141–172.

commercial activity between its two internal points on the basis of mutuality. The French word *caboter* and the Spanish word *cabotaje* mean basically to ship along the shore from foreland to foreland close to the coast within sight.[174] However, maritime cabotage differs from cabotage in air traffic deriving from the character of flying, although, considering their essential objective as an institution delimiting internal competition in the market, they are identical. Maritime cabotage means transport between two ports in the *same geographical unit* within a State on a territorial section surrounded by two different seas or oceans (for example, in the case of the coasts of France bordered by the Atlantic Ocean in the west and the Mediterranean Sea in the south). Whereas, cabotage in air traffic means operating between two airports in *the same political unit* of a given State[175] (for example, the air carrier leaves France behind and, having flown through the jurisdictional territories of several foreign States, lands on the airport of Papeete located on the island of Tahiti in French Polynesia, which is the territory of France).

Cabotage has preeminent significance in countries with large territories and national airspaces, where domestic traffic is far greater, and it is more attractive to engage in commercial activity here from the viewpoint of economic efficiency. Upon the negotiation of Air Services Agreements, the perspective of the permission of cabotage is a serious 'trump', which is not frequently dealt out, since this right has been one of the most treasured commercial privileges until these days. The Convention does not prohibit granting cabotage, but it emphasises that 'each contracting State shall have the right to *refuse* permission to the aircraft of other contracting States to take on *in its territory* passengers, mail and cargo carried for remuneration or hire and destined for another point within its territory' (Article 7).

The rights of cabotage are not always guaranteed even under liberalised Open Skies Agreements, although in these agreements the contracting parties open up their markets mutually to the largest extent before each other.

At the same time, the Convention stipulates that 'each contracting State undertakes not to enter into any arrangements which specifically grant any such privilege on an exclusive basis to any other State or an airline of any other State, and not to obtain any such exclusive privilege from any other State' (Article 7). The emphasis is expressly on exclusivity. This entails that cabotage may not be granted on the basis of exclusivity. Within the Member States of the European Union (EU), for example, the use of cabotage is completely permitted, which the airlines registered in EU Member States often resort to if it has economic potential or commercial opportunity. For example, any EU community air carrier has the right to operate between, for instance, Paris (CDG) and Lyon (LYS). While the air carriers of third countries cannot exercise cabotage within the EU, thus, they cannot enjoy this right.

[174] Mendes de Leon (1992), pp. 1–2.

[175] Cheng (1962), p. 314.

2.5.5 *The International Air Services Transit Agreement*

By accession to the so-called 'Two Freedoms' Agreement [the International Air Services Transit Agreement (IASTA)], the scheduled air carriers of the Member States became entitled to use transit rights. Since the Chicago Convention was concluded under peculiar historical circumstances and barely developed industrial and market conditions, the contracting States did not adopt basic rules on trade, since they entrusted the settlement of these important issues to the relations of the States between one another. Accordingly, all scheduled and commercial aircraft needed to obtain the preliminary consent or the permission of the foreign State to be able to fly into the sovereign airspace above the territory of the other State. Thereby, the States acquired the power to make decisions, which was supported by the international community and the law and was protected via its institutions.

The States which acceded to the IASTA, by reason of the fact of accession to the agreement, did not need further permissions or the conclusion of separate bilateral intergovernmental agreements (IGAs) for the exercise of transit rights by their scheduled flights. At the same time, the contracting States in the IASTA Agreement demanded such conditions for the exercise of transit rights which guaranteed restrictive rights for the countries acceded to the agreement vis-à-vis one another.

These rights promoted the protection of the national and commercial interests of the Member States. Thus, 'each contracting State reserves the right to *withhold* or *revoke* a certificate or permit to an air transport enterprise of another State

- in any case where it is *not satisfied* that the substantial ownership and effective control are vested in nationals of a contracting State, or
- in case of failure of such air transport enterprise to comply with the laws of the State over which it operates, or to perform its obligations under the Agreement' (Article I, Section 5).

The protection defined under Article I serves basically that another country or its air carriers or citizens by the acquisition of substantial ownership or the exercise of effective control cannot manage the airline of a foreign country on the basis of their own interests. Via this rule the sovereign States could also protect their national and economic interests, the domestic air transport industry and their international markets efficaciously. The rule is unequivocal: in bilateral Air Services Agreements between the parties, only those airlines may be appointed to physically carry out air transport between the two States which comply with the legal requirements of *substantial ownership* and *effective control*. Therefore, the Freedoms of the Air with extraordinary significance for airlines can only be exercised in the case of the complete prevalence of the '*national requirement*' (clause). The contracting States did not define the two conditions of the national clause precisely, they entrusted that to the interpretation of national law.

According to the terminology under company law:

- *Substantial ownership* is a primary, legal *(de iure)* condition, which requires quantitative ownership (above 50%) by the State, its citizens or both in the designated airline.
- *Effective control* is a predominant, factual *(de facto)* condition, under which the substantial national owner exercises the rights of ownership via qualitative management constituted by the citizens of the given State.[176]

If the airlines complied with the national requirements above, they were designated under Air Services Agreements.

For example, if Turkish Airlines (TK), as the national airline of Turkey, intends to operate commercially to another country of the world, it may carry out such activity as an airline designated by the Turkish Government only if the air carrier is under *substantial ownership*, in which the natural person of Turkey and/or its business association and/or the Turkish State itself has ownership, which entitles it to a minimum of 50% + 1 majority vote; and if it is under *effective control*, that is, in the management/board controlling the airline provably Turkish citizens are in majority, who may make final decisions freely without external influence.

The designation may be sole [in that case the national (flagged) air carrier is designated], or it may be dual or multiple depending on the market relations, commercial policy and peculiar interests of the designating country. By the designation the air carrier becomes entitled to exercise the commercial Freedoms of the Air.

At the same time, in the liberalised market of the European Union, the concept of the national air carrier has become emptied out. It has been superseded by the *community carrier*, the *principal place of business* of which is registered in any country of the EU and its ownership and control on the level of the Union complies with the clause of substantial ownership and effective control required under EU law.[177]

- The *community carrier* is an airline with traffic rights in the Member States of the European Union, which is in the substantial ownership (50% + 1) of EU Member States and/or the citizens thereof and is under their effective control. Effective control implies not only the preponderance of EU citizens, but also the capacity to make final decisions free from influence, their use of the assets of the company and their right to make business decisions.

[176] Sipos (2023), p. 98.

[177] Regulation (EC) No. 1008/2008 of the European Parliament and of the Council of 24 September 2008 on common rules for the operation of air services in the Community, OJ L 293, Article (1 *f*), 31.10.2008.

The reasons for the 'national requirements' are mainly based on the fact that the national air carrier is considered to be a strategic and economic asset, it serves national interest and defence or emergency needs, and during times of war, it is also necessary to know whether the ownership and control of the air carrier are in the hands of the 'enemy', or otherwise nowadays in a commercial context in the hands of the competitor.[178]

If the requirements of ownership and control are met, the other sovereign State accepts the designated airline as a partner and signs the Air Services Agreement depending on the strict inspection of the conditions. In other words, the traffic rights included in the bilateral Air Services Agreement may be exercised due to the conclusion of the Air Services Agreement by the designated airline to carry out commercial activity. The national clause is basically one of the instruments of power games permeating aviation, a kind of veto right, which provides a kind of protection vis-à-vis foreign ownership and influence. Furthermore, in an extreme case it provides an opportunity for the prevention of the airline of another country from carrying out commercial activity. This special national clause, which is so significant in bilateral agreements in the air transport industry, has become a real impediment to development. It immensely forestalls the privatisation and mergers of airlines, eventually, the evolution of market-based competition as well as the gaining ground of airlines organised on a multinational basis.

The Extra Charge of Transit Flights

The Chicago Convention expressly stipulates that 'no fees, dues or other charges shall be imposed by any contracting State in respect *solely of the right of transit over* or *entry into* or *exit from its territory* of any aircraft of a contracting State or persons or property thereon' (Article 15). This prohibition has been one of the most criticised provisions of the Convention up to now. Namely, some Member States for the use of certain designated routes of their airspace, beyond the determination of due air navigation charges, impose *extra transit charges*. All conditions are given when the aircraft of one Member State intends to use the national airspace of another Member State by exercising the right of transit, because it has the right of entry into and fly over the territory without landing. However, if the aircraft intends to indicate in the flight plan one of the separately designated routes in the national airspace of a Member State and to transit via that route, the aircraft will be obligated to pay further transit charge. It is an open question how this may be admissible despite the definite prohibition under the provision of the Convention.

By accession to the International Air Services Transit Agreement (IASTA), the scheduled airlines of the Member States have become entitled to avail themselves of the two transit rights as basic rights. Thus, the exercise of these rights in the case of scheduled flights did not necessitate the conclusion of bilateral Air Services

---

[178] The 'national requirements' have had disadvantages as well, for example, they represent an obstacle to foreign investment by air carriers and create a negative environment for fair competition. Giemulla (2011), pp. 180–181.

Agreements and the obtainment of special permissions by reason of accession. It is remarkable that among the 135 contracting States of the IASTA Agreement we cannot find a part of the large nation States with extensive continental territories such as Canada, China, Indonesia, Russia, Saudi Arabia (or Brazil, which finally ratified the Convention on 20 July 2022). By reason of the omission of accession, these States guarantee the transit rights for aircraft exclusively due to bilateral negotiations under strict State control. The cause of this is that the concerned States at the air services negotiations impose a special charge, a tariff for the exercise of transit rights, that is, for flights over their territories. Thereby, they obtain extra State revenues in addition to the basic charges due to air navigation services. Certainly, for this reason the States with larger territories did not ratify the IASTA Agreement, while bilaterally they have benefitted financially from their potentialities. Namely, the air carriers operating long-haul flights prefer paying for the shorter route to taking the longer route on their way to their destinations. Therefore, the omission of accession to the agreement in some cases provides broad scope for various business arrangements and deals under bilateral air services settlements between the negotiating parties. A part of the contracting States opts for this solution although the Chicago Convention expressly *(expressis verbis)* prohibits that the Member States 'exact a ransom' from the airlines. The loophole in the law gives rise to the *legal title*, since the concerned States demand this 'extra charge' obviously not under the exclusive pretext that the aircraft of another Member State flies over their territory. The legal title is a matter of legal creativity, then, a matter of agreement.

Trans-Siberian Overflights

At the dawn of aviation, it was impossible to fly from Europe to remote points of the world (and return) by direct flight. At least one stopover was necessary since the airplanes were not capable of flying longer distances. On the way to Asia, landing would usually take place in Moscow; therefore, Russian passengers could embark international flights since Aeroflot (SU) purchased and sold (so-called hard-block) seats on the flights of foreign airlines in the scope of commercial (so-called pooling) agreements. Later, more modern airplanes no longer landed, but the State and its airline did not renounce the revenue from such commercial activity and maintained it under another legal title.

Therefore, the national airline of Russia, Aeroflot (SU) imposes an extra charge on airlines registered in the European Union on their way from Europe to East Asia under the legal title of *royalty* (or 'special tax') for transit over its Siberian territory, which is booked as the revenue of Aeroflot. The Trans-Siberian routes reduce the travel distance by 4000 km and save the fuel and fee costs per flight significantly. Nearly 20 Community Airlines concerned pay extra charges annually at an estimated amount of approx. 350 million USD,

(continued)

which makes the Russian airline expressly profitable.[179] The procedure not only violates international law and is discriminative, but it is also an object of continual protest in international diplomatic and aviation relations. (The extra transit charge concerns all airlines, but it burdens mainly the European and Asian performers as the main users of these routes.)[180] Russia has not acceded to several international organisations, such as the European Civil Aviation Conference (ECAC), since it did not undertake the abolition of the payment of *royalty*, which was a condition of membership. Subsequently, Russia changed its point of view, and as a condition of membership in the World Trade Organisation (WTO), it undertook in 2012 to transform the payment mechanism after 2014. (The collection of the payment was entrusted to the air navigation service provider of the Russian Federation.) Furthermore, Russia envisioned the elaboration of a more transparent framework, as well as the gradual decrease of the amount of the payment, its attachment to the real costs and their abolition in the future.[181]

Unfortunately, due to the violent armed conflict between Ukraine and Russia commenced on 24 February 2022, this issue and many others will not be placed on the agenda for quite a long time.

The problems surrounding the two freedoms transit rights agreement sufficiently indicate the scope of action and the chances of ICAO vis-à-vis its sovereign Member States. By respecting the peculiar political and economic interests of the Member States, ICAO as an international organisation, proceeding from its derivative and limited legal personality, cannot always intervene efficiently and uniformly. This is one of the reasons why it could not achieve that all of its Member States acceded to the IASTA Transit Agreement, so important for the key performers of civil aviation, which was an indispensable condition of the further development of the industry. International civil aviation is in many cases the stage of the enforcement of the interests of the World Powers. The strategic objectives related to the aviation of the nations registering aircraft are determined basically by powerful national political interests, the economic processes of the regions and the effects of global economic competition.

---

[179] Trans-Siberian overflights, written question E-6399/09, 10 December 2009 (www.europarl.europa.eu/doceo/document/E-7-2009-6399_EN.html).

[180] In 2005, in an agreement (under a Protocol) concluded with the United States, Russia assumed the obligation to adjust the price of air transport services to the basic navigation charge due per flight. Havel and Sanchez (2014), pp. 77–78.

[181] Baur (2010).

2.5.6 The International Air Transport Agreement

The majority of the Member States did not accede to the so-called 'Five Freedoms' Agreement on International Air Transport (1944). The agreement was ratified by merely 11 States with smaller territories. The vital reason for under-ratification lies in the relations of Air Freedoms.

Owing to the protectionist economic policy widespread after World War II, the States did not intend to guarantee the exercise of any of the commercial traffic rights of 3 [A]–[B] or 4 [B]–[A], or of the valuable 5. [A]–[B]–[C] as basic rights for the airlines of other countries sheerly for accession to the International Air Transport Agreement. It is logical that as parties to the agreement, the scope of action of the acceded States would have decreased with respect to the allocation and negotiation of freedoms. Therefore, for the purpose of the more efficient enforcement of their interests, they reserved this privilege for themselves. Although the treaty-maker also bore the peculiar protection of the Member States in mind, since the agreement prescribes for the Member States compliance with the national system of the conditions of substantial ownership and effective control as basic requirements (Article I, Section 6).

Despite the above, the agreement did not become 'attractive' for the States since their majority favoured bilateral relations for understandable reasons. Consequently, the actual allocation of the Freedoms of the Air, vital from a commercial viewpoint, evolved as a result of diplomatic and commercial negotiations between the States and was embodied in bi- or multilateral agreements.

The rules of the Chicago Convention also reinforced this process. The recognition of the complete and exclusive sovereignty of the national airspace (Article 1), binding the commercial activity of scheduled flights to special permissions and other authorisations (Article 5) provided the Governments with a significant role in the protection of their markets. On the market the scope of action of airlines, in the beginning almost in complete or at least in substantial State ownership,[182] was determined under bilateral or multilateral Air Services Agreements by the States.

[182]The process that the States purchased the airlines in private ownership commenced during the Great Depression (1929–1933). The States generally maintained and designated one national airline under Air Services Agreements. However, the airlines of the United States were in private ownership from the beginning, therefore, of the great number of air carriers it was difficult to select the designated national airline. Eventually, the Government of the United States usually designated the Pan Am (PA) in Air Services Agreements until 1991, although Pan Am never had official flag carrier status. (The Pan Am Airline went bankrupt in 1991, subsequently, the well-established brand was sold.) Havel (2009), p. 176.

2.5.7 *Air Services Agreements*

The intergovernmental Air Services Agreements (ASAs) contain principles and rules not included in the Chicago Convention, which frequently restrict competition as well as reflect governmental policies and national economic interests. The Member States enter into Air Services Agreements in the form of international treaties on regional and multinational levels between themselves. In bilateral Air Services Agreements, the States agree on the conditions of scheduled air traffic: they designate the operating air carriers (the designation can be single, multiple or unlimited), determine the Air Freedoms that may be exercised, stipulate the routes (pairs of cities), and regulate the capacities, the frequency of flights and the applicable tariffs of the designated airlines. As the Convention highlights 'each contracting State may *designate* the *route* to be followed within its territory by any international air service and the *airports* which any such service may use' (Article 68).

Under the bilateral Air Services Agreements, in the beginning the governments agreed on the conditions of scheduled air traffic with a view to the need of enhanced protection of the domestic, primarily national airlines (Bermuda I),[183] later, they concluded agreements while somewhat clearing the way for market relations (Bermuda II). In practice, these days the number of these bilateral agreements reaches 4000; however, their number in the future will not considerably increase. One of the reasons is that bilateral Air Services Agreements have become an obstacle along the line for the air transport industry of developed countries, therefore, the intention to change has become constant, which has manifested itself in the initiation of the increasingly liberalised Open Skies Agreements arranged on the basis of market relations. Since in Air Services Agreements the States have granted rights and assumed obligations for themselves, therefore, all bilateral agreements have been concluded with different conditions. The agreements qualifying as special in a class by themselves can be categorised as such only by the simplification of the multifarious system of Air Services Agreements, therefore, they can be classified into three major groups based on their definitive features:

- Bermuda I Air Services Agreements;
- Bermuda II Air Services Agreements;
- Open Skies Air Services Agreements.

Bermuda I Air Services Agreements

The first such bilateral agreement was concluded between the United States and Great-Britain in Hamilton on the island of Bermuda, an overseas territory of Great-

[183] In the daily, *The New York Times* (1980) a historian, Walter Laqueur with reference to the 'outdated' role of national airlines comments satirically: 'The modern State must have four attributes: the operation of television channels, a police force of at least 100 people, a budget sufficient to maintain at least one delegate at the United Nations—and a national airline'. Gidwitz (1980), p. 21.

Britain in February 1946.[184] The conditions included in the agreement of the type of Bermuda I. offered a model for Air Services Agreements concluded on State level. The feature of these agreements is that they restrict especially the competition among airlines, they determine a single designation and limit the number of landing points designated on the basis of route rights indicated in the flight plan; furthermore, they apply a strict system of the approval of tariffs and schedule. The preliminary determination of capacity, frequency and the type of aircraft ensues under the strict control of the State and the authority. Besides the traffic rights of 3 [A]–[B] and 4 [B]–[A], they guarantee the freedom of 5 [A]–[B]–[C] exclusively on the basis of reciprocity, whereas, they do not mention right 6 [B]–[A]–[C] and prohibit the exercise of cabotage (8 or 9). It demands compliance with the national clause. These agreements do not facilitate that one airline is steadily granted better opportunities than its competitor, since pursuant to the agreement both parties can offer more or less the same capacity on the basis of the principle of reciprocity. In the case of the unilateral operation of flights, the growth of supply is impeded by compensation, the payment of the so-called *royalty,*[185] or high prices are maintained artificially.

Bermuda II Air Services Agreements

These agreements basically copy the system of Bermuda I, but to some extent they are guided by the competitive conditions of the fulfilment of the growing demand for air services. They increasingly apply the multiple designation of airlines, and the traditional capacity regulations are replaced by the principle of honest competition. Instead of the endorsement mechanism of all tariffs by both parties, the endorsement of departure tariffs tends to become established.

Open Skies Air Services Agreements

The first liberalised agreement in the world was concluded between the United States and the Netherlands in 1992. It was a historic step, since the two national airspaces were opened on a market basis above the territories of nearly ten million sq.km (USA) and 41,526 sq.km (NLD). The liberalised agreement between the European Union and the United States was concluded in 2007; then, in 2010, the contracting parties signed the second agreement granting even more rights. The agreement guarantees unprecedented rights for the airlines of the European Union and the United States. For example, any Community Airline from any airport of the EU

[184] *Final Act of the Civil Aviation Conference* held at Bermuda, United States Treaty Series, No. 3. 11 February 1946.

[185] The Annex to the Air Services Agreement contained the details of the application of *royalty*. If exclusively the airline of one contracting State flew on a specific route, it had to conclude a commercial agreement with the other country. Within the framework of the agreement, the operating airline paid a unit price on the route there (by foot) to the non-operating airline. Before the publication of all IATA tariffs to be found in the booking systems, the parties had renegotiated the extent of the amount, while the operating airline informed the other party transparently about the route statistics and the revenue figures. On the EU market, this solution collides with the rules of competition law, therefore, it is not applicable.

may fly without constraints to any point of the territory of the United States and vice versa.[186]

These days, the bi- and multilateral liberalised Open Skies Agreements (OS)[187] tend to gain ground. Approximately 100 countries can claim to be parties to such agreements. The United States disposes of the most, more than 130 liberalised agreements.[188] In these agreements, the contracting parties mutually open up their markets to each other; therefore, their airlines may exercise the majority of traffic rights freely without limitations of capacity and frequency. The States apply multiple airline designation, and the determination of the tariff is free. While the Bermuda I and II Agreements guaranteed essentially honest and equal opportunity for *operation*, the Open Skies Agreements have established honest and equal opportunity for *competition*. The latter presumes the multiple or unlimited designation of airlines as a basic condition, and the number of landing points connected to the network of flights is not restricted. It suffices to submit the schedules merely for the purpose of supplying information. The preliminary indication of the capacity, the frequencies of the flights and the type of aircraft is completely free.

Despite the above, it must be noted that the liberalised market is not completely open either, we still find limitations here as well. In the case of scheduled operations, the requirement of the national clause (substantial ownership and effective control) is still operative. Therefore, the availability of traffic rights 7 [B]–[C], and the cabotage 8 [A]–[C]–[C] or 9 [C]–[C] is generally not guaranteed and carrying out commercial activity in the other country is bound to further permissions. The events of September 2001 and the strengthening of terrorism have not affected the processes of liberalisation positively either. Consequently, State surveillance gained further strength, and the requirements and costs of aviation security have intelligibly multiplied. At the same time, the liberalisation of the market of the carriage of cargo

---

[186] 2007/339/EC Decision of the Council and the Representatives of the Governments of the Member States of the European Union, meeting within the Council on 25 April 2007 on the signature and provisional application of the Air Transport Agreement between the European Community and its Member States, on the one hand, and the United States of America, on the other hand. OJ L 134, 25.05.2007. The EU-US Air Transport Agreement, first implemented provisionally in March 2008, sparked what is undoubtedly the biggest regulatory development in the industry for 30 years and has directly affected economic and operational decisions and structures. Truxal (2013), p. 9.

[187] The first multilateral, international Open Skies Agreement, the MALIAT *(Multilateral Agreement on the Liberalisation of International Air Transportation)* open to other countries was concluded by the United States, Brunei Darussalam, Chile, Peru, New Zealand and Singapore in 2001. The agreement establishing a liberalised air services market was left open by the parties to other Member States of the Asia-Pacific Economic Cooperation (APEC), thus, later Mongolia (only for transporting cargo), the Cook Islands, Tonga and Samoa also acceded to the agreement (Later Peru and Samoa withdrew their membership). The parties liberalised the traditional requirements of ownership and control (the national clause). On such basis, they guaranteed that the effective control of the airlines concerned by the MALIAT Agreement can be exercised by any citizen of the States Parties (maliat.govt.nz/home/agreement).

[188] *Civil Air Transport Agreements, Open Skies Partners*. Released by US Department of Transportation 9 December 2021 (www.transportation.gov/policy/aviation-policy/open-skies-agreements-being-applied).

has taken place impressively because the States have been partners in opening up their markets, and the unambiguous impact of the carriage of cargo on the development of commerce occasioned less injury to national interests.

Although the legal and administrative differences between non-scheduled and scheduled flights are obvious, these differences in the liberalised domestic markets have lost their significance. For example, the rules of the internal market of the European Union are applicable equally and they are valid for both activities of operation uniformly, in modern terms, for flights engaged in international commerce. Essentially, this means that by close cooperation and the establishment of new forms (alliance systems, unified market requirements), the States and the performers of the industry have managed to undo step by step the negative effects of the Chicago system, limiting mainly commercial development and market-based operation, which were unforeseen at the outset.

Liberalised agreements tend to outnumber other agreements. Of the nearly 1000 Air Services Agreements concluded in the last decade, 70% were already liberalised. Almost 60% of international civil aviation in the world takes place in liberalised markets, mainly in a regional or multilateral framework.[189] One of the most successful regional integrations[190] has been accomplished by the European Union, owing to which Air Services Agreements between EU Member States have been terminated, while bilateral Air Services Agreements concluded with other States have been renegotiated and amended under so-called *horizontal agreements*. Essentially, horizontal agreements have harmonised existing bilateral Air Services Agreements with the rules of EU law pertaining to air transport, primarily with community designation. Thereby, only to a limited extent, but they have extended the opportunities of community air carriers to the market outside the EU. Thus, the benefits guaranteed by the EU air transport market have become available for other countries, perhaps regions pursuant to the so-called comprehensive Community Air Services Agreements concluded with the EU. Access to the EU air transport market with more than 500 million citizens undoubtedly affects the air transport of third countries positively. Simultaneously, this provides an excellent basis for negotiations for the EU upon the conclusion of Air Services Agreements on a community level. The comprehensive Air Services Agreements concluded by the EU Commission on behalf of the Member States supersede all bilateral agreements reached in the past. The EU Agreements not only settle legal issues, but beyond the opening of the market, they guarantee high-level regulatory harmonisation, and on demand, technical and educational assistance to the contracting parties.

[189] ICAO Secretariat: *Regulatory and Industry Overview, Regulatory Developments,* 20 September 2013, pp. 1–2.

[190] Such regional air transport agreements in the world include: the Trans-Tasman Travel Arrangement (TTTA 1983) between Australia and New Zealand; the Latin-American Andean Community (1991); the Caribbean Community Air Services Agreement (1996); the Latin-American Fortaleza Agreement (1996); the African Yamoussoukro Decision (1999); the Multilateral Kona Agreement (MALIAT 2001); the Pacific Island Air Services Agreement (2003); the Asian Single Aviation Market (ASEAN-SAM 2015), etc.

The European Union has gradually opened and liberalised its internal markets in three packages in the area of air transport. The cause of the gradual introduction was that especially because of ultraliberal changes, the threat of destabilisation had become realistic. Thereby, the reform was implemented in several phases, while the possibility of intervention by the States was maintained in all cases when the free play of market forces would have led to abnormal distortion. On 22 June 1992, the Community adopted the Third Package implying actual liberalisation. Its historic significance was that its taking effect terminated the system of bilateral Air Services Agreements between the Member States and guaranteed complete freedom for the airlines of the Member States to gain market share. The most important measure of the Third Package was that it granted the freedom of cabotage in the internal market of the EU for all airlines of the Member States as of 1 April 1997.[191] The free exercise of cabotage within the EU provides unlimited opportunities for all community air carriers in the domestic traffic of the Member States. This means that on the unified internal market of the EU, the community carriers of the Member States may freely perform any carriage of passengers or cargo for commercial purposes within the national territories of Member States. Thereby, the Member States of the EU eventually retreated from the system of economic decision-making in international air traffic with regard to capacities, tariffs, schedules and licensing flights. Thus, they entrusted themselves to the laws of the uniformly regulated market governed by the rules of competition law.[192] The special application of competition law in EU air transport was introduced by the first so-called Liberalisation Package in 1987.[193] At the outset, it provided broad exemption for groups from the general rules, then it gradually curtailed the existing exemptions in air transport. Competition law has advanced to become an important instrument of protection against dishonest market conduct with a view to a ban on anti-competition activity and on the abuse of economic dominance. Simultaneously, the States have further influence on the development of the processes of the air transport industry via the instruments and rules of competition law even in the most open markets, because politics and the enforcement of interests by the State will always be present markedly in aviation, even if merely in an indirect form.

---

[191] Council Regulation (EEC) No. 2408/92 of 23 July 1992 on access for Community air carriers to intra-Community air routes. Third Package OJ L 240 (24 August 1992). This Council Regulation consolidated into Regulation (EC) No. 1008/2008 of the European Parliament and of the Council of 24 September 2008 on common rules for the operation of air services in the Community. *OJ L 293, 31.10.2008*. Staniland (2008), pp. 87–106.

[192] Council Regulation (EC) No. 487/2009 of 25 May 2009 on the application of Article 81 (3) of the Treaty to certain categories of agreements and concerted practices in the air transport sector. O*J L 148, 11.6.2009.*

[193] Council *Directive 83/416/EEC* of 25 July 1983. OJ 1983 L 237.

2.6 General Rules

2.6.1 Facilitations

When travelling on increasingly more modern airplanes it may not be conspicuous from the viewpoint of travelling that there are other important areas undergoing constant development in order to deliver passengers, baggage and cargo safely and in a timely manner from the airport of departure to the destination. Due to the flight of always growing crowds, at international airports the customs, passport and security controls and the procedures of embarking and disembarking used to entail an increasing number of blockages. The necessary, mainly security controls still frequently imply inevitable obstacles in the rapid movement of passengers, the flight crew, the baggage and cargo; therefore, the ICAO Council regularly amends the rules and procedures of Annex 9 to the Convention on Facilitations adjusted to experience gained from practice.

Annex 9 to the Convention contains more than 300 Standards to be observed mandatorily by the Member States. The Member States assumed the obligation of the facilitation of formalities. In view of that, 'each contracting State agrees to adopt all practicable measures to *facilitate* and *expedite* navigation by aircraft between the territories of contracting States, and to prevent unnecessary delays to aircraft, crew members, passengers and cargo, especially in the administration of the laws relating to immigration, quarantine, customs and clearance' (Article 22).

The regulation of ICAO deals comprehensively with the faults of documentation, expired, lost, forged travel documents, the rescue of passengers, the equipment of search and rescue services, the monitoring of international health prescriptions, the extermination of bugs and rodents on the aircraft (for the prevention of malaria and other infections, as well as of the emergence of technical problems), the facilitation of clearance procedures and the related formalities. 'The laws and regulations of a contracting State as to the entrance into or departure from its territory of passengers, crew or cargo of aircraft, such as regulations relating to the entry, clearance, immigration, passports, customs and quarantine *shall be complied with* by or on behalf of such passengers, crew or cargo upon *entrance into* or *departure from*, or *while within the territory* of that State' (Article 13).

Upon embarkation the passengers are obligated to hand over their printed air tickets or the 'electronic confirmation' in the case of the electronic version of tickets, present their passports, certify their identity with a photo identification card, and comply with the prescriptions related to the journey. Before the commencement of the journey, the passenger needs to hold all the documents necessary for the flight (for entry or exit, health certificate, insurance and other documents required by any State concerned with the carriage), the air ticket or a confirmation, furthermore, the passenger needs to comply with the rules of the air carriers concerned by the carriage. The air carrier's responsibility for the existence, the lawful issuance and validity of the travel documents of the passenger or for the non-compliance of the passenger with legal requirements or the prescriptions of the authority is confined to its obligation to return this passenger having slipped through the controls to the airport of departure. To avoid this, apart from the competent authorities, the servant or agent of the air carrier must thoroughly inspect the documents of the passengers before embarkation.

If the passenger may only enter into or transit via any State concerned by the carriage with a valid visa, they must hold such a visa. Thus far as the passenger intends merely to transit in a State and transiting does not, whereas staying requires a visa, the passenger is obligated to prove their intention to transit and its duration. As long as the passenger fails to comply with the requirements of the statutes and other regulations or the conditions of admission to the State concerned by the carriage, and consequently, the air carrier develops the obligation of payment (e.g., fine, penalty), the passenger is obligated to reimburse these costs for the benefit of the air carrier (along with the cost of carriage from the State denying entry).

In September 2004, a passenger arrived in Budapest (BUD) from Moscow (SVO) on MALÉV (MA) Flight 103 and was heading in transit for Cairo (CAI). Before arriving at the transit lounge and before passport control, the passenger visited the toilet, where he flushed his passport and his air ticket. Some pages of the destroyed documents could be recovered from the drainpipe, and from the scraps it could be established that they originated in an Egyptian passport. Void of travel documents, the passenger could not continue his flight. Cairo could not admit the passenger, but he could not enter Hungary either, therefore, he was reversed. To postpone this, the passenger claimed to be a Palestinian citizen and immediately applied for refugee status, which the Hungarian Authority for Refugees considered unfounded and rejected after a week's examination. Owing to this decision, the obstacles before his return were averted. By making out a covering letter with reference to Annex 9 to the Convention, the reversed passenger was flown back to Moscow three times consecutively, where the 'readmission' of the passenger was denied by the competent Russian authorities each time. According to them, the passenger with a valid Egyptian passport and Russian visa had stayed in Russia lawfully, but after departing from their country, 8 days later, he could not enter Russian territory even if he was in possession of a covering letter.

Annex 9 to the Convention on Facilitations formulates lucidly that the person considered inadmissible and banished upon disembarkation shall be accepted by the contracting State for examination (in this case Russia), if, disregarding the direct transit stay, the person had stayed in the territory of the country before embarking the aircraft (Point 5.12).[194] Thus, the definite rejection by the Russian party was unlawful, furthermore, officially it did not notify the ICAO Council of derogation

[194] ICAO Annex 9 on Facilitations, 16th edn., July 2022, 5.12 of Chap. 5, B. Inadmissible persons.

from the rule stipulated by the ICAO, thus, Russia was obligated to observe that rule. Eventually, the parties on the basis of the provisions of international law initiated the admission of the passenger to a third country successfully, in this case Egypt designated as destination.

The passenger is obligated to submit to aviation security and customs controls carried out by the airport and other authorities, border guards and policing organs of the States concerned by air carriage and security examinations carried out by the airport operator and carriers (including the airlines actually implementing the carriage). As long as the passenger does not submit to aviation security examinations and checks (screening) carried out by the authorities of the concerned States, the operator of the airport and air carriers, the passenger (and their baggage) may be excluded from travelling. The damage and the arising costs deriving from the procedure and the examinations are shifted by the air carrier to the person concerned.

ICAO has elaborated and the majority of the Member States have introduced at their international airports the control by machines of travel documents (passports) provided with so-called biometric identifiers, the unique physical features of persons.[195] According to the ICAO standard, it is obligatory to introduce into the passport the biometric identifier [digitalised portrait, in case of stricter regulation (for example, in the EU), the digital fingerprint and the digital photo of the iris] readable and controlled by a computer scanner so as to establish a reliable connection between the travel document and its real owner. In the new procedure, the persons are reliably identifiable, while the authorities may track the whole process of the journey electronically. The appropriate identification of the person is a basic requirement of aviation security; it is indispensable, for example, from the viewpoint of the prevention of the commission of unlawful acts.

On 24 August 2004, the Tupolev TU-134 jet aircraft of the *Volga-Avia Express* Airline (G6) and the TU-154 aircraft of the Siberia Airline (S7) took off from the Domodedovo (DME) international airport in Moscow. With fake identification documents and the help of the ground staff, terrorists embarked the scheduled domestic airplanes, who, with the bombs fastened on their bodies, exploded themselves in the air. This was the first time in the course of the history of civil aviation that suicide-assailants destroyed civil airplanes during flight in the air.[196]

The Convention is not applicable to domestic flights, but proceeding from ICAO membership, all Member States, including Russia need to comply—in their national laws—with the rules of the Annexes to the Convention concerning the infrastructure and the security system of the airport. The examination of the above-mentioned

[195] ICAO Doc 9303 *Machine Readable Travel Documents (MRTD)*. 8th edn., 2021.

[196] ICAO AVSEC Panel, 18th Meeting, Agenda item 1, AVSECP/18–IP/3, 23 June 2006.; ICAO Assembly Resolution A35-1, Doc 10022.

events revealed all details. Owing to the tragic events, the whole system of the airport was modernised pursuant to the rules of Annex 9 and the specifications of aviation security under Annex 17 to the Convention.

To comply with ICAO rules, new technical equipment, procedures and training systems were introduced. The three-level baggage control and the 100% screening of all on-board supplies and mail have been accomplished. The X-Ray based screening of passengers was also introduced (not causing unnecessary delay for the passengers, since shoes and clothes do not need to be taken off, while the examined persons are affected by an extent of radiation which they are exposed to during flight at cruising altitude within 10–15 min); furthermore, a special system analysing human voice was also activated.

2.6.2 Using Airports and Air Navigation Facilities

The developed status of airports and their modern facilities are indispensably important for safe operation, but this also qualifies as one of the most amazing scenes of competition among the key performers of the industry. The contracting States guarantee equal and fair conditions in the competition among airports providing services of varying quality. Under the provisions of the Convention, 'each contracting State may designate the route to be followed within its territory by any international air service and the airports which any such service may use' (Article 68). The *airports* designated in a contracting State, which are open to public use by its national aircraft, shall likewise be open *under uniform conditions* to the aircraft of all the other contracting States. The like *uniform conditions* shall apply to the use, by aircraft of every contracting State, of all air navigation facilities, and any charges that may be imposed for the use of infrastructure by the aircraft of any other contracting State shall not be higher

- as to aircraft *not engaged in scheduled air services*, than those that could be paid by its national aircraft of the same class engaged in similar operations; and,
- as to aircraft engaged in *scheduled international* air services than those that would be paid by its national aircraft engaged in similar international air services (Article 15).

The intention of the contracting States has been to enforce the general principles of international law during access to airports and the use of the infrastructure thereof. The general principles of international law can be found in the entire norm-text of the Convention, primarily in the Preamble and in the general principles of the first Chapter. Under Article 15 and Articles 9, 11, and 44 *g)*, the prohibition of discrimination and the basic principles of equal treatment and equal opportunities need to prevail. The prevalence of basic principles is supervised via the national civil aviation authorities of the Member States. As a further guarantee, the treaty-maker demands just treatment creating identical conditions in the national procedure not only in legal terms but also in practice, expressly during the use of the airport infrastructure. The aircraft in national registry may not receive more prerogatives (may not be granted affirmative action) from the operator of the airport (which in many cases is State property) than the aircraft registered in another State, since both are entitled to service of the same class for identical charges.

The ICAO Council elaborated its policy pertaining to airport charges,[197] the basic principles of which include working ratio calculation, the prohibition of discrimination and the requirement of transparency. The principle of transparency requires that the organisation managing the airport and the airlines consult each other, share information about their activities and the quality of the received services, and mainly, comprehend the mechanism of the imposition of charges. For the purpose of safeguarding transparency, all such charges *shall be published* and communicated to ICAO. In the case of complaints, the ICAO Council *reviews* the imposed charges and drafts a report for the consideration of the State or States concerned, in which it makes recommendations (Article 15).

2.6.3 Airport Slots

The acquisition of airport slots is an essential aspect, since vainly do the air carriers of the Member States have permissions prescribed under Air Services Agreements for operation between two countries, if they cannot exploit their market opportunities in economic terms. The permissions required under the Convention guarantee merely the necessary framework, not the sufficient condition of the operation. In possession of the permissions, the air carrier also needs to obtain the airport slot at the destination necessary for the use of the specific airport at the planned times of arrival and departure. Namely, the effective Air Services Agreement is without avail, if the air carrier cannot participate under identical conditions in the competition of carriage with auspicious timetable, at the advantageous time from an economic viewpoint. (This generally holds true both for busy, congested and smaller airports with capacity problems as well.)

Slot means a period to take off or land at an airport.[198] The concept of and the need for airport slots (meaning gaps) became significant in the 1980s when capacity problems commenced at highly popular, busy airports, especially at times more favourable for air carriers. Such times are departures in the morning and arrivals in

---

[197] The ICAO Council differentiates airport charges from airport taxes. The *airport charge* is a levy that is designed and applied specifically to recover the costs of providing facilities and services for civil aviation. *Tax* is a levy that is designed to raise national or local government revenues, which are generally not reinvested in the civil aviation industry in their entirety or on a cost-specific basis. ICAO Doc 9082 ICAO's Policies on Charges for Airports and Air Navigation Services. 9th edn., 2012, Foreword 3. p. vii.

[198] Airport *slot* means the scheduled time of arrival or departure available or allocated to an aircraft movement on a specific date at an airport coordinated under the terms of the Council Regulation. (EEC) No. 95/93 of 18 January 1993 on common rules for the allocation of slots at Community airports. OJ L 14, 01.22.1993, [Article 2 *a)*].

the evening. It became necessary to launch an activity which manages the capacity of airports and guarantees equal treatment for the performers concerned. As a result, slot-coordination was established, which has undergone enormous technical, methodical and regulatory development and has had an important role until these days.

At the outset, on the basis of existing expertise, the operating experts of a specific airport or the experts of airlines flying to such airport carried out this activity. However, as demands for air services were growing to an extent highly surpassing the expansion of capacities, the independence of slot-coordination became increasingly urgent. This is comprehensible since if somebody is the employee of a performer commercially concerned (airport or airline), however fairly may they proceed, the unbiased nature of their decisions may be challenged. Recognising this, organisations specialising in slot coordination were established one after the other. Nevertheless, the uniform regulatory background to set out the applicable priorities and procedures was still missing.

The Convention left the commercial issues unsettled; it entrusted the Member States to regulate and resolve them. The Annexes to the Convention do not contain rules concerning the slots either, but we need to mention them here, since the requirement of equally open and available airports belongs to the issue of slots as well. Therefore, the regulatory background of slots is not uniform in the world although the Worldwide Airport Slot Guidelines (WASG) issued by IATA (to be applied only as recommendation by reason of its specificities) is generally observed worldwide.[199]

Since slots essentially impact business activities, for example, in the United States the sale and purchase of slots is completely established and encouraged. Elsewhere certain frequented airports hold *slot-auctions* or support start-up airlines by drawing lots operated as *slot-lottery*, which is completely unknown in many countries. The trade in slots also concerns Europe because with the central major hubs gradually becoming overloaded, the obtainable slots have become increasingly precious. What is precious, sooner or later will be the object of sale and this is valid here as well. A ‘grey zone’ has evolved, in which the airlines, by taking advantage of the technical instrument of the exchange of slots facilitated by the regulator, sold and purchased the precious slots in the background with considerable compensation. In particular, the airport of London Heathrow (LHR) had a ready sale in terms of business, where British Airways in itself possesses 40% of the airport slots. According to rumours, several million British Pounds have changed hands in this context. This was reinforced by the fact that British Airways (BA), in possession of significant traffic at this airport, entered the estimated value of its owned slots into its balance sheet as valuable rights and interests. It is a generally held view in the United Kingdom that

[199] *IATA Worldwide Airport Slot Guidelines (WASG)*, 1 June 2020. The WASG is jointly published by IATA, Airports Council International (ACI), and the Worldwide Airport Coordinators Group. The Worldwide Airport Slot Board provides recommendations on best practice. Truxal (2022), Point 5.

the trade in slots is well-established, or more precisely, it is not prohibited provided that an exchange is effected.[200] In the territory of the European Union, the forthcoming amendment of the uniformly valid rules contains and facilitates the sale of slots within limitations. It is a pressing interest of the key performers of the industry that this practice should be completely legal, and the already existent course of business verging on the grey zone should be settled with a realistic solution by the regulator. Indisputably, the current slot-mechanism is prone to be abused,[201] and as a well-established instrument of protectionist endeavours, it secures exceptional scope for the protection of markets.

2.6.4 Customs and Immigration Rules

'…every aircraft which enters the territory of a contracting State shall, if the regulations of that State so require, land at an airport designated by that State for the purpose of customs and other examination. On departure from the territory of a contracting State, such aircraft shall depart from a similarly designated customs airport' (Article 10). The passenger is obligated to submit to aviation security and customs controls carried out by the airport and other authorities, the border guard and policing organs of the States concerned by carriage as well as to the security examinations discharged by airport operators and carriers (including the airlines actually implementing the carriage). If the passenger upon departure does not submit to the controls carried out by the authorities of the concerned States, airport operators and air carriers, the passenger and their baggage may be excluded from the flight. For the proceeding damage, the air carrier does not assume responsibility. At the same time, if it is proven that the air carrier or its agent was careless during the control and this turns out at the airport of arrival (for example, the documents are not authentic, therefore, the passenger may not be admitted or the passenger carried prohibited objects), the responsibility of the air carrier is established.

The particulars of all designated customs airports shall be published by the State and transmitted to ICAO for communication to all other contracting States (Article 10).

The contracting States provide from the viewpoint of customs procedures separately for the following:

- the *aircraft*, which must be admitted provisionally duty-free, subject to the customs regulations of the State concerned; and
- the arrival *on board the aircraft* of fuel, lubricating oil, spare-parts, regular equipment and aircraft stores in the territory of another contracting State, which are exempted from the payment of customs duty, inspection fee or similar

[200] Balfour (1995), p. 112.

[201] Havel and Sanchez (2014), pp. 117–119.

national and local duties and charges provided that they are held on board the aircraft upon departure from the territory of the State concerned. This exemption does not apply to items unloaded from the aircraft.

The Convention does not permit the taxation of the fuel on board the aircraft. Air transport operates with the use of expensive equipment, while it makes use of the infrastructure and resources the most efficiently. On the one hand, air transport covers its own expenses, on the other hand, it pays taxes and fees, while it has privileges as to the payment of taxes and customs duties. Solely the airlines of the world annually (before the COVID-19 pandemic) paid more than 50 billion USD to airports and air traffic controllers under various legal titles, not to mention the high tax content of fuels. (The price of oil is always in the focus of attention because its increase influences the efficiency of the industry to a large extent.)[202]

'Spare parts and equipment imported into the territory of a contracting State for *incorporation in* or *use on an aircraft* of another contracting State engaged in international air navigation shall be *admitted free of customs duty*, subject to compliance with the regulations of the State concerned' (Article 24). ICAO has always supported the global achievement of freedom from taxes and customs duties in the international civil aviation industry and it continuously pronounces this commitment.[203] Otherwise, the provisions of the Convention facilitate the establishment of customs-free airports (Article 23).

2.6.5 Prevention of the Spread of Infectious Diseases

Airlines from time to time are faced with minor or major crises, starting from the oil price explosion and terrorist attacks via natural disasters and beyond the world economic depression to the spread of infectious diseases. Modern man rightfully figures that infectious diseases in the twenty-first century do not imply such a great threat to humankind as they did some decades before, but this is not in the vicinity of the truth. Air transport has crucial significance in the worldwide propagation of diseases. Therefore, it is both the responsibility and duty of ICAO and other specialised international organisations to prevent the spread of infectious diseases with comprehensive measures. To achieve this, 'each contracting State agrees to take effective measures to *prevent the spread by means of air navigation* of cholera, typhus (epidemic), smallpox, yellow fever, plague, and such other communicable diseases' (e.g., influenza) (Article 14). As a matter of course, the Member States do not need to cope only with the diseases enumerated under the Convention but also

[202] In the 1970s, several shocks struck the world economy. One of them was the oil crisis, as a result of which the price of 3785 litres (1000 gallons) of JET A1 fuel of kerosene increased from 100 USD to 1100 USD by 1980. Anderson and Eberhardt (2010), p. 8.

[203] ICAO Doc 8632 ICAO's Policies on Taxation in the Field of International Air Transport. 3rd edn., 2000 (Supplement to Doc 8632 on 24 September 2021).

with all infectious diseases which, by reason of their features, medicine considers apt to spread worldwide. They include a number of infectious diseases not known in 1944, such as atypical pneumonia (SARS-CoV), bird flu or the Ebola virus epidemic.[204]

Viruses and Civil Aviation

In 2003, the virus of a mysterious new disease, the Severe Acute Respiratory Syndrome (SARS-CoV), with its more familiar name, the atypical pneumonia jarred the nerves and roused worldwide panic considerably affecting international civil aviation. ICAO and the World Health Organization (WHO) reacted rapidly and made comprehensive recommendations to the Member States.[205] The Member States were obligated to check the passengers more rigorously at the airports of States concerned by the infection, to prohibit the departure of persons producing the symptoms of the disease despite their valid air tickets, to inform the passengers about the disease preceding embarkation, to carry out further check-ups in the case of passengers arriving from infected locations, to train both the crew members how to treat and separate patients producing the symptoms of SARS on board and the ground staff how to welcome the aircraft carrying passengers infected with SARS and how to disinfect the board efficiently.

In 2005, a more recent infectious disease deemed most dangerous, that is, the Highly Pathogenic Avian Influenza (H5N1), the bird flu capable of triggering a world pandemic demanded victims, which posed a new challenge to civil air transport. Upon the recommendation of WHO, the passengers had to be preliminarily informed about the health risks of the flight, while at the airports, in the interest of the detection of the disease, officially appointed healthcare employees asked the passengers directed questions and measured body temperature with heat cameras. At the airports special premises were opened for vectors, and for the case of the outbreak of an epidemic, ICAO and WHO recommended a procedure for the immediate closure of the airport.[206]

In 2009 the virus of the Swine Influenza (H1N1), in 2012 the Middle-East Respiratory Syndrome (MERS) coronavirus, in 2013 the novel virus of the

(continued)

[204] It is clearly seen that there have been different kinds of viruses affecting civil aviation activities worldwide: Communicable diseases (e.g., influenza pandemics in 1918, 1957, 1968); Serious Acute Respiratory Syndrome (SARS-CoV coronavirus) 2003; Highly Pathogenic Avian Influenza (bird flu) (H5N1) 2005; Swine Influenza virus (SIV) (H1N1) 2009; Middle Eastern Respiratory Syndrome (MERS-CoV coronavirus) 2012; Novel virus of the Avian Influenza (H7N9) 2013; Western-African Ebola-virus (EVD) 2014; Zika virus (ZIKV) 2016; Severe Acute Respiratory Syndrome Coronavirus 2 (SARS-CoV-2) 2019. Sipos (2022).

[205] Singh (2006), pp. 1–7.; ICAO Assembly A35–12 Resolution, 2004.

[206] *ICAO Report by Chief Aviation Medicine Section to the meeting at the WHO on avian (bird) influenza (flu) and human pandemic influenza.* ICAO Secretary General, SG 1862/05 AN5/24, 2005; ICAO Annex 9 on Facilitation 2.4.

Avian Influenza (H7N9), in 2014 the Western-African Ebola (EVD) virus, in 2016 the Zika virus (ZIKV) demanded victims worldwide. In the rapid spread of these and the formation of worldwide pandemics, air transport played a demonstrably prominent role. The Ebola-epidemic (2014)[207] is a perfect example, since the air passenger infected with Ebola implied only a slight danger for other passengers, yet, the sheer potential presence of the infected person caused grave anxiety in passengers. (The Ebola virus spreads with bodily fluids, not by inhaling or droplet infection. Although the common use of the toilet undoubtedly entails risks.) In such a critical period, plenty of people desisted from travel, since even the passenger who is wilfully coughing strongly, then crying out: 'I come from Africa, but I have only been joking' can cause real panic (entailing criminal liability), which can only be surpassed by the presence of the passenger truly infected with Ebola or another virus.[208]

In order to prevent the spread of diseases, ICAO continually consults international organisations[209] [such as the World Health Organization (WHO)[210] and the Food and Agricultural Organization (FAO)] competent in the elaboration of international health regulations to be applied on aircraft. With a view to the prevention of the propagation of epidemics via aviation, ICAO makes recommendations for its Member States. For the implementation of the recommendations, the Member States bear responsibility. Under the Convention from the outset, the States assumed the obligation to impede the spread of infections in every possible manner; for this purpose, they involve all concerned authorities, they stipulate regulations dependent on international recommendations, then they observe these entirely. The employees of airports and airlines are obligated to observe international and domestic health prescriptions, act preventively and intervene uniformly. If the employees proceed in compliance with the rules, they cannot be held legally responsible for events or damage deriving from the physical condition of the passenger. If a truly ill passenger could not be filtered at the airport (there is a medicine that temporarily brings down the fever of the sick person infected with Ebola), the infected passenger gets on board the airplane. The employees of the airport and the airline do not have either the

[207] Unfortunately, the Ebola virus, although only in an isolated manner, still demands victims in Africa. WHO—Ebola virus disease—Democratic Republic of the Congo. Disease outbreak news: Update 10 February 2020 (www.who.int/csr/don/16-April-2020-ebola-drc/en).

[208] Abeyratne, Ruwantissa: The Ebola Virus and Aviation. *Sri Lanka Guardian,* Montreal, 8 August 2014.

[209] In 2016, ICAO elaborated the CAPSCA Initiative (Cooperative Arrangement for the Prevention and Management of Public Health Events in Civil Aviation) (CAPSCA), in the framework of which ICAO regularly negotiates with the organisations concerned: WHO, FAO, UNWTO, IATA, ACI, UNDP, IFALPA, IOM, WFP (www.caspca.org).

[210] ICAO Annex 9 on Facilitation, Chap. 8 *E)* deals with the implementation of international health regulations and other provisions specified by the WHO. 'Implementation of international health regulations and related provisions' (8.12–15, 8.15.1 Recommended Practices). 16th edn., 2022.

qualifications or the practice to establish without doubt whether a passenger suffers from an infection or does not. It is exclusively the passenger who knows what their physical condition facilitates and whether they take the risk of travelling and the entailed responsibility [see, Part II, Chap. 10. 1.1].

2.6.6 The Search and Rescue of the Aircraft in Distress

The aircraft which has disappeared, is in emergency or suffered an air crash is in need of prompt assistance because the persons on board or on the surface may be exposed to immediate danger. Consequently, the Member States undertake to *render all possible help available for the aircraft in distress in their territories*. ICAO stipulates for its Member States to proceed according to the rules and prescriptions both under Annex 12 to the Convention on Search and Rescue and the International Aeronautical and Maritime Search and Rescue Manual (IAMSAR)[211] elaborated jointly with the International Maritime Organization (IMO). The Member States are obligated to elaborate procedures on national level and organise the search and rescue tasks by unifying the engageable domestic air and land forces in the territory of the Member State. The forces and means available for carrying out search and rescue are secured primarily by the military (air force), the disaster-prevention, the police, the fire guard, the ambulance (air rescue) and the experts of local governments and civil guard organisations. If the circumstances necessitate, it is possible that the Member State carrying out the search-rescue facilitates for the *owner of the aircraft* or *the authority of the State of registry* to take measures of assistance. External provision of help is admissible only under control by the authorities of the Member State.

In an extreme case, owing to the accident of a wide-body airplane, several hundreds of casualties may need medical help, which requires firm efforts, organisation and preparedness. As ICAO prescribes the units responsible for the implementation of search-rescue need to harmonise their tasks, work in close alliance, be in possession of equipment determined under the ICAO Standard and inform the aircraft using their airspace about the procedure to be followed in the state of emergency. The search and rescue activities along with accident investigation are very expensive and the cost has to be paid on national level as there is no relevant international regulation.[212]

---

[211] ICAO Doc 9731 International Aeronautical and Maritime Search and Rescue Manual IAMSAR, Volumes I. (2016), II. (2022), III. (2019).

[212] The cost is very high if the aircraft debris lies on the seabed. After the tragedy of Trans World Airlines (TWA) Flight 800 [New York (JFK)-Paris (CDG)] on 17 July 1996, the wreckage of the Boeing 747–131 aircraft spread over the high seas, but it was recovered from the Atlantic Ocean and reconstructed. The cost was a few times higher than the list price of a new version of that particular aircraft. The reason for the outstanding activity was not primarily safety but the fact that the Presidential Air Force One operated at that time a similar type of aircraft (Boeing 747-200B). Information during the visit at FAA Mike Monroney Aeronautical Center, Will Rogers Airport, Oklahoma City under the International Visitor Program (IVP), February 2004.

In the process, military and civil air traffic controls (ATC) have a prominent role. The reason is that in the overwhelming majority of cases, it is the air traffic control that first has cognizance of an aircraft in distress; furthermore, it is the air navigation service provider (ANSP) that informs the aircraft in the airspace about the services responsible for the coordination of search and rescue (align with their contact details) and their services provided in the concerned area under the Aeronautical Information Publication (AIP)[213] and NOTAM-reports.[214] 'Each contracting State, when undertaking search for missing or disappeared aircraft, will be obligated to *collaborate in coordinated measures*' (Article 25).

The basis of the successful implementation of the task is cooperation with neighbouring countries and other Member States, which is a basic requirement formulated by ICAO. ICAO regularly examines with what content and under what conditions the Member States and the neighbouring countries concluded cooperation agreements in the interest of the fulfilment of the obligations assumed under the Convention. In the case of a missing aircraft every minute matters, therefore, in the detection of endangered persons and material values it is only cooperation that may lead to success. A missing aircraft may be declared to have disappeared if the official search ended and the wreckage was not found.

2.6.7 *Investigation of Accidents*

The excellent aviation safety figures of air transport are grounded on the all-encompassing investigation of accidents and incidents. Aviation safety is never 100% since air transport is a complicated system to be construed in the interaction of man, machine and the environment, which in all cases contains error or at least the possibility of failure. Therefore, the operation system and the process of air transport have been designed for multiple errors. This implies that two or three simultaneous

---

[213] ICAO Annex 15 on Aeronautical Information Service.; ICAO Doc 8126 Aeronautical Information Services Manual, 7th edn., 2021.

[214] The Air Traffic Service (ATS) collects, collates, edits and issues air traffic information valid in the territory subject to the responsibility of the specific Member State. Aeronautical information is to be found in the Aeronautical Information Publications (AIP) and NOTAMs. AIPs, which contain continual information concerning air transport, are issued by the State or via State commission. NOTAM is a report broadcast via a tele-communication channel by means of the media. NOTAMs provide information concerning the creation, features and modifications of facilities, services, prescriptions, obstacles and concerning emergencies related to air transport. Familiarisation with these in time has serious significance and it is indispensably necessary for the participants of air transport. (SNOWTAM is a special NOTAM-series, which provides information about the presence or clearance of snow, ice, sludge or still water posing danger on the surface of mobility.).

errors in themselves do not entail calamitous consequences, because only the simultaneous occurrence of at least three or more (4–5) errors may result in an accident.[215]

The operation of the aircraft takes place in a strange and hostile environment for humans accustomed to terrestrial circumstances. Thus, the performers of the air transport industry cannot dispense with learning at the expense of others. Therefore, if an *accident* or *incident* occurs, the thorough investigation of the circumstances of the accident and drawing a lesson on an international level are of extraordinary importance, because the prevention of further similar accidents depends on this. There are two categories of accident investigation:

- Major accident investigation: 'Investigation into an accident involving a large aircraft usually involving fatalities'; and
- Minor investigation: 'Investigation into an incident involving any aircraft or into an accident involving a small aircraft'.[216]

There are some well-known reasons for accidents, such as equipment and/or mechanical failures, weather conditions, defective runways, piloting or other human errors (in which air traffic controllers, maintenance or ground handling staff and dispatchers play a role) or any combination of the previous ones. Most accidents occur because of piloting failures deriving from lack of training or experience, fatigue, intoxication, etc.

The following are not considered to be accidents: experimental test flights, sabotage, hijacking, terrorism, direct military action or the mental illness of the pilot.[217]

According to Annex 13 on Aircraft Accident and Incident Investigation, the definitions of accident, incident and serious incident are as follows:

---

[215]The investigation of flight accidents shows that accidents are generated by at least three to five system errors and failures. The probability of the occurrence of the first, second and following failures depends on the divergence of operational features and former failures. Rohács and Németh (1997), p. 203.;

Human errors are recognised to be the primary or secondary causes of more than 75% of aviation accidents/incidents (likewise in the maritime industry). Hollnagel (1993).

[216]ICAO Doc 9756 *Manual of Aircraft Accident and Incident Investigation.* 3rd edn., 2020. Chap. 1, 1.2.

[217]Unfortunately, the tragedy of the Germanwings Flight 9525 (2015) when the first officer committed suicide was not the only one. There were reports about the same intention or its suspicion on Japan Airlines (JL) Flight 350 (1982); EgyptAir (MS) Flight 990 (1990); Royal Air Maroc (AT) Flight 630 (1994); SilkAir (MI) Flight 185 (1997); Mozambique Airlines (TM) Flight 470 (2013); Malaysian Airlines (MH) Flight 370 (2014).

1. *Accident* is 'an occurrence associated with the operation of an aircraft which, in the case of a manned aircraft, takes place between the time any person boards the aircraft with the intention of flight until such time as all such persons have disembarked, or in the case of an unmanned aircraft, takes place between the time the aircraft is ready to move with the purpose of flight until such time as it comes to rest at the end of the flight and the primary propulsion system is shut down, in which:

   (a) a person is fatally or seriously injured as a result of:

   - being in the aircraft, or
   - direct contact with any part of the aircraft, including parts which have become detached from the aircraft, or
   - direct exposure to jet blast, *except* when the injuries are from natural causes, self-inflicted or inflicted by other persons, or when the injuries are to stowaways hiding outside the areas normally available to the passengers and crew; or

   (b) the aircraft sustains damage or structural failure which:

   - adversely affects the structural strength, performance or flight characteristics of the aircraft, and
   - would normally require major repair or replacement of the affected component, *except* for engine failure or damage, when the damage is limited to a single engine (including its cowlings or accessories), to propellers, wing tips, antennas, probes, vanes, tires, brakes, wheels, fairings, panels, landing gear doors, windscreens, the aircraft skin (such as small dents or puncture holes), or for minor damages to main rotor blades, tail rotor blades, landing gear, and those resulting from hail or bird strike (including holes in the radome); or

   (c) the aircraft is missing or is completely inaccessible'.

2. *Incident* is 'an occurrence, other than an accident, associated with the operation of the aircraft, which affects or could affect the safety of operation'.
3. *Serious incident* is 'an incident involving circumstances indicating that there was a high probability of an accident associated with the operation of an aircraft which, in the case of a manned aircraft, takes place between the time any person boards the aircraft with the intention of flight until such time as all such persons have disembarked, or in the case of an unmanned aircraft, takes place between the time the aircraft is ready to move with the purpose of flight until such time as it comes to rest at the end of the flight and the primary propulsion system is shut down'.[218]

Practicably the difference between an accident and a serious incident lies only in the result.

[218] ICAO Annex 13 on Aircraft Accident and Incident Investigation. 12th edn., July 2020, Chap. 1. pp. 1–1, 1–2, 1–3.

'In the event of an accident to an aircraft of a contracting State occurring in the territory of another contracting State, involving death or serious injury, or indicating serious technical defect in the aircraft or air navigation facilities, the State in which the accident occurs will institute an inquiry into the circumstances of the accident' (Article 26). ICAO obligates the Member States with jurisdiction to investigate the accident or the incident. The Member State where the accident occurred has jurisdiction. In the case of an accident on the high seas, the State which registered the aircraft has jurisdiction. Furthermore, the ICAO Council, at the request of any contracting State, has authorisation to investigate such situations and, 'after such investigation, issue such reports as may appear to it desirable' [Article 55 *e)*].

During the investigation of an accident, the Member State proceeds according to its national law, which must be in accordance with the requirements of Annex 13 to the Convention and of the *Manual of Aircraft Accident* and *Incident Investigation.*[219] In the case of a major accident, the national investigating organisation of the Member State does not attend to the complicated task of investigation on its own. The State registering the aircraft may be present at the investigation as an observer. Via the broad construction of the rule, beyond the observer of the State of registry, the following entities are entitled to be present at the investigation: the company manufacturing the aircraft, the operator of the aircraft and the representatives of the aviation authority and of the national transport safety organisation according to the citizenship of the deceased victims.

In the old times the only authentic witness used to be the wreckage of the aircraft. Even if there were witnesses from among the air passengers or the people in the vicinity, their testimonies frequently proved to be deficient or contradictory. The physical existence of the wreckage tells quite a great deal. Therefore, the inquiry into the accident commences with local inspection and collection of data, then it continues with the examination of the events preceding the accident. The information gained from these is analysed and the primarily presumed causes of the accident are determined. Subsequently to processing all the available data and information about the event, the investigating committee evaluates the complete system of relations of the accident, which it summarises and eventually publicises in a final report. The State holding the inquiry *shall communicate* the contents of the report and its findings in the matter to the State concerned (Article 26). The investigating committee makes comprehensive recommendations for the prevention of the occurrence of similar cases, which is essentially the main objective of all investigations.

The Member States are obligated to notify ICAO of all accidents occurring to aircraft with an ascending weight exceeding 2,250 kg. The flying accidents announced by the Member States in so-called ADREP reports[220] are regularly publicised by the ICAO Council in an electronic database. This knowledge base is one of the most important instruments of prevention. ICAO summarises the

[219] ICAO Doc 9756 *Manual of Aircraft Accident and Incident Investigation.* 3rd edn., 2020.
[220] ICAO Doc 9156 *Accident/Incident Data Reporting* (ADREP) *System.*

conclusions and lessons drawn from experiences and the recommended procedures in the Safety Management Manual.[221]

Annex 13 to the Convention defines the sole objective of investigation lucidly: *prevention*.[222] Indeed, the objective of this complex activity cannot be reduced to reproach and the establishment of responsibility. This is the case with the Flight Data Recorder (the Black Box) used on aircraft as well, which records not only the conversations of the cockpit crew (pilots) for nearly 2 h, but also the status and data of several devices and sensors for more than 24 h. The pilots are aware that anything they do can be traced back and used against them in a criminal procedure. Therefore, if during the flight they make a mistake and it is recorded, this awareness may inhibit them in a more open discussion and solution of the problem. Precisely for this reason, in Australia the data of the Flight Data Recorder may not be used as evidence against the cockpit crew in a criminal procedure.

At the same time, the lessons of the examined event must be drawn, while in cases of high priority, systematic transformation and organisational culture change need to be implemented. One element of the change familiar as 'Just Culture' is that the operational staff in aviation (flight crew, air traffic controllers, technical experts) can render an account of their commission of errors in a non-punitive procedure sincerely and free from sanctions. The concerned parties place the morals at the disposal of the competent parties. That flow of information is secured for all the parties concerned. The objective is unequivocal: the evasion of a later, perhaps graver consequence due to the revelation of the events. The inquiry into events related to aviation safety is notably supported, if the flight crew of the first line and the experts of the second line are not punished for voluntarily announced omissions and faulty decisions which are in accordance with their professional experience and level of education.

The most important guarantee for a procedure free from retorsion is voluntariness. This is valid vice versa; the most important guarantee for voluntariness is the freedom from retorsion. The information and data provided by the Member States influencing aviation safety, which can be evaluated, are protected according to the prescriptions of ICAO. The reporting party in an all-encompassing sphere of confidence needs to be encouraged to make an announcement related to aviation safety, but simultaneously, they need to be aware of the weight of their act and of the fact that their act may have criminal legal consequences.[223] However, the criminal legal consequences may only be neglected, if the conduct upon the commission of the act did not proceed from grave carelessness, deliberateness or destructive intention, as well as if the State relinquishes its demand to punish guided by the objective to familiarise with the most minute detail of the background of the incident

[221] ICAO Doc 9859 *ICAO Safety Management Manual* (SMM), AN/474, 4th edn., 2018.

[222] 'The sole objective of the investigation of an accident or incident shall be the prevention of accidents and incidents. It is not the purpose of this activity to apportion blame or liability'. ICAO Annex 13 on *Aircraft Accident and Incident Investigation*, 12th edn., July 2020, Chap. 3, 3.1.

[223] Improving Just Culture. CANSO, ICAO Assembly A39–WP/1931 TE/73 25/8/2016.

or the source of danger, and thereby, analyse its context. In this case, the enforcement of the interest of the community is stronger than the interest of the State to impose punishment.

References

Abeyratne R (2012) Air Navigation Law. Chapter 1, Civil and Military Aviation. Springer, pp 6–8

Abeyratne R (2014) Convention on International Civil Aviation: a Commentary. Springer, p 39

Anderson DF, Eberhardt S (2010) Understanding Flight. 2nd edn., McGraw Hill, p 8

Balfour J (1995) European Community Air Law. Butterworths, p 112

Bánk J (ed) (1993) 3500 Latin bölcsesség (3500 Latin Wisdoms). St. Gellért Church Publishing House, Budapest, p 10

Bartsch R (2018) International aviation law. A practical guide, 2nd edn., Routledge, p 225

Baur J (2010) EU-Russia Aviation Relations and the Issue of Siberian Overflights. Air Space Law 35(3):225

Baur M (2014) Planeten und Raumfahrt: Expedition ins all. Tesslof, pp 6–7

Bisignani G (2010) The Eruption of Eyjafjallajökull was a Wake-up Call for Change. Airlines International, IATA Magazine, 1 June 2010

Boschen AC, Jones RK (2004) Aviation Language Problem: Improving pilot-controller communication. In: Proceedings of 2004 International Professional Communication Conference; 29 September – October 2004, Minneapolis, United Sates. IEEE Press, Piscataway, pp 291–299. www.ieeexplore.ieee.org/abstract/document/1375313

Brownlie I (1979) Principles of Public International Law. 3rd edn., Oxford University Press, pp 512–513

Cheng B (1962) The Law of International Air Transport. University College, London, pp 7–9, 314

Cheng B (1985) The Destruction of KAL flight KE 007 and Article 3 *bis* of the Chicago Convention. In: Storm van's Gravesande JWE, Van der Veen Vonk A (eds) Air Worthy. Liber Amicorum Honouring Professor Dr. I.H. Ph. Diederiks-Verschoor. Kluwer, Denventer, p 47

Cheng B, Austin RHF (1973) Air Law. In: Bos M (ed) The present state of international law and other essays. Kluwer, Alphen aan den Rijn, p 183

Degani A (2004) The Crash of Korean Air Lines Flight 007. Chapter 4. Palgrave, New York, p 55. https://ti.arc.nasa.gov/m/profile/adegani/Crash%20of%20Korean%20Air%20Lines%20Flight%20007.pdf

Gál G (1969) Space Law. A. W. Sijthoff, Leiden, pp 59–116

Gidwitz B (1980) The Politics of International Air Transport. Lexington, p 21

Giemulla EM (2011) From Regulation to Deregulation, Chapter 4. In: Giemulla EM, Weber L (eds) International and EU Aviation Law: Selected issues. Kluwer Law International B.V., pp 180–181

Goedhart RFA (1996) The Never-ending Dispute: Delimitation of Airspace and Outer Space. Frontiéres 35:43

Gorove S (1978) Cosmos 954: Issues of Law and Policy. J Space Law 6(2):137–146

Haanappel PPC (2003) The Law and Policy of Airspace and Outer Space: a Comparative approach. Kluwer Law International, p 99

Havel BF (2009) Beyond Open Skies: a New regime for international aviation. Kluwer, The Hague, p 176

Havel BF, Sanchez GS (2014) Principles and Practice on International Aviation Law. Cambridge University Press, Cambridge, pp 77–78

Hawking SW (2005) The Theory of Everything. The Origin and Fate of the Universe. Phoenix Books, pp 4–5

Hollnagel E (1993) Human Reliability Analysis, Context and Control. Academic Press, London
Huyser R (2016) Flights Above Conflict Zones: Lessons learnt from the MH17 disaster. ECAC News 60:5–7
Jones KR (2003) Miscommunication Between Pilots and Air Traffic Control. Lang Probl Lang Plan 27(3):233–248
Kajtár G (2011) A terrorizmus elleni önvédelem a XXI. században (Self-defence Against Terrorism in the 21st Century). Kül–Világ, pp 1–2
Kajtár G (2017) The Use of Force Against ISIL in Iraq and Syria. A Legal battlefield. Wis Int Law J 34(3):572
Kajtár G (2018) Az erőszak tilalma (The Prohibition of Aggression). In: Jakab A, Fekete B (eds) Internet-based encyclopaedia of jurisprudence. Column of international law. Sulyok, Gábor, p 20
Kajtár G (2022) Fragmentation of Attribution in International Law. In: Kajtár G, Çali B, Milanovic M (eds) Secondary rules of primary importance – attribution, causality, standard of review and evidentiary rules in international law. Oxford University Press, pp 283–301
Kukis M, Arms K (2001) Bush to China: Return plane, crew. United Press International
Lachs M (1964) The International Law of Outer Space. In: Recueil Des Cours de l'Académie de Droit International, vol 113. Brill, p 55
Launius RD (2005) Sputnik and the Origins of the Space Age. NASA History Home Page, Anniversaries, Sputnik Anniversary. The American response to Sputnik
Lee E (1967) The Wind and Beyond: Theodore von Karman, pioneer in aviation and pathfinder in space. Little, Brown and Company, Boston/Toronto, pp. 300-301
Leich MN (1984) Destruction of Korean Airliner – Action by International Organizations. Am J Int Law 78(1):244–245
Mailer N (2010) Moonfire. Taschen, pp 266–267
Malone JL (1983) The United States and the Law of the Sea after UNCLOS III. Law Contemp Probl 46(2):29–36
Mendes de Leon P (1992) Cabotage in Air Transport Regulation. Martinus Nijhoff Publishers, The Hague, pp 1–2
Milde M (1986) Interception of Civil Aircraft v. Misuse of Civil Aviation. Annals of Air and Space Law XI:105–130
Mullany NJ (1989) The Legal Implications of Soviet Union's Assertions Concerning the Downing of KAL flight 707. West Aust Law Rev 19:430
Nagy L (2017) A helikopter-képesség fejlesztés lehetséges irányai (The potential directions of the development of helicopter-capacity). Repüléstudományi Közlemények 29(1):48
Palik M (2012) A pilóta nélküli légi járművek hazai szabályozói környezete fejlesztésre irányuló K +F projekt bemutatása (Introduction of the R&D project targeting the development of the domestic regulatory environment of unmanned aerial vehicles). Repüléstudományi Közlemények 24(2):486
Rohács J, Németh M (1997) Effects of Aircraft System Anomalies on Flight Safety. In: Soekkha MH (ed) Aviation Safety. VSP BV, Utrecht, p 203
Sagan C (1980) Cosmos. Random House, New York, p 365
Schmitt MN (2010) Air Law and Military Operations. In: Gill TD, Fleck D (eds) The Handbook on the International Law of Military Operations. Oxford University Press, New York, p. 307
Schnitker R, Kaar v h D (2013) Safety Assessment of Foreign Aircraft Programme - a European Approach to Enhance Global Aviation Safety, Chapter 8, EU Blacklist. Eleven International Publishing, The Hague, pp 92–94
Singh J (2006) Preparedness planning of the aviation industry for a pandemic crisis management. J Aviat Manag:1–7
Sipos A (1987) Mathias Rust esete (The case of Mathias Rust), Manuscript. Imre Madách Secondary School, Madách Cup Tournament, Budapest
Sipos A (2018) The Legal Status and Use of National Airspace. ELTE Ann 57:141–172

Sipos A (2022) Modernizing the Chicago Convention: The Challenge of 'Sicurity'! IAMC Proceedings, Emirates Aviation University, Dubai, November 2022, p. 203
Sipos A (2023) Milde's International Air Law and ICAO. 4th edn., Eleven International Publishing, The Hague, p 98
Smith P (2018) Cockpit Confidential: Everything you need to know about air travel: questions, answers, and reflections. Sourcebooks, pp. 20, 22, 38, 77
Staniland M (2008) A Europe of the Air? The Airline industry and European integration. Chapter IV, Negotiating the three packages. Rowman & Littlefield, pp 87–106
Sulyok G (2006) An Assessment of the Destruction of Rogue Civil Aircraft under International Law and Constitutional Law. In: Halmai G (ed) Hungary: Human rights in the face of terrorism. Vandeplas Publishing, Lake Mary, pp 5–30
Truxal S (2013) Competition and Regulation in the Airline Industry: Puppets in Chaos. Introduction. Routledge, p 9
Truxal S (2022) Slots. In: Garben S, Gormley L (eds) The Oxford Encyclopedia of EU LAW. Oxford University Press, Oxford, point 5
Tuck J (1986) High-tech Espionage. Sidgwick & Jackson, p 167
Tyson DN (2017) Astrophysics for People in a Hurry. W. W. Norton & Company, Inc, New York, p 45
Valki L (1999) Az Európai Unióhoz csatlakozó Magyarország szuverenitása (The Sovereignty of Hungary acceding to the European Union). Magy Tud 44(8), pp 1000–1007

Chapter 3
The International Civil Aviation Organization

3.1 Strategic Objectives and Mission

The unflagging development of aviation safety since World War II has been due to the extraordinarily thorough investigation primarily of accidents and incidents. The experiences gained from investigations and the drawn lessons have transformed into rules and materialised as technical solutions. All these have facilitated the worldwide spread of aviation. These days travelling by plane is at least twenty times safer than it used to be at the dawn of the era of jet propulsion. In the Magnum Opus of world aviation, that is, the Chicago Convention, the most important chapter about SAFETY was noted down with blood by the exceptional and casual heroes of aviation.[1] In this chapter the most significant challenge of the industry, aviation safety acquires sense and becomes manifest in an immensely rigorous and all-encompassing system of rules pertaining to all areas of aviation. This system of requirements is synthesised by a global summit organisation: ICAO.

ICAO as a specialised agency of the United Nations is the top intergovernmental summit organisation of international civil air transport. It is the only global organisation that, due to its regulatory and administrative functions, safeguards the highest general predominance of the safety and security of international civil aviation in the world, primarily depending on the cooperation of the Member States. The main objective of ICAO is the promotion of the complete observance of the uniform requirements of aviation safety via the establishment of a comprehensive international system of rules. Thus, an advanced stage of adherence to the rules by the Member States is constantly necessary in all areas of aviation for the safe planning and implementation as well as for the efficient development of international civil aviation. The significance of ICAO is universal both in the reduction of

[1] Otto Lilienthal (1848–1896), the German aircraft-engineer, inventor, pilot, a pioneer of aviation crashed owing to a sudden blast of wind while flying on a two-planed glider. His last words were: 'Victims are necessary'. Anderson and Eberhardt (2010), p. 20.

A. Sipos, *International Aviation Law*, https://doi.org/10.1007/978-3-031-39066-1_3

non-compliances proceeding from the technical differences between developed and less developed countries via the instruments of aviation and in the enforcement of the general principles of international law. The legitimacy of the organisation and its global leading role in the international community and civil aviation are acknowledged unanimously by all nations.

ICAO does its utmost to create an aviation environment in which aviation safety and security prevail at the highest possible level. In order to achieve these objectives, the performers of air transport in each Member State (prominently the airlines, the airports and the air navigation service providers implementing the flights) need to operate and cooperate efficiently besides the rigorous observance of the uniform rules.

Nevertheless, differences have always existed and will always exist among the States. These mainly economic, social and political differences have a significant impact on the processes undergoing in the air transport industry and on the formation of commercial activities. In the disrupted, fragmented world the economic divide is increasingly expanding. Therefore, the solution of new tasks awaits the international community, the performers interested in civil aviation and ICAO itself.

Such outstanding task is the unification of national airspaces. A perfect example for that is the truly developed, entirely liberalised, unified air transport market of the European Union, which is disjointed by the national airspaces of EU Member States. Since each time an aircraft enters the airspace of a State, it needs to continue its flight in cooperation with the air navigation service provider of the given State and in compliance with the requirements of operation based on the regulations of the given country in conformity with the prescriptions of ICAO and with its geographical features. The non-unified airspace is expensive, and it leads to problems of aviation safety and capacity. The inadequate efficiency of the system in the airspace of the European Union generates several billion euro (EUR) loss annually, which proceeds mainly from delays, the gradually increasing service charges and from the consequences of fragmentation itself.[2] It is exactly for this reason why ICAO on a global level supports the conception the final objective of which is the establishment of a unified global sky encompassing the whole world.

The primary objectives and the duty of ICAO include the development of the principles and technical standard of international air navigation and fostering the planning and development of international air transport.

With a view to reaching these goals ICAO has done its utmost to:

a) ‘insure the safe and orderly growth of international civil aviation throughout the world;
b) encourage the arts of aircraft design and operation for peaceful purposes;

[2]A total cost reduction across European Air Traffic Management (ATM) of 9 billion EUR per annum was achieved through structural and operational improvements in 2011. Blueprint for the Single European Sky (SES), Delivering on safety, environment, capacity and cost-effectiveness. IATA, AEA and ERA, 2011, p. 2.

c) encourage the development of airways, airports, and air navigation facilities for international civil aviation;
d) meet the needs of the peoples of the world for safe, regular, efficient and economical air transport;
e) prevent economic waste caused by unreasonable competition;
f) insure that the rights of contracting States are fully respected and that every contracting State has a fair opportunity to operate international airlines;
g) avoid discrimination between contracting States;
h) promote the safety of flight in international air navigation;
i) promote generally the development of all aspects of international civil aeronautics' (Article 44).

The Convention by asserting the general principles of international law formulates unequivocally on the principal objectives and tasks of the organisation.

The objective and mission of ICAO were formulated separately beyond the content of Article 44 of the Convention on an institutional level to influence the decision-making mechanism and have an impact on the ethos and ordinary work of the Secretariat of ICAO.[3] On this basis the *objective* of ICAO is to foster the realisation of the sustainable enhancement of the system of global civil aviation, whereas its *mission* is to function as a global forum of the States in international civil air transport. ICAO as the global forum of the States elaborates guiding principles, creates standards and carries out compliance audits examining the surveillance capacity of the Member States. Meanwhile, it provides assistance, prepares studies, analyses and contributes to the enhancement of the performance of air transport effectively via the cooperation of Member States and the performers of the industry.

The objectives and tasks formulated above highlight two important roles of ICAO: on the one hand, ICAO functions as the global forum of international civil aviation and in this quality it requires that the rules are observed by all Member States, then it monitors the implementation thereof and demands explanation if necessary, irrespective of the degree of development of the Member State; on the other hand, ICAO as the pledge of sustainable development and enhancement is the 'mentor' and 'supporter' of the States of the developing world.

Support is vital, since the less developed countries are not always capable of keeping up with rapid technical development and economic changes. ICAO as an international organisation means the ultimate guarantee for the enforcement and protection of their rights. Their expectations are comprehensible and legitimate since they may receive really efficient support and guidance solely from ICAO. Therefore, closing up the ranks and the support of these countries are crucial. Unity is the key to the development of the aviation industry.

A good example for the above-mentioned situation is the European Union, which has established the single (internal) market. If we theoretically removed the Member States of the EU from the global system of international civil aviation, the safe and

[3] Abeyratne (2012), p. 173.

secure operation and air navigation services within the EU would have to be further regulated. One of the reasons is that the EU has its own legal system, which is the achievement of centralised legislation. Furthermore, aviation safety in the EU is supervised by the European Aviation Safety Agency (EASA),[4] which in general prescribes more rigorous requirements for the Member States than ICAO. The EU constantly monitors the enforcement of rules, and in case of non-compliance, it coerces the rectification of the deficiency in several stages in a so-called infringement procedure. The European Commission as an institution based on supranational bureaucracy responsible for the enforcement and prevalence of EU regulations is truly capable of having non-compliances efficiently rectified and of demanding an account from the EU Member States not complying with the rules. ICAO contemplates these issues but it cannot enforce its willpower obligatorily to such high extent in its sovereign Member States. It is also an essential aspect that European aviation has a well-established organisational background: besides the European Civil Aviation Conference (ECAC), which as an intergovernmental organisation integrating 44 Member States (including EU Member States),[5] the European Organisation for the Safety of Air Navigation (EUROCONTROL) is also maintained on an intergovernmental level.[6] These European organisations harmonise the guiding principles and the practices of civil air navigation. In brief, a developed institutional background and a comprehensive regulatory system are operative, which would have the capacity to supersede the organisation of ICAO on a local level. (At this point it must be highlighted that EU law does not equal international law, but it is a new and self-sufficient legal regime.)[7]

This theoretical construction cannot be realised in practice, simply because aviation is a global industry. In the global world the international network of aviation can only be as strong as the strength of the weakest link is. That is, all Member States matter, the rules stipulated by ICAO need to be observed everywhere, this is the

---

[4]EASA, the agency of the European Union established in 2002 as an organ responsible for aviation safety is an autonomous legal entity subject to European public law. Regulation EU 2018/1139 of 4 July 2018 of the European Parliament and of the Council on common rules in the field of civil aviation establishing a European Union Aviation Safety Agency, *OJ L 212, 22.08.2018. (*www.easa.europa.eu*).*

[5]The ECAC (European Civil Aviation Conference) was established in Strasbourg in 1955 at the initiation of the European Commission and with the support of ICAO. The ECAC as an intergovernmental organisation based in Paris works under the auspices of ICAO. At present, the organisation has 44 Member States and the membership encompasses almost the whole of Europe. (www.ecac-ceac.org).

[6]EUROCONTROL is a Pan-European, civil-military intergovernmental organisation responsible for air navigation, which is dedicated to develop and secure the European system of air traffic control. The organisation was established by eight European countries on 13 December 1960, which at the moment has 41 European Member States and two Comprehensive Agreement States outside Europe (Morocco and Israel). (www.eurocontrol.int).

[7]EU law is the result of centralised legislation, which can be enforced mandatorily as opposed to decentralised international law. The legal sources of EU law differ from the legal sources of international law.

alpha and the omega of global aviation. If ICAO did not support the third countries outside the EU and did not require the observance of uniform rules, community airlines could operate in the less developed world only at the expense of immense risks. Obviously, nobody is interested therein. However, the several times more rigorous rules pertaining to the air navigation of the European Union than those of ICAO cannot be extended to the whole world unilaterally, since this could only be solved by a world organisation with proper authorisations such as ICAO.

So that ICAO achieved its set objectives, the Assembly (the main representative body of ICAO) determines the comprehensive, strategic objectives of the organisation every three years. These have clustered around three basic values for a long time: aviation safety, security and environmental protection.

More recently, ICAO has extended its strategic objectives and divided them into five larger groups:

Safety In air transport this is always and under all circumstances the most important aspect. Aviation safety is its top priority, which cannot be contested. It may not be the object of compromise. Aviation safety is based on facts, it can be measured and is one of the most important indices of the judgement of the industry. Aviation has unequalled safety indices in the world. Their basis is the comprehensive regulatory activity of ICAO, the transplantation of international rules to national level, their consistent implementation and the enhanced control of the surveillance capacity of Member State civil aviation authorities.

Air Navigation Capacity and Efficiency The saturation of the airspace and airports causes increasingly larger capacity problems for service providers and passengers. Therefore, ICAO insists on the introduction of new procedures for the purpose of the more efficient operation of air transport and airports as well as on the launch of infrastructural developments.

Security and Facilitation The maintenance of a high level of security implies an increasingly larger challenge for the Member States. Unlawful acts related to civil aviation occur in new areas with diverse ways of commission and perpetrator's conduct. The security programmes and audits of ICAO provide support in this continual battle for the Member States. Facilitation is an excellent instrument so that all procedures efficiently support the secure and obstacle-free implementation of operation.

Economic Development of Air Transport ICAO due to its regulatory function targets the establishment of a transport environment in which the service providers of variously developed countries with different market shares and opportunities are interested in the unfolding of competition, mutual access to the market, fair taxation and the establishment of efficient operation and cooperation.

Environmental Protection ICAO is interested in a global response to the problem of the pollution of the environment with respect to its character affecting the whole world. With a view to the realisation of this prominent strategic objective, ICAO institutes and requires increasingly stricter regulations in the areas of the reduction of the toxic emission of engines and of the noise-pollution of aircraft.

For the accomplishment of the common objective, 'each contracting State undertakes to collaborate in securing *the highest practicable degree of uniformity* in regulations, standards, procedures, and organization in relation to aircraft, personnel, airways and auxiliary services in all matters in which such uniformity will facilitate and improve air navigation' (Article 37). In the global world, the harmonisation and simplification of the complex system of the rules of civil aviation imply a basic requirement. Nevertheless, ICAO as an international regulatory forum within the special environment of air transport, interwoven by political and economic interests, cannot always adequately rise to these challenges. One of its reasons is that the peculiar political and national-economic sets of values of the States do not correspond to the market-based competition of the service providers of the air transport industry, which targets generating profit. The political willpower is still determining in air transport despite the increasingly widespread market openings. The influence of politics is unquestionable, its impact on the further development of the industry is obvious, and certainly, it frequently triumphs over the market-based effectiveness of commercial interests. In this complicated set of values, ICAO as the main performer of aerial diplomacy, as a kind of political performer and the highest representative of the profession has to create uniformity, keeping in mind the most important objective: the comprehensive safety of aviation.

ICAO achieves the well-formulated universal objectives by

1. *promoting the cooperation* of the Member States as an *international organisation*;
2. *creating the uniform* Standards and Recommended Practices for international civil aviation; and
3. *supervising the comprehensive implementation* of Standards and Recommended Practices.

In Chapters 4 and 5, following the Articles of the Convention, the implementation of the above-mentioned tasks, that is, the organisation and operation of ICAO will be introduced in a detailed manner based on the author's professional experience.

3.2 Legal Capacity

'The Organization (ICAO) shall enjoy in the territory of each contracting State such legal capacity as may be necessary for the performance of its functions. Full juridical personality shall be granted wherever compatible with the constitution and laws of the State concerned' (Article 47). ICAO as an international organisation may be the subject of rights and obligations to a limited extent. Its legal capacity is derivatively safeguarded under international law, primarily on the basis of the UN Charter, in which ICAO is mentioned as a specialised agency.[8] On such basis ICAO, maintaining its independence, is in a contractual relationship with the organisation of the UN and its Economic and Social Council and, proceeding from having its headquarters in Montreal, with the Canadian government, which safeguards the legal personality of the aviation organisation, its full diplomatic immunity and protection necessary for the performance of its functions.

3.3 Participation

At the Chicago Conference and after the closure of the conference, the States having acceded to the Convention became Parties to the then non-effective Convention because of the fact of accession. For the Convention to come into force, a statement of ratification made by the signatory States was needed. 'The instruments of ratification are deposited in the Archives of the Government of the United States of America' [Article 91 *a)*]. 'As soon as the Convention has been ratified or adhered to by twenty-six States it came into force between them on the thirtieth day after deposit of the twenty-sixth instrument. It came into force for each State ratifying thereafter on the thirtieth day after the deposit of its instrument of ratification' [Article 91 *b)*].

It was the government of Spain that acceded to the Convention as the 26th State on 5 March 1947, thus, it came into force after exactly 30 days on 4 April 1947. The Government of the United States as the designated depository of the Convention notified all signatory and adhering States about this fact [Article 91 *c)*].

After the taking effect of the Chicago Convention, the contracting States elaborated the operative mechanism of the organisation and chose Montreal, the largest town of Quebec in Canada, as the location of the headquarters of ICAO. Since only States may accede to the Chicago Convention, intergovernmental (IGO) or non-governmental organisations (NGOs) as well as regional economic integration organisations (REIOs)—such as the European Union—may only have observer status at the furthest. With respect to the wartime situation in those days, the contracting States stipulated special conditions for accession: 'the Convention was open for adherence by members of the United Nations and States associated with them, and States which remained neutral during the present world conflict' (see, World War II) [Article 92 *a)*]. What does this historically outdated rule, which is still in force, imply?

[8]Charter of the United Nations – International Economic and Social Co-operation, Article 57 of Chapter IX, and The Economic and Social Council, Article 63 of Chapter X on Function and Powers.

From a practical viewpoint it implies that the Convention drafted in the shadow of the war needs complete revision and modernisation.[9] This task of comprehensive amendment has been postponed for decades by the international community.[10] From a legal viewpoint, it implies that the States which are not members of the organisation of the UN may not gain membership in ICAO via the fact of accession. Thus, the States which are not members of the UN or associated with them or were not neutral during the war may accede to the Convention only with the approval of the UN and by means of a four-fifths vote of the Assembly of ICAO and on such conditions as the Assembly may prescribe: provided that in each case the assent of any State invaded or attacked during World War II by the State seeking admission shall be necessary [Article 93].

The former provision was essentially targeted against Spain governed by General Francisco Franco (1892–1975). However, Spain was strategically important, owing to its extensive range and advantageous position, so it has had a significant role in air transport. Therefore, it was unquestionable that Spain would accede to the Chicago Convention. At the same time, beyond the ICAO membership acquired in 1947, Spain could only obtain its UN membership later, in 1955 by reason of its commitment to Germany during World War II, the military dictatorship as well as the Falangist politics, which isolated Spain in the contemporary world. These were the main factors that accounted for the opposition and mistrust of the Member States of the UN vis-a-vis Spain.

At the first Assembly of ICAO (1947), the text of the Chicago Convention was amended for the first time, since ICAO became a specialised agency of the UN, therefore, the obligations proceeding therefrom needed to be manifest in the Convention. Furthermore, the Assembly supplemented the Convention with a new article *bis*[11] providing for the institutions of debarment and suspension: irrespective of the provisions of Articles 91, 92 and 93 above:

- 'A State whose government the General Assembly of the UN has recommended to be *debarred*[12] from membership in international agencies established by or brought into relationship with the UN shall automatically cease to be a member of ICAO;

  A State which has been expelled from membership in the UN shall automatically cease to be a member of ICAO unless the General Assembly of the UN

[9] Sipos (2023), pp. 210–222.; Likewise, there are concerns about the terminology of the Chicago Convention that may cause some confusion (see, Articles 1–15 of the Chicago Convention). Abeyratne (2012), pp. 12–14.

[10] Milde (1994), pp. 401–452.

[11] *Protocol Related to an Amendment of the Convention on International Civil Aviation* signed at Montreal on 27 April 1947 (came into force on 20 March 1961).

[12] A Member of the United Nations which has persistently violated the Principles contained in the present Charter may be expelled from the Organisation by the General Assembly upon the recommendation of the Security Council. Article 6 of the Charter of the United Nations.

attaches to its act of expulsion a recommendation to the contrary [Article 93 *bis a)* 1–2].

- A State which ceases to be a member of ICAO as a result of the provisions of paragraph a) above may, after approval by the General Assembly of the UN, be readmitted to ICAO upon application and upon approval by a majority of the Council [Article 93 *bis b)*].
- Members of the Organization which are suspended from the exercise of the rights and privileges of membership in the UN[13] shall, upon the request of the latter, be suspended from the rights and privileges of membership in this Organization' [Article 93 *bis c)*].

ICAO in these matters does not have a special sphere for action, because the application of the above provisions requires a prior according measure by the UN. As the practical application of the rules of Article 93 *bis* has never ensued in the history of ICAO, it has become a historical relic that has no further legal relevance.[14]

Chinese Membership of ICAO

Never has, despite the fact that the Republic of China was excluded both from the organisation of the UN pursuant to the resolution of the UN in 1971,[15] and pursuant to the rules above from ICAO as well. From the outset, China had been represented by the Republic of China both in the UN and ICAO. After the termination of the Chinese civil war (1945–1949), continental China was subdued to the people's governance, while the republican forces were driven back to the Island of Taiwan. Subsequently, Taiwan was replaced legally by the People's Republic of China representing the united China both in the UN and its Security Council as well as in ICAO. The membership and representation of China in international organisations remained legally continuous,[16] the depositary of the rights and obligations proceeding from membership became the People's China, therefore, the expulsion essentially did not ensue.

The Government of the People's Republic of China addressed a letter to ICAO on 15 February 1974, more than two years after the exclusion of

(continued)

[13] A Member of the United Nations against which preventive or enforcement action has been taken by the Security Council may be suspended from the exercise of the rights and privileges of membership by the General Assembly upon the recommendation of the Security Council. The exercise of these rights and privileges may be restored by the Security Council. Article 5 of the Charter of the United Nations.

[14] Sipos (2023), p. 33.

[15] *UN General Assembly Resolution,* 2758 (XXVI), 25 October 1971. Restoration of the lawful rights of the People's Republic of China in the United Nations.

[16] Status of Chicago Convention, list based on information received from the depositary, the Government of the United States of America. Para. 1, p. 4. (www.icao.int).

Taiwan, in which it informed the Secretary General that 'the Government of the People's Republic of China made a decision to recognise the Convention on International Civil Aviation, which had been signed by the Republic of China on 9 December 1944 and had been deposited for the purpose of ratification on 20 February 1946'.

Adherence to the Convention and the denunciation of the Convention takes place in a notification addressed to the Government of the United States.

- '*Adherence* shall take effect as from the thirtieth day from the receipt of the notification by the Government of the United States of America' [Article 92 *b)*].
- '*Denunciation* shall take effect one year from the date of the receipt of the notification and shall operate only as regards the State effecting the denunciation' [Article 95 *b)*].

Any contracting State may give notice of denunciation of the Convention three years after its coming into effect by notification addressed to the Government of the United States of America. About the fact of adherence or denunciation the United States shall at once inform each of the contracting States [Article 95 *a)*].

3.4 The Member States

Upon taking effect of the Chicago Convention (4 April 1947), ICAO had 26 Member States and its membership has extended to 193 States since then.[17] This growth clearly indicates the significance of the intergovernmental organisation shaping the future of air navigation in the world by framing its global rules. ICAO is one of the world's international organisations with the largest membership: between 1961–1970 as many as 54 States acceded to the institution of ICAO. The membership provided the acceded States opportunity for becoming wide-scale and all-out users of the internationally significant achievements of technological development and for active participation in the elaboration of the rules of international civil aviation.

Due to the dissolution of the Soviet Union, 14 new Member States acceded to the ICAO, then the disintegration of Yugoslavia and Czechoslovakia[18] increased the

[17] The 191st Member State acceded to ICAO was South Sudan on 11 October 2011, which had become independent on 9 July 2011. The fourth smallest state in the world, Tuvalu (Polynesia) situated on 26 sq.km joined the membership on 18 November 2017 as the 192nd Member State of ICAO. As the 193rd Member State the Dominican Republic acceded on 14 March 2019.

[18] Czechoslovakia solely from the Central-Eastern-European region was a founding party of ICAO, therefore, it had a serious role in ICAO. Solely from the region it had been a Member of the ICAO Council 11 times (for more than 30 years) before the dissolution of the country. Due to the

number of Member States considerably. Since the objectives of ICAO coincide with and follow the interests of the international community, almost all States have acceded to the Chicago Convention. Of course, there are exceptions, such as the Vatican, Kosovo, the State of Palestine, Taiwan and Liechtenstein, which are not Members of ICAO.

The sixth smallest State on the Earth, Liechtenstein, is officially not a Member of ICAO. According to its agreement concluded on 29 March 1923 with the Federation of Switzerland, Liechtenstein is represented in international organisations by Switzerland. The minister of the Swiss Government pronounced officially on 20 July 2014 that they had concluded an agreement with Liechtenstein with the objective that in the future the rules of the Chicago Convention would be applied in the territory of Liechtenstein. Liechtenstein does not have either an army or an airport, thus, the organisation of defence and administration related to air transport is discharged by the Federation of Switzerland.[19]

In comparison: The United Nations Organisation (UN) has 193 Member States and in a similar manner to the membership of ICAO, the Vatican, Kosovo and Taiwan (although the UN considers it represented by the People's Republic of China) do not feature among its Member States.

Taiwan with its 23 million residents has outstanding significance in international civil aviation and the air transport of the region (in 2018 it performed the navigation of more than 1.7 million flights and provided service to 70 million passengers in its airspace), nevertheless, it is not a member of ICAO and it does not have an observer status, either.[20] (Unfortunately, due to the COVID-19 pandemic the number of passengers flying to and from Taiwan fell to 1.02 million in 2021.)[21] Although ICAO has always endeavoured to unify and

(continued)

dissolution on 1 January 1993, the Czech Republic and Slovakia were elected to be two new Member States at the 30th Extraordinary Assembly of ICAO. Subsequently, the Czech Republic twice (1993–1995, 2001–2004), while Slovakia once (1998–2001) acquired the right of representation in the ICAO Council. With the dissolution of Czechoslovakia, the two new countries had increasingly slimmer chance to maintain their membership in the ICAO Council, therefore, in the interest of the further representation of the region, they formed successful alliance (Central European Rotation Group—CERG) with the countries of the region.

[19] Ndikum and Ndikum (2014), p. 654.

[20] Kao, Stanley: Time for Taiwan to Return to the ICAO Assembly. 25 September 2019. (www.nationalinterest.org/feature/rep-kao-time-taiwan-return-icao-assembly).

[21] Strong, Matthew: Airlines only flew 1.02 million passengers to and from Taiwan in 2021. Passenger traffic plummeted from 2019 to 2021, but the volume of cargo traffic grew. *Taiwan News*, 4 May 2022. (www.taiwannews.com.tw/en/news).

cooperate on the highest level, Taiwan does not have a role in ICAO. Its reason is the consistent adherence to the principle of 'only one China exists' by China, which on a political basis precludes the cooperation of Taiwan with the organisations of the UN including ICAO. The former President of the United States, Barack Obama supported under a statute[22] granting Taiwan the status of an observer at the ICAO Assemblies, furthermore, he initiated on a diplomatic level in alliance with Canada, Australia and the European Union the acceleration of the process at the President of the ICAO Council. As a result of the vast efforts, upon the amicable invitation of the President of the ICAO Council the representatives of Taiwan could be present as observers under the name of Chinese Taipei at the 38th Assembly of ICAO (2013) held in Montreal.[23] However, to the 39th Assembly of ICAO (2016) the representatives of Taiwan did not receive official invitation. Although the delegation of Taiwan travelled to Montreal and in front of the building of ICAO, they sharply criticised the civil aviation organisation contesting its main objective, that is, unification as well as the slogan that 'no country shall be left behind'.[24] The Taiwanese delegation faced repudiation at the 40th and 41st Assemblies (in 2019 and 2022) again.

3.5 The Headquarters

On 6 June 1947, the contracting States made a decision on the choice of the permanent headquarters of the organisation at the last session of the Provisional Assembly. Of the 44-Member States, 27 cast their votes in favour of Montreal, nine of Paris, four of Geneva and one of China (without the designation of the city),[25] thus, the permanent headquarters of ICAO became located in Montreal, the city of the Canadian province of Quebec. In the majority acceptance of Montreal by secret ballot proposed by the representative of Chile, the countries that had a major role and granted their overt support included the United States contributing a quarter of the budget, the United Kingdom, the members of the British Commonwealth such as Australia and Canada, and Peru in line with the Latin-American countries. It was an essential aspect of the choice that the centre of the United Nations in New York and the new headquarters of ICAO should be close to each other (533 km). The triumph of the Canadian city was also promoted by the fact that the country lies in a

[22] USA Public Law 113–17, 113th Congress. 12 July 2013 H.R.1151. Taiwan observer status.

[23] Glaser (2013).

[24] Taiwan hosts own event at the ICAO. *The China Post,* 1 October 2016.

[25] Sipos (2023), p. 124.

strategically prominent place not only geographically but also from the viewpoint of aviation. The fact that the city possessed outstanding aircraft manufacturing industry already at that time also backed Montreal.

Montreal is the second largest city (following Toronto) of Canada, the second largest country in the world. It is the capital and the centre of aviation since it is the sole city in the world, where more than 200 enterprises (with more than 40,000 employees) involved in the aerospace industry can be found within 30 km, which jointly have the capacity to manufacture all parts necessary to assemble an airplane (engines, wings, the fuselage, electronics etc.). Thence, Montreal is the third largest aircraft manufacturing city in the world following Toulouse in France (Airbus) and Seattle in the United States (Boeing).[26]

Besides ICAO, the main centres and offices of organisations with prominent role in international civil aviation can also be found in Montreal, such as the International Air Transport Association (IATA), the Airports Council International (ACI), the International Federation of Airline Pilots' Association (IFALPA), the International Federation of Air Traffic Controllers' Association (IFATCA) and the International Business Aviation Council (IBAC). Furthermore, the city of Montreal is also reputed for its higher educational institutions such as McGill University with a Master's Program in Air and Space law (LL.M.) and Concordia University awarding MBAs in Aviation Management.

Temporarily, the seat can be relocated pursuant to the decision of the ICAO Council. Permanently, the seat may be transferred by the decision of the Assembly, 'such decision is to be taken by the number of votes specified by the Assembly. The number of votes so specified will not be less than three-fifths (60%) of the total number of contracting States' (Article 45). Thus, the seat may be transferred as long as the Assembly votes for it.

In the history of ICAO, the transfer of the seat has been attempted informally without success several times, but none of the attempts reached the stage of voting. This has several reasons. International organisations agree with the accommodating State under an agreement on the conditions necessary for the exercise of legal capacity. ICAO concluded such an agreement, a so-called Headquarters Agreement[27] with the Canadian Government, in which the Parties stipulated all the conditions necessary for the full accomplishment of the duties of the international organisation specified in its mandate. Thus, they regulated among others the inviolability, the safeguard of the privileges and immunity of the permanent offices and their staff delegated to work beside ICAO, the extension of the exemption from taxes and customs duties, the out-of-turn management of diplomatic passports and visas, the diplomatic immunity of the staff of the ICAO Secretariat, and the settlement of emerging controversial issues.

---

[26] Dempsey (2013).

[27] *Headquarters Agreement Between the Government of Canada and the ICAO,* E101905 – CTS 1992 No. 7; supplementary E103232 – CTS 1999 No. 20; Supplementary E 105390.

Well before the time of the expiry of this long-term agreement and its renewal approaches, diplomatic harmonisation is commenced by the countries which are interested in the relocation of the headquarters. On such occasions informally, all presumed or real problems accumulate. For instance, issues of visas, customs, taxation and foreign policing, flaws of security, infrastructural problems, the extension of diplomatic privileges. In addition, unusual, certainly extremely cold weather also emerges as an ultimate argument. In fact, cold weather is a constant subject, but on that level, it cannot prove to be a crucial factor. This circumstance may particularly influence the representatives of the African community (55 Member States) with significant voting force. In winter -10 and -15° Celsius are quite frequent during the day, in the evening the temperature is between -20 and -30° Celsius. The largest volume of snow (279 cm/year) falls in this city in the world, but the extraordinarily high humidity and the extreme fluctuation of temperature do not create favourable circumstances, either. Global warming has its impact on the otherwise basically unbalanced climate; therefore, winters are getting milder, notwithstanding, it is still unbearably lengthy.[28]

At the beginning of the 1990s, the Government of Germany indicated unofficially that it would be a partner in the transfer of the headquarters of ICAO if the hosting country, that is, Canada is not capable of solving the capacity difficulties of the building and the problems deriving from the shortcomings of the technical standard. That is, the conference room of the main building of ICAO located at 1000 Sherbrook Street West seated merely 600 people, while it should have held more than 1000 people. Eventually, the Canadian Government decided on the construction of a new building, which was realised with a location at 999 University Street.[29] This state-of-the-art building fulfilled the expectations of the Member States in all respects.[30]

The Member State pressurising the relocation of the headquarters designates as an alternative the potential new location, which defies imagination. However, the possibility of an outclassing location means merely the basis for negotiations, in

---

[28] As the returning European visitor recounts to his friends: 'How was the summer in Montreal? I don't know, I spent only 11 months there' or, 'The winter lasted for eight months and in the other 4 months the circumstances were worse for skiing'. Fehérdy, Iván: *Montreal*. Budapest, 1976, pp. 12, 42.

[29] On the basis of the decision of the City Council of Montreal, on 15 March 2015, University Street was renamed to Robert-Bourassa Boulevard, whereas the numbers remained intact. Robert Bourassa (1933–1996) was a teacher and a lawyer, the 22nd Prime Minister of the Province of Quebec. Kelly, Amanda: University Street Name Change to Robert-Bourassa Boulevard is Official. *Global News*. Montreal. 18 March 2015.

[30] A perfect example for that was the 39th Assembly of ICAO (2016) organised in that building, during which totally 2200 delegates participated. Three years later at the 40th Assembly of ICAO (2019) 2600 delegates participated. At the 41st Assembly of ICAO (2022) the number of the delegates was over 5000, of whom 2000 delegates attended online. At this Assembly 184 Member States participated and 57 delegations with observer status were present. Pelsser, Albert: Accommodation. In Pelsser, Albert: *The Postal History of the ICAO*. (www.icao.int); (canso.org/canso-at-the-41st-icao-assembly-week-one-reflections); (unitingaviation.com/author/unitingaviation).

itself it is insufficient, since international diplomacy, the enforcement of interests by the World Powers does not depend on these aspects.

Attempts at Transferring Headquarters

In 2011, the Government of Singapore examined the possibility of the transfer of the headquarters informally, but after lengthy negotiations it abandoned its intention. No official initiation ensued, because during diplomatic inquiries, although a lot of States supported the Asian polis, the Singaporean leadership realised that at the elections it could not overcome the North American region with a leading role in aviation in the world and the aligning allied Member States.

In April 2013, the Government of Qatar raised a claim for the transfer of the headquarters and initiated officially for the first time in the history of ICAO that the capital of Qatar, Doha hosted the organisation of ICAO from 2016. In view of that objective the Government was planning the construction of a new, state-of-the-art building equipped with cutting-edge technology and assumed the total expense of its operation.

However, one month later Qatar withdrew its proposal, since its further suggestion that the 38th Assembly (2013) should be held in Doha instead of Montreal met with definitive rejection upon voting in the Council of ICAO (with 22 no and 14 yes votes). For Qatar, this oppositional voting projected ahead the further destiny of the proposal to transfer the headquarters, consequently, Qatar abandoned its plans.

In diplomacy the term defeat always has several interpretations. In this defeat ultimately the 'victory' of Qatar was manifest, since Qatar, by offering an alternative with proposals that generated competition, at the end of the day, achieved better conditions for the Member States and the organisation of ICAO. That is, the Canadian Government did its utmost to persuade ICAO to stay,[31] therefore, it put forward a by far more advantageous headquarters agreement offering solution for the emerged problems. The new Supplementary Agreement, which was signed by the Secretary General of ICAO and the Canadian Minister of Foreign Affairs on 29 May 2013, guarantees the operation of ICAO in Montreal for the following 20 years until 30 November 2036 (as the new Agreement came into force at the end of 2016).[32] Under this Agreement Canada assumed the obligation to allot 15 million dollars to the expenses of the building of ICAO and by relying on a significant amount, it undertook to renew the equipment of the conference rooms, to reinforce the security system as well as to introduce relief concerning visas and travelling.

[31] The presence of ICAO in Montreal implies its annual contribution of 100 million dollars to the economy of the city and eventually of Canada, furthermore, the direct and indirect creation of 1200 workplaces. Adams, Rick: How international aviation landed in Canada, ICAO was raised in Montreal. *Wings Magazine,* 5 November 2014.

[32] (www.icao.int/Newsroom/Pages/ICAO-and-Canada-sign-new-supplementary-agreement.aspx).

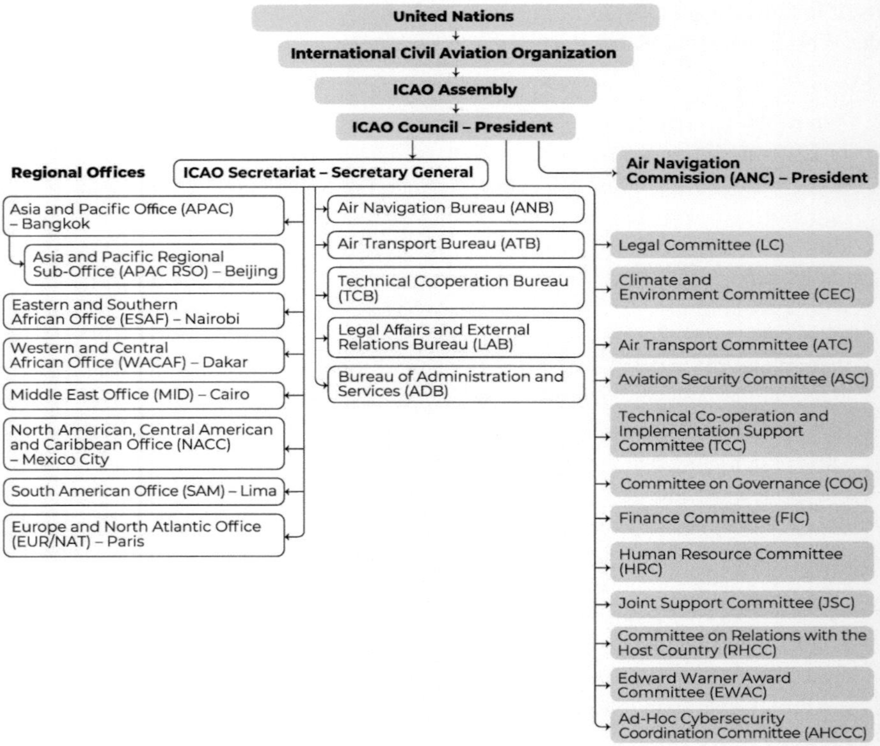

Fig. 3.1 The organisational structure of ICAO
The members of the organs and committees indicated in the grey area are delegated by the contracting States for the purpose of their representation. The employees of the offices in the white area are not the representatives of the Member States, but officials selected on a professional basis and according to other (e.g., geographical) principles

3.6 The Institutional System

Air transport is a conservative industry. It is not unproblematic to bring about changes in the well-operating system of checks and balances. This is valid not only for intergovernmental levels or international aviation policies, but also for the institutional system of ICAO itself. Under the Chicago Convention the contracting States formed 'an organization to be named the International Civil Aviation Organization, which is made up of an *Assembly*, a *Council*, and such other *bodies* as may be necessary' (Article 43). Thus, the triadic organisational structure marking the institutions of the UN 'family' prevails in the case of ICAO as well: it consists of the Assembly, the Council (with the Air Navigation Commission and Committees) and the Secretariat.

Each body in the institutional system of ICAO has an assigned competence and well-defined duty (Fig. 3.1):

- The main representative organ of ICAO is the *Assembly.*
- The permanent body of the *Council* is accountable to the Assembly.
- The *Secretariat* manages and arranges the administrative and official matters of the organisation of ICAO.

The Air Navigation Commission (ANC) is a main body of ICAO and accountable to the Council (see, in 3.9).

There are permanent Committees consisting of aviation experts operating under the control of the Council [see, in 3.10.1-2]:

- Legal Committee (LC); and
- Climate and Environment Committee (CEC).

Committees and the Ad Hoc Committee work subordinated to the Council, of which the Air Transport Committee (ATC), the Aviation Security Committee (ASC) and the Technical Co-operation and Implementation Support Committee (TCC) have prominent roles.

The Committees consist of the Council Members of ICAO:

- Air Transport Committee (ATC);
- Aviation Security Committee (ASC);
- Finance Committee (FIC);
- Committee on Governance (COG);
- Human Resources Committee (HRC);
- Joint Support Committee (JSC);
- Technical Co-operation and Implementation Support Committee (TCC);
- Committee on Relations with the Host Country (RHCC);
- Edward Warner Award Committee (EWAC)
- Ad Hoc Cybersecurity Coordination Committee (AHCCC).[33]

A Task Force was established after the WHO had declared COVID-19 to be a pandemic on 11 March 2020. The Task Force was designed to provide practical, aligned guidance to industry operators to restart the international air transport sector and to restitute it from the impacts of the pandemic on a coordinated global basis.

- Council Aviation Recovery Task Force (CART)

[33] In 2022, the ICAO Council adopted the creation of the Ad Hoc Cybersecurity Coordination Committee (AHCCC) and two separate Panels, under two different Committees. The new Cybersecurity Panel (CYSECP), as approved by the Aviation Security Committee during the 225th Session on 24 January 2022, held its first meeting in May 2022. Furthermore, the Air Navigation Commission created the Trusted Systems Panel (TSP) reinforcing perspectives of cross-coordination among the ICAO Bureaus, Committees and Technical Panels. ICAO Assembly Resolutions A40-10 (2019), A41-WP/64 (2022).

Fig. 3.2 The logo of ICAO
The first UN General Assembly in 1946 adopted its official emblem, which ICAO accepted and has changed several times during its history. The two main motives of the UN emblem are the world map positioned in the focus of five concentric circles and olive branches embracing the map as the symbol of peace. The logo of ICAO is also based on these two motives, which were supplemented by the globe depicted on a plane with its focus on the North Pole and wings to the east and west symbolising aviation manifestly and unequivocally all over the world surrounded by acronyms referring the multilingual character of ICAO. China insisted that in the Chinese inscription not only the acronym, but the whole name of the organisation appeared. The Arabic inscription consists of the Arabic graphs of the English letters of ICAO (The currently used official logo of ICAO was adopted by the Member States at the 31st Assembly (1995). Pelsser, Albert: ICAO Emblem and its History. *The Canadian Connection,* 1 September 1996; ICAO Assembly Resolution A31-1, 1995)

ICAO is the sole organisation within the framework of the UN family, in which the controlling body of ICAO, that is, the Council and its Committees have permanent sessions during the whole year. (Annually, the sessions of the Council are held on 26 occasions on average, while the sessions of the Committees jointly take place on 30 occasions.)

The official languages of the organisation are English, French, Spanish, Russian, Arabic and Chinese. The original Chicago Convention was drawn up in English. At the same time, the equally authentic versions in English, French and Spanish languages were opened for signature in Washington, D.C.[34] At the 16th Assembly of ICAO (1986) held in Buenos Aires, a decision was made (in the form of Protocol attached to the Convention) that the French and Spanish languages become official and equally usable. Upon the accession of the Soviet Union, it was formulated as a condition that the Russian language was also adopted as an official language, about which the 22nd ICAO Assembly (1977) ruled. On the adoption of Arabic, the 31st

[34] Chicago Convention, Chapter XXII, Signature of Convention.

Assembly of ICAO (1995) resolved, while the 32nd Assembly (1998) reached a decision on rendering the Chinese language official as well (Fig. 3.2).[35]

3.7 The Assembly

The *main representative organ* of ICAO is the Assembly, which 'shall meet not less than once in three years and shall be convened by the Council at a suitable time and place' [Article 48 *a)*]. Upon the formation of ICAO, the Convention prescribed annual sessions.[36] However, the Assembly held annually imposed significant financial burden on the Member States, therefore, this rule was amended at the 8th Assembly of ICAO (1954) by the Member States to sessions every three years. Due to this decision the representative function of the Member States in the most important organ of ICAO decreased, since although three years in the turn of the world is not regarded as a long time, but the Member States which are not represented in the permanent body of the Council essentially have the opportunity only every three years to formulate their opinion briefly about the subject on the agenda. Which indicates somewhat that the Assembly held every three years with less than two weeks' sessions does not fulfil entirely the criterion of the main representative organ.

In 2013, the representative of Saudi Arabia made a motion that Assemblies in the future should not be held every three years, but every two years. Furthermore, in the year of the Assembly, the number of Council sessions should be decreased, and the budget of ICAO should be earmarked for two years. However, the motion was repudiated, and it did not actually reach the Assembly, because the more frequent Assemblies would financially burden the budget considerably, while consequently, the elections to the Council would also have to be held every two years. All these would imply the amendment of the Chicago Convention, which the Member States are not interested in with respect to the specific balance of power having persisted for a long time *(status quo ante)* recognised by the majority.[37]

---

[35] *Supra* note 57 at Part I, Chap. 2. (See, ICAO Doc 8876; ICAO Doc 9208; ICAO Doc 9664, ICAO Doc 9722). The ICAO Doc 9664 and 9722 Protocols for Arabic and Chinese languages are not yet in force as the Protocols need certain number of ratifications (122 and 124 ratifications).

[36] ICAO Assembly Resolution A8-1, June 1954.

[37] ICAO Assembly Resolution A37-WP/305, Proposal to Hold ICAO Assembly Sessions Every Two Years, under Agenda Item 21: Increasing the efficiency and effectiveness of ICAO and Proposal to hold Assembly Sessions every two years. A38-WP/18 EX 13, Item 20, 2013.

'Extraordinary meetings of the Assembly may be held at any time upon the call of the Council or at the request of any ten contracting States addressed to the Secretary General' [Article 48 *a)*]. In the history of ICAO nine Extraordinary Assemblies have been convened, mainly by reason of the voting of organisational changes entailing the amendment of the Chicago Convention (e.g., the increase of the number of Members of the Council). Although the objective of the institution of the Extraordinary Assembly is decision-making on significant and urgent matters by the Member States, Extraordinary Assemblies have been convened related to such a situation only on two occasions for the time being.

Due to the drastic increase in the number of unlawful acts committed on board aircraft, an Extraordinary Assembly was convened in June 1970. The contracting States decided on the elaboration of a new Annex in order to tighten aviation security. A further Extraordinary Assembly was convened by the contracting States for the period between 24 April and 10 May 1984 because of the tragedy of KAL Flight 007, when Article 3 *bis* of the Convention was drafted and adopted on the prohibition of the use of weapons against civil aircraft in flight.[38]

3.7.1 The Powers and Duties of the Assembly

The Assembly is the supreme and plenary organ of ICAO, which in its competence determined under the Convention during discharging its duties primarily:

a) elects at each meeting its President and other officers;
b) elects the contracting States to be represented on the Council;
c) examines and takes appropriate action on the reports of the Council and decides on any matter referred to it by the Council;
d) determines its own rules of procedure and establishes such subsidiary commissions as it may consider to be necessary or desirable;
e) votes an annual budget and determines the financial arrangements of the Organisation;
f) reviews expenditures and approves of the accounts of the Organisation;
g) refers, at its discretion, to the Council, to subsidiary commissions, or to any other body any matter within its sphere of action;
h) delegates to the Council the powers and authority necessary or desirable for the discharge of the duties of the Organisation and revokes or modifies the delegations of authority at any time;
i) carries out the appropriate provisions of other international arrangements (Chapter XIII);

[38] ICAO Doc 8895 Resolutions adopted by the Assembly (1970): A17-Resolution; ICAO Doc 9437 Resolutions adopted by the Assembly (1984): A25-Resolution.

j) considers proposals for the modification or amendment of the provisions of the Convention and, if it approves of the proposals, recommends them to the contracting States;
k) deals with any matter within the sphere of action of the Organisation not specifically assigned to the Council (Article 49).

Although the Convention establishes that the Assembly is the most important organ of ICAO, in fact, it is not. The main reason for this can be found in one of the crucial sentences of the Convention concerning the delegation of duties: The Assembly 'deals with any matter within the sphere of action of the Organization not specifically assigned to the Council' [Article 49 *k)*]. This paragraph essentially restricts the role and competence of the Assembly, since it lays the emphasis on the Council; namely, the matters referred to the Council carry great weight and have significant impact on the organisation. Such matters include the issues decided within the powers of the Council, for example, the adoption of the Standard and Recommended Practices (SARPs), the management of the finances of ICAO, the election of the President of the Council, the appointment of the Secretary General, of the staff of the Secretariat, of the President and the members of the Air Navigation Commission (ANC) as well as the settlement of controversial issues. In these important matters the Assembly as the supreme organ may not make decisions. It is essentially the Council the decisions of which determine the sphere of action and the future of ICAO.

The delegation of the crucial duty, the function of regulation to the ICAO Council is not accidental, either. During the discharge of its mandatory duties, the ICAO Council adopts the international Standards and Recommended Practices [Article 54 *l)*]. Subsequently, the ICAO Council for convenience designates the technical rules adopted in its own right as Annexes to the Convention and notifies all contracting States of the action taken. The amendment of the Annexes to the Convention frequently ensues. The Assembly would not have the capacity to discharge such an intensive and time-consuming task. Therefore, exceptionally within the UN family, the ICAO Assembly is more of an institution making and reinforcing general decisions, determining the guidelines of the next three years, the decisions of which may not be reviewed.

3.7.2 The Meeting of the Assembly

'A majority of the contracting States is required to constitute a quorum for the meetings of the Assembly. Unless otherwise provided in the Convention, decisions of the Assembly shall be taken by a majority of the votes cast' [Article 48 *c)*]. The fact of the presence of the majority is established by the Administrative Committee after the inspection of the credentials. The procedure of the meeting of the Assembly is comprehensively determined by the Standing Rules of Procedure of the Assembly.[39]

The Assembly is opened by the President of the ICAO Council in the presence of the Secretary General of ICAO and a high-ranking representative of the Canadian Government. After the opening ceremony, the President of the Council conducts the meeting until the States with the right to vote at the Assembly with a quorum elect the acting President of the Assembly and his four Vice-Presidents. First, the speaking representatives make proposals for the requested candidates, who will be elected by open ballot in the Assembly. The proposal, then the election is formal since the Member States through diplomatic channels have already preliminarily agreed on the persons of the President and the Vice-Presidents to be elected. The President, who has in advance prepared for this honourable, but really difficult task, as a matter of course accepts the honouring request and expresses his thanks for the confidence. The Assembly continues under his direction and first the agenda compiled by the Council is adopted, then the Member States make decisions on the formation of the executive, co-ordinating and administrative Committees, Sub-Committees and Workgroups assisting the work of the Assembly. Subsequently, the Assembly continues with contributions preceding the agenda lasting for days. The representatives of the Member States accorded to speak initially congratulate the elected President, then, despite the time-limit defined by the acting President, in protocol statements, in lengthy and detailed presentations they enlarge upon the achievements of their State in aviation during the period between the two Assemblies and outline their prospective plans.

The generally at most two-week long session is conducted according to a well-prepared and pre-determined scenario. In its course, the Member States make decisions on the working-papers thoroughly elaborated during the preceding three years by the perpetually sitting Council and its Committees. Meritorious debates can be expected at the sessions of the Committees, Sub-Committees and Workgroups, but the plenary sessions with the participation of all Member States scarcely give rise to debates. Its reason is that the experts of the Member States prepare the working-papers motioned by them very meticulously, so these are tabled to the Assembly in a clear form, they have many times been preliminarily negotiated and reconciled on a regional level. The adoption of the working-papers by the Assembly is generally customary despite lesser or greater debates or corrections.

In the case of the points of the agenda, the contributions need to be focused and convey a clear message. This is a basic requirement since it is very risky to make further proposals on the points of the agenda at the plenary session. The reason for this is not the prevention of the boundless unfolding of the debate or of an irrelevant argument, but the obtainment of the support of the Member States is necessary for the adoption of new aspects. Gaining support in an Assembly debate is a really

[39] ICAO Doc 7600 Standing Rules of Procedure of the Assembly of the ICAO. Published by authority of the Secretary General (SG), 8th edn., 2014.

difficult task. Namely, before meritorious decisions, a large scope needs to be offered for diplomacy, political harmonisations and negotiations. This requires plenty of time and preliminary co-ordinations, but the Assembly does not allow enough scope for action and opportunity. A perfect example is that in issues unanimously supported by the Member States in the ICAO Council, which are professionally important and acceptable for everyone in full measure, the approval necessary for the decision may be granted only after prolonged debates maybe lasting for years. The pronouncement of yes needs to 'be born'. In many cases, the Member States attach their affirmative votes to gaining advantages and in consideration of their own interests they request something in return for their support.

In order to keep up with the tight pace of the Assembly, the opportunities for taking the floor at plenary sessions are firmly restricted. Here the representatives of all Member States cannot rise to speak, therefore, European countries and other countries belonging geographically to the same region always reconcile their standpoints preliminarily at their group meetings and negotiate about the strategy to be followed before the decisions. During reconciliations, they elaborate a joint standpoint, and abiding by the European example, they select the two European countries the representatives of which will make speeches on the given point of the agenda, essentially on behalf of the European countries. The representative of the European country taking the floor in the debate firstly justifies in their speech in detail why their government decided on the adoption or rejection of the recommendations formulated in the motion, what modifications they would make, and as a conclusion, they request the support of the Member States for this standpoint. The speeches follow each other, at the end of which the other European State takes the floor and in a brief speech with reference to what was said before they assure the first European speaker of their support. This scenario is more or less followed by the representatives of the African, the Arab, the Latin-American countries, and incidentally, the representatives of the States of the Asian region.

In Europe the Member States are integrated by the European Civil Aviation Conference (ECAC), the African States are united by the African Civil Aviation Commission (AFCAC), the Arab world is represented by the Arab Civil Aviation Commission (ACAC), while South America by the Latin American Civil Aviation Commission (LACAC). The Asian countries do not have such an intergovernmental regional organisation, but under the name of the 'Montreal Group', the representatives of the region regularly have sittings on strategic issues in the headquarters of ICAO. Of course, at all Assemblies there are agenda points which ultimately divide the Parties and trigger vibrant debates. Such critical subject was the launch of the Continuous Monitoring Approach (CMA), a procedure introduced at the 37th Assembly of ICAO (2010) as the reformation of the safety audit. Subsequently, the issue of the global extension of the environmental requirements demanded unilaterally by the EU also divided the parties at the 38th and 39th ICAO Assemblies in 2013 and 2016.

The protection of the environment is an important but sensitive area. Although all Member States and industrial performers support it, what is more, they deal with the issue of the protection of the environment on a level adequate to its significance, nevertheless, the standpoints essentially differ concerning the method of implementation. The main reason is that the specifications of the European Union are the most rigorous in the world, on the other hand, the system of requirements of the EU foregrounds the application of 'Market-Based Measures' (MBM). The majority of the ICAO Member States do not consider the latter solution to be a global response to be followed by all so as to address the problems emerging related to environmental protection, therefore, they repudiated this regional European solution. However, after protracted and tough debates a consensual solution was reached at the 38th Assembly (2013).[40] The MBM Agreement, in which the Member States consented to the further elaboration of the mechanism, was adopted. Eventually, at the 39th ICAO Assembly (2016) the Member States adopted the Global Market-Based Measure (GMBM) Scheme, which after 2020 requires the Member States to force back carbon dioxide (CO2) emissions in aviation in several phases (in the first phase voluntarily). Thus, the representatives of the air transport industry, for first time in the world, concluded a global agreement to reduce the pollution of the environment caused by the air transport industry.[41]

The decisions of the Assembly cannot be postponed to the next Assemblies (normally held every three years), thus, a consensus needs to be reached despite the limitations of time, which poses a real challenge for, and in case of success, gives credit to the acting President of the Assembly.

The budget is a constant object of debate. 'The Council shall submit to the Assembly annual budgets, annual statements of accounts and estimates of all receipts and expenditures. The Assembly shall vote the budgets with whatever modification it sees fit to prescribe' and apportions the expenses of the Organisation among the contracting States on the basis which it determines from time to time (Article 61). The budget does not include the financial expenses of the delegations, the Members of the Council, the Committees or of any other representatives. 'Each contracting State shall bear the expenses of its own delegation to the Assembly and the remuneration, travel, and other expenses of any person whom it appoints to serve on the Council, and of its nominees or representatives on any subsidiary committees or commissions of the Organization' (Article 63). Thus, each Member State contributes a membership fee to the budget of ICAO in proportion to the volume of its air traffic. The United States as the principal contributor to the budget of ICAO (20%) accounts for the largest civil air traffic, which is followed by China (about 15%). It is peculiar that these two countries, although they account for almost half of the total budget of ICAO and they are considered to be significant payers into open, voluntary financial funds, nevertheless, they are in a difficult situation upon the enforcement of their interests. The reason for this is that these countries do not

[40] ICAO Assembly Resolution A38-18, Consolidated statement of continuing ICAO policies and practices related to environmental protection – Climate change. September 2013.

[41] ICAO Assembly Resolution A39-3, Consolidated statement of continuing ICAO policies and practices related to environmental protection – Global Market-Based Measure (MBM) Scheme. September 2016.

belong to unified groups congregating regions, which carry numerous votes. In the case of China and Japan, these Asian countries are not formally rallied in a group, in most cases India proceeds separately as well. Consequently, these Member States (along with Russia, Canada and Australia) need to obtain the supporting votes individually.

3.7.3 Voting in the Assembly

In the organisational system of the UN, in compliance with the general principle of the equality of sovereign States under international law, 'all contracting States shall have an *equal right* to be represented at the meetings of the Assembly and each contracting State shall be *entitled to one vote*' [Article 48 *b)*].

Voting Systems
There are voting systems in which the votes have varying weight, have different force owing to the foundational intent by reason of the degree of economic development, the population, the range of the territory, the extent of contribution to the budget or for other reasons (for instance, political compromises).

A perfect example is the Council of the European Union, where the adoption of a qualified majority decision requires the support of 55% of EU Member States and the population of the Member States with yes votes needs to reach or exceed jointly 65% of the total population of the EU. In the decisions of the Administrative Board of the International Monetary Fund (IMF), the weight of the votes is determined by the extent of the paid quota. (The payment of the amount determined by the IMF entails a further Member State vote beyond the uniform basic vote due to each Member State.) On the basis of the principle of the 'unanimity of Five Powers', upon voting in the UN Security Council consisting of 15 Members (five standing and ten elected), the unanimous vote of the five standing Council Members (the United States, the United Kingdom, France, China and Russia) is necessary for reaching decisions concerning the international community.

At the sessions of the Assembly, each delegate may represent solely one State. The delegation consists of a chief delegate, an alternate chief delegate and advisors. The delegation is headed by the chief delegate. The legal status of the members of the delegation is contained by the letter of credence issued by the Member State, which needs to be submitted to the Secretary General of ICAO. The chief delegate appointed by the Member State, generally the Minister of Transport or the Director General of Civil Aviation (DGCA), casts votes and takes the floor at the Assembly. The alternate chief delegate and the advisors designated by the delegating State may participate in the sessions of the Assembly without the right to vote. The invited international organisations and the representatives of non-contracting States may also participate in the sessions in observer status with consultation rights, but without the right to vote.

Unless otherwise provided in the Convention, the decisions of the Assembly shall be taken by *a majority of the votes* cast [Article 48 *c)*]. The Convention derogates from the main rule in three cases and requires *qualified majority* in the following cases:

- The accession of certain States to the Convention shall require the approval of the UN and a *four-fifths vote* of the Assembly (Article 93).
- The headquarters may be relocated otherwise than temporarily only by the decision of the Assembly, which shall require *three-fifths of the votes* of all contracting States (Article 45).
- Any proposed amendment to the Convention shall be approved by a *two-thirds vote* of the Assembly [Article 94 *a)*].

If any Member State makes a motion for the amendment of the Convention, it needs to submit its written motion for the amendment to the Council at least six months before the opening day of the Assembly. The Council takes all such motions for amendments into consideration and forwards them with its comments and recommendations to the contracting States three months before the opening day of the Assembly. The amendment of the Chicago Convention [conforming to the Procedure of the Assembly[42] and to the decision made at the 4th ICAO Assembly (1950)][43] is admissible, if the purpose of the amendment complies with either or both of the following conditions:

– the established practice proves the necessity of the amendment; (and /or)
– the amendment is provably expected or useful.

The mechanism becomes more complicated after the approval of the amendment brought by majority, because the amendment does not come into force immediately despite its positive adoption. This requires the fulfilment of a further condition. Thus, the amendment comes into force in the States which have ratified such amendment when ratified by the number of contracting States specified by the Assembly. 'The number of the States so specified may not be less than two-thirds of the total number of contracting States' [Article 94 *a)*].

Abstention from voting is not considered to be a vote. Voting may take place verbally, by show of hands or standing up, but also by name following the English alphabet. The result of the latter option needs to be itemised under a protocol. If the chief delegates of two or more Member States request voting by secret ballot and their request is not objected, voting by secret ballot is admissible. In the case of

[42] ICAO Doc 7600 Standing Rules of Procedure of the Assembly of the ICAO. Published by authority of the Secretary General (SG), 8th edn., 2014. Section IV, 10 *d)*.

[43] ICAO Assembly Resolution A4-3, 1950.

objection, the Member States decide by majority vote whether they favour or repudiate voting by secret ballot.

Voting rights cannot be exercised in two cases pursuant to the Convention. The Member State that has 'not accepted

- the International Air Services Transit Agreement; or
- the International Air Transport Agreement,

shall not have the right to vote on any questions referred to the Assembly or Council under the provisions of the relevant Agreement' [Article 66 *b)*].

Pursuant to one of the general principles of international law and to the provision of the Vienna Convention on the Law of Treaties (1969), a treaty does not create either obligations or rights for a third State without its consent (Article 34).[44] The principle deriving from Roman law regards treaties as a two-party situation, which binds the parties and only the parties; it does not create prejudices or avails for a third State *(pacta tertiis nec nocent, nec prosunt).*

The exercise of the voting power may be suspended in two cases:

- 'the Assembly shall suspend the voting power in the Assembly and in the Council of any contracting State that during the settlement of controversial issues and the fulfilment of specified obligations violates the stipulated provisions' (Article 88, Chapter XVIII).
- 'the Assembly may suspend the exercise of the voting power in the Assembly and in the Council of any contracting State that fails to discharge within a reasonable period its financial obligations to the Organization' (Article 62).

The Secretary General of ICAO informs the Member States about the fulfilment or the omission of payment obligations annually. Before the commencement of the Assemblies, Member States that have failed to comply with the payment obligations due each year always crop up. With or without external assistance these States make payments for all arrearage in the last minute, thereby, they secure the opportunity of the exercise of voting power, the sustenance of the precious one vote. Not all of the 193 Member States appear at the Assembly, so not every Party exercises the powers of representation and voting. (At the same time, it may also occur that the representative of the Member State officially with the right to vote is not present upon voting, but settles other kinds of business in the city, nevertheless, they are finally present at the evening social events.)

Voting makes the Assembly intriguing and colourful. The voting process is well-regulated in the Standing Rules of Procedure of the Assembly of the International Civil Aviation Organization (ICAO) under Section VIII.[45] The voting rights, the method of voting, voting on motions, secret ballots, postponement of voting, the

---

[44] *Vienna Convention on the Law of Treaties* (1969), Article 34 of Section 4 of Part III.

[45] Standing Rules of Procedure of the Assembly of the International Civil Aviation Organization (ICAO), Doc. 7600/8, 8th edn., 2014.

vote itself and voting on amendments[46]—all these aspects are regulated precisely. Especially the amendment of the Convention and its voting as well as the election of the Members of the Council by secret ballot are special events awaited by all.

Voting on the Amendment of the Convention
From the outset, the Chicago Convention (1944) has been amended meritoriously in merely two respects, while the world has changed in its foundations: even the laws of physics have not remained the same. In addition, in these two cases not the existing text has been amended, but new norm-texts have been drawn up: Article 3 *bis* (1984) and Article 83 *bis* (1980). Other, minor amendments were related primarily to the organisational transformation of ICAO. Mostly, the Convention was amended pertaining to the increase in the number of the Members of the Council (upon its establishment the Council consisted of 21 Members, then in several stages the number of the Members changed to 40). By reason of changes in the official languages, the Convention has been amended several times (following English, French and Spanish languages, Russian, Arabic, then Chinese also became official languages) and related to the relocation of the permanent headquarters, the procedure of voting changed as well.

Why has the Convention not changed in major issues? One of the main reasons is to be found in the existing equilibrium *(status quo)*. The representatives have expressed their fear several times that once the amendment of the Convention commences, the changes in the future will not be restricted to the given motion, but the amendment motions arriving one after the other cannot be 'forestalled'.[47] Another basic reason for the limited number of amendments is that the contracting Parties bound the changes adopted with majority by the Member States at the Assembly to further ratification by the States. That is, despite its positive adoption, the new or amended rule does not take effect immediately, because its further condition is ratification by the number of States determined by the Assembly, and the number of these States cannot be less than two-thirds of all the contracting States [Article 94 *a)*]. In this special ratification regime, the amendment does not obligate all parties equally *(erga omnes)*, but exclusively those Member States which took the opportunity of the legal institution of ratification. This rule in many cases turns the whole procedure into absurdity, heterogeneous and lengthy with respect to its result, which explains why the Convention has remained 'unamended' for decades.

The situation becomes absurd because it may occur that the amendment adopted by two-thirds majority will not be ratified by two-thirds of the Member States, that is,

[46] Idem., the Procedure of Voting on Amendments is as follows: 'Any amendment to a motion shall be voted on before a vote is taken on the motion. When two or more amendments are moved to a motion, the vote should be taken on them in their order of remoteness to the original motion, commencing with the most remote. The presiding officer shall determine whether a proposed amendment is so related to the motion as to constitute a proper amendment thereto, or whether it must be considered as an alternative or substitute motion; this ruling may be reversed by a majority of votes cast' (Rule 49).

[47] ICAO Doc 8892 A 17-Min. Ex/1-8, 11, 16–30 June 1970.

there are Member States which voted for the amendment at the Assembly, however, they do not excel in its ratification. It may also occur that the Member State abstains from voting or objects to the amendment at the Assembly, but it ratifies the relevant rule subsequently. It has also occurred and has had primarily legal technical significance that certain Member States exercised voting rights at the Assembly in issues in which they did not ratify the relevant rules, therefore, the rule did not establish rights or obligations for them. A perfect example for that is the Member State which did not ratify the increase of the number of the Members of the Council from 33 to 36, but at the Assembly voted for the candidate Member States standing for these three seats. At the 34th Extraordinary Assembly of ICAO (2003), the acting President and the Director of the Legal Committee of ICAO decided in face of the facts that, in order to avoid diplomatic nuisances and with respect to the insignificance of the issue, all Member States would be granted the right to vote.

In view of the result, this special procedure makes the Convention heterogeneous, which further complicates the situation, since it disrupts the uniformity of the Convention and extinguishes faith in its universality. In fact, no amendment of the Convention has been ratified by all the Member States or by an equal number of Member States (for example, 157 Member States ratified Article 3 *bis*, while Article 83 *bis* was ratified by 177 Member States). All amendments of the Convention have essentially been ratified by different Member States. Simultaneously, the special procedure prolongs the enforcement of the will of the treaty-maker, since if we examine the amendments in the history of the Convention, we can see that their coming into force was awaited on average for a minimum of ten years.

It is not arguable: the Convention needs modernisation and reformation,[48] since the establishment of real uniformity logically requires the uniform application of the provisions of the Convention. It is thought-provoking why this is so since ICAO has authorisation proceeding from the Convention, pursuant to which it may 'find the strength' to demand uniform approval of the amendments by the Member States. If, according to the Assembly, the amendment is of 'such a nature as to justify this course, the Assembly in its resolution recommending adoption may provide that any State which has not ratified within a specified period after the amendment has come into force thereupon ceases to be a member of the Organization and a party to the Convention' [94 Article *b)*]. However, the ICAO Assembly has not taken the opportunity to apply the rule above in the intricate world of checks and balances offering alternatives and shaped by politics and diplomacy.

Voting about the Council

The most highlighted point on the agenda of the Assembly is the election of the Members of the ICAO Council. The election is a central event, which is demon-

[48] Sipos (2023), pp. 210-222.; Milde (1994), pp. 401-452.; Sipos (2022), pp. 203–211.

strated by the fact that the highest-ranking representatives of Member State delegations do not stay in Montreal after the election of the Council Members. They travel back to their homeland and entrust the Directors General or their deputies to attend to further representation. At the Assembly everything revolves around the Council elections. The Member States campaign (even those who do not stand for positions in the Council or their position in the Council is guaranteed) and as the closure of the campaign they arrange standing receptions. These offer topics for conversation for the participants besides the quality of the served meals, and the received presents manifesting the culture of the organising country. In some evenings as many as four receptions are organised almost simultaneously at different locations and it is good manners to turn up at each of them. (This needs proper time management but generally it can be realised.)

Upon voting for the Members of the Council at the Assembly, the significance of the legal institution of one vote due to each State guaranteed as a basic right in the UN family can be discerned. Irrespective of its degree of economic development or its influence, the largest and the tiniest Member State has equally one vote. In an extreme case it may occur that a Member State with no aviation industry determines whether a Member State developed in aviation wins or loses at the election. The voting for the Members of the Council takes place by secret ballot.[49]

In practice, nobody can be reassured about the realisation of the support promised in writing, then confirmed verbally because of the confidential character of voting. Pledging one's loyalty does not constitute a guarantee, therefore, the representatives of the Member States interested in nomination constantly endeavour to convince all Member States until the last minute. Even the allied is warned by its own allied Party lest they should have false expectations despite the preliminary diplomatic reconciliations. Based on the preliminary diplomatic exchange of notes, theoretically, the expectable result may be predicted but surprises may always befall.

In the decision-making mechanism of the Assembly, but mainly of the Council, we need to recognise that the first among equals deserves preferential treatment *(primus inter pares)*. That is, besides the equal votes there exists a firmer one: 'the more equal' vote. It is an unwritten rule that the so-called North-Atlantic formula has the strength to break through the equality of the votes of the Parties. This fact needs to be taken into consideration upon gauging the chances, since the capacity of the United States and of the Member States of the European Union to collect votes is significant on a world scale. It is worth conciliating with the above-mentioned countries preceding the submission of a motion, requesting their consent or acknowledgement. Namely, these countries can mobilise a lot of supporters and align a sufficient number of voters with themselves upon voting. Not to mention the fact that

[49]The election in each of the Groups I, II and III (candidates for Council membership) shall be conducted by secret ballot (Rule 59). The vote on any question shall be by secret ballot if the delegations of two or more Contracting States so request and the request is not opposed. In case of opposition the question whether there shall be a secret ballot shall be decided by a majority of votes cast in secret ballot (Rule 47). Standing Rules of Procedure of the Assembly of the International Civil Aviation Organization (ICAO), Doc 7600/8, 8th edn., 2014.

these countries contribute a considerable proportion of the budget of ICAO. The United States proceeding solely is not a member of the regional groupings, but as a World Power it has a great impact on the Latin American States. As opposed, the European countries, mainly Great Britain, France and Spain by reason of their historical traditions cultivate excellent diplomatic relations with their former colonies and can rally a sufficient number of supporters from other regions of the world. It is a basic principle that support entails support in return. This support in return is generally effectuated in the system of interests in aviation but in some cases the supporting Member State requests and receives assistance in another area (e.g., upon voting in another UN or other organisations).

3.8 The Council

The Council shall be a *permanent body* responsible to the Assembly. It shall be composed of thirty-six contracting States elected by the Assembly [Article 50 *a)*].

The Council is the controlling, the administrative organ, the governing body of the work of ICAO between Assemblies. The *permanent* character of the Council is an exceptional phenomenon in the specialised agencies of the UN. It is not inadvertent that several unsuccessful attempts have been made at the removal of this word from the Convention. Upon the adoption of the Convention, the permanent character was reasonable since the Council had to elaborate plentiful new technical standards, technical prescriptions under the Annexes. As time advanced and the initial far-reaching creative work was terminated, besides professional work, politics and specialised diplomacy gained predominance, nevertheless, the Council retained its permanent character. This facilitates that the Members of the Council in session three times for one month annually, often with several months' summer holidays spent in rented offices in the headquarters of ICAO, officially at the permanent diplomatic residences assigned to ICAO, may be convened at any time (within 48 hours upon Extraordinary Sessions).

The 16-storeyed headquarters of ICAO accommodates the majority of the permanent representative offices linked to ICAO (following American customs there is no 13th floor). Most diplomatic representative offices can be found on the 10th and 14th floors. The Member States with no space in the building by reason of the shortage of space, rent offices in the neighbouring office buildings. The Embassies of the delegating countries cannot provide assistance as to accommodation, since they are located in Ottawa, the capital of Canada. The concentration of the representative offices in one building facilitates extraordinarily intensive negotiations since within a couple of hours meritorious discussions can be held with the majority of the diplomats.

During the periods between the sessions of the Council, the ICAO Secretariat organises the major conferences related to civil aviation, high-ranking Ministerial Sessions, conferences and seminars initiated by the Directors General of Civil Aviation. In these periods, the permanent professional committees of the Council have sessions with the active participation of the Members of the Council (Fig. 3.3).

Fig. 3.3 ICAO Council Chamber
Opposite the entrance we can see the emblem of ICAO, the arms made of bronze with the flags of the UN and ICAO juxtaposed. The session is headed by the President of the ICAO Council, to the left the Secretary General of ICAO and an employee of the Secretariat are seated. In the middle we can see the present of the Netherlands, the stone work symbolising the Globe placed on a steel pedestal. The national banners of the 36 Council Member States can be found in the chamber, while the banners of other Member States can be seen in the reception hall. The Council Members sit facing each other in an order following the English alphabet. Directly behind them the colleagues of the representative office, while in the hindmost rows the representatives of the Member States with observer status are seated. On the right, we can see the office embracing the whole chamber seating the interpreters and the technical staff. About the discussions in the Council sessions, minutes are taken and an abstract is made. All speeches are translated into the official languages of ICAO. The red signals placed on the floor help adherence to the timeframe of the speeches

3.8.1 Functions of the Council

Fourteen obligatory and five optional functions of the Council are itemised under the Convention. The obligatory functions indicate clearly that the Council is essentially the most important and most efficient organ of ICAO.

During the implementation of its *mandatory* functions (highlighting the most important ones) the ICAO Council shall:

a) submit annual reports to the Assembly;
b) carry out the directions of the Assembly and discharge the duties and obligations which are laid on it the Convention;
c) determine its organisation and rules of procedure;

d) appoint and define the duties of an Air Transport Committee, which shall be chosen from among the representatives of the members of the Council, and which shall be responsible to it;
e) establish an Air Navigation Commission;
f) administer the finances of the Organisation;
g) determine the emoluments of the President of the Council;
h) appoint a chief executive officer who shall be called the Secretary General, and make provision for the appointment of such other personnel as may be necessary;
i) request, collect, examine and publish information relating to the advancement of air navigation and the operation of international air services, including information about the costs of operation and particulars of subsidies paid to airlines from public funds;
j) report to contracting States any infraction of this Convention, as well as any failure to carry out recommendations or determinations of the Council;
k) report to the Assembly any infraction of this Convention where a contracting State has failed to take appropriate action within a reasonable time after notice of the infraction;
l) adopt international standards and recommended practices; for convenience, designate them as Annexes to this Convention; and notify all contracting States of the action taken;
m) consider recommendations of the Air Navigation Commission for amendment of the Annexes and take action; and
n) consider any matter relating to the Convention which any contracting State refers to it (Article 54).

Thus, beyond its controlling, operative and administrative functions, the Council frames rules (as quasi-lawmaker) and settles controversial issues (has quasi adjudicating-functions). This substantiates its peculiarity, power and uniqueness within the framework of the UN family.

During the accomplishment of its *optional, permissive* functions the Council may

a) create subordinate air transport commissions on a regional or other basis;
b) delegate to the Air Navigation Commission duties additional to those set forth in the Convention;
c) conduct research into all aspects of air transport and air navigation which are of international importance;
d) study any matters affecting the organisation and operation of international air transport; and
e) investigate, at the request of any contracting State, any situation which may appear to present avoidable obstacles to the development of international air navigation (Article 55).

During the accomplishment of its optional functions, ICAO has yielded global solutions in several crucial areas, which actually overreached political interests and historical background.

Polar Routes as Strategic Routes

In 1995, at the Asian conference of the regional office of ICAO in Bangkok, a revolutionary idea came to the fore: the Polar Routes unused because of the Cold War, which, for reasons of defence and strategy were in the limelight, should be made adequate for international civil aviation, since this way the operation of airlines engaged in commercial air transport between North America and Asia could be shorter and swifter. Therefore, ICAO urged to render the air routes largely affecting the Russian airspace available by suitable technical development, by the technical and lingual preparation of air navigation control in close cooperation with the Russian Government. With a view to this, ICAO delineated four Polar Routes. Special rules were prescribed for operation with respect to extraordinary weather conditions, the temperature of the fuel, the evading airports and the procedures to be applied during the rescue of passengers.

The first official flight ensued on Polar Route in July 1998. The airplane of the Cathay Pacific Airline (CX) flew without interim landing within an hour's shorter time, in 16 hours between New York (JFK) and Hong Kong (HKG). By the present day, the Polar Routes have become the most important strategic routes (Fig. 3.4).

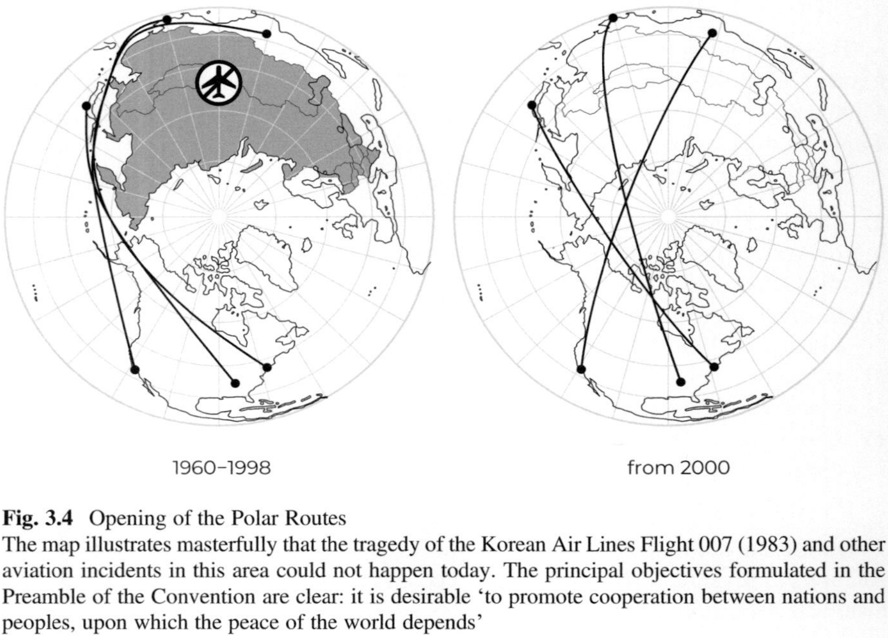

Fig. 3.4 Opening of the Polar Routes
The map illustrates masterfully that the tragedy of the Korean Air Lines Flight 007 (1983) and other aviation incidents in this area could not happen today. The principal objectives formulated in the Preamble of the Convention are clear: it is desirable 'to promote cooperation between nations and peoples, upon which the peace of the world depends'

3.8.2 Functions Related to Air Navigation Facilities

In conformity with the Standards and Recommended Practices adopted by the ICAO Council, each contracting State shall undertake, so far as it may find practicable, to

a) provide, in its territory, airports, radio services, meteorological services and other air navigation facilities;
b) adopt and put into operation unified and standard systems of communications procedure, codes, markings, signals, lighting and other operational practices and rules;
c) collaborate in international measures to secure the publication of aeronautical maps and charts (Article 28).

'If the Council is of the opinion that the airports or other air navigation facilities, including radio and meteorological services, of a contracting State are not reasonably adequate for the safe, regular, efficient, and economical operation of international air services, the Council shall consult with the State directly concerned, and other States affected, with a view to finding means by which the situation may be remedied and may make recommendations for that purpose. No contracting State shall be guilty of an infraction of the Convention if it fails to carry out these recommendations' (Article 69). At the same time, a contracting State may conclude an arrangement with the Council for giving effect to such recommendations. The State, if it decides so, bears all the costs involved in any such arrangement. If the State does not make a relevant decision, the Council may agree, at the request of the State, to provide for all or a portion of the costs of the construction of airports and other navigational facilities, the maintenance of radio equipment and meteorological services necessary for the enhancement of the safety, regularity and efficiency of international flights (Article 70). The Council in the territory of the State shall secure the conditions necessary for safe and efficient operation and provide, man, maintain and administer the necessary facilities. The Council shall specify just and reasonable charges for the services provided (Article 71). The Council may make current expenditures from the general funds of the Organisation (Article 73). From the revenues deriving from operation the concerned service providers pay charges.

Controlling the Somali Airspace
In the State of Somalia stricken by civil war from 1993, the control of air traffic ensued under the organisation of ICAO and the UN Development Programme (UNDP).[50] From May 1996, the Somali airspace was controlled from the neighbouring country, Kenya (Nairobi) by the air navigation service provider

(continued)

[50] ICAO Eastern and Southern African Office: *Workshop on the development of national performance for air navigation systems,* 2010, NPF/SIP/2010-WP/22.

called Civil Aviation Administrative Authority for Somalia established by ICAO. The main owner of the organisation was the Somali State. The activity was carried out by ICAO in close cooperation with the IATA, other UN agencies and the Somali civil aviation authority.

On 4 December 2014, the Secretary General of ICAO and the minister of the Somali Government signed an agreement on the implementation of a provisional programme,[51] which since January 2015 has facilitated the control of the Somali airspace for the State itself from the capital, Mogadishu. ICAO with several million Dollars supported the realisation of the necessary conditions, for which Turkey provided substantial help to Somalia.

'Where land is needed for facilities financed in whole or in part by the Council at the request of a contracting State, that State shall either provide the land itself, retaining title if it wishes, or shall facilitate the use of the land by the Council on just and reasonable terms and in accordance with the laws of the State concerned' (Article 72). A contracting State may at any time discharge any obligation into which it has entered under Article 70 and take over airports and other facilities which the Council has provided in its territory on condition that it pays to the Council an amount which in the opinion of the Council shall be reasonable in the circumstances. 'If the State considers that the amount fixed by the Council is unreasonable it may appeal to the Assembly against the decision of the Council. The Assembly may confirm or amend the decision of the Council' (Article 75).

3.8.3 Functions Related to Joint Operating Organisations

The provisions of the Convention facilitate for two or more contracting States to establish *joint air transport operating organisations* or *international operating agencies* and to pool their air services on any routes or in any regions.[52] All

[51] ICAO officially transfers control of Somali airspace to Government of Somalia. *Hiiraan Online,* 10 December 2014. (www.hiiraan.com).

[52] Several forms of pooling arrangements are known. In the beginning, one of the contracting airlines under a so-called *pool arrangement* made a payment of the difference between their revenues to the other Party. Before all timetable seasons, the parties agreed on the tariffs and the difference was paid by the Party generating larger revenue depending on the traffic. Later the so-called *code-share arrangements* also appeared, in which the participating airlines operate the flight jointly on agreed routes with a common flight number. In that case within the framework of the so-called *block-seat* arrangement, one party or both purchase(s) seat quotas on the aircraft operated by the other Party. The non-operating Party may purchase *hard-block* seats in fixed number and *soft-block* seats in flexible number on the given flight. The fixed number of seats has to be paid for in advance. If the contracting Party cannot sell the purchased quota, this causes damage. At the same time, if more seats are demanded, the revenue arises for the partner, since only

agreements with such purposes shall be announced to the ICAO Council for registration. Under the relevant provisions concerning the nationality of the aircraft (Articles 17–21), the Council shall provide for the application of the rules of registration in case of the pooled aircraft (Article 77). On this basis, in jointly operating organisations the States specify under separate agreements which State attends to registration, exercises the proceeding rights and undertakes obligations with regard to a specific aircraft.

Multinational Airlines

Air Afrique (RKA) operated between 1961 and 2002 after 11 Western-African countries established a joint air transport operating enterprise with headquarters in Abidjan (Ivory Coast) under the Yaoundé Agreement.[53] These countries would not have had the capacity to establish autonomous national airlines by themselves, therefore, the founders availed themselves of the opportunity guaranteed by the Convention. However, the joint enterprise did not survive the crisis following 11 September 2001 and went bankrupt. The majority of their routes were taken over by *Air France* (AF).

The most renowned multinational airline is the consortium of the *Scandinavian Airlines System* (SAS) established in 1951 and at that time owned jointly in a proportion of 50+1% by Sweden, Denmark and Norway.[54] Under an agreement, the Parties organised their national airlines into a new joint air transport operating organisation named SAS. The seat of the joint enterprise is located at the Arlanda International Airport of Stockholm (ARN).

'The Council may suggest to contracting States concerned that they form joint organizations to operate air services on any routes or in any regions' (Article 78). 'A State may participate in joint operating organizations or in pooling arrangements, either through its government or through an airline company or companies designated by its government. The companies may be State-owned or partly State-owned or privately owned' (Article 79). The rules of the Chicago Convention are to be applied to joint air transport operating organisations, international operating agencies or to pooled flights.

the operating Party may sell tickets exceeding the fixed number of seats. The sale of seats purchased in a flexible framework is less risky however, such contracts are seldom concluded.

[53] ICAO Circular 98-AT/19, 1970 – *Treaty relating to Air Transport in Africa.*

[54] ICAO Circular 99-AT/20, 1970 – *SAS Consortium Agreement and Related Agreements.*

3.8.4 Settlement of Disputes

In the history of ICAO, few controversial cases reached the final decision of the Council, since the President of the ICAO Council proceeding in his scope of competence, exerting his diplomatic and political influence persuaded the litigating parties to agree at their earliest convenience.[55] The Council shall exercise its dispute settlement functions indirectly pursuant to the Convention when it considers any matter relating to the Convention which any contracting State refers to it [Article 54 *n)*], or, when the Council reports to contracting States any infraction of the Convention, as well as any failure to carry out recommendations or determinations of the Council [Article 54 *j)*].

The Council can exercise its dispute settlement functions directly when it makes decisions on controversial matters relating to the interpretation or application of the Convention and its Annexes among the contracting States. No Member of the Council shall vote in the consideration by the Council of any dispute to which it is a Party (Article 84). The Council consisting of elected Member States has primarily political functions, which in disputes among the Member States aggravates making decisions on a purely professional basis. In order to eliminate this problem and to support the objective consideration of the case, the Council often employs internationally recognised experts.

Currently, there are ten cases in which the Council has proceeded under Article 84[56] in disputes between the States: India v. Pakistan (1952),[57] Lebanon v. Syria (1956),[58] the United Arab Republic v. Jordan (1958),[59] the United Kingdom v. Spain (1967),[60] Pakistan v. India (1971),[61] Cuba v. the United States (1998),[62]

---

[55] As ICAO became involved in a growing number of conflicts, the President on the Council gradually assumed a more prominent role as an arbiter and conciliator. The Convention is silent on the President's good offices. This activity has had much success, for example, in the dispute between Senegal and Cape Verde over flight information services for the north-west/south-east traffic flow between Dakar and North America and concerning the opening of the air corridor in the South China Sea after China had closed its airspace in the vicinity of Hainan Island, which affected traffic on the main air route to Hong Kong, etc. Sochor (1991), pp. 112–113.

[56] Dempsey (2017), pp. 851–870.; Abeyratne (2014), pp. 663–668.

[57] ICAO Doc 7367 Report of the Council to the Assembly on the Activities of the Organisation in 1952. A7-P1, 1953, pp. 74–76.

[58] ICAO Doc 7788, 49, 1956. ICAO Doc 2222, 14/5/56 and ICAO Doc 7739-C/894, pp. 18–19, 26–28.

[59] ICAO Council Working Paper/2661 at 5, 1958. Report of the Council to the Assembly; ICAO Doc 7960 A12-P/1, 1958, p. 60.

[60] ICAO Doc 8724 A16-P/3, August 1968; ICAO Doc 4582, 1/5/67, p. 1.

[61] Appeal relating to the Jurisdiction of the ICAO Council, Judgment, ICJ Reports 1972, pp. 46–179.

[62] Decision of the Council, C-DEC 154/16; C-WP 10864 (Restricted); C-DEC 147/9; C-DEC150/17; C-DEC 152/14; C-DEC 153/14.

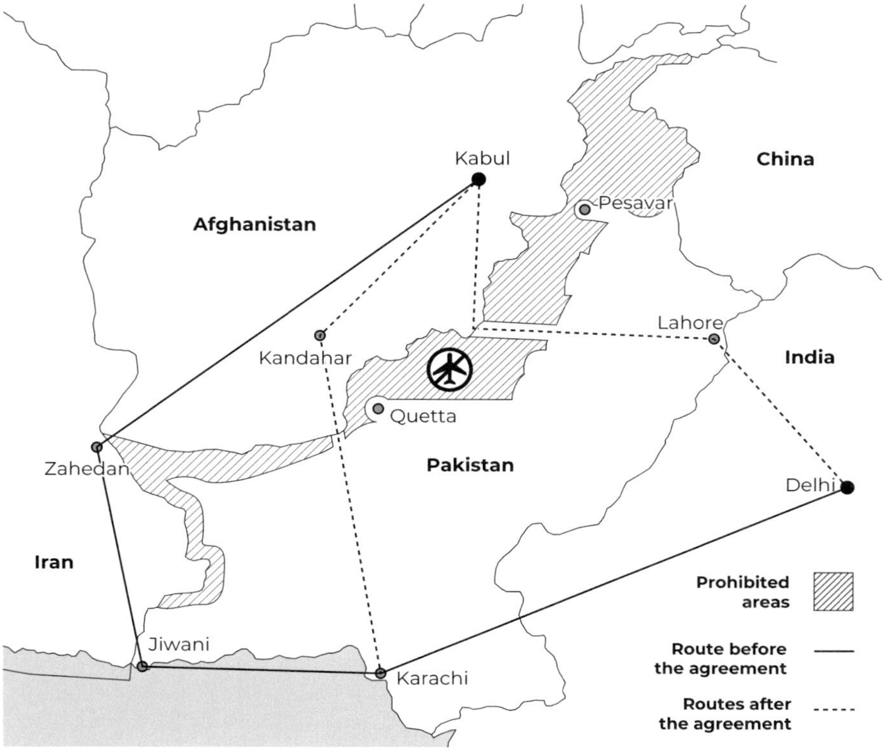

Fig. 3.5 Pakistan's transit dispute with India
Under the agreement Pakistan opened its prohibited airspace in two areas with a width of 12 miles, but this way it still did not secure the shortest direct route (through Peshawar the Delhi-Kabul or through Quetta the Delhi-Kandahar routes) for the designated Indian airline. Consequently, the Delhi-Kabul-Delhi flight travelling through Lahore had to cover a distance longer by 460 km (Cheng 1962, p. 102)

the United States v. the European Union (2000),[63] Brazil v. the United States (2016),[64] Qatar v. Bahrain, Egypt, the United Arab Emirates and Saudi Arabia (2017),[65] Australia and the Netherlands v. the Russian Federation (2023).[66] It is worth highlighting that a long-lasting opposition has evolved between India and Pakistan in the area of air transport as well (Fig. 3.5).

[63] C-DEC 170/16; C-WP/12075; C-DEC 152/14 and C-DEC 153/14.

[64] ICAO Annual Report 2019.

[65] Ivanov and Donakanian (2022), pp. 33–48.

[66] Australian Government: ICAO Council decision on jurisdiction in MH17 legal proceedings. 18 March 2023. (www.ministers.ag.gov.au/media-centre).

In the case *India versus Pakistan* (1952), the disputing parties first wished to dissolve their disagreement related to overflight within an informal scope. However, the parties could not agree, therefore, they requested the assistance of the ICAO Council officially. India made a grievance of not being able to use a large part of the airspace of the neighbouring country because Pakistan demarcated prohibited airspaces irrationally and unnecessarily. Whereas, in the airspaces closed before international air traffic, the scheduled flights of the Iranian airlines could demonstrably overfly and this discriminative conduct violated Articles 5, 6 and 9 of the Convention as well as the rules of the International Air Services Transit Agreement (IASTA). The ICAO Council settled the relations within a few months and in its decision it obligated the parties to secure unimpeded transit in their national airspaces for each other.

Any contracting State may appeal from the decision of the Council to an ad hoc arbitral tribunal[67] or to the Permanent Court of International Justice.[68] Any such appeal shall be notified to the Council within sixty days of receipt of notification of the decision of the Council (Article 84). The decisions of the Permanent Court of International Justice and of an arbitral tribunal shall be final and binding (Article 86).

[67] 'If any contracting State, party to a dispute in which the decision of the Council is under appeal, has not accepted the Statute of the Permanent Court of International Justice and the contracting States parties to the dispute cannot agree on the choice of the arbitral tribunal, each of the contracting States parties to the dispute shall name a single arbitrator who shall name an umpire. The arbitrators and the umpire shall then jointly constitute an arbitral tribunal. Any arbitral tribunal shall settle its own procedure and give its decisions by majority vote, provided that the Council may determine procedural questions in the event of any delay which in the opinion of the Council is excessive'. Article 85 of Chapter XVIII on Arbitration Procedure of the Chicago Convention.

[68] The International Court of Justice (ICJ) in The Hague is the Supreme Judicial Organ of the UN, the only permanent international judicial forum of universal character. The duty of the International Court of Justice is the adjudication of cases submitted thereto within the purview of international law. Article 92 of Chapter XIV on The International Court of Justice, Charter of the United Nations.

In the case *Pakistan versus India* (1971), a novel controversy emerged between the parties, therefore, they took recourse to the ICAO Council. In the background of the case, the war which had broken out in August 1965 between the parties caused anxiety, as a consequence of which India suspended the transit of the civil airplanes of Pakistan above Indian territories. The parties later agreed that transit flights (transit rights) may continue, however, the construction of this agreement differed.

Pakistan carried out transit flights in the specific region pursuant to (Article 5 of) the Chicago Convention and the rules of the IASTA Transit Agreement. Whereas, India permitted the Pakistani aircraft to fly into Indian airspace, within the special framework determined by itself, in possession of preliminary permissions. Notwithstanding, Pakistan insisted that its flights may transit over Indian territories in compliance with international rules, exercising Transit Rights 1 and 2 without preliminary permissions.

The dispute was exacerbated by the fact that two Kashmiri militiamen had hijacked the Fokker F-27 airplane of the Indian airline in India on 30 January 1971 and flew it to Pakistan. In response, India suspended all transit flights, therefore, Pakistan turned to the ICAO Council with a petition and a complaint with reference to Article 84 of the Convention and Paragraphs 1–2 of Article II of the IASTA Transit Agreement. As a result, India put forward preliminary reservations concerning the competence of the ICAO Council. The Council convened, and in its decision concerning its jurisdiction it established that it had the jurisdiction for the examination of the complaint. Against the decision of the Council establishing its own jurisdiction, the Indian Government already as a plaintiff appealed to the International Court of Justice. In the lawsuit *India versus Pakistan* (1971–1972),[69] the International Court of Justice in its decision rejected the petition of India and proclaimed the jurisdiction of the ICAO Council. Later the parties suspended the procedure before the Council and settled the dispute by themselves.

In its judgement, the International Court of Justice emphasised that the court always has to verify its jurisdiction and if necessary, it has to be examined *ex officio*. However, the preliminary decision concerning jurisdiction and the subsequent decision on the meritorious matters of the case may not be differentiated. Namely, the decision on jurisdiction, even if it does not determine the outcome of the case, may affect it on the merits (for example, the disavowal of the establishment of jurisdiction terminates the procedure). To the court which does not have jurisdiction, or the jurisdiction of which is ambiguous, neither party is obligated to give an explanation concerning the merits of the case. But in some cases, the issues of

[69] *India v. Pakistan* – ICJ Appeal Relating to the Jurisdiction of the ICAO Council, Judgement of 18 August 1972.

jurisdiction may affect meritorious matters and require the examination of specific meritorious parts.

The Convention authorises the Assembly and the Member States of ICAO to apply sanctions vis-à-vis a Member State and its airline, which does not adhere to the decision made in a controversial matter.

- In an intervention *vis-à-vis the Member State*, the Assembly may suspend the voting power in the Assembly and in the Council (provided that the contracting State is a Member of the Council) of any contracting State (Article 88).
- *Vis-à-vis the airline of the condemned Member State*, 'each contracting State shall undertake not to allow the operation of an airline of a contracting State through the airspace above its territory if the Council has decided that the airline concerned is not conforming' to the provisions of the Convention (Article 87).

While the application of the former rule has occurred several times, the application of the latter rule has not ensued, since it would probably have a great political resonance and it would divide the parties, therefore, the attached protected interest would be injured to a greater extent.

At the 15th Assembly of ICAO (1965), the Member States took a stand on the issues of racial discrimination and the apartheid vis-a-vis South Africa.[70] At the 16th Assembly of ICAO (1968), the Member States pronounced that the apartheid and other racial discrimination are the main sources of conflict among nations and peoples, furthermore, these political views and racial discrimination are contrary to the general principles formulated in the Preamble of the Chicago Convention.[71] At the 18th Assembly of ICAO held in Vienna (1971), the Member States confirmed the former decision and as a sanction they envisaged that South Africa will not receive invitation to ICAO Assemblies, in case it maintains its embraced politics condemned by the nations.

One of the most complex disputes growing ultimately acrimonious stemmed from the conflict of the States of the Arab region and generated grave economic, political, diplomatic and social tension in the region and all over the world. In 2017, the Qatar Government was accused of supporting terrorist groups and financing their activities by the leaders of Bahrein, Egypt, Saudi Arabia and the United Arab Emirates.[72] However, the Government of Qatar refuted the charges and failed to meet the demands itemised in 13 points by the countries to be fulfilled within ten days. In

[70] ICAO Assembly, A15-7 Resolution.

[71] Abeyratne (2019).

[72] Jamestown Foundation, Qatar's Role in the Libyan Conflict: Who's on the Lists of Terrorists and Why. 14 July 2017. (www.refworld.org/docid/596c92b64.html).

response, the countries participating in the dispute discontinued their relationship with Qatar on 5 June 2017.

The countries ordaining the blockade allowed 14 days for Qatari citizens living in their territories to leave,[73] furthermore, they cancelled all traffic (on water, land and in the air) with the renitent State. The closure of its airspace caused considerable damage to Qatar and led to the cancellation of numerous flights (Qatar lost more than 50 flights daily and its connection was terminated with 18 crucial destinations).[74] Because of the closure of the airspaces, the airplanes of Qatar could not use the airspaces of the neighbouring States, thus, they were obliged to fly towards Iran and Turkey, which occasioned the significant increase of flying time. (For instance, the one-hour-forty-minute flying time to Muscat, the capital of Oman increased by one hour due to using the Iranian airspace as a detour.) The growth of the duration of flights affected mainly the airplanes travelling to Africa and South America, in which more fuel needed to be filled, and in the case of multiple destinations, the narrow-body airplanes had to be replaced by wide-body ones since these are longer haul aircraft. Qatar instituted proceedings at the ICAO Council with reference to the Chicago Convention (Articles 1, 4, 57, 84) and to the IASTA Agreement (Paragraph 2 of Article II), while later in relation to the blockade, Qatar sued the United Arab Emirates before the International Court of Justice for the violation of human rights (mainly discrimination).[75] The four countries ordaining the blockade lodged a preliminary complaint vis-a-vis the proceedings to be conducted before the ICAO Council, which was dismissed by the overwhelming majority of the Council (23 affirmative votes, four votes against, six abstentions and the limitation of the right to vote of the concerned States). Against the decision of the Council, the boycotting countries took recourse to the International Court of Justice and pleaded for the establishment of the nullity of the decision. On 14 July 2020, the International Court of Justice dismissed the action of the plaintiffs unanimously and established that the final ruling can be brought by the ICAO Council as a body with jurisdiction.[76]

Let us evoke the lawsuit of *India versus Pakistan* with a feeling of *déjá vú* (1971–1972).[77] In that case the jurisdiction of the ICAO Council was established

---

[73] (www.bbc.com/news/world-middle-east-40173757).

[74] Mourad (2018).

[75] According to Qatar, these measures violate the prescriptions of the international agreement concerning racial discrimination, including the principle of the prohibition of discrimination on the basis of citizenship. Qatar sued solely the Emirates, since the United Arab Emirates and Qatar are parties to the Convention, whereas Saudi Arabia, Bahrein and Egypt are not. The State of Qatar institutes proceedings against the United Arab Emirates and requests the Court to indicate provisional measures. (Press Release, non-official). No. 2018/26, 11 June 2018. *International Convention on the Elimination of All Forms of Racial Discrimination* (ICERD). UN, New York, 21 December 1965.

[76] ICJ – Appeal Relating to the Jurisdiction of the ICAO Council under Article 84 of the Convention on International Civil Aviation (Bahrain, Egypt, Saudi Arabia and United Arab Emirates v. Qatar). The Hague, 14 July 2020. (www.icj-cij.org/en/case/173).; Sandeepa and Tushar (2022).

[77] *Gaver, Craig D.*: Déjà Vu All Over Again: ICJ Rules on the Jurisdiction of the ICAO Council in Relation to the Gulf Dispute. 29 July 2020. (www.opiniojuris.org).

as well, and the parties took pains to reach an agreement in both cases irrespective of the decision of the ICAO Council. In the more recent case, the mutual agreement titled 'Solidarity and Stability' was signed with Qatar in Al Ula, Saudi Arabia on 5 January 2021—during the Gulf Cooperation Council Summit.[78]

3.8.5 *Election of the Council*

The election of the currently 36 Members of the Council is always preceded by international diplomatic negotiations, an organised campaign. It is increasingly difficult to gain membership in the Council with respect to the fact that more and more countries wish to become Members of the Council with a limited membership. Upon the establishment of ICAO, 26 Member States could apply for 21 positions in the Council. The spectacular increase in the number of Member States and the reinforcement of the economic role of the air transport industry varying by regions resulted in the gradual growth of the number of Council Members.

The membership of the ICAO Council increased from 21 to 27 for the first time at the 13th Extraordinary Assembly of ICAO (1961), the reason for which was the massive accession of the countries liberated from colonial yoke to the UN and its agencies. At the 18th Assembly (1971), ICAO increased the number of Council Members from 27 to 30, since further Members including Hungary and the States of Central-Eastern Europe and the Soviet Union acceded to the organisation. With the accession of China, ICAO proposed the further increase of the number of Council Members at the 21st Assembly (1974), owing to which the membership increased to 33. Subsequently, the African, Arab and South-American countries urged for gaining membership, which they achieved and the 28th Extraordinary Assembly of ICAO (1990) raised the membership of the ICAO Council to 36.[79] Saudi Arabia proposed a further extension at the 37th Assembly of ICAO (2010). According to its reasoning, significant demand manifests itself on behalf of the countries of spectacularly developing regions in aviation (Arab, African and Asian) for the extension of the membership of the Council to 39.[80] The Assembly referred the Saudi Arabian

[78] Barakat, Sultan: Qatar-GCC Agreement: A victory for measured diplomacy. Qatar's reliance on international law and measured diplomacy paved the way for the amicable resolution of the Gulf crisis. Aljazeera, 8 January 2021. (www.aljazeera.com/opinions/2021/1/8/qatar-gcc-agreement-a-victory-for-measureddiplomacy).

[79] ICAO Doc 8970 Protocol Relating to an Amendment to the Convention on International Civil Aviation [Article 50 *a)*], New York, 12 March 1971; ICAO Doc 9123 Protocol Relating to an Amendment to the Convention on International Civil Aviation [Article 50 *a)*], Montreal, 16 October 1974.; ICAO Doc 9561 Protocol Relating to an Amendment to the Convention on International Civil Aviation [Article 50 *a)*], Montreal, 26 October 1990.

[80] ICAO Doc 9982 (A37-Min. P/6) Increasing the ICAO Council seats to 39, and Proposal to Amend Article 50 *a)* of the Convention on International Civil Aviation so as to increase the membership of the Council to 39 – ICAO Assembly 38th Session WP/17 EX/12, 2013.

proposal to the competence of the Council for further consideration, which did not support the adoption of the proposal. Eventually, after lengthy debates the Member States of ICAO at its 39th Assembly (2016) agreed to the increase of the membership of the Council to 40.[81] It may take a further decade for the new rule to take effect, since the ratification of a definite number of Member States, currently of 128 is necessary. This is a precarious and time-consuming process, since the number of places in the Council is the result of a political equilibrium, constant friction and diplomatic efforts.

The proposed amendments adopted at the Assembly by two-thirds majority of the contracting States are not enforced immediately. On the basis of the Convention the taking effect of amendments necessitates ratification by a definite number of States determined by the Assembly (Article 94). For example, at the Extraordinary ICAO Assembly on 26 October 1990, the Member States decided on the extension of the membership of the Council to 36 and this decision took effect in 12 years, on 28 November 2002 (then ratification by 108 Member States was necessary). In possession of this, the ICAO Council convened an Extraordinary ICAO Assembly (2003), at which the membership of the ICAO Council was extended by three new Members: in Group II South Africa and Singapore, while in Group III Chile acceded.[82] A legally interesting situation emerged when the countries not ratifying the amendment could also exercise their right to vote.

At the meetings of the Assembly, each contracting State is entitled to one vote [Article 48 *b)*]. The election is by secret ballot and has taken place with the use of an electronically closed system since 2010. The Assembly upon the election of the Members of the Council shall provide 'adequate representation to:

I. the States *of chief importance* in air transport;
II. the States not otherwise included, which *make the largest contribution to the development of facilities for international civil air navigation*;
III. the States not otherwise included, whose designation will insure that *all the major geographic areas of the world are represented on the Council*' [Article 50 *b)* 1–3].

The formation of the Groups is not carved in stone; its criteria were formulated in 1944. A lot of things have changed since then, but the essence has remained the same: becoming a member of the 'club', since via membership in the Council, the Member State may have a distinguished role in the formation of the future of air transport, while it may enforce its national interests related to air transport at the highest level. With a view to the most successful election result, the applicant States

[81] ICAO Assembly 39th Session Working Paper, A39-WP/18, EX/6, 31/05/2016; Resolutions adopted by the ICAO Assembly A39-4, October 2016, pp. 32–33.

[82] The 34th Extraordinary Assembly of ICAO – Election of three additional contracting States to be represented on the Council A34-WP/2 P/2, 24 January 2003 and Plenary meetings – Resolutions and Minutes A34, ICAO Doc 9820 Plenary Meetings – Resolutions and Minutes A34.

prepare for the election with nearly one year's diplomatic and professional campaign.

Group I

In the 'heavyweight' group with a leading role in air transport for the 11 positions determined by the Assembly essentially always the same countries apply, therefore, at first sight voting has no special stake. The odds are that 11 countries apply for 11 Members' positions. Nevertheless, all candidates go the extra mile to campaign and prepare for the elections, since the competition concerns the order in the list of 11 members. For them, the significance lies in the fact who are the first and the last ones. This order has a message, which of course we must not overrate.

The *standard* parties of Group I are as follows: Australia, Brazil, Canada, China, Germany, France, Japan, Italy, Russian Federation,[83] the United States and the United Kingdom.[84]

Obviously, the number of the States excelling in aviation cannot be reduced to a figure of tens, they amount to way above that number. Notwithstanding, there is no thronging in Group I, because the already established power relations are so significant that in the struggle for its reformation the new applicant may easily be overmatched. Consequently, the Member States are more ready to enter the competition in Group II, or even more in Group III, disregarding the Group criteria stipulated under the Convention.

Group II

In the Group contributing to the greatest extent to developments, the Member States can apply for 12 positions. Generally, for the 12 positions 12 Member States nominate themselves, despite that, the stake is by far larger, because a new contestant may appear at any time. In this Group, Member States unavoidable in their regions with stable positions feature, such as Argentina, Egypt, South Africa, India, Mexico, Nigeria, Spain, Saudi Arabia and Singapore.

For the purpose of persistence and the enhancement of chances, certain States have grouped in alliances and operate in a so-called rotational system. (In this order always the following State attends to the representation of the Members in the ICAO Council for three years.) We can mention the ABIS Group,[85] which congregates seven European countries, and the formation of NORDICAO,[86] which operates in the cooperation of also seven European countries. It is not difficult to see that the countries of the ABIS Group (Austria, Belgium, The Netherlands, Croatia, Ireland, Luxembourg, Portugal and Switzerland) could not stand successfully as a candidate

[83] At the 41st ICAO Assembly (2022) Russian Federation failed to win enough votes for re-election because political reasons, therefore, Russia lost its seat on the Council of ICAO for the period of 2022–2025. (www.simpleflying.com/russia-loses-icao-council-seat).

[84] Currently (2022–2025), there are ten States in Group I: Australia, Brazil, Canada, China, France, Germany, Italy, Japan, the United Kingdom and the United States.

[85] The ABIS Group. (www.abisgroup.org).

[86] NORD ICAO: Nordic and Baltic Cooperation on the ICAO. (www.nordicao.ca).

in the competition for membership separately, but as a unit they can, since they represent a significant territory, and they account for more than 5% of the ICAO budget. Consequently, they have seven votes and calculating with their capacity to enforce interests, this number is multiplied. NORDICAO consists of Denmark, Estonia, Finland, Iceland, Lithuania, Norway and Sweden. This Group is one of the most powerful ones as to its territory, since the largest island of the world also belongs here, i.e., Greenland under Danish suzerainty.

Venezuela and Columbia belong to Group II as well, which alternate each other in the Council on the basis of a cooperation agreement. Egypt, for example, weighs in the balance on its own. It can do so since numerous African countries and the increasingly influential Arabian countries line up with Egypt owing to its geographical position and its capacity to stabilise the region. For example, Nigeria as one of the most influential countries of the African community, establishing excellent diplomatic relations, has the power to enforce its interests.[87]

According to the rules, the Member State running in the elections in Group I or Group II, but not obtaining sufficient votes, may enter the competition in Group III. By reason of the high risk, the Member States usually do not avail themselves of this opportunity. Its reason is that if a newly nominated Member State underperforms in Group II, which is very likely in view of the prevalent stable power relations, in Group III it will finally fail with every likelihood. Namely, the participants in Group III have already agreed in advance on the conditions of supporting each other, therefore, the new entrant will not have enough time or opportunity to acquire sufficient support in the new Group. For the purpose of the avoidance of this, countries with important role in aviation, such as South Korea, Malaysia or the United Arab Emirates do not take the higher risk—they enter the election in Group III.

Group III

In the third Group the Member States can aspire to 13 seats.[88] Despite the usual formation of a competition, the chances here are the greatest, because the principle of the obtainment of representation by every significant geographical unit of the world facilitates the entry of all Member States in the elections. Furthermore, in this Group the votes scatter easily or agreements may be upset, in addition, the whole voting procedure is secret, which may cause further surprises. Despite this, the secret ballot provokes smiles among the representatives of countries well-versed in diplomacy, who can forecast the result. Namely, if the Member States adhere to the

[87] Currently (2022–2025), there are 12 States in Group II: Argentina, Austria, Egypt, Iceland, India, Mexico, Nigeria, Saudi Arabia, Singapore, South Africa, Spain and Venezuela.

[88] As Russia (in Group I) lost its seat on the Council of ICAO for the term 2022–2025, this extra seat was added to the seats of Group III, so one more State was elected as 14th for this three-year period. This country was the State of Qatar. The State of Qatar was elected first time in its history as permanent Member on the Council of ICAO between 2022–2025. Currently (2022–2025), there are 14 States in Group III: Bolivia, Chile, El Salvador, Equatorial Guinea, Ethiopia, Ghana, Jamaica, Malaysia, Mauritania, Qatar, the Republic of Korea, Romania, the United Arab Emirates and Zimbabwe.

diplomatically pre-arranged agreements, the final outcome of the election with every likelihood will coincide with the deals. However, this does not always happen.

Well-established power relations and protected interests underlie the positions in the Council, which can be changed only due to very tough work. A perfect example for this is Indonesia, which is one of the most rapidly developing countries, the fourth country with the highest population and one of the largest countries in the world (if we projected its territory onto Europe, it would range from London to the Ural Mountains). Since 1998 Indonesia has not been a Member of the ICAO Council. Despite entering the election on several occasions and diplomatic efforts, it has failed in Group III, although, if we consider merely the application criteria, Indonesia is one of the strongest candidates in this category. Nevertheless, the world has its unique logic. In 1998, Indonesia lost both its formerly stable position in the elections in the Council and simultaneously the possibility to regain it. The recovery of membership is often more difficult than entering as a new candidate. This has various reasons, mainly, that the Council Members during their three years' mandates form relationships, common stakes, occasionally friendships, owing to which the Members of the Council are interested in the maintenance of the *status quo*. It is not in vain that the saying goes: happy are the owners, the persons in possession *(beati possidentes)*.[89] The candidate can overcome this voluminous advantage only by way of a breakthrough strategy. On the other hand, the world is constantly changing, regions strengthen or weaken. When first in its history Malaysia with developed air transport ran for membership in the Council elections in 2007, it provided a regional alternative to Indonesia, while a part of the Indonesian airlines, among them the national airline, were blacklisted by the European Union. The outcome of the contest was not doubtable, Indonesia had only one chance, the conclusion of cooperation on a rotational basis with Malaysia (currently still an ICAO Council Member) for the joint representation of the region and for the common long-term retainment of the Council membership. Although, Indonesian civil aviation became much stronger and the Federal Aviation Administration (FAA) has upgraded Indonesia's status back to 'Level One' since August 2016, in spite of this fact Indonesia is still not a Member on the Council of ICAO.[90]

After elections, 'any vacancy on the ICAO Council shall be filled by the Assembly as soon as possible'. In such a case the Council convenes an Extraordinary Assembly pursuant to the rules of the Convention. 'Any contracting State so elected to the Council holds office for the unexpired portion of its predecessor's term of office' [Article 50 *b)*].

---

[89] Wrongly, this statement is attributed to Chancellor Otto von Bismarck (1815–1898). In fact, Ulpianus (170–223), the Roman jurisprudent noted it down as follows: *Possessores sunt potiores, licet nullum ius habeant,* Possessors are stronger irrespective of their legal title. Bánk: *3500 latin bölcsesség (3500 Latin Wisdoms).* Budapest, 1993, p. 38.

[90] Nugraha 2016.

3.8.6 The Composition of the Council

The composition of the Council is the result of an extremely balanced, broad consensus. In the Council the Member States strive to achieve their goals in a two-fold manner: solely or as a regional Member State congregated into unity. In the Council with 36 Members, eight European States are represented (all of them Members of the European Union), eight countries from the Latin-American region are represented, eight Members are the delegates of the African countries, the remnant positions are filled by Asian countries and the countries enforcing their interests independently, such as Australia, the United States, Russia, India, Japan, Canada and China.

The strength of the Member States congregated in unities is secured by regional alliance on an organisational level. These constitute the intergovernmental regional organisations of the ECAC, AFCAC, ACAC and LACAC. Asia does not expressly have such an organisation in aviation, here the dominance of the largest States and of Singapore prevails. (However, being clustered does not exclude that occasionally a Member State represents a diverging opinion and pronounces it at the session of the Council.)

The above entails that the future belongs to the regional enforcement of interests, that is, it is conceivable that one day the Council will not consist of Member States. Europe is an excellent example. The European countries often do not share the same standpoint, amidst the fierce debates they do not present a united front in specific matters, what is more, they are spectacularly discordant, which destabilises the advantageous position deriving from holding eight seats in the Council. In September 2005, the European Union opened a representative office in Montreal and examined the possibility of acquiring a powerful position, i.e., full membership in ICAO in a similar manner to the full membership of the European Community in the Food and Agricultural Organization of the UN (FAO). After prolonged debates and struggles, the EU received 'merely' an observer status, which guaranteed participation in open sessions, and exclusively on the basis of invitation, entitlement to contribution to matters directly concerning the EU. The Members of the Council understood that the *status quo* may be injured, if on behalf of a region an organisation superordinated on its Member States intervenes, therefore, they did their utmost to weaken the position of the EU.

The Convention formulates lucidly: only States may accede to the Chicago Convention (Article 92). Thus, the accession of the EU would be possible only via the amendment of the Convention, which would require the approval of two-thirds majority of all the contracting States [Article 94 *a)*]. This has realistically no chance. Simultaneously, the Convention grants opportunity, with a view to the formation of deeper cooperation, for the conclusion of agreements, the maintenance of common services and taking common measures concerning the Secretariat. The Council with the approval of the Assembly 'may enter into such other arrangements as may facilitate the work of the Organization' (Article 65). Within this framework, in September 2011, ICAO and the EU concluded a cooperation agreement with a view to the coordination of regulatory tasks during their work and to the establishment of closer work relations via the determination of common guidelines in the key areas of air transport.[91] The European Union, at the same time, has not abandoned its objective to represent the region with greater efficiency and broader authorisation by expanding its sphere for action. It is just a matter of time before another regional organisation raises a similar claim.

3.8.7 *President of the Council*

The ICAO Council elects its President for a term of three years. The President may be re-elected and is not entitled to the right to vote. The President is appointed by the contracting States. The President does not need to be selected from among the representatives of the Members of the Council, but, if a Council representative is elected, his seat is deemed vacant and it is filled by the State which he represented (Article 51). In 2006, the ICAO Council reformed the institutions of the election of the President and of selection.[92] While it avoided the amendment of the Convention, it incorporated the new rules in the Rules of Procedure for the Council.[93] The new procedure regulated the process of selection, introduced the institution of hearing[94] and limited the possibility of re-election only to one occasion. Thereby, it maximised the two terms of presidency in six years.[95] Pursuant to the Convention, the President could actually also be re-elected, but only on one occasion. The ICAO Council extended the institution of the limitation of re-election to one occasion to the office of the Secretary General as well, who at the same time fills the position of the Secretary of the Council.

The duties of the President include to 'convene meetings of the Council, the Air Transport Committee (ATC), and the Air Navigation Commission (ANC); serve as a representative of the Council; and carry out on behalf of the Council the functions which the Council assigns to him' (Article 51).

The office of the President of the Council is one of the most important positions. Another top leader of ICAO is the Secretary General directing the Secretariat. In an unusual way in UN organisations, the Convention assigns executive function to the President, because on behalf of the Council actually exercising power, the President

[91] European Council Decision of 31 March 2011 on the signing, on behalf of the Union, and provisional application of a Memorandum of Cooperation between the EU and ICAO providing a framework for enhanced cooperation. OJ L232 of 09/09/2011, p. 1.

[92] ICAO Assembly Resolution A36-28, Term limits for the Offices of the Secretary General and the President of the Council. September 2007. Election of the President of the Council. Presented by Austria and Hungary, C-WP/12494, 2005.

[93] ICAO Doc 7559 Rules of Procedure for the Council. 11th edn., 2022.

[94] Idem., Appendix A, Point 3.

[95] Resolution A36/28, Term limits for the Offices of Secretary General and the President of the Council. September 2007, Points 3 and 4.

shall be entitled to carry out the functions assigned to him by the Council [Article 51 *c)*]. Therefore, the President of the Council is manifested in a power position beside the Secretary General. This dual leadership is unusual and unique within the UN family, since the leadership of the UN and its specialised agencies is discharged either by the Secretary General (UN, IMO, WMO) or the Director General (IMF, ITU, WTO, WHO, WIPO, FAO, ILO, UNESCO, UNIDO).

The circumscription of the position of the President is superficial, since the Member States initially did not attribute major significance to the position. Essentially, the President represents the Members of the Council, in other words, the 'masters' of the President are the Members of the Council themselves. Nevertheless, in the history of ICAO it ensued that after filling the position of the Secretary General for six years, Assad Kotaite received the seat of the President in 1976. The new President informally exercised the Secretary General's powers further on and by relying on the Council and utilising the power and entitlements deriving from its adjudicating and dispute settlement functions, he acquired such central power which was unparalleled in the history of the UN. As a leader of the Council, Assad Kotaite (1924–2014)[96] attended to the office of the President for exactly 30 years, the longest term winning by unanimous vote in ten successive elections. Holding on to power democratically for such a long time required extraordinary skills and diplomatic talent.

The Council elects the President's deputy (deputies), the Vice-President(s) from among themselves. The term of the mandate is one year. The Vice-President is nominated by the Members of the Council. If the Council elects more than one Vice-Presidents, the first Vice-President will be the Member of the Council having worked for the longest time as a representative on the Council. While the President of the Council does not have the right to vote, the Vice-President always retains their right to vote and exercises it when attending to presidential duties. In practice, the Council elects three Vice-Presidents.[97]

The President of the Council may be removed from his office at any time due to the written motion made by one-third of the Members of the Council. The Council votes on the motion and its approval requires a majority decision adopted by the Members of the Council.[98]

---

[96] As an international lawyer representing Lebanon, Assad Kotaite gained a seat in the ICAO Council via election at the age of 33. Then did his unflagging and exceptional workmanship for 50 years commence in the service of international civil aviation. At the 38th Assembly of ICAO on 25 September 2013, he was awarded the highest-ranking Edward Warner Award in the air transport profession, which acknowledged his exceptional and outstanding achievement in international civil aviation. He became the President Emeritus of the ICAO Council and one of the most important and influential personalities of international civil aviation. MacKenzie (2010), p. 288.; Kotaite (2013), pp. 58–59.

[97] ICAO Doc 7559 Rules of Procedure for the Council. 11th edn., 2022. Articles 3, 6, 8–11, 19 *b)*, 60, Appendix B.

[98] Idem., Section II, Rule 6.

3.8.8 Voting by the Council

The Council may delegate authority on any particular matter to a committee of its Members. The decisions of any committee of the Council may be appealed to the Council by any interested contracting State.

As a main rule, the Council shall make its decisions by a majority of the votes of its Members (Article 52); that is, the decisions of the Council require the votes of 19 Members of the Council with 36 Members. An exception is the adoption of the Standards and Recommended Practices (SARPs) in the Annexes to the Convention by the Council, which shall require the vote of two-thirds, that is, of 24 Member States of the Council (Article 90).

The Council performs the joint representation of the 193 Member States for three years. At the same time, the Member States with no representation in the Council may take part in the work intensively. They may refer their opinions to ICAO via so-called State Letters, they may make presentations at ICAO events, in addition, they may be present at the sessions of the Council as observers, but they may not cast votes. It is a peculiarity that the 36 Member States essentially account for merely 18.65% of the 193 Member States. Upon a two-thirds majority decision, this proportion of 24 votes accounts for only a ratio of 12.43%. It is thought-provoking that such a creme de la crème representing such a low proportion of ICAO Member States frames the rules to be followed by all Member States. Upon the adoption or amendment of the SARPs rules, the Air Navigation Commission (ANC) carries out the work of professional preparation. Before passing a decision, the Air Navigation Commission (ANC) guarantees preliminary consultation with all the Member States, hearing the opinion of and integrating the professional recommendations of all parties concerned.

'Any contracting State may participate, without a vote, in the consideration by the Council and by its committees and commissions of any question which especially affects its interests. No member of the Council shall vote in the consideration by the Council of a dispute to which it is a party' (Article 53). 'No representative of a contracting State on the Council shall be actively associated with the operation of an international air service or financially interested in such a service' [Article 50 *c)*]. At the same time, the incompatibility rule does not prohibit that representatives receive passenger cards granting allowances within an official agreement from airlines registered in their home country, which entitle them to flights at reduced prices upon purchasing tickets.

3.8.9 Official Presents to ICAO

In diplomacy it is customary for Member States to bestow presents to international organisations with all due solemnity. Following the wide-ranging custom within the UN family, Hungary donated a statue to ICAO in 2006. The present of Hungary can

Fig. 3.6 The statue titled Generations
The statue raises a monument to 'the youngest generation of human transportation and delivers the message that aviation is impossible without assistance from the Earth'

be found directly beside the entrance of the conference room of the ICAO Council, which is a bronze statue titled *Generations*, a masterpiece of an Artist named Róbert Csíkszentmihályi (1940–2021), who lived in Szentendre (Fig. 3.6).

The Secretariat of ICAO publishes the collection of objects bequeathed to ICAO by the Member States catalogued in a special publication.[99]

[99] Available at ICAO Shop. Headquarters, Canada, Montreal.

3.9 The Air Navigation Commission

The Air Navigation Commission (ANC) is a matchless main body of ICAO, which is constantly in session and carries out professional work. It is composed of 19 members appointed by the Council from the candidates nominated by the contracting States. At the 39th Assembly of ICAO (2016), the Member States raised the number of the members to 21, which will take effect following ratification by 128 Member States.[100] The members of the Commission need to have 'suitable qualifications and experience in the science and practice of aeronautics. The Council requests all contracting States timely to submit nominations' (Article 56). As one of the basic requirements in the UN, upon nomination it is an emphatic element besides expertise that *the principle of equal geographical representation* is safeguarded. This means that in vain is one of the most outstanding experts nominated, he will not be appointed in case the region of the nominating State is overrepresented in the Commission. It is characteristic of the competition that at the elections the members of the Commission are elected in several rounds. The members of the Commission are elected by the Council and its President is appointed by the Council as well. The mandate of the Commission is two years.

During the implementation of its tasks 'the Air Navigation Commission shall

a) *consider*, and *recommend* to the Council *for adoption* modifications of the Annexes to the Convention;
b) establish technical sub-commissions on which any contracting State may be represented, if it so desires;
c) advise the Council concerning the collection and communication to the contracting States of all information which it considers necessary and useful for the advancement of air navigation' (Article 57).

For the accomplishment of its tasks, the Commission receives constant support from the Air Navigation Bureau of ICAO (ANB). The principal task of the Commission is the elaboration of Standard and Recommended Practices (SARPs) and of Procedures for Air Navigation Services (PANS), furthermore, the modification of further procedures and the elaboration of recommendations for the Council. While the Members of the Council hold the title of *permanent representative*, the members of the Commission are designated as *commissioners*. Besides the commissioners, the experts of international aviation organisations (IATA, ACI, CANSO, FAI, IAOPA, IBAC, ICCAIA, IFATCA, IFALPA) holding permanent observer status may

[100] At the outset, the Air Navigation Commission was composed of 12 members. During the history of ICAO, the contracting States raised the number of the members of the Commission three times: for the first time at the 18th Assembly in Vienna (1971) to 15 members, for the second time at the 27th Assembly in Montreal (A27-2, 1989) to 19 members and for the third time at the 39th Assembly in Montreal to 21 members. The change in the number of members entailed the amendment of Article 56 of the Convention. Resolution adopted by the ICAO Assembly A39-6, October 2016, p. 34.

participate in the sessions, and the representatives of the Member States and other international organisations may also be present as observers.

3.10 Committees

The Legal Committee (LC), the Climate and Environment Committee (CEC) and the Council Committees have evolved to become professional workshops through many decades with central roles of discharging special tasks under the direction of the Council.

3.10.1 The Legal Committee

ICAO is one of the greatest treaty-makers both in public and private law (conventions, protocols, agreements) within international aviation law, the motor of unification and as such it deserves imperishable credit for its regulatory activity. The Convention does not provide for legal tasks, either for aviation security, or for environmental protection, or for comprehensive audits. This can be traced back to historical reasons since these tasks were introduced into the task list of civil aviation posteriorly. However, legal work has always been prevalent and has permeated the everyday life of ICAO from the outset. Why does the Convention not mention legal work either among the tasks of the Assembly or of the Council, why is it not a highlighted strategic objective like other tasks?

The reason for this is simply the fact that work in aviation law had always been discharged formerly by an autonomous organisation, therefore, it was not necessary to provide for it separately. In the beginning, this task had been comprehensively discharged by the Comité International Technique d'Experts Juridiques Aériens (CITEJA) established in 1926, which had worked on the uniform international regulation of private aviation law and had made efforts to compile an aviation law code with general effect. The expert members of CITEJA had been delegated by the States and the committee had attended to the tasks of the development and regulation of private international aviation law for nearly two decades. Upon the formation of ICAO, it became unambiguous that CITEJA would dissolve and continue its work as a permanent body within the organisation of ICAO, that is, as the Legal Committee (LC) under the direction of the Council.[101]

The Legal Committee is permanently in session and its procedure prescribes the convocation of one session annually. In reality, the convocation of the Committee ensues more scarcely. In the beginning, the Committee was subordinated to the Assembly, then gradually the Council took over its direction. The Committee is

[101] ICAO Doc 4411 ICAO Assembly Resolution A1-46, Appendix A, 6–27 May 1947.

accountable both to the Assembly and the Council. Any Member State may delegate legal experts or representatives to the Committee. However, an expert working at the Secretariat of ICAO may not be a member of the Committee. At the request of the Council, the Legal Committee makes a statement concerning the amendment or the construction of the Convention and prepares studies and recommendations for the Assembly or the Council. During its work, the Committee studies private legal issues affecting international aviation law and international civil aviation for the purpose of the elaboration of the drafts of international aviation law treaties and of the preparation of related reports and recommendations.[102]

During the drafting of treaties (e.g., conventions), the Legal Committee

- in its own competence unifies the materials elaborated by legal experts and incorporates them in the draft of new treaties and refers it to the Council;
- for the purpose of reporting on the draft, the Council refers it to the Member States, then on the basis of the collected recommendations, the Legal Committee prepares the final draft;
- besides referring the final draft, the ICAO Council convokes an international aviation law or diplomatic conference, at which the representatives of the Member States discuss the draft of the treaty;
- at the end of the conference, the parties adopt the convention in its final form, which is opened for ratification by the acceding States.

The Legal Committee in close cooperation with the ICAO Council participates actively in framing the most important international aviation law treaties regulating international civil aviation.

3.10.2 The Climate and Environment Committee

The Climate and Environment Committee (CEC) was established in 1983 by the ICAO Council.[103] This specialised committee operates under the supervision of the ICAO Council with the involvement of nearly 450 experts of more than 23 Member States. The main functions of the CEC are formulating new policies and adopting new SARPs, making recommendations and reports mostly concerning noise pollution and pollutant emission by aircraft as well as preparing drafts for the amendment of SARPs rules for the ICAO Council.

The CEC and ICAO itself work with increasingly greater intensity to produce outstanding results in forcing back environmental pollution by the air transport

[102] ICAO Doc 7669 Legal Committee (LC/139/5). Edn. 6. Constitution, Procedure for Approval of Draft Conventions, Rules of Procedure. 2018.

[103] At that time its name was Committee on Aviation Environmental Protection (CAEP).

industry. Consequently, at the 37th Assembly of ICAO (2010)[104] the Member States adopted an international intergovernmental agreement concerning the reduction of pollutant emission in the sector. Hence, air transport became the first industry in the world to enter into such global obligation.

Pursuant to the Resolution, the Member States undertook to increase the efficiency of used fuels by 2% before 2020, while since 2020 they have endeavoured to achieve a 2% annual increase in efficiency by 2050 as well as not to raise the level of emissions deriving from air transport after 2020 (so-called carbon-neutral expansion). The Member States are authorised to institute more ambitious measures. According to the Resolution, the obligations of certain countries related to the limitation or reduction of emissions need to be determined in consideration of the extent of their contribution to environmental pollution and of their financial and technical capacity to reduce harmful effects. This facilitates the lower contribution of developing countries and the higher contribution of developed countries to the attainment of the objectives under the Resolution. The countries the air transport activity of which is insignificant (does not reach 1% of global air transport) are not obligated to frame provisions designed to reduce emissions and their airlines are exempt from the scope of the Market-Based Measures (MBMs). In the future, the Member States are going to introduce and apply the Market-Based Measures according to the guidelines under the resolution. In the interest of the efficient fulfilment of the requirements, ICAO is going to elaborate the conditions of the technical and financial support of less developed countries.

The protection of the environment is an extremely sensitive area. Although all the performers of the industry support and deal with the issue of the protection of the environment at a level proper for its significance, the standpoints differ basically concerning the method of implementation. The principal reason for this is that the prescriptions of the European Union are the most rigorous ones in the world and the system of requirements of the EU foregrounds the Market-Based Measures and their application. However, the majority of the Member States of ICAO regard this solution for the emerging problems as an example initially to be followed voluntarily, not to be extended mandatorily to countries with more basic infrastructure.

3.10.3 The Council Committees

'The Council may delegate authority with respect to any particular matter to a committee of its members' (Article 52). The following are permanent working

[104]ICAO Assembly Resolution A37-19, *Consolidated statement of continuing ICAO policies and practices related to environmental protection – Climate change.* October 2010. ICAO Assembly Resolutions A38-18, A39-2, A40-18, A41-21.

committees (and Task Force) set up by and subordinated to the Council, which consist of the representatives of the countries with membership in the Council:

- Air Transport Committee (ATC)
- Aviation Security Committee (ASC)
- Finance Committee (FIC)
- Human Resources Committee (HRC)
- Joint Support Committee (JSC)[105]
- Technical Co-operation and Implementation Support Committee (TCC)
- Committee on Governance (COG)
- Committee on Relations with the Host Country (RHCC)
- Edward Warner Award Committee (EWAC)
- Ad Hoc Cybersecurity Coordination Committee (AHCCC)

Merely the Members of the ICAO Council are accommodated by the committees. The countries represented in the Council nominate the members of the committees and the Council elects them with a mandate for one year. While the representatives at the sessions of the Council may address the meeting on behalf of their countries (the President of the Council accords them the right to speak by the designation of their countries), at the sessions of the committees they do not state their views on behalf of their countries, but in their own name. The Member States delegate the Council representatives to the different committees on the basis of political interests and professionalism. The membership of the committees is limited; therefore, serious diplomatic conciliations precede the election of the committee members, then, of their chairmen and deputies. At the sessions, the representatives do not participate primarily as diplomats, but they address the specific issues on the basis of their professional experience. The composition of the Members of the ICAO Council and of the members of committees is extraordinarily varied. Generally, career diplomats are nominated,[106] whereas the larger countries appoint ambassadors,[107] but mostly specialised diplomats, pilots, economists and lawyers with a background in aviation become representatives.

So that the Council and its committees can perform their duties at a high standard, they need to have at their disposal appropriate data and up-to-date information about

[105] The Joint Support Committee (JSC) was first established in 1947, the main objective of which was the provision of technical, administrative and financial support to ensure the availability of technical equipment, facilities and services required for the safe implementation of flights in the problematically accessible regions of the Earth, oceanic regions, which the major international air routes pass through (mainly in the region of the Atlantic Ocean in air traffic between America and Europe). The Member States have concluded multilateral agreements to achieve their objectives and the Council supervises the accomplishment of these via the JSC. Such agreements have been reached for the joint financing of stations set up in the northern region of the Atlantic Ocean and of the meteorological, tele-communicational, radio-navigational and search-rescue services in Greenland (Denmark), Iceland and the Faroe Islands. ICAO's North Atlantic Joint Financing Agreements. pp. 1–8. (www.icao.int/sustainability/Documents/jf_accord_en.pdf).

[106] South Korea and Italy usually nominate the head of their consulate in Montreal.

[107] For example, France, the United States and Germany.

the situation of air traffic in the Member States. With a view to that 'each contracting State undertakes that its international airlines, in accordance with requirements laid down by the Council, shall file with the Council traffic reports, cost statistics and financial statements showing among other things all receipts and the sources thereof' (Article 67). 'Decisions of any committee of the Council may be appealed to the Council by any interested contracting State' (Article 52).

3.11 The Secretariat

The Convention does not provide for the Secretariat itself. The Secretariat with more than 900 staff members, representing 108 nations[108] is the principal administrative organ of ICAO headed by the Secretary General as a Chief Executive Officer. The Secretariat is an international administrative body consisting of the Secretary General and the staff of officials. The officials are selected based on the aspects of performance, expertise and moral integrity pursuant to the requirement of the UN that selection should be made from the most extensive possible geographic territory.[109]

Adherence to the basic principle of geographic proportionality strictly required by the UN is an important aspect of selection, which means that it is an advantage if the expert is from a geographically non-represented or underrepresented Member State. Each year ICAO makes a statement: the citizens of which Member States work at the Secretariat and ideally how many people could be employed from the Member States with respect to proportionality. If the citizens of a specific Member State are overrepresented at the Secretariat (for example, Canada, Russia), consequently, the chance of their new candidate to join the Secretariat of ICAO will be next to nothing. The basic principle of geographic proportionality prevails upon the election of the President, the Secretary General of ICAO and upon the selection of the Directors of the Secretariat. If, for example, the mandate of the Director from the continent of Asia expires, the fundamental aspect of the selection of the new Director will be geographical: which region will delegate the successor. It is obvious if the forthcoming region is Europe, the new Director will be selected from here, irrespective of the fact that candidates from other continents may be professionally more prepared.

In the organisations of the UN family another highlighted aspect during the selection process is the support of female candidates. It is an objective prescribed by the UN that the proportion of male and female employees should be balanced at 50%. ICAO has fulfilled that requirement.[110] In the interest of the achievement of

[108] Annual Report of the Council, Human Resources Management and Gender Equity. 31 December 2021.

[109] Charter of the United Nations (1945), Chapter XV, Article 3. Secretariat, 101.

[110] Female employees held 32.28% of posts in the Professional and higher categories and the percentage of female employees in the General Service category was 75% at the end of December

this objective, initially, of the candidates with almost the same preparedness always the female candidate needs to be chosen. At the same time, in the work of the organisation men and women always work under the same conditions. On their participation in work, neither the UN nor ICAO sets a limitation.

Several other aspects are considered during the selection process, but this much is certain: anyone who can join the organisation of ICAO is really fortunate, because may the candidates be professionally well-prepared, their selection is not merely professionally based. In fact, several further conditions and individual aspects are considered during recruitment, which derive from the operational specificities of the UN and its agencies.

The scope of activity of the Secretariat encompasses the discharge of administrative and organisational tasks necessary for the work of the Assembly and the Council, such as the collection and collation of aviation data provided by the contracting States, establishing and keeping contact with intergovernmental and other international organisations, the issuance and distribution of ICAO publications and documents, administrative work and the settlement of the current affairs of the organisation. The accession to (or the ratification of) an international aviation law treaty by the Member States is registered by the Secretariat, specifically, by the Legal Affairs and External Relations Bureau (LEB). Every year the Secretariat of ICAO publicises the list of the Member States having acceded to international treaties (conventions, protocols, agreements) in a so-called State Letter in tabled form (with the official reservations of the Member States). The document containing the fact of accession is generally presented to the Secretary General of ICAO by the ambassador of the referring country accredited to Canada, whose residence is usually in the capital of Canada, in Ottawa. An official photograph is taken of the presentation of the document, which is published in the monthly of ICAO (ICAO Journal) by the Secretariat. If the President of the ICAO Council or the Secretary General pays an official visit to a Member State, the list containing the accessions to international treaties (if not acceded, why not) is generally put on the agenda of negotiations and it is an object of inspection upon the audit of the Member State carried out by ICAO (if the Member State has acceded, does it comply with the requirements?).

The Secretariat consists of five large organisational units:

- Air Navigation Bureau (ANB);
- Air Transport Bureau (ATB);
- Technical Cooperation Bureau (TCB);
- Legal Affairs and External Relations Bureau (LEB);
- Bureau of Administration and Services (ADB).

2021. Review of Management and Administration in the International Civil Aviation Organization (ICAO), JIU/ REP/2019/1, (www.unjiu.org/news/jiurep20191-review-management-and-administration-international-civil-aviation-organization).

The offices are headed by the Directors, who are simultaneously the Deputies of the Secretary General, and their selection ensues with the complete enforcement of the principle of geographical proportionality.

3.11.1 The Secretary General

The Secretary General is completely accountable to the ICAO Council. The Secretary General as the Chief Executive Officer of the organisation of ICAO is directly accountable for the work of the Secretariat and for its management as well as for the direction of the seven regional offices. Simultaneously, the Secretary General attends to the secretarial tasks of the ICAO Council. For the person of the Secretary General, the Member States make recommendations, and the ICAO Council elects the Secretary General from among the candidates and appoints him for a definite term of three to four years (generally for three years since a four-year term would only apply in exceptional cases).[111] The Secretary General can be re-elected once in his office. ['A Secretary General who has served for two terms shall not be appointed for a third term' (Rule 12)].[112] The Council in its Rules of Procedure determines the conditions of nomination, the method of the election and the term of the appointment of the Secretary General. The provisions of the Convention authorise the Council to determine the training, the salaries, allowances and the conditions of service of the Secretary General (Article 58). Owing to the written motion of one-third of the members of the Council, the Secretary General can be removed from his office any time. The Council casts votes on the motion and its approval requires a majority decision by the Members of the Council.

As a sole organisation in the UN family, ICAO is subject to dual leadership. The division of work between the President of the ICAO Council and the Secretary General of the Organisation of ICAO is not properly regulated. The Convention does not provide for the position of the Secretary General under a separate article; however, it makes mention of the appointment of the Secretary General among the mandatory functions of the Council [Article 54 *h)*] and of the conditions of the appointment and of the termination of appointment under the Chapter pertaining to the Personnel (Chapter XI, Article 58).

[111] Resolution A36/28, Term limits for the Offices of Secretary General and the President of the Council. September 2007. Point 1.

[112] ICAO Doc 7559 Rules of Procedure for the Council. Section II., Rules 12–15, App. C, 11th edn., 2022.

3.11.2 Professional Staff

The Council stipulates the method of the appointment and the termination of appointment, the payment and allowances, the qualification and the conditions of service of the Secretary General and the professional staff. The Council may employ or make use of the services of the nationals of any contracting State (Article 58). The remuneration of the personnel accounts for 80% of the budget of ICAO. The number of the positions to be filled is limited and depends on the budget, while the Technical Cooperation Bureau (TCB) of ICAO employs several hundreds of experts for special tasks under contracts of agency. It is also possible for ICAO to employ the external expert full-time, while the expert receives his salary and remuneration from the referring Member State.

'The President of the Council, the Secretary General, and other personnel shall not seek or receive instructions in regard to the discharge of their responsibilities from any authority external to the Organization. Each contracting State shall undertake fully to respect the international character of the responsibilities of the personnel and not to seek to influence any of its nationals in the discharge of their responsibilities' (Article 59). In the interest of safeguarding the equal geographical representation, the nationality of the candidate is an important and considered element upon selection, however, during employment only the manifested expertise and attitude to work matter.

'Each contracting State shall undertake, so far as possible under its constitutional procedure, to accord to the President of the Council, the Secretary General, and the other personnel of the Organization, the immunities and privileges which are accorded to corresponding personnel of other public international organizations' (Article 60). For the purpose of the protection of the personnel, the UN provides the leaders and outstanding members of ICAO with diplomatic passports issued by the UN. All UN Member States grant diplomatic immunity and privileges to the holders of such documents.[113] The immunities and privileges are due to the representatives in the interest of guaranteeing the independent discharge of their functions related to the Organisation.

3.11.3 Regional Offices

The Convention does not mention regional cooperation, although this is one of the clues to the successful operation of ICAO. Regional offices being familiar with local circumstances have the capacity to solve current tasks, they provide assistance to the implementation of SARPs rules and maintain intensive relationship with the experts of governmental and administrative aeronautical organs of regional Member States. The regional offices distant from the centre carry out expressly professional work

[113] Charter of the United Nations (1945), Articles 104–105.

and provide assistance exclusively in matters related to aviation. The experts of regional offices discharge their functions in a somewhat isolated manner taking advantage of having to focus exclusively on their profession.

Seven regional offices work under the direction of the Secretary General. Geographically, the metropolises accommodating the offices are located on the main continents: Bangkok, Dakar, Nairobi, Cairo, Lima, Mexico City and Paris. With respect to the spectacular development of civil aviation in the Asian region, the Secretary General of ICAO with the consent of the Council decided on 5 November 2012, for the first time in the history of ICAO, to open a regional branch office in Beijing under the supervision of the regional office in Bangkok.

The regional offices have a crucial role in regional integration. Their common objective is unification in the region, the accomplishment of which is the predominant task of the offices. This entails a lot of work even in the developed European region, which may seem to be unified, but under the surface vast differences can be discerned among the supervisory capacity and the preparedness of the authorities of the different States in Europe. Yet, the future of civil aviation considerably depends on the capacity to integrate the underperforming regions falling behind into the network of the global industry of air transport. The African region indicates the engagement of ICAO perfectly: in the past the developed countries used to deal with Africa only to the extent their interests required. If their business interest required operation in Africa, they examined whether the conditions of the safe implementation of flights were available in the national airspace and at the international airports of the recipient country. The prevalent situation in the airspaces of the African countries has caused a lot of trouble for ICAO, since it is characterised by neglected airports (with the occurrence of mammals and birds on the runways and taxiways), unreliable air navigation control service (the control towers do not transfer flights to each other), the high rate of fatal accidents and the frequent disregard of operational specifications. For the settlement of the African situation, ICAO has provided assistance and launched a separate comprehensive settlement programme (AFI Plan),[114] for the implementation of which the African regional offices are responsible. The African continent accounting for merely a fraction of global air transport awaits immense development. Due to international civil aviation, the economies and air navigation of this region may commence to develop rapidly, for which the support of ICAO is indispensable.

[114]ICAO Assembly Resolution A36-1, *The comprehensive regional implementation plan for aviation safety in Africa.* September 2007.

References

Abeyratne R (2012) Aeronomics and Law. Fixing Anomalies. Springer, Berlin-Heidelberg, p 173

Abeyratne R (2014) Convention on International Civil Aviation: a Commentary. Springer, pp 663–668

Abeyratne R (2019) The Legal Status of ICAO. In: Legal priorities in air transport. Springer, pp 13-26

Anderson DF, Eberhardt S (2010) Understanding Flight, 2nd edn., McGraw Hill, p 20

Cheng B (1962) The Law of International Air Transport. London, p 102

Dempsey PS (2013) Why it's important to keep ICAO here. McGill, The Montreal Gazette, 14 May 2013. www.mcgill.ca/law/channels/news/paul-dempsey-keep-icao-in-montreal-226780

Dempsey PS (2017) Public International Air Law. 2nd edn., William S. Hein & Company, Incorporated for the Centre for Research of Air and Space Law, McGill University, pp 851–870

Glaser BS (2013) Taiwan's quest for greater participation in the international community. A Report of the CSIS Freeman Chair in China Studies. Lanham-Boulder-New York-Toronto-Plymouth, U.K.

Ivanov DV, Donakanian VG (2022) The ICAO Council as a Dispute Settlement Body: Theoretical and Practical Issues. Moscow J Int Law 3, pp 33–48

Kotaite A (2013) My memoirs: 50 years of International Diplomacy and Conciliation in Aviation. Montreal, pp 58–59

MacKenzie D (2010) ICAO: a History of the International Civil Aviation Organization. Toronto, p 288

Milde M (1994) The Chicago Convention – are major amendments necessary or desirable 50 years later? Annals of Air and Space Law, XIX, pp. 401–452

Mourad D (2018) To analyse the feasibility of business diversification as a mitigation strategy to compensate impact of GCC crisis within the aviation industry: a case study on Qatar Airways. Metropolitan University, Cardiff

Nugraha RA (2016) Improving Aviation Safety in Indonesia: How Many More Accidents? Halrev 2(3):328

Ndikum PF, Ndikum S-D (2014) Encyclopaedia of International Aviation Law. Vol 2. Trafford, p 654

Sandeepa BB, Tushar K (2022) Jurisdiction under Article 84 of the Chicago Convention 1944 in the Context of Middle East Conflict. Centre for Aviation and Space Laws, Vol 2, 30 January 2022

Sipos A (2022) Modernization of the Chicago Convention: Challenge of 'Sicurity'! Proceedings of 4th International Aviation Management Conference (IAMC-2022), Emirates Aviation University, Dubai, November 2022, pp 203–211

Sipos A (Rev.) (2023) Milde's International Air Law and ICAO. 7.4 Does the Chicago Convention require modernization? 4th edn., Eleven International Publishing, The Hague, pp 210–222

Sochor E (1991) The Politics of International Aviation. MacMillan Press, pp 112–113

Chapter 4
ICAO Standards and Recommended Practices (SARPs)

Diverse national rules and procedures increase the aviation safety risk of air transport considerably. Already in the beginning, the international community was aware of the fact that international civil aviation can operate safely and efficiently only if the States frame uniform rules and procedures to be followed by all performers. It is obvious that if a flight of an airline takes off at any point in the world, every concerned entity (not only the pilot-in-command) needs to be assured that during the overflight of national borders the aircraft and its flight crew will encounter adherence to uniform international rules (standards), order of traffic and procedures. This is the basic and paramount foundation of the operation of international civil aviation. The international regulatory framework is guaranteed by ICAO—in which the Council on the ICAO adopts the rules—generally known as the Standards and Recommended Practices. SARPs is a complex regulatory mechanism, which ensures uniform rules and provisions for the civil aviation industry worldwide.

4.1 The Evolution of the System of Rules

The first milestone of *unification* consisted in the Paris Convention Relating to the Regulation of Aerial Navigation (1919) as the first international aviation law treaty.[1] Although the Paris Convention was designed to frame uniform public aviation law valid for the whole world, uniform standardisation as the main objective 'missed the mark' immediately. That is, the majority of its chapters promoted chiefly the safeguard of the supremacy of the victorious States and were practically targeted

[1] Convention Relating to the Regulation of Aerial Navigation. Signed at Paris, 13 October 1919 (Paris Convention). Journal of Air Law and Commerce 94 (1930). (https://scholar.smu.edu/jalc/vol1/iss1/6.)

A. Sipos, *International Aviation Law*, https://doi.org/10.1007/978-3-031-39066-1_4

against the defeated States, which is comprehensible in view of the historical situation.[2]

Apart from the historical situation, the Paris Convention divided the nations from a legal point of view as well. The main reason was that under the convention the contracting States adopted a new regulatory method, according to which the Paris Convention and its Annexes[3] had the same binding force. While the 8 Annexes could be amended by the International Commission for Air Navigation permanently sitting in Paris in its own competence within an expeditious and flexible procedure, the amendment of the Paris Convention itself required a decision by the Member States, which lengthened and complicated the procedure. Since both had the same binding force, the contracting States could react to industrial challenges and changes in the regulatory environment simply by prompt amendments under the Annexes.[4]

A part of the States criticised this legal solution since during the amendment by the Commission of the technical rules specified under the Annexes and during the drafting of new Annexes the party States were not involved, therefore, their participation was reduced to their signature. Regarding this the Commission for Air Navigation held regulatory function. Consequently, the United States did not ratify the Paris Convention, in addition Spain did not accede to the convention either, because it did not receive the same right to vote. As a diplomatic measure to hold its ground in view of this shortfall of prestige, Spain in a leading role established the Madrid Convention on Aerial Navigation on 1 November 1926, which finally did not take effect.[5]

The Paris (1919), Madrid (1926) and Habana (1928)[6] Conventions were not recognised internationally, since allowing for mainly political objectives, they

---

[2]Fortunately, the development of air navigation and its intellectual achievements cannot be restricted so that they should not be accessible for the community of nations in the hour of need. As early as after World War I, a process commenced, which matured by our days, due to which the aviation industry has become the safeguard of the power of the modern State, a firm pillar of the national economy, while it has also met indispensable cultural needs and demands of traffic. Szentnémedy (1933), last page (mek.oszk.hu).

[3]The Convention Relating to the Regulation of Aerial Navigation signed at Paris on 13 October 1919 had eight Annexes elaborated by the Technical Sub-Committee: Annex (A): The Marking of Aircraft; Annex (B): Certificates of Airworthiness; Annex (C): Log Books; Annex (D): Rules as to Lights and Signals. Rules of the Air; Annex (E): Minimum Qualifications Necessary for Obtaining Certificates as Pilots and Navigators; Annex (F): International Aeronautical Maps and Ground Markings; Annex (G): Collection and Dissemination of Meteorological Information; Annex (H): Customs Regulations.

[4]MacKenzie (2010), p. 11.

[5]The Madrid Convention [Convencion Ibero-Americana de Navigacion Area (CIANA)] was ratified by 21 States, among them 19 Central- and South American countries, whereas from Europe only by Spain and Portugal. However, accession to the Madrid Convention was ratified by merely seven States, thus, by reason of under-ratification it did not take effect. Shawcross and Beaumont (1951), Para. 34.

[6]Convention on Private International Law. Signed at Habana, 20 February 1928. League of Nations Treaty Series Publication of Treaties and International Engagements Registered with the Secretarial of the League of Nations. No. 1950. Vol. LXXXVI 1929, Numbers 1, 2, 3. (https://treaties.un.org).

contributed to a wider divide in the world. Therefore, it devolved on the Chicago Convention to discontinue with peaceful instruments the harmful processes deriving from dividedness and to incorporate an international system of rules to be followed by all Member States, thereby unifying the world via the instruments of aviation law. The practical experience gained from the regulatory system of the Paris Convention supported the Member States in the creation of a more advanced and efficient system of rule-making and implementation under the Chicago Convention.

4.2 The Rules Established by ICAO

The principal function which guarantees ultimately the central and unparalleled role of ICAO recognised by the Member States is rule-making itself. This function is discharged by the ICAO Council, which from the viewpoint of rule-making has unequalled authorisations among the organisations of the UN, since its mandatory functions (Article 54) include the examination and adoption of standards to be applied worldwide. These encompass standards pertaining to the airspace over the high seas, which without exception need to be applied mandatorily by all States (pursuant to Annexes 2, 6, 11 and 12), since 'over the high seas the rules in force shall be those established under the Chicago Convention' (Article 12). This is the sole example among international organisations for the authorisation of an executive organ (of ICAO) to make legally binding rules for more than 43% of the surface of the Earth.[7]

The rules and provisions framed in the scope of the rule-making activity of ICAO are as follows:

***Standards and Recommended Practices* (SARPs)** The principal objectives of the SARPs rules are the enhancement of the safety of international air navigation and the unification of rules and procedures on a world scale. The application of SARPs rules is a basic requirement for the Member States worldwide.

***Procedures for Air Navigation Services* (PANS)** PANS provide operative guidance including practical regulations, which are too detailed in comparison with SARPs, therefore, they function as special rules for SARPs.[8]

***Regional Supplementary Procedures* (SUPPs)** The regulatory scope of SUPPs coincides with the scope of SARPs, but their application is not wide-scale and their territorial scope applies only to one specific ICAO region.

---

[7] Sipos (2023), p. 157.

[8] PANS: ICAO Doc 8400 ICAO Abbreviations and Codes (ABC); ICAO Doc 4444 Air Traffic Management (ATM); ICAO Doc 8168 Aircraft Operations (OPS).; ICAO Doc 9868 Training; ICAO Doc 7030 Regional Supplementary Procedures.

Documents, Manuals and Guidance Materials **(Docs, GMs)** Manuals provide help and detailed guidance for the application of SARPs, while Guidance Materials are designed to supplement and facilitate the application of SARPs and PANS (generally as supplements to Annexes or as separate documents).

The up-to-date status of ICAO publications is guaranteed by the summary published annually under the title 'Product and Services Catalogue'. The ICAO Council shall adopt SARPs (designated for convenience as Annexes to the Convention) requiring the vote of *two-thirds* of the Council at a meeting called for that purpose (Article 90). Whereas, PANS and SUPPs Documents, regional air navigation plans, Manuals and Guidance Materials shall be adopted by the Council requiring approval by a *majority* of its members (Article 52).

4.3 Standards and Recommended Practices

'Each contracting State shall undertake to collaborate in *securing the highest practicable degree of uniformity* in regulations, standards, procedures and organization in relation to aircraft, personnel, airways and auxiliary services in all matters in which such uniformity facilitates and improves air navigation. To this end, ICAO shall adopt and amend from time to time, as may be necessary, International Standards and Recommended Practices and Procedures dealing with:

(a) Communications systems and air navigation aids, including ground marking;
(b) Characteristics of airports and landing areas;
(c) Rules of the air and air navigation control practices;
(d) Licensing of operating and mechanical personnel;
(e) Airworthiness of aircraft;
(f) Registration and identification of aircraft;
(g) Collection and exchange of meteorological information;
(h) Log books;
(i) Aeronautical maps and charts;
(j) Customs and immigration procedures;
(k) Aircraft in distress and investigation of accidents; and

such other matters concerned with the safety, regularity, and efficiency of air navigation as may from time to time appear appropriate' (Article 37).

The framework rules of SARPs are publicised in 19 separate Annexes to the Convention. The Annexes of at least 4000 pages contain more than 12,000 Standards. It is the elementary interest and obligation of the contracting States to incorporate the SARPs rules, set forth under the Annexes encompassing all major areas of civil aviation, into their national law. The Standards and Recommended Practices have two-fold functions, thus, the marked differences between them can be inferred from their definitions:

- *A Standard* implies any *specification* for physical characteristics, configuration, material, performance, personnel or procedure, the *uniform application* of which is recognised as *necessary* for the safety or regularity of international air navigation, and to which the contracting States will *conform* in accordance with the Convention (in the event of the impossibility of compliance, notification to the Council of ICAO is compulsory).
- *A Recommended Practice* is any *specification* for physical characteristics, configuration, material, performance, personnel or procedure, the *uniform application* of which is recognised as *desirable* in the interest of the safety, regularity and efficiency of international air navigation, to which the contracting States will *endeavour to conform* in accordance with the Convention.[9]

Thus, the Standard is a specification, which stipulates a minimum requirement, therefore, its content cannot be emptied out or implemented with less obligations. However, diversion into a more rigorous direction in national legislation or international treaty-making is admissible any time. The uniform observance of standards is recognised by the Member States as necessary and practicable.

The Recommended Practice is also a specification, the uniform observance of which by the Member States is recognised as practicable and desirable, but conformity thereto is not mandatory. A Recommended Practice is less demandable. ICAO provides the Member States an opportunity for option in case of Recommended Practices, therefore, the text of the regulation itself offers alternatives. The Member State has to indicate that it adopts the specifications set forth under the Recommended Practice and conforms thereto. The Recommended Practice takes effect only in this case, via active commitment and *opting in provision* by the Member State.

4.4 The Uniformity, Reliability and Admissibility of Standards

The SARPs rules need to comply with the triadic, closely interrelated basic requirements of *uniformity, reliability* and *admissibility*.

Uniformity

Uniformity is the most important criterion of the Standards stipulated by the ICAO. The objective of the stipulation of SARPs rules is securing the 'highest practicable degree of uniformity' in international civil aviation on a world scale (Article 37). Uniformity is achieved by the prevalence of SARPs rules in national regulations. The contracting Parties formulate clearly and obligate each contracting State that in compliance with the Convention, it 'undertakes to keep its own regulations in these

[9] Annex 19 to the Chicago Convention on Safety Management. Foreword, 2nd edn., July 2016, pp. x-xi.

respects uniform, to the greatest possible extent, with those established from time to time under this Convention' (Article 12). The stipulation of the greatest possible extent indicates that the sovereign Member State is authorised to determine maximally to what degree it has the capacity to fulfil the requirements. Namely, the accomplishment of the impossible is no legal obligation *(impossibilium nulla obligato est)*. In reality, complete uniformity is unfeasible, because in practice it is impossible to unify all aviation rules of all Member States, this is instantiated abundantly in life. Precisely because of this, the standards constitute minimum requirements, 'the lowest degree' (Article 33); therefore, the Member States are permitted, actually get the go ahead to demand the observance of more rigorous specifications. Nevertheless, it would be unreasonable to define the standards of Annexes 1, 6 and 8 more rigorously in practice, since these norms are considered to be basically uniform by the international community.

Reliability

Conformity to the criterion of reliability is necessary for the systematic introduction of new procedures and achievements stemming primarily from technological and technical development. The history of aviation has proved that even the boldest dreams may come true, but this is only meaningful if they become accessible and available for every person. This requires, beyond engineers, scientists and courageous aviators, the institution of ICAO itself. ICAO examines the reliability of the new procedure or achievement via the system of aspects of aviation safety.

For example, thanks to technical development, a paradigm shift ensued in the mid-1980s when ICAO and the American Federal Aviation Administration (FAA) permitted twin-engine wide-body aircraft to fly intercontinentally over oceans without landing. The problem is simple: what happens if one of the engines stops working in the middle of the ocean far from an airport suitable for landing? Will the airplane be capable of flying for hours and landing safely with one engine? The answer is: yes. The basis of the licensing of Extended-Range Twin-Engine Operations Performance Standards (ETOPS) is the reliability examination, which by analysing the statistical data of the operation safety of engines established that the chance of the halt of working[10] by both engines separately in the same hour is 1:10 billion.[11]

[10] *FAA Advisory Circular. Extended Operations (ETOPS and Polar Operations),* 120–42, 6 June 1985, Para. 6, p. 4.; Mortimer (1984), no. 4.

[11] This is an excellent ratio. This chance is next to nil. Merely for the sake of demonstration, according to the scientist-researcher Carl Sagan (1934–1996), the chance of finding extraterrestrial life is 1:1 million based on theoretical calculations. Sagan (1980). no. 1190.; Nowakowski, Tomasz: We could find aliens any day now – SETI scientists discuss extraterrestrial life hunting. 9 July 2015. (https://phys.org/news/2015_07_aliens-day-nowseti-scientists-discuss.html).

Admissibility

The SARPs rule needs to be suitable for implementation in all regions. In vain is the new rule established, if the Member States in less developed regions cannot afford its implementation, since they cannot conform to the specifications in the absence of financial, technical or professional resources. For example, it is impossible to confine aircraft exceeding the noise level specified by ICAO immediately to the ground, since it is necessary to provide opportunity for the performers of the concerned Member States and of the industry to obtain more modern aircraft which conform to the prescribed noise levels. ICAO always takes these impediments into account and tends to secure a transitional period, or, if necessary, it introduces the requirements gradually.

4.5 The Binding Effect of the Standards

From a legal viewpoint the most important question is whether the standards have legally binding effect. The question is the object of constant, frequently academic debates, while practice and life itself answer the question unambiguously.

It is among the mandatory duties of the ICAO Council to adopt the principal rules of civil aviation: the Standards and Recommended Practices (SARPs), and for convenience, designate them as Annexes to the Convention [Article 54 *l)*]. Owing to this provision, the Annexes are removed from the norm-text of the Chicago Convention with binding effect, they become the *non-integrated part of the Convention*, thus, their legal status changes as they do *not have binding effect*, while from a professional viewpoint they remain closely related. Therefore, the SARPs rules are in fact not regarded as prescriptions to be followed under all circumstances, but this holds true only at first sight.

The provisions of the Convention allow for differences from SARPs rules in certain cases. This is admissible if any State finds it impracticable to bring its own regulations or practices into full accord with any such international standard or procedure (Article 38). The Member States frequently resort to the legal institution facilitating differences from SARPs rules. However, in case of the Standards the potential differences applied by the Member States may be only provisional, since although the Member States may freely decide on the degree of differences, they are obligated to eliminate such differences posteriorly and after full compliance incorporate the Standards into their national law.

Despite the provision facilitating differences, the Member States attribute acknowledged binding effect to Standards without reservations. With respect to the fact that the Convention establishes a general legal framework for the performers of international civil aviation, this framework will be substantiated only if the Member States integrate the Standards into their national law, thereby, they make them legally enforceable therein. The Standards with binding force are made via a majority decision by the ICAO Council while exercising its regulatory function as it receives authorisation to do so from the Member States. The Member States have guaranteed authorisation for the organisation of ICAO to make laws, and thenceforth, they have endowed the international organisation with competence to establish rules binding them.

In possession of the delegated authorisations, ICAO creates Standards

- which guarantee rights and prescribe obligations for the contracting States;
- which are framed and approved of by a competent professional organisation; furthermore,
- the institutional implementation of which is required mandatorily and can be controlled at national audits.

Thus, the *Standard adopted by the ICAO Council* on grounds of the Convention [Article 54 *l)*] consists in every *specification* the *uniform observance* of which is recognised as *practicable* and *necessary* for the safety and regularity of international air navigation, which the contracting States *conform to* pursuant to the Convention (with the reservation that of any non-compliance with the Standard, the Member State shall notify the ICAO Council without delay). The definition diplomatically contains the word *observance* instead of the more emphatic expression *needs to be observed*, but this does not have special significance. From the objective and spirituality of the Convention the conduct to be followed can be clearly inferred, since the establishment of the uniformity of international air navigation, its formation on the basis of equal opportunities can be attained by the Member States solely via the mandatory observance of the Standards. ICAO demands the consistent prevalence of the Standard. The Standard becomes effective without the consent of the Member State, even implicitly—without passive commitment or ratification *(opting out provision)*. Thus, Standards are legally effective *erga omnes*, that is, they have binding effect for all Member States (they are valid in case of provisional differences communicated by the Member States to, and publicised by the ICAO). The binding effect of this legal institution proceeds primarily from the entirety, the spirituality of the Convention and the commitment of the Member States, not from continued practice followed as law or from customary law.

4.6 The Creation of SARPs Rules

In 24 hours of all the 365 days of the year and in every second of a minute at some point of the Earth an airplane ascends or descends (even under the circumstances of the COVID-19 pandemic). During operation in air traffic, each aircraft receives equal treatment due to uniform procedures. Via the SARPs specifications, ICAO can ensure the entire regulatory background of all technical and operative elements of international civil aviation, of all moments of operation starting from licensing procedures to the investigation of the causes of incidents or accidents.

We can understand the complex procedure of the creation of SARPs lasting for several years illustriously via the ‘birth’ of a Standard. We are going to observe the way of the recommendation formulated by professionals from the beginnings to its

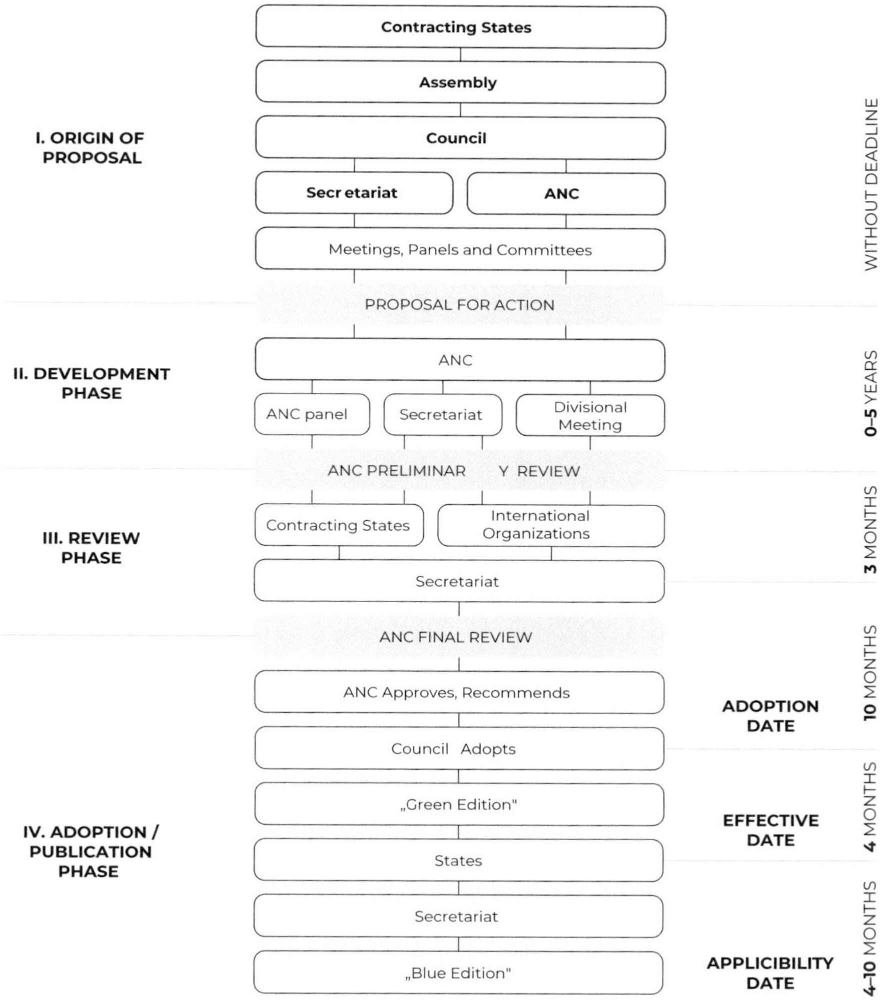

Fig. 4.1 The making and amendment of Standards and Recommended Practices

adoption, since only this way can we become familiar with the systems of instruments and arguments used in the profession and diplomacy. Of the many potential examples, we present one which at first sight seemed acceptable and reasonable for all contracting States, nevertheless, it divided the parties to the utmost, although it concerned merely the change of an age limit (Fig. 4.1).

The case concerned the rule of Annex 1 to the Convention on Personnel Licensing, which among others provides for the upper limit of the age of pilots of aircraft. The rule-maker aimed at the raise of the upper age limit of pilots from the age of 60 to 65. Annex 1 contains the international requirements concerning the qualification of the professional personnel of civil aviation and its official acknowledgement. Owing to the risk deriving from dangerous operation it is necessary that professionally prepared, qualified and physically suitable professionals implement the tasks releted to flying, since this is certainly an important requirement and simultaneously a guarantee for the maintenance of the safety of flights.

4.6.1 Initial Phase: The SARPs Recommendation is Made

The recommendation may target either the making of new SARPs or the amendment of already adopted SARPs. The recommendation commences with the submission of the draft presenting the life-situation to be regulated, which arrives from the contracting State, or the organisation of ICAO or another international organisation. The recommendation needs to be based on reality and to address a real problem. Furthermore, already upon drafting the recommendation it needs to be examined whether it will meet the requirements of cooperation, agreement, compliance and commitment (as conditions of the issuance of all SARPs). During rule-making, ICAO and its Member States expect mutual *cooperation*, *agreement* on the issues regulated by SARPs, the *compliance* of national statutes with SARPs rules and the *commitment* of the Member State to the observance of the requirements specified by SARPs.

The raise of the pilots' age limit to 65 was necessitated by social processes and economic aspects. Therefore, the recommendation was based on reality, it addressed a real problem and complied with the basic criteria above. Due to the growth of air transport, a heightening shortage of well-qualified, experienced professionals, especially pilots manifested itself, while in the majority of countries changes in welfare and healthcare systems, the development of medicine, the increase in average age led to the raise of the age of retirement. If we set out from the fact that the development of air transport will result in the doubling of the number of passengers in the foreseeable future, it is superfluous to possess the philosophers' stone to forecast that in the near future plentiful new pilots, air navigation controllers and technical staff will be needed. According to Boeing, the aircraft manufacturer merely in the next 20 years, also calculating with the effects of the COVID-19 pandemic, the training of at least 649,000 new pilots, 690,000 new maintenance technicians and 938,000 cabin crew members will be necessary.[12]

[12] Pilot and Technician Outlook (2023–2042). Flight Operation Solution, Boeing. 2023. (www.boeing.com/commercial/market/pilot-technician-outlook).

With respect to the fact that the demand for qualified pilots had increased in an unprecedented manner, it was reasonable to initiate the change of the age limit regulated under Annex 1 to the Convention on Personnel Licensing, due to which the shortage of pilots became easier to handle.

4.6.2 *Elaboration Phase: Consultation of the SARPs Recommendation*

With the elaboration of the recommendation a complex consultation process commences, which as to its duration may be protracted for five years, but even in a basic case it may also last for years. The technical recommendations are examined by the Air Navigation Commission (ANC), and for the purpose of obtaining further information, it refers the recommendation to a competent workgroup. Subsequently, the ANC organises several professional meetings, which have crucial significance during making the SARPs, since the agreement necessary for adoption is essentially reached at such forums. All Member States are authorised to attend the sessions. International organisations are authorised to address the subject as solicited parties in an observer status. At the meetings, expertise is guaranteed by the ANC consisting of the experts of the Member States, by other experts of the Member States and the employees of the ICAO Secretariat.

The raise of the age limit from 60 to 65 in itself seems to be a simple task. During the consultation, all aspects of the issue are examined: to what extent is it an aviation safety issue or a social, economic issue, to what extent is the recommended measure discriminative or compatible with the retirement policy of the Member States? To what extent does the system of requirements of the pilots' doctors support this step? According to Argentina, this raise should be introduced in tiers in line with the stricter medical check-up of pilots, while Canada recommended that by reason of discrimination, instead of the upper age limit, exclusively the pilots' valid medical licences should determine how long the pilots serve actively. Obviously, the medical requirements do not concern merely the physical condition, but also human factors and mental preparedness, which have very significant role in the occurrence of accidents. The United States insisted on the maintenance of the age limit of 60 years, since above this age the proportion of the risk of the occurrence of various diseases, especially cardio-vascular cases is multiplied. The experts of the Air Navigation Commission rejected this, since in the former 40 years they had not heard of an accident which had become fatal by reason of the sudden death of the pilot.

As a conclusion of the process of consultation, a report is made on the review of already existing SARPs or the preparation of new SARPs in the form of technical recommendations.

4.6.3 Review Phase: The Finalisation of the SARPs Recommendation

The Air Navigation Commission refers the recommendation elaborated in the form of a preliminary examination in line with alternative solutions to the Member States and international organisations in a so-called State Letter for the purpose of the statement of their opinions. The States have three months for rendering their opinions. In the interest of the most comprehensive elaboration of the opinions, ICAO renders accessible all technical details that arose during the elaboration of the recommendation.

The Secretariat processes the incoming opinions and prepares a final review material on the basis of its own recommendations and of the received opinions.

On the basis of the incoming responses, the raise of the upper age limit of pilots was supported by 83% of the Member States. It is remarkable that the pilots' professional community, the International Federation of Airline Pilots' Associations (IFALPA) with reference to professional reasons, primarily to the heightened psychological overload at that age, did not support the raise of the age limit.

4.6.4 Adoption Phase: Adoption of the SARPs Recommendation

The Air Navigation Commission makes a recommendation for the *amendment* of the Annexes, which is considered by the Council in its function [Article 54 *m)*]. It is important to highlight that the Air Navigation Commission does not carry out the professional elaboration of each Annex, since it is the Air Transport Committee (ATC) that is in charge of Annex 9 on Facilitation, whereas the Aviation Security Committee (ASC) is competent in Annex 17 on Security. Pursuant to the rule of the Convention, the Air Navigation Commission (ANC) refers the final recommendation and its attachments to the Council for adoption, where the last great debate takes place.

Council of ICAO Meeting and Decision
The debate of the Council is moderated by the President of the Council. In the first round the representatives of the Council Member States pronounce their opinions and standpoints on the final material (often to 'the minutes').

According to Canada, the essential point is actually not the specification of an age limit (which otherwise is discriminative), but the professional guaranteeing of the physical suitability of the professional staff over the age of 60.[13] Since it is possible to differ from the amended regulation, several countries are likely to apply difference, since their national law does not permit the limitation or specifies a different limit. According to France, the subject is rather social than a matter of aviation safety. Since the principal objective of the Convention is the increase of the level of aviation safety, the Council is to decide on an issue which has a significant effect on aviation safety. According to Egypt, the experienced pilot is an asset in aviation, therefore, supported by other Member States, it declared that the age limit of 68 may also be a realistic objective. According to Nigeria, the pilot-in-command can fly until the age of 65 on condition that the age of the co-pilot (first officer) in charge is below 60.

According to the United States, the rule on the age limit of 60 does not need to be changed, therefore, in case of the adoption of the change, the US will apply a difference from ICAO. The United States insisted on the perpetuation of the age limit of 60 years, since it was not assured that the raise of the age limit entailed the increase of the level of aviation safety. Simultaneously, it envisioned that although it would differ from the international standard, this does not imply that pursuant to the Convention (Article 33) with respect to flight above its territory, it would deny the inflight of another State with reference to the fact that the age of the pilot navigating the aircraft of another State exceeds 60 years.

According to India, the raise of the age of pilots brings up financial issues, since the shortage of pilots facilitated negotiating for better payment conditions. Nevertheless, owing to the amendment, more pilots would be available on the market, which may affect the amount of salaries adversely. This context was evoked by IFALPA from the outset as the main reason for opposition. This also implies that the raise of the age limit may result in a decline in the training of new pilots, therefore, later the number of qualified pilots will not be sufficient to replace the retiring ones. According to St. Lucia, in their country more problems arise with the physical condition of pilots between the ages of 40–45 than of those between 60–65, thus, the tightening of the system of medical check-ups is necessary in the case of all age groups.

(continued)

[13] ICAO Doc 8984 Manual of Civil Aviation Medicine. AN/895, 3rd edn., 2012.

At the end of the debate, the President of the ICAO Council summarised the opinions, in view of which he made a textual recommendation, which he put to vote. The 36 members of the Council adopted the amendment of the Standard with 27 affirmative votes, four votes against (e.g., France and the United States) and four abstentions under the following conditions: all pilots over the age of 60 (to the age of 65) are obligated to undergo medical check-ups twice a year and upon the navigation of the aircraft the age of the other pilot in charge may not exceed 60 years.[14]

Nota bene: Annex E to the first international public aviation law treaty, the Paris Convention (1919) determined the upper age limit of pilots to be 45 years.[15]

The submitted and negotiated recommendation is adopted by the Council at its session convened for that purpose with two-thirds majority. The decisions of the Council related to SARPs rules are mostly reached unanimously due to the prolonged and thorough preparatory work as well as the efficient conciliatory and negotiation mechanism. After its adoption, any such Annex or any amendment of an Annex becomes effective within three months after its submission to the contracting States or at the end of such longer period of time as the Council may prescribe. The Council refers the final decision to the Member States in the form of a so-called Green Edition. The Member States shall be allowed to register their disapproval of the decision with the Council within three months [Article 90 *a)*]. If more than half of the Member States approve, the recommendation becomes valid automatically after the expiry of the determined deadline and takes effect after the expiry of the appropriate time.[16] In the history of ICAO in this phase no objection has been put forward, which is due to the wide-scale and efficient conciliatory process.[17]

After the expiry of three months, a further one month's period is at the disposal of the Member States to prepare for the application of the norm, thus, between adoption by the Council and taking effect a period of four months has to pass. According to the main rule, a period of further four months passes between the day of taking effect and the applicability of the norm, although the curtailment or extension of this period is admissible depending on the circumstances. One month before the day of the commencement of applicability, the deadline expires for notifications to the Council by the Member State of the differences between its national regulation and the adopted SARPs rule (Article 38). The notified differences are publicised in the supplements to the Annexes.

[14] ICAO Council Working Paper/12615, Adoption of Amendment 167 to Annex 1. 23 February 2006.

[15] Annex E to the Paris Convention on the Minimum Qualifications Necessary for Obtaining Certificates as Pilots and Navigators. The Operating Crew. Chapter I, Section III.

[16] Sipos (2023), p. 158.

[17] Huang (2009a), p. 55.; Huang (2009b).

'The Council shall immediately notify all contracting States of the coming into force of any Annex or amendment thereto' [Article 90 *b)*]. Subsequently to the day of taking effect, the Secretariat elaborates the statute in the form of a so-called Blue Edition, which is adequate to be incorporated under the Annexes or the PANS. On the day of the commencement of applicability, the Member States are obligated to implement the new regulation.

4.7 Annexes to the Chicago Convention

Under the Annexes the technical, operational and professional rules of the constantly changing and developing air transport industry are publicised, which reflect today's demands and tomorrow's necessities influencing aviation safety and all performers of the air transport industry. Drawing on the Paris Convention (1919), the Chicago System maintained the system of the institution of the Annexes, but it transformed their legal regulation basically. It is a mandatory function of the Council to adopt the SARPs rules, and for convenience, designate these as Annexes to the Convention [Article 54 *l)*]. The intention of the rule-maker was the uniform incorporation of the collection of the Annexes into the Convention. Nevertheless, the most important regulatory constraints contained in the Convention concern the legal status of ICAO Annexes.[18] The formulation of the rule-maker is not inadvertent: the SARPs rules are designated for convenience. Thus, the special legal status of the Annexes diverging from that of the Convention facilitates both the flexible amendment of the SARPs rules incorporated under the Annexes and difference therefrom as well. At the same time, we need to emphasise that the Convention and the Annexes are practically inseparably and closely related, therefore, the interpretation and implementation of the existent 19 separate Annexes may ensue only in accordance and uniformity with the Convention.

The Annexes imply comprehensive systems of rules of great volume. (According to specialists, the processing, comprehension and practical utilisation of each Annex 'in themselves equal to the completion of an academic degree'.)[19] The Annexes of the Chicago Convention contain Standards and Recommended Practices in the following areas (Fig. 4.2):

[18] Sochor (1991), p. 156.

[19] The Presentation of Jiefang Huang (ICAO Senior Legal Officer, later Legal Director) at ICAO and CERG (Central European Rotation Group) Air Law Conference, Warsaw, 2012.

1. Personnel Licensing

2. Rules of the Air

3. Meteorological Service for International Air Navigation

4. Aeronautical Charts

5. Units of Measurement to be Used in Air and Ground Operations

6. Operation of Aircraft
Part I – International Commercial Air Transport – Aeroplanes
Part II – International General Aviation – Aeroplanes
Part III – International Operations – Helicopters
Part IV – International Operations – Remotely Piloted Aircraft Systems

7. Aircraft Nationality and Registration Marks

8. Airworthiness of Aircraft

9. Facilitation

10. Aeronautical Telecommunications
Volume I – Radio Navigational Aids
Volume II – Communication Procedures including those with PANS status
Volume III – Communication Systems
Volume IV – Surveillance Radar and Collision Avoidance Systems
Volume V – Aeronautical Radio Frequency Spectrum Utilization

11. Air Traffic Services

12. Search and Rescue

13. Aircraft Accident and Incident Investigation

14. Aerodomes
Volume I – Aerodromes Design and Operations
Volume II – Heliports

15. Aeronautical Information Services

16. Environmental Protection
Volume I – Aircraft Noise
Volume II – Aircraft Engine Emissions
Volume III – Aeroplane CO_2 Emissions
Volume IV – Carbon Offsetting and Reduction Scheme for International Aviation (CORSIA)

17. Aviation Security
Safeguarding International Civil Aviation against Acts of Unlawful Interference

18. The Safe Transport of Dangerous Goods by Air

19. Safety Management

Fig. 4.2 Annexes of the Chicago Convention

Annexes 1, 2, 6, 8, 11 and 14 are of extremely great significance by reason of the operative implementation of the flight, therefore, they mainly consist of Standards. Within the regulatory framework of the Convention, the Member States may differ from the Standards on grounds of justification and a compliance plan. The most recent Annex to the Convention, that is, Annex 19 on Safety Management has been applied worldwide since 14 November 2013. From the viewpoint of regulation, Annex 19 does not contain new elements, but summarises the safety prescriptions which were applicable formerly in the relevant areas of air transport under all the Annexes concerned by aviation safety (with the exception of Annex 17).

4.8 Differences from the SARPs Rules

Standards need to be incorporated into national law. However, the Convention facilitates differences from the new Standards.

'Any State which *finds it impracticable*

- to comply in all respects with any such international standard or procedure;
- to bring its own regulations or practices into full accord with any international standard or procedure; furthermore, which
- deems it necessary to adopt regulations or practices differing in any particular respect from those established by an international standard, *shall give immediate notification to ICAO of the differences between its own practice and that established by the international standard*' (Article 38).

Pursuant to Annex 15 to the Convention on Aeronautical Information Services, the Member State is obligated to publicise the most important differences from SARPs-, PANS- and SUPPs rules in the national Aeronautical Information Publication (AIP). With respect to SARPs rules, the Member State is obligated to notify the organisation of ICAO of all the differences. In its notification the Member State is obligated to justify the differences and simultaneously make a suggestion for the time and method of the elimination of the situation causing the difference. Thus, the differences are sheerly provisional, the Member States do not have another option but to comply. Essentially, pursuant to the Convention there are two admissible options, both of them leading in the direction of implementation: (1) the implementation of the SARPs rule, or (2) notification of the difference until prospective compliance. The Member States are obligated to justify the differences and the background of relevant decisions owing to the burden of proof,[20] thus, it is not worth interpreting the phrase of 'finds it impracticable' under the Convention literally and broadly. However, there are Member States which do not give notice of their differences or do not posteriorly rectify the notified differences, therefore,

[20] ICAO Assembly Resolution A36-13, Consolidated statement of continuing ICAO policies and associated practices related specifically to air navigation. September 2007.

these facts are established as non-compliance upon Member State audits carried out by the ICAO. The Member States may give notification of the differences electronically as well.[21]

If the ICAO Council makes amendments to an existing Standard, within 60 days of its adoption the contracting State needs to amend its own regulation and practice in compliance with the Standard. In case it fails to do so, the contracting State shall give notice of this fact or the proposed national action to the Council. 'In any such case, the Council makes immediate notification to all other States of the difference which exists between one or more features of an international standard and the corresponding national practice of that State' (Article 38).

However, there are basic Standards from which no difference is allowed because of their significance. Of course, the ICAO Council did not mark these ones, but the Member States need to know what consequences any difference from the specific Standard may entail. For example, it is vital to comply with the rules specified under Annex 17 to the Convention on Security, since in vain are the security systems of the international airports of London excellent if the perpetrator departs from a less secured airport and after circumventing its security system, they arrive in London. In order to prevent this, if ICAO during the audit forms the opinion that the security system of the examined airport is defective, this may entail that the passengers will undergo meticulous new control and search at the recipient airport.

A perfect example of mandatoriness is that subsequently to the events of 11 September 2001, the ICAO Council amended Annex 6 to the Convention on Operations of Aircraft.[22] In this Standard it tightened up and prescribed the fortification of the door of the pilots' cabin on the aircraft, its closure for the period from embarking to disembarking and introduced a special procedure for handling suspicious situations. Later, these prescriptions were extended by the ICAO Council in the form of a recommendation to aircraft discharging domestic flights and to smaller airplanes as well.[23] It is inadmissible to differ from this Standard and it would not be worthwhile either, since with regard to non-compliance with this strict rule a situation may develop when the recipient Member State denies entrance into its territory by that aircraft. Compliance with the SARPs rules is an obligation assumed by accession to the Convention by the Member States (Article 12). It is not accidental that the Member States endeavour to comply with the SARPs rules

---

[21] At its 192nd Session on 4 March 2011, the ICAO Council affirmed the possibility of submission to the Council of SARPs compliances and differences (with the exception of Annexes 9 and 17) electronically via the so-called EFOD (Electronic Filing of Differences) System. Hitherto, the Member States have given notification of 17,000 differences. ICAO State letter – AN 1/1–11/28.; ICAO Council Working Paper/13954.; ICAO Doc 10055 Manual on Notification and Publication of Differences. 1st edn., 2019.

[22] ICAO Council Working Paper/11757, Adoption of Amendment 27 to Annex 6 – *Operation of Aircraft,* Part I – *International Commercial Air Transport – Aeroplanes,* 28 February 2002.

[23] ICAO Doc 9809-Cl/1142, Council Min. 166/1–14, 2002.; ICAO Doc 9802 ICAO's Policies on Charges for Airports and Air Navigation Services. 9th edn., 2012.

completely, since this is one of the conditions of equal participation in international air traffic and of the universal establishment of aviation safety and security.

The Council has adopted Annex 2 in the form of international Standards, without any Recommended Practices.[24] This means that there may be no difference from the Standards established under Annex 2 to the Convention on Rules of the Air (similarly to the rules of the Highway Code pertaining to traffic on public roads), especially during the implementation of flights and manoeuvres over the high seas as well as during transit in the airspace of another State. In this case, the value to be protected is the safe implementation of flights, which cannot be overridden under any circumstances by any Member State. Therefore, the Standards established under this Annex may not be disregarded.

4.9 The Implementation of SARPs Rules

The paramount objective of ICAO is guaranteeing the constant and effective safety of international civil aviation. Its primary instrument is the transplantation and implementation by the Member States of aviation safety requirements into their national law. Compliance with SARPs rules is the duty of the Member States due to accession to the Convention. ICAO is authorised to control implementation by the Member States. As a forum of the Member States, ICAO does not only draft rules in order to guarantee aviation safety to the greatest possible extent, but it also operates an institutional mechanism supporting the national implementation of rules made by the community, and if necessary, ICAO requires it, and in an ultimate case, it coerces implementation. Coercion is not to be construed literally, since ICAO is not an authority, it does not have supervisory authorisation, for the enforcement of its will it has limited executive authorisations. Although, these facilitate the indirect enforcement of the interests of ICAO, they do not allow for making decisions by ICAO via avoiding the sovereign Member States or restricting the Member States in exercising their domestic rights.

4.9.1 Compliance with Uniform Requirements

Air transport is transboundary and is an integral part of the global world. In this system, the activity of air transport within the borders is closely related to such activity over the borders, thus, the level of safety and the supervisory capacity of the Member State are not matters of internal affairs, but international requirements and obligations. With respect to the fact that aviation safety is the primary interest of all the performers of air transport, in practice the Member States are interested in the

[24] Joyner (1997), p. 77.

implementation of SARPs rules. However, this was not always the case. The global development of air transport coerced the less developed Member States to implement the SARPs rules completely, since only in that case could they get access to markets and get engaged in world trade via aviation, if they guaranteed safe operation in their national airspaces and at their international airports. Not to mention that in the new examination system of ICAO, any non-compliance with SARPs rules entails the application of adverse legal consequences.

For the purpose of the most efficient support of implementation and familiarisation with problems deriving from the deficient implementation of SARPs rules, ICAO has set up the Universal Safety Oversight Audit System and later the Universal Security Audit Programme. All Member States are obligated to participate in the oversight audit system. Therefore, ICAO concludes a bilateral agreement with the audited Member State, in which the sovereign Member State undertakes both submission to systematic aviation safety and security controls and the provision of the conditions of the successful conduct of the audit. The objectives of the wide-scale control process set up by the ICAO are the control of the complete process of the implementation of SARPs, and in view of that, making recommendations for the development of aviation safety. The audit process also provides feedback for ICAO on the existence of the real-life relations designed to be regulated by SARPs rules and on the quality of the Standards, which may substantiate the framing of new SARPs rules or the amendment of the existing ones.

4.9.2 Oversight of the Implementation of SARPs Rules

ICAO has elaborated an exceptional and unique oversight system. The Member States have granted supervisory competence to ICAO in several tiers, which authorises ICAO, while being 'superimposed' over the Member States, to control their aviation safety and security preparedness during audits on the basis of uniform aspects, and in the case of deficiencies, to obligate them to comply with the rules. The audit is designed to examine the status of national regulations and the supervisory capacity of the authorities of the Member State. ICAO audits exclusively its Member States. During the examination, it is possible to examine indirectly the main performers of the air transport industry of the Member State, but only with respect to the extent of the compliance of licences issued by the aviation authority, of the licensed procedures with SARPs rules, and whether the quality of the supervision of the operation of service providers by the authorities complies with SARPs rules. Thus, ICAO during its aviation safety audit examines the difference of the national rules from SARPs rules constituting the basis of the system of the rules of civil aviation as well as the supervisory capacity of the aviation authority of the Member State.

The supervisory capacity indicates whether the Member State has the capacity to guarantee

- the effective implementation of SARPs rules;
- the operation of the supervisory system (eight critical elements); and
- the practical application of aviation safety procedures.

Guaranteeing the supervisory capacity is the responsibility of the Member States. If the supervisory capacity is absent or weak, it implies unambiguously hazard and threat to the stakeholders of international civil aviation. If the supervisory capacity of the aviation authority of the Member State is weak, for example, it is incapable of making international rules observed, or the issued licences do not conform to the Standards of ICAO, then the aircraft of a foreign State, while using the airspace or the airports of such Member State, cannot be assured of receiving treatment conforming to international norms, thereby, it submits to higher risk. This is valid vice-versa: the airline of the specific Member State, while operating to another country, may be the object of constant examination. Namely, there is no guarantee for the correctness of the authority licences of the aircraft and the personnel, of the documents held mandatorily on the aircraft or for the appropriateness of the airworthiness of the aircraft in compliance with international specifications. It is not inadvertent that the institution of the Flags of Convenience could not gain ground in civil aviation. To put it simply, it is not worthwhile registering the aircraft with the authority of a State the supervisory capacity and preparedness of which are weak. With the increase of risk, the concerns regarding the safety of the aircraft may injure the interests of other Member States related to safety; thus, the authorities of these States may rightfully deny operation thereto. At the same time, there are examples to demonstrate that the service providers (airlines, airports, air navigation service providers) of the Member State with an underperforming authority have outstanding indicators, comply with the highest-level international specifications since the profession and the management pay great attention to achieving full conformity to international and national rules and procedures stipulated for service providers.

Aviation oversight is a function which enables States to ensure the "Effective Implementation" (EI) of SARPs, in the areas of (1) Legislation, (2) Organisation, (3) Licensing, (4) Operations, (5) Airworthiness, (6) Accident investigation, (7) Air Navigation Services and (8) Aerodromes (www.icao.int/safety/pages/usoap-results.aspx). The basis for the EI system of examination is the complete control of the so-called Critical Elements (CE) as applied assessment aspects. These elements encompass the broad spectrum of civil aviation. ICAO summarises the results of the assessment in a chart.

Critical Elements 7 and 8 are the most important. These indicate whether the national aviation authority has the capacity to identify deficiencies which directly or indirectly (may) affect safety. In vain is compliance full in the first 6 elements, if grave deficiencies occur in respect of these Critical Elements. Via the exercise of rights and the fulfilment of obligations deriving from supervisory functions, the aviation authority needs to have the capacity to analyse the extent of the deficiency, to make recommendations, and if necessary, to enforce effective implementation (Fig. 4.3).

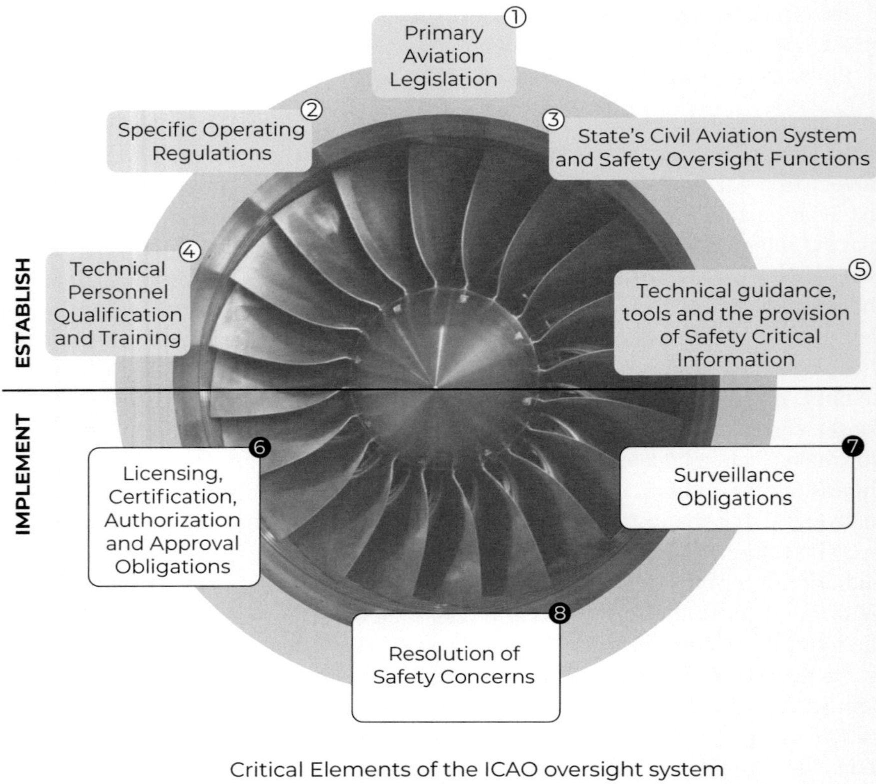

Fig. 4.3 Critical Elements of the ICAO oversight system
The Critical Elements 1–5 present the introduction and establishment of rules. They introduce primarily the extent of the harmonisation of the internal rules of national law with the requirements of the Chicago Convention and its Annexes as well as of the international aviation law treaties. The Critical Elements 6–8 represent the implementation of the former elements. The Critical Elements need to be examined in their relations. The requirements of Critical Elements 1 and 2 are closely related to Critical Element 6. Critical Element 4 needs to be construed together with Critical Elements 6, 7 and 8

4.10 The Development of the System of Oversight

The Member States of ICAO under the Convention assumed the obligation to elaborate, introduce, maintain and continually develop the institutional system of supervision, which completely guarantees the achievement of the highest possible level of aviation safety in compliance with international requirements. The complete fulfilment of obligations is supported by the oversight system elaborated by ICAO.

The audit system has been accomplished in three closely related, gradually developed phases.

4.10.1 *The Universal Safety Oversight Audit Programme (1999–2004)*

At the end of the last century, considerable remissness and lack of consequences were discernible in the implementation of SARPs rules by the Member States. This process led to the emergence of grave issues of aviation safety, which jeopardised universal trust in ICAO and mutual recognition.[25] At the 29th Assembly of ICAO (1992)[26] the Member States took firm steps. At the Assembly a resolution was made, which granted opportunity for the organisation of ICAO to examine the supervisory system of Member States tackling deficiencies in aviation safety on a voluntary basis in the claimant Member States. The programme commenced in 1996, but more drastic intervention was necessary.

Therefore, at the conference of Directors-General of Civil Aviation held in Montreal (1997), the delegated representatives formulated the strategy of an entirely new oversight system, which transcended its shadow and triggered real change. In this new system the Member States undertook obligatorily the audit carried out by the experts of ICAO in their territory and accepted that the implementation of the audit entailed the limitation of the sovereignty of Member States. The international group of auditors set up by the ICAO could examine compliance with the rules under Annexes 1, 6 and 8 in the Member States, for which the Convention did not grant authorisation. This new initiative familiar as the Universal Safety Oversight Audit Programme (USOAP) was revolutionary. At the 32nd Assembly of ICAO (1998)[27] the majority of the Member States adopted the new oversight system, and thereby, the universal safety supervisory audit programme could commence in the Member States in 1999. Thenceforth, ICAO was granted quasi transboundary supervisory competence by the Member States, and as a consequence, it was authorised to effect enforcement.

The Member States at the 33rd Assembly of ICAO (2001) extended the number of areas to be examined to Annexes 11, 13 and 14 to the Convention.[28] Since the audit programme progressed vigorously, a number of conclusions could be drawn from the values revealed due to the examinations. In the audit calculation system of USOAP, the examined country which completed the requirements of the Critical Elements and the SARPs rules without any differences was assessed at 0%.[29] In

[25] Dempsey (2004), p. 20.

[26] ICAO Assembly Resolution A29-13, Improvement of Safety Oversight. September 1992.

[27] ICAO Assembly Resolution A32-11, Establishment of an USOAP. September 1998.

[28] ICAO Assembly Resolution A33-8, Expanded the USOAP to include audits of Annexes 11, 13 and 14. September 2001.

[29] The best result was achieved by South Korea in 2006 with a difference of 1.11%, while a part of the African countries was positioned in the category over 80%. The method of calculation could be misleading for non-professionals, since 80% suggests a ‘good’ result, whereas, the 80% does not show the value of compliance but the opposite, the value of difference from SARPs rules. Subsequently, this method of calculation was replaced by ICAO and the proportion was adjusted

reality, such a country does not exist, since there are always factors to be rectified, new requirements to be met. This is a basic feature and an essential attribute of the air transport industry. Just as the revealed faults do not imply problems in themselves, since they are to be corrected. Problems appear if the revealed fault is categorised as '*non-compliant*' upon the next audit (for example, after five or six years), that is, no meritorious work took place, no endeavour to rectify the faults can be identified on the part of the State or the profession. Notwithstanding, there are countries where State will and commitment exist, but the infrastructure is basic, by reason of the shortage of finances or experts, there are insufficient resources for the implementation of SARPs rules, for training and development. Therefore, for understandable reasons, these countries cannot fully comply with the prescriptions of ICAO.

4.10.2 The Comprehensive Approach Audit Programme (2005–2010)

In August 2005, five tragic aviation accidents took place in the world,[30] therefore, the governments of the Member States demanded that the top organisation of international civil aviation took urgent measures. ICAO made a list on the basis of their experiences and assessments at safety audits immediately, but it did not publicise the list with regard to the confidentiality of the information therein. However, in August 2005 via *Le Figaro,* the French daily newspaper, France, the Government of which knew these results (within ICAO the audit database was accessible for experts) unexpectedly came up with a 'blacklist' involving 30 countries. It could do so, since owing to the accidents which had happened to French citizens,[31] the French Parliament with reference to the protection of its residents issued an official statement about the States in which air traffic was not safe enough.

to compliance. Thus, the two extremities of the percentage scale, 0% became the value of non-compliance, while 100% became the category of 'completely implemented'.

[30] In the aviation accidents of 'Black August' 339 people lost their lives: [(1) 1 August 2005 – Calvi (France) CL-415; (2) 6 August 2005 – Palermo (Italy) ATR-72; (3) 14 August 2005 – Athens (Greece) Boeing 737; (4) 16 August 2005 – Machiques (Venezuela) MD-82; (5) 23 August 2005 – Pucallpa (Peru) Boeing 737], which demanded urgent measures. The developed countries increasingly pressurised the organisation of ICAO and demanded that ICAO publicised the results of audits, since this information needs to accessible for the citizens of all Member States, because people have the right to know which countries have grave aviation safety deficiencies. Essentially, according to the justification they intended to inform the passengers and the performers of the industry about the degree of risk to be expected during recourse to air services in the territory of a given State. ICAO News Release PIO 10/2005, *ICAO Council President calls for increased global transparency in sharing of aviation safety information.*

[31] On 3 January 2004 the Boeing 737-300 of the Egyptian *Flash Airlines* (7K) crashed into the Red Sea causing the death of 148 people. Of the 135 passengers 133 were French citizens. On 16 August 2005 the charter flight McDonnell Douglas MD-82 of the Columbian *West Caribbean Airways* (WCW) crashed above the mountainous territory of Venezuela causing the death of 160 people.

With regard to the evolved situation at its 35th Assembly, ICAO (2004)[32] Member States introduced the so-called Comprehensive Systems Approach (CSA), in which ICAO extended the USOAP programme to all the Annexes to the Convention. An exception from this was Annex 17 on Security, which did not imply that the comprehensive examination of the rules under Annex 17 did not ensue. On the contrary, owing to the events of 11 September 2001, ICAO, following the model of safety audits, set up the Universal Security Audit Programme (USAP), which was prescribed for the Member States mandatorily. However, by reason of confidentiality, the security audit demanded a more secluded form of oversight.

However, experience showed that the majority of Member States did not take every necessary measure to correct the faults. Moreover, they did not report their differences from SARPs rules within the bounds of the Convention, therefore, ICAO resolved to take a further step. In possession of increasingly more negative experiences and audit results to be collated, the organisation decided to publicise the data and information deriving from audits to pressurise the Member States performing under the global average.

At the Conference of Directors-General of Civil Aviation (2006)[33] held in Montreal on 23 March 2008, the delegates decided that ICAO should publicise the summarising reports on audits and the results in tables.[34] The step of ICAO was dictated by logics. Since sovereign Member States may not be blacklisted, the basic principle of transparency was foregrounded. This served as an excellent instrument, which could persuade the Member States performing under the average by resorting to the power of publicity directly so that they should rectify the deficiencies and raise the degree of aviation safety. The Member States of ICAO rejected the blacklist and affirmed the encouragement of implementation in this form. The objective was to encourage the States under the global average to do their utmost to belong to the other half of the list, to the scope of countries performing above the global average. Of course, of the 193 Member States there will always be States under the average, which is as it should be.

The main point was that the figure of the average could approach the results of the foremost countries as closely as possible. The production of results below the average, sitting on the 'dunce's seat' names and shames the examined Member State. Everyone can see this position and mark its price; therefore, it is extremely

---

All the 152 passengers were French citizens, except for the Italian citizen who had organised the journey.

[32] ICAO Assembly Resolution A35-6 USOAP/CSA.

[33] ICAO Doc 9866 *ICAO DGCA Conference on a global strategy for aviation safety.* Report, 2006.

[34] The full report is qualified as confidential; thus, it is not completely accessible for the public. The reason is that the deficiencies therein should not be available for incompetent persons. Nevertheless, the shortened public report and its figures in tables provide plentiful information for experts. On the website it is possible to compare the results of other countries, and infer to the safety standards of the given region or Member State. *Integrated Safety Trend Analysis and Reporting System* (iSTARS). www.icao.int/Meetings/APSD-HLPF17/Documents/iSTARS flyer donor profile FINAL.pdf (icao.int).

important to budge from this place. This necessitates making massive efforts, which should be based on professional commitment and political will. We need to be aware of the fact that the performers of the aviation industry already know everything about one another. Today the degree of the supervisory capacity of the Member States or the level of the preparedness of the civil aviation authority of the given State is no secret any longer. It suffices to have a look at the public results of an ICAO audit, to cast a glance at the summarising table issued by ICAO or by another international organisation. It does not suffice to pretend professionalism, in this system talking big is not appreciated, since you cannot argue with or twist the facts.

4.10.3 The Continuous Monitoring Audit Programme (2010–)

In possession of experiences, the system of examination needed to be further developed. The USOAP programme, although, it was obligatory and every performer could be audited at least twice and re-examined, had a deficiency. Audits could ensue only after five to six years' intervals, which worsened efficiency and reduced the commitment of the Member States. Therefore, at the 36th Assembly of ICAO (2007),[35] the Member States, after reforming the USOAP system, adopted the Continuous Monitoring Programme (CMP). The introduction of the new procedure ensued on 1 January 2013, subsequently to securing a two years' transitional period.

The new procedure terminated the former practice, in which audits took place in two stages.[36] First, the full audit was carried out, which consisted in the comprehensive examination of the aviation safety supervisory capacity of the Member States. Then, the follow-up audit ensued, during which the experts of ICAO examined the implementation of corrective measures. Subsequently, no control took place for a long time. It is no wonder that after the closure of the audit a lot of performers laid back, and due to an attitude of biding their time, they did not do their utmost to rectify the faults despite the opportunity for Member States to send the partial results of corrective measures to ICAO for validation between the two audits. If ICAO found the correction justified and accepted it, the audit result was modified accordingly, thereby, the public result of the Member State improved. Nevertheless, the Member States did not concern themselves about the urgent correction of the faults, which ICAO attributed to the fact that there was no entity in charge of this new and special area.

[35] ICAO Assembly Resolution A37-5, the USOAP Continuous Monitoring Approach (CMA). October 2010.

[36] ICAO Doc 9735 *Universal Safety Oversight Audit Programme Continuous Monitoring Manual.* 4th edn., 2014.; ICAO Doc 9734 *Safety Oversight Manual* (Parts A, B) and *Oversight Manual* (Part C). Part A, 2nd edn., 2006; Part B, 2nd edn., 2011 and Part C, 1st edn., 2007.

Learning from experience, ICAO demanded the designation of a *national coordinator* under bilateral agreements concluded with the Member States for carrying out the audits. The main tasks of the national coordinator are the organisation of the implementation of the measure plan prepared via the operation of the supervisory system of the Member State for the correction of the deficiencies revealed during the so-called Continuous Monitoring Approach (CMA) and drafting reports to ICAO and other Member States about the status of the implementation of the measure plan via questionnaires demonstrating constantly the current circumstances. Via the activity all Member States are continuously controlled. In the area of aviation safety spectacular results, achievements cannot be attained, therefore, no prominent performance or swiftly worsening status is discerned, only continuously changing processes. There is no stagnation, only constant change, in which, if the indicator is not increasing, it is in decline. Improvement can be achieved via steady performance and work. An extremely important institution of this process is the Continuous Monitoring Programme, the reports and corrective measures of which are in all cases public and the results can be continuously monitored on the website of ICAO.

In this system the examined Member States are differentiated in three categories:

- the most auspicious category (non-compliance is under 30%);
- the moderate category (non-compliance is between 30% and 50%);
- the least auspicious category (non-compliance is above 50%).

Due to its constancy, the Continuous Monitoring Programme supports the objective control of the capacity of the State to appropriately implement the international safety requirements and prescriptions determined by ICAO. Its significance is rendered by the constant pressurising of Member States and the encouragement of the more efficient distribution of resources, while it provides a solution with guaranteed results in the long term. The CMA is a versatile and complex system, the significance of which is that the States are continuously audited due to the enforcement of the obligatorily applied basic principle of transparency. This entails that the efforts made in the interest of the improvement of aviation safety by the States can be continuously monitored. Due to constancy, the audit results are always up-to-date and become accessible for everyone. Thus, the CMA continuously monitors the capacity of the supervisory system of the State to appropriately guarantee the discharge of the tasks proceeding from the implementation of the requirements of aviation safety. This has a huge advantage from the viewpoint of the State, that is, under the token of regularity the State can exercise continuous self-control, it can immediately correct its determined deficiencies, and via active reporting to ICAO, the State can participate in the sharing and popularisation of aviation safety principles.

ICAO discharges the CMA-tasks in four steps. First, the audit department collects, validates and approves of the aviation safety information. Then, ICAO evaluates, and via processing the Critical Elements, it assesses in eight columns the supervisory capacity of the examined Member State. In the next step, in possession of the results, ICAO reveals and ranks the deficiencies, since the difference is measurable in the case of the determination of a 'significant safety concern' (SSC) or of a minor deficiency. Since the preponderance of the problems is different, it matters whether the issue is the absence of the complete system of supervision in an area or merely minor faults (for example, the amendment of an international agreement has not been harmonised with national law). In the case of a significant safety problem, if the Member State does not correct it before the given deadline, this is publicised by the ICAO on its public website. Finally, ICAO processes the experiences of the audit, and according to the drawn conclusions, it develops and renews its oversight system.

The CMA audit results of ICAO have great significance, since the up-to-date and objective statements have a serious impact on the judgement of the role of the examined country in international air transport. ICAO has also examined the extent to which the repeatedly controllable, electronic and paper-based audits carried out by its experts, providing consultative (explanatory) opportunity for the States contain subjective elements. This was necessitated by the informal insinuations of some Member States according to which their results deriving from the statements of the audit did not meet the expectations due to partiality and not to highly appreciated rigorousness. Anyone who has an insight into the whole audit process is aware that the system is not 100% objective, that is, there are subjective elements, however, their proportion is not worth mentioning.

An unexpected consequence of the audits was that certain ICAO Member States, which operated to geographical areas contestable from the viewpoint of aviation safety, guided by their own best interests, provided assistance to Member States producing a high extent of differences.[37] The audit results are transparent. Their display in charts in percentages (www.icao.int/safety/istars) (with no exaggeration) is a measure (an index) of the aviation industry of the ICAO Member State and symbolically is a 'business card' of State commitment.

Despite the unequalled nature of the comprehensive audit system in the modern history of aviation, the Convention observes silence about it. Its mentioning would require the amendment of the Convention, which the Member States resort to only scarcely in exceptional cases, nevertheless, the regulation of the new system of oversight having exceptional effect on the performers of international civil aviation deserves to be on the pages of the Convention. Despite these, the oversight carried out by the experts of ICAO affecting all Member States has developed into a decisively successful programme. The reasons are the commitment of the Member States and confidence in the oversight system, because it is in the best and

[37] After the accident of Garuda Indonesia (GA) Flight 200 on 7 March 2007, the Government of Australia made the decision that firstly it would support the development of aviation safety in Indonesia with an amount of 24 million Dollars within the framework of a three-year program. The support encompassed the establishment of an independent air navigation service provider, the training of air traffic control officers (ATCOs) and the organisation of search-rescue operations. Australia launched a similar programme also in Papua New Guinea. Furthermore, Belgium has provided assistance to the Democratic Republic of Congo since 2011 for the reformation of air navigation rules, education, the issue of operation-related licences and carrying out examinations. *ICAO Safety Partnership Meeting.* States' Reports, Montreal, 20 November 2012.

elementary interest of all Member States that the establishment of the highest level of aviation safety and security should be supported by external and objective examination carried out by the experts of ICAO. Drawing upon this, the organisation of ICAO has been authorised legitimately to control the supervisory activity (surveillance) of the civil aviation authority of its sovereign Member States comprehensively, to demand the implementation of rules and to apply sanctions indirectly in the event of the prevalence of deficiencies.

References

Dempsey PS (2004) Compliance & Enforcement in International Law: Achieving global uniformity in aviation safety. N C J Int Law Commer Regul 30(1):20

Huang J (2009a) Aviation Safety and ICAO. Montreal, p 55

Huang J (2009b) Aviation Safety Through the Rule of Law: ICAO's mechanisms and practices. Kluwer Law International, The Hague

Joyner CC (ed) (1997) The United Nations and International Law. ASIL and Cambridge, p 77

MacKenzie D (2010) ICAO: a History of the International Civil Aviation Organization. Toronto, p 11

Mortimer LF (1984) New ICAO Rules considered for Long-range Twin-engine Aeroplane flights. ICAO Bulletin 39

Sagan C (1980) Carl Sagan, Science Populariser, Star-Gazer and Intellectual Gadfly Talked with Roger Bingham. New Scientist 85, no. 1190, pp 152–154

Shawcross CN, Beaumont KM (1951) Air Law. 2nd edn., London, p 34

Sipos A (Rev.) (2023) Milde's International Air Law and ICAO. 4th edn., Eleven International Publishing, The Hague, pp 157–158

Sochor E (1991) The Politics of International Aviation. MacMillan Press, p 156

Szentnémedy F (1933) A repülés (Aviation). Magyar Szemle Társaság, Budapest

Chapter 5
Aviation Security

Nearly all paragraphs of the Chicago Convention concern aviation safety and its wide-scale accomplishment. At the same time, the Convention barely mentions aviation security. Moreover, the word '*security*'—in a completely different sense—appears only once[1] in the provisions of the Convention, although aviation security following safety figures is the second most significant strategic pillar and a constant challenge for ICAO. Today it is barely conceivable but, at the time of drafting the Convention, issues of security did not generate special concern in the world of civil aviation. At that time nobody could seriously envisage that one day terrorists would hijack airplanes or use them as weapons, or unruly passengers would cause everyday problems. Therefore, the contracting States, bypassing the amendment of the Convention, regulated security constituting a prominent area of civil aviation under Annex 17, taking effect in the summer of 1975.[2]

Aviation safety and security, despite their close relationship, differ from each other fundamentally. Although in both areas the dual purpose of the contracting States has been preventing or averting danger and thereby saving lives as well as protecting property, we are dealing with two sharply distinct areas.

- Aviation *safety* means a system of capabilities, owing to which the performers in the industry can react effectively and competently to eventual emergencies related to operation and upkeep, as a result of which no accidents or incidents occur. (Due to the fact that safety is never 100%, from a practical viewpoint it is more pragmatic to use the phrase 'no avoidable or as few as possible accidents or incidents occur'.)[3]

---

[1] See, in the Preamble of the Chicago Convention: '. . .yet its abuse can become a threat to the general security'.

[2] ICAO Annex 17 on Security was adopted by the ICAO Council in March 1974. ICAO Annex 17 on Security – Safeguarding International Civil Aviation Against Acts of Unlawful Interference. 11th edn., March 2020.

[3] Wassenbergh (1998), p. 83.

A. Sipos, *International Aviation Law*, https://doi.org/10.1007/978-3-031-39066-1_5

- Aviation *security* is a system of capabilities, due to which the performers of the industry can provide effective and competent protection to aircraft on the ground or in the air, to the passengers and crew members on board the aircraft or on the grounds of airports, to the ground staff and third persons on the ground vis-à-vis unlawful acts endangering their security.

Unlawful acts include all acts or attempts committed by a person endangering the security of international civil aviation. Such acts include unlawful seizure, sabotage, taking hostages, violent intrusion (on board, at the airport, or in an air navigation facility) and the placement of weapons, a dangerous tool or material for the purpose of the commission of a crime.[4] Furthermore, what frequently occur are threats of bomb attacks, imparting misleading, false information or refusing to cooperate with staff during the flight.

It is broadly accepted that recourse to safety and security as a marketing tool is inadmissible. This is justified when the presumption of air safety and security in general are designed to be undermined, in addition, the presumption that a particular airline is safer than others or the presumption of danger aboard become a matter of competition. According to protocol, any airline may designate itself safe or secure, however, not safer or more secure.

Beyond the difference between the notions, aviation safety prevails via the completion of mainly international and transparent regulatory tasks, while aviation security, although its effect is global, consists primarily of tasks of protection to be tackled nationally. The system of rules of aviation safety is accessible and knowable for everyone, whereas the security rules constitute a closed system, excluding access to the internal confidential information for those not concerned. However, the safety and security of international civil aviation may only be effective if these two prominent areas cooperate continually and support each other unconditionally.

5.1 The Tokyo Convention (1963)

Although in the early phase of aviation unlawful acts against staff, or devices used during flights also occurred, no social demand prevailed for their international regulation due to their isolated character and low number.[5] In our days, the presence

---

[4]The enumeration is not complete. Several crimes and criminal conducts will be introduced, which are atypical and occur in cumulative offences or have become relevant for criminal law as new commission conducts.

[5]Jacques Charles (1746–1823), a French inventor and mathematician released a (pilotless) balloon filled with hydrogen, the lightest gas (with 14.4 times less density than air) for the first time in the world on 26 August 1783, which, after one of its successful landings, was destroyed by the startled inhabitants of the settlement of Gonesse guided by their terror of the device. Later, the name of Gonesse near Paris was written in black in the history of civil aviation, since it was its territory on which a Concorde, a supersonic airplane of Air France crashed on 25 July 2000. Lechter (2003), pp. 35–36.

of people in the air has become constant; it is therefore not accidental that, along with the incessantly growing number of passengers, the number of unlawful acts committed on board aircraft has also increased. Although, the States had applied developed punishment systems as early as at the beginning of the twentieth century, none of them could effectively respond to the challenges of international air traffic. The acts committed on board the aircraft, their increasingly and obviously unique situation and peculiar management coerced the rule maker to take a different approach. Undoubtedly, any minor, insignificant act occurring with various frequencies and committed on board an aircraft in flight (e.g., smoking despite prohibition, fighting or verbal harassment) has a great impact on aviation safety, however, its gravity clearly differs from similar acts committed on the ground. Moreover, at an altitude of 10 km (33,000 feet), unlawful acts committed on board aircraft overflying the sovereign airspace of various countries raise several issues, the solution of which on an international level became inevitable. For instance, during the enforcement of the territorial principle, it was difficult to determine in which country's airspace the crime was committed and, due to this uncertainty, which country could be entitled to proceed against the perpetrator of the crime. It also occurred that the country having jurisdiction did not conduct the criminal proceedings or did not request the extradition of the perpetrator.[6] In the worst scenario, States could not proceed in the absence of jurisdiction, and therefore, the perpetrator's crime remained unpunished.

Although jurists had dealt with the criminal legal aspects of unlawful acts committed on aircraft from the 1910s, the first comprehensive response was formulated in 1963 under the first international treaty dealing with aviation security.[7] The *Convention on Offences and Certain Other Acts Committed on Board Aircraft*, adopted in Tokyo[8] under the auspices of ICAO, was framed as a result of ten-year concerted work by the international community. In the Convention, the international community as a whole responded with proper determination primarily to *international terrorism* as the gravest danger, threatening civil aviation and damaging its interests.

The Tokyo Convention shall apply to offences against penal law of the contracting States as well as to acts which, whether or not they are offences, may or do jeopardise the safety of the aircraft or of persons or property therein or which jeopardise good order and discipline on board irrespective of whether the acts qualify as crime pursuant to the national rules of substantive criminal law of the contracting States [Article 1 (1) *a)–b)*]. The essence of the Convention is contained in this provision, since the wide-scale extension of the substantive scope of

In March 1784 Jean-Pierre Blanchard (1753–1809) a pioneer in gas balloon flight was compelled by a young man named Dupont de Chambon with a sword to take him into the clouds. The attempt was thwarted by reason of the application of physical strength. Encyclopaedia Britannica. New York, 11th edn., 1910, p. 264.

[6]Mankiewicz (1971), pp. 195–196.

[7]Shubber (1973), p. 5.

[8]ICAO Doc 8364 Tokyo Convention on Offences and Certain Other Acts Committed on Board Aircraft (1963).

application facilitates holding anyone responsible for any act jeopardising aviation safety as an objective to be protected to the utmost by all contracting States.

The Convention has fulfilled its most important objective, since it unified and standardised the legal relationships that needed to be regulated on the international level. This was absolutely urgent, since in the early days of commercial aviation there were several examples of unlawful acts severely jeopardising safety on board the aircraft where the perpetrator was not called to account under criminal law due to the deficiencies of relevant national rules.

In the *United States versus Cordova*[9] lawsuit, the defendant could not be prosecuted due to the absence of jurisdiction. On 2 August 1948, a scuffle broke out on board a United States registered DC-4 passenger plane travelling from the capital of Puerto Rico, San Juan (SJU) to New York (LGA) between the heavily inebriated Mr. Cordova and the cabin crew in the tail of the plane while it was flying above the (high seas of the) Atlantic Ocean. Due to the weight of the flight attendants and passengers hastening to help to restrain Mr. Cordova, the airplane became tail-heavy. Thanks to the rapid interference of the pilots, the resulting loss of altitude and speed could be corrected and the unruly passenger, restricted in his personal freedom, waited for landing and his transfer to the authorities. The accused, whose culpability was beyond doubt, was committed for trial, but he could not be prosecuted under the federal law then in force, since, in the event of a crime committed on the high seas, the court of the United States only had jurisdiction if the crime was committed on board a ship registered by US authorities, so the case had to be dismissed.[10]

5.1.1 Jurisdiction

The contracting Parties to the Tokyo Convention settled the above-mentioned deficiencies deriving from diverse national rules and dealt with the issue of jurisdiction with high priority. The establishment of the system of the institutions of jurisdiction was carried out along the principle that the criminal liability of natural entities under international law due to an infringement of the rules of international law could be prosecuted and punished by the State in the territory of which the crime was committed. With respect to the fact that national penal codes primarily apply the territorial principle, its enforcement was not impeded by a legal obstacle.

As a main rule, 'the State of registration of the aircraft is competent to exercise jurisdiction over offences and acts committed on board' jeopardising safety [Article

---

[9] *United States v. Cordova,* US District Court E.D. New York, 1950.89 F. Supp. 298.

[10] Havel and Sanchez (2014), p. 185.

3 (1)]. The contracting Parties demand that 'each contracting State shall take such measures as may be necessary to establish its jurisdiction as the State of registration over offences committed on board aircraft registered in such State' [Article 3 (2)]. The purpose of the contracting Parties was to prevent the lack of jurisdiction as a consequence of the lack of State sovereignty while flying over the high seas (as a territory to be freely used by all). Therefore, the Convention needs to be applied 'in respect of offences committed or acts done by a person on board any aircraft registered in a contracting State while that aircraft is in flight or on the surface of the high seas or of any other area outside the territory of any State' [Article 1 (2)]. This also entails that *exclusive jurisdiction* is only applicable with respect to the registering State if the registered aircraft is flying over the high seas or Antarctica. This way, the contracting Parties created a situation in which the people on board are subject to the jurisdiction of at least two States (one securing its national airspace and the State of registration) at the same time. 'Offences committed on aircraft registered in a contracting State shall be treated, for the purpose of extradition, as if they had been committed not only in the place in which they have occurred but also in the territory of the State of registration of the aircraft' [Article 16 (1)].

However, it is not at all unlikely that not only 'the State of the flag' and the State of the national airspace, but other States also have jurisdiction vis-à-vis the perpetrator of the crime. The equitable interest of the States to avail themselves their rights is narrowly constructed and guaranteed as an exception by the Convention. As such, a specific State may have jurisdiction if:

a) 'the offence has effect on the territory of such State;
b) the offence has been committed by or against a national or permanent resident of such State;
c) the offence is against the security of such State;
d) the offence consists of a breach of any rules or regulations relating to the flight or manoeuvre of aircraft in force in such State;
e) the exercise of jurisdiction is necessary to ensure the observance of any obligation of such State under a multilateral international agreement' (Article 4).

The contracting Parties also grant jurisdiction to the 'State of first landing', provided that the aircraft commander may 'disembark in the territory of any State in which the aircraft lands any person who he has reasonable grounds to believe has committed, or is about to commit on board the aircraft' an offence (Article 8). At the same time, 'the aircraft commander may deliver to the competent authorities of any contracting State in the territory of which the aircraft lands any person who he has reasonable grounds to believe has committed on board the aircraft an act which, in his opinion, is a serious offence according to the penal law of the State of registration of the aircraft'. Related to this fact the aircraft commander shall notify the authorities of such State of his intention to deliver such person and shall furnish the authorities to whom any suspected offender is delivered with evidence and information (which are lawfully in his possession) under the law of the State of registration of the aircraft (Article 9).

While establishing a broad scale of forums of jurisdiction, the contracting Parties were attentive to the legal preferences manifest in the major legal regimes:

- to the Anglo-Saxon (common law) legal system, which favours the *territorial principle*, according to which the proceedings should be conducted in the country where the act was committed (over which the aircraft was flying); and
- to the Continental (civil law) legal system, which favours the *personal principle*, according to which the close relation of citizenship between the State and its citizen requires that the person (in the present case the passenger) has to observe the law of their State, even in the territory of another State.

The resolution of the vast differences between the two basic systems of law under international treaties and in debates presented a major challenge and frequently qualified as a great achievement. Beyond the reconciliation of differences, we need to consider the fact that international law cannot and does not intend to regulate everything, but it grants frameworks, and therefore, national law has an indispensable role as expressly permitted by the contracting Parties. The Tokyo Convention formulates clearly that it 'does not exclude any criminal jurisdiction exercised in accordance with national law' [Article 3 (3)].

Let us presume that, on board an Austrian Airlines aircraft registered in Austria in flight from Vienna (VIE) to Madrid (MAD), a Czech and a Dutch passenger commence to scuffle in Swiss airspace. The Dutch passenger is severely injured and, following the entry of the airplane into French airspace, the injured party loses consciousness. The aircraft commander decides to interrupt the flight and lands on French territory. Related to the case, several rivalling jurisdictions emerge. According to the main rule, the registering State, Austria, may have jurisdiction on the basis of the *principle of the flag* (quasi territorial principle). Furthermore, a claim for jurisdiction may also be submitted on the basis of the *territorial principle (principium territoriale)* by Switzerland and France; the latter may invoke *the principle of the first landing*, but the intention of the Czech Republic and the Netherlands to lodge a criminal action may also be recognised on the basis of the *personal principle (principium personale)* as well. Finally, Spain, as the *place of destination,* may also request the recognition of its jurisdiction with reference to its national rules.

The example vividly demonstrates that a combined system of jurisdictions was introduced.[11] The objective is unambiguous: it is better if multiple jurisdictions need to be applied than none. At the same time, it is important to highlight that although the contracting Parties itemise taxatively the possibilities of the enforcement of jurisdiction (Articles 1, 3–4, 8–9), they omit guidance as to which of the rivalling jurisdictions has priority. If several rivalling claims for jurisdiction exist, it is

[11] Gutierrez (1965), pp. 3–4.

essentially the circumstances that determine which of the authorised parties is recognised as the best and the safest to adjudicate the case. The body proceeding in the case is obliged to accept the support and intervention of the other parties authorised for jurisdiction. To guarantee legal certainty, the proceeding authorities should be highly attentive to the non-commencement of parallel proceedings, because that would injure one of the most important general principles of criminal law, the prohibition of dual proceedings *(ne bis in idem).*[12]

5.1.2 The Competence of the Aircraft Commander

In the interest of the uniform safeguarding of aviation security beyond the issues of jurisdiction, the contracting Parties paid close attention to the rights and obligations of the aircraft commander. The aircraft commander (pilot-in-command or captain) is the member of the specialised staff with special authorisation appointed by the aircraft operator for the standard and safe attendance to the tasks of flight and operation. The aircraft commander [even if the first officer (co-pilot) navigates the plane][13] is authorised and simultaneously obligated to guarantee security on board the aircraft and make a final decision on all issues related to operation. While in flight, the commander is entitled to deviate from the rules, if that is unquestionably essential and reasonable in the interest of security.

The commander directs the crew members of the aircraft. The Convention is to be applied in the event of crime or unlawful acts committed on board the aircraft in flight.[14] The aircraft commander may, when he has reasonable grounds to believe that a person has committed, or is about to commit, an offence or other act on board the aircraft, impose reasonable measures, including restraint, upon that person. The objective of such measures is to protect the safety of the aircraft, or of persons and property therein; to maintain good order and discipline on board; or to enable the aircraft commander to deliver that person to the competent authorities or to disembark him [Article 6 (1)].

In the interest of the earliest restoration of order and discipline on board, the resolute intervention of the crew, and depending on the evolved situation, of the

---

[12]No one shall be liable to be tried or punished again for an offence for which he has already been finally convicted or acquitted in accordance with the law and penal procedure of each country. UN International Covenant on Civil and Political Rights (ICCPR), adopted and opened for signature, ratification and accession by General Assembly Resolution 2200A (XXI) of 16 December 1966, entered into force on 23 March 1976 [Article 14 (7)].

[13]First officers (co-pilots) are fully qualified to operate the plane in all regimes of flight, and they perform just as many take-offs and landings as captains do. Pilots take turns at the controls. The captain (pilot-in-command) has ultimate authority over the flight. Smith (2018), p. 83.

[14]'For the purposes of the Convention, an aircraft is considered to be in flight from the moment when power is applied for the purpose of take-off until the moment when the landing run ends' [Tokyo Convention, Article 1 (3)].

passengers may be necessary vis-à-vis unlawful acts. The aircraft commander may *require* or authorise the assistance of other crew members and may *request* or authorise, but not require, the assistance of passengers to restrain any person he is entitled to restrain (by tying up, shackling or holding down). 'Any crew member or passenger may also take reasonable preventive measures without such authorisation when he has reasonable grounds to believe that such action is immediately necessary to protect the safety of the aircraft, or of persons or property therein' [Article 6 (2)].

The treaty-maker endeavours to encourage this frequently indispensable intervention by guaranteeing exemption (from liability under criminal, civil and administrative law) for all conduct, aimed at the restitution of order, that would qualify as unlawful conduct under normal circumstances. 'For actions taken in accordance with the Convention, the aircraft commander, any other member of the crew, any passenger, the owner or operator of the aircraft, or the person on whose behalf the flight was performed shall not be held responsible in any proceeding on account of the treatment undergone by the person against whom the actions were taken' (Article 10).

The aircraft commander is not only entitled to restrain personal freedom on board the airplane via the application of measures, but he may also disembark the person having committed or about to commit an unlawful act in the territory of any contracting State. The aircraft commander shall notify the authorities in advance, may deliver the offender and shall provide evidence and information concerning the fact of and the reasons for the disruption of the flight and disembarkation to the competent authorities of the contracting State (Articles 8–9). At the same time, 'any contracting State shall allow the commander of an aircraft registered in another contracting State to disembark any person' (Article 12). 'In taking any measures for investigation or arrest or otherwise exercising jurisdiction in connection with any offence committed on board an aircraft, the contracting States shall pay due regard to the safety and other interests of air navigation and shall so act as to avoid unnecessary delay of the aircraft, passengers, crew or cargo' (Article 17).

In summary, the aircraft commander has the right to maintain good order and discipline on board:

- to restrain reasonably any persons on board;
- to require crew members to take action to restrain an unruly passenger;
- to request fellow passengers to assist to restrain an unruly passenger;
- to disembark a passenger having committed or about to commit an unlawful act;
- to deliver a person to the competent authorities in the territory of any contracting State.

In practice, the pilot-in-command has to fulfil numerous obligations related to security; he is thus not only obligated to take all the necessary measures if the persons aboard or the aircraft is endangered, but also to help other endangered aircraft (or ocean liner or ship) as necessary and practicable in the given situation.

The popularity of the convention is indicated by its ratification by 187 States. This high figure can be attributed to the fact that the Tokyo Convention only reformulated the already existing international practice under an international treaty. However, the

Tokyo Convention after a while could not keep up with the changes surrounding air transport and previously unknown criminal methods, all of which required the treaty-maker to provide more developed and subtler international regulation.

5.2 The Hague (1970), Montreal (1971), New York (1979) and Montreal (1991) Conventions and the Montreal Protocol (1988)

Mainly due to the strained political ambience related to the Cold War, the number of hijacks rose dramatically from the late 1960s onwards. According to statistics, the pinnacle of hijacks was between 1968 and 1972 (because of hijacked aircraft registered in the US alone, more than 130 interventions were necessary). The most hijacks in the history of civil aviation occurred in 1969, on 86 occasions.[15] Although the objective of terrorists was not the destroyal of the aircraft, but being granted political asylum or the liberation of others, these terrorist acts left behind many victims. By seizing the aircraft and becoming the focus of the attention of the international public, the usually armed terrorists manifested their will and endeavoured to achieve their political objectives. These included requesting asylum in a country designated by the terrorists or demanding the release of prisoners convicted for political or other reasons, taking hostages and receiving financial or other benefits. Seizing or taking control of an in-flight aircraft is always distressing since it endangers the safety of persons and property, seriously disrupts air traffic and undermines the confidence of the public in the security of civil aviation. Therefore, with a view to driving back the criminal practice of using aircraft as an instrument for unlawful purposes, the international community held a diplomatic conference in The Hague in December 1970. The conference, organised by ICAO, was concluded by the ratification of the *Convention for the Suppression of Unlawful Seizure of Aircraft.*[16]

Pursuant to The Hague Convention (1970) all contracting States assumed the obligation to impose '*severe penalties*' against 'any person who on board an aircraft in flight[17] unlawfully, by force or threat thereof, or by any other form of intimidation *seizes*, or exercises control of that aircraft' (Articles 1–2). The contracting Parties

[15] In our days this occurs very rarely; in 2013, 2015 and 2017 such a crime did not occur at all. Morris, Hugh: The strangest stories from the golden age of plane hijacking. *Travel News Editor*, 5 July 2019. (www.telegraph.co.uk/travel).

[16] ICAO Doc 8920 Convention for the Suppression of Unlawful Seizure of Aircraft. The Hague, 6 December 1970.

[17] 'For the purposes of the Convention, an aircraft is considered to be in flight at any time from the moment when all its external doors are closed following embarkation until the moment when any such door is opened for disembarkation. In the case of a forced landing, the flight shall be deemed to continue until the competent authorities take over the responsibility for the aircraft and for the persons and property on board' [Article 3 (1)].

envisage severe penalties, while the lowest penalties are subject to national jurisdiction and facilitate the exercise of criminal jurisdiction in accordance with national law [Article 4 (3)].

The rules related to the exercise of jurisdiction basically complied with those of the Tokyo Convention, whereas, the contracting Parties secured a further forum besides the existing ones. The Hague Convention extends jurisdiction to the State of the operator of the aircraft. Due to the features of the aviation industry, the State of registration is in many cases different from the State of the operator. The main reasons for this include the increasingly extensive use of leased airplanes, while the institution of forum shopping is popular with aircraft operators. Thus, with respect to any act of violence committed by the alleged offender vis-à-vis the passengers or the crew members, 'when the offence is committed on board an aircraft leased without crew, that State in which the lessee has his principal place of business has jurisdiction or, if the lessee has no such place of business, his permanent residence, in that State' [Article 4 (1) *c)*].

Apart from the introduction of the new forum of jurisdiction, the contracting Parties tightened the freedom of the State with jurisdiction to proceed: if the contracting State in the territory of which the alleged offender has been arrested does not extradite the alleged offender, it shall take such measures as may be necessary to establish its *universal jurisdiction* over the offence, 'whether or not the offence was committed in its territory, and to submit the case to its competent authorities for the purpose of prosecution' (Article 7). Therefore, via the consistent observance of the *aut dedere, aut judicare* (either extradite or prosecute) principle, the perpetrator either needs to be extradited to a State that shall conduct the criminal proceedings or needs to be punished in the State in which he is held; a third way is not applicable. The objective of the contracting Parties is explicit: the States may not provide asylum to the perpetrators; their punishment, being the enemies of humankind *(hostis humani generis)*, is inevitable. Therefore, The Hague Convention provides the greatest measure of mutual assistance among States in the criminal proceedings (Article 10). The contracting State needs to report promptly to the ICAO Council any relevant information on the circumstances of the offence and the measures taken (Article 11).

Because of the alarming proliferation of unlawful acts, in parallel with and almost copying The Hague Convention, with the involvement of ICAO, the *Convention for the Suppression of Unlawful Acts against the Safety of Civil Aviation* was framed as the Montreal Convention, adopted in 1971.[18] The Montreal Convention (1971) prescribes the punishment of acts jeopardising the security and safety of aircraft and the infrastructure of ground air navigation service providers. Considering that unlawful acts against the safety of civil aviation jeopardise the safety of persons and property, seriously affect the operation of air services, and undermine the confidence of the peoples of the world in the safety of civil aviation, the contracting Parties

[18]ICAO Doc 8966 Convention for the Suppression of Unlawful Acts against the Safety of Civil Aviation. Montreal, 23 September 1971.

enumerate taxatively the broad scope of the methods of terrorist acts infringing the safety of air transport.

Under the Convention, 'any person commits an offence if he unlawfully and intentionally:

a) performs an act of violence against a person on board an aircraft in flight if that act is likely to endanger the safety of that aircraft; or
b) destroys an aircraft in service or causes damage to such an aircraft which renders it incapable of flight or which is likely to endanger its safety in flight; or
c) places or causes to be placed on an aircraft in service, by any means whatsoever, a device or substance which is likely to destroy that aircraft, or to cause damage to it which renders it incapable of flight, or to cause damage to it which is likely to endanger its safety in flight; or
d) destroys or damages air navigation facilities or interferes with their operation, if any such act is likely to endanger the safety of aircraft in flight; or
e) communicates information which he knows to be false, thereby endangering the safety of an aircraft in flight' [Article 1 (1) *a)–e)*].

In comparison with The Hague Convention, the basic difference was the shift of the central element of the perpetrator's conduct from seizing the aircraft to rendering it incapable of flying.

The main provisions of the Montreal Convention (1971) concerning civil airports were extended by the Montreal Protocol (1988).[19] The *Protocol for the Suppression of Unlawful Acts of Violence at Airports Serving International Civil Aviation,* in comparison with the Montreal Convention, extended the conducts to be criminalised by acts (probably) jeopardising the safety of airports serving international civil aviation. The Protocol was drawn up following the simultaneous terrorist attacks against the airports of Rome and Vienna on 27 December 1985.[20] This Protocol supplements the *Convention for the Suppression of Unlawful Acts against the Safety of Civil Aviation;* therefore, the Convention and the Protocol shall be read and interpreted together as one single instrument (Article 1). [Remark: As between the States Parties, the *Beijing Convention on the Suppression of Unlawful Acts Relating to International Civil Aviation* (2010) shall prevail over the previous international contracts, that is, the Montreal Convention (1971) and its Protocol (1988) (Article 24)].

The ink had not dried on the Montreal Convention pertaining to security when the trend in the seizure of aircraft became incidental to taking hostages from among the

[19] ICAO Doc 9518 Protocol for the Suppression of Unlawful Acts of Violence at Airports Serving International Civil Aviation, Supplementary to the Convention for the Suppression of Unlawful Acts against the Safety of Civil Aviation. Montreal, 23 September 1971.

[20] At the Leonardo da Vinci Airport in Rome (FCO) four armed terrorists fired at the passengers waiting at the counter of the Israeli Airline (EL AL). At the Schwechat Airport in Vienna (VIE) 3 armed terrorists fired shots also at the counter of the Israeli Airline and flung a hand grenade into the waiting crowd. In the attacks 17 innocent people lost their lives and 117 people were injured. The Pittsburgh Press: *Terrorist raid 2 Europe airports*. Vol. 102, No. 184, 27 December 1985, p. 1.

civil aviation passengers. Drawing on their experience, terrorists realised that it was simpler and less risky to seize a passenger airplane and threaten the governments with exterminating the hostages than kidnapping figures symbolising the given regime (for example a protected person or an important businessman). The perpetrators, in return for the hostages, demanded the release of convicts (frequently political prisoners) or, according to the citizenship of the hostages, demanded the States concerned to fulfil political demands or several times to grant financial or other benefits.

Hijacking

On 13 October 1977 the terrorists of the Popular Front for the Liberation of Palestine hijacked the Boeing 737-200 operated by Lufthansa, the German airline on route between Palma de Mallorca (PMI) and Frankfurt (FRA). The Flight 181 was flying over Marseilles, in French airspace when two male and two female perpetrators armed with hand grenades and pistols seized control. The airplane first landed in Rome, then over the next 5 days, for the purpose of constant mobility, it touched down at several international airports such as Larnaca, Bahrein, Dubai, Aden and Mogadischu. The leader of the hijackers, named Zohair Youssif Akache, identifying himself as 'Captain Martyr Mahmud', came to the fore with his demands: the release of 10 imprisoned leaders of the far-left Red Army Fraction (RAF) and of their two other faithful comrades imprisoned in Turkey, furthermore, that they should be given 15 million dollars. During their stay in South Yemen, the terrorists executed the pilot-in-command of the airplane.

Vis-a-vis the hijackers, the German Government put its Bundesgrenzschutz GSG-9 commando unit into action, formed after the hostage drama terminated in bloodshed at the 1972 Olympics in Munich. The operation with the cover name 'Feuerzauber' (Magic Fire) took place in Mogadishu in Somalia. The country's President, Sziad Barre (1919–1995) consented to the mission to be carried out, while the German Chancellor Helmut Schmidt (1918–2015) assumed complete responsibility for its outcome. While Somalian soldiers set fire to the runway in front of the cockpit as a distraction, simultaneously, the German and British SAS (Special Air Service) commando units blew open the doors and threw intoxicating and noise grenades into the passenger compartment, then after entering it, they opened fire. The special tactical operation met with complete success after 5 min and all the hostages were released physically unharmed.[21]

The international community, in the interest of the security of civil aviation, concluded a new international treaty: the *International Convention against the*

[21] Lufthansa Flight 181. Updates on 22 November 2022. (www.alchetron.com/Lufthansa-Flight-181).

Taking of Hostages, which was adopted by the contracting States in New York in 1979.[22] 'Anyone who seizes or detains and threatens to kill, to injure or to continue to detain another person in order to compel a third party, namely, a State, an intergovernmental organization, a natural or juridical person, or a group of persons, to do or abstain from doing any act as an explicit or implicit condition for the release of the hostage commits the offence of taking of hostages' [Article 1 (1)]. 'Any person who attempts to commit an act of hostage-taking, or participates as an accomplice of anyone who commits or attempts to commit an act of hostage-taking likewise commits an offence' [Article 1 (2)].

'Each State Party shall take such measures as may be necessary to establish its jurisdiction over any of the offences committed:

a) in its territory or on board a ship or aircraft registered in that State;
b) by any of its nationals or, if that State considers it appropriate, by those Stateless persons who have their habitual residence in its territory;
c) in order to compel that State to do or abstain from doing any act; or
d) with respect to a hostage who is a national of that State, if that State considers it appropriate' [Article 5 (1) *a)–d)*].

If 'the circumstances so warrant, any State Party in the territory of which the alleged offender is present shall, in accordance with its laws, take him into custody or take other measures to ensure his presence for such time as is necessary to enable any criminal or extradition proceedings to be instituted. That State Party shall immediately make a preliminary inquiry into the facts. The custody or other measures shall be notified without delay directly or through the Secretary General of the United Nations' [Article 6 (1–2)].

As the 1980s wore on, it seemed that the Tokyo Convention (1963), The Hague Convention (1970), the Montreal (1971) and New York (1979) Conventions, joined by the Montreal Protocol (1988) had encompassed the complete area of civil aviation from the viewpoint of criminal law. Unfortunately, that was not the case. On 21 December 1988, above the Scottish town of Lockerbie, Pan Am Flight 103 suddenly disappeared from the radar screen due to the explosion of 312 grammes of Semtex plastic explosive.[23] The plastic explosive annihilating the airplane had been placed by Libyan terrorists. Subsequently, the Libyan government assumed responsibility for the manoeuvre and paid 10 million USD as compensation for each victim.[24] In response to the situation, namely, the significant increase in the number of sabotage actions against airplanes during the 1980s,[25] the Legal Committee of

[22] International Convention against the Taking of Hostages, 34th Sess., Supp. No. 46, at 245, U.N. Doc. A/34/46 1979; UN Doc A/Res/34/146.

[23] Semtex is an extraordinarily dangerous and powerful explosive developed in Czechoslovakia in the 1960s. It is difficult to find, dogs cannot smell it, X-Ray does not detect it, the density of the material is low; finally, it is plastic and heat and water resistant. It can be used for 20 years. Glenn (1990), p. A15.

[24] Seenan, Gerard: Lockerbie Deal to End Libya's Isolation. *The Guardian*, 15 August 2003.

[25] In 1985, 13 sabotage actions caused the death of 473 people, while in 1989, 279 people fell victim to such offences. (www.unodc.org/pdf/crime/terrorism/Commonwealth_Chapter_11.pdf).

ICAO drafted a *Convention on the Marking of Plastic Explosives for the Purpose of Detection*. The Convention was adopted by ICAO Member States on 1 March 1991 in Montreal.[26]

The Convention does not apply to the 'authorities of a State Party performing military or police functions' [Article III (2)]. The main objective of the treaty-makers was that the Member States banned and prevented the production and distribution of unmarked explosives (without chemical fingerprints) so that unauthorised persons could not have access to them. The technical supplement to the Convention contains a detailed description of plastic explosives, their marking material and molecular formulae as well as the minimum concentration of markings, thereby assisting unified and concerted State intervention for driving back the use of such explosives.[27] In principle, each Party shall take the necessary measures to ensure that the existing stock of unmarked explosives are in due course destroyed or consumed, marked or rendered permanently ineffective (within a period of three years from the entry into force of the Convention for private devices, for military or police functions within 15 years) (Article IV).

5.3 The Modernisation of the International Aviation Security Treaties

Following the adoption of the Explosives Convention, no convention was drawn up in the area of criminal law related to international air traffic for nearly 20 years. However, the twenty-first century offered new morals and shocks. Civil air transport had to face unprecedented acts of mass violence: the tragic events of 11 September 2001 with the loss of 2977 lives in the United States and the airplanes exploded by suicidal assassins on 24 August 2004 in Russia shattered the world and its assumptions, which revised our views on the safety of aviation for good reason. The Man Portable Air Defence Systems (MANPADS) also present serious risks and threats for civil aviation, as due to the first reported attack,[28] there were more than 40 civilian victims on an aircraft hit by MANPADS, causing about 28 crashes and more than 800 deaths worldwide.[29] The conventions adopted in the

[26] The international treaty is also called: MEX Convention (or 'Explosives Convention'). ICAO Doc 9571 Convention on the Marking of Plastic Explosives for the Purpose of Detection. Montreal, 1 March 1991. The Convention entered into force on 21 June 1998.

[27] Consequently, the Czech manufacturer currently produces Semtex, the plastic explosive so that its detection should be easier and the duration of its usability should be shorter. (www.explosia.cz/en/products-2/explosives/special-application-explosives, Special applications explosives).

[28] In Italy, in Rome at the Fuicimino (FCO) Airport on 5 September 1973 the attack targeted an EL AL flight but it was not successful as the terrorists were arrested in time.

[29] US DoT MANPADS: Combating the Threat to Global Aviation (2009–2017.state.gov/t/pm/wra/c62623.htm).

past became outdated since they were unable to rise to all the challenges affecting the security of air transport.[30]

5.3.1 *The General Risks Convention (2009)*

A major challenge was related to compensation for persons on the ground, especially if the aircraft in flight caused damage to third persons due to unlawful conduct on board. As a modernisation of the Rome Convention on Damage Caused by Foreign Aircraft to Third Parties on the Surface (1952)[31] the Member States of ICAO adopted the Convention on Compensation for Damage Caused by Aircraft to Third Parties, the so-called *General Risks Convention* on 2 May 2009,[32] and, due to unlawful acts, the Convention on Compensation for Damage to Third Parties Resulting from Acts of Unlawful Interference Involving Aircraft, the so-called *Convention on the Compensation for Unlawful Acts.*[33] This latter convention establishes the International Civil Aviation Compensation Fund, the objective of which is the provision of a considerable amount by raising the liability limit of the aircraft operator with absolute responsibility in cases subject to the Convention. During an international flight, the operator is liable for the occurrence of death, physical injury, damage to property or the environment. The liability of the operator is restricted on the basis of the weight of the aircraft. The payment of compensation ensues via the Supplementary Compensation Mechanism. The absolute liability and the raised liability limitation encumbering the aircraft operator, as it was determined under the Convention, guarantee that the aggrieved victims of terrorists are granted higher compensation and can enforce their compensation claims more efficiently in the future [see, Part II, Chap. 14. 2].

5.3.2 *The Beijing Convention and Protocol (2010)*

In 2010, at the Diplomatic Conference on Aviation Security organised in Beijing by ICAO, two new international treaties were adopted following several years' legal

---

[30] ICAO Doc 8973 Aviation Security Manual (Restricted). Appendix 16 contains technical recommendations and procedures to minimise the risk of an aircraft hit by MANPADS.

[31] ICAO Doc 7364 Convention on Damage Caused by Foreign Aircraft to Third Parties on the Surface (1952). If the General Risk Convention takes effect, it will replace the Rome Convention.

[32] ICAO Doc 9919 Convention on Compensation for Damage Caused by Aircraft to Third Parties, done at Montreal, 2 May 2009.; Two New Treaties Adopted by International Conference on Air Law. ICAO News Release, PIO, 12 May 2009. (www.icao.int).

[33] ICAO Doc 9920 Convention on Compensation for Damage to Third Parties Resulting from Acts of Unlawful Interference Involving Aircraft. Montreal on 2 May 2009.

and diplomatic background work, for the purpose of the reform and modernisation of the system of rules governing aviation security.

- The Beijing *Convention on the Suppression of Unlawful Acts Relating to International Civil Aviation*,[34] which prevails over the Montreal Convention (1971) and its supplementary Protocol (1988), is a much more detailed uniform regulation adjusted to the requirements of the age; and
- the Beijing *Protocol Supplementary to the Convention for the Suppression of Unlawful Seizure of Aircraft*,[35] which supplements The Hague Convention (1970) by guaranteeing that legal entities are called to account and that the accessory conduct of accomplices related to the preparatory and the main act is punished.

Via these sources of law, the number of the international treaties regulating international criminal aviation law has risen to seven.[36]

The principal innovation of the Beijing Convention is the criminalisation of conducts of the modern age. Within the purview of the Beijing Convention, the acts to be punished include:

- the use of a civil aircraft as a weapon for the purpose of causing death, serious personal injury or considerable material damage;
- using a civil aircraft so that biological, chemical and nuclear (so-called BCN—Biological, Chemical, Nuclear) weapons reach their destinations with the purpose of the extermination of lives, causing injury or incurring damages;
- assault on civil aircraft using BCN weapons;
- unlawful delivery of BCN weapons using civil aircraft;
- unlawful delivery of explosives and fissionable materials by civil aircraft for terrorist purposes; and
- attack against the IT infrastructure of airports or air navigational services (Article 1).

The punishment of these unlawful acts has become even more important since the worldwide spread of the COVID-19 pandemic. The utilisation of viruses as weapons is not a novelty, we are familiar with several cases,[37] nevertheless, it has been in the focus of attention since terrorists in possession of these instruments are terribly difficult to screen and the attack produces an effect well after the commission. The contracting Parties also provide scope for the regulation of cyberattacks against IT infrastructure, which may include the communication of false information via info-

---

[34] ICAO Doc 9960 Convention on the Suppression of Unlawful Acts Relating to International Civil Aviation. Beijing. 10 September 2010. The Beijing Convention took effect on 1 July 2018.

[35] ICAO Doc 9959 Protocol Supplementary to the Convention for the Suppression of Unlawful Seizure of Aircraft. Beijing, 10 September 2010. The Beijing Protocol took effect on 1 January 2018.

[36] *ICAO Journal,* Vol. 66. (2011) No. 1, p. 8.

[37] Abeyratne (2010), p. 23.

technology or attack against airports, against air navigation service providers or in-flight aircraft via manipulative acts. Among the responses to diverse new forms of conduct, the restriction of liquids, gels and aerosols (LAGs) and the screening of instruments containing chemical and toxic materials are notable.[38]

As a further novelty, the contracting Parties render attempts at acts of commission punishable and prescribe the punishment of conduct that hinders calling the perpetrator to account [Article 1 (4) *a)–d)*]. Thus, one of the most significant changes regarding the former Conventions consists in the increased efficiency of enforcement due to the demand to call perpetrators to account. Pursuant to the Convention, the State of a national not only may, but is obligated to establish its jurisdiction and enforce its due process against the perpetrator. Furthermore, the jurisdiction of the State may also be established if the victim is a national (Article 8). The Convention shall not apply to aircraft used in military, customs or police services; it solely applies to aircraft used for international civil aviation (Article 5).

The Beijing Protocol was drafted with the intention of extending the community interests against international terrorism. The terrorist attacks of September 11th, 2001 made it abundantly clear that a civil airliner with full fuel tanks can cause destruction comparable to that brought about by armed military aircraft. The States started analysing the legal framework of the destruction of rogue civil aircraft under international law and constitutional law.[39]

In order to prevent the unlawful seizure of aircraft more effectively, the contracting Parties amended and supplemented The Hague Convention (1970). Its substantive scope of application was accordingly extended; it now ordains the punishment of other forms of hijack, hence commission with the use of modern technology: 'any person commits an offence if that person unlawfully and intentionally seizes or exercises control of an aircraft in service by force or threat thereof, or by coercion, or by any other form of intimidation, or by any technological means' [Article 1 (1)]. Furthermore, it extends criminal liability to accomplice and preparatory activities [Article 1 (3) *c)–d)*]. It prescribes that each State Party, in accordance with national law, holds legal entities criminally liable for the crime they committed (2 *bis*): in accordance with its national legal principles, each State Party may take the necessary measures to enable a legal entity located in its territory or organised under its laws to be held liable when a person responsible for management or control of that

---

[38] The threat is well-known for the public since 2006 when a London-based group planned to blow up jetliners using liquid explosives. After the act was revealed, ICAO took serious steps to prevent this kind of terrorist attack against civil aviation. Previously there had been a successful attack against Philippine Airlines (PR) Flight 434, a Boeing 747-283B en-route from Manila (MNL) via Cebu (CEB) to Tokyo (NRT) on 11 December 1994. The detonation of the bomb (made from nitroglycerin, sulfuric acid, acetone and other chemicals) aboard—killing one and injuring 10 passengers—was a test-run for the so-called 'Bojinka Plot', the long-forgotten al-Qaeda scheme to destroy simultaneously 11 wide-body airplanes over the Pacific Ocean from Asia to the United States. Hatzadony, John: Oplan Bojinka Revisited: The Plot and its Legacy. 16 October 2019. (www.tsi-mag.com/oplan-bojinka-revisited-the-plot-and-its-legacy).

[39] Sulyok (2006), pp. 5–30.

legal entity has, in that capacity, committed an offence. Such liability may be criminal, civil or administrative [Article 4 (1)].

The role of national law remains definitive further on in the Convention, so the legislator, as in the international treaties previously established, does not exclude any criminal jurisdiction exercised in accordance with national law.

5.3.3 The Montreal Protocol (2014)

The Montreal Protocol (MP14)[40] was designed to amend the Tokyo Convention (1963) to offer a comprehensive response to the problems caused by the constantly growing number of unruly passengers. The Protocol was not expressly drafted with the intention of intervention against international terrorism, but basically with the objective of extending the possibilities of criminal intervention against violent passengers not motivated by terrorism but who defy the instructions of staff. Accordingly, the contracting Parties specified and supplemented the elements in cases of delinquency.

According to the main rule, the Tokyo Convention grants the opportunity of the exercise of jurisdiction for the State of registration over offences and acts committed on board. The State of landing had not always been authorised to conduct proceedings; therefore, unruly passengers had often gone unpunished. The Montreal Protocol was designed to eliminate this defect in law, since it guaranteed jurisdiction to the authorities of the State of landing to conduct proceedings vis-à-vis the delivered passenger [Article 1 (1)]. The contracting Parties further extended the variety of forums of jurisdiction by granting jurisdiction to the State of the operator [Article 3 (2) *bis b)*].[41]

The Montreal Protocol extends the scope of application of the Tokyo Convention, so that the effect of its provisions concerns offences and acts jeopardising safety on board 'an aircraft in flight at any time from the moment when all its external doors are closed following embarkation until the moment when any such door is opened for disembarkation' [Article 1 (3) *a)*]. That is not inadvertent, since the majority of unlawful acts are committed by unruly passengers during taxiing before the commencement of take-off.

To lighten the tasks of the aircraft commander, the Protocol factually enumerates instances of unruly behaviour, such as physical assault or a threat to commit such assault against a crew member and as refusal to follow a lawful instruction given by the crew for the purpose of protecting safety [Article 15 *bis* (1) *a)–b)*]. Each

[40] ICAO Doc 10034 Protocol to Amend the Convention on Offences and Certain Other Acts Committed on Board Aircraft, Montreal, 4 April 2014. The Montreal Protocol took effect on 1 January 2020.

[41] The designation of articles follows the Consolidated text of the Tokyo Convention and Montreal Protocol. DCTC Doc No. 33., International Conference on Air Law, Montreal, 4 April 2014.

contracting State is encouraged to take such measures as may be necessary to institute appropriate criminal, administrative or any other forms of legal proceedings against any person who commits an offence on board an aircraft. On financial aspects, the Protocol expressly emphasises the Freedoms of the Air to claim compensation from the offending passenger (Article 18 *bis*).

In the Montreal Protocol, the States extended the jurisdiction opportunities boldly, by which they supported that as many unlawful acts as possible would actually be adjudicated in criminal proceedings. However, the contracting Parties took something of a risk[42] when they dealt with the other highlighted area of the Tokyo Convention and juxtaposed the scope for action of the In-Flight Security Officer (IFSO),[43] that is, the Air Marshal, besides the rights and obligations of the aircraft commander. The question immediately arises: if the aircraft commander is the ultimate decision-maker, may the IFSO take over the competence of the aircraft commander in preventing or handling unlawful activities occurring on board the aircraft? To what extent may the IFSO make decisions in such situations, thereby lightening the burden on the commander pilot? Obviously, the highly trained specialist IFSO may take measures according to his or her obligations proceeding from his or her sphere of activity with reasonable grounds without special authorisation [Article 6 (3)], but he or she may not surpass the competence of the aircraft commander. The contracting Parties also stipulated that the 'aircraft commander may require or authorize the assistance of other crew members and may request or authorize, but not require, the assistance of in-flight security officers or passengers to restrain any person whom he is entitled to restrain' [Article 6 (2)].[44] Exemption is also granted to the IFSO from being held responsible for the consequences of his lawful acts (Article 10).

With respect to the fact that the aircraft itself is considered quasi-State territory, the registering State thus has jurisdiction pertaining to the mobile territory,[45] therefore, the activity of the IFSO in the national system of rules can be construed as that of the protector of the quasi territory of the State. Upon the definition of their situation besides the national regulation and programs,[46] the bilateral or multilateral agreements[47] concluded among the States concerned have significance due to the international character of aircraft [Article 6 (3)–(4)].

---

[42] Jennifer (2016), pp. 739–740.

[43] ICAO Annex 17 on Security. Standards, Preventive Security Measures. 11th edn., March 2020, Chapter 4., 4.7.5 and 4.7.7–8.

[44] Authority in Handling Offences and Certain Other Acts Committed on Board Aircraft. International Conference on Air Law (Montreal, 26 March to 4 April 2014) – Presented by Indonesia, DCTC Doc No. 24. 21 March 2014, p. 3.

[45] The right of the flag does not mean territorial sovereignty (since in reality it is not the territory of the State), but definite jurisdiction.

[46] More than forty States have IFSO programs. International Conference on Air Law, Authority and Protections for In-Flight Security Officers, at 1, DCTC Doc. No. 7., 23 January 2014. 2.3, p. 1.

[47] For example: 'Agreement on the employment of Air Marshals' concluded between many States and the United States of America on bilateral level.

5.4 The Result of Modernisation

It is obvious that criminality will not be prevented by law in itself; unlawful acts will always be committed by people. We may question whether the new conventions pertaining to security drafted under the auspices of ICAO and designed to renew the comprehensively prevalent international system of treaties concerning security will be able to forestall these transboundary crimes and impose legal consequences. To what extent will these rules prevail in practice? The question is justified, because the renewal of treaties pertaining to security arises not only because the world has changed considerably and new forms of commission have emerged, or an increasing number of unlawful acts (mostly committed by unruly passengers) occur, but simply because the content of basic conventions had not prevailed in international practice, despite numerous ratifications. National law has retained a great scope for action, which impeded unification,[48] implying that the authorities of the competent State did not always intend to exercise jurisdiction; they did not wish to become engaged in matters in which furnishing evidence was problematic (the crime was committed in foreign airspace, on board an aircraft registered in another State by a foreign citizen), the questions of liability were ambiguous, while they imposed a financial burden on the proceeding State.

In the interest of the observance of security rules and following the model of aviation safety audits, ICAO has established the Universal Security Audit Programme (USAP), which is prescribed for the States as mandatory. This auditing programme has been carried out in the framework of the Continuous Monitoring Approach (CMA) since 2015.[49] The essence is that, during the audit, ICAO examines the extent to which the Member State is party to the international treaty, and whether the rights and obligations stipulated therein have been incorporated into and harmonised with national law; furthermore, to what extent these rules and procedures prevail in practice and in the course of operation. The examined State regularly reports on the implementation of the measure plan designed to rectify the revealed deficiencies, in which it presents the current circumstances. Via the implementation of the activity, all Member States are under continuous surveillance, which supports the enforcement of the rules of international conventions and of the Standard and Recommended Practices (SARPs) adopted by the ICAO Council.

This much is certain: via the Beijing Convention and Protocol (2010) as well as via the Montreal Protocol (2014), ICAO and its Member States regulating international air transport convey an unequivocal message to the world: all acts related to or

[48] The Tokyo Convention does not exclude any criminal jurisdiction exercised in accordance with national law [Article 3 (3)]. The rule that criminal jurisdiction should be exercised in accordance with national law hindered the achievement of the objective of uniformity. Gutierrez (1965), p. 13.

[49] ICAO Doc 9807 Universal Security Audit Programme Continuous Monitoring Manual. 3rd edn., 2021.; ICAO Assembly Resolution A37–17, Appendix E refers.; ICAO Doc 10010-C/1172 Council Decision, 197th Session. C.MIN 197/1, Subject No. 52.1. 2013, pp. 11–12.

jeopardising aviation security, wherever committed, will have criminal legal consequences under all circumstances.[50]

References

Abeyratne R (2010) Aviation Security Law. Springer, p 23

Glenn F (1990) Havel Details Sale of Explosive to Libya. Washington Post Foreign Service, London, 23 March 1990, p A15

Gutierrez JJL (1965) Should the Tokyo Convention of 1963 be ratified? J Air Law Commerce 31(1), pp. 3-4

Havel BF, Sanchez GS (2014) Principles and Practice on International Aviation Law. Cambridge, p 185

Jennifer AU (2016) The Protocol to Amend the Convention on Offences and Certain Acts Committed on Board Aircraft: a Missed opportunity or a sufficient modernization? Indiana Law Rev 49:713

Lechter P (2003) Eccentric France, the Bradt guide to mad, magical and marvellous. Bradt Travel Guides, UK, pp 35–36

Mankiewicz RH (1971) The 1970 Hague Convention. J Air Law Commerce 37:195–196

Sandeepa Bhat B (2023) Dealing with civil aviation crimes (Chapter 10). In: Sandeepa Bhat B, Ukey D, Variath A (eds) Handbook on international aviation law, 1st edn., Thomson Reuters, pp 183–209

Shubber S (1973) Jurisdiction over Crimes on Board Aircraft. The Hague, p 5

Sipos A (2020) The Dogmatics and Modernisation of International Conventions on Aviation Security. Eötvös University Press, ELTE Law J 1:147–167

Smith P (2018) Cockpit Confidential: Everything you need to know about air travel: questions, answers, and reflections. Sourcebooks, p 83

Sulyok G (2006) An Assessment of the Destruction of Rogue Civil Aircraft under International Law and Constitutional Law. In: Halmai G (ed) Hungary: human rights in the face of terrorism. Vandeplas Publishing, Lake Mary, pp 5–30

Wassenbergh H (1998) Safety in Air Transportation and Market Entry. J Air Space Law 23(2):83. The Hague, p 83

[50] Sipos (2020), pp. 147–167.; Sandeepa Bhat (2023), pp. 183–209.

Chapter 6
Closing Words for Public Aviation Law

In 1944, nobody could foresee the unparalleled future of air navigation defying description, although back then neither audacious thoughts nor revolutionary ideas had been scarce, which had become reality before the majority of the readers of this book were born. In the 1960s, the supersonic Concorde civilian airplanes (1969) traversed the aerial ocean at twice the speed of sound, while the Blackbird SR-71 military spy planes (1964) flying at a speed of 3500 km/h outspeeded the missiles targeting them, humankind entered outer space (1961) and the 'envoys of mankind', the astronauts took a walk on the surface of the Moon (1969). Doubtless, if the vision of the future is put down in writing, one chapter therein indisputably concerns Aviation. In view of the fact that the future can be predicted via retrospection into the past, we can by this time be aware that we are heading for amazing development.

In 1944, statesmen, diplomats and aviation experts—the contracting States of the Chicago Convention shown in a little faded photograph at the entrance of the Council Chamber of ICAO—were well aware that they were creating something special, which was in a class by itself. They established the universal framework and constitutional bases of international aviation. They created the sole global intergovernmental organisation of international civil aviation, bestowed it with regulative and administrative powers, furthermore, they agreed on the international basic principles and rules of aviation. They did so in the interest of promoting cooperation among nations and peoples, but particularly of guaranteeing the safety of aviation worldwide.

The overall establishment of aviation safety first required the international elaboration of technical requirements. The elaboration of the uniform system of rules and procedures of the aviation industry had commenced as early as after the World War I, but the establishment of uniformity in the fragmented world of winners and losers was not feasible. While approaching the end of the World War II, the historic moment of December 1944 can be identified in the extent to which the makers of the Chicago Convention, the prospective winners could transcend the world interwoven by politics and belligerent redress upon the enforcement of their interests to create an actually uniform and just system of international civil aviation. They had to wait for

A. Sipos, *International Aviation Law*, https://doi.org/10.1007/978-3-031-39066-1_6

its success, which did not fail to come about. However, hardly had the Convention been signed, when humankind returned afresh to the battlefield: to the scene of the Cold War, which divided the world once again, thereby, it forestalled the creation of the insomuch longed-for peace and unity. In the course of time, aviation overstepped the politically determined system of interests based on protectionism safeguarding domestic markets to the utmost. Thus, the peculiar feature of civil aviation encompassing the global world and the primacy of aviation safety did not tolerate the persistence of the way of thinking based on outdated views and customs.

It is a well-known fact: aviation is dangerous operation. At the dawn of the jet era, the chances of the passengers of airplanes did not bid fair prospects. Everyone had to undertake the grave risk entailed by the flight, therefore, solely the considerable increase of the level of safety could secure the future of the industry. Consequently, the establishment of aviation safety all over the world became an emphatic and essential task of the performers of the air transport industry. The transparent system of aviation safety has been guaranteed jointly by the Member States clustered in the international organisation of ICAO. The Member States, by acceding to the Chicago Convention, assumed the universal obligation of the complete observance of the rules of aviation safety. It is not accidental that, as one of the most regulated industries in the world, civil aviation has become the safest branch of modern transportation in some decades.

The modern means and achievements of aviation frequently amaze and enthuse people, although civil aviation despite all its innovative manifestations has remained an old-fashioned conservative world, which was tailored by the Chicago Convention. The general framework based mainly on political considerations incorporates legal principles and legal institutions prevalent until this day. The Convention has restricted civil aviation within bounds, the posterior consequences of which the contracting States could not foresee. The framework implied a world arranged around bilateral relations. In this world aviation was predictable, national markets were protected, competition was not so remarkable. In bilateral Air Services Agreements, the Party States conserved these idyllic circumstances in their domestic regulations, political and commercial relations, by the designation of their flagged national airlines.

However, sinister shadows started to appear, and the overregulated world called for the dismantling of the obstacles created by itself. Meanwhile, the system of bilateral relations became an impediment to aviation and functioned as a strait jacket against further development, since the prevalent complex system of rules outgrew itself and was unable to track down the rapid changes. Therefore, the initial process of regulation was superseded by a new trend in the 1970s. The deregulation and harmonisation of the law of the overregulated, up and down regulated air transport industry commenced, which established the basis of the evolution of a new regulatory culture. This culture favoured regulations suitable for the demands of the market and the changing environment. At the beginning of the 1990s, the course of history changed, and a new world order was born subsequently to the unification of the binary world of the two World Powers and the aligned States, which promoted the unfolding of the uniform world trade and the concomitant global competition, allowing free scope for liberalisation in air transport. The opening of domestic markets has expedited to an unprecedented extent the consolidation of the industry currently still in high gears, making spectacular progress from the world of States to a market-based world. The policy supporting the overall protection of domestic markets has been forced back and the new regulatory principles have transformed aviation into regular business. The increasingly frequent secession of the States from the airline business, the operation of airports, and more recently, from the monopolised world of air navigation services has led to the rearrangement of the tasks of management, operation and proprietorship and this process has coerced the States to discharge their regulatory and supervisory tasks at a qualitatively higher standard.

The dismantling of the binary monopolised world is advancing step by step, is currently making progress vigorously, while everything is in transformation. Dogmas are undermined on the level of the industry generating a revolutionary situation, illustrious airlines disappear or merge, budget airlines or rather their business model gain the upperhand, private airports unify, and the solid monopoly of air navigation services is shaken by the Single Sky initiative. The policy of liberalisation has been rewriting the history of aviation by demolishing taboos such as the system of bilateral relations, which had determined the framework and the operational basic principles of the air transport industry in its bases from the coming into force of the Chicago Convention.

As a matter of course, the world has not changed in its foundations, it has remained disjointed and fragmented despite all endeavours. We could think of the world of airports, which has opened up before the States, but this fact in itself does not entail carrying out commercial shipment among the Parties. That is, in vain does the air carrier of the given Member State receive the right to operate flights, in case it cannot make business-like use of the proceeding opportunity in economic terms. For example, if the recipient State introduces an obligatory visa-system, or its aviation safety and security indicators do not conform to the international norms, if the supervisory capacity of the aviation authority is null and void, if by reason of the low degree of technical, financial or infrastructural development the performers are not competitive, or the airlines do not get access to proper slots at the airports important in respect of their schedule. These impediments aggravate efficient operation financially and commercially as well as the provision of high-standard service in the given market.

The other constant problem and simultaneously the challenge of international civil aviation are to be found in the low-level implementation figures of Standards and Recommended Practices (SARPs), since even the most rigorous rules prove to be futile if a part of the Member States do not adhere thereto. This is one, maybe the most important task of the industry, which is designed to be addressed globally, primarily by ICAO as a multilateral organisation. ICAO as the regulator of aviation in the world is the guardian of safety. However, the establishment of unity on the wide scale of interests is by far not a simple task, therefore, the decisions of ICAO are substantiated by a consensus, which implies a guarantee for adherence to the rules by the Member States and authorises ICAO to demand law-abiding conduct.

This institutional stability originates in the confidence manifested by the Member States and is founded on high-level cooperation by the sovereign Member States. Therefore, ICAO can uniformly intervene, allowing little scope for unilateral measures and problem-solving guided by peculiar interests. The special system of the rules and institutions of ICAO elaborated uniquely does not coerce, it rather encourages compromises and consensus.[1] Its objective is the unification of the rules of aviation in different legal systems.

ICAO has unequivocally achieved its objective: it guarantees aviation safety worldwide and has created uniformity on the level of regulations. The constitutional basis of the Convention is incontestable. Nevertheless, the activity of ICAO, the Convention establishing the organisation and its system of rules are frequently criticised. There is need for ICAO's leadership in harmonising (not in 'fostering') the air transport regulatory framework.[2] In certain periods and situations, ICAO makes its decisions slowly, since the majority of the Member States guided by their own interests intend to sustain the status quo. Obviously, the less developed countries are not interested in swift changes, in the opening of markets, since with good reason they are afraid of being outclassed by stronger parties in a more open competition. In addition, the power and interest relations, the equilibrium of the status quo would be threatened by every change. We need to assert: for the majority of Member States, ICAO means a protective basis, a real forum, where they can express their opinions and are protected vis-à-vis more developed Member States. The developing world needs help instead of sanctions, which ICAO does provide for them. It is not inadvertent that ICAO has become a 'centrepiece' in the less developed world. Moreover, the Convention does not provide for essential commercial issues since it entrusts them to Member State regulation and relations. Therefore, ICAO has to keep an issue of vital importance in view: to what extent can State will and an array of obligations, deriving from commitment to ICAO, be reconciled with the financial (commercial) interests of the service providers? In written form, the response is indisputable: the primacy of aviation safety and security may not be jeopardised by the interest in profits or any other market-based viewpoint.

At the same time, criticism is justifiable in respect of the fact that the rules of the air many times cannot keep up with dynamic development. Sometimes a part of the prevalent rules have been emptied out, practical life has left them behind, just like the Convention has not been amended either to accord with the demands of the age. A justification for the Chicago Convention is that it has stood the test of time, its treaty-makers abided by the old saying: 'the enemy of good is the best'. Despite these, after such a long time, the Convention needs complete review and modernisation, since the original text of the Convention does not regulate areas which in our age basically determine the development of civil aviation. Back then, nobody could foresee that one day hijacking, sabotage, attacks against airports, renitent passengers would disturb the longed-for peaceful ordinariness, or noise pollution and pollutant

[1] Buergenthal (1969), p. 229.

[2] Abeyratne (2016), p. 9.

emission would jar the mood of city-dwellers. Of the three major strategic areas ranked by ICAO, that is, aviation safety, security and environmental protection, about the latter two ones the Convention keeps silent. Consequently, neither the Assembly, nor the Council has related obligatory tasks defined by the Convention. Nonetheless, life goes on, thus, ICAO, with an excellent solution in legal technical terms, framed Annexes 16 and 17 to the Convention, which contain Standards and Recommended Practices pertaining to the highlighted areas of environmental protection and security without the amendment of the Convention.

At the same time, the fact must also be considered that in the national implementation of the rules of international civil aviation and in the exercise of the supervisory rights by national aviation authorities responsible for their observance, significant deviations and considerable differences can be discerned, which can never be dissolved to full extent. It is impossible to establish complete uniformity in the world, there will always be deviations and deficiencies. Despite these, the elimination of differences as well as the formation of consensus from the increasingly complex, many times state-level interests are constant endeavours. In this work, ICAO has an extraordinary and central role more and more demanded and recognised by the contracting States.

In the twenty-first century aviation has become a progressively accelerating, multinational enterprise in a global environment, which makes demands on the Member States of ICAO and the performers of the industry in terms of new rules, directions and principles. These principles surpass the policy of Open Skies, overstep it, since it is not enough to liberalise and open markets, more than these need to be done. Global planning and complete cultural change are necessary for entrance into a new dimension, possibly with less, but more applicable aviation rules. By this day it is certain that full liberalisation may only be accomplished in a uniform market. Therefore, these markets need to be extended, allowing scope for the proliferation of multinational airlines. We are just witnessing that process. Soon, fewer but even more efficient airlines operated unilaterally will thrive. Although these airlines will be registered in different regions and continents, they will travel with one commercial image, under consolidated management and a uniform system of regulations, under the auspices of harmonised competition law prescriptions, uniformly benefitting from the opening domestic markets expanded by the interested States.

Liberalisation is irresistible, undoubtedly efficient and encouraging, although on an industrial level it has progressed more slowly than expected. This process has realised the consolidation of the industry, the evolution of unified markets and the development of competition. Meanwhile, it has given way to the comprehensive enforcement of radical changes and the realisation of new commercial and industrial solutions. The multilateral transition to the Open Skies has been in progress for decades. This process was forestalled by the COVID-19 pandemic, which launched comprehensive changes we are witnessing now. This is a milestone for all of us. One of the most important consequences of this process has been that the long-awaited paradigm shift ensues not only in our lives, but inevitably in civil aviation as well. We are on course for a new era, which will revise in its foundations the congestion stemming from fierce competition on the surface and in the air. It is possible that the bygone bilateral world will strengthen once again, nevertheless, what has more chance is that subsequently to the ruthless consolidation of the market, the world and air transport therein will become more uniform. We need not doubt that humankind will realise its novel dream and create a more peaceful world via the instruments of civil aviation and cooperation among peoples and nations. A world in which 'the Ocean of the Air Unites All People!'[3]

References

Abeyratne R (2016) Competition and Investment in Air Transport. Legal and Economic Issues. The Role of ICAO in Air Transport. Springer, p 9

Buergenthal T (1969) Law-making in the International Civil Aviation Organization. New York, p 229

Noppen RK (2016) Foreword. In: Noppen RK (ed) Blue Skies, Orange Wings. The Global reach of Dutch aviation in war and peace, 1914–1945. Grand Rapids, Michigan/Cambridge

[3] Albert Plesman (1889–1953), KLM Royal Dutch Airline—the famous sentence of the founder of the first commercial airline of the world turned into an adage (1919). Noppen (2016).

Part II
The Private Law of International Civil Aviation

Chapter 7
Liability in Transportation

The massive transportation of persons and objects takes place via recourse to the technical means of road, railway, water and air transport. Transportation is a branch of production, although owing to its peculiar features diverging from other productive activities, no new material goods proceed therefrom, since its main task is the transportation of goods itself. Transportation increases the price of material goods since the costs of carriage are included in the price of each delivered product. In the system of market-based air transport, the party paying for the carriage (the passenger or the consignor of goods) and the entrepreneur performing the carriage establish a contractual relationship, in which the legislator obligates the air carrier to adhere to its liability rigorously.

The demand for more rigorous liability than general is justified by the dangerous operation of air transport (public transport) and by the vulnerable position of passengers upon their transportation. In this hazardous environment the life, the safety of the obligee and the protection of their property are to be safeguarded by law.

7.1 Dangerous Operation

Air transport is an activity involving extreme danger both on the surface and in the air in all the processes of operation. If the activity involving extreme danger is carried out carelessly and negligently, it can be foreseen that significant damage may be caused, even the occurrence of a slight fault may cause disproportionately grievous damage. Despite that, banning this activity in consideration of the hazards

A. Sipos, *International Aviation Law*, https://doi.org/10.1007/978-3-031-39066-1_7

is not viable by reason of its general social and national economic significance. As the Romans put it: ‘navigating is necessary, while living is not’.[1]

The institution of dangerous operation can be found in Roman law as well. The facts of the case of delinquent responsibility without fault appeared already in ancient Rome. The *edict of the praetor* guaranteed the right to file action against anyone on whose house or flat a protrusion overhanging the public road (e.g., the balcony), an object menacing with falling was hung. In the action *(actio de posito et suspenso)* the occurrence of damage was not necessarily required.

In universal legal history, the legislator qualified railway as dangerous operation for the first time. Its rigorous liability rules were laid down as early as in the nineteenth century. The legislator prescribed the objective liability of the party causing damage.[2] The railway company was only exonerated from liability if it could prove that the death or physical injury was caused by an unavoidable event *(vis maior)*, or the unavoidable act of a third person, which the railway company was unable to avert or if the damage proceeded from the fault of the claimant. Judicial practice extended the substantive liability of steam-driven railway to all other traffic with similarly dangerous operation: steamships, horse-driven or electric public railway, then after a while, to automotive vehicles.

According to judicial practice, in our days typical dangerous operation encompasses: motorised vehicles, mechanised businesses, electric power generating and transforming plants (mines, gas works, water plants), explosives and pyrotechnics (open fire is not included), radiating and poisonous materials and their use (for example, spraying), furthermore, keeping wild animals, game farming, the production, keeping and use of fire-arms, construction, roofing, digging ditches and wells, extraction of rubble and sand, even logging. Chemical spraying from aircraft, damage occasioned by sound effects of aircraft or by flight models driven by radio-waves (drones) also belong to this category.

Owing to the development of law and the evolution of new means of traffic, the States realised that traffic on public roads needs to be differentiated from railway, water and air transport from a legal point of view. That is, in the case of the occurrence of emergency, catastrophic consequences can be expected in branches of public transport mainly on waters and in the air, that is, in hostile environment for humans, where it is more difficult to flee or escape. Therefore, the legislator considered it reasonable to demarcate the boundaries of criminal legal defence in a broader scope.

---

[1] Plutarch, the Greek biographer (46–119 A.D.) took down the sentence of Pompeius Magnus (106–48 B.C.), the Roman General, which became an adage: *Navigare necesse est, vivere non est necesse*. The General addressed the sailors who, having unloaded the wheat, did not want to leave the port in Sicily for the stormy sea. The genuine profession does not only demand humbleness and reverence, but also superhuman sacrifices (e.g., the doctor departs to heal the infectious ill person). Bánk: *3500 latin bölcsesség (3500 Latin Wisdoms),* (1993), p. 205.

[2] See, the Preußisches Eisenbahngesetz (Prussian Railway Law) of 1838.

7.2 Criminal Liability

According to the general rule, the person who *endangers the life* or *safety of others* by breaking the rules of railway, water or air transport commits a crime. (Note that criminal law is part of public law, mentioned here specifically for better understanding of the liabilty consequencies of unlawful acts.)

- The endangerment of railway, water and air transport can be committed *intentionally* and *negligently* (subjective side). As opposed, in the case of traffic on public roads endangerment can be committed only intentionally, since endangerment on public roads cannot be committed in a negligent form.
- The object of crime is the life and safety of persons participating in railway, water and air transport (objective side). In the interest of the efficient protection of these objects of law, the legislator stipulates holding criminally responsible in the case of *indirect*, distant endangerment in itself as well. Whereas, in the cases of endangerment on public roads only the prevalence of *direct* danger entails criminal liability.

The situation of emergency evolving during dangerous operation is the outcome of a process. The establishment of criminal liability requires the launch of the process of change. This implies that the conduct of the perpetrator mobilises the accident factors otherwise in quiescent condition. The criminal offence is realised even by the breach of one sole rule. Its indispensable objective condition is the prevalence of a cause–effect relationship between the act contrary to the rules and the commencement of the process of change directed at the occurrence of personal injury. By unlawful conduct, the perpetrator of the criminal offence engenders a situation of emergency, which implies the remote possibility of personal injury (the possibility of the extinction of human life or the infliction of physical injury). This process launches a change, which may easily lead to a detrimental situation. At the same time, if the pilot of the aircraft deliberately breaches the rules in order to prevent an accident, it does not matter that by carrying out the activity the pilot has brought about emergency since in the absence of culpability or by reason of extreme necessity no crime has been realised.

7.3 Civil Liability

7.3.1 General Liability

General liability for damages prevails for damage proceeding from the *breach of contract* or *tortious conduct*. The legislator has differentiated the rules of (contractual) liability for the breach of contract from the (tort) liability for damage caused by unlawful conduct (delictual). The justification for the distinction of the two forms of liability is that while the party assumes responsibility in the contract voluntarily and consciously, we cannot identify the assumption of obligation upon tort liability. Consequently, the legislator narrows the scope of exemptions from contractual liability. The cause of exemption may only be a circumstance surpassing the scope of control unforeseen at the time of the conclusion of the contract, that is, the norm will not consist in attributability. Furthermore, the legislator restricts the scope of reparation for damage foreseeable upon the conclusion of the contract.

The basic requirement of both liabilities for damage proceeding from Roman law is as follows: the person who causes damage to another party unlawfully is obligated to indemnify it. The legislator prohibits causing unlawful damage. For the establishment of liability, the joint fulfilment of the following criteria is necessary:

(a) The damaging party breaches the contract/manifests unlawful conduct.
(b) The unlawful conduct causes damage which affects

1. the property as damage to property; or
2. the person as injury but not the property related to a damaging event.
   The damaging party is obligated to indemnify the entire damage

   - to property rights, the actually emerging decrease in the value of the property of the claimant *(damnum emergens),* furthermore, the lost financial gain *(lucrum cessans)* and the reasonable costs necessary for the elimination of the pecuniary injury of the claimant, with the formerly mentioned limitation that in the case of damage caused by breaching the contract, merely the foreseeable damage needs to be indemnified.
   - in the case of non-pecuniary damage, the compensation for the injury shall be determined after individual judgement and the consideration of all aspects jointly, however, in this scope the evidence of the fact of injury of the law suffices, while the occurrence of damage does not need to be proved.

(c) Between the unlawful damaging conduct and the occasioned damage, a *cause-effect relationship* needs to prevail.

If the three objective conditions above (*a*–*b*–*c*) conjunctively materialise, in the case of tort liability the socially expectable nature of the damaging conduct needs to be examined as a fourth (*d*) subjective condition. If this conduct was attributable, that is, the damaging party did not proceed as it would have been generally expectable in the given situation, the liability for damages is established. However, if this conduct provenly may not be attributable, the damaging party is exempted from liability (subjective liability). In the case of contractual liability, the condition of exemption is not the absence of attributability, but the fact that the breach of contract was caused by a circumstance which was beyond the scope of control of the defaulting party and unforeseen at the time of the conclusion of the contract. Thus, the avoidance of the circumstance or averting the damage could not be expected.

7.3.2 Increased Liability

In comparison with the rules of general liability for damages, the legislator determines more rigorous requirements vis-a-vis the performer of highly dangerous activity. The performer of highly dangerous activity is obligated to indemnify the damage proceeding therefrom.

The liability for damages prevailing upon carrying out such activity has paramount significance among the forms of liability for damages under civil law. Liability for damages proceeding from dangerous operation differs from general liability for damages, since the definition of increased liability for dangerous operation does not imply attributable conduct. Increased liability is objective in character. This means that liability for damages prevails even if the damaging party proceeded innocently, but the cause-effect relationship is demonstrable between the highly dangerous activity and the caused damage.

The establishment of increased liability has two conditions:

- the damage must be in a *cause-effect* relationship with the highly dangerous activity; and
- the damage should not be occasioned by an inevitable external cause (vis maior, interference by the claimant, act by a third party or other inevitable external force). The damaging party needs to prove that the damage proceeded from an inevitable external cause.

The production of evidence of the existence of a cause-effect relationship devolves on the claimant. The causation is an essential condition that is absolutely necessary, in other words, a condition without which the damage would not have occurred *(condition sine qua non)*. If no connection exists between the occurrence of the damage and the activity as dangerous operation, the establishment of the liability will be governed by the rules of general liability for damages.

The operator is accountable for the damage proceeding from a highly dangerous activity. As a general criterion, it is usually the operator that maintains or runs the dangerous operation and that makes the basic decisions. The operator does not always coincide with the person of the actual damaging party (e.g., the pilot causing the accident) and is not necessarily the same as the owner of the dangerous operation.

The main activity of airlines is the commercial carriage of persons, baggage, cargo and mail performed for reward on the international and domestic aviation market. In the entire process of carriage, the liability of the air carrier for damages is extraordinarily manifold with prominent significance towards the passengers, the consignors and consignees of the cargo, but it also prevails towards the ground service providers, the on-board catering service providers, the maintenance, repair and overhaul companies, the lessors of the aircraft, the operators of the airports, the border guards, the customs and tax authorities, what is more, the liability prevails as a consequence of noise and air pollution as well. The comprehensive international conventions regulating the liability of air carriers for damages, i.e., the Warsaw Convention (1929) and the Montreal Convention (1999) were concluded to regulate the relations between air carriers and consumers (passengers or consignors/consignees). However, no international and uniform regulation of the liability for damages to international airports, air navigation service providers (ANSPs), maintenance, repair and overhaul organisations (MROs), or to aircraft manufacturers has been drafted. The actions for damages vis-a-vis these outstanding performers of the industry are governed by national law despite the significant number of elements with international aspects.

7.4 The Legal Sources of Private Aviation Law

The principal objective of the rules of the private law of international civil aviation is the realisation of the uniformity of law in the system of international relations, especially giving rise to rightful and equitable *(ex aequo et bono)* balance concerning the rights of the claimant.

1. In the system of the rules of liability for damages in international civil aviation, the rules of liability for damage caused to the *second party* (passengers or consignors/consignees) by air carriers are incorporated by the following sources of law:

- multilateral international treaties
  [e.g., the *Warsaw Convention* (1929) and its amendments; as well as the *Montreal Convention* (1999)];
- the decisions of international organisations;
- the universally recognised general legal principles of international law;
- judicial decisions made by the appliers of the law;
- agreements concluded between the State and the air carriers;
- agreements among the air carriers;
- so-called *soft law*[3] provisions and agreements.

Besides international treaties, what have great significance upon the adjudication of damage caused to a second party include internationally recognised legal practice (cases constituting precedents), the resolutions of the International Air Transport Association (IATA), its agreements concluded with the member airlines and the professional requirements therein. Among the legal sources, the universally recognised Warsaw Convention and the Montreal Convention as well as the legal cases founded on their rules are prominent.

[3] On the basis of the works of international legal commentators, the norms of soft law are divided into three groups: (1) resolutions, guidelines, programs, directives, declarations, recommendations of international organisations concerning extra-organisational relations; (2) (legally not binding) bilateral or multilateral agreements and declarations concluded jointly among the States (e.g., the joint final acts of conferences, accords, recommendations and comments); (3) regulations shaped by non-intergovernmental organisations, which in certain areas may be definitive in international practice (e.g., the International Red Cross). Blutman (2008), p. 29.

2. In international civil aviation, for damage caused to *third parties* (persons on the surface) by foreign aircraft, the rules of liability are incorporated under

- the *Rome Convention* (1952) (on Damage Caused by Foreign Aircraft to Third Parties on the Surface) and its amendment, the *Montreal Protocol* (1978);

The Rome Convention and its amendment were replaced by the Conventions below:

- the *General Risks Convention* (2009) (Convention on Compensation for Damage Caused by Aircraft to Third Parties);
- the *Unlawful Interference Compensation Convention* (2009) (Convention on Compensation for Damage to Third Parties Resulting from Acts of Unlawful Interference Involving Aircraft) [see, Chap. 9].

3. The protection of the international recognition of rights in aircraft and mobile equipment and its liability background are established by the *Geneva Convention* (1948), furthermore, the *Cape Town Convention* and its *Aircraft Equipment Protocol* (2001) [see, Chap. 10].

This book prioritises the rules of liability for damage sustained primarily by the second party (the passenger and the consignor/consignee). Its reason is mainly that these are the most frequently arising cases in international civil aviation. The passengers and consignors need to be aware that wherever they travel or send cargo and parcels in the world, they do so within the framework of a uniform system of general rules regulating optimally the liability of the air carrier for damages.

References

Bánk J (ed) (1993) 3500 Latin bölcsesség (3500 Latin Wisdoms). St. Gellért Church Publishing House, Budapest, p 205

Blutman L (2008) Nemzetközi soft law: hagyjuk dolgozni Occam borotváját (International Soft Law: Let Occam's razor work). Közjogi Szemle 1:29

Preußisches Eisenbahngesetz (Prussian Railway Law) 1838

Chapter 8
The Air Carrier's Liability for Damages Caused to the Second Party

For 70 years, the Convention on the Unification of Certain Rules Relating to International Carriage by Air, more commonly known as the Warsaw Convention (1929), had been the most important treaty regulating the relations of private international aviation law, until it was replaced by a new international treaty, the Montreal Convention for the Unification of Certain Rules for International Carriage by Air (1999). Of the international aviation law treaties drafted under the guidance of the International Civil Aviation Organization (ICAO), the Montreal Convention is at present the most important treaty of private international aviation law. Its specialty is hidden in its legal institutions, which support the universal predominance of the Montreal Convention. The legal institutions introduced by the contracting Parties are familiar and transplanted from the Warsaw Convention or utterly new ones, all of which aim at its ratification by as many States as possible so that private international legal unification can be accomplished in the broadest possible scope.

The contracting States opened a new chapter in the history of the liability of air carriers for damages since they obligated air carriers to assume unlimited liability for damages in the event of an accident sustained by passengers, they also simplified the documentation of carriage, facilitated the electronic issuance of air tickets and the air waybill, and, by the introduction of the fifth forum of jurisdiction, they extended the scope of optional proceeding courts for the plaintiffs; furthermore, they obligated air carriers, if their national law so requires, to make advance payments following an accident sustained by a passenger. The requirement to maintain adequate insurance by the air carriers (Artcile 50) covering their liabilty is also a new element in the Montreal Convention, just like the provision that the person liable for damage has a right of recourse againt any other person (third parties) (Article 37).

Instead of a fragmented and complex system consisting of six international treaties (Warsaw System), the Montreal Convention offers the alternative of a uniform and homogenous system of rules. This reinforces the intention of the States and regional economic integration organisations to accede. Although there are some States which are Parties only to the Warsaw Convention, it can be established that, as reflected by the ratifications of the new Montreal Convention hitherto, the

A. Sipos, *International Aviation Law*, https://doi.org/10.1007/978-3-031-39066-1_8

contracting Parties have successfully laid the foundation for the unification of the system of the liability of the air carrier for damages. Legal harmonisation on international level can be realised merely via the actual prevalence of the rules and procedures set forth under the Montreal Convention since there are still numerous collisions deriving from diverse national regulations and conflicts arising during the adjudication of private legal disputes.

8.1 The Warsaw Convention (1929)

The first international commercial flight travelling between Paris and London took off on 8 February 1919 with 12 revenue passengers on board. The airplane, an F.60 Goliath, was navigated by Henry Farman (1874–1958), a reputed aviator, pilot, and airplane architect at that time. All of the passengers were soldiers, as non-military flying was still prohibited following the First World War.[1] After the transition to peacetime and the establishment of civil airlines, the French Government soon realised that rules and regulations on the liability for damages need to be formulated on an international level. Therefore, the French President, Raymond Poincaré (1860–1934) convened an International Conference on Private Air Law in 1925. At the conference held in Paris, the delegates of the invited countries set up an International Technical Committee of Experts in Air Law (CITEJA). In the beginning, the objective of the Committee was the examination of the feasibility of the establishment of a uniform international regime of liability, whereas later the goal became the elaboration of the system and elements of an international treaty regulating liability for damages. The body, at its first and second sessions (1928), deliberated on the liability of air carriers, the system of jurisdiction, and the issues of combined and successive carriage. At the third session of CITEJA, the final draft of the treaty was approved; therefore, the Committee made a recommendation for organizing a new conference on international aviation law. On the basis of the recommendation, the second International Conference on Private Air Law was convened in Warsaw on 4–12 October 1929, to which 33 countries sent their delegates. The United States participated in the conference as an observer. The final recommendation put forward by the presidium was adopted by the Parties as an International Convention on the Unification of Certain Rules Relating to International Carriage by Air, which later became known as the Warsaw Convention. The Convention was drafted in French and it had a sole original; therefore, the Polish Government, as the depositary of the Convention, took steps so that the Governments of the contracting Parties received an authentic copy. The only genuine version of the Warsaw Convention was lost during World War II; merely the copies received by the representatives of the States that acceded to the Convention remained

[1] DeMace, Kayleigh: Farman F.60 Goliath – The Plane of the Week. (Theflightblog.com).

intact. Having been ratified by five acceding States, the Warsaw Convention took effect on 13 February 1933.

As air transport had been gaining significance, it became increasingly problematic that the amount of compensation, mainly for personal injury, varied from State to State, and the legal grounds for liability were not the same in different legal systems. Therefore, the Warsaw Convention focused on the uniform regulation of the liability of air carriers for damages. For the compensation of pecuniary claims arising from damages caused by air carriers, the Convention established a system of private law rules, which applied directly both to natural and legal entities.[2] One of the prominent merits of the Warsaw Convention consisted in its endeavour to resolve the contradictions between the Continental and the Anglo-Saxon legal systems:

- In the Continental (civil law) legal system, laws are constituted by statutes, which regulate life circumstances in detail. The jurists work essentially from the collection of statutes, regulations and case-law and in the education of lawyers teaching the theoretical bases and the acquisition of the knowledge of the dogmatics of law have definitive roles.
- On the other hand, in the Anglo-Saxon (common law) legal system, law is established by way of analogy inferred from case-law. Therefore, the appliers of law first determine whether a decision on a similar case has been made by the courts, and if so, what the decision established. If a similar case exists, it can be invoked as a precedent. In the Anglo-Saxon legal system, judicial decisions have more weight than statutes. Of course, there are statutes, but they do not regulate in detail and only set out basic principles. Common juries participate in the administration of justice, while the training of lawyers is emphatically practice-oriented.

It was primarily the legal experts from countries following the Continental legal system who drafted the Convention, but working open-mindedly, they offered scope for Anglo-Saxon case-law as well. As a consequence, mainly internationally recognised Anglo-Saxon legal cases as precedents and judicial practice have given guidance for the interpretation of the main rules and concepts of the Warsaw Convention and its successor, the Montreal Convention. The treaty-makers of the Warsaw Convention, drawing on the institutional system of maritime law, created one of the most significant international treaties of international law. The Warsaw Convention was ratified by 152 States; thus, we can rightly state that the Convention achieved the goal set by its drafters since it:

- *unified* the specific statutes pertaining to international carriage by air;
- *limited* the liability of air carriers for damages; and
- *harmonised* the contents and the formal requirements of the documents of carriage.

The high number of acceding countries to the Warsaw Convention indicates that it has been the most widely recognised private international law treaty in the history

[2] Landry (1975), pp. 372–374.

of aviation. The number of acceding States will no longer increase, despite the fact that the Warsaw Convention is still in effect, since it has been completely replaced by the Montreal Convention, which in a way 'superannuated' it. For countries that have acceded to the Montreal Convention, the Warsaw system of rules has been entirely invalidated. At the same time, in the case of countries that have not acceded to the Montreal Convention but had ratified the Warsaw Convention and its amendments, the Warsaw regime remains guiding.

8.1.1 Limited Liability

At the outset, in the Warsaw System, the contracting States counterbalanced the rigorous liability of the air carrier for damages by limiting the amount of compensation to be paid in the event of accidents sustained by the passengers, thereby alleviating the situation of the air carrier. The limitation of the liability for damages as an institution had been adopted from maritime law. Its introduction was justified mainly by the financial protection of air carriers since, upon the occurrence of graver accidents, they had become obligated to compensate for damage to such an extent that it could entangle them in financially difficult situations and crises in extreme cases. Therefore, one stakeholder group in the air transport industry, namely, the airlines needed an adequate safeguard for their liability for damages, its protection by the regulator. Aviation is a capital-intensive and financially risky activity. Owing to the increasing competition in the market, a great majority of the airlines became financially vulnerable, and their profit-generating capacity in the passenger-forwarding segment remained low.[3] Although the States have, since then, tended to liberalise their domestic markets and to withdraw from regulating them, they are still interested in safeguarding, via the instruments of law, the stability of airlines, which has yielded measurable domestic economic benefits and served national interests in many respects. Such a regulatory instrument, that is, creating an

[3]The main activity of airlines is the carriage of passengers. In the passenger carriage segment, airlines generate low revenues due to fierce competition, the price of kerosene, high tax burdens and many other factors. In other areas, such as the consignment of cargo or charter activities, airlines realise by far higher profits. In 2012 the IATA member airlines on average made profits of 2.56 USD per passenger on one-way flights. According to the report by IATA, between 2004 and 2011, airlines made profits of 4.1 percent on average, which, in comparison with the profitability of other industries, is extremely low. In view of the fact that, in the inventory of a larger airline, the total value of its modern airplanes alone is several billion dollars, compared with the huge operational risk, this profit is not really prominent. Such enormous capital would yield much higher profits in other investments. At the same time, between 2015 and 2019, the IATA member airlines achieved quite high profits, of above 8.4 percent. However, during the COVID-19 pandemics (2020–2022) the airlines lost 186.9 billion USD, which means that the profits of the previous 5 years practically extinguished. Pearce (2013), p. 18.; IATA Annual Review. 2019, p. 44.; IATA Economics' Chart of the Week. A return to industry profitability in 2023. 9 December 2022.

advantageous situation for the air carriers, was the comprehensive limitation of the liability of airlines for damages under an international treaty (the Warsaw Convention).

The introduction of the limitation protected not only the air carriers but also facilitated the uniformisation both of the assertion of the right to compensation and of the due extent of payments, as well as the reduction of the number of frequently circumstantial and protracted lawsuits between the subjects of the legal relation of carriage.[4] The limitation of liability for damages also diminished the high financial risk arising from the activity of carriage by air. In this way financing the insurance became cheaper and the financial consequences of causing damage became more predictable. These manifested themselves in decreasing operating costs and the falling price of air services. As a consequence of the limitation, before the commencement of the journey, the passenger or the consignor of cargo was obliged to take out insurance for a considerably higher amount than the limited amount of compensation to be paid by the airline.

With good reason, the question arises whether the passenger or the consignor of the cargo was aware of the circumstance that, in the event of an accident, the air carrier did not compensate for the value of the whole damage, but only for its fraction. Pursuant to the Warsaw Convention, the answer is unequivocally yes. Namely, on the basis of the provision of the Convention, the airline, before the commencement of the flight, was obligated to warn each passenger of this condition indicated on the air ticket proving the contractual relationship. The air ticket needed to contain an unambiguous warning that the carriage may be covered by the Warsaw Convention, which in most cases limited the liability of carriers for death or personal injury and in the case of the loss of or damage to the baggage [Article 3 (1) *c)*].

However, in practice, the majority of passengers would not read the contractual conditions indicated on the air ticket, but this essentially did not affect the limited liability of air carriers. If an air carrier fulfilled its obligation to communicate the information lawfully, it could maintain its advantageous situation deriving from the limitation. If the passenger did not read the warning publicised on the air ticket, this fact did not have any implication for the air carrier since, pursuant to the Roman legal maxim, ignorance of the law does not exempt anyone from bearing responsibility *(ignorantia iuris neminem excusat)*. Although the contracting States strictly demanded the communication of such information, however, they excluded its application to passengers with sight defects, to the illiterate, and to those who did not understand the conditions of the contract written in a foreign language.

[4] Drion (1954), pp. 36–41.

8.1.2 *The Signification of Documentation*

The documents of carriage (the passenger ticket, the air waybill upon the consignment of cargo) have probative force. In the absence of evidence to the contrary, the passenger ticket, as main evidence, shall constitute *prima facie* evidence [5] of the conclusion and conditions of the contract of carriage [Article 3 (2)] and, consequently, of the route as agreed upon by the parties without any doubt whatsoever. The international character of the carriage may be established according to the exact route (the place of departure and the place of destination) accepted by the contracting parties [Article 1 (2)], which is important since the Warsaw Convention is applicable only and exclusively to cases of *international carriage*, not to domestic carriage.

The Warsaw Convention strictly demanded notification on the passenger ticket of the limited liability of the air carrier. The passenger needed to be aware of the fact of the limitation in time so that they could take out supplementary insurance with more favourable conditions in order to gain greater protection. The absence, irregularity, or loss of the passenger ticket in itself did not affect the existence or validity of the contract of carriage [Article 3 (2)], but it had an entirely detrimental legal consequence for the carrier. Namely, if, with the consent or awareness of the air carrier, the passenger embarked the aircraft without a passenger ticket made out in advance or if the ticket did not include the general warning pertaining to the limitation of liability and an accident happened, the air carrier forfeited its right to determine the upper limit of the compensation and was liable for the damage caused *without limitation*. The air carrier could also forfeit the applicability of the limitation clause if, in the lawsuit, the passenger (in the case of their death, their relative) proved successfully that they could not avail themselves of the opportunity to purchase extra insurance because the condition pertaining to the limitation was ineligible or incomprehensible.

In the lawsuit *John Lisi versus Alitalia*,[6] the plaintiff took recourse to the court with the claim that the airline should pay total compensation for the damage instead of that of about 8300 USD (this was the normative amount at that time) deriving from limited liability for the fatally injured passenger on board the airplane travelling from Rome (FCO) to New York (JFK), which crashed close to Shannon Airport. In the lawsuit, the plaintiff founded his claim on the fact that the notification on the passenger ticket had been printed in modern typeface letters sized 4. Consequently, before the flight, the passenger had

(continued)

[5] A Latin expression meaning on its first encounter or at first sight. It is based on first impression; accepted as correct until proved otherwise.

[6] *John Lisi v. Alitalia,* US Court of Appeals Second Circuit, Nos. 91–95, Dock. 30543–30547, 1966. pp. 510–514.

been unable to read and construe the warning on the ticket appropriately; therefore, he had not been able to take prudent steps in order to supplement his insurance. The court sustained the action, highlighting that by printing the notification in Lilliputian letters, the airline concealed the conditions of the flight; therefore, the air carrier had to compensate for the entire damage.

The *Lisi* case did not become a precedent to be followed by other judicial forums, it is rather an interesting example of the struggle for breaking through the limitation from the position of the plaintiff.

In the lawsuit *Chan Elisa versus Korean Air Lines*,[7] the plaintiff took recourse to the court with the claim that, in the case of the passenger who had been killed in the tragedy of Flight 007 of Korean Air Lines (KE), the airline should compensate for the entire damage instead of the limited amount specified in the Warsaw Convention, which had been raised to 75,000 USD under the Montreal Agreement applicable in the event of death. While issuing the air ticket, the airline used modern typeface letters sized 8 instead of the modern characters of size 10 prescribed under the Montreal Agreement (1966) (see, 8.2.3) concluded among the airlines. Thus, the passenger could not read clearly and interpret the warning, consequently, they did not take due steps to purchase supplementary insurance. Nevertheless, the court ruled that by the use of letters of size 8, the defendant airline did not forfeit its advantage deriving from limited liability guaranteed under the Warsaw Convention, therefore, the court dismissed the plaintiff's action. Although the reference to the size of the letters was unsuccessful, the plaintiff (a relative of the passenger), not long after the ruling, broke through the limitation of liability for damages in another way. Subsequently to the end of the Cold War, an international team of experts examined the flight recorder (black box) of the crashed aircraft, which revealed that the pilots had been unambiguously responsible for the occurrence of the tragedy. Consequently, *Korean Air Lines* was denied the protection of the limited liability for damages guaranteed by the Warsaw Convention, therefore, it had to pay damages in full to the heirs of the victims.

[7] *Chan Elisa v. Korean Air Lines,* Supreme Court Reporter, 490 U.S. 122, 104 L. Ed. 2d 113, 1989.

Thenceforward, the crucial factor in judicial practice consisted not in the size of the letters, but a much more practical aspect: the delayed receipt of the passenger ticket (for example, the passenger received their air ticket while embarking,[8] or they gained access to their air ticket on board in their seat).[9] In these cases it is unequivocal that the passenger could not read the warning, or if they did, they could do so in the moment preceding departure, thus, they did not have time to take steps in the interest of the further reinforcement of their protection.

The majority of passengers do not pay attention to the contractual conditions written on the air ticket; their attention is obviously focused on the time of departure and arrival. If any of the passengers did read the warning attentively, generally, they did not arrive at the conclusion to turn to an insurance company in order to supplement the low amount determined for the occurrence of an accident under the contractual conditions. However, the contracting States provided the opportunity for the passenger before the commencement of the flight to purchase insurance entitling them to an amount of compensation deemed sufficient and favourable, or to agree to a higher limit of liability with the air carrier under a special contract [Article 22 (1)] and, in the case of registered baggage of high value, a special declaration of interest in delivery at destination for a supplementary sum [Article 22 (2) *a)*] could be made under the Warsaw Convention.

Although it safeguarded the limited liability of the airlines by all means, in certain cases the Warsaw Convention provided scope for the forfeiture of the limitation. In the system of the Warsaw Convention, liability became unlimited, if pursuant to the provisions of the Convention, the intentional conduct of the airline as damaging party was established. For this to apply, the claimant needed to prove that the damage resulted from an act or omission of the carrier, his servants, or his agents, which was done negligently/recklessly *(luxuria)* or with intent to cause damage and with knowledge that damage would probably result from it (Article 25).

[8] *Warren v. Flying Tiger Line Inc.*, US Court of Appeals ninth Circuit, 352 F. 2d 494, 1965.

[9] *Mertens v. Flying Tiger Line Inc.*, US Court of Appeals second Circuit, 341 F. 2d 851, 1965.

In the lawsuit *Marjorie Zicherman versus Korean Air Lines*,[10] the plaintiff took recourse to the court with the claim that, in the case of a passenger who died in the tragedy of Flight 007 of Korean Air Lines (KE), the airline should compensate for the entire damage instead of the limit specified in the Warsaw Convention and raised to 75,000 USD in the Montreal Agreement (1966) applicable in the case of death. The plaintiff submitted the claim with reference to the fact that the pilots, while proceeding in their duty, caused the tragedy via wilful misconduct and negligence, which was proved. Consequently, the limitation of the liability for damages was broken. The court established the liability of the airline and emphasised in its judgement that the heirs, on the basis of international maritime law, may claim further pecuniary compensation as a consequence of the loss of life occurring above the high seas. The court obligated the airline to pay the plaintiff (the relatives) compensation of 70,000 USD for the loss of companionship, 161,000 USD for the grief to be borne during their lives, 16,000 USD for the omitted support and inheritance and 100,000 USD for the pain and suffering of the deceased during their fall.

The Death on the High Seas Act (DOHSA) is integral to the national law of the United States, and it is applicable solely if the jurisdiction of an American court has been appointed to adjudge the case. The main objective of the act adopted in 1920 by the Congress of the United States is that, in accidents on the high seas and due to deaths therefrom, the heirs (child, wife, husband, parents, or relatives) will receive compensation from the owner of the ship. The statute also applies to aviation accidents but pertains only to commercial flights (does not extend to helicopters, State or military planes, or corporate or private airplanes). This rule is applicable only to accidents taking place beyond 12 nautical miles from the coast of the United States.[11]

Since the airlines paid unreasonably low compensation of a fixed amount for the loss of life, before the court, the relatives and heirs resorted to the only method of breaking through limited liability: pursuant to Article 25 of the Warsaw Convention, they endeavoured to prove the responsibility of the crew of the aircraft for the event. The array of solicitors saw evidence in all cases for the fact that the accident had ensued due to the wilful misconduct of the flight crew or the agent of the air carrier with malice aforethought, but mainly due to the deliberate negligence or recklessness *(luxuria)* of the pilot-in-command proceeding in their scope of duties. They did so with consideration to demand the highest possible amount of compensation for their clients from the airlines. This is the origin of the saying that in aviation it is not the safety risk that is high, but the membership of the Bar Associations.

[10] *Marjorie Zicherman v. Korean Air Lines, Co. Ltd.*, Supreme Court reporter 510 U.S. 217, 133 L. Ed. 2d 590, 1996.

[11] *Death on the High Seas Act* (DOHSA). *Code of Laws of the United States of America*. 46 U.S.C. appx. (Articles 761–768).

8.2 The Modernisation of the Warsaw Convention

With the passage of time, the Warsaw Convention became obsolete, although the contracting States amended it several times via further treaties and supplementary protocols. The continual revision of the Warsaw system of rules ensued primarily because of the reconsideration of liability limitations. The Member States did not always keep up with inflation, furthermore, the economic differences and divergences of the standard of living among the countries made the payments of the amounts of compensation disproportionate. The saying according to which 'the American passenger is the most expensive passenger' well described the evolved situation. The rulings passed by the courts of the United States one after the other secured the highest pecuniary and non-pecuniary compensation for the claimants, which encompassed all the elements of the damage, such as suffering, the loss of support and inheritance, the grief and pain of the relatives, the loss of paternal care, child-rearing, the absence of the loved person and the loss of an affectionate life. Since the quality of life and the cost of living vary by country, this fact was taken into consideration by the courts upon the calculation of the amount of damages.

For example, if in the United States a 45-year-old wage earner (having an administrative position) died in an air accident and left behind a wife and one child, the family would receive a compensation of approx. 4.5 million USD. The amount of compensation would be, under the same circumstances, equal to 1.7 million USD in Canada, 1.2 million USD in Great Britain, 1.4 million USD in France, and 450,000 USD in Eastern Europe, whereas in Asia, it would be between 250,000 and 650,000 USD.[12]

Claimants therefore generally filed their claims to US courts in the hope of the award of higher amounts of compensation due to the additional benefits deriving from the more effective protection of consumers. They did so even if the US courts did not have jurisdiction for the adjudication of the case, since the headquarters or the principal place of business of the air carrier was not registered in the territory of the US or the place of destination (the last destination on the air ticket) was not in the US. In such cases, the US courts rejected the action due to lack of jurisdiction to adjudicate.

---

[12] Harakas (2014), p. 7. (Note that these figures are presented for demonstrative rather than scientific purposes.)

In the case of *Klos versus Polish Airline* (LOT),[13] the passenger purchased a return ticket for the route Warsaw (WAW)–New York (JFK)–Warsaw (WAW) in May 1987. The real objective of the flight was not sightseeing, but the passenger wished to start a new life in New York. The passenger bought the return air ticket only with the intent to disguise his plan. However, the Ilyushin Il–62M airplane, Flight 5055 of the airline crashed shortly after take-off, and all persons on board lost their lives. The heirs-at-law relatives (plaintiffs) submitted the case to a US court with reference to the fourth forum, since the ultimate end of the journey of the deceased passenger, his destination was New York. Although in this case the first three forums secured the jurisdiction of a Polish court, the plaintiffs opted for the American forum of jurisdiction. However, the US court established that it could not proceed with the case due to lack of jurisdiction since the final destination of the journey was not New York but Warsaw, therefore, it dismissed the action. Undoubtedly, the air ticket attests the real objective of the journey (the place of departure and the place of destination were both Warsaw, whereas the agreed stopping place was New York). The subjective goal of the passenger in the contractual relationship was not relevant, hence it was a non-considerable circumstance in the judgment of the case.

If the responsibility of the air carrier was proved, it was by all means liable to the upper limit of the amount of compensation determined under the Warsaw Convention. Although the limitation of the amount of compensation implied measurable advantage for the air carrier, nevertheless, the contracting States precluded the possibility that the air carrier in an extreme case could settle unilaterally on a lower value than the determined amount of liability, or, exonerate itself from the obligation of compensation. All clauses with the objective of exoneration of the air carrier or the determination of a lower limit of liability than that prescribed under the Convention were null and void, but the nullity of any such clause did not entail the nullity of other provisions of the contract.

The main objective of the amendments to the Warsaw Convention was to raise the limits of liability and the amount of compensation. The increases in themselves did not solve all problems but they were conducive to achieve the accession of as many countries as possible to the international treaties amending the Convention, as well as the accession of as many airlines as possible to the agreements on carriage by air. Namely, the most important objective further on remained the same: should the parties entitled to compensation take action anywhere, the statutes to be applied in their cases and the judgments they are awarded need to be the same.

[13] *Stefania Klos v. Polskie Linie Lotnicze,* No. 379, Docket 97–7073, US Court of Appeals, Second Circuit 1997.

The modernisation of the Warsaw Convention ensued in several steps, of which the most important ones are the following:

- The Hague Protocol (1955);
- The Guadalajara Convention (1961);
- The Montreal Agreement (1966);
- The Guatemala City Protocol (1971);
- Montreal Additional Protocols Nos. 1, 2, and 3, and Montreal Protocol No. 4 (1975);
- The Japanese Initiative (1992);
- The IATA Intercarrier Agreements (1995–1996);
- The Regulation of the Council of the European Union (1997).

8.2.1 The Hague Protocol (1955)[14]

The objective of the ICAO Legal Committee (LC) was that, rather than drafting a new Convention, the content of the Warsaw Convention should be validated with the necessary amendments. The members of the Committee focused on counterbalancing the excessive protection of the airlines and on the assertion of the interests of the less protected passengers using the service. On this basis, the contracting Parties doubled the upper limit of the amount of compensation to be paid in the event of the death or injury of a passenger, thus, it was increased from 8300 to 16,600 USD (this amount did not include the cost of legal proceedings). While the majority of the States ratified the Protocol, the Government of the United States, with reference to the excessively low limit, refused to accede. (This is interesting because, as a consequence, in the United States, being a party to the Warsaw Convention, the upper limit of 8300 USD remained authoritative until 1966).

8.2.2 The Guadalajara Convention (1961)[15]

In the Guadalajara Convention, the States Parties extended the liability rules to relations where the passenger does not establish a contractual relationship with the air carrier actually operating the carriage (the airlines conclude so-called "code-share" agreements with one another (one is contractual carrier and the other one is

---

[14] Protocol to Amend the Convention for the Unification of Certain Rules Relating to International Carriage by Air, signed at Warsaw on 12 October 1929, done at The Hague on 28 September 1955.

[15] Guadalajara Convention, Supplementary to the Warsaw Convention, for the Unification of Certain Rules relating to International Carriage by Air performed by a person other than the contracting carrier. Signed Guadalajara at 18 September 1961.

the actual, operating carrier), that is, the flight on a specific route is operated jointly (see, Part II, Chap. 9. 4.5]. With this step, besides the contracting carrier, the actually operating carrier was also included in the scope of regulation.

8.2.3 *The Montreal Agreement (1966)*[16]

The Montreal Agreement is not an intergovernmental treaty but an agreement concluded by and between the airlines. The agreement raised the amount of compensation for death and bodily injury to 75,000 USD in the case of flights[17] departing from, arriving at in, or flying over the United States. The agreement was applicable in the case of the death or bodily injury of a passenger, but it did not contain provisions concerning baggage and consigned cargo. Airlines that intended to operate in the United States needed to accede to the Agreement in order to be granted permission to carry out commercial activity in the territory of the country. The United States encouraged the air carriers interested in cooperation and pressurised them commercially, since at that time 25% of international passenger carriage in the world was implemented through the US, and simultaneously, it had the largest number of domestic flights in the world.[18] Under the Montreal Agreement, airlines also assumed the obligation to print air tickets (with the warning of limited liability thereon) in Modern typeface letters sized 10 (Article 2).

8.2.4 *The Guatemala City Protocol (1971)*[19]

As a principal objective, the States concerned made an attempt to review the Warsaw Convention to raise the limits of liability and enhance the responsibility of the air carriers, but the Protocol never took effect as it was ratified by merely seven States. However, it became a historical document.

---

[16] Montreal Intercarrier Agreement. Agreement relating to Liability Limitations of the Warsaw Convention and The Hague Protocol. 31 Fed. Reg. 7302, Civil Aeronautics Board Order No. E–28680 approving CAB 18900, 13 May 1966.

[17] The amount of 75,000 USD contained all costs of the assertion of rights. If the claim was enforced before a court in a Federal State in which the costs of legal proceedings were reimbursed separately, the upper limit of pecuniary liability was 58,000 USD, which did not include the legal expenses. The territorial and personal scopes of the Agreement were restricted to air carriers which operated carriage departing from, flying over or arriving in the territory of the United States. *Montreal Intercarrier Agreement* (CAB18900), 1966. I (I).

[18] Wells and Chadbourne (1992), p. 83.

[19] ICAO Doc 8932 Guatemala City Protocol.

8.2.5 *Montreal Additional Protocols Nos. 1, 2, and 3, and Montreal Protocol No. 4 (1975)*[20]

The contracting Parties participating in the Diplomatic Conference convened in Montreal set the objective of addressing the questions left open by the Guatemala City Protocol. The Warsaw Convention had determined the limits of liability in the currency of the French gold francs.[21] After the Vietnam War, the United States and other countries devaluated their currency as a consequence of the war. Therefore, the determination of some new stable measurement was necessary. It became a unit designated as Special Drawing Rights (SDR).[22] The SDR is a supplementary international foreign exhange reserve asset, determined and maintained by the International Monetary Fund (IMF), an independent organisation belonging to the UN family. During the proceedings, the conversion of these amounts to the national currency was discharged by the court upon passing its judgment on the basis of the value of SDR prevalent in the given currency. Furthermore, the States Parties modernised and simplified the rules concerning the documentation of carriage, which resulted in serious changes, since the Parties could accept lawfully the (paperless) air waybill made out electronically. In addition, the air cargo could depart even if its complete documentation had not been prepared. The contracting Parties supplemented the limited liability of the air carrier for damage caused to the cargo with the clause that the upper limit of the liability for damage could not be surpassed [unbreakability (inviolability) of the liability limits], with the exception if a higher value had been stipulated in advance.

[20] In Montreal, the Additional Protocols Nos. 1–3 and a Protocol No. 4 were signed, which are jointly designated as the "Montreal Protocols." The Additional Protocol No. 3 did not take effect. The Additional Montreal Protocols Nos. 1., 2., 3.; ICAO Doc 9148 Montreal Protocol No. 4 to Amend the Convention for the Unification of Certain Rules Relating to International Carriage by Air signed at Warsaw on 12 October 1929 as amended by the Protocol done at The Hague on 28 September 1955. Montreal, 25 September 1975.

[21] The sums mentioned in francs shall be deemed to refer to a currency unit consisting of sixty-five and a half milligrams of gold of millesimal fineness nine hundred. These sums may be converted into national currencies in round figures. Conversion of the sums into national currencies other than gold shall, in case of judicial proceedings, be made according to the gold value of such currencies at the date of the judgement. Warsaw Convention, Article 22 (4).

[22] The amounts manifest in SDR pertain to a unit determined by the International Monetary Fund (IMF). The determination of the SDR is effected so that the major international currencies used in international transactions are united in a currency basket. The SDR (the currency code of which, according to the ISO–4217 Standards, is XDR) derives its value from a basket of five currencies: the Euro (EUR), the Japanese Yen (JPY), the United States Dollar (USD), the British Pound Sterling (GBP) and the Chinese Yuan Renminbi (CNY). The weight of the given currency manifest in SDR is determined by the weight the given national currency carries in international transactions. *IMF Review of the Method of Valuation of the SDR*. Executive Summary, July 2015, pp. 1–2.

8.2.6 *The Japanese Initiative (1992)*[23]

The Initiative encompassed ten Japanese airlines, which incorporated a special provision into their conditions of carriage. For its legal grounds, they drew on the Warsaw Convention, which facilitated that the airlines and the passengers could agree on a higher limit of liability under a special contract [Article 22 (1)]. According to the conception of the Japanese airlines, in the event of an accident sustained by the passenger, the air carrier acceded to the Initiative would be liable in a two-layered system:

- below the amount of 100,000 SDR, the air carrier cannot preclude or limit its liability; therefore, it shall be entirely liable for the damages;
- in the event of damages exceeding 100,000 SDR, the air carrier shall be liable for the amount of proven damage if it cannot exonerate itself.

Via the Initiative, the Japanese airlines made history, because their recommendation consisting of three paragraphs on barely half a page established the *unlimited* liability of the air carrier with respect to accidents sustained by the passenger. Although an upper limit was applied, its significance was that the air carrier could only exonerate itself from liability above that amount. It is incredible: what the States had been unable to reach an agreement on for 40 years, some airlines could resolve after 7 years' negotiations. (Note: this two-layered system will appear later in the Montreal Convention.)

One of the most grievous catastrophes of the history of civil aviation underlay the commitment of the Japanese, which demonstrated in reality that the low level of the limits of liability for damage could not be tenable any longer. On 12 August 1985, 12 min after take-off the vertical stabilizer of a Boeing 747–400 Jumbo Jet airplane detached explosively due to a maintenance-repair fault on the Tokyo–Osaka Flight 123 operated by Japan Airlines (JL). The unnavigable plane crashed on the mountains. Of those on board, 520 persons lost their lives, and only two persons survived the accident. Since the flight was domestic, the Warsaw Convention was inapplicable. Therefore, the payment of compensation was determined pursuant to national law. However, these amounts considerably exceeded the Warsaw limits, so it became unambiguous that, had this been an international flight, the relatives of the victims would have received much less compensation.

[23] Japan Airlines' Conditions of Carriage; "The Japanese Initiative". *Lloyd's Aviation Law* (11). 1995/22.

8.2.7 The IATA Intercarrier Agreements (1995–1996)[24]

In June 1995, Washington, D.C. accommodated the IATA international conference, where two agreements were drawn up (IIA/MIA) by the member airlines. The majority of air carriers accepted the "two-layered system" (see, Part II, Chap. 12.2) of the Japanese Initiative (1992) guaranteeing higher liability limits and agreed that the Warsaw system inevitably needed a complete review besides the preservation of its bases. The review of the Warsaw system was necessitated by the rigorous liability rules and the low value limits, which were unfair towards the claimants.

8.2.8 The Regulation of the Council of the European Union (1997)

Although the law of the European Union does not constitute international law (therefore, it does not belong to the international treaties reforming the Warsaw system), we need to make mention of it here since the institutions of the European Union were among the pioneers in the modernisation process of the system of liability for damages governing air carriers. The European Union also deemed the value limits of the liability of air carriers low, so it urged that uniform liability rules be prescribed within the Community. The legitimacy of the regulation within the Union was justified mainly because the Warsaw Convention contained rules exclusively concerning international air carriage; on the other hand, in the internal market of the EU, the legislator abolished, on 1 April 1997, the distinction between domestic and intra-EU carriage as part of the Third Package.[25] Consequently, in the internal market of the Community, liability rules based on the same regulations were necessary. A further intent of the legislators of the European Union was to reinforce the protection of passengers involved in air accidents, therefore, an unlimited liability system in the event of the death or bodily injury of passengers was introduced.

---

[24] The Intercarrier Agreement on Passenger Liability (IIA) and the Agreement on Measures to Implement the IATA Intercarrier Agreement (MIA) adopted at the 51st General Assembly of IATA organised in Kuala Lumpur in October 1995.

[25] The Third Package (HL L 240.) consisted of Council Regulation (EEC) No. 2407/92 on licensing of air carriers; Council Regulation (EEC) No. 2408/92 on access for Community air carriers to intra-Community air routes; Council Regulation (EC) No. 2409/92 on fares and rates for air services.

The before-mentioned Council Regulations are no longer in force. The new Regulation replaced all of them by one, that is, Regulation (EC) No 1008/2008 of the European Parliament and of the Council of 24 September 2008 on common rules for the operation of air services in the Community. Official Journal L 293, 31/10/2008, pp. 3–20.

As a result of legislation, the European Parliament and the Council of Europe adopted Council Regulation (EC) No. 2027/97 on air carrier liability in the event of accidents,[26] which was amended under Regulation (EC) No. 889/2002 of the European Parliament and of the Council 5 years later.[27] The latter measure was necessary since on 5 April 2001, the Council of Europe made a decision on the approval of the accession of the European Union to the Montreal Convention and on the harmonisation of EU regulations with its rules.[28] According to the justification of the Council, the Community and its Member States had parallel competence concerning the issues encompassed by the Montreal Convention, therefore, for the purpose of its uniform and comprehensive application, the simultaneous ratification of the Montreal Convention by the EU and its Member States was inevitable.

Council Regulation (EC) No. 2027/97 is to be applied in the event of the death or bodily injury suffered by a passenger, if the accident that caused the damage so sustained took place on board an aircraft or in the course of any of the operations of embarking or disembarking (Article 1). Following the models of the Japanese Initiative and the IATA Intercarrier Agreements, the European Union on the Member State level introduced the unlimited liability of Community air carriers for damages in the event of the death or bodily injury of passengers. The Community air carrier,[29] for any damages up to the sum of the equivalent of 128,821 SDR (ca. 155,000 EUR), may not challenge the claim for compensation or exclude or limit its liability [Article 3 (2)]. Up to this amount, the air carrier is absolutely liable, therefore, it shall provide compensation in all cases. Above the amount of 128,821 SDR, fault liabity prevails, which means that the air carrier shall be liable for the damage caused, but may resort to defence against the claim (may be exonerated wholly or partly from its liability), if it can prove that the damage derived from the negligence of the injured or deceased passenger or the passenger contributed to the occurrence of the damage [Article 3 (3)]. The burden of proof shall be borne by the Community air carrier; as a consequence, the passenger is granted greater opportunity to enforce their claim for damages more successfully.

As the above-mentioned regulatory solutions demonstrate the 'Warsaw system' outgrew itself. Due to increased traffic and the changed commercial circumstances, it no longer served the purpose for which it had actually been established. The modernisation of the Warsaw Convention had constantly been on the agenda and, as a consequence of the previous amendments and accessions to them in various numbers, it gradually became a rather complex and heterogeneous system of rules. It was not by chance that the international community coordinated by ICAO, as a result

---

[26] *Official Journal L 285, 17/10/1997*, pp. 1–3.

[27] Council Regulation (EC) No. 889/2002 of 13 May 2002 amending Council Regulation (EC) No. 2027/97 on air carrier liability in the event of accidents HL L 140, 30 May 2002, p. 2.

[28] Council Decision 2001/539/EC of 5 April 2001 on the Conclusion by the European Community of the Convention for the Unification of Certain Rules for International Carriage by Air.

[29] The *community carrier* is an airline with air traffic rights in the Member States of the European Union, which is in the substantial ownership (50% + 1) of EU States and/or the citizens of the Member States and is under effective control (see, Part I, Chap. 2. 5.5).

of the work and deliberations of 33 years, reached the ultimate and all-encompassing destination of the process: the Montreal Convention.[30]

8.3 The Warsaw System and the Montreal Convention

The Montreal Convention summarises the results of flatly 70 years' treaty-making, and it retains certain provisions from the original text and the subsequent amendments of the Warsaw Convention while meeting the most recent demands of regulation. The Montreal Convention, is not a 'successor' of the Warsaw regime; it is a new international treaty, which was designed to create complete uniformity in the liability relations between air carriers and their passengers as well as between air carriers and consignors under private law. However, the establishment of such uniformity requires as many accessions by the States as possible. The Montreal Convention 'predominates' over the outdated Warsaw System, replaces the Warsaw Convention and its amendments in all respects, and *prevails over* any other rules that apply to international carriage by air (Article 55).

Nevertheless, the Warsaw Convention is still in effect; it was ratified by 152 States. At the same time, the Montreal Convention has been ratified by 139 States and a regional economic integration organisation, the European Union itself.[31] Thus, there are still States, although in a diminishing number, where the Warsaw Convention and its amendments are still in effect. This fact further complicates the adjudication of cases on the basis of the Warsaw system. The situation is also aggravated by the fact that certain States may have ratified different amendments of the Warsaw Convention, thus, it is very likely that the passengers on the same airplane are subject to different rules and different jurisdictions. In the case of one passenger, the Montreal Convention is applicable, in the case of the other one, the Warsaw Convention and its amendments apply, while the third passenger's situation (in the absence of the ratification of the before-mentioned conventions by their States) is governed by national law; therefore, in the event of an accident, their claims for damages will be adjudged on the basis of different rules of liability. A strange situation may also emerge where if the airline sustains a catastrophe, less compensation will be due to the relatives of the deceased passenger than to a less injured person surviving the accident. The reason is that the heir of the deceased passenger is entitled to compensation on the basis of the Warsaw Convention and its

[30] Milde (2003).; ICAO *Special Meeting on Limits for Passengers under the Warsaw Convention and The Hague Protocol,* Montreal, 1–15 February 1966.

[31] The European Community as a regional economic integration organisation deposited the ratifying document with the Secretary General of ICAO on 29 April 2004, as a consequence of which the Convention took effect for the EU on the 60th day afterwards, that is, on 28 June 2004; Council Decision 2001/539/(EC) of 5 April 2001 on the Conclusion by the European Community of the Convention for the Unification of Certain Rules for International Carriage by Air (the Montreal Convention 1999). Official Journal L 194, 18/07/2001 P. 0038–0038.

amendments (its version amended by The Hague Protocol and the Montreal Agreement) and may in the first step claim compensation of at most 75,000 USD, whereas the passenger subject to the Montreal Convention may claim compensation, with respect to the degree of the injury, of at least SDR 128,821 (ca. 170,000 USD).[32] If the damage is lighter, the demand of the claimant shall be fulfilled under this amount. If the damage is more severe, i.e., it exceeds the equivalent of SDR 128,821 and the air carrier cannot exonerate itself above this sum, it shall indemnify the entire amount of the proven damage to the passenger.

The different practice of the application of law under the Continental and the Anglo-Saxon (case-law) legal regimes founded on each other permissively by the Warsaw regime gave rise to a special situation. The voluminous case-law practice under the Warsaw System became a knowledge base in the course of time, which the treaty-maker saved for posterity with a unique legal technical solution: several legal institutions and concepts of the Warsaw Convention (e.g., limited liability, the exclusivity of the Convention, the four jurisdictional forums, the limitation of liability, the concepts of accident and international carriage) were transplanted into the new Montreal Convention in some places with minor modifications, which did not affect their substance. Consequently, the relevant legal cases in this scope will have further significance in the application of law, they provide guidance for the judges and shape the law. Therefore, the proceeding courts of the States that acceded to the Montreal Convention may refer to and rely on former case-law (judicial precedent) and legal practice constituting precedence on the basis of the Warsaw Convention and its additional Protocols.

This way, the contracting States resolved the sustained differences and the consequently deriving conflicts persisting between the old and the new systems by framing an entirely new international treaty, i.e., the Montreal Convention (not by the amendment of the Warsaw Convention, although drawing thereon), which as a whole replaced all the former private aviation law (air carrier liability) conventions, protocols and agreements in the relations among the contracting States. The comprehensive uniformisation of aviation law is unequivocally only a matter of time, and the Montreal Convention will eventually predominate as being observed by the decisive majority of the international community.[33]

---

[32] The amount of 100,000 SDR per passenger determined in 1999 and all other amounts in Articles 21–23 of the Convention, for the purpose of the offset of the inflation, have been raised by the States Parties pursuant to the rule of Article 24 of the Montreal Convention. The upper limit in the case of passengers became 113,100 SDR in 2009, then 128,821 SDR in 2019. The limit, revised at 5-year intervals did not change in 2014, then, in 2019 it was amended again, and the raised amounts have been applied since 28 December 2019. *Revised Limits of Liability Under the Montreal Convention of 1999* (www.icao.int/secretariat/legal/Pages/2019_Revised_Limits_of_Liability_Under_the_MC).

[33] Sipos (2019), pp. 101–119.

8.4 The Montreal Convention (1999)

The ICAO Council convened a Diplomatic Conference in Montreal for the period between 10–29 May 1999 for the purpose of the finalisation and adoption of the draft of a new international treaty resting on the 70-year-old Warsaw System, which would eliminate the faults of the latter system and replace it. At the Conference held in the ICAO headquarters, 121 ICAO Member States participated, the envoy of the Vatican (not an ICAO Member), and the representatives of 11 international organisations were present as observers. As a result of successful treaty-making and cooperation, on 28 May 1999, the Final Act of the Conference was signed by 107 Member States, whereas the *Montreal Convention for the Unification of Certain Rules for International Carriage by Air* was signed by the representatives of 52 States.[34] The contracting Parties opened the Montreal Convention for signing by all States and regional economic integration organisations, whereas they did not provide this opportunity for international organisations. 'For the purpose of this Convention, a "Regional Economic Integration Organisation" means any organisation which is constituted by sovereign States of a given region which has competence in respect of certain matters governed by this Convention and has been duly authorised to sign and to ratify, accept, approve or accede to this Convention' [Article 53 (2)].

The taking effect of the Montreal Convention required further ratification by the signatory States and regional economic integration organisations. 'The Convention shall enter into force on the 60th day following the date of deposit of the thirtieth instrument of ratification, acceptance, approval or accession with the Depositary[35] between the States which have deposited such instrument' [Article 53 (6)]. The Depositary of the Convention is the International Civil Aviation Organization. The Government of the United States symbolically handed over the 30th instrument of ratification to the Secretary General of ICAO (the Depositary), consequently, the international treaty, under the name Montreal Convention (hereinafter: Convention), took effect on 4 November 2003 and simultaneously commenced its 'conquering' journey. Namely, the Convention is superimposed on all other private international rules on carriage by air. However, its universal enforcement can be realised entirely only if an increasing number of States and regional economic integration

[34] ICAO Doc 9740 Convention for the Unification of Certain Rules for International Carriage by Air. Montreal, 28 May 1999.

[35] The Depositary (the Secretary General of ICAO) shall promptly notify all signatories and States Parties of: (a) each signature of this Convention and date thereof; (b) each deposit of an instrument of ratification, acceptance, approval or accession and date thereof; (c) the date of entry into force of this Convention; (d) the date of the coming into force of any revision of the limits of liability established under this Convention; (e) any denunciation [Montreal Convention, Article 53 (8)].

organisations accede to the Convention since only this way shall the unification of certain rules for international carriage by air be comprehensively accomplished.[36]

Air transport is a specifically transboundary activity. Thus, compliance with international regulations and their implementation in and harmonisation with the national legal system are the obligations and basic interests of the States. Owing to the diverse degrees of social and economic development and political establishment of the countries of the world, the national economic role of the air transport industry is considered and gauged differently by the States, which affects, even if indirectly, the regulatory, industrial, and professional standard of the country. In certain regions (e.g., the European Union), the future of the sector is shaped by open competition, thus, traditional air carriers have been compelled, one after the other, to relinquish the market. In other regions, it is recognised that competition has priority, but it is a step-by-step process in which the strategic character of air transport providing public service needs to be retained as far as possible. In some countries, the air transport industry is a strategically highlighted and marked part of the national economy. Today, almost all countries agree that the excellent opportunities integral to air transport need to be exploited since in the modern world it is obvious that competition in a global environment is impossible without meritorious recourse to the air transport industry. This circumstance does not primarily focus on the maximisation of profits but on guaranteeing aviation safety and security on the highest practicable level, which means the protection of the life and safety of passengers, of the flight crew and of third persons on the surface, as well as on safeguarding significant material values.

The principal objective of the contracting States is the unification of the rules of international carriage by air but not of all of them, merely of really important regulations. These major rules of private international law are not only operative as collision norms, but they also include law governing legal relations, and they partly refer to or rely on national law (e.g., in the establishment of jurisdiction, in the conduct of legal proceedings, or in the calculation of damages). Namely, the legislator cannot unify all rules; therefore, it allows a broad scope for the application

[36]One of the reasons for the lengthy ratification process prevalent in international law is that several times the international community awaits ratification by the World Powers. Therefore, maybe long years or decades pass before the taking effect and gaining ground of an international treaty in broader scope. This holds true even if the majority of the international community evaluate the rule itself positively. If the World Powers do not ratify the international treaty or bide their time, this fact apparently decelerates or blocks the accession of other States to the specific international treaty. At the same time, if the Government of the United States ratifies an international treaty related to, for example, air navigation, owing to its crucial role and weight in aviation, the number of accessions will without doubt soar. Several international treaties exist, such as the Paris Convention (1919) or the Moon Agreement (1979), which did not achieve their objectives (they were considerably under-ratified) since the majority of the developed World Powers did not accede thereto with regard to their own best interests.

of national law. The following provisions of the Convention expressly refer to the application of national law:

- The national law of the court having jurisdiction and proceeding in the case shall govern the procedural issues [Article 33 (4) and Article 45].
- The action for damages may be filed within a period of 2 years. The method of calculating the 2 years' period shall be determined by the law of the court seized of the case [Article 35 (2)].

The contracting States do not define important concepts; thus, their precise definition and the clarification of their conceptual elements devolve on the application of national law. From the viewpoint of the Convention, one of the most important concepts, i.e., *accident*, is not precisely circumscribed, which may imply a problem in the process of unification with respect to the application of different interpretations under national laws.[37] Of course, the differences in interpretation affect adjudication as well, therefore, situations may arise which later cannot be remedied. For instance, if in the lawsuit the court seized of the case makes a decision detrimental to the claimant as a consequence of its interpretative method significantly derogating from international practice, an appeal against the decision may be lodged to a higher judicial forum, but this forum of legal remedy will also be on the national appellate level of the given country. Private law does not have an international judicial forum [unlike public law, where the International Court of Justice (ICJ) adjudges disputes between States]; therefore, despite the broadly applied international system of rules of the Convention, the national element will remain decisive.

The Convention was drafted in the official languages used in aviation and accepted by ICAO: in English, Arabic, French, Chinese, Russian, and Spanish languages. The texts of the Convention formulated in these languages are all uniformly authentic. However, the English version is somewhat 'more authentic' since the official language of the conference was English and the final draft of the Convention itself was also formulated in English, the world language of civil aviation.

The Convention consists of 7 Chapters and 57 Articles and focuses closely on four major areas:

- The format and conditions of documents of carriage and their layout (Articles 3–11);
- The liability regime (objective liability) (Articles 17–18);
- The limitations of liability (unlimited liability) (Articles 21–22); and
- Jurisdiction (five forums) (Articles 33, 46).

> Any State Party may denounce the Convention by written notification to the Depositary. The denunciation shall take effect one hundred and eighty days following the date on which notification is received by the Depositary (Article 54).

[37] Sandeepa (2016), pp. 1–17.

In the present part of the volume on private law, each provision of the Montreal Convention (1999) will be explicated in detail.

8.4.1 The Objectives of the Convention

In the Preamble to the Convention, the contracting States explicate lucidly the objective of framing the regulation and its most important basic principles. The principal objectives of the Convention are unification, the harmonisation of regulations, and the elimination of legal conflicts. These guarantee that the claims for damages of the injured passengers or the consignors of goods, irrespective of their nationality, the place of damage, or the competent court, will be adjudicated pursuant to the same rules anywhere in the world.

The contracting Parties recognised both the necessity of the modernisation and unification of relevant legal instruments and the importance of safeguarding the interests of the parties engaged in international carriage by air. With a view to that, equitable compensation based on the principle of restitution of rights is necessary. The contracting States of the Convention formulate unambiguously: they prioritise the protection of the interests of the customers participating in international carriage by air. The protection of customers was foregrounded to such an extent that upon drafting the Convention one of the drafters made the following remark not inadvertently: The solicitors of the claimants will be really pleased with the Convention![38]

The Montreal Convention is unequivocally in favour of customers since the customer became the 'Master'.[39]

- The *Warsaw System* favoured air carriers. Air carriers practically 'demanded' that they could pay compensation pursuant to the rules of the Warsaw Convention since they were protected by limited liability.
- In contrast, the *Montreal System* favours customers (passengers/consignors). The main example is that in the case of the death or bodily injury of a passenger, the liability of the air carrier for damages is unlimited; therefore, in the event of an accident, now the passenger 'demands' the air carrier with unlimited liability to pay compensation pursuant to the rules of the Convention.

Accordingly, after a long time costumers eventually landed in a more advantageous situation, since the treaty-maker harmonised the interests of the subjects of the contractual relationship via equitable compensation, painstakingly guarding the dispute resolution between the damaging party and the claimant as well as the proportional balance of their interests. In the Preamble of the Convention, the contracting States declare the significance of the Chicago Convention on International Civil Aviation (1944), in harmony with the principles and objectives of which

[38] Whalen (2000), p. 15.

[39] Caplan (1999), p. 193.

they intend to safeguard both the orderly development of international air carriage operations and the smooth flow of passengers, baggage, and cargo.

8.4.2 The Liability System of the Convention

In the next part of the book, I will introduce via legal cases the whole process from filing the action to the actual adjudication of the damage. Consequently, the reader can familiarise themselves more thoroughly with the cause-effect relations underlying the decisions reached during the court proceedings. For the adjudication of a legal case pursuant to the rules of the Convention, the judge needs to consider several elements and the circumstances of the case. If all the essential elements/requirements of the examined case fulfil the conditions stipulated under the Convention, the court awards the indemnity of the damage on the basis of the rules of the Convention. If a condition or an element of the facts of the case is missing, the court dismisses the action because it cannot settle it pursuant to the provisions of the Convention. Obviously, the passenger (plaintiff), in this case, does not remain without legal assistance since their action can be adjudged on the basis of national law.

The establishment of the liability of the air carrier for damage and the process of the determination and indemnification of damage are introduced in the following five Phases (I–V), and within these, in closely related questions of the examination. In these Phases, taking into account their importance, the rules on the carriage of passengers and baggage or cargo are expounded more emphatically and in detail.

8.4.2.1 Phase I: The Scope of Application of the Montreal Convention

In the first Phase, the primary task of the court is the establishment of the applicability of the Montreal Convention, of the personal and substantive conditions necessary to bring a claim, and of other procedural issues (e.g., jurisdiction, international carriage, limitation periods).

1. Examination of the *documents of carriage* (air ticket and air waybill).
2. Does the court have *jurisdiction* for the adjudication of the case?
3. Does the given legal relation fall under the *substantive scope* of the Convention?
4. Does the *personal scope* of the Convention cover the parties concerned?
5. Was the claim for damages submitted within *the prescribed time limit*? Was the complaint against the air carrier filed within *the prescribed time limit*?

8.4.2.2 Phase II: Examination of the Liability of the Air Carrier

If in the first Phase the court finds that everything is appropriate, the court, on the basis of the facts of the specific legal case, shall examine the matter meritoriously. The court shall examine the liability of the air carrier or its absence.

6. Is the air carrier liable for the injury suffered by the passenger?
7. Is the air carrier liable for the damage to the baggage of the passenger?
8. Is the air carrier liable for the damage to air cargo?
9. Is the air carrier liable for the damage caused by the delay of passengers, baggage, or air cargo?

8.4.2.3 Phase III: Exoneration of the Air Carrier from Liability

If in the second Phase the liability can be established, the court shall examine whether the air carrier can adduce a circumstance that exonerates it wholly or partly from the obligation of indemnification.

10. Can the air carrier be exonerated from liability according to the provisions of the Convention on the possibilities of exoneration?
11. In case the air carrier is wholly exonerated from liability under the provisions of the Convention, can it be held accountable later under national or other laws?

8.4.2.4 Phase IV: Limited or Unlimited Liability of the Air Carrier

If in the third Phase the air carrier cannot exonerate itself, the court shall establish its limited or unlimited liability and shall obligate the air carrier to indemnify the damage. As a main rule, the air carrier has limited liability for the destruction, loss of, or damage to baggage or cargo as well as for the delayed carriage of passengers, baggage, or cargo, whereas it has unlimited liability for the death or bodily injury of passengers.

12. In which cases can the air carrier limit its liability?
13. When does the air carrier's liability become unlimited?

8.4.2.5 Phase V: Compensation

If on the basis of the fourth Phase the court obligates the air carrier to indemnify the damage, it shall determine the precise sum of indemnity in consideration of the rules, of the limited amount under the Convention, and of all the circumstances of the case.

14. Which elements of the damage caused to the claimant can be remedied by the indemnity and how?

During adjudication, the judge assesses each essential condition required under the Convention because only in the case of the joint prevalence of conditions may the satisfaction of the demands of claimants for damages ensue on the basis of the rules of the Convention.

References

DeMace K (n.d.) Farman F.60 Goliath – The plane of the week (Theflightblog.com)
Caplan H (1999) Novelty in the New Convention 1999. Aviat Q 4:193
Drion H (1954) Limitation of Liabilities in International Air Law. Springer, Dordrecht, pp 36–41
Harakas AJ (2014) Aviation Issues in the US. McGill University, Lecture, p 7
Landry JE (1975) Swift, Sure and Equitable Recovery. A Developing Concept in International Aviation Law. N Y State Bar J 47:372–374
Milde M (2003) From Warsaw 1929 to Montreal 1999. In: IASL/McGill Symposium, UAE, Dubai, 13–14 December 2003
Pearce B (2013) Profitability and the Air Transport Value Chain. In: IATA Economics Briefing, Vol 10. IATA, p 18
Sandeepa BB (2016) Air Carrier Liability for Passenger Death or Injury under Carriage by Air Act 1972. Nima Univ Law J 5(2):1–17
Sipos A (2019) The Modernisation of Air Carrier Liability. Is the New Montreal Convention the Humble Successor to the Warsaw System? ELTE Annals 58:101–119
Wells AT, Chadbourne BD (1992) Introduction to Aviation Insurance and Risk Management. Krieger, Melbourne, p 83
Whalen TJ (2000) The New Warsaw Convention: The Montreal Convention. Air and Space Law J 25(1):15

Chapter 9
The Scope of Application of the Montreal Convention

International treaties may be established among international legal entities (States, international organisations). States are entities of international law with full powers, and their capacity to conclude agreements is complete. States may manifest their recognition of the binding effect of international treaties by signing, ratification, approval, and accession. These acts give rise to rights and obligations proceeding from international treaties for the contracting States. The applicability of the Convention depends on several factors, first and foremost on the fact whether the sovereign State has acceded to the treaty, in this case to the Montreal Convention. If so, by reason of this fact the Convention integral to national law has binding effect and is applicable. Of course, this does not suffice in itself because in a specific situation, although the country has acceded to the Montreal Convention, it is not applicable to the judgement of specific cases. For the establishment of the applicability of the Convention, the primary tasks are the determination of the personal and substantive conditions, of major procedural issues such as jurisdiction and the examination of the limitation periods.

9.1 Examination of Documentation

Initially, in the first phase, the documentation of carriage is examined because it is indispensable for the establishment of the personal and substantive scopes of application and of jurisdiction. We can learn the most important information from the documents of carriage, namely, what the real intent of the passenger or the consignor was concerning the final destination of the flight or the carriage of cargo. Namely, it can be unambiguously established owing to familiarisation with the geographical connecting points, *the places of departure* and *destination* indicated in the documents of carriage, whether the carriage qualifies as *international carriage* within the purview of the provisions of the Convention. If the carriage qualifies as international, the Convention is applicable, but if pursuant to the Convention the

A. Sipos, *International Aviation Law*, https://doi.org/10.1007/978-3-031-39066-1_9

carriage is not international, the liability for damages shall be adjudged under national law. This implies that the claims for damages by the passengers of a specific flight are adjudged individually and differently (depending on the applicability of the Convention) in consideration of the *place of departure* and the *place of destination* and, if this applies, of the *agreed stopping places* indicated on the air ticket. Consequently, on a specific flight, there may be passengers to whom different rules of liability pertain for the simple reason that they were travelling under different contractual relations. For instance, one passenger is just arriving at their destination, while for the other passenger this stopover is an agreed stopping place, from where they travel further or return.

It may have been simpler if the drafters of the Convention had not demanded the examination of the applicability of the Convention according to contracts from passenger to passenger, but if they had taken into account the specific aircraft itself upon the occurrence of damage. This can be conceived as follows: all the passengers participating in the flight subject to the Convention upon the occurrence of damage would without exception be indemnified under the same regime of liability for damages, that is, on the same flight at all times the same private legal rules of liability would apply to each passenger. The legal status of the aircraft subject to the scope of the Convention would be determined by the fact whether the State the aviation authority of which registered the aircraft is party to the Convention. However, the drafters of the Convention did not opt for this opportunity, but they chose a more complicated form, according to which the emphasis is laid on the persons and the contractual relations relevant in the air ticket or the air waybill.[1]

The documents of carriage have probative force: they attest the conclusion of the contract by the parties, proving without doubt the route acknowledged by the parties, which is necessary for the establishment of the applicability of the Convention.

The documents of carriage made out in writing include:

- in the case of the passenger: the *air ticket* and the *baggage identification tag* (Article 3);
- in the case of the consignment of cargo: the *air waybill* or the *cargo receipt permitting identification* (Article 4).

The provisions of the Convention simplify and renew considerably the specifications concerning the documentation of the carriage of passengers, baggage, and cargo. If, for some reason, the document of carriage is missing, the common intent of the contractual parties is attestable: the fact of the journey, the itinerary, and the route between the geographical connecting points. Air waybills are designed and distributed by IATA. There are two types of air waybills: an airline-specific one and a neutral one. Each airline-specific air waybill must include the air carrier's name, its head office address, its logo, and an air waybill number. Neutral air waybills have a similar layout and format to airline-specific air waybills. An air waybill has 11 digits and contains eight sheets of varying colours. However, paper-based air waybills are

[1] Dempsey and Milde (2005), p. 75.

no longer required, namely, e-air waybills have been in use since 2010.[2] Owing to a strategic objective, IATA has made the documents of carriage paperless within a simplification programme. In the modern, paperless world, in the reality of electronic tickets, it suffices to send a message from an iPhone, a fax, or email address, or to produce either an invoice or a memorandum made out by an agent, furthermore, it is satisfactory merely to be registered by IATA or the airline, all of which prove the conclusion of the contract.[3]

On 31 May 2008, the air transport industry took leave of paper-based air tickets officially. Paper-based air tickets had been used from the 1920s, the contents and the layout of which had been unified in the 1930s. The first electronic tickets were issued in 1994 and IATA adopted rapidly the global standards for electronic air tickets.[4] Being paperless does not mean the disappearance of air tickets and air waybills from our lives, since documents testifying the contractual relationship are necessary. Namely, air tickets have significance not only in legal disputes, but they may be subject to frontier policing checks, they provide unambiguous information about the times of departures and arrivals, they contain the price (taxes) paid for the carriage and provide help with clearing accounts, etc. At the same time, for damage by reason of the loss, forgery, theft or annihilation of air tickets, the air carriers do not assume responsibility. In legal practice in a significant percentage of cases, the lack of these evidences does not cause problems, because a printable, tangible version always exists.

The Convention provides opportunity for air carriers to operate modern and efficient systems for handling tickets, such as the purchase of tickets via the Internet. Any other instrument which contains the indication of the places of departure and destination or the designation of the agreed stopping place may substitute the document. This way, the regulator facilitated the use of paperless, electronic documents of carriage. For instance, checking in for a specific flight is possible via the identification of a two-dimensional QR code appearing on the electronic ticket saved on a smartphone.

This new system not only entails considerable financial and administrative relief for the industrial performers, but it also made access to air services substantially easier both for the passengers and the consignors.

9.1.1 Contractual Relationship

Within the framework of civil law, between the *air carrier* and the *passenger* as well as the *air carrier* and the *consignor* of the cargo, as an expression of their mutual and

[2] IATA Resolution 672: Multilateral Electronic Air Waybill Agreement (www.iata.org/e-awb).

[3] Tompkins (2015), p. 153.

[4] While in 2007 the cost of the issuance of paper-based air tickets was 10 USD on average, the electronic air ticket cost 1 USD. The advantages are numerical, the issuance of 400 million paperless air tickets annually yielded savings of minimum 3 billion USD. Bisignani (2008).

unanimous intent, a written contract is concluded, which contains the designation of the places of departure and destination as well as the agreed stopping place(s). According to the air passenger's contract of carriage, the air carrier delivers the passenger on an aircraft from the airport of departure to the airport of arrival. The air carrier may diverge from the route indicated on the air ticket for reasons related to air traffic. The contract between the parties is concluded if

- the passenger makes payment of the fare offered by the air carrier (including authority taxes, dues, and other contributions); and
- the air carrier issues the air ticket.

The air ticket, until the contrary is proved, attests at first sight acceptably *(prima facie)* to the content of the legal declaration made by the air carrier and the passenger, that is, the conclusion of the contract. The sections of the journey indicated in one air ticket or connecting air tickets constitute the parts of one contract. A separate air ticket qualifies as a separate contract. However, the air ticket and the air waybill are more than a contract of carriage; they are rather documents attesting to the conclusion of a contract and the existence of a contractual relationship between the parties.[5] No formal specification exists for the contract of carriage, it can be entered into freely without the coercion of a form.

Nothing in 'the Convention shall prevent the carrier from:

- refusing to enter into any contract of carriage,
- waiving any defences available under the Convention, or
- laying down conditions which do not conflict with the provisions of the Convention' (Article 27).

Pursuant to the above, the air carrier may refuse to enter into a contractual relationship with any person whom, for some reason, it does not wish to see aboard its aircraft, for instance, a passenger who was unruly on the airline's other flights or does not hold an appropriate visa or travel documents or who does not produce them or has a physical condition or mental state that does not facilitate their safe carriage. At the same time, the contracting States expressly formulate that 'any clause contained in the contract of carriage and all special agreements entered into before the damage occurred by which the parties purport to infringe the regulations laid down under the Convention, whether by deciding on the law to be applied, or by altering the rules as to jurisdiction, shall be null and void' (Article 49).

The Convention only generally provides for the formal requirements and the content of the documents of carriage; therefore, the numerous and complex issues emerging during the carriage of passengers shall be settled according to the General Conditions of Carriage or other separate rules specified by the airlines. Under these rules, the air carriers explicate the rights and obligations of the passengers and the conditions of the carriage of persons and baggage in detail.

---

[5] Margo (2001), p. 10.

9.1.2 The General Conditions of Carriage

The detailed conditions of the contract of carriage by air concluded between the air carrier and the passenger not prescribed under effective regulations are stipulated under the General Conditions of Carriage. The provisions of the General Conditions of Carriage constitute a part of the contract between the air carrier and the passengers. The General Conditions of Carriage containing the conditions integral to the contract is not qualified as a legal statute, but it stipulates the servicing strategy of the airline, which is predetermined unilaterally by one party (the air carrier) for the purpose of the conclusion of several contracts via the establishment of the servicing framework, whereas the other party (the passenger) is not involved in the determination of the conditions part of the contract.

Therefore, it is a basic legal requirement that the air carrier may not determine the rights and obligations of the contracting parties proceeding from the contract unreasonably and disproportionately to the detriment of the passenger. This is guaranteed by the obligation of the party applying the General Conditions of Carriage to furnish evidence for the fact of the contingent violation of the law, furthermore, the General Conditions of Carriage is to be drafted by the airlines in consideration of international and EU regulations, the IATA specifications and recommendations, and national statutes and authority prescriptions in line with the approval of the authority. The General Conditions of Carriage may not be contrary to statutes, but apart from this, the air carriers decide themselves, maybe differently, what services and under what conditions they provide for their passengers. For reasons of safety, the air carrier may prohibit or restrict the use of various electronic devices (mobile phones, laptops, portable recording devices, portable radios, CD players, electronic toys, re-recording equipment, radio-controlled toys). However, the use of hearing aids and pacemakers is permitted on board aircraft.

The General Conditions of Carriage becomes part of the contract if its applier has facilitated that the other party familiarised themselves with its content preceding the conclusion of the contract and the other party consented thereto. Therefore, the specifications of the General Conditions of Carriage, for the purpose of familiarisation with them, are made accessible for the passengers by the airline both in the customer service premises or electronically. IATA prescribes the notification of the passengers of the fact that the detailed and all-encompassing system of the conditions of carriage is contained by the General Conditions of Carriage of the airline.

IATA determined the minimum conditions of the contract to be applied by its member airlines as recommended practices in Carrier Agreements.[6] Since in the air ticket the indication of the complete system of conditions is impossible because of limited place, in the air ticket the airlines inform the passengers about the basic conditions of the contract, primarily about the limited liability of the air carrier. If the General Conditions of Carriage and the contract conflict with each other, the latter prevails and becomes the guideline.

[6] IATA Recommended Practice 1724: *General Conditions of Carriage, Passenger Services Conference Resolutions Manual* (PSCRM). 42nd edn., 2022.

Breach of the obligations provided under the Carrier Agreement entails legal consequences. The air carrier is authorised to take measures considered necessary, if the passenger on board the aircraft manifests conduct which, according to the grounded judgement of the crew members, jeopardises the aircraft, the safety of persons and property on board or aviation safety, or via which they verbally or physically harass the crew members or hamper them in discharging their duty, or if the passenger does not follow the instructions of the crew, or occasions inconvenience, nuisance, or injury to the persons on board, or causes damage to the property on board.

During the complete time of carriage, the passenger is obligated to manifest conduct in conformity with the instructions of the airline employees, not only on board but during embarking and disembarking as well.

9.1.3 Passenger Documentation: Air Ticket and Baggage Identification Tag

Upon the carriage of the *passenger*, the documents of carriage may be made out in writing or in electronic form, or by any other means. However, the air carrier needs to issue a written declaration for the passenger in all cases, which has to contain:

- an indication of the places of departure and destination; and
- if the places of departure and destination are within the territory of a single State Party, one or more agreed stopping places being within the territory of another State, an indication of at least one such stopping place [Article 3 (1)].

The Convention prescribes merely the former two basic conditions, the indication of the geographical connecting points (of departure and destination) as a compulsory content element of the air ticket. Its reason is that upon causing damage, the establishment of the international character of carriage and the real destination of the journey should be possible on the basis of the geographical connecting points without doubt. In practice, the airlines indicate the abbreviated IATA designation of the airports of departure and destination in three letters, furthermore, the flight number and the number of the baggage identification tag. The air ticket does not need to be printed out as the electronic form is valid as well. The air ticket entitles for journey only on routes, flights, at times and for reservation classes indicated therein.

The fare for the air ticket purchased by the passenger is determined by the entire route indicated on the air ticket. Consequently, the sections of the flight may be utilised only in the sequence the tickets specify, departing from the place of departure indicated in the air ticket. With the exception of the first section of the flight, the utilisation of other sections of the flight may be omitted, but the omitted section shall not entitle for posterior journey and its value may not be reimbursed. The air ticket forfeits its validity if the first section of the flight was not utilised by the passenger who intends to commence their flight from an agreed stopping place.

From a legal point of view, it does not matter who purchased the air ticket. It is all the more essential, however, that the air ticket may not be transferred unilaterally. IATA does not recommend its member airlines the practical introduction of unilateral transfer primarily for reasons of security and foreign policing (for example, an increasing number of countries demand prior information about the passengers), secondly, because of the practical considerations of market protection, since the secondary market of the sale of air tickets facilitating abuses would soon take shape.[7]

Thus, exclusively the person designated on the air ticket as passenger is entitled to take recourse to carriage, therefore, the identity of the passenger needs to be verified with photo ID. The Warsaw Convention (1929) demanded a great deal more content elements in the documents of carriage, because it implemented the practice adopted from maritime law[8] with all its formalities. If the air carrier committed a formal or procedural error (for example, it did not issue the air ticket in time or the air ticket was handed over to the passenger promptly before or in the midst of boarding the airplane with the awareness or consent of the air carrier, or the air ticket did not contain the warning about the limitation of the liability of the air carrier), the air carrier forfeited its protection via limited liability for damages.

Learning from experience, the drafters of the Montreal Convention (1999) handled this issue with flexibility. Considering merely the former decades, numerous actions had been lodged vis-à-vis the airlines with reference to the rigorous formal rules for the purpose of breaking the limited liability. Therefore, the treaty-makers introduced several reliefs, which do not facilitate any longer breaking the limitation of liability for damages by the plaintiffs during judicial proceedings with reference to formal or procedural faults.

As a main rule, 'the passenger shall be given written notice to the effect that where the Convention is applicable it governs and may limit the liability of carriers in respect of death or injury and for destruction or loss of, or damage to, baggage, and for delay' [Article 3 (4)]. 'Non-compliance with this provision by the airline shall not affect the existence or the validity of the contract of carriage, which shall, nonetheless, be subject to the rules of the Convention including those relating to limitation of liability' [Article 3 (5)].

The treaty-maker does nor stipulate sanction for the case of the omission of warning, in addition, it does not expand on the detailed rules of warning, nor does it mention the ultimate time of imparting the information, it merely stipulates that the warning has to be communicated in writing. Thus, the requirement that communication must be in writing does not extend to the air ticket, that is, it is not necessary that the warning appears on the air ticket because it suffices if the information is displayed on the website or billboard of the air carrier, or at an airline counter of the airport or in the airline ticket office. With respect to the fact that the Convention does

[7]IATA Transferability of Tickets. IATA Position Paper, 2012 (www.iata.org).

[8]Aviation law has adopted from maritime law such as the registration of aircraft, innocent (peaceful) passage, the eighth and ninth commercial rights of cabotage, the freedom of passage on the high seas, licensing procedures and administrative requirements.

not attach legal effect to non-compliance with the stipulation, therefore, in legal terms the disregard of the requirement above does not have legal consequences for the air carrier. Thus, the question arises: what is the point of the provision? In fact, via the provision, the legislator communicates expressly that an international regulation is in effect for the limitation of liability for damages and no derogation is admissible in the cases adjudged pursuant to the rules of the Convention in national legal systems.

On the basis of the contract of air carriage of passengers, the air carrier transports the passenger's baggage from the airport of departure to the airport of destination via aircraft. The contract is concluded after the passenger has paid the fare specified by the air carrier and after the air ticket and baggage identification tag have been issued. Upon the carriage of the *baggage*, 'the air carrier shall deliver to the passenger a baggage identification tag for each piece of checked baggage' [Article 3 (3)].

No formal requirement under the Convention applies to the separate baggage identification tag, thus, in practice the airline decides on the data appearing on the tag generally made out electronically. For security reasons, such a tag needs to be attached to each baggage, and only the baggage of a passenger on board may be loaded on the aircraft. On international flights upon the procedure of passenger-baggage matching in all cases if the passenger is not on board (misses the flight despite the warning about the closure of the boarding gate), or was on board, but for example, they were sick, and consequently, were disembarked from the airplane, the air carrier may not transport such passenger's baggage. In such cases the search for the concerned passenger(s)'s baggage in the storage space of the plane and its removal may cause more or less delay. This is an obligatorily prescribed rule: 'Each contracting State shall ensure that commercial air transport operators do not transport the baggage of persons who are not on board the aircraft unless that baggage is identified as unaccompanied and subjected to appropriate screening'.[9] This is the guarantee that no more accidents similar to the tragedy of Pan Am Flight 103 may occur.[10]

[9] ICAO Annex 17 on Aviation Security. Measures relating to hold baggage, 4.5, 4.5.3.

[10] Similar accidents were the following: (1) Air India Flight 182 from Montreal (YMX) to London (LHR) continuing to Bombay (BOM) on 23 June 1985 was destroyed with 329 fatalities, the bomb was planted in a baggage checked in at Vancouver airport, whose owner did not board the Boeing 747–237B aircraft. (2) At Tokyo Narita Airport (NRT) a bomb exploded on 22 June 1985, while luggage was being transferred from Canadian Pacific Airlines (CP) Flight 003 to Air India (AI) Flight 301 to Bangkok (BKK), owing to which two baggage handlers were killed and four other baggage handlers were injured. (3) Korean Air Flight 858 from Abu Dhabi (AUH) to Bangkok (BKK) on 29 November 1987 was destroyed with 115 fatalities, after two passengers had disembarked and left a radio/alarm clock and liquor bottles with explosives in the overhead compartment of the Boeing 707–300 aircraft. Canadian Aviation Safety Board (CASB) Final Report about Air India flight (aviation-safety.net/database/record.php?id=19871129-0).; ICAO Adrep Summary 4/88 (#11); ICAO Circular 259–AN/153 (234–243).; Rea, Bob: Lessons to be learned (www.publicsafety.gc.ca/cnt/rsrcs/pblctns/lssns-lrnd/index-en.aspx).

Pan Am (Pan American World Airways) Airline Flight 103 took off from London Heathrow (LHR) on 21 December 1988. The Boeing 747–121 airplane travelling to New York (JFK), with 243 passengers and 16 crew members on board, disappeared from the screen of the radio locator shortly after take-off and crashed onto the ground near the outermost houses of the Scottish village of Lockerbie. In the disaster, 11 persons on the ground also lost their lives. The airplane was exploded by Libyan terrorists with the use of a Semtex explosive. The plastic explosive blowing up the wide-body airplane was hidden in an unaccompanied checked baggage, the owner of which (the passenger) did not travel on board. This tragedy was the second gravest catastrophe of the air navigation of the United States caused by a terrorist act (the gravest disaster was the terrorist attack of 11 September 2001).

9.1.4 Cargo Documentation: Air Waybill and Cargo Receipt

"In respect of the carriage of cargo, an *air waybill* shall be delivered" [Article 4 (1)].

The most important functions of the air waybill include an emphasis on the limited liability provision, furnishing evidence of the terms and conditions of the contract of carriage, an acknowledgement of the receipt of cargo by the air carrier, furthermore, it verifies the description and the condition of the cargo when it was received by the air carrier.[11]

Upon the carriage of cargo, the consignor transfers the cargo to the air carrier so that it is unable to influence meritoriously either the process of carriage or the conduct of the air carrier during the consignment. Therefore, all circumstances of the carriage need to be documented regularly. The Convention permits the air waybill to be substituted by any other instrument that records the carriage to be carried out. Its issuance in electronic form had already been facilitated under the Montreal Additional Protocol 4 (MAP–1975).[12] 'If such other means are used the carrier shall, if so requested by the consignor, deliver to the consignor a *cargo receipt* permitting identification of the consignment and access for the consignor to the information contained in the record preserved by such other means' [Article 4 (2)]. The Montreal Convention incorporated all relevant provisions of the Montreal Additional Protocol 4 (e.g., paperless air waybill, inviolability of the liability limits, simplification, jurisdictions, etc.).

[11] Bartsch (2018), p. 200.

[12] ICAO Doc 9148 Montreal Protocol No. 4 to Amend the Convention for the Unification of Certain Rules Relating to International Carriage by Air signed at Warsaw on 12 October 1929, as amended by the Protocol done at The Hague on 28 September 1955. Montreal, 25 September 1975.; Sipos (2019), pp. 101–119.

As the Convention provides, upon the carriage of *cargo*, 'the air waybill and the cargo receipt as *prima facie* evidence proves the conclusion of the contract, the acceptance of the cargo and the conditions of carriage mentioned therein' [Article 11 (1)]. The air waybill and the cargo receipt prove the route agreed on by the parties without doubt, therefore, it contains three obligatorily prescribed elements:

(a) an indication of the places of departure and destination;
(b) if the places of departure and destination are within the territory of a single State Party, one or more agreed stopping places being within the territory of another State, an indication of at least one such stopping place; and
(c) an indication of the weight of the consignment (Article 5).

The contracting States significantly simplified the requirements pertaining to documents of carriage under the Convention. The Warsaw Convention required the mandatory indication of 17 pieces of information and data, of which the failure of the indication of 10 entailed the forfeiture of the application of limited liability guaranteed under the Convention for the air carrier, which consequently had to perform unlimited liability for any contingent damage to cargo.[13]

Air carriers may obligate the consignor to submit, if necessary, to 'the formalities of customs, police and similar public authorities by delivering a document indicating the nature of the cargo. This provision creates for the carrier no duty, obligation or liability resulting therefrom' (Article 6). This new rule gives rise to the air carrier's obligation merely to furnish information, which they otherwise need to fulfil towards the proceeding customs, police and other public authorities pursuant to national law. 'The consignor must furnish such information and such documents as are necessary for the examinations carried out by the customs, police and any other public authorities before the cargo can be delivered to the consignee. The consignor is liable to the carrier for any damage occasioned by the absence, insufficiency or irregularity of any such information or documents, unless the damage is due to the fault of the carrier, its servants or agents. The carrier is under no obligation to enquire into the correctness or sufficiency of such information or documents' [Article 16 (1–2)].

The carriage of cargo poses a triangular legal relationship, in which the consignor, the air carrier, and the consignee are involved. 'The air waybill shall be made out by the consignor in three original parts':

– 'The first part shall be marked 'for the carrier' and shall be signed by the consignor.
– The second part shall be marked 'for the consignee'; it shall be signed by the consignor and carrier.
– The third part shall be signed by the carrier, who shall hand it to the consignor after the cargo has been accepted'. [Article 7 (1–2)].

[13] Dempsey (2005), p. 99.

The signature of the carrier and that of the consignor may be printed or stamped. If, at the request of the consignor, the carrier makes out the air waybill, the carrier shall be deemed, subject to proof to the contrary, to have done so on behalf of the consignor [Article (3–4)].

If cargo consisting of multiple packages or pieces needs to be consigned and upon the issuance of the air waybill a document (other instrument) made out electronically is used

(a) the carrier of cargo has the right to require the consignor to make out separate air waybills;
(b) the consignor has the right to require the carrier to deliver separate cargo receipts (Article 8).

However, if the before-mentioned basic requirements concerning the documents of cargo carriage are not observed pursuant to the specifications of the Convention, 'non-compliance with the provisions of Articles 4 to 8 shall not affect the existence or the validity of the contract of carriage (in a similar manner to air tickets), which shall, nonetheless, be subject to the rules of the Convention including those relating to limitation of liability' (Article 9). 'The consignor is responsible for the correctness of particulars and statements relating to the cargo. The consignor shall indemnify the air carrier against all damage suffered by it, or by any other person to whom the carrier is liable, due to the irregularity, incorrectness or incompleteness of the particulars and statements furnished by the consignor or on its behalf. At the same time, the carrier shall indemnify the consignor against all damage suffered by it, or by any other person to whom the consignor is liable, by reason of the irregularity, incorrectness or incompleteness of the particulars and statements inserted by the carrier or on its behalf in the cargo receipt or in the record preserved by other means referred to in (2) of Article 4' [Article 10 (1–3)].

'Any statements in the air waybill or the cargo receipt relating to the weight, dimensions and packing of the cargo as well as those relating to the number of packages are *prima facie* evidence of the facts stated. The statements relating to the quantity, volume and condition of the cargo do not constitute evidence against the air carrier except so far as they both have been, and are stated in the air waybill or the cargo receipt to have been checked by it in the presence of the consignor, or relate to the apparent condition of the cargo' [Article 11 (2)]. The furnishing of correct data and the clarification of real circumstances are legal obligations beyond the confidential relationship between the contracting parties, because, if they carry special cargo which requires distinct attention and care (for example, baby chicks, perishable products), a factual statement concerning its condition is necessary and with its due consideration an agreement on the conditions of carriage needs to be reached. These pieces of information have significance with respect to the establishment of the scope of liability for damage caused during the carriage.

Basically, the modern information-based society requires that clients should get access to services with less administration, more rapidly and simply. We cannot lose our air tickets any longer, they are easy to change, to overwrite, while we do not have to fetch our air ticket from the seller, furthermore, the purchase of last-minute tickets before departure and online check-in via smartphone are also practicable. In the future the passenger will meet all administrative requirements via electronic systems from checking in to the check-in of baggage, from taking out insurance to passport control, except for customs, security controls and foreign policing checks, which necessitate the presence of the organs of the competent authority and of the examined person.

9.1.5 Documentation of Carriage Performed in Extraordinary Circumstances

The provisions concerning the documentation of the carriage of passengers, baggage, and cargo 'shall not apply in the case of carriage performed in *extraordinary circumstances* outside the normal scope of a carrier's business' (Article 51). The treaty-maker does not define flight in extraordinary circumstances. It may include experimental test-flights, air navigation flights (e.g., the airline flies over a polar route), calibrating flights, when the devices and the navigation system of the airport are checked as well as when the devices of the aircraft are set during the flight. Similar flights encompass the rescue of refugees from war zones by aircraft or flights in discordance with the operation of the aircraft by reason of safety risks or meteorological circumstances, as well as flights because of events external to ordinary operation by the air carrier.

In these cases, no legal consequences (sanctions) are set forth by the treaty-maker vis-a-vis the air carrier that is non-compliant with the content and formal requirements of the documents of carriage.

9.2 Jurisdictions

In international legal disputes, jurisdiction (scope of competence) is always a principal issue, namely, which State is vested with judicial power to proceed and make judgement in a specific case. Jurisdiction *(iurisdictio)*[14] implies the competence of the States, according to which the cases under dispute are allocated. In the case of the prevalence of international jurisdiction, the case is referred to the administration of justice of one or the other State. Therefore, it is a primary

[14] Random House Webster's Legal Dictionary: 'The power and authority of the court or administrative tribunal to decide legal issues and disputes.' Jurisdiction is the legal authorisation of State organs (the court, arbitration tribunals, the notary public, the court of guardians, etc.) on the basis of which they may proceed in the adjudication of legal disputes or conduct legal proceedings in the area of conflicting laws.

procedural legal condition to establish which country has jurisdiction, authority, competence and the capacity to sue and be sued.

In concrete legal disputes deriving from international conflicts, it is necessary to establish the court of which country has jurisdiction over the action for damages in order to avoid the collision of several rivalling jurisdictions.

Let us imagine a modern wide-body Airbus airplane manufactured in France, registered by the German aviation authority, which takes off from London Gatwick (LGW) Airport, and its destination is the Istanbul Ataturk (IST) Airport. While travelling to its destination, the aircraft traverses the sovereign airspaces of several countries. The passengers, who are of various nationalities, purchased their air tickets from travel agents registered in different countries. Apparently, the transferring passengers are flying to diverse destinations. The crew members are of different nationalities as well, the operator and owner of the leased aircraft are registered in different countries. For technical reasons, the aircraft makes an emergency landing on the Vienna Schwechat (VIE) Airport. Some passengers get injured during the manoeuvre. Immediately, a crucial question arises concerning the adjudication of the case: the law of which State applies? The passenger injured in the accident needs to know at the court of which country the action for damages should be lodged; in other words, where to initiate the legal proceedings? Then the court needs to decide whether it is authorised to proceed in the specific case.

Pursuant to the Convention, 'an action for damages must be brought, at the option of the plaintiff, in the territory of one of the States Parties, either

1. before the court of the *domicile of the carrier* or of its *principal place of business*; or
2. where the carrier has a *place of business*; or
3. through which the *contract has been made (lex loci contractus)*; or
4. before the court at the *place of destination*' [Article 33 (1)]; or
5. 'where the passenger has his or her *principal* or *permanent residence* and to or from which the carrier operates services for the carriage of passengers by air' [Article 33 (2)].

Exclusively that court may establish its jurisdiction the State of which acceded to the Convention. If the Convention is to be applied, law-enforcement has five forums (fora) at disposal:

- Forums 1–4 apply in the case of the initiation of *any action* (delay, destruction, loss, damage to baggage, or cargo, and in case of accident).
- Forum 5 can be opted only in the case of *the death* or *bodily injury of the passenger* (in case of accident).

In the case of forums with jurisdiction, the passengers (or their heirs) or the consignor of the cargo may make a choice: at the court of which contracting State with jurisdiction they file their action for damages.

In the lawsuit *Renton Swaminathan versus SwissAir Transport Company,*[15] the plaintiff purchased an open-ended return ticket for the route Dakar–Geneva–New York–Geneva–Dakar. Upon arriving in New York, when fellow passengers were preparing for disembarking, as they opened the overhead lockers, a metal box fell on the head of the plaintiff passenger, who got injured. The plaintiff filed an action for damages against *Swissair* (SR) in the court of the State of Texas. The court established that although pursuant to the Convention the flight qualified as international carriage, the final destination of the trip was not New York, even if the passenger left the date of the return open. Therefore, the court dismissed the action of the plaintiff due to lack of jurisdiction. Namely, the air ticket, as a document of carriage proving the existence of a contract, expressly manifests the intention of the passenger. Without doubt, the passenger wanted to return to Dakar since the place of departure and destination on the air ticket were Dakar (DKR), while New York (JFK) was only an agreed stopping place. The principal place of business of *Swissair* is in Zurich; therefore, from the viewpoint of the case, it is legally irrelevant that the airline has a representative office in New York. Relinquishing the hope of being awarded a higher amount of compensation, the plaintiff could file the action at one of the courts of Switzerland (on the basis of forums 1–2) or Senegal (on the basis of forums 3–4) with actual jurisdiction.

The before-mentioned four forums adopted from the Warsaw Convention were supplemented with the option of a fifth forum by the contracting States. The fifth forum could be opted for in the case of accidents sustained by passengers (death or bodily injury) but not in the event of damage to the baggage or cargo or the delayed carriage thereof. The United States had supported the introduction of a new forum for a long time, because by all means, among others by envisioning their secession from the Montreal Diplomatic Conference,[16] it had intended to grant the opportunity for its citizens to bring an action in the United States in the event of an accident outside the frontiers of the country, anywhere in the world, even if the flight did not concern the territory of the United States at all. The majority of the drafters of the Convention did not support the citizen-based approach *(lex patriae)*, nevertheless, a

[15] *Renton Swaminathan v. Swiss Air Transport Company,* US Court of Appeals, fifth Circuit No. 91–2897, 962 F. 2d 387—Federal Reporter, 10 June 1992.

[16] Tompkins, George N., Jr.: The New Era of International Legal Liability and What It Is Likely to Mean for the Airlines, Manufacturers and Insurers. *IATA Airline Insurance Rendezvous 2001,* NYDATA: 93389. p. 14.

compromise was reached with similar effect,[17] thus, the fifth forum guaranteed the institution of action according to the principal or permanent residence of the passenger *(lex domicilii).*

Thereby, the treaty-maker facilitated that the plaintiff lodged the action for damages in the territory of a State Party:

- where the passenger has their *principal* or *permanent residence*; and
- to or from 'which the air carrier operates services for the carriage of passengers by air, either on its own aircraft, or on another carrier's aircraft pursuant to a commercial agreement;[18] and
- in which the carrier conducts its business of carriage of passengers by air from premises leased or owned by the carrier itself or by another carrier with which it has a commercial agreement' [Article 33 (2)] at the time of the accident.

Pursuant to the Convention, principal and permanent residence means the fixed and permanent residence of the passenger at the time of the accident. The existence of a fixed and permanent residence needs to be proved beyond doubt before the court by the plaintiff. It does not suffice to spend some months in a specific country, staying in residence habitually is necessary, and the court is obligated to consider this fact upon the determination of jurisdiction.

In the case *Rahila Razi versus Qatar Airways,*[19] the passenger was travelling with a transfer in Doha (DOH) from Karachi (KHI) to Houston (IAH) and then back to Karachi. On the overseas flight the passenger asked for a cup of tea, but the boiling water offered by the flight-attendant on a tray was spilt on the passenger, who suffered burns. The passenger brought an action against the airline before the court of the United States since she chose the option guaranteed by the fifth forum. However, the court dismissed the action because of lack of jurisdiction, namely, the conditions required under the Convention were not fulfilled by the period of 4 months the passenger had spent in Houston on the basis of a visa to the United States permitting several entries into the United States for the duration of 5 years. The situation of the passenger was basically determined by the destination of the return air ticket (Karachi according to the fourth forum) purchased in Karachi (third forum), that is, the plaintiff intended to return to her home country, to her permanent residence (fifth forum). Therefore, the passenger could exercise her right to bring an action in Qatar (forums 1–2) or Pakistan (forums 3–5).

---

[17] Balfour (2003), p. 2.

[18] Pursuant to the Convention: *commercial agreement* means 'an agreement, other than an agency agreement, made between carriers and relating to the provision of their joint services for carriage of passengers by air' [Article 33 (3) *a)*].

[19] *Razi v. Qatar Airways,* 36 Avi. 15,501 (S.D.Tex.)—United States District Court Southern District of Texas Houston Division. Case 4:12-cv-02073 Document 25 Filed in TXSD on 6 February 2014.

Pursuant to the rule of the Convention, 'the nationality of the passenger shall not be a determining factor in this regard' [Article 33 (3) *b)*]. This results in the fact that if the principal and permanent residence of a citizen of the United States is abroad, they will not find jurisdiction on the basis of the fifth forum in the United States. The court will carefully and thoroughly examine whether the principal and permanent residence is indeed the stated place and whether the passenger uses it habitually for residence.

In the case of *Hornsby versus Lufthansa German Airlines*,[20] the plaintiff (the passenger) travelling from Frankfurt (FRA) to Los Angeles (LAX) suffered an accident owing to strong turbulence at flight altitude. The plaintiff had purchased a return ticket and had designated Frankfurt as a place of destination. The claimant intended to enforce his claim for damages in his home country as a citizen of the United States. Since the passenger had spent almost all his life in California but at the time of the accident he lived and worked in Germany, the question arose whether the United States had jurisdiction. During the proceedings, it was proved that the plaintiff's tax and social security numbers and his fixed residence were in Germany (he had sold his house in California 2 years before); even his pets were expecting him in his home in Germany. For the court it became unambiguous that the plaintiff, against proof to the contrary, was staying habitually in Germany as a place of residence rather than in the United States. At the same time, the court weighed that the plaintiff regularly returned to his home country (renewed his driving licence, announced his abstention from voting, he had a post-box and filed tax returns), but what mattered most was that he never intended to settle down in Germany. The court was satisfied on this evidence, therefore, having weighed up everything, it found that the home of the plaintiff was California, so he could enforce his legal claim in his home country.

Obviously, most of the citizens of the United States dwell habitually in their home country, so their protection by the national courts is guaranteed. The protection of access to national courts also covers all the persons having permanent residence in the United States, who are not US citizens. The rule benefits the citizens of other nations in their home countries as well, since may the accident occur anywhere in the world, the claimant may enforce their claim for damages at their national court (if their principal and permanent residence is in that country). A further advantage of resorting to a local court is that this level can calculate the amount of full indemnification most of all according to local living circumstances, standard of living and other conditions.

---

[20] *Hornsby v. Lufthansa German Airlines,* US District Court, C.D. California, 593 F. Supp. 2d 1132, 6 January 2009.

Simultaneously, the fifth forum provides scope for the practice of the so-called *forum non-conveniens*, formerly also widespread in Anglo-Saxon law. This institution facilitates that the courts of the States do not proceed, even in the case of the existence of their jurisdiction, if, with respect to all the circumstances of the case, the legal dispute can be adjudged before another court having jurisdiction more successfully, or, if the other court is more suitable to adjudge the legal dispute. It may be more suitable because it may be easier to obtain evidence, to hear the witnesses, to opt for the governing law, it may be more cost-efficient and entails less administration. In such a case the judge deliberates and requests the plaintiff of the legal dispute to file the action at another court, or the judge in his competence initiates the conduct of the proceedings before the court chosen by them. If the judge fails to do so, eventually, they have to adjudge the case.

This much is certain: the claimant always finds a proceeding court, since the logic of the system is that there will necessarily be a State which has jurisdiction. If the responsibility of the damaging party is established, it cannot shirk being called to account. If the court having jurisdiction or other organs of a specific State may proceed in a case with an essential foreign element, this does not mean that the substantive law of the State concerned has to be applied in the solution of the legal case. However, 'questions of procedure shall be governed by the law of the court seized of the case' [Article 33 (4)].

The treaty-maker guarantees further jurisdiction for passengers on *code-share* flights. This is not a new forum of jurisdiction, but it is the extension of the opportunity of the first forum (where the *domicile* or *the principal place of business* of the air carrier is located) to another air carrier actually performing the flight not being in contractual relation with the passenger. Simply, practice itself requires that besides the numerous forums related to the contracting carrier, a proceeding forum in the case of the actual carrier should exist as well. The treaty-maker guarantees the possibility of bringing an action for damages against the actual carrier according to the domicile or the principal place of business of the actual carrier.

'In relation to carriage performed by the actual carrier, an action for damages may be brought, at the option of the plaintiff, against that carrier or the contracting carrier, or simultaneously against both together or separately. If the action is brought against only one of those carriers, that carrier shall have the right to require the other carrier to be joined in the proceedings, the procedure and effects being governed by the law of the court seized of the case' (Article 45).

Any action for damages must be brought, at the option of the plaintiff, before the court having jurisdiction in the territory of one of the States Parties:

- either before a court in which an action may be brought against the contracting carrier according to the five forums of jurisdiction (as provided in Article 33); or
- before the court having jurisdiction at the place where the actual carrier has its domicile or its principal place of business (Article 46).

9.2.1 Arbitration

Arbitration organised by the parties is increasingly widespread, which is due to the claim that the dispute is resolved rapidly and efficiently by competent persons proficient in the subject-matter. The decision is made secretly at a closed session, and it is legally binding in the first instance, the opportunity for legal remedy is very rare. The rules of procedure are flexible, which the parties may determine themselves; they can decide on the language to be used, on the venue for the proceedings, and on the persons of the arbitrators as well.

The parties to a contract of carriage for cargo may stipulate, exclusively in cases of the legal relation of the carriage of cargo, to settle any dispute arising with respect to the liability of carriage by way of arbitration.[21] The clause needs to be made out in writing. The clause or agreement on arbitration contains the following provisions mandatorily:

- The arbitration proceedings shall, at the option of the claimant, be conducted in the concerned territories in compliance with the Convention.
- The arbitrator or the arbitration tribunal shall apply the provisions of the Convention during the proceedings (Article 34).

The scope of arbitration does not encompass accident to the person of the passenger, therefore, arbitrators may be elected only in relation to the first four forums of jurisdiction.

9.2.2 States with Different Systems of Law

'If a contracting State has two or more territorial units in which different systems of law are applicable in relation to matters dealt with in this Convention, it may at the time of signature, ratification, acceptance, approval or accession declare that this Convention shall extend to all its territorial units or only to one or more of them and may modify this declaration by submitting another declaration at any time. Any such declaration shall be notified to the Depositary and shall state expressly the territorial units to which the Convention applies' [Article 56 (1–2)]. In practice, however, this case does not often ensue, because on the one hand, the world is not governed by colonial establishment any longer, on the other hand, such unification of different legal systems in an issue of private law is atypical.

In fact, the treaty-maker granted this opportunity for China with respect to special administrative regions such as Hong Kong and Macao. The People's Republic of China ratified the Montreal Convention on 1 June 2005. It indicated in its ratification document that it extends the scope of application of the Convention to the territory of Macao but did not make such a statement in the case of Hong Kong. However, not

[21] ICAO Legal Committee, 30th Session, LC/30–WP/4 (A-19) 5.4.22.

much later, on 15 December 2006, the Government of the People's Republic of China permitted the application of the Convention to Hong Kong as well.[22]

9.2.3 Parallel Jurisdictions: Forum Shopping

Since the plaintiff may choose the proceeding forum, it is essential in the choice of the several parallelly existing jurisdictions to bring the action in the territory where the highest indemnification of the damage of the obligee can be expected. The possibility of a more advantageous legal outcome has established the selection among parallel forums, the institution of the so-called *forum-shopping* (opting for the most favourable law). Solicitors specialised in aviation law know where the highest amount of indemnification can be claimed. Therefore, availing themselves of the opportunities provided by the forums of jurisdiction, the action is lodged at the most suitable court adjudging the case 'the most open-handedly'.

The Convention limits this opportunity to some extent, so far as solely the court the country of which acceded to the Convention may establish its jurisdiction. Owing to the unification of the main regulations pertaining to air carriage any judicial forum proceeding in the specific case applies the same rules. The determination of the law governing the adjudication of the concrete case does not depend on the proceeding forum or its collision rules any longer, since the relating identical rules in a specific case, may it be in the hands of any forum, lead to the same legal regime. Thus, the plaintiff may expect similar judgement pursuant to the Convention before all proceeding forums. Furthermore, the treaty-maker expressly prohibits 'any clause contained in the contract of carriage or all special agreements entered into before the damage occurred, by which the parties purport to infringe the rules laid down by the Convention whether by deciding the law to be applied or by altering the rules as to jurisdiction'. Such written clauses or agreements contained in the contract of carriage 'shall be null and void' (Article 49).

With regard to the fact that no uniform regulation of liability for damages on an international level has been established pertaining to airports, aircraft manufacturers, maintenance, repair and overhaul companies (MROs), or to air navigation service providers (ANSP), in these areas the phenomenon of *forum-shopping* is absent. The solicitors in the Warsaw System wished that all parties were present in the court room, since they were seeking further resources in order to relieve the damage. Eloquent examples for this were the cases when disaster struck airplanes manufactured in the United States by reason of some technical fault, the solicitors of the passengers concerned grasped all opportunities to institute proceedings so as to enforce the manufacturer's product liability beyond the liability of the airline for damages. If, for example, the accident originated in the failure of the aircraft or its

[22] ICAO Secretariat: *Status of Montreal Convention 1999 and Declarations*. Point 18, p. 6. (www.icao.int/secretariat/legal).

parts, and this fault could be traced back to manufacturing, assembly, repairs or design, under the legal title of product liability the manufacturer of the aircraft was held liable. Likewise, if the aircraft's engine stopped working and an accident occurred, the claimants could sue the manufacturer of the engine. (Aircraft manufacturers do not attach warranty to their engines since they do not manufacture them.)

Product Liability Case

From the fuselage of a DC-10 airplane carrying out Flight 981 of the Turkish Airline (TK), travelling between Paris (CDG) and London (LHR), the left cargo door ripped off on 3 March 1974. Consequently, the wide-body airplane became unnavigable at an altitude of 4000 metres and crashed into the forest of Ermenonville, where it exploded. All of the 346 persons on board lost their lives. The accident was caused by the defective planning and construction fault of the cargo door as well as by the fault of the ground handling staff in Paris, that is, the improper closure of the cargo door.[23]

Owing to the limited liability of the air carrier for damages, it was not worth suing the Turkish Airline for a larger amount of damages. Therefore, the solicitors of the British claimants took action in the United States for the establishment of the liability of the aircraft manufacturer. Their purpose was to prove the improper planning of the catcher of the cargo door by the aircraft manufacturer.[24] The solicitors were well-aware of the fact that in the United States the liability of the aircraft manufacturer is absolute, and a larger amount of indemnification is attached to the title of product liability in the case of an evidence of the fault.

Eventually, a group of the British claimants achieved that the proceedings were conducted at a Californian court. The liability of the manufacturer was established, thus, for the relatives of the passengers deceased in the disaster, the American company manufacturing the airplane, *McDonnell Douglas* and *General Dynamics Corporations* paid an indemnity of 62 million USD beyond the compensation by the airline.[25]

The Montreal Convention forecloses the practice of litigation against aircraft manufacturing companies popular in the Warsaw System by the stipulation of the unlimited liability of the airlines. The States Parties to the Warsaw Convention were essentially interested in the protection of the evolving aviation industry serving public interest, therefore, they guaranteed limited liability for the air carriers. Since

[23] Final Report. Secretariat of State for Transport, Accidents Investigation Branch, LTS 2291/75, London, February 1976.

[24] Varley (1978), pp. 22–23.

[25] Business Insurance, 29 May 1978 (www.businessinsurance.com/article/20190531/STORY/912328805/May-1978-$62-million-handed-out-in-wake-of-DC10-crash).

then, the world has changed considerably, the industry has gained strength and is decreasingly in need of protection, or more correctly, it is in need of another kind of protection. While in the age of limited liability for damages the plaintiffs, for the purpose of the supplementation of the indemnification deemed to be low, and being really low to be paid by the air carrier, engaged other concerned companies in the chain of liability (an array of potential payers). This is not necessary any longer owing to the new rule of the Montreal Convention because the air carriers are obligated to indemnify the full extent of damage proved by the passenger (or the relative) in the case of an accident sustained by the passenger.

9.3 The Substantive Scope of the Convention

The air carrier's liability extends 'to all *international carriage of persons, baggage or cargo* performed by aircraft *for reward*' [Article 1 (1)].

As a matter of course, air carriage can be divided into the carriage of persons and cargo with two differences in principle:

- Upon the carriage of cargo, the object of carriage is removed from the disposal of the consignor, obviously, this does not take place in the case of the transport of passengers.
- Upon the carriage of cargo, a triangular legal relation is established (consignor, air carrier, and consignee), while the carriage of passengers posits a bilateral legal relation (passenger and the air carrier), with the exception of *code-share* carriage, which also implies a triangular legal relation: the passenger, the contracting carrier and the actual carrier. (The Montreal Convention contains general and specific provisions: the *general* provisions apply to passengers and baggage, while the *specific* provisions apply to cargo.)

A consignor is a person/company sending the cargo (freight) and may act through a *cargo forwarder* (or its agent), which engages the carrier to ship the cargo. Consignors usually intend the cargo to be delivered to another person. This person, to whom the cargo is sent, is the consignee acting as a customer or client. The drafters of the Convention did not avail themselves of the opportunity to define baggage or cargo, therefore, the airlines circumscribe the scope of objects falling in this category under their General Conditions of Carriage. Accordingly, in the practice of air carriers, cargo includes, for instance, double coffins containing the mortal remains of a deceased person. This category also pertains to carried pets and livestock (for instance, dogs and race horses).[26] For this reason, injuries to animals must be considered based on the provisions on cargo under the Montreal Convention.[27] Live animals may be forwarded pursuant to industry prescriptions and the

[26] Dempsey and Milde (2005), p. 67.

[27] *Aya v. Lan Cargo*, S.A. (1:14-cv-22260) District Court, S.D. Florida, 18 September 2014.

prior consent of the air carrier. The conditions of transporting live animals include their confinement in a regular, portable, escape-proof carrier (not hindering the movement of the animal, in compliance with industry specifications and the limitations of size and weight prescribed by the air carrier), the production of valid official, veterinary and vaccination certificates and entry permits as well as other documents required by the prescriptions of the States concerned by the carriage.

From the enumeration of classical objects (baggage, cargo, mail) postal goods forward were omitted, the reason for which is that the provisions of the Convention do not apply to the carriage of postal items. In the case of the carriage of postal items (letters, parcels, postal orders) the lawmaker merely requires that the air carrier shall be liable only to the relevant postal administration in accordance with the rules applicable to the relationship between the carriers and the postal administrations [Article 2 (2–3)].

9.3.1 International Carriage

According to the nature of carriage, it can be divided into international and domestic carriage. The Convention encompasses exclusively international air carriage, not domestic carriage. The treaty-maker defines the concept of international air carriage precisely, since this is one of the basic conditions of the applicability of the Convention. In the establishment of the international character, the precise definitions of the *document of carriage* proving the existence of the contractual relationship and of *international carriage* provides help:

The document of carriage is the first manifestation and proof of a contractual relationship, which could refer to

- the *air ticket* and the *baggage identification tag* upon checking the baggage; and
- the *air waybill* and the *cargo receipt* upon the consignment of cargo.

The contractual relationship established between the customer and the air carrier for reward is unambiguously attested by the air ticket and the air waybill, which undoubtedly indicate the places of departure and destination, as well as the agreed stopping place(s), which are significant for the carriage to qualify as international.

'For the purposes of the Montreal Convention', the expression *international carriage* means any carriage in which, according to the agreement between the parties,

- *the place of departure* and *the place of destination*—whether or not there be a break in the carriage or transhipment—are situated within the territories of two States Parties; or
- *the place of departure* and *the place of destination* are within the territory of a single State Party if there is an agreed stopping place within the territory of another State, even if that State is not a State Party.

> Carriage between two points within the territory of a single State Party without an agreed stopping place within the territory of another State is not international carriage for the purposes of this Convention [Article 1 (2)].

In the interest of the achievement of unification in the broadest practicable scope, by taking a bold step, the treaty-maker extended the scope of the Convention, under the prevalence of certain circumstances, to those international carriages which target the territories of States which did not ratify the Convention. Initially, the documentation of the carriage is examined, because that is indispensable for the establishment of the personal and substantive scopes of application and jurisdiction. If the carriage qualifies as international, the Convention is applicable; if, pursuant to the Convention, the carriage is not international, liability for damages shall be adjudged under the national law of the State that has jurisdiction.

In air transport flying over borders is unequivocally deemed to be international carriage, although this fact in itself under the Convention, and emphatically merely here, does not imply the qualification of the carriage as international. Cambodia has not acceded to the Montreal Convention but has ratified the Warsaw Convention (just like, for instance, Iraq, Iran, or Yemen); thus, the passengers on a flight travelling one way from Phnom Penh to London (PNH–LHR) or from London to Phnom Penh (LHR–PNH) are not governed by the Montreal Convention. But in case the flight takes place between Phnom Penh–London–Phnom Penh (PNH–LHR–PNH), it is governed by the Warsaw Convention, therefore, the flight shall be international. At the same time, if the destination is Funafuti (FUN), the capital of Tuvalu in the Pacific Ocean, on the route connecting Funafuti–Phnom Penh–-London–Funafuti (FUN–PNH–LHR–FUN) or on the one-way route to London from Funafuti (FUN–LHR), the passengers shall be subject to the rules of liability for damage under the national law of Tuvalu, since the flights are not deemed to be international given that Tuvalu has not ratified either the Montreal Convention or the Warsaw Convention.[28]

Pursuant to the rules of the Convention what is and what is not deemed to be an international flight is determined solely and exclusively by the geographical connecting points designated under the contract of carriage. For instance, in a return air ticket, the following geographical connecting points need to be indicated:

- *The place of departure*: the town or airport indicated *as the first place* on the air ticket (or air waybill);
- *The place of destination*: the town or airport indicated *as the last place* on the air ticket (or air waybill);
- *The agreed stopping place*: all towns or airports indicated *between the first place and the last place.*

If we consider a one-way journey: in the relation between town [A]—town [B], town [A] means the place of departure, town [B] means the place of destination. If

[28] Sipos (2020), pp. 155–184.

we consider a return flight en route [A]–[B]–[A], town [A] means the place of departure and simultaneously the place of destination because the passenger departs from and arrives in town [A],[29] while the agreed stopping place is the airport of town [B]. (The agreed stopping place may imply more than one geographical connecting point if on the air ticket several landing or transfer points are indicated.) The places of departure and destination are of crucial importance. Whether the States of the geographical connecting points have acceded to the Montreal Convention is a further essential aspect. Let us consider an example to understand its significance in practice.

The country of town [A] acceded to the Montreal Convention, whereas the country of town [B] did not. Pursuant to the definition under the Convention, this results in the following:

- on route ([A]–[B]), between town [A] and town [B] (one-way ticket); or
- on route ([B]–[A]) between town [B] and town [A] (one-way ticket), the carriages are not deemed to be international;
- the return flight on route town [A]—town [B]—town [A], the carriage is deemed to be international;
- the return flight on route town [B]—town [A]—town [B], the carriage is not deemed to be international.

In the case above, the flight travelling on route [A]–[B]–[A] qualifies as international carriage, irrespective of the fact that the country of town [B] did not accede to the Convention. This applies even in the event the damage occurs in the territory of the country of town [B], or, when the flight is operated by the airline of a country not having acceded to the Convention, with its own flight crew, and if exclusively the citizens of the country of town [B] are on board. Despite these circumstances, the Convention is governing, since the citizenship of the passengers, the geographical point of the occurrence of the damage or the place of business, the headquarters of the airline performing the carriage or the State of registration of the airplane do not matter in the least, nor does the fact whether the flight is non-scheduled or operated according to schedule. What matters is merely one aspect: the route delineated by the geographical connecting points indicated on the document of carriage. Precisely, this positively determined route may qualify the carriage, according to the criteria stipulated under the Convention, as international or non-international. The international character of the carriage is a key issue because this is one of the basic conditions for the applicability of the Convention.

If the aircraft of the contracting State lands in a State that did not accede to the Convention and then it continues its flight to another State that acceded to the Convention, the Convention shall be applicable. Pursuant to the provision of the Convention, this carriage qualifies as international since, for instance, on route [A]–[B]–[C], the country of town [C] indicated as the place of destination acceded to the Convention (Fig. 9.1).

---

[29] *Jones v. USA 3000 Airlines*, 33Avi. 17,442 (E.D.Mo.), 2009.; Larsen et al. (2012), pp. 242–346.

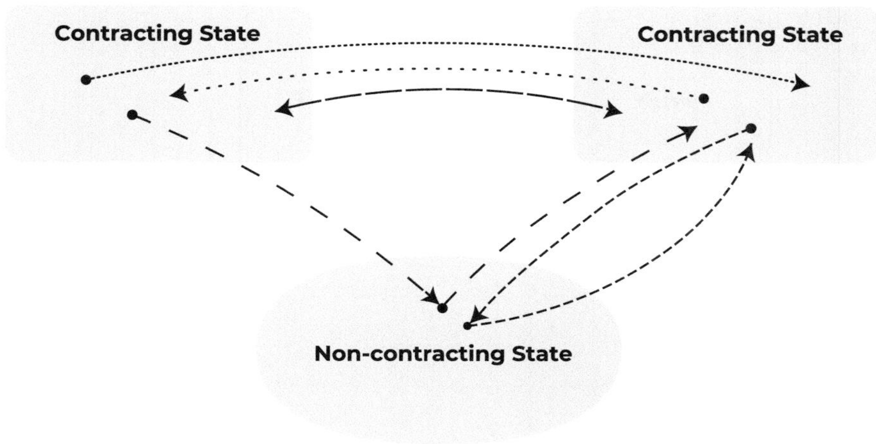

Fig. 9.1 International carriage

Pursuant to the Convention, the carriage does not qualify as international carriage in six basic cases, including domestic carriage. Within the purview of the Convention, the carriage does not qualify as international either if the carrier travelling between two points of a contracting State lands in another State as well when the parties *did not designate an agreed stopping place* [Article 1 (2)]. If the aircraft performs domestic carriage but for technical, meteorological, or other extraordinary reasons (e.g., hijacking, forced landing, medical aid) it is forced to land in the territory of another State, the carriage furthermore qualifies as domestic because the place of landing was not specified jointly and preliminarily by the parties to the contract as an agreed stopping place (Fig. 9.2).

The examination of the international character of carriage would lose its significance if all ICAO Member States ratified the Convention, which is utopian. Since this is likely to ensue none too soon, it will continue further on that, in the actions for damages by two passengers or the consignors of two different cargo units on the very same flight, depending on the route for which their air tickets or air way bills entitle them, irrespective of the citizenship of the passenger or the consignor and of the nationality of the operating airline, different rules of liability for damages will be applicable.

For instance, the passenger who travels with an air ticket for route [A]–[B]–[A], on their return flight from town [B] may happen to travel with a passenger holding an air ticket for route [B]–[A]–[B] or just for the relation [B]–[A], so the first passenger is returning to town [A] from town [B], while the other passenger is just departing for town [A]. In the event of an accident, the two passengers, even if they suffer the same injuries, shall be entitled to different indemnification: the returning passenger shall receive compensation pursuant to the Montreal Convention due to the international character of the carriage, while the passenger departing from town [B] shall be indemnified pursuant to the national rules of the country of town [B].

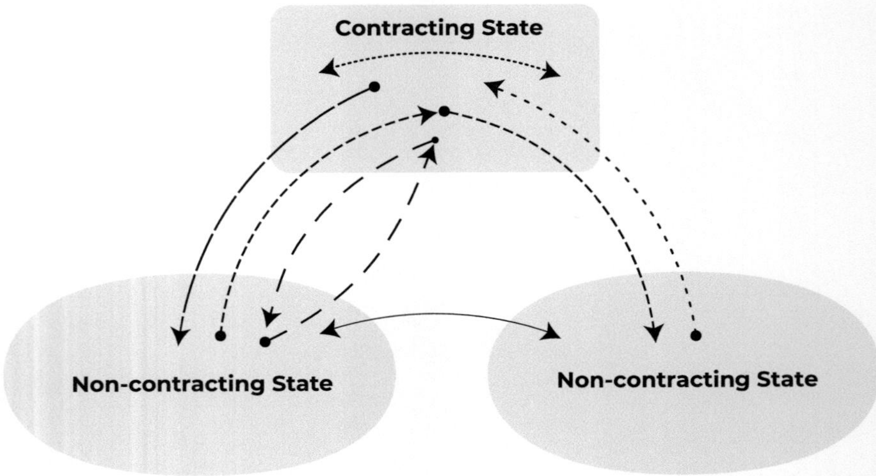

Fig. 9.2 Non-international carriage

It may also occur that in the case of another passenger sitting beside them, the Warsaw Convention and its amendments are applicable because this passenger, after landing in town [A], is heading for a State that acceded to the Warsaw Convention but not yet to the Montreal Convention. It is easy to comprehend: it may arise that the passenger suffering a minor injury is indemnified more on a different scale than the heir of the deceased passenger. Therefore, it is important that the Montreal Convention achieves its goal and 'prevails' in as many Member States as possible because only this way shall its rules be capable of forging real unformity in the still fragmented system of liability for damages.

The Montreal Convention provides scope for national law, guiding case-law, and the IATA resolutions because it intends to unify the system of the liability of air carriers for damage only in the most important issues. At the same time, it will be capable of establishing uniform regulation worldwide solely if all, but at least as many States as possible accede to the Convention.

9.3.2 *Reservations*

The Montreal Convention applies to all carriage performed by the State or by legally constituted public bodies provided that this carriage is international, and it is performed for reward by the aircraft [Article 2 (1)]. That is, the contracting Parties extend the scope of the Convention both to civil and State flights. In the latter case, the treaty-maker allows the contracting States to make reservations.

The reservation *(réserve)* is a unilateral declaration by a State upon its accession to a multilateral international treaty, on the basis of which the State accedes to the international treaty so that it assigns predetermined sense to, or precludes, amends one or more provisions in its relations with other contracting Parties. Reservation as a concept in international law has significance only in relation to multilateral treaties. In the case of bilateral relations, the Parties as a matter of course do not need to make such declarations since the challenged parts are corrected on the spot.

As a main rule, vis-à-vis the rules of the Montreal Convention, the Parties cannot make reservations, but in two cases the treaty-maker allows the Member States to apply the legal institution of reservation. 'A State Party may at any time declare by a notification addressed to the Depositary that the Convention shall not apply to:

(a) international carriage by air performed and operated directly by that State Party (by State aircraft) for non-commercial purposes in respect to its functions and duties as a sovereign State; and/or
(b) the carriage of persons, cargo and baggage for its military authorities on aircraft registered in or leased by that State Party, the whole capacity of which has been reserved by or on behalf of such authorities' (Article 57).

Essentially, both exceptions serve the differentiation of carriage by State aircraft from the system of private law.[30] Here we need to highlight that in a basic case, the applicability of the Convention to State (military) flights is not excluded, but the treaty-maker exceptionally provides opportunity for the Member States to make reservations since as sovereign Member States, they have this right.

Substantive Scope of MC 1999
In summary, the substantive scope of the application of the Convention extends to relations deriving from the following activities of air carriage:

- *international civil* carriages and carriages *by the State* or *legally constituted public bodies;*
- all scheduled or non-scheduled *international carriages* performed by an aircraft of an air carrier for reward;
- *gratuitous* carriages performed by an air carrier free of charge; and
- the carriage of *baggage* and *cargo.*

The substantive scope of application of the Convention does not extend to the following:

- domestic carriages;
- flights without a preliminary stipulation by the Parties of an agreed stopping place;
- gratuitous amicable flights performed by private aircraft;
- the carriage of postal items; and
- State/military flights in the case of which the Member States made reservations.

---

[30] Milde (2008), pp. 7–8.

9.4 Personal Scope of the Convention

With respect to the personal scope, the Convention 'applies to all international carriage of *persons*, baggage or cargo performed by aircraft for reward'. It 'applies equally to *gratuitous carriage* by aircraft performed by an air transport undertaking' [Article 1 (1)]. The treaty-maker does not unfold the scopes of persons, the air transport undertaking, or of the air carrier.

9.4.1 Persons

The personal scope of the Convention encompasses expressly *persons*, although the contracting States meant primarily the passengers consistently referred to in the Convention.

The scope of persons includes everybody on board the aircraft (or engaged in the operations of embarking or disembarking), furthermore, everybody in contractual relation with the air carrier concerning the carriage, that is, holding an air ticket. Nevertheless, the scope of persons does not include the flight crew (pilots, flight attendants, contingently the flight engineer, the mechanic travelling on board indicated in the flight document) because they are subject to an employment (labour) contract with the air carrier. Pursuant to the Convention, the crew cannot sue the airline for damages caused by an accident, therefore, in their case the rules of national law stipulated under the employment contract are applicable.

The category of persons, however, includes the airline staff seated among the passengers,[31] who travel, for example, in order to participate in a simulator training or to bring home an airplane stranded abroad or to serve on another airplane flying back from its destination. These employees (mainly the members of the staff, technical experts) travel on the airplanes of the parent company or often of another airline to take on work in another part of the world. For their journey, the airline provides chiefly free air tickets; thus, the staff who are not on duty are governed by the rules of the Convention during the flight. As the scope of persons is not circumscribed under the Convention, the concrete scope of subjects in this category is defined under the General Conditions of Carriage or the internal regulations.

Stowaway passengers (free riders) are not covered by the Convention because the contractual relation does not exist between the parties. In most cases free riders 'are seated' in the baggage compartment of the airplane or in the passenger compartment by circumventing the security system of the airport, but it may also happen that they hide in the under-carriage cabinet of the airplane (where their chance for survival is practically zero).

---

[31] Danko (2012).

In the case of persons forced to travel (for example, juniors abducted violently because of divorce),[32] the Convention is not applicable either. In spite of the fact that they travel with valid air tickets, we cannot posit a contractual relation in this case since they are forced to 'sustain' the flight disregarding their will.[33] Human trafficking is also subject to this issue as the conduct is exploitative and non-consensual.[34]

In the case of *Ko versus EVA Airways Corporation*,[35] the divorced father was supposed to take his and the plaintiff's twins to a piano lesson, but instead thereof, he drove to the airport with the children and travelled to Singapore (SIN). Later, the former husband was arrested, and the children, after 1.5 years, returned to their mother. The mother, as plaintiff, sued the airline, claiming that it had not prevented the abduction and that its negligence had been contributory to the successful implementation of the act. The plaintiff alleged that, in the practice of airlines, proof concerning the right to supervision should be furnished if the child travels with only one parent. At that time, a written consent of the other parent is necessary. The court dismissed the plaintiff's action because it found that the boarding procedure of the airline had been in compliance with the usual practice (the case did not fall under the Montreal Convention).

The treaty-maker stipulates that the liability of an air transport undertaking applies to free carriage as well. Usually, airline employees and their family members get access to free or special priced air tickets,[36] in addition, there are persons for whom the air transport undertaking has granted free air tickets under some legal title. For example, the member airlines of IATA for flights among each other provide open and special priced air tickets not entitling to seat reservation pursuant to the relevant rules of IATA and within the framework of the so-called Interline Staff Agreement (ISTA). These air tickets may generally be used if there are empty seats on the specific airplane. The scope of beneficiaries includes the employee and their family members, the wife, the children and the parents, as well as the siblings of the employee. Gratuitousness is symbolic, so far as airport taxes and duties generally have to be paid by the grantees of free air tickets.

[32] Annually, the number of children violently abducted (kidnapped) by the parents via air transport may reach several thousands. Abeyratne (2001).; On the Proclamation of the Convention on the Civil Legal Aspects of International Child Abduction dated 25 October 1980, The Hague; Decree no. 14. 1986.

[33] Goldhirsch (2000), p. 13.

[34] 'Human trafficking' is not the same as 'human smuggling', since the people transported by human smugglers participate of their own free will. Kearns (2018), pp. 203–206.

[35] *Ko v. EVA Airways Corporation,* 42 F. Supp. 3d 1296, February 2012.

[36] IATA *Interline Staff Travel Agreement.* Version 15. 1 June 2019.

The price of the air ticket is irrelevant, therefore, the liability of the air carrier for damages is always sustained in the case of free or special priced air tickets as well. Liability may not be foreclosed in advance, nor may the due amount of indemnification be unilaterally reduced or the claim of the passenger who sustained damage be rejected with reference to the gratuitousness or the low price of the air tickets. Under the Convention, the airline owes equal liability for damage deriving from delay, the loss of baggage, the injury or death of the passenger to be indemnified for the benefit of each passenger suffering damage in case the relevant legal conditions prevail. Airlines shall mandatorily maintain adequate insurance for each passenger in order to cover their liability for damages (Article 50).

The persons participating in the journey in contractual relation, whom the personal scope of the Convention extends to, from the viewpoint of liability for damages, have equal rights and are equally insured, may they travel in economy or business class. Law, in compliance with the principle of equal treatment, does not distinguish the business models of the industry (traditional or discount airlines), even if there are actually considerable differences between them. All passengers and consignors, if they suffer damage and the liability of the air carrier is established pursuant to the Convention, will receive equal treatment and uniform adjudication.

9.4.2 Air Transport Undertaking

The Warsaw Convention mentions 'air transport undertakings' [Article 1 (1)], that is, international airlines operating unequivocally for commercial purposes. The Montreal Convention also mentions 'air transport undertakings' [Article 1 (1)]; however, its precise meaning is not defined by the contracting States. The air transport undertaking is a broader term than the airline, because the undertaking, while maintained or leased by an international, multinational organisation or company, is authorised to transport passengers and cargo, that is, costumers, employees or products and spare parts in international air traffic, maybe gratuitously, but obviously for commercial purposes (e.g., in the scope of barter agreements). For such carriage, the Convention is to be applied.

In the handling and carriage of baggage or cargo, other economic performers also participate, such as ground service provider companies and security organisations, which are responsible for the protection of the cargo transported by an airline. Therefore, the term of the air carrier encompasses not only the airline as an obligor liable for damages but also the proxies and agents of the airline.

At the same time, a free amicable excursion or a pleasure flight abroad on a private airplane is not subject to the Convention. Namely, the carriage is neither implemented for reward, nor does the aircraft operate for commercial purposes or within the framework of a contractual legal relation.[37]

[37] *Lavergne v. ATIS CORP.*, Civil No. 09–1421 (SEC). Cite as 767 F. Supp. 2d 301, 2011.

9.4.3 Air Carrier

The term of the air carrier is not defined under the Montreal Convention. According to the contracting States of the Chicago Convention: an *airline* is 'any air transport enterprise offering or operating international air service'. *Air service* means 'any scheduled air service performed by an aircraft for the public transport of passengers, baggage, mail, or cargo' (for reward) [Article 96 *a), c)*]. Primarily, the air carrier operates its flights in its own sphere of activity, but the scope of the Convention encompasses cases when the carrier takes recourse to the services of several other air or surface carriers in order to accomplish the flight.

9.4.4 Carriage Performed by Successive Carriers

Upon successive air carriage, different airlines in their own right perform the carriage consisting of several phases under their own flight number. 'Carriage to be performed by several successive carriers is deemed, for the purposes of the Convention, to be one undivided carriage if it has been regarded by the Parties as *a single operation*, whether it had been agreed upon under the form of a single contract or of a series of contracts, and *it does not lose its international character* merely because one contract or a series of contracts is to be performed entirely within the territory of the same State'. [Article 1 (3)].[38]

International Carriage with Successive Carriers
For instance, *Lufthansa* (LH) Airline issues a ticket for the route Munich--New York–Oklahoma City–New York–Munich (MUC–JFK–OKC–JFK–MUC). In the United States, despite the Open Skies Agreement concluded with the European Union, it is not possible to implement a domestic flight by an aircraft of a foreign airline since the exercise of the right of cabotage is not permitted. Therefore, the passenger on the domestic route between JFK–OKC–JFK flies on the airplane of the *Delta* (DL) Airline. All phases of the entire journey including the domestic section qualify as undivided carriage considered to be a single operation, and as international carriage it is subject to the scope of the Montreal Convention.

At the same time, if a passenger purchases an air ticket for the route Munich–New York–Munich (MUC–JFK–MUC) and while in New York decides to purchase a return ticket to Dallas (DFW) and back, this separate journey shall qualify as domestic carriage; therefore, it is not subject to the scope of the Montreal Convention.

---

[38] *Kathleen Robertson v. American Airlines*, US Court of Appeals, District of Columbia Circuit, No. 03-7129, 18 March 2005.

In the case of successive carriages, it may occur that for passengers travelling on domestic flights different rules of liability for damages are applicable upon the occurrence of an accident of the same or different severity. This is possible if the case of one passenger is governed by the Convention while the case of another passenger, who availed themselves merely of domestic flight services, is not.

'In the case of carriage to be performed by various successive carriers, and falling within the definition set out in Paragraph 3 of Article 1, each carrier which accepts passengers, baggage or cargo is subject to the rules set out in the Convention'. The air carrier under the supervision of which the carriage is performed is 'deemed to be one of the parties to the contract of carriage in so far as the contract deals with that part of the carriage which is performed under its supervision' [Article 36 (1)].

Upon successive carriages:

- In the case of *the carriage of passengers*, the passenger or any other person entitled to compensation can take action only against the carrier that performed the carriage during which an accident or delay occurred, save in the case where, by express agreement, the first carrier has assumed liability for the whole journey [Article 36 (2)].
- As regards *baggage*, the passenger will have a right of action against the first carrier, and the passenger who is entitled to delivery will have a right of action against the last carrier.
- With regard to *cargo*, the consignor will have a right of action against the first carrier, and the consignee who is entitled to delivery will have a right of action against the last carrier.

Essentially, 'each may take action against the carrier which performed the carriage during which the destruction, loss, damage or delay took place. These carriers will be jointly and severally liable to the passenger or to the consignor or consignee' [Article 36 (3)]. So far as the consignor or the consignee does not take action for various reasons, and the entity of the owner of the cargo (or baggage) is different from these obligees, since the contracting States do not expressly designate the owner as a person entitled to take action, they may only sue for damages, if they can prove that a real legal relation prevails with any of the Parties concerned.[39]

9.4.5 Carriage Performed by the Contracting or Actual Carrier

It was under the Guadalajara Agreement (1961) that for the first time special rules were formulated pertaining to the contracting and the actual carrier, which were also incorporated into the system of rules set forth under the Montreal Convention by

[39] *Gatewhite v. Iberia Lineas Aereas de Espana*, 1989, 1 All E.r. 944 1 Lloyd's Report 160, 225, 226; *Western Digital Corp. v. British Airways*, 2 Lloyd's L. Report, 380 (1999), 266.

the contracting Parties. The provisions of the Convention are to be applied to the so-called *code-share* carriage performed by an actual (operating) carrier instead of the contracting (marketing) carrier. *Code-share* carriage is carried out via an agreement between two or more airlines. Within the agreement, the air carriers operate the specific flight jointly under a common flight number on a route determined by them, and they sell the seats jointly as well, but on the determined route the whole or part of the carriage shall be performed by the actual carrier.[40] The provisions of the Convention apply when a *contracting carrier* 'as a principal makes a contract of carriage governed by the Convention with a passenger or consignor or with a person acting on behalf of the passenger or consignor, and the *actual carrier* performs, by virtue of authority from the contracting carrier, the whole or part of the carriage'. 'Such authority shall be presumed in the absence of proof to the contrary' (Article 39). Despite the fact that in such a relation two or more air carriers are concerned, the legal relation between the parties remains bipolar, since the passenger or the consignor is involved in legal relation merely with the contracting carrier. In this case, no contractual legal relation exists with the actual carrier. However, this fact does not mean that the carriage does not qualify as international, and consequently, the Convention would not be applicable.

In the following cases, both the contracting carrier and the actual carrier shall be subject to the rules of the Convention:

- the *contracting carrier* for 'the whole of the carriage contemplated in the contract'; and
- the *actual carrier* 'solely for the carriage it performs' (Article 40).

The treaty-maker serves the interests of the passengers by providing for the joint liability of the contracting and actual carriers for each other's acts and omissions:

- The acts and omissions of the *actual carrier* and of its servants and agents acting within the scope of their employment shall, in relation to the carriage performed by the actual carrier, be deemed to be also those of the *contracting carrier* [Article 41 (1)].
- The acts and omissions of the *contracting carrier* and of its servants and agents acting within the scope of their employment shall, in relation to the carriage performed by the actual carrier, be deemed to be also those of the *actual carrier* [Article 41 (2)].

[40] In the so-called *code-share agreement,* the participating airlines operate the flight jointly on agreed routes with a common flight number. In that case, within the framework of the so-called *block-seat* arrangement, one Party or both purchase(s) seat quotas on the aircraft operated by the other Party. The non-operating Party (marketing carrier) may purchase *hard-block* seats in fixed number and *soft-block* seats in flexible number on the given flight. The fixed number of seats has to be paid for in advance. If the contracting Party cannot sell the purchased quota, this causes damage. At the same time, if more seats are demanded, the revenue arises for the partner, since only the operating Party may sell tickets exceeding the fixed number of seats. The sale of seats purchased in a flexible framework is less risky; however, such contracts are seldom concluded.

The treaty-maker creates the balance of mutual liability by protecting the carrier performing the air carriage vis-à-vis the contracting carrier. The essence of the protection is that the treaty-maker attaches the contract of the contracting carrier with the customer to conditions, thereby restricting its content.

Thus, the contracting carrier may not conclude a special agreement

- on the basis of which the contracting carrier assumes obligations not imposed by the Convention; or
- that pertains to waiving rights or defences conferred by the Convention; or
- under which a separate declaration of interest in delivery at destination with respect to baggage and cargo affects the actual carrier unless agreed to by it [Article 41 (2)].

No act or omission may subject the actual carrier to liability for an amount exceeding that referred to in Articles 21–24 of the Convention [Article 41 (2)]. 'Any complaint to be made or instruction to be given under the Convention to the air carrier shall have the same effect whether it is addressed to the contracting carrier or to the actual carrier'. Nevertheless, instructions concerning the right of disposal over the cargo 'shall only be effective if they are addressed to the contracting carrier' (Article 42). This rule of the Convention does not pertain to the case when Airline A concludes a *code-share* agreement with Airline B. The passenger purchases the air ticket from Airline B and the complete route is covered by Airline B. Thus, the passenger is in contractual relation with Airline B, which as the actual carrier performs the flight. Obviously, the liability of Airline A for damages in this relation cannot be established since solely and exclusively Airline B bears responsibility. The contracting carrier and the actual carrier in the *code-share* legal relation cannot be qualified as successive carriers.

Liability of Code-Share Carriers

In the case of *Best versus BWIA West Indies Airways*,[41] the plaintiff purchased an air ticket from BWIA (BW) Airline, intending to travel from New York to Grenada. From the flight of BWIA Airline departing from New York she landed on the airport of Port of Spain (the capital of Trinidad and Tobago), then the passenger wished to continue her journey on board an airplane of a Caribbean airline called LIAT (LI). However, the flight was cancelled, therefore, the LIAT Airline rebooked the passenger on another, later flight, so Ms. Best boarded the airplane. Before departure, a man working at the airport requested the plaintiff to disembark the plane because an administrative fault had occurred. Since she refused to comply, the employee of the airline also called upon Ms. Best to disembark the plane, who failed to cooperate with reference to fatigue and hunger. A minor scuffle flared up, and eventually, the

(continued)

[41] *Best v. BWIA West Indies Airways Ltd.*, No. 06 581 F. Supp. 2d 359, 2008.

airline cabin crew dragged the passenger out of the plane with force, then she was conveyed down the stairs. Meanwhile, Ms. Best got injured, lay down on the concrete ground and complained about a pain in her leg. Another employee of the airline, trying to save the day, took the passenger back on the plane, which left for Grenada.

Upon the adjudication of the case, it was unambiguous that international carriage had taken place and in its course the passenger had suffered an accident. However, the question arose which air carrier was liable for the damage caused. Pursuant to the provision of the Convention, the contracting carrier is liable for causing damage during the whole of the carriage, while the actual carrier is liable merely for events during its own carriage provided that the airlines were in a *code-share* legal relation. The examination established that the BWIA and LIAT Airlines had not concluded a *code-share* agreement, this fact was not indicated on the air ticket or in the flight numbers either. LIAT Airline flew under its own code, thus, the carriage qualified as *successive*, not a *code-share* cooperation between the contracting and the actual carrier. Consequently, the full liability of LIAT Airline was established by the court.

9.4.6 Combined Carriage

In the case of combined carriage performed partly by air and partly by any other mode of carriage, the provisions of the Convention shall apply only to the carriage by air, provided that the carriage by air qualifies as international carriage and the aircraft performs the carriage for reward [Article 38 (1)].

Different rules are applicable to carriage by other sub-branches of transport. If for technical or meteorological reasons, or because of strike, the aircraft does not land at its destination and is not capable of continuing its journey or the flight is cancelled, the airline may offer the passengers an alternative mode of carriage (land) within a certain distance if it cannot perform carriage by air. For instance, if the passengers travel from Amsterdam (AMS) with transfer in Paris (CDG), but the flight to Paris is cancelled, the connecting flight can be reached by train. The journey by train, or limousine, bus or boat, etc. does not qualify as air carriage,[42] since the Convention by its own strength *(ex proprio vigore)* does not encompass other transport sub-branches. Thus, the damage caused in this period of the journey is adjudged pursuant to the rules of national law pertaining to the concerned sub-branch of transport.

[42]Ground Carriage—Article 16., General Conditions of Carriage, Air France, March 2022 (www.airfrance.us).

At the same time, the Convention facilitates that in the case of combined carriage the contracting parties may insert 'in the document of air carriage conditions relating to other modes of carriage, provided that the provisions of the Convention are observed as regards the carriage by air' [Article 38 (2)]. Upon the carriage of cargo, if the consignor and the carrier of the cargo stipulate in advance in the air waybill that the carrier for certain sections will take recourse to means of land (public road or railway) or water transportation (ship), these modes of carriage will be governed by the rules of the Convention.[43] Nevertheless, if the parties do not stipulate in advance the possibility of using other modes of transportation in the air waybill, the period of carriage by air does not extend to any carriage by land, sea, or inland waterway performed outside the airport.

In the case of *Siemens versus Schenker International*,[44] the plaintiff demanded the defendant to indemnify the damage caused to its manufactured products during consignment. The electronic products manufactured in Germany were delivered to Australia by the Schenker consignment company. The cargo arrived at the airport in Melbourne (MEL), from where it was delivered by lorry to a warehouse at a distance of 4 km and stored there temporarily. However, during the transportation of the cargo back to the airport, some of the products fell from the plateau owing to the fault of the lorry driver, and significant damage was caused to the cargo.

As the carriage was deemed international, the case needed to be adjudged pursuant to the provisions of the Convention. Nevertheless, the damage was caused during the section performed outside the area of the airport, when the Convention was not applicable. However, the carriage by air can be extended in writing in the air waybill to consignment on other modes of transportation for the purpose of loading, delivery or transhipment. In such a case, the Convention is governing, because this section is also deemed to be air carriage.

The Court established that the limited liability indicated in the air waybill had been extended by the parties to the whole carriage, thereby, to consignment to the warehouse as well. Therefore, according to the rules of the Convention the carrier, sustaining its limited liability, was liable on the basis of weight for the damage worth 1.7 million Australian Dollars (AUD). On the basis of weight, the carrier made a payment of 74,680 USD as damages calculated with 20 USD per kilogram.

[43] *Masudi v. Brady Cargo Services Inc.*, No. 1:2012cv02391—Document 44 (E.D.N.Y.), 8 September 2014.

[44] *Siemens Ltd. v. Schenker International (Australia) Pty. Ltd.*, High Court of Australia, S158/2003, HCA 11, 9 March 2004.

Essentially, the liability of the air carrier is maintained during the time of storage in the warehouse as well, if the disposal over the cargo in the warehouse is deemed to be part of the carriage by air by the contracting parties. The treaty-maker extends the section of air carriage to cases, when upon the performance of a contract of carriage by air for the purpose of *loading*, *delivery* or *transhipment*, carriage takes place using other modes of transport. Any damage caused during this period is presumed, subject to proof to the contrary, to have been the result of an event that took place during the carriage by air.[45]

> If a carrier, without the consent of the consignor, substitutes carriage by another mode of transport for the whole or part of a carriage intended by the agreement between the parties, such carriage by another mode of transport is deemed to be within the period of carriage by air [Article 18 (4)].

Personal Scope of MC 1999

Thus, the personal scope of the Convention extends to the following legal entities:

- *persons* (the contracting parties: *passengers*, *consignors*) and the *staff travelling as passengers;*
- *air carriers*, to wit, airlines and the *agents* of airlines and, in the case of free carriage, air transport *undertakings;*
- *consecutive* carriages performed by several air carriers;
- *combined* carriages performed partly by aircraft[46] and partly through any other mode of transport;
- *actually performing* carriers instead of the contracting carrier.

The personal scope of the Convention does not extend to the following:

- the flight crew on duty serving on board (pilots, flight attendants, the flight engineer, technical experts);
- stowaway passsengers (free riders); and
- kidnapped persons.

[45] *Fuller v. Amerijet International Inc.*, 273 F. Supp. Ed 902, Civil Action H-03–1128, 22 July 2003.

[46] The Montreal Convention does not contain the concept of aircraft. However, ICAO Annex 7 to the Chicago Convention quotes the definition of the ICAO Council, according to which aircraft includes airplanes in the traditional sense, helicopters, balloons, airships, gliders and ultralight aircraft, etc. [see, Part I, Chap. 2. 3].

9.5 The Limitation of Actions

The deadline for the submission of the claim for action, that is, the term of preclusion of the enforcement of the claim is *2 years*. The court considers the deadline *ex officio*.

In the case of *Fishman by Fishman versus Delta Air Lines*,[47] the plaintiff mother's 2-year-old daughter suffered from extremely strong earache during landing by reason of the change in cabin pressure. In order to alleviate the pain of the child, the flight attendant dipped a hot hand towel into a cup then pressed it to the ear of the child. However, the hot water spilt from the cup and burnt the neck and shoulder of the child. The parent requested first-aid, which was rejected by the flight attendants. The plaintiff filed an action against the airline after 2 years and 3 months following the case, which was dismissed by the court with reference to the term of preclusion.

> The right to damages shall be extinguished if an action is not brought within a period of 2 years, reckoned
> - from the date of arrival at the destination; or
> - from the date on which the aircraft ought to have arrived; or
> - from the date on which the carriage stopped.

'The method of calculating that period shall be determined by the law of the court seised of the case' [Article 35 (1–2)]. After the expiry of 2 years from any of the dates above, the claim for indemnification cannot be enforced. No exemption is admissible since this is an objective deadline which does not include contingent abeyance or interruption of the term of limitation.

[47] *Fishman by Fishman v. Delta Air Lines, Inc.*, NOS 1818, 2038, Dockets 96–9345, 96–9457, 132 F.3d 138, 1998.

In the case *Duay versus Continental Airlines,*[48] the plaintiff with Swiss citizenship paralysed under his waist noticed upon arriving in Dallas (DFW) on 2 December 2007 that his wheelchair made to measure had been damaged and became unusable due to careless lading by the ground handling staff. The passenger received a wheelchair for his 2-week stay in the United States from the airline, but the wheelchair did not fit the figure of the claimant. Consequently, Mr. Duay's skin became so irritated that when he returned to Switzerland, his doctors thought he needed hospitalisation and surgery.

The plaintiff passenger filed an action against the Continental Airline (CO) (the defendant) with reference to carelessness and breach of contract after 2 years and 1 day following his return to Switzerland, on 18 December 2009 in the State of Texas. The court established that the plaintiff overrode the 2 years' term of preclusion. The plaintiff argued that he calculated the 2 years' deadline from the time of the discovery of his illness and of consulting a doctor.

With respect to the fact that the method of calculation of the period of the enforcement of the claim is determined by the court seized of the case, the plaintiff expected the court in Texas to do justice to him. Nevertheless, the court repudiated the claim, because it held that the main objective of the Montreal Convention, that is, unification cannot be injured in this case either, furthermore, the Convention undoubtedly and clearly determines the calculation of the deadline, which in this case was 2 years after arrival in Dallas.

In case during the carriage damage is caused to baggage or cargo, furthermore, if the flight is delayed, the clients may make a claim for damages or make a *complaint* to the air carrier for the purpose of the examination of the case. 'In the case of damage, the person entitled to delivery must complain to the air carrier forthwith after the discovery of the damage':

- In the case of checked baggage, within 7 calendar days from the date of receipt;
- In the case of cargo, within 14 calendar days from the date of receipt at the latest [Article 31 (1)].

'In the case of delay, the complaint must be made at the latest within 21 calendar days from the date on which the baggage or cargo have been placed at his or her disposal' [Article 31 (2)].

[48] *Philippe Duay v. Continental Airlines,* INC., United States District Court Southern District of Texas, Houston Division, Civil Action No. H-10-cv-1454 Doc.13, 2010.

'Receipt by the person entitled to delivery of checked baggage or cargo without complaint is prima facie evidence that the same has been delivered in good condition and in accordance with the document of carriage or with the record preserved by other means' (electronically) [Article 31 (1)]. 'Every complaint must be made in writing and given or dispatched to the air carrier within the times aforesaid' [Article 31 (3)]. The omission of the deadline entails forfeiture. If no complaint is made within the times aforesaid, no action shall lie against the carrier, save in the case of fraud on its part [Article 31 (4)]. This means the delayed initiation of action may not be exempted, with the exception of the case when the air carrier for the purpose of the evasion of its obligation of indemnification commits fraud (for instance, by marking time).

References

Abeyratne RIR (2001) Aviation Trends in the New Millennium. Transportation of Abducted Children. Routledge, Part 17, pp. 297–311

Balfour J (2003) Aviation Legal News and Views. Beaumont Bull Special Issue:2

Bartsch R (2018) International Aviation Law: a Practical guide. 2nd edn., Routledge, p 200

Bisignani G (2008) IATA Press release (No. 25, 31 May 2008). IATA's Director General and CEO, Istanbul

Danko M (2012) Montreal Convention Does Not Apply to Crew Members. Aviation Law Monitor 18. www.aviationlawmonitor.com

Dempsey PS, Milde M (2005) International Air Carrier Liability: the Montreal Convention of 1999. McGill University Centre for Research in Air & Space Law, Montreal

Goldhirsch LB (2000) The Warsaw Convention Annotated: a Legal Handbook. Wolters Kluwer, The Hague, p 13

Kearns KS (2018) Fundamentals of International Aviation. Routledge, pp 203–206

Larsen PB, Sweeney JC, Gillick JE (2012) Aviation Law: Cases, laws and related sources. Martinus Nijhoff, Leiden, pp 242–346

Margo RD (2001) Liability and Damages. IATA Training and Development Institute, Montreal, p 10

Milde M (2008) 'Rendition Flights' and International Air Law. In: REDRESS seeking reparations for torture survivors, pp 7–8

Sipos A (2019) The Evolution of Air Carrier Liability. Is the new Montreal Convention the humble successor of the Warsaw System? ELTE Ann 58:101–119

Sipos A (2020) The Air Carrier's Liability for Damage Caused to Cargo. ELTE Ann 59:155–184

Tompkins GN Jr (2015) 2014 Summary of MC99 Court Decisions. Air and Space Law J 40(2):153

Varley H (ed) (1978) The Air Traveller's Handbook. The Complete guide to air travel, airplanes, and airports. Simon et Schuster, New York, pp 22–23

Chapter 10
Examination of the Liability of the Air Carrier

If the court has jurisdiction to adjudicate the claim meritoriously as well as the personal and substantive scopes of the Convention encompass the case, and if the claim for action or complaint has been filed in due time, the court shall examine on the basis of substantive law via the elements of the facts of the legal case whether the liability of the air carrier prevails. During the adjudication, the judge assesses each essential condition required by the Convention, since merely in the case of the joint prevalence of the conditions may the fulfilment of the demands of the claimants for damages ensue pursuant to the rules of the Convention.

The liability of the air carrier for damages during international carriage can be established in cases when

1. the death or bodily injury of the *passenger* was caused by *an accident*,
2. the *baggage* was destroyed, lost, or damaged,
3. the *cargo* was destroyed, lost, or damaged,
4. the carriage of the passenger, baggage, or cargo was *delayed*.

10.1 Liability for Damage Caused to Passenger

'The air carrier is liable for damage sustained in case of death or bodily injury of a passenger upon condition only that the accident which caused the death or injury took place on board the aircraft or in the course of any of the operations of embarking or disembarking' [Article 17 (1)]. For the establishment of liability, the joint fulfilment of the conjunctive conditions below is necessary:

- *the occurrence of an accident*; and
- the accident causes the *death or bodily injury* of the passenger; and
- the accident takes place *on board* an aircraft or in the course of any of the operations of *embarking* or *disembarking*.

A. Sipos, *International Aviation Law*, https://doi.org/10.1007/978-3-031-39066-1_10

In case one condition or a conceptual element of a condition is missing, the air carrier is not liable, therefore, the clarification of the concept of accident is important. Although minor or major accidents often occur during flights, an accident that gives rise to the liability of the air carrier rarely happens. Its reason is that an accident consists exclusively in what the Convention interpreted by case laws circumscribe as such. The contracting States transplanted the provision concerning the accident from the Warsaw Convention wholly, with minor differences in phrasing not related to the essential content of the provision.[1] This means that judicial guidance and judgements made under the effect of the Warsaw Convention having become precedents integral to the system of case-law related to accidents suffered by passengers have been applicable up to these days, thus, they directly affect the cases under the scope of the Montreal Convention and the practice of the judges. Judgements on damage deriving from accidents constitute an inexhaustible repository of the regime of case-law, since the great majority of relevant lawsuits belong to this group of cases.

10.1.1 Conditions and Definition of Accident

The first essential condition is that an *accident* should occur.

One of the most important keywords in the Convention is accident. The term of 'accident' appears in the original French text of the Warsaw Convention as well. Due to the fact that the Warsaw Convention was originally adopted in French, the States Parties needed to have the complete text of the Convention translated from the original French language. Consequently, in debates concerning interpretation, experts always take the French version into consideration (since the British and American translations slightly differ from the original context, for example, in the case of the word 'accident').[2]

Although the concept of accident is a weighty and simultaneously the most important element of the Convention, the contracting Parties omitted to define the concept in the drafting phase of the Convention. In spite of the fact that the guiding judgements of international aviation law constituting precedents settle this issue basically in the majority of States, the absence of a uniform definition renders scope for the courts of the Member States to interpret the conceptual elements of accident creatively in their judgements. The quality of the interpretation is essential since this determines whether the judge in the specific legal dispute reaches a decision pursuant to the Convention. Namely, if, according to the discretion of the judge,

[1] "The carrier is liable for damage sustained in the event of the death or wounding of the passenger or any other bodily injury suffered by the passenger, if the accident which caused the damage so sustained took place on board the aircraft or in the course of any of the operations of embarking or disembarking". Warsaw Convention (Article 17).

[2] Lowenfeld and Mendelsohn (1967), pp. 497–692.

the ensued event of damage for some reason is not subject to the conceptual scope of accident circumscribed under the Convention, the action will be dismissed.

During the concrete construction of the word of accident, several factors need to be taken into consideration: the dangerous operation of air transport with inherent risks, the content underlying the written rules, the treaty-maker's will, the historical, economic and social situation prevalent during the preparation of the draft-law, the conciliations between the concerned parties and the practical context of the outlined legal solutions. Considering all these factors, mainly the judges of Anglo-Saxon countries have had pioneering role in the concrete definition of the concept of accident.

The generally acknowledged concept of the accident has been shaped by the following complementary legal cases establishing legal practice to be followed in the larger part of the world.

In the lawsuit *DeMarines versus KLM Royal Dutch Airlines,*[3] the Supreme Court of the United States made a verdict for the first time, in which it exhaustively enlarged upon the elements and unique criteria of the concept of accident. The plaintiffs (husband and wife) departed from Pittsburgh (PIT) to Europe on a charter flight of the KLM Airline in May 1972. During the return flight, the plaintiffs flew to Philadelphia (PHL) from Zurich (ZRH) via Amsterdam (AMS). On route between Zurich and Amsterdam, Mrs. DeMarines felt an explosive pain in her head. Consequently, her speech became unintelligible, and she was overcome with complete obtuseness. After the case, the physical condition of the passenger considerably deteriorated, persistent disturbance of equilibrium emerged in her organism. In their action, the plaintiffs tried to find and explain the causes of the bodily injury with reference to the faulty operation of the air pressure control system and the rapid fall of pressure (dehermetisation). Apart from the plaintiffs, further seven passengers indicated that in this section of the journey they had similar problems, mostly unpleasant earache. As opposed, the lawyers of KLM invited eight passengers as witnesses, who did not feel anything special and found that everything had been in order during the whole journey. The technical experts of KLM could prove in the lawsuit that all the equipment of the aircraft had operated normally, and no fault occurred.

In the case of *DeMarines* the court sought for an interpretation of the concept of accident acceptable in judicial practice. Eventually, it aligned with the standpoint that 'an accident is an occurrence or event, a physical circumstance, which contrarily to the usual course of events occurs unexpectedly'. If the event on board the aircraft was an expectable, usual occurrence, the case obviously cannot be conceived as an accident. For the event of an accident, the following elements should be present: the

[3] *DeMarines v. KLM Royal Dutch Airlines,* 580 F. 2d 1193 (3 Fed. R. Evid. Serv. 5753), 1978.

occurrence or *event* should be *unexpected*, *unusual*, or *unforeseeable*. The operational decrease of pressure on the aircraft is not an unexpected occurrence or unusual event, therefore, it does not qualify as an accident.

In the lawsuit *Air France versus Valerie Hermien Saks*,[4] the passenger brought an action against the French national airline because on its flight travelling between Paris (CDG) and Los Angeles (LAX), she, by reason of the change of cabin pressure, suffered complete loss of hearing in her left ear. The Supreme Court emphasised during the legal construction of accident (under Article 17) that all circumstances leading to the injury sustained by the passenger need to be examined. The flight was in all respects ordinary, upon disembarking nothing noteworthy happened. The passenger did not complain about pains, nor did she ask the staff of the airline for help, but 5 days later, after her medical examination and the communication of the fact of her deafening, she turned to her lawyer. Then as a claimant she justified the injury of her left ear by the fact that the maintenance by the airline was negligent and the badly set air pressure control system on the airplane contributed to the occurrence of the irrecoverable damage to her ear. However, the legal representatives of *Air France* entered a counterclaim, thereby, as plaintiffs *(reus in exceptione fit actor)*,[5] they demanded that the passenger as defendant proved that she had suffered an accident in relation to flying on the aircraft. The defendant, however, was not able to prove this fact.

The case is quite simple, nevertheless, it is historic. It has greater significance than the *DeMarines*-Case, since the judicial attempt to define the word *accident* in the adduced reasoning achieved its aim and became normative in a broad scope. In the course of the interpretation of the law, the court ruled that an accident which causes the bodily injury of the passenger needs to be an unexpected or unusual event, which is *external to the passenger*. Therefore, this new approach is essential, since the bodily injury does not arise in the regular course of flying as an internal reaction in the passenger, but it arises as a consequence of an accident, because the accident is the cause of the injury.[6]

[4] *Air France v. Valerie Hermien Saks,* US Supreme Court Reports, 470 U.S. 392, 105 S.Ct. 1338, 84 L. Ed. 2d 289, 1985.

[5] If the accused (the defendant) counterpleads, in this respect they become a plaintiff.

[6] *Sakaria v. Trans World Airlines,* 8 F.3d 164, 170 (fourth Cir. 1993), cert. denied, 114S.Ct. 1835, 1994.

Sexual Harassment on Board Aircraft
In the lawsuit *Brandi Wallace versus Korean Air*,[7] the plaintiff, on board Flight 61 of *Korean Air* (KE) on route from Seoul (ICN) to Los Angeles (LAX), became a victim of sexual harassment. Miss Brandi Wallace was seated in economy class beside an unfamiliar Korean passenger, Kwang-Yong-Park. They did not communicate with each other during the flight. After 3 h following take-off, Mr. Park carefully unfastened the belt of the trousers of Miss Wallace, who was fast asleep in her window seat. After some minutes, he managed to undo the button on the trousers of Miss Wallace, then carefully undid the zip. All this time, the claimant Miss Wallace did not wake up; only when Mr. Park was already stroking her. Upon realising what was happening, the claimant hit the perpetrator and fled from the tight spot she was in, jumping over the seats in front of her while shouting. Miss Wallace immediately notified the flight attendants of the incident; thus, Mr. Park was arrested by the airport police in Los Angeles. The United States criminal court found the perpetrator guilty in the commission of the crime of 'unwelcome sexual conduct' vis-à-vis another passenger and sentenced him to imprisonment suspended for a 2 years' probationary period.

In the first instance, her action for damages against the airline was dismissed. According to the judgement of the court, during the complete flight there was no act or negligence on the part of the cabin crew, which in the context of the operation of the aircraft could substantiate the establishment of an accident and the event was not considered to be a 'risk-factor characteristic of air travel'. This explanation of the judgement is important in the evolution of the definition of accident.

In the second instance, however, the court established the occurrence of an accident with respect to the extraordinary circumstances of the case. According to the reasoning of the court, Miss Wallace did not know that she was sitting next to a 'sexual predator' and that 'the uncontrolled sexual predator breaks loose in darkness'; therefore, the incident, from that viewpoint, was in fact unexpected and unusual. Since this unlawful act in itself is insufficient for the establishment of the liability of the air carrier, the solicitors of the plaintiff emphasised that the sexual harassment took a longer time. In this context, the activity could not be carried out inconspicuously in secret, thus, the cabin crew should have noticed it. The negligent behaviour of the cabin crew substantiated the claim of the plaintiff. It is interesting and thought-provoking that, despite the judgement establishing the liability of the airline, the reasoning of the judgement in the first instance became a further stage of the interpretation of the law, because the statement therein was conducive to the interpretation of accident. On these grounds, the act or assault (fight, libel, and in this

[7] *Wallace v. Korean Air*, No. 98 Civ. 1039, 1999 WL 187213 (S.D.N.Y.), 1999.

case, harassment) of a passenger vis-à-vis another passenger does not qualify as accident, because these acts are not related to a *risk characteristic of air travel*.

In the lawsuit *Husain versus Olympic Airways*, the conceptual scope of accident defined in the preceding legal case was extended and amplified by an essential phrase, and thereby, it became complete.

Death on Board Aircraft

In the case of *Husain versus Olympic Airways*,[8] Dr. Abid Hanson, a 52-year-old passenger on board an aircraft travelling from Athens (ATH) to New York (JFK), suffered an asthma attack due to a large amount of secondary cigarette smoke and died. In 1998, smoking was not prohibited on all flights;[9] in practice, the passengers could choose between smoking and non-smoking sections on international flights.

The wife of the victim, plaintiff Mrs. Husain, claimed that although her husband was seated in the non-smoking section in second class, he was only three rows away from the smoking section. Because of the bad physical condition of her husband, Mrs. Husain requested the flight attendants, on three occasions, to seat her husband farther away from the smoking section. However, all her three requests were denied, stating that all the seats were full. In fact, however, there were 11 empty seats on the flight, and 28 seats were occupied by airline staff travelling with free tickets; thus, it would have been possible to seat the passenger elsewhere. The passenger could also have had the chance to request his fellow passengers to exchange seats. The condition of the passenger being allergic to cigarette smoke was exacerbated by his asthma attack, and his life could not be saved despite the medical help provided on board.

The plaintiff with the charge of causing death resorted to a Californian court, which established the facts of the case of causing an accident. The court awarded an indemnification of 2.8 million USD, which was halved since the physical condition and the conduct of the passenger contributed partly to the occurrence of the accident. Thus, the court obligated the airline to pay a compensation of 1.4 million USD.

[8] *Husain v. Olympic Airways,* 316 F.3d 829 (ninth Cir.), 2002.

[9] On the domestic flights of the United States smoking has been prohibited since February 1990, while on international flights it has been prohibited by law since the summer of 2000. Today the smoke-free world is natural, but at that time the prohibition of smoking provoked huge debate and opposition. The prohibition did not have reasons related to aviation safety, but positively the side-effects of secondary cigarette smoke detrimental to health justified it, however, further aspects also emerged, such as the irretrievable discolouration (yellowness) of the interior of the aircraft and the time-consuming cleaning of the ash-trays and its costs also arose.

US DoT, Office of the Secretary 14 CFR Part 252, Federal Register/Vol. 65, No. 112/9 June 2000/, Rules and Regulations, Prohibition of Smoking on Scheduled Passenger Flights; Final Rules.

The solicitors of the airline based their defence on the allegation that the occurrence of an accident requires real physical impact, which, in their opinion, did not occur. At the same time, the negative conduct of the flight attendants did not contribute to the occurrence of the accident either because the passenger did not die as a result of it but due to the secondary cigarette smoke, which was not an unexpected or unusual event on an open-plan international flight packed with smokers. However, the court held that the abruptness of the flight attendants conflicted with the General Conditions of Carriage of the airline, furthermore, it violated the industrial prescriptions, which is discordant with the requirement of ordinary and expected operation. The plaintiff felt with good reason that the denial of help by the crew member who is trained to help and provides service on board the aircraft mainly for this purpose gives rise to such an unexpected situation, which is external to the passenger. In other words, in the causal chain leading to the accident, in its context, the conduct of the flight attendants was a link of chain, which directly contributed to the death of the passenger, therefore, the accident occurred *in connection with the activity of operation*. Thereby, the judgement of the court extended the scope of the concept of accident. Consequently, an accident may ensue not only owing to the unusual or unexpected event *related to the airline's operation of the aircraft*, but it may occur proceeding from the unusual or unexpected act of the *flight crew* as well.

The Definition of Accident

On the basis of the legal cases above and pursuant to the rule of the Convention, an accident is

- an *unexpected* or *unusual or unforseeable event;*
- *external to the passenger*;
- *related to the airline's operation of the aircraft* (risk characteristic of air travel, thus, risk proceeding therefrom);
- due to which the passenger *dies* or *gets bodily injured*.

Thus, according to legal practice, the following events do not qualify as accident:

- tripping on a piece of hand luggage protruding from the rows of aisle seats;[10]
- tumbling down or slipping on a pillow or blanket on the floor;[11]
- injuries or inconveniences caused by adjustable seats;[12]

---

[10] *Sethy v. Malév Hungarian Airlines*, US District Court, 2d 2012.

[11] *Vanderwall v. United Airlines, Inc.*, F. Supp. 3d, 2015 WL 309094 (S.D. Fla.), January 2015.

[12] However, if owing to pushing (tilting back not strongly) the seat, the hot tea from the tray on the back of the seat is plunged into the lap of the other passenger, this may qualify as an accident. In such a case an unexpected and irregular event external to the passenger ensues, which is related to the activity of flying, since the tea on the tray should not spill owing to a minor push or bump. If the event is attributable to the defect of the tray (the tray was instable), the relationship between the activity of flying and causing damage can be established, because the main function of the tray is to hold the tea, the served drinks and the meals. *Wipranik v. Air Canada,* No. CV 06–3763 AHM, May 15, 2007.

- backache, sprain, or strain deriving from packing hand luggage;
- any event or occurrence deriving from the disease or physical condition of the passenger.

The poor quality of service provided by the airline and the deriving inconvenience do not fall under the scope of the conduct of causing damage circumscribed by the Convention. Nor does communication in a language unfamiliar to the passenger instead of the usual bilingual provision of information on board cause damage.[13] Furthermore, accident does not include the case when the entitlement of the passenger to business class is downgraded to economy class and then the passenger complains about swollen feet,[14] neither does accident extend to problems arising during the serving of food or drinks because of their substance, quality, nor to the allergy, disease and other complaints of the passenger. Obviously, the claims for damages related to the quality of the service are not founded on the scope of accident, even if consequently, damage is caused to the passenger (with the exception when in this context the accident emerges in a cause-effect relationship). In the case of a passenger rejected because of the overbooking of the flight, although the air carrier breaches the contract, its adjudication is not subject to the Convention. If the passenger cannot enforce their claim for damages directly against the airline, they may sue the party causing the damage but only within the framework of national civil law (see, Part II, Chap. 11. 4). The treaty-maker does not distinguish damage from damage, but it requires that the claim for damages is satisfied in the case of the fulfilment of the conditions of the Convention and exclusively within the purview of the Convention (Article 29).

Likewise, the injuries caused by objects falling from the overhead compartment on the passengers do not qualify as accident, but they give rise to a lot of disputes, because they are difficult to adjudge uniformly.[15] Depending on the circumstances, the court may in some occasions rule that such case qualifies as accident.[16]

In the lawsuit *Maxwell versus Aer Lingus*,[17] after the halt of the aircraft bottles purchased in the duty-free shop tumbled on the head of the plaintiff passenger (who was not the owner of the alcohol) after the passenger in the next seat had opened the overhead compartment. According to the court, this extraordinary event was in relation to the activity of flying, which qualifies as accident. In its reasoning, the court expounded that airlines announce in advance what items and in what size may be carried as unchecked baggage on board by the

(continued)

[13] *Thibodeau v. Air Canada*, SCC 67, 3 S.C.R. 340. 2014.

[14] *David v. United Airlines*, WL 1573423, C.D. Cal., 18 April 2016.

[15] Truitt (2015), pp. 449–470.

[16] *Smith v. American Airlines, Inc.*, No. 09–02903 WHA, 2009 WL 3072449, 22 September 2009.

[17] *Maxwell v. Aer Lingus Ltd.*, 122 F. Supp. 2d 210, November 2000.

passenger for reasons of safety and passenger comfort. Packing takes place under the surveillance of the cabin crew, who help the passengers to pack in the racks and before take-off they close the compartment doors left open. The flight attendants may request the passenger to place their hand luggage elsewhere, but they may also place it themselves if its size or other feature justifies it, even if the cabin crew does not always attend thereto the warning of the airline concerning falling objects is a prescription, a simple routine activity, which in itself does not protect the airline from liability for damages. This provides protection for the air carrier vis-à-vis the passenger exclusively if the passenger upon opening the compartment causes damage to themselves,[18] but it may not be helpful if another passenger suffers such damage because of the negligence of another passenger. The event must be unexpected or unusual for the injured passenger, because people generally do not reckon that something is going to fall on their heads on board an airplane.

However, it does not qualify as accident if the passenger does not follow the instructions of the flight crew. An example is when a passenger refuses to fasten their seat belt, even when it is obligatory, and as a consequence, upon a slight braking, they get injured. In such cases, courts dismissed the actions of the injured passengers since it was the negligence of the passengers that caused the damage and it was proved that the airline 'has taken all the necessary measures to prevent the damage'. Neither was an accident established when a passenger, despite the displayed warning of the necessity to fasten seat belts, did not comply with the instruction but instead stood up and dashed to the still-open door to wave goodbye. The passenger fell out of the airplane because she did not notice that the passenger stairs had formerly been removed by the ground service provider staff. Pursuant to the Convention, no accident happened in this case despite the fracture in the passenger's leg and her hospitalisation.[19]

As opposed, if the flight crew directly or indirectly contributes to the emergence of an unexpected or unusual event, for example, the flight attendant serves plenty of alcohol to the passenger several times (for safety reasons only the alcoholic drinks served on board may be consumed), who, in an inebriated condition, starts kissing the woman in the next seat and biting her lips, thereby, he causes bodily injury, the case is subject to the conceptual scope of accident. In such a case, the cabin crew do unambiguously not comply with the strict regulations, and due to this negligent conduct, the passenger behaves unlawfully, which is already related to the activity of flying.[20] If a member of the flight crew carries out their work under the influence of alcohol, drugs or any substance inducing stupor affecting their capacity to act detrimentally, and this is proved during the establishment of the facts of the case,

---

[18] *Wright v. American Airlines Inc.*, WL 446077, 2010.

[19] *Chutter v. KLM Royal Dutch Airlines*, US District Court, 132 F. Supp. 611, 1955.

[20] *Tsevas v. Delta Airlines*, WL 767278 (N.D.III.), December 1997.

in each case beyond criminal legal and labour legal consequences, the court will establish the fact of an accident and the liability of the airline for damages. The flight crew discharging crucial activity from the viewpoint of the safety of air transport may not breach their obligations, because this way they may easily bring about emergency, even the negligent form of which is punishable.

Unequivocally, accidents are related to the activity of air travel when the passengers get injured upon the emergency landing of the airplane [e.g., the fuel runs out, because the pilots filled up with less fuel with a view to saving costs by carrying less weight, or the under-carriage (nose gear) does not open].

However, the conceptual scope of accident does not extend to the death or bodily injury of stowaway passengers (free riders). Most frequently, free riders occupy the baggage storage space, or, by outwitting the security system of the airport, they travel in the passenger compartment, but it has also happened that the free rider hid in the under-carriage compartment (where the chance for survival on long-haul or even short-haul flights is practically zero). Upon the adjudication of the accident suffered by the free rider, the Convention is not applicable in the absence of a contractual relationship.

The Medical Condition of the Passenger

On flights, events deriving from some illness occur on a daily basis. This is not astonishing since on average far more than one million passengers flew in every minute of the day before the worldwide proliferation of the SARS-CoV-2 virus. (Daily 12 million passengers and cargo of a value of 18.8 billion USD are carried on 120,000 flights in the world.)[21] Despite the high numbers, it is surprising that annually on average more than 1000 passengers[22] die on board aircraft, as a consequence of some cardiovascular unforeseen event [mainly heart attack or haemorrhage of the brain (stroke), thrombosis].

These accidents do not fall under the scope of liability of the air carrier. For that matter, the air carrier does not have appropriate information about the physical condition of the passenger, and the staff cannot be expected to 'examine' the passengers and take measures dependant on the 'findings' before the flight.

Heart Attack on Board Aircraft

In the lawsuit *Fülöp versus Malév Hungarian Airlines*,[23] the plaintiff suffered a heart attack on MALÉV Flight 090, travelling from Budapest (BUD) to New York (JFK). In relation to this, the passenger suffered irreversible damage to his heart muscle, and his life could be saved only by the incorporation of a triple pacemaker. According to the plaintiff, despite his heart attack

(continued)

[21] *Aviation Benefits Beyond Borders. Executive Summary.* ATAG report, October 2018, p. 7.

[22] Charles (2011).

[23] *Fülöp v. Malév Hungarian Airlines,* 175 F. Supp. 2d 651 (S.D.N.Y.) 2001; WL 202958 (S.D.N.Y.), 2003.

and severe pains, the pilot-in-command refused to make a forced landing, and the flight crew did not comply properly with the prescriptions to be followed in such emergencies stipulated under international standards and the General Conditions of Carriage.

The airplane was flying above the British coastline when the passenger felt severe pain in his chest. He knew that he was in trouble since 4 years before, he had experienced such a case and, therefore, was familiar with the symptoms. On board the airplane among the passengers a doctor was also travelling, who attended to the passenger. He found that his blood pressure was in order, so he alleviated the passenger's pain with painkiller. The passenger felt better, but later during the flight, the precordial pains recurred several times. After a consultation with the passenger doctor and the crew members, the pilot-in-command (captain) decided not to disrupt the flight. Upon landing at the place of destination, the passenger was instantly taken to a hospital, where it was established that he had had a heart attack; therefore, a life-saving heart operation was performed.

In its judgement, the court ruled that a heart attack did not fall under the conceptual scope of accident pursuant to Article 17. The flight crew had taken every necessary step that could be expected in the specific situation. Solely the passenger had been aware of their physical condition, and the heart attack was not related to flying; therefore, the liability of the airline was not established in this case.

It is the pilot-in-command who has an outstanding legal status among the flight crew, who, during his commandment, is authorised to make a final decision on each issue related to aviation safety on board.[24] The pilot-in-command is responsible for the operation of the aircraft according to rules, whether he navigates the airplane or not. Generally, the airplane is navigated by alternating pilots (one of them on the route there, the other pilot on the route back), so that both of them stay in practice. The pilot-in-command is obligated in relation to the physical condition of the passenger:

- to attend to the provision of first aid to the person who has fallen ill or suffered an accident on board the aircraft, furthermore, if necessary and justified, land on the first suitable airport and transfer the patient to a healthcare organ for the purpose of expeditious medical care;
- to take records of births, deaths, accidents on the aircraft and the related measures;
- upon death on the aircraft to take care of the preservation of the belongings of the deceased person until their transfer to the authority.

The pilot-in-command is authorised to deviate from the rules of the air, but only in case the deviation is unconditionally necessary and justified in the interest of the maintenance of aviation safety. Thus, he is authorised to make a decision, after

[24] ICAO Annex 2 on the Rules of the Air. Chap. 2, 2.4.

weighing up all the known circumstances of the case, on the disruption of the flight and landing on the nearest airport. May the pilot-in-command decide anyhow, the psychic or mental problems emerging in themselves, not entailing the bodily injury of the passenger, or, physical and behavioural disorders deriving from the disease of the passenger shall not result in the liability of the airline for damages.

In the case *Rónai versus Delta Airlines*,[25] the claim of the plaintiff for damages was related to a flight of the *Delta* Airline on route from Budapest (BUD) to New York (JFK). The case, which was similar to the situation in the legal case of *Fülöp versus Malév Hungarian Airlines,* evolved on board the aircraft with the distinction that the passenger did not suffer an actual heart attack. Despite this, according to the allegation of the plaintiff, he suffered irrecoverable bodily injuries and psychic trauma since the possibility of rapid medical treatment was omitted due to the decision of the pilot-in-command not to disrupt the journey via forced landing. However, mental injury and psychic trauma do not fall under the conceptual scope of accident circumscribed under Article 17 of the Convention, as the court expounded in its ruling dismissing the action of the plaintiff.

The rules of the Convention do not give rise to liability for damages on the basis of the physical condition of the passengers, since unexpected events related to the physical and mental condition of the passenger such as heart attack, asthma attack, pulmonary embolism, stroke,[26] deep vein thrombosis, etc. are not *the characteristic risk factors of air travel*, they *do not arise in relation to air travel* and *are not external to the passenger*, thus, they do not qualify as accident. Therefore, the scope of liability of the air carrier does not encompass events or occurrences arising from the disease or the physical condition of the passenger.

The essential content of the former statement is well explained by the risk of Deep Vein Thrombosis (DVT) frequently occurring on long-haul flights. The journeys spanning continents are already performed by direct (non-stop) flights thanks to modern airplanes. During the many times 13–15 h' flights the passengers are limited in their free movement, which provenly increases the chance of the development primarily of deep vein thrombosis due to the lengthy sedentary position. (As early as in World War II, it was observed in the United Kingdom that during air raids among the people sitting in shelters the chance of developing thrombosis was five times higher than among those lying in beds.)[27]

---

[25] *Rónai v. Delta Airlines,* US District Court, Eastern District of N.Y. No. 99 CV 6793 (SJ), 21 December 2000.

[26] *Singh v. Caribbean Airlines Ltd.,* 36 Avi. 16,127 (S.D.Fl.), 2014.

[27] Tompkins (2001), p. 232.

The low humidity (15–20%) on board and cabin overpressure[28] in comparison with the external circumstances produce a relative oxygen-deficient condition *(hypoxia)* and that circumstance induces, beyond many other symptoms, complex biochemical changes in the lower limbs.[29] Owing to several hours' sitting and constant vibration, blood circulation in the legs slows down, the blood stagnates in varicose veins. The most endangered persons are the elderly, expectant mothers and people suffering from cardiovascular diseases, who may easily develop thrombosis. In civil aviation, related legal cases have proliferated in great numbers[30] and the symptom has become familiar as the 'economy class syndrome'.[31]

In the lawsuit *D. Wrobel versus Air France*,[32] the plaintiff travelled on route from Rome (FCO) through Paris (CDG) and San Francisco (SFO) to Portland (PDX). The total travelling time on these flights is altogether 18.5 h. The plaintiff had a stroke on route between CDG and SFO. He justified the emergence of the stroke by the journey being lengthier than planned (indeed, the flight reached its destination with a 3 h' delay) and by being limited in movement on board. Therefore, he demanded indemnification (of 180,902 Euros and 20 cents, a total of 152,000 SDR, furthermore, the payment of litigious and other expenses) by the airline with reference to moral and biological damage. According to the court, it is undoubted that on long-haul flights the several hours' sedentary position increases the risk of the evolution of diseases, but to the occurrence of disorders the current physical condition of the passenger, their contingent alcoholic affectedness or the consumption of sedatives, similar occurrences in the past necessitating medical intervention and their complications may have contributed as well. The court in Rome held that the passenger could not prove beyond doubt the cause-effect relationship between the suffered injury and the lengthier journey because of the delay, therefore, it dismissed the action with reference to its factually and legally unfounded character.[33]

[28] Keeping the pressure all the way at sea level is unnecessary and would put undue stress on the airframe, so the atmosphere in a jet is actually kept at the equivalent of 1500–2400 m, meaning that the persons on board are breathing the same air as they would in Denver or Mexico City (minus the pollution). The cockpit crew (pilots) are breathing the same air as everybody else. An aircraft fuselage does not contain separate compartments with different pressure settings. The entire vessel is pressurized equally from front to back. This includes the cabin, the cockpit (flight deck), and the lower-deck cargo holds. Smith (2018), pp. 41, 122.

[29] Sándor (2008).

[30] For example, *Van Luin v. KLM* (New South Wales) 1 DCLR, (NSW) 25, 2002.; *McDonald v. Korean Air* (Ontario Superior Court of Justice), Docket 29708, 2003.; *Rynne v. Lauda Air Luftfahrt Aktiengelsellschaft* QDC 004 (01/5586) Boulton DCJ, 2003.

[31] Tompkins (2001), p. 232.

[32] *Wrobel v. Air France,* Tribunal of Rome, ninth Civil Law Section, Decision No. 9153, 28 March 2009.

[33] Guerreri (2010).

Deep vein thrombosis unequivocally develops because of lengthy and monotonous sitting, not in relation to the activity of flying. Thus, if the flight is not the cause of the health problem, logically, the air carrier may not be held liable. The air carrier is responsible for aviation safety, but the air passenger is responsible for their own physical condition. Only the passenger and their doctor can reassuringly decide how the flight may affect the passenger's physical condition. What the airline can do during the long-haul flight is restricted to warning the passengers of the importance of bodily movement as well as the dangers of motionless posture and to the publication of magazines to be made available on board for free to everyone about the special exercises to be done in a sedentary position in order to minimise the risk of thrombosis.

In the case of *Hu versus Air China Limited*,[34] the plaintiff arrived in Milan (MXP) from Shanghai (PVG) by direct flight. After disembarking he was queuing up for passport control, which did not take place since he suddenly died because of pulmonary embolism. The plaintiff's relatives sued the airline with reference to the facts that the deceased passenger needed to sit in an uncomfortable seat during the long-haul flight as well as that the airline omitted to warn the passengers of the dangers of immobile position and the entailed risks. The court dismissed the action in all of its points.

In such cases, everywhere in the world generally the defendants (the airlines themselves) are in a favourable position. Although, there are situations and circumstances when the court makes a decision in favour of the plaintiff.[35] If the air passenger can prove that, for instance, the development of the deep vein thrombosis is a consequence of the narrow, uncomfortable seats and the health risk increased in relation to the activity of flying, they have a chance that the court regards the facts of the case as accident pursuant to the Convention and obligates the air carrier to pay indemnification. Related to the health problems of the passenger, the flight crew on duty obligated to be liable can be called to account, only if they did not conform to the international industrial regulations pertaining to first aid.[36] It is important to highlight: if the flight crew (in the absence of medical knowledge) does not provide the most appropriate 'treatment' to the patient, or the help does not support the cure of the patient, the passenger cannot refer to accident. Even if the Automatic External Defibrillator (AED), which can save lives in the case of the sudden stop of blood circulation, is missing from the aircraft owing to the fault of the air carrier, this is not deemed to be an accident.[37] However, if the flight crew breaches international

[34] *Hu v. Air China Limited,* Judgment. No. 399/2009, Tribunal of Busto Arsizio in Case No. 1118 of 2007.

[35] Ehlers (2004), pp. 493–500.

[36] ECAC *Air Passenger Health Issues.* WG, 2005.

[37] *Aziz v. Air India,* 658 F. Supp. 2d 1144, C.D. Cal., 2009.

requirements or the internal rules and procedures based on them (e.g., does not use or misuses the tools necessary for first aid carried on board mandatorily and mishandles the medicines), this qualifies as accident since the event is in cause-effect relationship with negligence related to the airline's operation of the aircraft.

In the case of *Safa versus Deutsche Lufthansa Aktiengesellschaft,*[38] the passenger collapsed on board the plane due to cardiac failure. After consultation with the doctors, the cockpit crew continued the flight without disruption. After arrival, the passenger was taken to hospital immediately, where the doctors established that the condition of the passenger had deteriorated considerably by reason of the delay in medical help. The court held that the flight crew conformed to the international regulations and the internal rules of the airline, therefore, the liability of the airline for damages was not sustained in the absence of accident.

When during the flight a situation deriving from a health condition evolves, in a favourable case, somebody among the passengers on board has a doctor's qualification, which implies great assistance to the patient and the flight crew. At the same time, futile is the benevolent and professional help, if the condition of the patient despite care exacerbates, or in an extreme case, the patient dies. In such a situation the case is generally brought up for a trial. Therefore, before the commencement of the provision of assistance, the doctor may request the flight crew of the airline to declare whether the airline holds third-party insurance for medical intervention, in which the air carrier fully assumes the contingent damage deriving from medical activity. If the necessary and sufficient conditions of the provision of assistance do not exist (the airline does not hold such insurance), the doctor on board may deny the provision of help, since they are not obligated to participate in the rescue. It may also occur that the passenger, who has a medical background, does not come forward, does not take the legal risk when the flight crew is seeking a person with medical qualifications (doctor, nurse or paramedic), rather remains in incognito because they do not want to swell the number of those who, despite providing professional care, found themselves in the midst of a litigious procedure. However, this conduct is most risky, since in such a case the criminal legal facts of the case of the omission of the provision of help may be realised.

The air carriers are unambiguously interested in the provision of appropriate and expeditious medical aid for the passengers during the flight. Therefore, they do their utmost in order not to plunge the doctor on board into a legally vulnerable situation. There are airlines which well in advance contact doctors as their prospective passengers, and besides the full assumption of legal responsibility, they provide other benefits for them.[39] It is increasingly widespread among the airlines that the

[38] *Safa v. Deutsche Lufthansa Aktiengesellschaft, Inc.*, 36 Avi. 16,148 (E.D.N.Y.), 2014.

[39] Doctor on Board Program (www.lufthansa.com/us/en/doctoron-board).

doctor or the person with medical qualification providing help receives a travel voucher to be redeemed for the next journey or other travel allowance besides being guaranteed complete legal protection.

Nowadays, a global medical emergency service exists, which provides ‘phone-in’ medical help for the flight crew in service all over the world. If the passenger or a crew member on the surface or in the air gets into trouble, a contracted company can be called, in which qualified doctors expect calls, provide professional advice and precise instructions for taking care of the patient. If the pilot-in-command decides on forced landing, the service provider arranges that well-prepared ambulance staff knowledgeable about the specific situation picks up the patient. This service can be subscribed.[40]

Passengers with Special Needs

The Convention does not mention passengers with special needs separately, and it does not need to, since the personal scope of the Convention encompasses all persons in contractual relationship with the air carrier under private law. With respect to the fact that air services need to benefit all people, therefore, for the physically handicapped or people with special needs for some other reason, access to air transport needs to be guaranteed, irrespective of the fact whether the limitation of motion originates in a handicap, age, disease, or any other factor. The increasing primacy of passenger rights necessitates that the air carrier provides its services for all passengers on equal terms. At the same time, air carriers may stipulate special rules under their General Conditions of Carriage.

Prior to the scheduled departure time, the passenger or person paying for the carriage is obligated to inform the air carrier about the fact that the carriage of the physically handicapped passenger or a serious patient with limited motility needs care on a stretcher, or uses an oxygen bottle for breathing, or their physical size necessitates the booking of more than one seats. The communication of such information is important not only because this way the air carrier can carry the passenger with the best quality, professionally and safely, but this way the air carrier also has the chance to limit, attach to conditions, or eventually deny the carriage of these persons in compliance with rules of aviation safety and technical specifications. The principal reason is that in the case of emergency, the rescue of passengers with special needs requires extra effort, which cannot jeopardise the implementation of the rescue operation disproportionately.

For instance, the number of passengers in wheelchairs is limited depending on the type and capacity of the airplane and on the General Conditions of Carriage. The number of passengers necessitating the booking of more than one seats because of their physical size is also limited, and the placement of seeing-eye dogs of asthenopic passengers is also possible only in a definite number. Expectant women after the 28th week of pregnancy may travel only in possession of a filled out

[40] Such service is provided by companies such as MedAire’s, MedLink and Stat MD. Medical Emergencies—Guidance for Flight Crew (www.skybrary.aero/index.php/Medical_Emergencies_Guidance_for_Flight).

Medical Information Form (MEDIF) and under special circumstances with a medical report (certificate or a letter signed by the doctor). In general, pregnant women are not allowed to fly after the 32nd week of a multiple pregnancy (with twins or triplets) or after the 36th week of a single pregnancy.

With respect to the fact that the natural process of childbirth may be expedited by the flight, in addition, for the reception of the baby there are, of course, no suitable conditions on board, therefore, the airlines may exclude the expectant mother from the flight, so far as their pregnancy is at an advanced stage and they have failed to notify the airline thereof preliminarily. These rules for the carriage of pregnant women vary from one air carrier to the other.[41] Likewise, infectious sick persons may not travel or stay on board the aircraft at all. Air carriers specify these special, simultaneously obligatory rules in their General Conditions of Carriage.

The Infectious Sick Passenger

The infection of other passengers by the sick person suffering from corona or other virus in itself does not qualify as accident. The reason for this is that infection these days is the most widespread risk factor; therefore, it is not an unexpected, unusual, or unforeseeable event or occurrence. Infection is part of our lives since in our lifetime, everybody has caught an influenza or has been exposed to an infectious disease. Many times, in real life we do not know surely either, or not in the least, from whom we contracted the virus, still less on the airplane in a situation when we can get infected by touching objects. Thus, it is difficult to prove that a passenger, infected with the virus, has infected another passenger or the flight crew on board the aircraft, or, if it happened during embarkation or disembarkation. The passengers are not easily found posteriorly, and it is time-consuming to withdraw the aircraft for thorough inspection from traffic, and the procedure requires immense effort (for example, in a specific case the spread of tuberculosis on board the aircraft was inspected by more than 30 experts working for nearly 8 months for 1200 h).[42]

---

[41] For example, Qatar Airways after the 36th week of gestation does not allow pregnant women to travel. British Airways has the same rule, but in case of multiple pregnancy, the 32nd week is the limit. Some airlines request medical certificate after the 36th week (e.g., Lufthansa, American Airlines). Emirates Airline requests customers located in the United States to furnish a medical report after the 28th week with multiple pregnancy, and it is possible to travel after the 32nd week exclusively with prior clearance from the air carrier's medical department. After the 36th week it is only possible to fly in the case of an uncomplicated single pregnancy and if prior clearance from the air carrier's medical department has been issued.

[42] The Hawaii State Healthcare Department of the United States announced in June 1994 that a 32-year-old Korean woman died of tuberculosis. Before the diagnosis, the victim had travelled from Honolulu (HNL) by flight of nearly 8 h to Chicago (ORD), then further on to Baltimore (BWI), and finally, after 1 month back to Honolulu. The investigation of the authority revealed that during the journey the woman could have infected several passengers. Later, the passengers became symptom-free, but the investigation clarified several real problems. During the journey, the passenger had met 925 persons on board the aircraft, which gave rise to concern because the multidrug-resistant tuberculosis (MDR–TB) spreads quietly and insidiously in the air, primarily via droplet infection (via coughing, speaking and sneezing). Kenyon et al. (1996), pp. 933–938.; Global Plan to End TB: 2018–2022. Stop TB Partnership, Geneva, 2019.

Nevertheless, there can be situations in which the judge establishes the event of an accident and the liability of the air carrier. This requires the existence of a cause-effect relationship between the occurrence of the accident and the negligent conduct of the air carrier. Such relationship may prevail if:

- the air carrier does not deny the carriage of the passenger manifesting COVID–19 symptoms upon the operation of embarkation, or, if it does not take precautionary steps to ensure that the passenger is free from symptoms;
- the air carrier neglects to separate the passenger manifesting COVID–19 symptoms on board, or, in the case of the already separated passenger, the air carrier fails to wait for the arrival of medical help before the commencement of the operation of disembarkation;
- despite a trustworthy notification, the air carrier does not check the passengers for the purpose of the separation of the infected passenger;
- the air-conditioning equipment of the aircraft (the air filter) does not work or is faulty,[43] or during the surface stay of the aircraft, the air conditioner [the ground or the auxiliary power unit (APU)][44] is not switched on professionally.[45]

Obviously, if it is proved that the passenger caught the infection during the service of the airline, and the flight crew or the agent of the air carrier discharged their duties by breaching the industrial regulations, there is a chance to sue the airline. This, however, is not realistic, since the course of business requires that during epidemics, besides the observance of extraordinarily rigorous rules and double security, the airlines do their utmost so that the hygienic circumstances of the passenger are the best possible from embarkation to the end of disembarkation.[46] However, this activity costs a pretty penny. Apparently, this drives up the prices, the surplus cost of which will eventually be paid by the passengers. The challenge of the COVID–19 lays substantial financial burden on the stakeholders (not only regarding lost profits), thus, it poses challenge to the States and insurance companies as well,

---

[43] In the case *Dias versus Transbrazil Airlines Inc.*, the ruling was passed pursuant to the Warsaw Convention on 13 October 1998. According to the allegation of the plaintiff, the passenger en route from Brazil to the United States (NYC) was taken ill with pneumonia, which later caused her death. As stated by the court, the pneumonia could have been caused by the poor quality of the air, as a result of which the fatal respiratory disease developed. According to the court, such event qualifies as accident, therefore, the case was adjudicated under Article 17. *Dias v. Transbrazil Airlines* Inc. 26. Avi (CCH) 16, 048 (S.D.N.Y.), 1998.; Prager et al. (2020).; Onianwa and Agbonze (2020).

[44] The auxiliary power unit (APU), a small jet engine is used to supply electricity and air conditioning when the main engines are not running, or to supplement them when they are working. All modern airliners have an APU, and it is typically located in the rear of the fuselage under the tail. Smith (2018), p. 18.

[45] Coles (2020).

[46] According to the IATA, in respect of the spread of infections on board, flying is the safest means of travel. IATA Guidance for Cabin Operations During and Post Pandemic. 4th edn., 8 September 2020, pp. 1–35.

since the expenses of persons (air passengers) stranded in quarantine, related to accommodation, to travel but chiefly to hospitalisation and medical care need to be settled.

Infectious diseases propagated as pandemics, especially the COVID-19 disease bind the cooperation of industrial performers even closer,[47] especially of airlines, airports and ground service providers. The new regulations are at least as strict as the numerous aviation security requirements introduced after 11 September 2001, which have transformed former travel habits. Although the system of the rules of aviation safety and security has been developing and taking shape for a long time, now a familiar, but unregulated area needs to be regulated comprehensively, with regard to changing and diverging national rules. Besides national regulations, procedures determined and simultaneously required by international organisations have important roles. Retaining confidence will necessitate constant attentiveness, which will be combined with more administration and licensing procedures as well as with authority supervision, which will render the journey more closed. New travel requirements minimising human contact such as keeping distance in all the phases of the journey, systemic controlling, and if necessary, the separation of passengers, the application of modern technology (biometric face recognition systems, procedures based on the scanning of the retina), the introduction of uniform testing, all of these ultimately purport the decrease of the liability of the air carrier.

With respect to the facts that in the rapid and efficient spread of viruses, the air carriers have a responsible role, and that the passenger, many times foregrounding their interests, generally misjudges or disregards their physical condition, it is necessary, beyond the recommendations of international organisations, for the industrial performers in cooperation with each other to introduce a new, internationally acknowledged and uniform testing system, which assesses the physical condition of the passenger and the involved risks. This examination system preceding the journey would consist of two stages: the presentation of a preliminary medical certificate based on uniform requirements to be furnished by the passenger and upon arrival at the airport a rapid and efficient examination in a medical test facility. If, despite all rigorous international requirements, controls and internal regulations, owing to the imputable conduct of the air carrier or its agents, the infected sick person provably boards the airplane and infects other passengers, or jeopardises other passengers' safety and lives by their presence, this circumstance would substantiate the liability of the air carrier for damages.

Medical Certificate

With respect to the fact that the air carrier cannot check the physical condition of the passengers, therefore, it is necessary to elaborate, besides several already introduced

---

[47] The most important industrial performers of civil aviation are the air carriers, airports and air navigation service providers (ANSPs), furthermore, the States' civil aviation authorities (CAAs), aircraft manufacturers, maintenance, repair and overhaul companies (MROs), travel, telecommunication and consignment service providers, and last but not least, the passengers themselves. In the performance of the activity of air transport, insurance, aircraft financing and ground handling service providers also have important roles.

other measures, a strict system of requirements decreasing the risk of the embarkation of infected persons. From the outset, air carriers, mainly in their General Conditions of Carriage, have prohibited the travelling of infected sick persons. However, the systematic check and documentation of this requirement have not ensued, at present this as a matter of course supervenes. However, the idea is not novel in the least. We could think of passengers with special needs, who are obligated to request their doctors' advice concerning the extent to which their air travel is risky. Precisely because of the risks involved in the travelling of such persons, the air carrier reserves the right to demand any passenger to produce a medical certificate issued at least in English [in compliance with the prescriptions of the International Air Transport Association (IATA) and the World Health Organisation (WHO)] concerning their transportability by air, and if necessary, accompaniment by a qualified doctor or nurse. The medical certificate shall unambiguously contain that on the specific day(s) of the journey(s), the air travel of the passenger is risk-free, and under what conditions it is risk-free, and that the passenger may or may not travel without an attendant. The air carrier may deny the confirmation of the booking and the carriage if

- the passenger or their representative fails to comply with any of the requirements determined by the air carrier; or
- the presented medical certificate is deficient; or
- on the certain type of the airplane operated on the specific route, the conditions specified in the medical certificate cannot be guaranteed; or
- the transfer of the passenger to another flight cannot be secured.

If the passenger has not requested medical advice or support or has requested but does not comply therewith during the journey, the air carrier shall not be liable for the resulting accident, bodily injury, impairment of health, or its deterioration, or, eventually, for the death of the passenger. The employees of airports and airlines are obligated to act preventively and intervene uniformly vis-a-vis the propagation of diseases in compliance with international and national health prescriptions. If the employees proceed according to the rules, they cannot be held legally liable for events or damage deriving from the physical condition of the passenger, even if at the airport the screening of an actually infected person was not efficacious (a certain medicine temporarily reduces the high temperature of the sick person infected with virus) and this person boards the airplane. The employees of the airport do not have the qualification or the practice to establish with certainty whether the passenger suffers from an infectious disease or does not. Nor does the air carrier itself have precise information related to the physical condition of the passenger (with the exception of the passenger with special needs) and the staff cannot be expected to 'examine' the passengers professionally or to proceed depending on the 'medical findings' (constat) before the journey.[48] This is not realistic. It is exclusively the

[48] Few people know that in the beginnings of aviation it was a basic requirement for flight-attendants to have qualifications as nurses. Anderson and Eberhardt (2010), p. 33.

passenger who knows what their physical condition facilitates and to what extent they can undertake the risks involved in the journey and the entailed responsibility.

Since exclusively the passenger is aware of their physical condition, the responsibility devolves exclusively on them and their doctors. The air carrier could only be liable for the damage deriving from the health problems of passengers if it could obligate each passenger to submit a medical aptitude document (conforming to international standards) 48 h before the journey. On the basis of medical certificates, the air carrier could decide unilaterally on whom and under what conditions it allows to board the plane. Obviously, this idea in practice seemed unfeasible for a long time regarding all passengers, however, these days there seems to be no wizardry in it. Air carriers need to respond to the growing number of cases and drive them back, primarily, when passengers in poor physical condition venture air travel irresponsibly or they undertake travelling with a disease, thereby, they jeopardise others' safety and lives. It is in the best interest of each air carrier that accidents do not happen, and if they do, they should not qualify as accident pursuant to the Convention.[49]

10.1.2 Death and Bodily Injury of the Passenger

The second essential condition of the application of the Convention is that the accident must cause the death or bodily injury of the passenger.

Between the accident and the death or bodily injury of the passenger, a cause and effect relationship needs to exist. While death is unambiguous, meaning the end of human life, bodily injury offers a much broader scope for interpretation. The meaning of bodily injury, its precise circumscription is of outstanding importance during the work of the appliers of the law since the relationship between *bodily injury* and *psychic injury* is a significant aspect. Therefore, the question arises: to what extent does bodily injury involve psychic injury? At the Diplomatic Conference, upon drafting the Convention, the representatives of the States had the opportunity to unfold the conceptual scope of bodily injury by drawing on the case-law of the Warsaw regime. However, the parties did not grasp the opportunity, thus, the Convention does not define the conceptual scope of bodily injury. In void of a definition, the precise interpretation devolves on national legal systems. This, just as other cases of the absence of definitions, involves the danger that the diverse national approaches may easily jeopardise the legislative expectation of the identical judgement of legal cases.

Bodily injury consists in the tangible, perceptible injury causing change in the human body, with harsh simplification: when the bone fractures, the muscles are strained, a cut or bruise occurs, etc., that is, the human body is injured. This unambiguously proves injury, a bodily injury caused by an accident.[50] However,

[49] Sipos (2021), pp. 105–106.

[50] *Uthuppan Jacob v. Korean Air Lines Co. Ltd.*, Case No. 14–11663, 11th Cir., 20 March 2015.

the ambiguity of the concept is often exploited by the plaintiffs filing action in order to improve their position, so that psychic injuries developing during the flight shall be adjudged as physical, bodily injuries by the court. At the same time, in its text the Convention does not make an express distinction, it grants opportunity unambiguously, solely and exclusively for the assertion of rights by reason of bodily injuries. Psychic problems, anxiety, mental injuries, and even behavioural disorders or traumas, if they do not directly entail bodily injury (even if the journey takes place on an airplane attacked and hijacked by terrorists), shall not qualify as accident.

Fear of flying (panic, stress, or claustrophobia) and mental shock in themselves do not fall under the concept of bodily injury. Thus, for instance, the passenger whose handbag with her medicines had been stolen in the transit lounge at the airport, and was faced with this fact on board the airplane, got obviously into an agitated state of mind. As a matter of course, she asked the flight crew to return, because taking her special medicines brooked no delay. The medicines (Alprazolam) remedy panic attacks and are designed to reduce anxiety and fear of flying. The request of the passenger was rejected several times, the pilot-in-command decided to continue the journey, thereby, the passenger was psychically even more pressurised. The passenger then, losing control, called the police in despair. Eventually, the plane taxied back to its stand, and the passenger was arrested by the police, only for a short time. After the prompt 'arrival', the case was filed with court. It was established that the passenger had not suffered bodily injury, physical damage, or internal organic lesion. According to the allegation of the passenger, breathing difficulties and sleep disorders evolved in relation to the case, furthermore, her ability to concentrate also decreased. However, these psychosomatic symptoms do not constitute an accident under the Convention, therefore, the court dismissed the action of the plaintiff.[51]

A situation may also occur when not only one passenger or a group of passengers but all the passengers are overcome by panic attack. This case does not constitute an accident either.

[51] *Turturo v. Continental Airlines,* 128 F. Supp. 2d 170 (S.D.N.Y.), 2001.

Panic on Board Aircraft

A passenger carrier aircraft was making its way through a weather front between two thunder clouds. In this situation, extremely strong turbulence hits the aircraft,[52] which may be conceived as if we speeded by car on an unpaved road in bad condition, full of potholes at 100 km/h into infinity. The passengers were filled with terror because of the unusual weather circumstances, mainly by the frequently striking lightening. Therefore, the pilot-in-command informed the passengers via the on-board loudspeakers that such extreme weather (despite the inconvenience) would not threaten the flight, but his announcement, instead of diminishing the terror, rather heightened it. Although the crew members were in control of the situation, some passengers started writing 'farewell letters', since they were convinced that they were in huge trouble.

The pilot-in-command was informed about the evolved situation by the cabin crew, who, in order to reassure the passengers, requested the chief flight attendant to call out to the flight attendant in the rear of the plane so that the passengers could hear: 'In 8 min the Captain requests his supper!'

While the flight attendants were reassuring the alerted passengers, the chief flight attendant called back loudly to the flight attendant: 'In 8 min heat up the Captain's supper; the last one!' Upon hearing the words 'last' and 'supper', panic overwhelmed the passengers.[53]

Nor do mental and psychic damage occasioned on board the aircraft (or during the operations of embarkation or disembarkation) qualify as accidents if they proceed from

- technical failure (forced landing, unusual flight manoeuvres);
- the unstable psychic condition of the passenger;
- threat or harassment of a passenger by a fellow passenger;
- assault or threat by a third person; or
- extreme weather conditions (for instance, strong turbulence, storm, or lightning strike).

[52]For all intents and purposes, the airplane cannot be flipped upside-down, thrown into a tailspin, or otherwise flung from the sky by even the mightiest gust or air pocket. Conditions might be annoying and uncomfortable, but the plane is not going to crash. Turbulence is an aggravating nuisance for everybody, including the crew, but it's also, for lack of a better term, normal. From a pilot's perspective it is ordinarily seen as a convenience issue, not a safety issue. Smith (2018), p. 35.

[53]Kiss, Kálmán: Memoirs. Manuscript. November 2015.

In the lawsuit *Eastern Airlines versus Floyd Marie*,[54] the plaintiffs litigated because on route from Miami (MIA) to the Bahamas one of the three engines of the aircraft, because of the problem of oil pressure, stopped working. The airplane turned back to return to Miami, but in the meantime the other two engines also broke down. As a consequence, the airplane lost altitude really rapidly since the tractive force, which moves the mass of the aircraft in the direction of the flight, ceased to exist. The pilot-in-command of the plane notified the passengers that they were going to land on the ocean, but during the emergency fall, the three engines could be restarted in a manner bordering on the miraculous and the airplane could land safely. After arrival in Miami, the pilots were celebrated as heroes. In spite of that, a group of the passengers filed an action against the airline. However, the court dismissed their plea because the psychic trauma or injury in itself, not causing bodily injury, does not fall under the conceptual scope of accident circumscribed under Article 17 of the Convention.

Travelling in itself is a factor entailing heightened stress. The lightest manifestations of psychic troubles related to travelling include phobias and abruptly strengthening panic reactions. While travelling, all apprehensive illnesses may easily aggravate. Unstable mental condition or starting psychosis may entail the commission of violent acts on board. Unrestrainable aggressiveness evolving on the airplane or at the airport has various origins. The most frequent causes are alcohol, drugs, or unstable mental state, but sometimes even completely normal, properly socialised adults take leave of their senses and can become furious and aggressive.[55]

On Malév Flight 210 on route from Budapest (BUD) to Tel Aviv (TLV), one of the passengers behaved strangely upon embarkation; he was unwilling to take his seat, tore his headphones apart, pulled down his trousers, and kept showing his bottom. He came to high words with the passengers and threatened to kill them several times. After about half of the journey, he went to the forefront and in an unguarded moment rushed into the pilot's deck, and after being conveyed out, he set upon the 3 L door in order to open it. He behaved aggressively with the intervening male flight attendant, spat on him, and hit him with the Coke can in his hand, thereby, causing bodily injury. Then with the can of Coke in his hand, he engaged in a fight with the fellow passengers. He rushed several times from the front of the plane to its back, flinging his

(continued)

[54] *Eastern Airlines v. Floyd Marie,* Supreme Court Reporter, 499 U.S. 530, 113 L.Ed. 2d 569, No. 89–1598, April 17, 1991.

[55] Felkai and Kurimay (2017).

body among the passengers. The hard core of a 22-member American group headed by a county sheriff travelling on the plane attempted to tame the unruly passenger, but he stretched them in moments. At that time, fighting commenced in the crowd, which ended in the temporary holding down of the riotous passenger and restraining him in his personal freedom. The airplane landed safely. During disembarkation on the stairs, the perpetrator kept kicking, then pounded a passenger leaving the plane. The passenger was then rowdy on the concrete grounds and 'thrashed' whoever he could.[56]

The damage deriving from injuries caused by fighting among the passengers is usually not indemnified by the airline, because it is not occasioned in relation to the activity of flying. The establishment of bodily injury, may it derive from weather conditions, technical failure, careless or deliberate behaviour of the passengers or from terrorist attack, does not pose a special problem, since the bodily injury has to have an objectively distinct, physical manifestation. The damage deriving from bodily injury has to be indemnified by the airline if it emerges in relation to flying. For example, in the 'fight' of passenger versus passenger, the liability of the air carrier may be established on condition that a member of the crew, maybe only indirectly, but contributed to the emergence of damage (the fight), that is, they did not discharge their tasks in compliance with the prescriptions, thereby jeopardising safety.

The passenger during the entire carriage is obligated to manifest behaviour in compliance with the instructions of the flight crew. If the passenger on board the aircraft behaves in such a manner that they

- jeopardise the aircraft, the safety of persons and property thereon or of the flight according to the grounded judgement of the crew;
- harass the crew verbally or physically or prevent them from discharging their tasks;
- do not observe the instructions of the crew;
- cause inconvenience or trouble, damage or injury to the persons on board or effect damage to the property on board;

the air carrier is authorised to take measures deemed to be necessary.

With respect to the fact that an armed in-flight security officer (IFSO), a so-called air-marshal, who attends to the safety of the passengers and the crew members and would interfere with routine in such a situation, does not travel on each international flight, therefore, the flight crew is obligated to take steps. Within the purview of the Tokyo Convention,[57] the aircraft commander may, when he has reasonable grounds

[56] Lautner (1998).

[57] Convention on Offences and Certain Other Acts Committed on Board Aircraft, signed at Tokyo, on 14 September 1963 (Tokyo Convention). Article 6 of Chap. III on the Aircraft Commander's Competence.

to believe that a person has committed or is about to commit, on board the aircraft, an offence or other unlawful acts, impose upon such person reasonable measures, including restraint. The aircraft commander may *require* or authorise the assistance of other crew members and may *request* or authorise, but not require, the physical assistance of passengers to restrain any person whom he is entitled to restrain. Any crew member or passenger may also take reasonable preventive measures without such authorisation. When the aircraft commander has reasonable grounds to believe that the conduct of a passenger jeopardises aviation safety and security or the safety of other passengers and the flight crew, the aircraft commander may deny the carriage of the said passenger. The passenger is obligated to reimburse the damage and expenses engendered by their conduct and the coercive measures to the air carrier.

In the case of *Sedigh versus Delta Air Lines, Inc.*,[58] the passenger on board the aircraft (after the neutralisation of the smoke detector) smoked several times in the toilet, insulted the cabin crew verbally, and agitated the passengers. He triggered such tension that the aircraft commander deemed the presence of the passenger on board to be risky, but he did not disrupt the flight on route from Istanbul (IST) to Frankfurt (FRA), then to New York (JFK), since nine armed federal air marshals were also on board the airplane. After consultation with their head, they applied the procedure regular at such times, and the American passenger (heading for New York), restrained in his freedom, was transferred to the German authorities. As usual in the case of the denial of carriage, the checked baggage of the passenger was also removed from the baggage storage space of the airplane. The passenger demanded an indemnification of more than 4 million USD, but his action was dismissed by the court.

The breach of the rights and obligations determined in the contract of carriage entails legal consequences. For reasons of aviation safety, the air carrier may prohibit or restrict the use of various electronic devices (e.g., mobile phones, laptops, portable recorders and radios, CD players, electronic toys, re-recording equipment, radio-controlled toys). (The use of hearing aids and pacemakers is permitted on aircraft.)

Safety Measures on Board Aircraft
Before the departure of the aircraft, the head of the flight attendants announced that electronic devices should be switched off. Despite a further request by the flight attendant, a passenger refused to switch off his portable personal

(continued)

[58] *Sedigh v. Delta Air Lines, Inc.,* 850 F.Supp.197 (E.D.N.Y.), 1994.

computer, therefore, the flight attendant reported the emerged situation to the pilot-in-command. The cabin crew summoned the passenger several times, but he did not comply and insisted on speaking to the cockpit crew. Then the airplane was preparing to take off. The pilot-in-command informed the passengers via the on-board loudspeakers that one of their fellow passengers does not follow the instructions of the flight attendant, therefore, the last call would be heard. 'Hereby I request the honoured passenger to relinquish the activity jeopardising safety within a minute, otherwise, I must refuse to carry him.'

The passenger started to rant and defied, thus, the security service took the shouting man down from the board. Then the Captain informed the passengers as follows: 'Dear Passengers! In the interest of your safety, I presume that if in such a calm and peaceful situation somebody does not follow the instructions of the flight attendant, in a contingent emergency, when your life may depend on compliance or non-compliance with the instructions of the flight attendant, they will refuse to obey as well. Therefore, in the interest of aviation safety and your safety I had the passenger removed from the airplane. Currently, the removal of the passenger's checked baggage is in process and afterwards, only afterwards may the departure commence.' (The passengers applauded.)[59]

The example shows perfectly what a situation the rule-breaking conduct of an 'innocent' passenger may evoke already in the initial phase of the journey. Therefore, it is much safer to take measures to exclude the problematic passenger from the flight already on the surface. Let us imagine theoretically an extreme situation: a heavily inebriated passenger is not excluded from the flight, then after take-off, he starts smoking in the toilet, owing to which the fire alarm goes off. The cockpit crew assesses the momentary situation well and does not implement an emergency drop, thus, it does not cause further complications in the airspace (the activation of the fire alarm would require an emergency drop and immediate fire extinguishment). The passenger denies his act and gets entangled in a conflict with the flight crew. The passenger panics and starts shouting, then hurls away the pacifying person, who gets injured. A fellow passenger hurries to help out the hurled person and a fight flares up, while intensifying the situation, somebody has a stroke as an effect of the events, etc. All this ensues because the ground staff or the flight crew did not make the right decision. The situation is not simple since the passenger does not share their personal motivation, sensitive data concerning their person (e.g., physical condition, addictions) or give unambiguous indications of how they will react to unforeseeable events and situations.

The treaty-maker lays emphasis exclusively on bodily injuries and wounds. However, judicial practice in the cases of bodily injury, in void of a definition, is divided since, if the injuries are related, they cannot make a sharp distinction

[59] Kiss (2009).

between psychic and bodily injury. National legal systems have been shaping the legal boundary between bodily injury and psychic injury up to these days, which the courts interpret depending on the developed character of the national legal order. Although in legal practice the Convention is generally applicable only in the cases of bodily injury, in legal development it is increasingly discernible that the judge deals with psychic injuries deriving from extreme cases such as sexual harassment on board, terrorist acts[60] or extreme weather conditions as accidents.

Harassment on Board Aircraft

In the case of *Morris versus KLM Royal Dutch Airlines*,[61] a young 15-year-old female passenger on board a plane travelling from Kuala Lumpur (KUL) to Amsterdam (AMS) was awakened suddenly to being molested by an unfamiliar man sitting next to her. The female passenger immediately informed the cabin crew about the incident, who took the necessary measures. The passenger suffered grave trauma, necessitating that she immediately saw a doctor. After examination, the doctor established that clinical depression had developed in the patient. In the court of first instance, the action of the plaintiff was dismissed since, according to the court, this event does not fall under the conceptual scope of accident under the Convention.

However, the Supreme Court obligated the airline to pay full indemnification and noted: although, bodily injury pursuant to the Convention did not happen, the crime triggered a process in the plaintiff, which led to persistent psychic trauma entailing the deterioration of abilities in the activities of daily life. It was established that in the conceptual scope of accident, the clause according to which the event needs to be a 'risk characteristic of air travel', does not always have to be considered.

In these extreme cases a post-traumatic stress disorder (PTSD) evolves easily, and this psychic illness may certainly entail bodily consequences, which fall under the conceptual scope of accident.

Terror on Board Aircraft

Trans World Airlines (TWA) Flight 741 operated by a 707–331B Boeing airplane on route between Tel-Aviv (TLV) and New York (JFK), with agreed stopping places in Athens and Frankfurt, was hijacked after take-off in Frankfurt by the terrorists of the People's Front for the Liberation of Palestine

(continued)

[60] *Husserl v. Swiss Air Transport Co.,* 388 F. Supp.1238 (S.D.N.Y.), 1975.; *Borham v. Pan American World Airways,* U.S. Dist. Lexis 28554 (S.D.N.Y.), 1986.

[61] *Morris v. KLM Royal Dutch Airlines,* UKHL 7, 2002.; Judgement of the British Supreme Court of Judicature, case no. B3/2000/3820, 17 May 2001.

(PFLP) on 6 September 1970.[62] The terrorists forced the pilots to land on the former military airport of the British Royal Air Force (RAF) in the area of Dawson's Field (its current name is Zarqa) in the desert of Jordan. The terrorists held the passengers, among them the 17-year-old Miriam Herman, in custody on the airplane, stranded in the desert for 6 days, but they did not hurt the hostages.

In the lawsuit *Herman versus Trans World Airlines*,[63] the claimant turned to the court with a claim for compensation for damage by reason of insomnia, depression, loss of weight, nightmares, extreme anxiety arising as a consequence of the terrorist act. Of the passengers on the airplane, Mrs. Edith Rosman also filed a claim by reason of suffering several traumas, although she and her children were not hurt physically. During the terrorist act, the detained passengers were exposed to considerable stress because of confinement, the strong fluctuation of temperature, improper nutrition and hygienic circumstances. In the lawsuit *Rosman versus Trans World Airlines,*[64] just like in the *Herman* case, the Supreme Court established that mental torment and distress in themselves do not substantiate compensation pursuant to the Convention. For this, objective bodily injury assessable in itself needs to be proved, but if the psychic injury triggers bodily injury directly, as in these cases it really occurred, the air carrier shall be held liable.[65]

Generally, terrorist attacks (hijacks, taking hostages) cause injuries and death; however, even in these grave cases, the liability of the air carrier is not always established. Namely, its liability is only sustained if the accident suffered by the passenger is external to the passenger; it is an unexpected, unusual or unforeseeable event, which emerged as a risk characteristic of air travel and ensued in relation to the airline's operation of the aircraft.[66]

---

[62] In that month, "the Black September" four further airplanes were hijacked by terrorists, altogether 600 passengers and crew members were held in custody, but nobody died of them. Later, the hijacked airplanes of the British Overseas Airways Corporation (BA), the Trans World Airlines (TW) and the Swissair (SR) Airlines were exploded by the terrorists, which were broadcast live as "shows" by the invited (admitted) TV channels.

[63] Newman and Burrows (2013), pp. 60–61.; *Herman v. Trans World Airlines, Inc.,* Court case 40. App. D. 2d 850. 337 N.Y.S. 2d 827, 830 (NY AD 2 Dept.), 1972.

[64] *Rosman v. Trans World Airlines, Inc.,* US Court of Appeals Second Circuit 314 N.E. 2d 848, 1977.

[65] Barnett (1975), pp. 191–204.

[66] Lowenfeld (1992), pp. 83–84.

Turbulence on Board Aircraft

In the case *Spielberg versus American Airlines*,[67] the plaintiffs (13 passengers) were litigating because on route from Los Angeles (LAX) to New York (JFK) they experienced fear of death for a time of 28 s by reason of extremely strong turbulence arising unexpectedly. The plaintiff, Nancy Spielberg was litigating by reason of nightmare experienced with her children and irreversible psychic injury. The lawyers were well aware: the airline was not liable pursuant to the Montreal Convention because of the domestic journey, nor because of the mental suffering owing to atmospheric turbulence tossing the airplane, therefore, they emphasised mainly that the extreme situation could develop by reason of the negligence of the pilots. Before flying through the storm zone, the cockpit crew (pilots) had not activated the weather-sensitive radar appropriately, which could have been conducive to the evasion of the actually invisible turbulence, but other acts breaking rules were also elucidated, which exacerbated the situation of the airline. For instance, in spite of the fact that the pilots had been warned of the storm, the signal reminding of the necessity to fasten the seat belts had not been switched on. Therefore, due to the rapid vertical loss of altitude, several passengers quasi in the condition of 'weightlessness' so to say started 'flying in the passenger compartment'.

Although bodily injury did not occur and the life of the passengers returned to the old routine, this out-of-the-ordinary case left a timeless mark on the lives of the plaintiffs. Owing to the psychic effect, for example, in the elder child of passenger Spielberg hyperventilation developed, although this was not proved. Finally, the court obligated the defendant airline to pay indemnification of 2.2 million USD, which was allocated among the 13 plaintiffs (the three minor plaintiffs received proportionately higher indemnification).

By these days, it has evolved in practice that for injuries deriving from large turbulence the airline is liable, particularly when the passengers suffer so-called swish injury deriving from the sudden strain of tendons linking the cervical vertebras due to the lashing of the head here and there. In the case of medium or minor ordinary turbulence, the air carrier is not liable. At the same time, as the above legal case demonstrated, if bodily injury or organic lesion develops from mental suffering or mental injury, and a cause-effect relationship exists, the air carrier shall be liable for damages. This new trend[68] has provoked many legal disputes, which is capped by the fact that damages deriving from psychic injuries are very difficult to calculate

[67] *Spielberg v. American Airlines Inc.*, United States District Court, S.D. New York, 105 F. Supp. 2d 280, 2000.

[68] It is worth mentioning that the contracting States of the Guatemala City Additional Protocol (1970) endeavoured to settle this issue and replaced the term of bodily injury for personal injury, thereby, they extended the conceptual scope of injury, but they did not achieve their goal since the Protocol did not take effect.

financially. But this eloquently illustrates a new social expectation: in the cases of mental injuries, psychic traumas emerging under extreme circumstances, the applier of the law should not be passive, should not interpret the statute literally and should not follow the standard legal practice at any rate. Undoubtedly, the observance of the letter of the law, and thereby, the breach of its spirit results in the injury of the law.[69]

10.1.3 Location of the Accident (Embarkation or Disembarkation)

The third essential condition is that the accident has to take place *on board* the aircraft or during the operations of *embarkation* or *disembarkation*.

The contracting States do not apply exact definitions, so it is not irregular that the operations of embarkation or disembarkation are not concretely defined either, therefore, it is legal practice that shall be guiding in this respect as well. The board of the aircraft does not necessitate special explanation, but the operations of embarkation and disembarkation do. The demarcation of the operations is legally significant, since during the processes of embarkation and disembarkation the passenger is subject to the Convention, that is, the circumscription of the operations determines when the liability of the air carrier commences and terminates. The passenger before the commencement and after the termination of the operations spend their time at the airport, therefore, the legal problems arising in this period are governed by national law in the absence of a uniform system of rules pertaining to liability for damage caused at international airports. For instance, the passenger may tumble over in the parking lot of the airport, may get injured at the lifts or may be assaulted in the area of the terminal building not during the operations of embarkation or disembarkation. In legal practice, different interpretations exist concerning the commencement and termination of the operations.

It is generally accepted that the *operation of embarkation* commences when the passenger becomes subject to the supervision of the servant (or agent) of the airline and follows their instructions. (For instance, when the passenger ultimately sets out to the boarding gate with the actual intent of embarking the flight, or finishes waiting before the boarding gate and answers the call of the servant of the airline by setting forth to the gate and joining the queue.). The *operation of disembarkation* finishes when the passenger reaches the terminal building, and leaves behind the surveillance of the airline, that is, the farther the passengers advance from the aircraft, the less chance they have to render the airline liable for the occurrence of an accident pursuant to the Convention.

---

[69] *88th legal principle of Part Regula Iuris of the Liber Sextus Code*, 1298. In: Pallas Nagylexikon (Pallas Encyclopaedia), Pope VIII. Boniface (1235–1303), entry. Pallas Irodalmi és Nyomdai Rt., Budapest, 1893–1897.

The Operation of Embarkation

The passenger is obligated to appear at the airport, or at an external location of passenger reception designated by the air carrier 1.5 hours before the scheduled departure time at the latest for the purpose of submission to the necessary official, air ticket and baggage check, security and customs procedures. With respect to the fact that the time of the termination of passenger reception and embarkation is varied at different airports, the air carrier may change the time of appearance, thus, the passenger needs to appear at the time determined and announced thereby. The passenger is obligated to hold a boarding card, and so far as the passenger travels with checked baggage, a baggage identification tag before the time determined by the air carrier, or, if the air carrier does not determine such time, 30 min before the scheduled departure time at the latest. The passenger is obligated to appear at the boarding gate before the time indicated on the boarding card, 20 min before the scheduled departure time at the latest.

The air carrier is not liable for the damage and expenses deriving from non-observance of the rules pertaining to the time of appearance or from non-compliance with the authority prescriptions necessary for boarding, furthermore, from non-appearance at the aircraft or the boarding gate at the time indicated on the boarding card.

According to the decision of the British Supreme Court, the operation of embarkation commences with checking in for the flight.[70] After the passenger has received their boarding card at the check-in desk of the airport, they undergo passport and security controls; after that, they proceed immediately to the departure gate of the airplane and maybe they stop for a short time at the toilet—these activities are continually related to embarkation. However, if the passenger starts dining and having coffee in the airport restaurant, if they do shopping in the duty-free shops, or use the airline departure lounge for at least an hour while waiting for the flight, then the process of embarkation is disrupted.[71] The airline is not liable for events of damage caused during this period. Obviously, the process of embarkation takes place in a distinguishable period related to the precise departure time of the aircraft, because if the passenger gets injured in front of the departure gate an hour before departure time, the accident cannot be evaluated as part of the operation of embarkation. When the passenger from the places mentioned above eventually heads for the boarding gate with the actual intent of embarking the flight, or, when finishing waiting before the departure gate, the passenger answers the call of the airline servant and joins the queue, we can again speak about the operation of embarkation.

[70] *Susan Philips v. Air New Zealand Limited,* EWHC 800, DMC/Sand T/09/2002.

[71] *Ramos v. American Airlines, Inc.,* WL 5075674, (W.D.N.C.), October 2011.

In the case of *Walsh versus Koninklijke Luchtvaart Maatschappij* (KLM),[72] the plaintiff, while heading for the boarding gate during embarkation, tripped over a protruding metal bar (of the same colour as the floor), and as a consequence, he broke his elbow. The court established that pursuant to the Convention an accident happened, and owing to the accident bodily injury occurred, which ensued during the operation of embarkation. Although the passenger had not handed over his boarding card to the staff waiting at the gate, he took firm steps towards the gate, where other passengers were waiting. On such basis the court established the liability of the air carrier and obligated KLM Airline to pay a high amount of indemnity.

According to the court proceeding in the case *Okeke versus Northwest Airlines, Inc.*,[73] staying in an area designated for waiting by the passengers in order to check in at the gate qualifies as embarkation. So does the case when the majority of passengers are already queuing up, while some passengers still remain sitting because they are tired to queue up.

As examples of diverging legal practice, the courts generally adjudge differently the commencement and the termination of the operations of embarkation and disembarkation. In the diverging interpretation of the operations, the court of the United States laid down a new direction for legal cases evaluated as precedents. The court examined the process of the operations of embarkation and disembarkation via a test consisting of three interrelated parts.

Criteria of Embarkation

In the lawsuit *Day versus Trans World Airlines, Inc.* (TWA),[74] the passengers of the airline were waiting for boarding Flight 881 travelling from Athens (ATH) to New York (JFK) at the Hellenikon Airport in Athens. The passengers waiting in transit, having undergone passport and baggage controls, were lining up with their boarding cards at the boarding gate, where they were about to undergo further personal and hand luggage control. However, at that time, two terrorists threw three bombshells at the passengers and opened fire. Three persons died and more than 40 persons got injured. The plaintiff, Aristedes A. Day, was among the injured.

Essentially, the court focused on the point whether the passengers, in the moment of the attack, standing at the point of the control of hand luggage,who

(continued)

[72] *Walsh v. Koninklijke Luchtvaart Maatschappij (KLM),* 09-civ-01803 (RKE) N.V. (S.D.N. Y.), 2011.

[73] *Okeke v. Northwest Airlines, Inc.,* No. 1:07CV538, *WL 780167 (M.D.N.C.), 26 February 2010.*

[74] *Day v. Trans World Airlines, Inc.,* US Court of Appeals, Second Circuit.528 F. 2d 31, 1975.

after this were making their way to the bus to take them to the airplane, were carrying out the operation of embarkation. For the precise establishment of this, the court set up a three-step system of supplementary criteria:

1. *Act:* What was the passenger doing in the moment of the accident?

   The plaintiff, with the intent of embarkation, was actively trying to get through the hand luggage and personal controls.

2. *Direction:* Under whose direction and supervision was the passenger?

   The plaintiff was waiting in the queue in the presence of the entrusted representative of the airline.

3. *Definition of the location:* Where was the passenger in the moment of the accident?

   The plaintiff was standing before Boarding Gate 4 (from where a bus would have taken him to the flight).

   The court defined the complete process of embarkation in 11 steps, without which the passenger could not have boarded the airplane waiting further away from the terminal building on the concrete grounds. For boarding, in this process, the following moments are necessary: the production of the air ticket, the reception of baggage identification tags and the boarding card, reception of the seat number, passing passport and security controls, checking the boarding card, getting on the bus, travelling on the bus, getting off the bus, and finally, approaching the airplane. The court established that the embarkation was continuous, and the passenger had fulfilled the first five conditions indispensable for boarding. The passenger in the examined period was already under the supervision of the airline, not of the airport, and the fulfilment of these conditions is sufficient for the establishment of the facts of the case of an accident during embarkation and of the liability of the airline.

The application of the three-step test elucidates whether the plaintiff, in the moment of the occurrence of the accident, was performing an operation of embarkation or disembarkation. In the case of *Hunter versus Lufthansa*,[75] the court took further aspects into account: was the passenger restricted in their movement, had embarkation commenced, and how close was the passenger to the boarding gate physically? The point remains the same: for how long and to what extent was the passenger subject to the supervision and direction of the air carrier upon the occurrence of the accident?

[75] *Hunter v. Deutsche Lufthansa AG,* 863, F. Supp. 2d 190 (E.D.N.Y.), 2012.

The Operation of Disembarkation

The judgement of the operation of disembarkation is somewhat easier than of the complex process of embarkation because it takes much shorter time and generates less disputes, although in legal practice it sometimes arouses surprise. Legally, the precise definition of disembarkation, just like of embarkation, has crucial significance because this determines whether the facts of the case falls under the conceptual scope of accident. Namely, futile are all the endeavours of the claimant for the establishment of the liability of the air carrier for damages if the court rules that the passenger had abandoned the operation of disembarkation a long while before the event, therefore, the case does not qualify as accident pursuant to the Convention.

Why is it all the same important that the case of the claimant should be adjudged pursuant to the Convention? The objective of the plaintiff is to receive the highest possible amount of indemnification, even though the pain and loss they suffered can never be fully remedied by any amount of compensation. The claimant is most likely to receive the highest expectable amount from the airline. The claimant may sue the airport or other third party pursuant to national law, but even in the case of the effective enforcement of their claim, the compensation will not reach such a high amount as in the case of the liability of the air carrier.

For instance, upon attacks committed by terrorists, it is especially difficult to receive a high amount of indemnification from airports (many times enjoying protection and exemption deriving from State ownership) pursuant to national law, not to mention the terrorists causing damage, who have unlimited liability in every respect, but a claim for damages vis-à-vis them is impossible to enforce. By reason of the above, the solicitors of the passengers generally put their faith in the establishment of the liability of the air carrier.

The termination of disembarkation is construed by many from stepping out of the airplane and leaving the board of the aircraft, but according to judicial verdicts that is not the case. In fact, the operation of disembarkation terminates when the passenger reaches the building of the airport and leaves behind the scope of supervision by the airline.

- In case the passenger bridge (jetway) is mounted and the passenger leaves the airplane and proceeds through the corridor of the passenger bridge or maybe uses its lift,[76] the operation of disembarkation is in progress. The passenger moves along a closed area, where merely the servants of the airline, the ground servicing staff, the security experts and passengers are allowed to pass. When the passenger reaches the terminal building and makes their way to passport and customs controls, then in the direction of the connecting flight or of baggage reclaim,[77] the operation of disembarkation has been terminated.
- If the aircraft is parking in an external stand and the passenger stumbles while descending the stairs, or if the passenger after leaving the passenger stairs is

[76] *Ugaz v. American Airlines, Inc.*, 576 F. Supp. 2d 1354 (S.D. Fla.), 2008.

[77] *Fedelich v. American Airlines*, 724 F. Supp. 2d 274, 284 (D.P.R.), 2010.

injured while getting on or travelling on the bus waiting on the concrete grounds to deliver the passengers to the airport terminal, the event qualifies as an accident during the operation of disembarkation.[78] After the passenger has left the bus and arrives at the terminal building and the 'accident' occurs there, this cannot be construed as an accident pursuant to the Convention since it takes place after the termination of the operation of disembarkation.

In the lawsuit *Malcolm Paterson versus Air Link Pty Ltd.*,[79] the overweight plaintiff, suffering from knee problems, with two pieces of luggage in his hands, somewhat aggravating his movement during disembarkation, while going down the stairs of the *Piper Navajo Chieftain* airplane, tripped and fell down on the concrete grounds of the Australian Dubbo Airport (DBO) smashing his knees. Namely, the ground servicing staff had placed a light aluminium stair grade under the stairs of the airplane to facilitate more comfortable and safer disembarkation. When the plaintiff stepped from the last grade of the stairs of the airplane on this separate piece, the structure suddenly shifted, and the accident occurred. Other passengers did not have a problem with disembarkation on the additional light aluminium grade of stairs. There was no evidence that the additional stair was faulty, damaged, or unstable.

The court of appeals of the Australian New South Wales established in the lawsuit that the passenger was not responsible for the use of the portable extra stair. During the operation of disembarkation, the plaintiff did not manifest an act owing to which the stair could have moved away. The passenger could not be obligated to prove what and why caused the accident, that is, what the cause of the dislocation of the stair structure was. The claimant needed to prove only that the damage (injury) was caused by an accident, that is, an external, unexpected, and extraordinary event that led to the occurrence of the injury.[80] The court awarded the plaintiff an indemnity of 439,500 Australian Dollars (AUD).

The legal case originated in a domestic flight, therefore, the Convention was not applicable since this was not a case of 'international carriage'. In any case, upon the clarification of the circumstances of the accident, the court unambiguously drew on international legal practice, to wit, standard case-law.

Obviously, the ordinary observer considers the events entailing damage, which inflicts loss of life or bodily injury, to be accidents. However, in international aviation law an accident, even if it unambiguously and apparently has occurred, is not always qualified as an accident under the Convention, since for the establishment

[78] *Ricotta v. Iberia Lineas Aereas De Espana,* 482 F. Supp. 497 (E.D.N.Y.), 1979.

[79] *Paterson v. Air Link Pty Ltd.*, NSWDC 241, 1 November 2008.

[80] Tulloch and Shaw (2010), pp. 81–82.

of the liability of the air carrier for damages the fact of the injury in itself is insufficient. The examination of the complete process preceding the occurrence of the accident is necessary on the basis of the system of aspects of the Convention, since solely in this case can we answer the question on the basis of what rules the party causing damage will be obligated to indemnify the damage. Considering the process of the above-mentioned legal case, we can conclude that the further the passenger moves from the aircraft, the more likely it is that they forfeit the opportunity for making the airline liable for the occurrence of an accident pursuant to the Convention.

The precise circumscription of the operations of embarkation and disembarkation is the headstone of adjudication by the court, therefore, the circumstances are to be examined case by case, revealing the facts one by one. All cases differ from each other, and each detail, however minute it may seem, matters upon the establishment of the facts of the case. In judicial practice, the triadic test has become widespread, which in the course of time has developed further and included other aspects as well in the scope of scrutiny.[81] Namely, in the application of law the time factor and the position of the passenger in relation to the airplane have become increasingly important. The structured questions have been supplemented with a view to the precise positioning of the operation and the following questions have become subject to examination: upon the occurrence of the accident, how much time was left until the departure of the plane, until the concrete boarding, how far the departing or the arriving aircraft was from the location of the accident.

10.2 The Air Carrier's Liability for Damage Caused to the Baggage

The contracting States do not define the meaning of baggage. Thus, it is reasonable to presume that everything that the passenger carries with them falls under this term. In practice, the airlines circumscribe in their General Conditions of Carriage what they mean under this term (for instance, what they permit to be carried, in what quantity, size and weight on board or in the storage space). On such basis, the air carriers determine diverging limitations on the number of the pieces, the size and weight of the baggage.

The baggage needs to be packed so that the packaging protects the content of the baggage during the complete time of carriage by air. The air carrier may deny the reception of baggage not packaged according to prescriptions, exceeding the specified size or of damaged baggage for the purpose of air carriage. The air carrier carries the passenger and their baggage as far as possible on the same flight, but meanwhile, it may reserve the right to place the checked baggage of the passenger not on the flight carrying the passenger for reasons of safety or operation. In this

[81] *Buonocore v. Trans World Airlines, Inc.*, 900 F. 2d 8, 11 (2d Cir.), 1990.

case, the air carrier shall deliver the baggage of the passenger on the next flight on which this is feasible without impediment. In such a case, the air carrier shall notify the passenger of the expectable time of the arrival of the baggage at the latest upon their arrival at the place of landing.

10.2.1 Checked Baggage and Unchecked Baggage

The provisions of the Convention differentiate baggage checked upon check-in for the flight from unchecked hand baggage retained and carried by the passenger on board. The difference lies in the different methods of the carriage of the baggage (the hand-baggage is under the supervision or in charge of the passenger throughout the flight):

- In the case of *checked baggage,* 'the carrier is liable for damage sustained in the case of destruction or loss of, or of damage to *checked baggage* upon condition only that the event which caused the destruction, loss or damage took place on board the aircraft or during any period within which the checked baggage was in the charge of the carrier. However, the carrier is not liable if and to the extent that the damage resulted from the inherent defect, quality or vice of the baggage' [Article 17 (2)].
- 'In the case of *unchecked baggage*, including personal items, the carrier is liable if the damage resulted from its fault or that of its servants or agents' [Article 17 (2)]. In spite of the fact that the unchecked baggage is in possession of the passenger, it requires further care since in the world of public transport, the passenger may be robbed on board the aircraft as well.

It may also occur that the determination of the character of the baggage is prima facie not unambiguous. In the cases when the passenger presents their suitcase at the check-in desk and it is registered (it receives a baggage identification tag), but finally it is not put on the carousel carrying baggage since the passenger takes the checked baggage on board the aircraft, the baggage is qualified as unchecked baggage. It may also happen that in the moment preceding boarding, the ground service staff takes the hand baggage of the passenger (for reasons of aviation safety, for example, the limited capacity of baggage racks in the passenger compartment of a full airplane), therefore, the hand baggage is placed in the baggage storage space of the aircraft. In such a case, the hand baggage is removed from the supervision of the passenger and qualifies as checked baggage.

10.2.2 Delivery of the Checked Baggage

The passenger is obligated to collect their baggage upon the arrival of the flight without delay.

In the practice of the airlines, solely the passenger holding a baggage receipt corresponding to the baggage identification tag is entitled to reclaim the baggage, but the air carrier may transfer the baggage to a third person, so far as this third person proves their entitlement to receipt trustworthily. At the same time, the air carrier may reserve the right to compare the baggage receipt held by the passenger with the number of the baggage identification tag on the baggage of the passenger for the purpose of control upon the release of the baggage.

So far as the passenger receives their baggage without complaint or without filling in a baggage irregularity record, the air carrier presumes that it has delivered the baggage of the passenger intact according to the content of the contract concluded for the carriage of the baggage. If the checked baggage of the passenger is removed from the carousel in arrivals illegally by another passenger, the air carrier is not liable for the damage.

So far as the airline does not carry the passenger and their checked baggage on the same flight, it shall deliver the baggage to the address of the passenger free of charge, with the exception if the passenger is obligated to appear at customs control pursuant to applicable law. If the passenger is staying at a hotel, the baggage can be handed over to the staff of the hotel. With the exception of the cases of deliberateness and grave negligence, the air carrier does not assume responsibility for transferring the baggage not to the person entitled to receipt.

10.2.3 Limited Liability

In the carriage of baggage, the liability of the air carrier extends to the destruction, loss, damage, or delay of the baggage, which is limited to 1288 Special Drawing Rights for each passenger, irrespective of the nature of the damage and the method of compensation [Article 22 (2)]. 'Unless otherwise specified, the term *baggage* in itself means both checked and unchecked baggage' [Article 17 (4)]. It is a novelty in the Convention that the treaty-maker did not favour the weight-based system of liability, but introduced a procedure maximised in 1288 SDR determined for all baggage per person.

In the Warsaw System, the compensation was determined on the basis of the weight of the checked baggage, the basis of the compensation was the entire measured weight of the baggage. This meant that if the passenger's checked baggage weighing 15 kg was destroyed or lost during air carriage, the air carrier paid 250 francs per kilogramme, that is, about 20 USD as damages at the then rate of exchange. Calculating precisely, in the case of the loss of baggage this amounted to 15 × 250 francs, that is, about 300 USD. The original Warsaw Convention (1929) used French francs, but later the Montreal Additional Protocol No. 1 (1975) amended it and introduced the supplementary foreign exchange reserve asset SDR (Special Drawing Rights) [see, Part II, Chap. 8. 2.5]. This means, in the case of checked baggage, the compensation limit changed for 17 SDR per kilogramme at that time. If the passenger also had left the ignition key of their car and the key to their flat in the baggage (for which the air carrier compensated as a weight of 20 dkg), consequently, the claimant could not open their car parked at the airport, then later their home, for the deriving further damage the air carrier was not liable. The passenger was entangled in a similarly difficult situation, if they packed their light and valuable clothes (silk or a mink coat) and belongings of higher value into a high-quality suitcase purchased for a high price and did not make a special declaration of interest in delivery at destination, thus, their damage was never recovered according to the rules of the Warsaw system.

The amount of compensation determined on the basis of weight (in our case 300 USD) differs significantly from the current person-based upper limit, which initially amounted to 1000 SDR, while later, following the inflation, its amount changed to 1288 SDR (ca. 1715 USD) under the Montreal Convention. The airline does not indemnify the damage above the limited amount, and within the limited amount, it indemnifies the extent of the proved damage. This implies that under the amount of 1288 SDR, the claim for damages is fulfilled up to the amount of the proved damage (for instance, if the baggage is damaged and the damage equals 200 SDR, after the judgement of the rightfulness of the claim, 200 SDR will be refunded). Thus, the airline does not indemnify all damages at an amount of 1288 SDR, since this amount is an upper limit, which plentifully covers the total value of an average baggage and of the personal belongings therein. The airlines make these payments, but if the journey becomes inconvenient or entails suffering because of the loss or destruction of the baggage, which causes damage above the amount of 1288 SDR, for further sustained material damage or psychic injuries the airline with limited liability is not liable.

Beyond the higher amount of liability for damages, the Convention, upon the carriage of highly valuable objects in checked baggage, provides opportunity for the passenger to make a special declaration of interest in delivery at destination (declaration of excessive value). The object of higher value shall be insured for the fixed amount determined under the declaration. The condition of making the declaration of excessive value is that the passenger determines the real value under the declaration and makes the payment of the contingent extra charge. If the passenger calculates the values indicated in the declaration maliciously, and the airline proves this fact, the air carrier will not pay the amount above the real value [Article 22 (2)].

In the case of *Titona Arini versus Eurofly*,[82] the plaintiff travelled from Rome (FCO) to the Mexican town of Cancun (CUN) for her honeymoon. At the airport, while waiting for her baggage, the passenger was shocked to realise that it did not arrived since it had been lost. The plaintiff sued the airline for an indemnity of 8715 EUR, which contained the cost of the new clothes, the total

(continued)

[82]Tompkins (2009), p. 425.; *Titona Arini v. Eurofly,* Tribunal of Marsala, Judgement of 14 April 2007.

expense of the journey, the damage deriving from the breach of contract, and mainly, the decrease of the pleasure value of the honeymoon. According to the court, the claim of the plaintiff was excessive and disproportionate, thus, she could in fact claim merely the purchase price of the new suitcase and the new clothes (personal belongings). With respect to the fact that the liability of the airline per person in the case of damage to the baggage was limited to 1000 SDR (according to the then guiding rule), in the absence of a differing agreement with the airline (the plaintiff had not made a special declaration of interest in delivery at destination before the flight), her claim for damages could be fulfilled only within this amount. In its judgement, the court obligated the airline to indemnify the then maximum amount of 1000 SDR (ca. 1411 EUR).[83]

If the arrival of the baggage of the passenger is delayed, their complaint related to the damage deriving from the delay needs to be made in writing within 21 days following the receipt of the baggage. The deadline is preclusive. In the case of the omission of the deadline, the passenger may not make a claim vis-à-vis the air carrier. Pursuant to the provision of the Convention, the checked baggage needs to be regarded as lost

- 'if the carrier admits the loss of the checked baggage; or
- if the checked baggage has not arrived at the expiration of 21 days after the date on which it ought to have arrived'.

In such cases, 'the passenger is entitled to enforce against the carrier the rights which flow from the contract of carriage' immediately after the declaration of the acknowledgement of the fact of loss by the carrier or after the expiry of 21 days as of the due date of the arrival [Article 17 (3)].

The stipulation of 21 calendar days is lifelike, since after its expiry the lost baggage is unlikely to be recovered. If the checked baggage is recovered on the 20th day, we regard it as a delay, when the liability of the air carrier can likewise be established.

[83] The amount of 1000 SDR and all other amounts in Articles 21–23 of the Convention, for the purpose of the offset of the inflation, have been raised by the States Parties pursuant to the rule of Article 24 of the Montreal Convention. The upper limit in the case of baggage became 1131 SDR in 2009, then 1288 SDR in 2019. The limit reviewed at 5-year intervals did not change in 2014, then, in 2019 it was amended again and the raised amounts have been applied since 28 December 2019. *Revised Limits of Liability Under the Montreal Convention of 1999* (2019). (www.icao.int/secretariat/legal/Pages/2019_Revised_Limits_of_Liability_Under_the_MC).

In the case of *Nastych versus British Airways*,[84] the plaintiff travelled from New York (JFK) to Budapest (BUD) and then to London (LHR). On arriving in Budapest, the plaintiff did not find his checked baggage, therefore, he could not continue his journey. Finally, the baggage was found as delayed. On his return journey, the claimant once again transferred in Budapest and headed for New York, where after arrival, he was shocked to realise that his checked baggage was again missing. The baggage was not recovered later either. Nastych, the plaintiff demanded the air carrier to indemnify altogether 25,000 USD for the two consolidated cases. In its ruling, the court established the international character of the journey, the fact of causing damage deriving from the delay, then the loss of the checked baggage and obligated the defendant airline to be liable. The airline admitted its liability and indemnified the limited amount of 1000 SDR (1411 USD) in both cases.

Checked baggage undoubtedly involves risks. Experience demonstrates that a great deal of checked baggage disappears at the bustling airports of the world, and thefts from baggage occur in uncountable cases. Drawing on such experiences, air carriers prescribe that the checked baggage of the passenger should, for reasons of the protection of property, safety and security, not contain the following:

- Cash, securities, and bank or credit cards;
- Watches, jewellery, clothes and accessories of high value, precious metal, gems, or semi-precious stones;
- Notebooks, video cameras, cameras, mobile phones, other electronic devices, musical instruments, technical items, and their parts;
- Instruments, documents, and product samples;
- Travel documents and other documents of identification;
- Keys;
- Fluids, medicines, and medical aids;
- Personal property of artistic value and works of fine arts;
- Any other valuable objects.

In so far as the checked baggage contains the objects enumerated above, the air carrier cannot be made liable for the delayed delivery of, loss of, or damage to the baggage. Upon checking the baggage, the passenger declares that the baggage to be checked does not contain any of the enumerated objects. The passenger makes that declaration by the implicit conduct of transferring their baggage to the air carrier. Posteriorly, the passenger may not revoke this declaration. So far as the air carrier becomes aware that the passenger's baggage contains objects excluded from carriage or conditionally carriable objects, it may demand that the passenger removes these objects from the baggage. The air carrier does not preserve the objects removed

[84] *Nastych v. British Airways Plc.*, US District Court, S.D. New York. 09 Civ. 9082 (AJP). February 2010.

from the baggage. The search of the baggage may be extended to the person and personal belongings of the passenger. The air carrier, its staff and agents do not assume responsibility for damage caused by the search, X-ray or other scanning of the baggage, with the exception of the cases of deliberate or gravely negligent conduct.

The unchecked baggage of the passenger may not contain alcohol, medicine or cosmetics products beyond the amount determined by IATA, furthermore, matches, cigarette lighter or its fuel. The passenger may not carry on board stabbing or cutting tools or sharp objects, which, according to the opinion of the air carrier or the airport security service, may be used as weapons. Real weapons may only be carried on board, if the persons, carrying weapons during their service discharging official or special security duties, hand over their weapons to the pilot-in-command before the commencement of the journey. During the time of the flight, the pilot-in-command takes care of safeguarding the weapons, storing them separately so that they are inaccessible for passengers, and after arrival, they are handed over solely to the entitled persons.

The occurrence of an essentially more voluminous damage can be precluded by the passenger via making a declaration of excessive value or not packing valuable objects in the checked baggage. If, nevertheless, they do so, yet do not grasp the opportunity for making a declaration of excessive value, and for instance, their '*moai kavakava*' wood carving purchased for 1500 USD on the Island of Rapa Nui mysteriously disappears, they may easily come off as badly as the respondent Wali Mohammed, whose box containing valuable works of art on route from Paris to New York disappeared and was finally awarded a minute indemnity of 10 USD.[85]

10.3 The Air Carrier's Liability for Damage Caused to Cargo

'In the carriage of cargo, the liability of the air carrier in the case of the destruction, loss, damage or delay is *limited* to a sum of 22 SDR per kilogramme', with the exception if the consignor, upon transferring the consignment to the carrier, has made a special declaration of excessive value and paid a supplementary sum charged for this [Article 22 (3)].

The meaning of *cargo* is not defined by the contracting States, thus, its interpretation is restricted to a national level. Air cargo includes essentially all portable and valuable objects forwarded by the air carrier. With respect to the fact that in the event of the destruction, loss of or damage to the cargo, it can always be replaced, repaired, or reproduced, the legislator is less rigorous in this area, rather focuses primarily on accidents sustained by persons (of course, this is not valid for priceless works of art

[85] *Mohammed v. Air France,* NY Slip Op 50462 (U) [11 Misc. 3d 1071(A)]. Decided on 28 March 2006.

or treasures, which are generally forwarded by aircraft, but these objects are forwarded with separate, special insurance from the outset). In addition, the cargo does not miss the flight, does not cause damage 'purposefully', does not act unlawfully, in legal terms there are not so many related problems, by reason of which it would require enhanced protection or attention. It is not accidental that in the event of damage to cargo, the liability of the air carrier for damages is weight-based and limited, while in the case of accidents sustained by passengers, the liability is unlimited.

At the same time, here we also need to mention that the claimant cannot transgress limited liability (unless they make a declaration of excessive value), and the destruction of the cargo is not restricted to the physical annihilation of the cargo, but it also involves the change of the features or the substance of the cargo by force, therefore, due to its damage it cannot be used in compliance with its original designation.[86] The similarity between the loss and the destruction of the cargo is that in both cases the cargo forfeits its financial value or utility.[87]

10.3.1 The Time Period of Air Carriage

'The air carrier is liable for damage sustained in the event of the destruction or loss of, or damage to, cargo upon condition only that the event which caused the damage so sustained took place during the carriage by air' [Article 18 (1)]. Air carriage implies the time period during which the cargo was under the supervision of the air carrier. Its duration, as a main rule, does not extend to any carriage performed outside the airport by land, sea, or inland waterways.[88]

If, however, such carriage takes place during the performance of the contract for carriage by air for the purpose of the loading, delivery, or transhipment of the cargo, any damage is presumed, subject to proof to the contrary, to have been the result of an event that took place during the carriage by air. The air carrier may substitute air carriage with another mode of transport, for instance on public roads by lorry or truck, but this possibility shall be agreed upon in advance by the parties in the air waybill. In such cases the liability of the air carrier prevails during the whole section of road transport with respect to the fact that the parties deemed consecutive forwarding to be one carriage.[89]

The carrier may also resort to other modes of transport without the consent of the consignor. 'If a carrier, without the consent of the consignor, substitutes carriage by

[86] Mankiewitcz (1982), p. 168.

[87] *Dalton v. Delta Air Lines*, U.S. Court Appeals, Fifth Circuit, 7 April 1978. 14. Avi. 18.425.

[88] *Victoria Sales Corporation v. Emery Air Freight Inc.*, 917 F.2d, 705 at 707 2d Circ., 1990.; *Railroad Salvage of Connecticut v. Japan Freights Consolidators*, 556 F. Supp. 124 (E.D.N.Y. 1983), aff'd mem. 779 F2nd 38 (second Cir.), 1985.

[89] *Commercial Union Insurance Co. v. Alitalia Airlines*, 347 F. third 448 (second Cir.), 2003.

another mode of transport for the whole or part of a carriage intended by the agreement between the parties to be carriage by air, such carriage by another mode of transport is deemed to be within the period of carriage by air' [Article 18 (3–4)].

If the cargo is deposited in a bond store outside the area of the airport, but it remains under the control of the airline and its agent,[90] this time period is deemed to be part of carriage by air. Essentially, in all the three cases the liability of the air carrier prevails, because upon the establishment of liability for damages supervision has legal preponderance, not the location.

The rules of the Convention pertaining to cargo guarantee less legal protection for the consignor, regarding that the majority of objects can be reproduced, remanufactured. Therefore, the contracting States stipulate that the liability of the air carrier for damages in the case of the loss of, or damage to the cargo is low and limited. Thus, the air carrier cannot be obligated to pay more indemnity than the maximum amount. This is a fixed amount binding the parties. It cannot be exceeded even if the conduct of the servant of the air carrier caused the loss of or damage to the cargo.

If the consignor intends to have the air carrier forward cargo of higher value, it may make a special declaration of excessive value. The fixed amount determined in the declaration provides sufficient guarantee for the consignor so that it can be reassured of its cargo. The condition of making a special declaration of interest in delivery at destination is that the consignor of the cargo should indicate the real value in the declaration and pay a supplementary sum if the case so requires. If the consignor declares the value in the declaration in bad faith and the air carrier proves the fact that the declared sum exceeds the actual interest of the consignor in delivery at destination, the air carrier will not pay the sum exceeding the real value [Article 22 (3)].

In the event of the destruction or loss of, damage to, or delay of the consigned cargo, for the purpose of the establishment of the upper limit of the liability of the air carrier, exclusively the total weight of the package or packages concerned shall be taken into consideration. Nevertheless, when the damage of a part of the cargo, or of an object contained therein, affects the value of other packages covered by the same air waybill, or the same receipt, the total weight of such package or packages shall also be taken into consideration in determining the limit of liability [Article 22 (4)].

In calculating liability, the weight of the package(s) concerned is taken into account. If only some parts of the cargo are damaged, the question arises: for which part is the air carrier liable? In the *Motorola versus Federal Express* case, the defendant could not provide evidence that the damage to several mobile telecommunication station modules did not affect the value of the whole station, so the court awarded full restitution to the injured party based on the weight of the entire shipment.[91] In the *Deere & Co. versus Deutsche Lufthansa* case, the shipment consisted of various components together comprising a mainframe computer. The

[90] *Vigilant Insurance Company v. World Courier*, WL 2332343 (S.D.N.Y.), 4 June 2008.

[91] *Motorola Inc. and Fireman's Fund Insurance Company v. Federal Express Corporation and Kuehne & Nagel, Inc.*, No. 00–17374. US Court of Appeals, Ninth Circuit. Argued and Submitted, 13 February 2002.

damaged package contained one of those components, namely the 'directors frame'. These damaged computer parts are not easily replaceable by similar parts, so upon adjudication, the total weight of the shipment was taken into account by the court.[92] In these cases, the damage to a part of the cargo resulted in the consideration of the weight of the entire shipment as a basis of indemnification.

'The carrier may stipulate unilaterally that the contract of carriage shall be subject to higher limits of liability than those provided for in the Convention or to no limits of liability whatsoever' (Article 25). This new opportunity of application and the client-friendly step manifested on the part of the air carrier rarely ensues in practice.

The contracting States expressly prohibit provisions aiming to exempt the air carrier from liability or impose a lower limit of liability than that laid down in the Convention. This way, the air carrier cannot evade the prevalence of the limits of liability stipulated in the Convention. If the air carrier still sets out such a limiting provision, it is null and void, but the nullity of the contested provision does not entail the nullity of the whole contract. Its provisions, apart from the contested part, remain effective (Article 26).[93]

The drawback of the limited liability for damages is that the amount of compensation to be paid to the obligees is generally deemed low since it is not always in proportion to the extent of the damage sustained. Therefore, the consignor needs to purchase supplementary insurance so that, in the event of damage, besides the indemnity to be paid by the air carrier, they can receive further compensation depending on the amount paid and the conditions set out in the insurance contract. This conception does not conform entirely to the basic principle of compensation deriving from the liability for damages, the essence of which is that the claimant needs to be restituted to such a situation as if the damage had not occurred. The entity liable for the damage is obliged to restore the original state *(in integrum restitutio)*. Obviously, the phrase of the original state has a literal, but also a metaphorical meaning. If the consignor recovers the object stolen from the cargo unit, the original state is reinstated, indeed. However, if the cargo is destroyed, restitution to its former state becomes impossible. In this case, the damaging party indemnifies the adversely affected party for the damage caused. If the actual damage does not exceed the upper limit, the air carrier indemnifies the damage of the claimant within the limited amount with respect to the extent of the proven damage.

---

[92] *Deere & Co. v. Deutsche Lufthansa Aktiengesellschaft*. 621 F. Supp. 721 (N.D. Ill. 1985), US District Court for the Northern District of Illinois, 26 April 1985.

[93] The contracting States prohibit the application of a limiting clause in the relations of contracting (marketing) and actual (operating) carriers *(code-share)* and attach the nullity of the contested part of the contract as a legal consequence of its breach. Montreal Convention (1999), Article 47.

10.3.2 *Liability for Live Animals*

In practice, airlines also deal with live animals (livestock) as cargo. Live animals may be forwarded pursuant to the IATA prescriptions and with the prior consent of the air carrier. The condition of transporting live animals is their confinement in a regular, portable, escape-proof carrier (not hindering the movement of the animal, in compliance with the industry specifications and the limitations of size and weight prescribed by the air carrier), and the production of valid official, veterinary and vaccination certificates and entry permits as well as other documents required by the prescriptions of the States concerned with the carriage. Further conditions of the carriage of live animals are the payment of appropriate charges for excess weight and the assumption of responsibility for the live animal.

The passenger carrying the animal is liable for the damage to or the soiling of any part of the aircraft or the baggage of other passengers as a consequence of the carriage of the animal, and the air carrier may enforce a claim for damages against the passenger as well. With the exception of seeing-eye dogs and disaster-rescue dogs, live animals and their portable carriers, in all cases (including carriage on board), qualify as excess weight and, as such, can be carried only for extra charge. In case of damage to the live animal, the financial liability of the air carrier shall be determined on the basis of the weight of the live animal and its portàble carrier.

10.3.3 *The Delivery of Cargo*

The consignor has a right of disposition over the cargo. This right is due to the consignor if it carries out all its obligations under the contract of carriage. The consignor in possession of the right of disposition may:

- *recall* the cargo at the airport of departure or destination; or
- *stop* the cargo in the course of the journey on any landing; or
- call for the cargo to be delivered in the course of the journey *to a person other than the consignee* originally designated*;* or
- *require* the cargo *to be returned* to the airport of departure.

'The consignor must not exercise this right of disposition in such a way as to prejudice the carrier or other consignors and must reimburse any expenses occasioned by the exercise of this right. If it is impossible to carry out the instructions of the consignor, the carrier must so inform the consignor forthwith' [Article 12 (1–2)]. 'If the carrier carries out the instructions of the consignor for the disposition of the cargo without requiring the production of the part of the air waybill or the cargo receipt delivered to the latter, the carrier will be liable, without prejudice to its right of recovery from the consignor, for any damage which may be caused thereby to any person who is lawfully in possession of that part of the air waybill or the cargo receipt.' The right conferred on the consignor is terminated at the moment the carrier delivers the cargo to the consignee. 'Nevertheless, if the consignee declines to accept the cargo, or cannot be communicated with, the consignor resumes its right of disposition' [Article 12 (3–4)]. As long as the consignor has not exercised its right of disposition over the cargo, that is, the cargo has arrived at its destination, the consignee, after the payment of the due charges and in compliance with the conditions of carriage, becomes entitled to require the air carrier to transfer the delivered cargo and to receive it. Unless otherwise agreed upon, the air carrier is obligated to notify the consignee of the arrival of the cargo. Notification needs to take place at the earliest possible time. Although the Convention does not prescribe a concrete time, action needs to be taken as early as possible according to the situation. For instance, in the case the consignee was notified with a delay of 19 h after the arrival of the expiring cargo, the court did not deem the duration between the arrival and the notification to be suitable, therefore, it obligated the carrier to pay indemnity.[94]

If the cargo was lost and the carrier admits this fact or 'if the cargo has not arrived at the expiration of 7 days after the date on which it ought to have arrived, the consignee is entitled to enforce against the carrier the rights which flow from the contract of carriage' [Article 13 (1–3)]. The obligees, 'the consignor and the consignee during the enforcement of their rights proceed each in its own name whether it is acting in its own interest or in the interest of another, provided that it carries out the obligations imposed by the contract of carriage' (Article 14). The provisions above do not affect the relations of the consignor and consignee with each other or the mutual relations of third parties whose rights are derived either from the consignor or the consignee. If the consignor or the consignee intends to derogate from the rules above, they can do so through an express provision in the air waybill or cargo receipt concerning an intention of modification [Article 15 (1–2)].

10.4 The Air Carrier's Liability for Damage Caused by Delay

'The air carrier is liable for damage occasioned by delay in the carriage by air of *passengers*, *baggage* or *cargo*' (Article 19). In the case of damage caused by delay, 'the liability of the carrier for each passenger is limited to 5346 SDR' [Article 22 (1)]. In the carriage of baggage, the liability of the carrier in the case of destruction, loss, damage, or delay is limited to 1288 SDR for each passenger. These limitations (5346 SDR for passenger, 1288 SDR for baggage) are breakable, 'if it is proved that the damage resulted from the act or omission of the air carrier, its servants or agents, done with intent to cause damage or recklessly and with knowledge that damage would probably result, provided that, in the case of such act or omission of a servant or agent, it is also proved that such servant or agent was acting

[94] *Wea Frams, Lima Peru v. American Airlines, Inc.*, 31 Avi 18,739 (S.d. Fla), 2007.

within the scope of its employment' [Article 22 (5)]. In the case of the delay of cargo, the limitation is based on 22 SDR per kilogramme and this limit is unbreakable.

There are numerous acknowledged reasons for the delay of flights, most often, technical failures and various meteorological circumstances cause problems. At the same time, increased waiting time because of deficient airport infrastructure [boarding gates or passenger bridges (jetways)] or the saturation of the airspace brings about delays. The unique tasks related to aviation security and their implementation, but even the inappropriate handling of cargo or baggage may also lead to delays. Delayed connecting flights contribute to further delays, but if the passenger purchases air tickets for several sections within a single transaction from the same airline, it may also happen that the flight ready to depart waits for the transferring passengers of the flight arriving delayed. At the same time, the reasons deriving from the faults of administration are not scarce either. The contracting States include delays under the scope of liability of the air carrier for damage, since the passengers and consignors opt for air transport as a mode of carriage not only because of its safety, but chiefly because of its speed. The quality of the service is determined essentially by rapidity and punctuality; punctual departure is simultaneously the pledge of arrival on time. If the air carrier cannot adhere to the timetable, the quality of its service suffers and damage calculable in numbers arises.

In the case of *Chendrimada versus Air India*,[95] the passengers arriving from New York were waiting at the Delhi Airport (DEL) on board the airplane travelling to Bombay (its current name is Mumbai) (BOM) because of foggy weather for 11.5 h. While waiting, the passengers could not return to the terminal building because, in the hope of the improvement of weather conditions, the cockpit crew wished to be ready for quick departure. During the waiting time, the cabin crew did not serve food, only beverages. The extreme circumstances, as alleged by the plaintiff, caused physical injury. The court established that the airline did not breach the contract. By reason of the clauses of contractual conditions, the carrier was not liable for the delay, nor did the passenger sustain bodily injury (accident). At the same time, the court emphasised that waiting because of weather conditions is not an unexpected or irregular event, whereas, waiting on board by the passengers for a lengthy time, indeed is.

Delay is a very controversial area. The object of controversy used to be mainly the content of former standards of the General Conditions of Carriage recommended by IATA. The airlines favoured to use these standards, according to which 'the times of departure and arrival do not constitute part of the contract, the timetable can be altered by the air carrier without notification any time,[96] the air

[95] *Chendrimada v. Air India,* 802 F. Supp. 1089 (S.D.N.Y.), 1992.

[96] IATA Resolution 724: *Passenger Ticket. Notices and Conditions of Contract*, 2000.

carrier does not guarantee the times of departure and arrival indicated in the timetable, furthermore, the airline is not liable if the passenger misses the connecting flight or any other flight operating according to schedule'. These rules with the strengthening competition and the prevalence of passengers' rights have become unacceptable by our days and do not constitute part of the contractual conditions any longer. It has also been the subject of disputes that the community law of the European Union, based on the rules of the Montreal Convention, provides for the liability of community carriers for damages more rigorously and specifically.[97] Thereby, the community regulation lays more burden on carriers operating in the area of the European Union, while it hinders the principal objective of the Convention, the accomplishment of unification.[98]

The Convention does not define the concept of delay either. We think of delay, in general, when the passenger, the baggage, or the cargo fails to arrive at its destination on time. The concept provides broad scope for interpretation; in addition, when the passenger, the baggage, or the cargo of the consignor is delayed, all of these have different effects. The Convention does not remedy psychic injuries in the case of delays either, although situations that are hard to process occur on a daily basis: for example, the passenger is unable to arrive at wedding, a recital, or other important events or take an entrance examination. Likewise, if the passenger's flight is delayed owing to which the long-haul connecting flight is missed, its consequence is generally a lengthy waiting time, financial loss, and a form of psychic suffering.

[97] Uniformly booked, directly connecting aircraft departing from one EU Member State, travelling via a third country to a destination in a further third country: the air carrier implementing the first section of the flight is obligated to indemnify the passengers sustaining significant delay upon the arrival of the second section of the flight implemented by an air carrier external to the Community. The decree reserves the right for the operating air carrier to intervene in the interest of the compensation of this financial burden vis-à-vis the other air carrier. Court of Justice of the European Union, Press Release No. 95/19 Luxembourg, 11 July 2019. Judgment in Case C-502/18 CS and Others v České aerolinie a.s. ECLI:EU:C:2019:604,

[98] In the European Union, the legislator, upon the occurrence of delay, adjusts the assistance to be provided and the extent of indemnification to be paid upon the occurrence of delay to the relation between the length of the flight and the time spent waiting. In the case of the cancellation or significant delay of the connecting flight, the indemnity to be provided for the passengers needs to be calculated on the basis of the air distance between the airports of departure and arrival, even if in the case of a connecting flight the passenger has already covered half of the route. Regulation (EC) No. 261/2004 of the European Parliament and of the Council of 11 February 2004 establishing common rules on compensation and assistance to passengers in the event of denied boarding and of cancellation or the long delay of flights, and repealing Regulation (EEC) No. 295/91 – Commission Statement. *Official Journal L 046, 17/02/2004 P. 1–8*; *Birgit Bossen, Anja Bossen* and *Gudula Gräßmann v. Brussels Airlines,* SA/NV, C-559/16. case, Court of Justice of the European Union (CJEU), Luxembourg, 7 September 2017.

In the case of *Fangbeng Fuondjing versus American Airlines, Inc.*,[99] the plaintiffs (family members) were travelling from the United States to Cameroon to attend the last honours of their deceased relative. The passengers missed the connecting flight in New York, so they stayed in a hotel for 4 days, did not get access to their baggage, and eventually they were late for the memorial services. The travel agent had warned them in writing well in advance that the timetable had been changed, consequently, they should drive to the airport in New York, since the chance for catching the long-haul flight with the domestic flight was slim. Eventually, the passengers took the domestic airplane and were indeed late for the connecting flight. The court held that according to the provision of the Convention a delay occurred. The delay was factual, since even at the expense of 4 days' waiting, the air carrier finally took the passengers to Cameroon (if it had not acted so, a breach of contract would have been established). The agent of the airline had warned the passengers of the risk in time, and the airline performed the service undertook under the contract and it took all reasonably necessary steps to prevent damage. The plaintiffs lost the lawsuit as the liability of the airline was not established.

It is important to separate the conceptual scope of delay from all other situations which the applier of the law does not wish to adjudge under the legal title of delay pursuant to the provisions of the Convention.

The separation is necessary since some legal cases not falling under the category of delay shall be adjudged under the legal title of *the breach of contract* on the basis of national law.

- The category of delay does not extend to the case of non-departing, that is, cancelled flights.

The cancellation of the flight may have several reasons, mainly technical failure, accident, extreme weather circumstances, the act of a third person, or strike.[100] From a legal viewpoint, it is essential that the airline does not carry the passenger to the place of destination or to the agreed stopping place, to the next stop stipulated under the contract (because booking on another flight was not feasible, there is no connecting flight, etc.). In such a case, the airline breaches the contract, therefore, it is liable to indemnify the passenger pursuant to the rules under national law.

- The denial of the embarkation of the passenger by the airline despite a valid air ticket does not fall under the category of delay.

Denied boarding has been an evergreen problem as the consequence of the practice of selling tickets surpassing the capacity of seats on the given flight by the

[99] *Fangbeng Fuondjing v. American Airlines, Inc.*, WL 1375606 (D. Md.), April 2011.

[100] *Mullaney v. Delta Airlines, Inc.*, 33 Avi. 12,819 (S.D.N.Y.) 2009.

airlines, that is, of overbooking flights. They do so with the knowledge that generally not all passengers arrive in time for the flight (because of missing the connecting flight, falling ill, being stuck in a traffic jam, sustaining an accident, travelling further on other modes of transport, overlooking the time, etc.). This method has guaranteed that the place of the passenger not turning up in time (the so-called no-show passenger) can always be taken by a revenue passenger. The problem emerges if more people wish to travel at the same time than the number of seats facilitates. According to the prescription of ICAO, as many passengers may travel on board an aircraft as the number of seats with seat-belts is available.[101] No standing places are available on flights. In an exceptional case, the passenger may travel in a so-called *jump seat* with seat-belt reserved for a crew member, if it is empty and the passenger undertakes the flight this way as well as if the pilot-in-command grants his permission. Although denied boarding deriving from overbooking has become a practice in aviation, there have not been many relevant legal disputes.

The Convention does not provide for cases of denied boarding. It deals with the cases of denied boarding as non-contractual performance (not in the least as delays), therefore, claims for damages are adjudged essentially on the basis of national law.[102] In such a situation the airline does its utmost to alleviate the damage, and firstly, it tries to find volunteers among the passengers who undertake to fly on a later flight. Volunteering passengers resign their booked seats on full flights in return for definite (financial and travel-related) advantages. It has also occurred that university students in the hope of access to allowances entailed by compensation favoured to purchase tickets for full, sought after flights in the summer season, and upon overbooking they had a propensity for voluntary resignation. However, if there are not enough volunteers, the ground staff chooses the persons who will stay despite their intention, in consideration of proper compensation.

The passenger has the right to desist from the flight. The passenger may exercise this right if there are reasonable grounds to think that elementary problems manifest themselves in the observance of the requirements of safety on the aircraft. For example, if the airplane does not depart for technical failure, then mechanics appear and repair the fault, then the pilot-in-command announces that the flight is going to take off, but not much later new problems occur and the whole procedure starts again. In an extreme case, the passenger may deny boarding, if they deem that there are serious problems with the aircraft on the concrete grounds (it releases smoke, some liquid is dripping from it or the member of the crew is inebriated). If the passenger is right, the air carrier is obligated to indemnify the passenger for damage. However, the passenger receives indemnity not by reason of delay, but under the legal title of the breach of contract, since the service was not realised, the passenger eventually did not travel on the aircraft of the airline.

---

[101] ICAO Annex 6 on Operation of Aircraft, Part I – *Commercial Air Transport Aeroplanes, Cabin/ Safety* B 6. *Seat belts,* 6.2.2.

[102] *Weiss v. EL AL Israel Airlines, Ltd.*, United States District Court, S.D. New York, 433 F. Supp. 2d 361, 2006.

For reasons of safety, the air carrier may request the passenger any time to facilitate the search, scanning or other safety control of their checked and unchecked baggage. If the passenger does not fulfil the request, the air carrier may deny forwarding the baggage. The concerned service provider of the airport carries out the search of the baggage in the presence of the passenger and a representative of the authority in their procedural order with entry on record. The concerned service provider of the airport registers the implementation of the control in the baggage control record, in which they indicate the weight and the contingent damage of the baggage, the circumstances of the examination and the measures taken. During the carriage of the passenger by air, if the regulations of the concerned State require the presence of the passenger at the examination of their baggage, and therefore, the passenger misses their flight or sustains any other damage, the air carrier is not liable for the damage caused this way.

Hence, the Convention does not include in its scope of regulation the cases of the cancellation of flights or denied boarding; it deals solely with delays. In practice, these cases are not so easy to adjudge. It is not inadvertent that judicial practice is divided in these issues. Although the cases of the cancellation of flights and denied boarding entail loss of time and constitute breaches of contract, delay only implies performance at a later time. According to judicial practice, by denied passenger we mean the cases (disregarding overbooking) when the passenger is late for boarding, or they develop health problems, or an expectant mother at an advanced stage cannot be carried, or the behaviour of the passenger does not facilitate their safe carriage. In these cases, the liability of the air carrier is not established because, although these are cases of breach of contract, they result from the behaviour or condition of the passenger. It is essential that these situations occur immediately before departure. If the passenger is already on their way and has arrived at the first agreed stopping place and only subsequently, on the connecting flight or on the return flight does the denial of boarding ensue, practice evaluates that as delay and the rules of the Convention will be governing.[103] Despite the cancellation of the flight or denied boarding, the passenger in the decisive majority of cases reaches their destination. If the passenger covers the distance on the same flight or another relief flight, although later, but under the same conditions as indicated on the original air ticket, we speak of delay. If the journey takes place on a new route under amended contractual conditions with different departure time, another airline or flight, we do not speak of delay.[104]

Delay does not occur either in the case when the passenger reaches the boarding gate in time but cannot board because the ground staff for some reason is not present, or the ground staff is present, but denies boarding for administrative or other, frequently security reasons. In this case, the passenger may demand compensation not for delay, but for denied boarding (thus, for breach of contract).[105]

---

[103] Clarke (2010).

[104] Dempsey and Johansson (2010).

[105] *Amtsgericht Erding* (Court of Small Claims) Case No. 4 C 309/06, 5 July 2006.

In the case of *Kamanou-Goune versus Swiss International Air Lines*,[106] the plaintiff wished to travel with her daughter from Douala in Cameroon (DLA) to Zurich (ZRH). During the operation of embarkation, the representative of the Swiss International Air Lines (LX) did not permit the plaintiff's daughter to board with reference to the fact that, on the basis of the passport photograph, the little girl present was not the same person. The representative directed the passengers to the local police, who instituted an examination and requested the plaintiff to obtain an official document concerning the identity of the little girl from the Embassy of the United States in Cameroon. The plaintiff travelled to the capital, Yaoundé, and turned to the Embassy, which refused to issue the document since the passport was valid and suitable for travelling. However, the representative of the Swiss International Air Lines still did not permit the boarding of the little girl. Consequently, the plaintiff purchased air tickets from another airline, whose representative did not find such a problem and was instead ready to carry the two passengers to Europe.

The plaintiff sued the Swiss International Air Lines mainly for breach of contract, malicious slander, and psychic anguish. The court established that the airline committed a breach of contract since they refused to carry the passenger despite her valid air ticket.

The passenger may request the reimbursement of the air ticket or rebooking in cases of significant delay, cancellation of the flight, or the denial of boarding. The passenger may choose between the reimbursement of the purchase price of the air ticket and recourse to other modes of transport (e.g., rents a car or travels further by train or bus) and the request of rebooking on a flight securing the earliest or later arrival at the destination under comparable conditions of carriage. If the passenger opts for rebooking, the air carrier shall provide meals and refreshments in proportion with the waiting time. In the cases when one or more nights' stay is necessary, the airline shall provide accommodation in a hotel and arrange transportation between the airport and the hotel.

If the checked baggage or cargo is delayed, the person entitled to receipt (the passenger or the consignee) shall make a complaint to the air carrier 'at the latest within twenty-one (21) days from the date on which the baggage or cargo have been placed at his or her disposal' [Article 31 (2)]. On the basis of the complaint, the claim of the obligee for damages is adjudicated.[107]

---

[106] *Kamanou-Goune v. Swiss International Air Lines,* WL 874600 (S.D.N.Y.), 2009; US Supreme Court, NY Slip Op 08100, 2012.

[107] Sipos (2020), pp. 155–184.

References

Anderson DF, Eberhardt S (2010) Understanding Flight. 2nd edn., McGraw Hill, p 33
Barnett JF (1975) Case Comment: Rosman versus Trans World Airlines Inc. Brook J Int Law 2(1): 191–204
Charles RA (2011) Cardiac Arrest in the Skies. Singap Med J 52(8):582
Clarke MA (2010) Contracts of Carriage by Air. Taylor & Francis, London
Coles P (2020) COVID–19 Aviation: Liability implications arising from coronavirus. Market Insight, Clyde & Co. Asia Pacific. www.clydeco.com/en/insights/2020/02/coronavirus-2019
Dempsey PS, Johansson SO (2010) Montreal v. Brussels: the Conflict of Laws on the Issue of Delay in International Air Carriage. Air and Space Law J 35(3):207–224
Ehlers NP (2004) Aviation in Europe. A Multiple-challenge Industry. Carswell, Toronto. Ann Air Space Law XXIX:493–500
Felkai P, Kurimay T (2017) Patients with Mental Problems – the Most Defenseless Travellers. J Travel Med 24(5):tax005
Guerreri G (2010) Italian Court Denies Recovery for Cerebral Haemorrhage Following 18.5 hour Aircraft Journey. Air Space Law 35(1):79
Kenyon TA et al (1996) Transmission of Multidrug-resistant Mycobacterium Tuberculosis During a Long Airplane Flight. N Engl J Med 334:933–938
Kiss K (2009) Report on Unlawful Interference on Board, Selection from a Report. Capt. Kálmán Kiss, Pilot-in-command and instructing pilot. Malév Hungarian Airlines
Lautner E (1998) Report on Unlawful Interference on Board, Selection from a Report, Erzsébet Lautner, Chief flight-attendant. Malév Hungarian Airlines
Lowenfeld AF (1992) Liability of Airlines for Injury Caused by Terrorism. In: Air and Space Law: De lege ferenda, essays in Honour of Henri A. Wassenbergh. Martinus Nijhoff, Dordrecht
Lowenfeld AF, Mendelsohn AI (1967) The United States and the Warsaw Convention. Harv Law Rev 80(3):497–692
Mankiewitcz RH (1982) The Liability Regime of the International Air Carrier. Kluwer, Deventer, p 168
Newman LW, Burrows M (2013) Legal Remedies Available to Hijack Victims of TWA Flights 847. In: Newman LW, Burrows M (eds) The Practice of International Litigation (Part I, Chapter 7), 2nd edn., Juris Publishing, New York, pp 60–61
Onianwa K, Agbonze KA (2020) The Coronavirus (COVID-19) Pandemic – the Liability of Air Carriers. Ajumogobia and Okeke Law Firm. www.ajumogobiaokeke.com/associates/kelly-a-agbonze
Prager S et al (2020) COVID-19 and the Aviation Industry: Turbulent times ahead? Chancery Lane 1. Lexology, 7 May 2020. www.lexology.com/library/detail.aspx
Sándor T (2008) Travel Thrombosis: Pathomechanism and Clinical Aspects. Pathophysiology 15(4):243–252
Sipos A (2020) The Air Carrier's Liability for Damage Caused to Cargo. ELTE Ann 59:155–184
Sipos A (2021) The Liability of the Air Carrier for Damages and the State of Health of the Passenger. Accidents and Diseases (COVID-19). Hung J Leg Stud 61(1):85–112. www.akjournals.com/view/journals/2052/61/1/article-p85.xml
Smith P (2018) Cockpit Confidential: Everything you need to know about air travel: questions, answers, and reflections. Sourcebooks, pp 18, 35, 41, 122
Tompkins GN Jr (2001) Deep Vein Thrombosis (DVT) and Air Carrier Liability. The Myth and the Law. Air Space Law 26(4–5):232
Tompkins GN Jr (2009) The 1999 Montreal Convention: Alive, well and growing. Air Space Law 34(6):425
Truitt RD (2015) Plain talk about plane claims: an air carrier claims examiner's handbook. Overhead bins – a hard case. J Air Law Commer 80(2):449–470
Tulloch A, Shaw M (2010) Report from Australia. Air Space Law 35(1):81–82

Chapter 11
Exoneration of the Air Carrier from Liability

After it has been decided that the Convention is applicable and the legal case may be adjudged pursuant to the Convention, the meritorious adjudication of the legal case follows. In its course, the court examines to what extent the air carrier is liable for the damage, whether there are any circumstances on the basis of which it can be exonerated. It is important to highlight that the air carrier, as a matter of course, does not have to indemnify the damage deriving from the intervention or own fault of the claimant, that is, the damage caused or contributed to by the negligence or other wrongful act or omission of the person claiming compensation or of the person from whom the claimant derives their right to claim compensation. This rule applies to all provisions related to liability, that is, to cases of the death or bodily injury of the passenger, of damage to the baggage or cargo, as well as of delays. Thus, the air carrier shall be exonerated from its liability to the claimant to such an extent to which such negligence or wrongful act or omission caused or contributed to the damage. When by reason of the death or injury of the passenger, the compensation is claimed by a person other than the passenger, the carrier shall likewise be wholly or partly exonerated from its liability to the extent to which it proves that the *negligence* or other *wrongful act* or *omission* of the passenger caused or contributed to the damage (Article 20).

In so far as no own fault prevails and the responsibility of the claimant cannot be established, the air carrier shall be liable, provided that further reasons for exoneration, expounded below, do not prevail.

If on the basis of the provisions of the Convention the air carrier is not liable since it exonerates itself or its liability is not established on the basis of the provisions of the Convention, the air carrier cannot be, in the concrete case, in any other way called to account any longer. This implies that in the specific case, the plaintiff cannot enforce their claim for damages vis-à-vis the air carrier pursuant to national law or any other legal regime (Article 29). The institution of exclusive remedy is a special protective stronghold, which, to all intents and purposes, provides ultimate protection for the air carriers of the States Parties.

A. Sipos, *International Aviation Law*, https://doi.org/10.1007/978-3-031-39066-1_11

11.1 Exoneration from Indemnity of Damage Caused to the Passenger

The air carrier may exonerate itself from the payment of damages deriving from the death or bodily injury of the passenger in a two-step (absolute and fault liability) system (see, Part II, Chap. 12. 2):

I. 'For damages – arising under [Article 17 (1)] – not exceeding 128,821 SDR for each passenger, the carrier shall not be able to *exclude* or *limit* its liability' [Article 21 (1)].

   In the case of damages not exceeding the limit of 128,821 SDR, the air carrier shall, by all means, be liable. As a consequence of the absolute ('no fault') liability of the air carrier, it is liable even if it did not cause the accident because a cause-effect relationship does not necessarily have to exist between the accident and the injury of the passenger.

II. In the case of damages—arising under [Article 17 (1)]—exceeding the limit of 128,821 SDR, the air carrier may exonerate itself from liability solely if it '*proves* that

   - such damage *was not due to* the negligence or other wrongful act or omission of the carrier or its servants or agents, or,
   - such damage *was solely due to* the negligence or other wrongful act or omission of a third party' [Article 21 (2)].

In so far as the exoneration is successful, as a consequence of fault liability, the air carrier shall not be liable for damages and shall not be called to account in the given case pursuant to the provisions of the Convention or other national law by reason of the exclusivity of the Convention.

The contracting States, beyond the general rule, guarantee the air carrier further opportunities for exoneration from damage arising during the carriage of passengers, baggage, or cargo and because of delay.

11.2 Exoneration from Indemnity of Damage Caused to the Baggage and Cargo

'The air carrier is liable for damage sustained in the case of the destruction or loss of, or of damage to, checked baggage upon condition only that the event which caused the damage took place on board the aircraft or during any period within which the checked baggage was in the charge of the carrier', with the following exception: if 'the damage resulted from the inherent defect, quality or vice of the baggage' [Article 17 (2)]. Thus, the air carrier is exonerated from damage to the baggage if the damage was occasioned by the inherent defect, quality, or vice of the baggage. On such basis, the air carrier does not assume responsibility for damage, such as scratches, dents, abrasion, soiling, traces of cuts, torn straps, missing lifting handles or wheels, etc., ensuant during the regular use of the baggage. Furthermore, the air carrier does not assume responsibility for damage deriving from the overload of baggage, for the damage to or loss of packages fastened to the baggage, or for the damage to or loss of the lock or the brace fitted on the baggage.

For the damage 'to unchecked baggage, including personal items, the air carrier is liable if the damage resulted from its fault or that of its servants or agents' (culpability) [Article 17 (2)].

However, the carrier is not liable for damage to the cargo if and to the extent it proves that the destruction, or loss of, or damage to, the cargo resulted from one or more of the followings:

(a) inherent defect, quality or vice of that cargo;
(b) defective packing of that cargo performed by a person other than the carrier or its servants or agents;
(c) an act of war or an armed conflict;
(d) an act of public authority carried out in connection with the entry, exit or transit of the cargo [Article 18 (2)].

For the damage to the baggage or cargo, the air carrier's liability is limited unless the passenger or the consignor has made, at the time when the checked baggage or cargo was handed over to the carrier, a special declaration of interest in delivery at destination and has paid a supplementary sum to the air carrier. In that case, the carrier will be liable to pay a sum not exceeding the declared sum. The air carrier shall not be liable if it proves that the sum stated in the declaration does not correspond to the facts since it is greater than the passenger's or the consignor's actual interest in delivery at destination [Article 22 (2–3)]. In this case, upon the carriage of cargo, the extent of indemnification is adjusted to the weight of the cargo, not to the value stated in the declaration.

11.3 Exoneration from the Indemnification of Damage Caused by Delay

The carrier shall not be liable for damage occasioned by delay if it *proves* that

- it and its servants and agents took all measures that could reasonably be required to avoid the damage; or,
- it was impossible for it (air carrier) and for them (servant or agents) to take such reasonable measures (Article 19).

Under the Convention, the contracting States prescribe that the air carrier, its servants, and agents merely *take all measures reasonably required* for the avoidance of damage in contrast to the more rigorous requirement of the Warsaw System, in which the basic expectation *was taking all the necessary measures*. There are situations when the air carrier cannot fulfil its obligation since its servants and agents are not able to avert the unforeseeable, external, and compelling circumstance or impediment and its consequences. On such occasions, it is impossible to take appropriate measures because one is powerless vis-a-vis the superior power *(vis maior)*, such as wars and emergencies, natural disasters (e.g., volcanic ashes, earthquakes, tornados), catastrophes, and even strikes.[1] It is worth emphasising that the Convention does not mention the legal institution of *vis maior*, hence, it entrusts the judgement relevant for the case to national courts.

The eruption of the Icelandic Eyjafjallajökull volcano and the volcanic ashes hanging over a large part of Europe created severe chaos in air traffic in April 2010. In a matter of minutes, the natural phenomenon impeded the journey of more than ten million people, and at least 100,000 flights were cancelled. Consequently, the air transport industry of the world suffered a loss of approx. 1.7 billion USD. The insurance companies, with reference to a situation of *vis maior*, denied the fulfilment of claims for damages.[2] The air carriers took all reasonably necessary measures in the interest of the prevention of damage by not taking off; therefore, their exoneration from liability for damages was deemed justified.

A further important aspect of the exoneration of the air carrier in the case of delay is that the delay should be justified. If the flight is performed on another airplane by the air carrier since the change of aircraft is justified by technical or safety reasons, its position based on the requirements of aviation safety despite the delay remains defensible if it can prove that it took all the reasonably necessary measures in order to prevent damage. Beyond taking the reasonably necessary measures, the air carrier does not only need to do its utmost to remedy the situation (the prevention of damage) but also to prevent any delay. If the delay had been preventable or the recklessness and negligence of the air carrier underlie the technical failure, in vain is the fault repaired, the air carrier cannot exonerate itself; therefore, it shall be entirely liable.

A further requirement of the exoneration of the air carrier from liability for delay is that the passenger does not contribute to the avoidance of delay. If the passenger does not follow the instructions of the air carrier and contributes to occasioning the damage, for instance, upon boarding, the passenger does not arrive at the boarding gate despite the last call, and as a consequence, the aircraft gets delayed, the passenger may not sue the airline since the delay did not occur due to the fault of the air carrier.

---

[1] *Tismanariu v. Societe Air France,* QCCQ 2847, 2014.; Force Majeure Trumps Delay Claim in Québec Aviation Case. *Transportation Notes,* 10. (2014) 5. p. 2.

[2] Bisignani (2010).

11.4 Exclusive Remedy

A special and highly important legal institution of the Convention is the exclusive remedy. The contracting States promote the achievement of the objective of unification among others via this unique provision. In diverging national legal systems, exclusivity safeguards the primacy of the Convention and its comprehensive predominance.

'In the carriage of passengers, baggage and cargo, any action for damages, however founded, whether under the Convention or in contract or in tort or otherwise, can only be brought subject to the conditions and such limits of liability as are set out in the Convention without prejudice to the question as to who are the persons who have the right to bring suit and what are their respective rights. In any such action, punitive, exemplary or any other non-compensatory damages shall not be recoverable' (Article 29).

This intricately formulated, but all the more significant rule has been transplanted into the Montreal Convention from the Warsaw Convention[3] without substantial changes; therefore, a considerable amount of case law pertaining to exclusive remedy is available. The two legal cases below have become guiding principles because of their consequence, and they have had a momentous impact on the practice of the legal application of the institution of exclusive remedy and on the procedural legal strategy of the contending parties.

In the case *Sidhu versus British Airways*,[4] the passenger brought action because the airplane on route from Kuala Lumpur (KUL) to London (LHR) landed on the international airport of Kuwait (KVI) for refuelling. During refuelling, Iraqi armed men invaded the airport and held the passengers and the crew members back. The passengers of the flight were transported to Baghdad, where they were detained for a month. Later, the armed men released the hostages, who could travel home safely. In the lawsuit, the plaintiff passenger contended that the airline had landed in a war-stricken zone and had been or should have been aware that 4 hours before landing, Iraq had commenced wartime operations. During his confinement for a month, the passenger suffered grave psychic injuries, which also led to bodily injuries. The passenger was taken ill, developed eczema, and lost a lot of weight. These injuries caused

(continued)

[3] In the cases of the carriage of passengers and baggage, any action for damages, however founded, can only be brought subject to the conditions and limits set out in this Convention without prejudice to the questions: who are the persons who have the right to bring suit and what are their respective rights. Warsaw Convention [Article 24 (1–2)]. See, the effect, *Paradis v. Ghana Airways Ltd*. 348F. Supp 2d 106 (S.D.N.Y.) 2004, affirmed 194 Fed. Appx. 5 (2d Cir.) 2006.; Larsen et al. (2012), pp. 335–342.

[4] *Sidhu v. British Airways*. Lloyd's Law Reports. 76. (1997), 2. p. 84.

damage to the plaintiff, therefore, he finally turned to the court. The court, however, held that pursuant to the Convention, no accident happened. Thus, the main question did not consist in: under what conditions and to what extent may the psychic injury be deemed to be an accident pursuant to the provisions of the Convention? Instead, the court sought an answer to the question: if the action of the plaintiff is unsubstantiated vis-a-vis the air carrier, vis-a-vis what party and under what law can the passenger enforce his claim for damages for the purpose of the indemnification of the truly sustained damage?

According to the House of Lords, the Convention regulates the most important issues of private law so that the liability of the air carrier for damages should be uniform and exclusive, superimposed over the national legal systems. The institution of exclusive remedy also serves the objective that if the enforcement of the claims vis-à-vis the air carrier is impracticable, national law should not entitle the claimant to sue the airline either under national law or any other system of rules. That is, if the action is not enforceable pursuant to the Convention, it should not be substantiated under national or other legal systems either.

At the same time, exclusive remedy does not mean that the passengers do not have opportunity to enforce their rights solely for the reason that they cannot claim compensation from the air carrier itself. The claimants may, in their own right, lodge civil legal or criminal legal action vis-à-vis the tortfeasor third party (generally the other passenger) pursuant to the rules of national law. Civil legal and criminal legal responsibility are separated by a sharp boundary. Nevertheless, in the practice of case-law, the question may arise to what extent a specific offence gives rise to criminal legal (public legal) or to civil legal (private legal) liability for damages. The reason for indistinctness consists in the supplementary character of the two legal branches since they jointly provide complex protection vis-à-vis offenders. For example, the victim of crime, beyond the criminal legal claim of having been strongly hit, then spat by the perpetrator on board, realising the facts of the case of forceful libel, may also enforce, via the instruments of civil law, a pecuniary claim for damage to their clothes, hand baggage or other personal belongings.

In the case *EL AL Israel Airlines Ltd. versus Tseng*,[5] the passenger wished to depart from New York (JFK) to Tel Aviv (TLV), when upon the strict security control, several factors on the basis of the passenger's answers were found illogical by the experts, who deemed the passenger risky; therefore, she was subjected to serious examination. In a separate room designed for this purpose,

(continued)

[5] *EL AL Israel Airlines Ltd. v. Tsui Yuan Tseng,* US Court of Appeals for the Second Circuit, No. 97–475, 122 F. 3d, 1999.; Larsen et al. (2012), pp. 324–334.

the female security official carried out body search on the plaintiff, then examined the objects in her checked and unchecked baggage as well as the content of her wallet one by one before the passenger; then she did so in another closed room as well. The examination revealed that everything was in order, so the woman could depart with evident annoyance, nervously and in a state of humiliation. Upon arriving at the hotel, her condition deteriorated since she noticed that her Rolex watch, ring, a part of her clothes, furthermore, 1000 USD in cash had disappeared. Pursuant to the rules of the Convention, the court did not find legal remedy for the claimant's psychic injury, but it awarded her 1034 USD and 90 cents as pecuniary compensation. The passenger lodged an appeal, but the court of appeal approved of the judgement in the first instance. The court established, related to the primacy of the Convention, that if the Convention does not substantiate the compensation of the emerged damage, in the same case, the claim of the passenger for damages vis-à-vis the airline cannot be enforced in any other way.

In summary, if the Convention is applicable in the given case but, pursuant to its provisions, the award of compensation is not substantiated and, as a consequence, the liability of the air carrier is null and void, this claim cannot be enforced, that is, the airline cannot be sued on any other legal grounds proceeding from national or other laws.

The majority of the courts construe this rule rigorously, and according to established judicial practice, the claimant is ultimately deprived of the opportunity of compensation by the air carrier, if in the absence of legal grounds pursuant to the Convention, they cannot enforce their claim. At the same time, in some places, for instance, in South American countries, the provision of the Convention concerning exclusive remedy is construed permissively and is more scarcely observed in practice.[6]

Despite the above, the Convention essentially dictates exclusive remedy and emphasizes its primacy; thereby, it evades conflicts deriving from different national legal systems and creates uniformity.

[6] Wegter (2006), pp. 133–148.

References

Bisignani G (2010) The Eruption of Eyjafjallajökull was a Wake-up Call for Change. Airlines International, IATA Magazine, 1 June 2010

Larsen PB, Sweeney JC, Gillick JE (2012) Aviation Law: Cases, laws and related sourches. Martinus Nijhoff, Leiden, pp 324–334

Wegter JJ (2006) The ECJ Decision of 10 January 2006 on the Validity of Regulation 261/2004: Ignoring the Exclusivity of the Montreal Convention. Air and Space Law J 31(2):133–148

Chapter 12
The Liability of the Air Carrier

In the case of the destruction, loss of or damage to baggage or cargo as well as upon the delayed carriage of passengers, baggage, or cargo, the liability of the air carrier is *limited*, whereas, in the case of accidents sustained by passengers, the liability of the air carrier is *unlimited*.

12.1 Limited Liability

The liability of the air carrier for damages is maximized; therefore, the amount to be indemnified is essentially limited under the Convention. At the same time, 'an air carrier may stipulate unilaterally that the contract of carriage shall be subject to higher limits of liability than those provided for in the Convention or to no limits of liability whatsoever' (Article 25). This new opportunity for application and the passenger-friendly step manifested on the part of the air carrier ensue relatively scarcely in practice.

We can find several 'passenger-friendly' provisions of consumer protection in the Montreal Convention such as the following:

- The review of the upper limits of liability corresponding to the rate of inflation at five-year intervals (Article 24);
- In the case of the occurrence of an accident, the obligation of the air carrier to make an advance payment if required by national law (Article 28);
- The absolute liability of the air carrier in terms of accident up to an amount of 128,821 SDR [Article 21 (1)]; or
- Upon the exoneration of the air carrier, the placement of the burden of proof on the air carrier [Articles 20, 21 (2)].

The contracting States expressly prohibit provisions with the purpose of the exoneration of the air carrier from its liability or of the imposition of a lower limit of liability than what is laid down in the Convention. This way, the air carriers cannot

A. Sipos, *International Aviation Law*, https://doi.org/10.1007/978-3-031-39066-1_12

	Warsaw Convention	Montreal Convention
Damage sustained in case of death or bodily injury of a **passenger**	125,000 francs	**128,821 SDR** Above this amount unlimited
Destruction, loss, damage with respect to **checked baggage**	250 francs/kg	**1288 SDR**
Damage with respect to **unchecked baggage**	500 francs/passenger	**1288 SDR**
Destruction, loss, damage in relation to the carriage of **cargo**	250 francs/kg	**22 SDR/kg**
Damage with respect to **delay**	passenger: no regulation baggage: 250 francs cargo: 250 francs	passenger: **5346 SDR** baggage: **1288 SDR** cargo: **22 SDR/kg**

Fig. 12.1 The upper limits of the liability of the air carrier for damages

evade the prevalence of the limits of liability stipulated in the Convention. If the air carrier still sets out such a limiting provision, it is null and void, but the nullity of the contested provision does not involve the nullity of the whole contract. Its provisions, apart from the contested part, remain effective (Article 26).[1]

The drawback of the limited liability for damages is that the amount of compensation to be paid to the obligees is generally deemed low since it is not always in proportion with the extent of the sustained damage. Therefore, the passenger or the consignor needs to purchase supplementary insurance so that in the case of the occurrence of damage, besides the indemnity paid by the air carrier, they can receive further compensation depending on the paid amount and the conditions set out in the insurance contract. This conception does not entirely conform to the basic principle of compensation deriving from the liability for damages, the essence of which is that the claimant needs to be reinstated to such a situation as if the damage had not occurred. The entity liable for the damage is obligated to restore the original state *(in integrum restitutio)*. Obviously, the phrase *original state* has a literal and also a metaphorical meaning. If the passenger recovers the object stolen from their checked baggage, the original state is reinstated, indeed. However, if the passenger's baggage is destroyed, restitution of the former state becomes impossible. In this case, the damaging party indemnifies the caused damage. If the actual damage does not exceed the upper limit, the air carrier indemnifies the damage of the claimant within the limited amount with respect to the extent of the proved damage (Fig. 12.1).

[1]The contracting States prohibit the application of a limiting clause in the relations of contracting and actual carriers *(code-share)* and attach the nullity of the contested part of the contract as a legal consequence of its breach. Montreal Convention (1999), Article 47.

12.1.1 Limited Liability of the Servants and Agents

A lawsuit may be filed vis-à-vis the servant or agent of the air carrier on account of causing damage regulated under the Convention. In that case, the servant or the agent, if they can prove that they acted in the scope of their employment upon the occurrence of damage, shall 'be entitled to avail themselves of the conditions and limits of liability which are applicable under the Convention to the carrier whose servant or agent they are'. If it is proved that the servant or agent did not act in the scope of their employment, that 'prevents the limits of liability from being invoked in accordance with this Convention' (Article 43). In that case, the aggregate of the amounts recoverable from the carrier, its servants, and agents shall not exceed the limits stipulated under the Convention.

'In relation to the carriage performed by the actual carrier, the aggregate of the amounts recoverable from that carrier and the contracting carrier, and from their servants and agents acting within the scope of their employment, shall not exceed the highest amount which could be awarded against either the contracting carrier or the actual carrier under the Convention, but neither the contracting nor the actual carrier shall be liable for a sum in excess of the limit applicable to that person' (Article 44). Thus, the plaintiff cannot claim more compensation from the servant or agent than from the air carrier itself.

If an action is brought against a servant or agent of the carrier arising out of damage to which the Convention relates, such servant or agent, if they prove that they acted within the scope of their employment, shall be entitled to avail themselves of the conditions and limits of liability which the carrier itself is entitled to invoke under the Convention. The aggregate of the amounts recoverable from the carrier, its servants, and agents, in that case, shall not exceed the said limits [Article 30 (1–2)]. Such a case emerges, for instance, when the servant does not hinder the irregular act of the passenger; despite the display of the 'fasten your seatbelts' warning, they allow the passengers to walk on board, or upon disembarking, they navigate the passengers in the wrong direction. It is not necessary that bodily injury ensues since the manifestation of conscious negligence in itself entails liability without the occurrence of the result. At the same time – in respect of the carriage of cargo – the previous provisions [Article 30 (1–2)] shall not apply 'if it is proved that the damage resulted from an act or omission of the servant or agent done with intent to cause damage or recklessly and with knowledge that damage would probably result' [Article 30 (3)].

12.1.2 Breaking the Limited Liability

If the plaintiff breaks through the limited liability of the air carrier related to delay and damage to baggage (in the case of cargo, this limit is unbreakable), the court obligates the damaging party to indemnify the total damage. Limited liability may be broken by the plaintiff if they prove that the 'damage resulted from an act or omission of the carrier, its servants or agents, done with intent to cause damage, or recklessly and with knowledge that damage would probably result. So far as the servant or agent of the air carrier commits such an act or omission, the air carrier is fully liable provided that it is also proved that such servant or agent was acting within the scope of its employment' [Article 22 (5)]. Such a case arises, for example, if the pilots purposefully carry out an irregular flight manoeuvre, lands on the wrong runway, or, despite the weather conditions, does not opt for an alternate airport.

The air carrier may resort to the enforcement of a claim vis-à-vis a third person if, according to its judgement, the person contributed to the occurrence of the damage. 'Nothing in the Convention shall prejudice the question whether a person liable for damage in accordance with its provisions has a right of recourse against any other person' (Article 37).

12.2 Unlimited Liability

The contracting States intend to create an equilibrium in the damaging party's and claimant's systems of interests because in the beginnings (see, the Warsaw regime), it shared the risk disproportionately by limiting the liability deriving from causing damage between the service-providing air carrier and the parties using the service. In the course of time, this equilibrium loosened because the low amounts of damages deriving from limited liability generated dissatisfaction, and the limitation of liability hindered the achievement of the unification of private law on an international level. The cause of this was that the system of limited liability could not handle diverging economic circumstances in a righteous manner. This situation was solved by the treaty-maker via returning to the 'Japanese Initiative' of 1992 and the IATA Intercarrier Agreements (1995–1996) [see, Part II, Chap. 8. 2.6-7], which introduced unlimited liability on the level of air carriers in the scope of accidents sustained by passengers.

Unlimited liability for damages has a lot of advantages. The principal advantage is that the extent of the compensation reflects the loss properly because it takes the actual loss of property into account, and thereby, it mitigates the actual damage much more fairly. Furthermore, it also encourages the parties to agree on the amount of the compensation as soon as possible, even in an out-of-court settlement, because the contracting States do not intend to provide scope for lengthy litigious disputes. The institution of unlimited liability was elevated to an international level by the Convention; thereby, it made a momentous impact on the more expeditious conduct of legal proceedings and on the process of the conclusion of an agreement between the parties.

The Convention establishes the unlimited liability of the air carrier for accidents sustained by passengers. The air carrier honours its liabilities in a two-step system of liability for damages.

Step I

'For damages – arising under [Article 17 (1)] – not exceeding 128,821 SDR for each passenger, the air carrier *shall not be able to exclude* or *limit* its liability' [Article 21 (1)]. This implies that up to 128,821 SDR (ca. 170,000 USD), the liability of the air carrier is absolute, thus, it is unconditionally liable. The liability prevails from the moment the accident occurs pursuant to the Convention. Upon the establishment of absolute liability, it does not matter whether the damage was caused by the air carrier, its servant or agent, the ground service provider, or another passenger. What matters is the following:

- *accident* happened and it was proved;
- the accident causes *damage*;
- the damage caused is *death* or *bodily injury* (exceptionally mental injury); and
- the accident occurs *on board* the aircraft or during *the operations of embarking* or *disembarking*.

For the establishment of absolute liability, it is necessary that a cause-effect relationship exists between the accident and the deriving damage. If the occurrence of the accident is proved and the air carrier cannot exonerate itself from liability, it shall honour liability by all means, even if it did not cause the accident. On the basis of the provision, the claimant shall receive compensation as a civic right, and they do not have to, in a strained manner, assert the presumed or real fault of the air carrier, the flight crew, the manufacturer, or somebody else in a post-accident state of mind. It is also reassuring that in the case of the death of the passenger, the plaintiff, in the interest of positioning themselves better in the lawsuit, does not have to know the details of what and exactly how the accident happened. Notwithstanding, it is not permitted to make unfounded and false accusations vis-à-vis the air carrier. In addition, by enforcing its right to recourse, the air carrier can take up the position of the plaintiff vis-à-vis the claimant.

If the emerged damage is less than the amount of 128,821 SDR, as a matter of course, the proved share of the damage is indemnified. The amount of 128,821 SDR indicated in the first step is a legal technical limitation, however, it does not mean that the liability of the air carrier is limited. By the introduction of that barrier, the contracting States purported to favour the air carrier because in the case of claims for damages exceeding that amount, although shouldering the burden of proof, the air carrier has the opportunity to exonerate itself.

Step II

The air carrier shall not be liable for damages—arising under Article 17 (1)—to the extent that they exceed, for each passenger, 128,821 SDR if the carrier 'proves that:

- such damage was *not* due to the negligence or other wrongful act or omission of the carrier or its servants or agents; or
- such damage was *solely* due to the negligence or other wrongful act or omission of a third party' [Article 21 (2)].

In this stage, if the extent of the damage exceeds the amount of 128,821 SDR, the air carrier still owes unlimited liability, but at this point, it has the opportunity to exonerate itself from liability. The burden of proof is shouldered by the air carrier; it needs to prove that the circumstances resulting in its exoneration prevail. This is a heavy burden because even a minor negligence by the air carrier favours the plaintiff. The lawmaker shifts this burden on the defendant, consciously setting out from the basic tenet of Roman law asserting that anybody who affirms something is obligated to prove it *(affirmanti incumbit probatio)*. The exoneration of the air carrier is a difficult task because the court, during its proceedings, on the basis of the legal principle of 'the thing speaks for itself' *(res ipsa loquitur)*, deems the cause of the damage to be almost proved proceeding from the occurrence of the event of damage in itself.

Pursuant to the above-mentioned provision of the Convention, the air carrier may be exonerated if it proceeded appropriately or the damage was caused solely by a third party. The term 'solely' delimits the chances of the air carrier rigorously, while the negligence, other wrongful act, or omission of a third party is difficult to prove from the outset (especially if the airplane was destroyed).

In case the actual damage exceeds the amount of 128,821 SDR and the air carrier cannot exonerate itself, the parties shall commence negotiations. The plaintiff needs to prove their pecuniary damage (e.g., medical and funeral costs, the loss of the source of income and salary, the number of dependants, etc.). Depending on national legal systems, the loss of parental help or partner, the loss of the enjoyment of life as well as the shortening of life prospects and life expectancy may be calculated as non-pecuniary damage. Thus, in the case of a young passenger who was otherwise the breadwinner, the material damage may be higher for the family members than, for example, in the case of a pensioner. If the "person" in the accident loses their ability to work, their former income needs to be considered; therefore, for example, a surgeon who suffered an accident may receive a higher amount of compensation than a public servant.

Chapter 13
Compensation

If the system of criteria under the Convention is in accordance with the elements of the facts of the legal case, the court adjudicates the claim for damages. The objective of the contracting States is unambiguous: may the verdict or the out-of-court settlement be made in any part of the world, the claimants may expect, with regard to the proved damage, the similar judgement everywhere provided that the Convention is applicable. The establishment and justification of liability are crucial elements of the judgement. If the liability of the air carrier is established, the court obligates the air carrier to provide indemnity for the caused damage. The exact amount of the indemnity is calculated and established by the court with regard to the limits stipulated under the Convention and to all the circumstances of the case.

The amount of the indemnity to be paid are as follows:

- in the case of limited liability it will be generally the same amount owing to the uniform system of liability for damages in the cases adjudged pursuant to the Convention;
- in the case of unlimited liability (if an accident happens or the claimant breaks through limited liability), it will always be different depending on the unique circumstances and judicial practice.

Several legal solutions (already introduced in this book) can be found in the Convention, which promote proper indemnification and the protection of clients' interests. Related to the present chapter we mentioned that the upper limit of limited liability follows the inflation (if justified, it is raised at 5-year intervals), in the case of an accident sustained by the passenger, the air carrier is obligated to make an advance payment, the coverage of payments is guaranteed by the mandatorily prescribed insurance, the exchange of the indemnity determined in SDR into national currency is regulated under the Convention.

A. Sipos, *International Aviation Law*, https://doi.org/10.1007/978-3-031-39066-1_13

13.1 The Measure of Compensation

It is highly important for the concerned parties in the action for damages what scope of pecuniary damage or non-pecuniary damage the compensation pertains to and under what conditions it will be paid. The contracting States define neither the concept of damage, nor the method of compensation. At the same time, the claimant needs to know what claim for damages they can enforce and which parts of the pecuniary or non-pecuniary elements of the damage they may demand from the damaging party.

- *Pecuniary damage* includes the decrease in value actually determinable in the property of the claimant, including missed income and reasonable costs. It does not include the surplus value attributed to an object for moral or emotional reasons, to wit, the so-called affection value *(pretium affectionis)*, because only the market value of the object is decisive. Let us think, for example, of the memorabilia received from ancestors or loved ones, inherited belongings, and adventurously acquired objects, which are as worthy as treasures for those concerned.
- *Non-pecuniary damage* cannot be measured in finances; thus, it implies injury to the so-called personal rights (e.g., the right to safety, life, dignity, or good reputation). Thus, the grievance fee is destined to compensate for the legal consequences of damage which do not influence directly the property of the claimant, but in other ways they make an impact on the claimant's prospective life.

The contracting States essentially shift the settlement on the scope of rules pertaining to damage to national law, therefore, its substantiation and the determination of the method of compensation are accomplished on a national level.[1] In order to avoid unwelcome differences deriving from national regulations, the courts endeavour to construe the concept of damage uniformly. The Vienna Convention on the Law of Treaties (1969)[2] sets forth, in the general rules of interpretation, that international treaties are to be construed in good faith, in the context of their phrases, according to their ordinary meaning, as well as with

[1] Points 16–22 of the Motion no. C–63/09 of Judge Ján Mazák, the Slovakian Advocate General of the Court of Justice of the European Union on 26 January 2010 in the case *Axel Walz v. Clickair S. A.*

[2] Vienna Convention on the Law of Treaties (1969), [Part III, Section 3, Article 31 (1)].

regard to their subject-matter and purpose. In interpreting the concept of damage,[3] the Court of Justice of the European Union, in the case of *Axel Walz versus Clickair*,[4] initiated by the plaintiff by reason of the loss of his baggage, concluded that the Montreal Convention, which defines the limitation of the liability of the air carrier, needs to be interpreted in such a way as to include indemnification of both pecuniary and non-pecuniary damages. The judge's interpretation elucidated that under the Convention, the States Parties did not intend to interpret the concept of damage differently from the general rules.

At the same time, the contracting States expressly provide that in the case of any action for damages related to the carriage of passengers, baggage, and cargo, however founded, whether under the Convention or in contract or in tort or otherwise, can only be brought subject to the conditions and such limits of liability as are set out in the Montreal Convention. 'In any such action, punitive, exemplary or any other non-compensatory damages shall not be recoverable' (Article 29).

In the *Lukács versus United Airlines* case,[5] the plaintiff wished to set off from Winnipeg, Canada (YWG) to the town of Columbus (CMH) in the United States for a 1-day conference, but because of technical failure on the part of the airline, the flight was cancelled. The airline could provide travelling opportunity for the next day, but the passenger did not make use thereof, since this way he would have been late for the conference. The professor of mathematics raised a claim for damages in the amount of 6080 USD, although he was able to recover the full price of the air ticket, and the airline reimbursed the costs charged by the travel agent as well. He calculated that the missed the opportunities of gaining experience, studying, and research amounting to 5000 USD. The passenger intended to have the

(continued)

[3] In the interpretation of the concept of damage, the Court of Justice of the European Union was supported by a common statement recognised universally by international law elaborated by the International Law Commission of the UN and adopted by the 56th UN General Assembly (2001). Pursuant to international law, in the case of damage deriving from the commission of wrongful acts, the liability of the State is complete and its reparations extend to all "pecuniary and non-pecuniary damage." UN General Assembly Resolution 56/83 of 12 December 2001 corrected by document A/56/49 (Vol. I)/Corr. 4 (Reparation—Article 31. 1. 2.).

[4] *Axel Walz v. Clickair S. A.*, C 179/15, 2010.

[5] *Lukács v. United Airlines, Inc.*, MBCA 111 (CAN LII). November 2009.

damage deriving from psychic anguish refunded at a value of 1000 USD because he missed the never recurring opportunity of professional development offered by the conference because of the 'wrongdoing' of the airline. However, the plaintiff could not substantiate through evidence the (intricately calculable) damage deriving from nuisance and anxiousness. Therefore, the court dismissed the action.

The treaty-maker prohibits the punishment of air carriers, that is, the imposition of punitive damages, by reason of an accident or delay ensuing due to the fault of the airline. In more serious cases (such as accidents), the courts permit the inclusion of the loss of life and the termination of the prospective acquisition of property into the pecuniary damages, while into non-pecuniary damages, they include physical pain, suffering, torment, and in the case of survivors, the loss of pleasure in life.

Flight 191 of Delta Airline (DL), operated by a Lockheed L–1011 TriStar airplane, crashed while landing on the airport in Dallas (DFW) on 2 August 1985 as a consequence of extremely severe *microburst* (windshear).[6] *Microburst* is wind with devastating power, which, by gaining external energy, is directed towards the earth and triggers an unusually strong circular current downwards. Its range may be as extensive as 5 km, and its lifecycle is merely a couple of minutes. It may contain eddies revolving around a horizontal axis, which may reach the power of a tornado, thereby implying exceptional threat to ascending or descending airplanes.[7] In order to compensate the 137 victims coming to grief, the insurance companies deposited 125 million USD. One of the victims was the 47-year-old Estridge D. Philip (1937–1985), who had become famous as the father of the IBM personal computer, whose heir was awarded a compensation of eight million USD.[8]

[6] A *microburst* is generally an intense downward draft, while *windshear* can occur in any direction, any rapid change in the direction and/or speed of the wind. Therefore, every microburst is windshear, but not every windshear is a microburst.

[7] Caracena et al. (1989), pp. 1–35.

[8] Wells and Chadbourne (1992), p. 69.

Lost income	25 yrs x 100,000 USD	2,500,000 USD
Lost services	35 yrs x 10,000 USD	350,000 USD
Loss of inheritance		250,000 USD
Funeral / Burial expenses		15,000 USD
Grief / anguish	Spouse and children	500,000 USD
Lost guidance / care	Children 2 x 250,000 USD	500,000 USD
Loss of care, comfort & companionship	Spouse and children	1,000,000 USD
Deceased's pre-death pain	Suffering approx. 10 minutes	1,000,000 USD
Total Compensatory Damages		**6,205,000 USD**

Fig. 13.1 Compensation for loss of life in the United States

The figure below demonstrates that before the courts of the United States, the family of a 40-year-old man who dies these days in an air accident, leaving behind his beloved wife and two minor children, may expect the compensation below[9] (so far as the man had at his disposal an annual salary of at least 100,000 USD) (Fig. 13.1).

The unequivocal purpose of the contracting States is to provide fair and equitable compensation for everyone concerned and the persons sustaining damage (or their relatives) on the basis of the 'something for something' *(quid pro quo)* principle should really recover "something" in return.

13.1.1 Advance Payments

In the case of aircraft accidents resulting in the death or injury of passengers, the carrier shall, if required by the national law of its country, make advance payments without delay. The party causing damage is obligated to meet *the immediate economic needs* (emerging as a consequence of the accident) of a natural person or persons who are entitled to claim compensation (Article 28). The advance payment covers, for example, in the case of the death of the passenger, the travelling costs of the relative to the place where the accident happened or, in the case of bodily injury, the delivery of the injured passenger and their hospitalisation. Such advance payments in themselves shall not constitute a recognition of liability by the air carrier. If the liability of the air carrier is maintained, the advance payment may be offset against the amount subsequently paid as damages by the carrier. The determination of the amount of advance payment and the elaboration of the detailed rules of the institution devolve on national law. This rule does not pertain to damage to the baggage or cargo.

[9] Harakas (2014), p. 8. (Note that these figures are presented for demonstrative rather than scientific purposes.).

The introduction of advance payment under the Convention is a new element, which was also urged expressly by the European Union in accordance with the provision of 2027/97/EC of the Council on air carrier liability, which in such cases obligates the community air carrier to make an advance payment of 18,096 SDR (ca. 22,000 EUR) without delay.[10] In differing national legal systems there is opportunity for reaching decision on how grave the accident should be to require making the advance payment and on what amount it should equal to be in proportion with the sustained troubles and to cover urgent financial needs. The international introduction of advance payment somewhat injured the spirit of unification since it provided scope for diverging national practice.

If the national law[11] requires making advance payments, the air carrier has to effect the payment to the obligee without their express according claim. The advance payment is legally enforceable, although the payments in practice raise questions. Namely, real relatives may appear, who outstripping each other demand the advance payment, but false relatives may also turn up, who abuse the newly introduced institution. It is not inadvertently a basic requirement that in all cases only subsequently to the identification of the natural entity entitled to compensation may the advance payment be made. If the advance payment is utilized by an unauthorised person, or, the air carrier exonerates itself, and consequently, it is fully exempted from liability, the advance payment is to be refunded, if it is not recovered, it may be revindicated. From the person who was entitled to the advance payment the received amount may not be revindicated.

13.1.2 The Cost of the Proceedings

In the case of the judgement of the award of upper limits of liability for the death or the bodily injury of the passenger or damage to the baggage or cargo shall not prevent the court from awarding, in addition, the whole or part of the court costs and of the other expenses of the litigation incurred by the plaintiff, including interest. At the same time, 'the foregoing provision shall not apply if the amount of the damages awarded by the court, excluding court costs and other expenses of the litigation, does not exceed the amount which the air carrier has offered in writing to the plaintiff within a period of 6 months from the date of the occurrence causing the damage, or before the commencement of the action, if that is later' [Article 22 (6)]. In fact, the rule compels the air carrier to make a proposal to the plaintiff for the amount of

[10] Regulation (EC) No. 889/2002 of the European Parliament and of the Council of 13 May 2002 on air carrier liability in the event of accidents amending Council Regulation (EC) No. 2027/97/EC of 17 October 1997 on air carrier liability with regard to the air carriage of passengers and their baggage. Official Journal HL L 140, 30/05/2002, pp. 2–5.

[11] The reference to "national law" shall be construed as referring to the law of the relevant territorial unit of that State. Montreal Convention [Article 56 (3) *b)*].

compensation. Namely, if the court determines a lower sum than the amount offered by the air carrier, the airline does not have to pay the court costs and other expenses incurred by the plaintiff.

13.1.3 The Conversion of Monetary Units

The currency of Special Drawing Rights (SDR)[12] mentioned and indicated in the Convention is defined by the International Monetary Fund (IMF), freely utilizable by its Members. Conversion into national currencies[13] shall in case of judicial proceedings be made according to the value of such currencies in terms of the Special Drawing Right at the date of the judgement.

- 'The value of the national currency, in terms of the SDR, of a State Party which is a Member of the International Monetary Fund, shall be calculated in accordance with the method of valuation applied by the International Monetary Fund, in effect at the date of the judgement,[14] for its operations and transactions.
- The value of a national currency, in terms of the SDR, of a State Party which is not a Member of the International Monetary Fund, is calculated in a manner determined by that State' [Article 23 (1)].
- Nevertheless, the States that are not Members of the International Monetary Fund and whose law does not permit the application of the conversion from SDR may, at the time of ratification or accession to the Convention, or at any time thereafter, declare a fixed amount for the upper limit of the liability of the air carrier per passenger in judicial proceedings conducted in their territories [Article 23 (2)].

'The monetary unit corresponds to 65.5 mg of gold of millesimal fineness nine hundred'. These sums may be converted, in round up figures, into the national currency concerned, and the conversion of these sums into national currency shall be made according to the law of the State concerned. The above-mentioned calculation and the conversion method shall be made in such manner as to express in the national currency of the State Party as far as possible the same real value for the amounts determined in the Convention. States Parties shall communicate to the Secretary General of ICAO (Depositary) the manner of calculation or the result of the conversion according to the rule of the Convention, when depositing an instrument of ratification, acceptance, approval of or accession to the Convention and whenever there is a change in either [Article 23 (2–3)].

---

[12] *Supra* note at 22 in Part II, Chap. 8.2.5.

[13] The reference to "national currency" shall be construed as referring to the currency of the relevant territorial unit of that State. The Montreal Convention [Article 56 (3) *a)*].

[14] In the case *Ekufu v. Iberia Airlines,* one piece of the checked baggage of the plaintiff arrived after a week's delay and with deficient content. The court obligated the airline to indemnify an amount of 1131 SDR awarded to the plaintiff, the conversion of which to an amount of 1730 USD was made on the day of the judgement. *Ekufu v. Iberia Airlines*, 36 Avi. 15,372 (N.D.Ill.), 2014.

Montreal Convention	1999	After 2019
Damage sustained in case of death or bodily injury of a **passenger**	100,000 SDR/passenger	**128,821** SDR/passenger
Destruction, loss, damage with respect to **checked** and **unchecked baggage**	1000 SDR/passenger	**1288** SDR/passenger
Destruction, loss, damage in relation to the carriage of **cargo**	17 SDR/kg	**22** SDR/kg
Damage with respect to **delay**	4150 SDR/passenger	**5346** SDR/passenger

Fig. 13.2 Change of upper limits

13.1.4 Review of Limits

The contracting States of the Convention prescribe for the Depositary (Secretary General of ICAO) to review the upper limit of compensation determined under the Convention at 5-year intervals. The treaty-maker provides that the first such review has to be effected at the end of the fifth year following the date of entry into force of the Convention. With respect to the fact that the Convention took effect on 4 November 2003, the first such review was carried out in November 2009, thus, the amount of liability determined under the Convention was raised by the States Parties (Fig. 13.2).[15]

The additional review took place in November 2014, but the amounts remained unchanged. In 2019, the contracting States increased the limit by nearly 14 percent. When raising the amounts, the changes in inflation rates are to be considered so that the amounts do not lose their value and problems similar to those with the Warsaw Convention do not occur. 'The measure for the rate of inflation to be used in determining the inflation factor shall be the weighted average of the annual rates of increase or decrease in the Consumer Price Indices of the States whose currencies [the Euro (EUR), the Japanese yen (JPY), the United States Dollar (USD), the British Pound Sterling (GBP), and the Chinese Yuan Renminbi (CNY)] comprise the SDR' [Article 24 (1)].

'If the inflation review concludes that the inflation factor has exceeded 10 percent, the Depositary shall notify the States Parties of a revision of the limits of liability. Any such revision shall become effective 6 months after its notification to the States Parties' [Article 24 (2)]. This process is special in international law, since the Convention is amended so that the consent of the States Parties is not necessary. 'If within 3 months after its notification to the States Parties a majority of the States Parties register their

[15] Inflation Adjustments to Liability Limits Governed by the Montreal Convention Effective, 30 December 2009, 74 Fed. Register 59017, 16 November 2009. 74 Fed. Register 59017, 16 November 2009. 2019 Revised Limits of Liability Under the Montreal Convention of 1999. (www.icao.int/secretariat/legal/pages/2019_Revised_Limits_of_Liability_Under_the_MC).

disapproval, the revision shall not become effective, and the Depositary shall refer the matter to a meeting of the States Parties.' In such a case, an extraordinary Diplomatic Conference is convened, which the Secretary General of ICAO is entitled to initiate. If the revision is adopted, 'the Depositary shall immediately notify all States Parties of the coming into force of any revision'. The revision procedure shall be applied at any time provided that one-third of the States Parties express a desire to that effect and upon the condition that the inflation factor has exceeded 30% since the previous revision. Subsequent reviews will take place at 5-year intervals, or if the revision procedure took place in a different period, the next revision will start at the end of the fifth year following the date of the review [Article 24 (1–3)].

As a matter of course, the review is not affected if certain air carriers apply unilaterally higher limits of liability than the upper limits stipulated under the Convention or do not prescribe any limitation of liability in the contracts of carriage concluded with the passengers or consignors.

13.2 Insurance

Generally, insurances are divided into 'hull' and 'liability'.

- Hull insurance provides coverage to the owner of the aircraft in the case of physical damage or loss of the aircraft as a result of various perils (including war and terrorism).
- The air carrier insurance for liability provides limited coverage for damage to the property of third parties on the ground and it also covers liability for passenger death or bodily injury (accident) and other damages related to the passenger or the consignor (baggage, cargo) in international carriage.[16]

---

[16]The main forms of insurance encompass the body of the aircraft, the passenger, the cargo and liability. (1) *Hull insurance covers the owners and operators of aircraft against losses arising from the physical damage to the aircraft. It has two types:* (a) *Total Loss Only* (TLO), which is a cheaper form of insurance and pertains to the insurance of old aircraft bodies, but only total damage is considered to be an insurance event; (b) *All Risks Insurance is more expensive, and it is applied to modern airplanes, but in this case the insurance company assumes the indemnification of all damage to the body of the aircraft.* (Both include war and terrorism insurance.); (2) *Third Party Liability* (TPL) gives rise to liability insurance vis-a-vis persons on the ground or on board relating to the body of the aircraft.; (3) *Ground Risk Only* (GRO) is the reduced risk application of the Hull and TPL forms of insurance for the case when the aircraft is not in flight (e.g., it is under repair).; (4) *Passengers Legal Liability* (PLL) is a liability insurance related to the aircraft, which is purchased on the basis of the number of passenger seats for the protection of the passengers.; (5) *Mail and Cargo Liability* is the liability insurance of the consignment, which is generally purchased on the basis of the weight-capacity of the aircraft.; (6) *Ground Handling Insurance* provides coverage for bodily injuries and damages to property occasioned during ground service.; (7) *Aviation Products Liability for Manufacturing and Design Defect* is a product liability insurance pertaining to the body of the aircraft, which is purchased by the manufacturer for the coverage of the cases of bodily injury and damage to property proceeding from the defect of the aircraft or its parts, and this defect can be traced back to manufacturing, assembly, repairs or planning.

The Warsaw Convention does not require air carriers to be insured. The Warsaw system follows the limited liability concept; therefore, the insurance cost was calculable and could be planned. As opposed, the Montreal Convention, although provides limited liability (e.g., for cargo or baggage destruction, loss, damage or delay), it ensures unlimited liability benefitting the passenger in the case of accident (Article 17). The treaty-maker places the burden of proof on the plaintiff, thus, if there is an accident, and especially, if the claims exceed 128,821 SDR, the air carriers face increased insurance costs, which is now unavoidable and legally required.[17] For this reason, the requirement of purchasing adequate insurance appears as a new element in the Montreal Convention.[18]

States Parties shall require their carriers to maintain *adequate insurance* covering their liability under the Convention. A carrier may be required by the State Party into which it operates to furnish evidence that it maintains adequate insurance covering its liability under this Convention (Article 50).

Since, in practice, liability insurance is mandatory in the industry, without which an air carrier may not operate, the new rule, in some respects, seems somewhat meaningless.[19] Meaningless, since the air transport industry is governed by a developed system of rules concerning insurance, which is extraordinarily rigorous and is covered by some insurance companies interested in air transport, based on serious traditions and enormous capital. At the same time, the treaty-maker touches a sore spot, because in vain do the air carriers take out liability insurance so that instead of them the insurance companies shall be liable to an extent determined under the contract, if even this is insufficient in some cases.

[17] In terms of liability for baggage (1288 SDR) or cargo (22 SDR/kg) the liability is limited, unless the passenger or consignor has made a "special declaration of interest" [Article 22 (2–3)].

[18] In private international law, the mandatory insurance requirement is acknowledged by the Rome Convention (1933) on Unification of Certain Rules Relating to Damage Caused by Foreign Aircraft to Third Parties on the Surface, and its successor, the Rome Convention (1952) on Damage Caused by Foreign Aircraft to Third Parties on the Surface (ICAO Doc 7364) and also contains provisions stipulated by its successor, the "General Risks Convention" 2009 (ICAO Doc 9919). There is a regulation to ensure a proper minimum level of insurance to cover the liability of air carriers (operators) in respect of passengers, baggage, cargo and third parties. Regulation (EC) No 785/2004 of the European Parliament and of the Council of 21 April 2004 on insurance requirements for air carriers and aircraft operators. OJ L 138, 30.4.2004, pp. 1–6.; Furthermore, there are provisions regarding insurance in bilateral Air Services Agreements (ASAs) as well.

[19] Whalen (2000), p. 25.

After the terrorist attack against the United States on 11 September 2001, the community of international air insurance companies, with a limited number of members, was invaded by demands for payments, which was unforeseen before. This led to the uniform nullification by the insurance companies of the clause 'coverage for violent acts' without exception, enforcing their right guaranteed under the policies, with a 7-day deadline. For the reinstatement of this coverage into the policies, all airlines in the world were obligated to pay 1.25 USD/passenger extra charge for each carried passenger. This amount implied considerable burden for the industrial performers in the period economic situation, therefore, the States, supporting their airlines, guaranteed to be liable for the compensation of damage caused to third parties deliberately by the airplanes of the designated airlines in the case of unlikely "terrorist and wartime" events.

The contracting States leave the precise interpretation of adequate insurance open. Thus, adequate insurance may be interpreted differently by the States. Although, the treaty-maker's intention is clear: the provision of coverage for the occurrence of any kind of accident (even for unlimited liability) by the amount of the insurance. The raise of the coverage implies higher insurance charges for air carriers in less developed countries in comparison with air carriers in more developed countries, which have modern fleets and excellent accident indices. The treaty-maker extends the rule, since it authorises all States Parties to require the air carrier operating in its territory to adduce evidence of disposing of adequate insurance to cover its liability proceeding from the Convention. In practice, the aviation authorities of the States attach the issuance of operating licenses to the attestation of the existence of liability insurance. The existing, valid, and adequate insurance provides protection against risks, furthermore, protecting the parties in contractual relations, at the same time, it is definitely a safety issue which is a number one priority for the insurance companies as well. Therefore, the States have an outstanding role in the examination of the existence of insurance and of adherence to all other legal requirements in their supervisory competence.

References

Caracena F, Holle RL, Doswell CA (1989) Microbursts: a Handbook for Visual Identification. US Department of Commerce, pp 1–35

Harakas AJ (2014) Aviation Issues in the United States. p 8

Wells AT, Chadbourne BD (1992) Introduction to Aviation Insurance and Risk Management. Melbourne, Krieger Pub Co, p 69

Whalen TJ (2000) The New Warsaw Convention: the Montreal Convention. Air Space Law 25(1): 25

Chapter 14
The Air Carrier's Liability for Damage Caused to Third Parties on the Surface

14.1 The Rome Convention (1952)

In the universal history of international civil aviation, it has occurred several times that the aircraft in flight caused the death or injury of persons on the surface. The States have obligations with respect to the protection of the lives and safety of air passengers and their properties, which is a rightful expectation of society. The protection also encompasses third parties, being in an exceptional situation from the viewpoint of law. Obviously, the chance of the affectedness of third parties is a lot stronger if the aircraft hits people on the ground. The highest number of fatal victims on the surface was demanded by the terrorist attack of 11 September 2001, when officially 2977 persons died and thousands of persons got injured. Previously, on the surface of Lockerbie (Sherwood Crescent) 11 persons fell victim to the terrorist attack on the flight of the Pan Am Airline (21 December 1988). The cargo plane of *Africa Air* (Antonov-32) crashed into a market made of wood and iron shacks, killing more than 300 people on ground in Kinshasa, Zaire,[1] on 8 February 1996. Then, the disaster of a Concorde airplane (25 July 2000) demanding four fatal victims on the surface ensued, and subsequently, 44 victims lost their lives due to the crash of the *EL AL* cargo shipping airplane, which fell onto residential buildings 13 km away from Schiphol airport (4 October 2002).[2] The list is not complete, for example, 35 persons died under such circumstances in 2017;[3] thus, the enumerated incidents demonstrate adequately that third persons on the surface are really exposed to danger.

The air carrier is liable for the damage caused to passengers during international carriage pursuant to the rules of liability set forth under the Montreal Convention (1999), the legal grounds of which is the contractual relationship established

[1] Now, this State is called the Democratic Republic of Congo.

[2] Mauritz (2003), pp. 1–3.

[3] Supra note 15 at Part I, Introduction 1.1.

A. Sipos, *International Aviation Law*, https://doi.org/10.1007/978-3-031-39066-1_14

between the parties (in which the passenger voluntarily accepts the risks deriving from the carriage), however, the third party sustaining damage due to an incident is not subject to a legal relationship with the operator of the aircraft causing the damage. The third party is an external, innocent victim of the incident who did not take risks or is not involved in the process of carriage since they stay on the surface, nevertheless, they become the victims of an activity qualified as dangerous operation.

The *Rome Convention on Damage Caused by Foreign Aircraft to Third Parties on the Surface* (1952)[4] and its amendment, the Montreal Protocol (1978),[5] provide for the rules of third-party liability. Merely 51 States have ratified the Rome Convention. The major reasons for under-ratification were that the liability of the operator of the aircraft for damages was restricted to a low and limited amount, the number of the optional jurisdictions proved to be low, and national regulations pertaining to such tort guaranteed essentially better conditions and protection to injured third parties claiming compensation.

The scope of application of the Rome Convention encompasses damage caused by civil aircraft in flight, damage by aircraft above the high seas, and damage to third persons on the surface caused by aircraft, persons, or falling objects in the territory of States Parties. The damage needs to be occasioned in the territory of a State Party by an aircraft registered in another State Party [Article 23]. The Convention encompasses aircraft in flight and an aircraft is considered to be in flight from the moment power is applied for the purpose of actual take-off (from switching the engines to maximum performance for the purpose of take-off) until the moment the landing run ends (until taxiing) [Article 1 (2)]. The contracting States obligate the operator of the aircraft to assume liability vis-à-vis a third party. The person who uses the aircraft at the time of causing the damage qualifies as an operator (the registered owner of the aircraft is considered to be the operator as long as it is proved that another person is the operator) [Article 2 (3)]. The Convention is based on the principle of absolute (Article 1) and limited liability [Articles 3, 4, 7]. The liability of the operator is established if, owing to the accident, the damage is caused by the aircraft to the life or property of a third party, which means that the

[4]The predecessor of the Rome Convention (1952) was the *International Convention for the Unification of Certain Rules relating to Damage Caused by Aircraft to Third Parties on the Surface*, opened for signature at Rome on the 29 May 1933. The Rome Convention (1933) did not receive broad recognition and was expressly superseded by the Rome Convention (1952) (Article 29). The Convention on Damage Caused by Foreign Aircraft to Third Parties on the Surface (1952), namely the Rome Convention (ICAO Doc 7364), was then replaced by the General Risks Convention (2009).: ICAO Doc 9919 Convention on Compensation for Damage Caused by Aircraft to Third Parties, Montreal, 2 May 2009.

[5]The Montreal Protocol (1978) raised the low amounts of limited liability for damages adjusted proportionately to the mass of the aircraft stipulated under the Rome Convention, but it was ratified only by 12 countries. ICAO Doc 8932. Protocol to Amend the Convention on Damage Caused by Foreign Aircraft to Third Parties on the Surface as adopted and signed at Montreal on 23 September 1978. The Protocol took effect on 25 July 2002.

aircraft operator will be absolutely liable for damages even if it is proven that the flight crew did not commit fault but was unable to prevent the accident or that the duty of proceeding with care was fulfilled.[6]

In case the incident occurs in a State not having ratified the Convention, the national law is applicable upon the adjudication of damage caused to third parties. In this area, the States (as treaty-makers) did not manage to create an international regime of liability for damages to be followed universally, although they did their utmost to balance the rights of the operator of the aircraft and of the claimants as well as to unify the liability system under private law in these cases.

14.2 The General Risks Convention and the Unlawful Interference Compensation Convention (2009)

In August 2000, the ICAO Legal Committee, at its 31st Session, put the reformation of the Rome Convention on its agenda. In June 2001, the ICAO Secretariat sent a questionnaire to the Member States in connection with the Convention. The events of 11 September gave a severe boost to rethinking the Convention. The contracting Parties explicated that via the amendment, they intended to make the Convention 'attractive' and thereby achieve the accession of the States in great numbers, which is a basic condition for the predominance of an internationally uniform system of liability for damages. In the professional work commencing on an international level, the majority espoused the creation of a completely new Convention instead of amendments and supplements.[7] Eventually, the ICAO Council and the Secretariat, in close cooperation with each other, established the workgroup, which laid the foundations for two completely new conventions.

At the International Air Law Conference held in Montreal, the Member States discussed the drafts of the new Conventions, and on 2 May 2009, they signed two Conventions:

1. Convention on Compensation for Damage Caused by Aircraft to Third Parties,[8] which is called the 'General Risks Convention'; and
2. Convention on Compensation for Damage to Third Parties Resulting from Acts of Unlawful Interference Involving Aircraft,[9] which is called the 'Unlawful Interference Compensation Convention'.

---

[6] Bartsch (2018), p. 134.

[7] Report of the *Latin-American Air Law Association* (ALADA), September 2004.

[8] ICAO Doc 9919 Convention on Compensation for Damage Caused by Aircraft to Third Parties, done at Montreal, 2 May 2009.; Two New Treaties Adopted by International Conference on Air Law. *ICAO News Release – PIO,* 12 May 2009. (www.icao.int).

[9] ICAO Doc 9920 Convention on Compensation for Damage to Third Parties Resulting from Acts of Unlawful Interference Involving Aircraft, done at Montreal on 2 May 2009.

The latter Convention makes use of the same terms, and its legal institutions are similar to those in the foundational General Risks Convention, but there is an essential difference between them. Namely, the Unlawful Interference Compensation Convention establishes the International Civil Aviation Compensation Fund, the purpose of which is the reinforcement of securing a blanket amount of a maximum of 3 billion SDR (approx. 4.3 billion USD) per event, thereby raising the limit of liability for damages caused by the air carrier, bearing absolute liability in cases subject to the scope of the Convention. The event occurs if the damage was caused by an aircraft in flight via acts of unlawful interference. In this case, the compensation for the damage ensues via the supplementary compensation mechanism. The absolute liability shouldered by the air carrier and the raised upper limit of liability determined under the Convention guarantee that the claimants falling prey to terrorist attacks gain access to higher amounts of compensation and can enforce their claims for damages more effectively in the future.

The General Risks Convention modernised with time replaced the Rome Convention applicable if the damage is caused in the territory of a State Party by an in-flight civil aircraft discharging international carriage. The rules of the Convention are also applicable to non-international flights if the State Party extends the rules of the Convention to domestic flights and declares this fact to the Depositary (the Secretary General of ICAO) [Article 2 (1–2)]. The Convention is applicable to the death or bodily injury of a third party, or exceptionally, to mental injuries if they are caused by a psychiatric illness probably resulting from bodily injury, and to the damage to the property of the claimant. The Convention is applicable to environmental damage (with the exception of nuclear damage) on condition that the claim for damages is enforceable pursuant to the law of the State Party in the territory of which the damage occurred [Article 3 (5)].

The damage to third parties caused by the aircraft in flight may not be a result of purposeful unlawful conduct. The Convention further on makes the operator of the civil aircraft liable, which has absolute (objective) responsibility and limited liability for the damage caused by the aircraft in flight. The IATA airlines espoused the maintenance of limited liability for damages because, this way, the protection by the State, secured under an international treaty, guaranteed that an airline does not go bankrupt by reason of its lack of capacity to meet the claims for damages arising because of terrorist acts, not mentioning the fact that terrorist acts are directed not against the airlines themselves but principally against the States. The indemnification of the damage is practicable if, owing to the accident, the third party dies or gets injured (including psychic injury as well if it has bodily consequences) furthermore, if material and environmental damages ensue on the surface. At the same time, the Convention does not include the regulation of nuclear damage, punitive or other non-compensatory indemnity, or compensation exceeding the actual amount of damage, and damage directly resulting from armed conflict or civil disturbances.

The treaty-maker defines several concepts: for example, it circumscribes the concept of maximum mass as a new element [Article 1 *e)*], which has significance in the calculation of the limits of liability since the heavier the aircraft that causes

Aircraft having a maximum mass of 500 kg or less	**750,000 SDR**
Aircraft having a maximum mass of more than 500 kg but not exceeding 1,000 kg	**1,500,000 SDR**
Aircraft having a maximum mass of more than 1,000 kg but not exceeding 2,700 kg	**3,000,000 SDR**
Aircraft having a maximum mass of more than 2,700 kg but not exceeding 6,000 kg	**7,000,000 SDR**
Aircraft having a maximum mass of more than 6,000 kg but not exceeding 12,000 kg	**18,000,000 SDR**
Aircraft having a maximum mass of more than 12,000 kg but not exceeding 25,000 kg	**80,000,000 SDR**
Aircraft having a maximum mass of more than 25,000 kg but not exceeding 50,000 kg	**150,000,000 SDR**
Aircraft having a maximum mass of more than 50,000 kg but not exceeding 200,000 kg	**300,000,000 SDR**
Aircraft having a maximum mass of more than 200,000 kg but not exceeding 500,000 kg	**500,000,000 SDR**
Aircraft having a maximum mass of more than 500,000 kg	**700,000,000 SDR**

Fig. 14.1 The upper limit of damage inflicted on third parties

damage is, the larger the compensation the claimant may expect is. The maximum mass is the maximum certificated take-off mass of the aircraft, which is considered since by reason of the fuel consumption of the aircraft, it may lose as much as 70 tons from its weight [for instance, the Boeing 747 (Jumbo Jet)[10] on a London–New York route]. An aircraft is considered to be 'in flight' at any time from the moment all its external doors are closed following embarkation or loading until the moment any such door is opened for disembarkation or unloading [Article 1 *c)*] (Fig. 14.1).

The amounts are to be understood per events and aircraft. The Convention obligates the operator of the aircraft to make advance payments for persons sustaining damage or their relatives in order to meet their immediate economic needs (Article 8).

For an event causing damage, the liability of the operator shall not exceed the limit of 700,000,000 SDR (about 1 billion USD) based on the mass of the aircraft involved [Article 4 *a)–j)*]. The amounts follow inflation since the rules of the Convention facilitate the review of the limits of liability. The right to compensation shall be extinguished if an action is not brought within 2 years from the date of the event that caused the damage (Article 19).

The General Risks Convention is not in effect yet; its entry into force requires ratification by 35 States. When this ensues, the new Convention will replace the Rome Convention and its amendment with respect to the acceded countries. The structure and the legal institutions of the Convention, although they settle varied life circumstances and pertain to different legal entities, undoubtedly resemble the system of rules of the Montreal Convention, which has created uniformity successfully. Will the new Convention be successful with respect to the number of

[10]The Boeing 747 airplane needs top off its tanks at just over a total of 170,325 litres. As a consequence of the COVID–19 pandemic, the "Queen of the Skies" was withdrawn from traffic by most airlines, and it was replaced by more economical airplanes with two engines. The Boeing 747 is unarguably the most impressive and inspirational work of art—call it industrial art, if you please—ever produced by commercial aviation. *Flight International*: Retirements, Jumbo Regrets. BA, Qantas Bid Farewell to "Queen of the Skies". 28 July–3 August 2020, p. 5.; Smith (2018), pp. 31, 44.

accessions? It is not likely since the higher and fair amounts of limited liability and the adequate number of forums of jurisdiction secured for the claimants, as well as the new legal institutions supporting mainly the third party may be ineffective, provided that the majority of sovereign States still deem that the adjudication of the cases of tort inflicted by a civil aircraft in flight vis-à-vis a third party is more suitable and fairer pursuant to the rules of national law.

References

Bartsch R (2018) International Aviation Law, a Practical guide. 2nd edn., Routledge, p 134

Mauritz AJ (2003) Liability of the Operators and Owners of Aircraft for Damage Inflicted to Persons and Property on the Surface. Leiden University, Maastricht, pp 1–3

Smith P (2018) Cockpit Confidential: Everything you need to know about air travel: questions, answers, and reflections. Sourcebooks, pp 31, 44

Chapter 15
The Liability of Interests in Mobile Equipment

In the sharpened competition in the global world, we can accept responsibility solely via the rational and joint dismantling of obstacles and regulatory differences deriving from diverse social, economic, and legal systems. The comprehensive international unification in the relations of public law and private law has outstanding importance. With respect to the fact that the rules concerning economic rights, registration and ownership requirements vary significantly from country to country,[1] the contracting States of the Vienna Convention (1980)[2] on Contracts for the International Sale of Goods removed 'ships, vessels, hovercraft and *aircraft*' from its scope [Article 2 *e)*]. This deficiency was rectified by the Convention adopted in Cape Town on 16 November 2001, which laid the foundations of a new, uniform legal system of trade.

15.1 The Cape Town Convention and its Aircraft Equipment Protocol (2001)

The Institute of UNIDROIT promoting the unification of private international law treaties,[3] the ICAO Council, and its Legal Committee (LC) jointly drafted the Cape Town Convention on *International Interests in Mobile Equipment* and its Protocol

[1]For example, in the United Kingdom, the Sale of Goods Act (1979); in France, the Code Civil and the Code in Civil Aviation; in the United States, the Uniform Commercial Code apply.

[2]United Nations Convention on Contracts for the International Sale of Goods. Vienna, 1980. Its entry into force: 1 January 1988. The international treaty known as the Vienna Convention was elaborated by the United Nations Commission on International Trade Law (UNCITRAL), the legal organisation of the United Nations established for the legal unification of international trade.

[3]The International Institute for the Unification of Private Law (UNIDROIT) is an independent intergovernmental organisation with its seat in Rome, which studies the possibilities and methods of the harmonisation of private law, in particular of commercial law. The Institute founded in 1926 operates on the basis of its Statute under a multilateral agreement concluded in 1940. Its purposes

A. Sipos, *International Aviation Law*, https://doi.org/10.1007/978-3-031-39066-1_15

on *Matters Specific to Aircraft Equipment*[4] attached to the Convention. Besides the Protocol on aircraft, three other Protocols are integral to the Convention: the Railway Rolling Stock Protocol (2007), the Space Assets Protocol (2012), and the Mining, Agricultural, and Construction Equipment Protocol (2019).

The purpose of the intergovernmental, multilateral Cape Town Convention was the establishment of a system necessary for the creation of an independent, internationally acknowledged, and legally protected interest via the institution of a transboundary legal regulation, which protects international interests in valuable mobile equipment and the associated rights. The protection is due to the holder, which assigns the use of its valuable mobile equipment (airplane or helicopter) to another party.

In national legal systems, the regulation of such transactions is quite complicated and accurate, which aggravates the validation of an interest established in one country in another country. In the majority of European States, the main problem is that getting access to adequate securities for the repayment of credits granted for movables is not always possible. The most effective security formerly had been that the pledged property needed to be assigned to the disposition over the pledgee under hypothecary law. However, in the global economic environment, this legal construction did not in every respect fulfil the expectations of the performers of the business world, therefore, the harmonisation of the rules of various legal solutions securing transactions became imperative.

Hitherto, 86 contracting States and one regional economic organisation, namely, the European Community[5] have acceded to the Cape Town Convention.[6] The

include the unification of the private law of the States and groups of States, studying the methods of legal harmonisation, and the support of the adoption of international treaties (embraced as a result of legal harmonisation) by the Member States. Of the work of regulation carried out in the framework of the UNIDROIT, uniform model laws elaborated for general problems of international commercial treaties stand out, as well as the treaties in connection with representative transactions related to the international sale of movables and with international financial leasing and factoring contracts elaborated for the international unification of the rules of specific kinds of contracts. The Institute of UNIDROIT has 65 Members including the Member States of the European Union. (www.unidroit.org/about-unidroit/overview).

[4]ICAO Doc 9794 Protocol to the Convention on International Interests in Mobile Equipment on Matters Specific to Aircraft Equipment. 16 November 2001.

[5]The preparation of the accession of the Member States of the European Union to international treaties takes place on a community level. On the basis of the authorisation of the Council of Europe, the representative of the European Union concludes international treaties on behalf of the Member States. Thus, on 28 April 2009, the European Community ratified the Cape Town Convention on International Interests in Mobile Equipment and its Protocol on Matters Specific to Aircraft Equipment (Aircraft Equipment Protocol—AEP), which took effect on 1 August 2009, except in Denmark. Council Decision No. 2009/370/EC of 6 April 2009 on the Accession of the European Community to the Convention on International Interests in Mobile Equipment and its Protocol on Matters Specific to Aircraft Equipment were adopted jointly in Cape Town on 16 November 2001.

[6]ICAO Doc 9793 Convention on International Interests in Mobile Equipment, and its Protocol on Matters Specific to Aircraft Equipment, 16 November 2001.

Convention took effect on 1 March 2006. In order to establish real international uniformity, the States that ratified the Cape Town Convention accepted that the Cape Town Convention 'shall prevail over the United Nations Convention on the Assignment of Receivables in International Trade (2001) as it relates to the assignment of receivables, which are associated rights related to international interests in aircraft objects, railway rolling stock and space assets' (Article 45 *bis*).

Besides ratifying the Cape Town Convention, the States also adopted its *Aircraft Equipment Protocol* (2001), which superseded the Rome Convention on the *Unification of Certain Rules Relating to the Precautionary Attachment of Aircraft* (1933),[7] and also replaced the *UNIDROIT Convention on International Financial Leasing* (1988)[8] as it relates to aircraft objects (as defined in Articles XXIV and XXV).

The Aircraft Equipment Protocol (2001) shall, for a contracting State that is Party to the *Geneva Convention on the International Recognition of Rights in Aircraft* (1948),[9] supersede the latter Geneva Convention as defined in the Protocol, it relates to aircraft and aircraft objects. However, with respect to rights or interests not covered or concerned by the Cape Town Convention, the Geneva Convention shall not be superseded (Article XXIII).

The Cape Town Convention and its Protocol shall be read and interpreted together as a single legal instrument, and in case of inconsistency, the rule of the Protocol shall prevail (Article 6). The Cape Town Convention and its Protocol shall be known as the *Convention on International Interests in Mobile Equipment* [Article II (2)]. This international treaty furthers the financing of the valuable equipment of aircraft by securing extraordinarily strong international guarantees while protecting the interests of creditors comprehensively. The wider adoption is absolute desirable due to its 'real benefits in terms of providing for contractual certainty in allowing parties to agree, for example, what constitutes a default, and in terms of allowing the parties certain contractual freedom to agree on remedies in the case of default.'[10]

15.1.1 The Remedies of the Creditor

Aircraft Financing is the 'art' of financing aircraft assets.[11] Aviation experts need to specialise in this field as this is a complex and risky cross-border financing transaction with many jurisdictions involved. In these contractual relations, the Parties can

[7] (www.mcgill.ca/iasl/files/iasl/convention_for_the_unification_of_certain_rules_relating_to_the_precautionary_attachment_of_aircraft_1933.pdf).

[8] Signed in Ottawa on 28 May 1988. (www.unidroit.org/instruments/leasing/convention).

[9] ICAO Doc 7620 Convention on the International Recognition of Rights in Aircraft. 19 June 1948.

[10] Hanley (2021), p. 183.

[11] Scheinberg (2018), p. 1.

purchase from the seller new or used aircraft and can also lease from the lessor new or used aircraft. The involved Parties are mainly the following:

1. The aircraft buyer or lessee (the air carrier/operator);
2. The aircraft seller or lessor (the owner);
3. The aircraft lender (creditor/capital lender).

Aircraft Financing encompasses a multi-billion USD market.[12] Aircraft are definitely very expensive vehicle. The aircraft is defined, from a financial point of view, as a *movable chattel* and a *device* (includes not only the aircraft but also the airframes, engines, parts, and spare parts) of personal *property* with *nationality*. *Nationality* is determined by the place of registration[13] and not by the nationality of the aircraft's owner or operator. ICAO does not focus on the foreign ownership of aircraft but rather on the safety oversight capabilities of the States in which the foreign aircraft are registered. This is the 'genuine link' between an aircraft and its State of registry [see, Part I, Chap. 2.3.5-7)] (for example, in the United States, the aircraft's registration must be renewed every 3 years).

Aircraft Financing is based on mandatorily written contractual relation. Before established, it requires a 'Term Sheet' [Letter of Intent (LOI) or Heads of Agreement or Memorandum of Understanding (MOU)] till the aircraft purchase (sale) or leasing contracts have been written. These are very rigorous contractual relations and are based not only on rights and obligations but also on trust. If one of the parties (mainly the debtor) fails to comply with a contractual obligation expressed or implied, in this case, the suffering party is entitled to some remedies. The remedies are guaranteed to restitute the party that has suffered the loss (mainly the creditor) to the position it would have enjoyed had the other party performed its obligations, or, to restore the creditor to its original position before the breach ensued.

The most significant and complex provisions of the Cape Town Convention[14] pertain to the remedies for the omission of performance, which are applicable if the debtor does not satisfy any of its obligations. In that case, different international remedies attached to 'mobile equipment' protect the interests of the lessor and creditor. The legal consequences applicable against the debtor depend on such remedy. Thus, the seller (or in the case of title reservation, the conditional seller) or the lessor is authorised to denounce the contract and to take possession of the object. The Convention secures concrete remedies for the financial institutions or sellers acting in the contracting States, granting credit for the acquisition of civil aircraft and their engine.

---

[12] According to the survey: "Aviation Asset Management Market to Hit USD 300 billion by 2030, says Global Market Insights Inc.", Global Market Insight, 10 October 2022. (www.globenewswire.com/en/news-release/2022/10/10).

[13] Chicago Convention (1944) Article 17: Aircraft have the nationality of the State in which they are registered. The registration is a unique alphanumeric string that identifies a civil Aircraft. The registration must be transparent, single, valid and subject to various obligations (Rules of the Air, Radio Equipment, Certificates of Airworthiness, Insurances, Taxes, etc.).

[14] Havel and Sanchez (2014), p. 357.

The Malév Hungarian Airline (MA), having been placed under insolvency proceedings, suspended its flying activity at 06:00 a.m. on 3 February 2012. Eighteen modern Boeing 737 Next Generation airplanes, constituting the backbone of the fleet were seized forthwith by the lessor, the International Lease Finance Cooperation (ILFC), with headquarters in Los Angeles, since the airline had defaulted on the lease charges. The lease contracts grant extensive opportunities for the lessor to take possession of its airplane nearly any time (if merely the suspicion arises that the airline will not manage to perform its obligation to make payments in the future is sufficient reason in itself). Under the contract, the lessor has almost solely rights, while the lessee has uncountable obligations. It is not inadvertent that the basis of lease contracts is mutual trust. At the same time, the lessor is well aware that although they have numerous rights, they are vulnerable since by reason of physical, legal, and financial obstacles, they cannot always enforce their rights immediately vis-à-vis the airline as a partner. Therefore, beyond the private legal requirements of lease contracts, the Cape Town Convention guarantees on a State level to protect international creditors' interests much more effectively.

The creditor is authorised to take possession of the leased object, check its condition, sell it or lease it to another entity and may collect the revenues or profits arising from the management or use of the object. For the purpose of the settlement of the debt, as an alternative solution, the pledging of the object may ensue, but such a solution may be applied solely with the consent of the Parties concerned. In the interest of the exercise of their rights, granted under the Convention, the creditor may proceed by themselves or may have recourse to relief by the court having jurisdiction (Article 13). Jurisdiction is a principal issue; its role is well-known both in international and national laws. Jurisdiction implies 'the power and authority of the court or administrative tribunal to decide legal issues and disputes'.[15] Jurisdiction is crucial in public and private international[16,17] aviation laws. Aircraft financing is a matter of contract law. It covers many issues, such as contractual, legal, business, documentation filing, insurance, tax, technical, risk and priority issues, etc. In addition, it has to be governed by proper law. Various property laws that should apply are chosen by the Parties (as a contractual relationship allows the Parties to have the freedom of choice), or, if the Parties have not chosen an applicable law, the contract shall be governed by the law of

[15] *Supra* note 14 at Part II, Chap. 9.2.

[16] See, Chicago Convention (1944), *Jurisdiction*: Rules of the Air (Art. 12); Nationality of aircraft (Art. 17); Search of aircraft (Art. 18); Aircraft in distress (Art. 25); Disputes and Default (Chap. XVIII), etc., or the Tokyo Convention (1963), *Jurisdiction*: The State of registration of the aircraft is competent to exercise jurisdiction over offences and acts committed on board (Art. 3. 1). [see, Part I, Chap. 5.1.1].

[17] Montreal Convention (1999), *Jurisdictions*: 5 Forums (Fora) [Art. 33 (1) (2)]. [see, Part II, Chap. 9.2].

the country 'with which it is most likely to be connected'.[18] There are also a great number of conflict of laws rules applicable in Aircraft Financing:

- Lex situs—the law of the place where the aircraft was located at the relevant time;
- Lex debitoris - the law of the country in which the debtor is located or has its place of business;
- Lex domicili—the law of the place of the owner of the aircraft;
- Lex actus—the law of the place where the transfer of the instrument was executed;
- Lex registri—the law of the place where the aircraft is registered (the right of the flag, Lex bandi).[19]

The Cape Town Convention and its Aircraft Equipment Protocol (AEP) provide for these various jurisdictions (Chap. XII, Articles 42–45) to protect international creditors' interests. The international interest shall pertain to a uniquely identifiable object, which falls within one of the next three categories:

- Airframes, aircraft engines, and helicopters;
- Railway rolling stock;
- Space assets [Article 2 (3)].

15.1.2 Validation of the Remedies of the Creditor

Registration secures an effective coercing instrument for the validation of remedies since it basically defines the order of rivalling interests in one given object. In fact, registration is not a condition for validity; it is merely an instrument that provides help for the obligee to enforce their rights. Upon granting credits necessary for the acquisition of aircraft, the numerous diverging national regulations raise obstacles, which do not favour the creditor wishing to validate the obligation of the defaulting debtor to pay. Via international registration, the creditor acquires security for absolute priority over all other creditors upon reclaiming the debt.

---

[18] Major manufacturers typically insist on the governing law of their "home" jurisdiction (e.g., Boeing, Airbus). The majority of the aircraft operating lease contracts are governed by British or New York law (some Québec or Californian law). The reason is that there are well-elaborated commercial legal precedents in these jurisdictions. See, the European Union's practice: The Rome I Regulation [Regulation (EC) No 593/2008] (successor to the Rome Convention 1980 on the law applicable to contractual obligations) of the European Parliament and of the Council of 17 June 2008 on the Law Applicable to Contractual Obligations; The Rome II Regulation [Regulation (EC) No 864/ 2007] of the European Parliament and of the Council of 11 July 2007 on the Law Applicable to Non-Contractual Obligations. OJ C 27, 26.1.1998, p. 34–53.; OJ *L 177, 4.7.2008, p. 6–16.;* OJ L 199, 31.7.2007, p. 40–49.

[19] In the Geneva Convention (1948), the Lex Registri prevails [Art. 1 (1) *i)*]; it contains a clear reference to this: The contracting States undertake to recognise: a) rights of property in aircraft. . .; [*b)*; *c)*; *d)*]; (i) in accordance with the law of the contracting State in which the aircraft was registered as to nationality at the time of their constitution, and (ii) are regularly recorded in a public record of the contracting State in which the aircraft is registered as to nationality".

Under the Cape Town Convention, the order of the priority of security interests is as follows:

- A registered interest has priority over an unregistered interest.
- A formerly registered interest has priority over any other interests subsequently registered *(prior tempore, potior iure).*

This order prevails even if the holder's interest was registered with actual knowledge of pre-existing, unregistered other interests (Article 29). (The latter rule differs from the domestic civil legal norm of most countries.)

The principal element of the regime of the Cape Town Convention grants opportunity for the international registration of internationally recognised interests. Under the direction of ICAO, the Member States established a sole registry system, and in compliance with the Cape Town Convention, they founded the International Registry. During its proceedings, the Registry registers internationally recognised holders' interests and extends, amends, or terminates interests.

The Registry implementing the rules of the Cape Town Convention is directed by the *Aviareto* company operating in the joint ownership of Ireland and SITA SC (*Société Internationale de Télécommunications Aéronautiques*)[20] in Dublin. *Aviareto* is in contractual relationship with ICAO. The public legal and supervisory rights over the Registry are exercised by the ICAO Council.[21] The clients have to pay for registration. Since the company does not produce profits, the fixed charges secure the finances necessary for the operation and maintenance of the company. Aviareto surpassed one million registrations in 2019.[22] The registration of interests ensues electronically. If interests are registered in compliance with the rules of the Convention, these guarantee immediate and valid legal protection for the creditors. The registration of an international interest remains effective until discharged or until the expiry of the period specified in the registration (Article 21). The Registrar is liable for compensatory damages for the loss suffered by a person that directly results from an error or omission of the Registrar or from a malfunction of the international registration system [Article 28 (1)].

15.1.3 The Effect of the Cape Town Convention

Via the establishment of a new international legal framework, the Convention reduces the risks attached to property-based financing and leasing transactions as

---

[20] The company SITA was founded by 11 airlines in February 1949. Nowadays, SITA has become a multinational information technology company, which provides IT and telecommunications services for its more than 2500 customers. (www.sita.aero).

[21] ICAO Doc 9793 Cape Town Convention, The Supervisory Authority and the Registrar (Article 17).; ICAO Doc 9864 Regulations and Procedures for the International Registry. 9th edn., 2022.

[22] www.aviareto.aero/celebrating-one-million-registrations.

well as the risks of the acquisition of civil aircraft or engines. Due to the slackening of risks, the availability of aviation-related credits can be increased, and their costs and interest rates can be reduced; thereby, the financing opportunities available with more favourable conditions for the operators of aircraft can be extended. The Convention exerts a positive effect on all the performers of the air transport industry.

Furthermore, the Convention affects States Parties that finance the acquisition of aircraft via underwriting State guarantees, while the decrease of risks extends the scope of export credits granted to Governments for purchased aircraft. The profit proceeding from the decrease of costs and the mitigation of external levels of debt may benefit the less developed economies since the economic regimes of these countries are currently not founded on the basic principles of property-based financing. The profit related to fleet planning, export activities, and employment is produced in developed economies.

The airlines benefit from the fall of financing costs by at least 30% since with the extension of their opportunities for access to funds and financing resources, their operational efficacy and profitability may also improve. According to calculations, as a consequence of the impact of the Convention, the airlines in the world may achieve annual joint savings of about 5 billion USD[23] from reduced leasing charges. The winners of the new regulation are the manufacturers of commercial aircraft and their suppliers, as well as the investors in the air transport industry, since with the growth of sales, the performance and employment levels are rising and the returns on investments are also increasing. The key performers of air transport, the passengers can also appreciate these benefits via transmitted reduction in prices and the rise in the standard of services.

The Cape Town Convention demonstrates thoroughly how a uniform international regulation can be implemented in a relatively brief time with the cooperation of international organisations. The new system does not collide with a single basic principle, nor does it threaten with the disregard of national legal systems, and it does have an especially beneficial impact on the performers of the industry. The principal virtue of the Convention is that it unified the rules of financing aircraft; therefore, it will be significantly conducive to the satisfaction of the demand for new aircraft.

References

Hanley DP (2021) Aircraft Operating Leasing. A Legal and practical analysis in the context of public and private international air law. 3rd edn., Wolters Kluwer, p 183

Havel BF, Sanchez GS (2014) Principles and Practice on International Aviation Law. Cambridge University Press, Cambridge, p 357

Scheinberg R (2018) The Commercial Aircraft Finance Handbook. Part 1, 2nd edn., Routledge, p 1

Wool J (2012) Treaty design, implementation, and compliance benchmarking economic benefit – a framework as applied to the Cape Town Convention. Unif Law Rev 17:13

[23] Wool (2012), p. 13.

Chapter 16
Closing Words for Private Aviation Law

Of the international treaties of private law drafted under the guidance of ICAO and presented before, the Montreal Convention (1999) is the most important treaty of private international aviation law. Its peculiarity consists in its legal institutions, which support the universal predominance of the Convention. The treaty-maker introduced legal institutions partly familiar and transplanted from the Warsaw Convention (1929), partly utterly new ones, all of which purported the accession of as many countries as possible so that private international legal unification in aviation law could be accomplished in the broadest possible scope.

The contracting Parties opened a new chapter in the history of the liability of air carriers for damages since in the case of an accident sustained by a passenger, it obligates the air carriers to assume unlimited liability for damages, furthermore, it simplifies the documentation of carriage, facilitates the electronic issuance of the air ticket and the air waybill, and, via the introduction of the fifth forum of jurisdiction, it extends the scope of optional proceeding courts for the plaintiffs, and finally, it obligates the air carriers, if the national law so requires, to make advance payments upon accidents sustained by the passengers. The requirement of the purchase of adequate insurance by the air carrier is also a new element in the Convention, just like the provision stating that against a claimant third party, the air carrier may enter a counterclaim.

By replacing a fragmented, complex system consisting of six international treaties, the Convention offers the alternative of a uniform, homogenous system of rules. This reinforces the intention of the States and regional economic integration organisations to accede. Although there are still States that are parties only to the Warsaw Convention, it can be established that, as reflected by the accessions to the new Convention hitherto, the contracting Parties have laid the foundation for the unification of the system of liability of the air carrier for damages successfully. International legal harmonisation can be realised only via the actual prevalence of the rules and procedures set forth under the Convention since there are still numerous collisions deriving from varied national regulations and conflicts arising during the adjudication of private legal disputes proceeding from the legal relation of carriage.

A. Sipos, *International Aviation Law*, https://doi.org/10.1007/978-3-031-39066-1_16

Therefore, at the General Assemblies of ICAO, the States Parties to the Montreal Convention regularly call upon the States not having acceded to ratify the Convention at their earliest convenience.[1]

Although the Convention guarantees several benefits for the performers of air carriage, undoubtedly, it favours the passengers and consignors by protecting the customer. The treaty-maker lays emphasis primarily on the protection of the interests of the passengers: on the protection of the life and safety of passengers and partly of their property. What underlies the treaty-maker's intent is the affirmation of the basic principle that human life and the right to dignity cannot be restricted since they are absolute, inviolable basic rights. At the same time, the protection of objects in the carriage of cargo is not given distinctive attention since the product is substitutable and less valuable despite its preciousness; thus, it does not represent privileged value to be protected. Since, as a new rule in the case of the carriage of cargo, the upper limit of limited liability for damages cannot be transgressed (in the case of a declaration of interest in delivery at destination, the designated amount is guiding), upon the loss or destruction of the cargo, generally no litigious proceedings are initiated because the damage can be established easily and settled forthwith.

However, for accidents sustained by the passenger, the air carrier has to accept unlimited liability. Therefore, for the passengers and their relatives, litigation is not a perspective any longer since they do not have to transgress the limited liability instituted under the Warsaw Convention because the air carrier, upon the establishment of its liability, will indemnify the actual damage. The introduction of unlimited liability has transformed the practice of the enforcement of rights in its foundations. Namely, neither do the plaintiffs have to participate in lengthy and circumstantial legal proceedings, nor do the solicitors have to wheedle every minute detail out of the clients or ponder, in the borderland of creativity of the applier of the law, on the question for what reason they could transgress the low limit of limited liability.

The introduction of the new forum of jurisdiction has repositioned the passenger claiming compensation so that they can settle their claim for compensation in their own country for an accident occurring in any part of the world. Since the passengers claiming compensation belong to the same regime of liability for damages, this has given rise to the opportunity for the uniform application of the law by the Member States. Thus, should the adjudication of the claim for damages take place anywhere, the claimants will receive approximately the same treatment and final judgement. Nor do the claimants have to sue the manufacturer of the aircraft or of the engine since the air carriers settle the accounts of the damages deriving from the fault of the manufacturer between each other.

The treaty-makers do not define the major concepts. The contracting Parties delegate their interpretation to national law (at the same time, they construe certain concepts peculiarly). The reason for this is that the contracting Parties could not disregard national laws and their role in shaping the law, thus, the Convention

[1] ICAO Resolution A41–4, Appendix C: Ratification of ICAO International Instruments. October 2022.

unified merely the most important rules on the liability of air carriers. Like all international treaties, this Convention also has less elaborated points and deficiencies, which can be remedied meritoriously only after decades. Obviously, in the course of time, new questions will arise and new life circumstances diverging from the regulated ones will appear; nevertheless, we can await the decades ahead of the Convention with composure. Namely, the Montreal Convention arising from the foundations of the Warsaw Convention is a pragmatic and efficacious new international treaty abundant in legal institutions, which, by replacing six effective international treaties, consolidates the complex private legal regime of international aviation law impressively, all along with the endeavour not to be the last but to be 'the first Mohican'.

Part III
Book Summary

Chapter 17
Book Summary

Air transport is one of the safest modes of transport and results from the combination of prominent human intellect, cutting-edge technology and engineering. The complexities of aviation law must be understood in order to master the principles of the regulation of aviation. In fact, aviation law is a particular area of international law and represents a novel and modern development from centuries-old maritime law, now constituting a separate legal discipline engendered by the stringent demands of aviation safety and security.

This book is based on the author's aviation experience and embodies his academic achievement, which contains more than 100 legal cases and 31 illustrations. Its aim is to familiarise readers interested in aviation with aviation law, which is one of the most intriguing fields of international law. It also intends to help the work of aviation experts as well as to expand the knowledge of jurisprudents and practitioners by broadening their horizons.

This book addresses the two fundamental treaties of international aviation law—the Chicago Convention (1944) on International Civil Aviation and the Montreal Convention (1999) on the Unification of Certain Rules for International Carriage by Air, furthermore, it explicates other highly momentous treaties of international civil aviation.

After coming into force in 1947, the Chicago Convention has only been substantially amended twice, while none of the substantive clauses of the Montreal Convention have been amended since its entry into force in 2003. Therefore, the analysis and commentary contained in this volume can supply the reader with up-to date information even after decades as they will not rapidly become outdated.

The volume consists of two major parts:

I. Public International Aviation Law;
II. Private International Aviation Law.

In the first part, the provisions of the Chicago Convention are expounded, with special emphasis on sovereignty, the legal status and regulation of international and national airspaces, on the requirements of the performance of scheduled and

A. Sipos, *International Aviation Law*, https://doi.org/10.1007/978-3-031-39066-1_17

non-scheduled flights, and the legal issues related to aircraft. The author does not always follow the structure of the Convention; he sheds light on the correlations among provisions dealing with the same topics contained in different places in the norm text. He positions the analysis of intergovernmental legal norms in the context of the underlying international reality and pays special attention to the clear explanation of public international law.

Although aviation safety is a central issue in the Chicago Convention, the word 'security' does not appear therein (although security was posteriorly regulated under Annex 17 on Aviation Security). Security—after safety—is the second most important strategic pillar of the activity of, and also a challenge to the International Civil Aviation Organization (ICAO); therefore, the book also expands on all the treaties related to public aviation law on security [such as the Tokyo (1963), The Hague (1970), the Montreal (1971), the New York (1979), and the Beijing (2010) Conventions and the Montreal (1988, 2014) and Beijing (2010) Protocols].

ICAO is one of the top international intergovernmental organisations and a specialised agency of the United Nations. Its specific operation and its professional and diplomatic activities are expounded in depth in the first part. The author also worked as a permanent representative on the Council of ICAO (2004–2007), thus, he offers insight into his practical and diplomatic experience.

He bestows particular attention on the following aspects of ICAO:

- the close co-operation of the Member States in institutional mechanisms;
- the creation of Standards and Recommended Practices (SARPs), which establish uniform standards for civil aviation worldwide; and
- the implementation of SARPs (introduction to the regulatory process with specific decisions) as well as the audit procedure of control systems, which plays a crucial part in implementation.

The second part of the book presents the complex field of air carrier liability. The Montreal Convention (1999) is the most important international treaty of private law within international aviation law; it updates and replaces the regulatory system of the Warsaw Convention (1929), both of which purport to create a standardised liability system concerning damage caused to air passengers and consignors.

The Montreal Convention is a comprehensive international treaty, which addresses the liability of air carriers for damage arising from international carriage by air, the paramount goals of which are the modernisation and consolidation of the previous Warsaw System in order to achieve global uniformity in private international aviation law and to enhance the protection of the interests of air passengers and consignors of cargo. Certainly, the Montreal Convention eliminated the expressly low limit of liability previously applicable to cases of death and bodily injury (accident) and introduced the unlimited liability of air carriers. The air carrier is liable for damage sustained in the case of the death or bodily injury of the passenger caused by an accident on board an aircraft or during either of the operations of embarking or disembarking. If the bodily injury (mental injury is generally not included) falls within that scope and the carriage was international pursuant to the Montreal Convention, the air carrier has strict liability up to 128,821

SDR and fault liability thereover. It has to be pointed out that the liability in this case is unlimited solely to the extent of proven and recoverable damage. Carriers are liable exclusively if the death or bodily injury of the passenger was caused by an accident and a considerable body of case law is introduced on what constitutes an "accident" for such purposes.

Thus, the author examines the Montreal Convention through legal cases—from filing the claim to the binding judgement—so that the grounds for the judgements and the conditions necessary for a successful claim become easier to understand. He explores the aspects emerging throughout the legal proceedings and the necessary and sufficient conditions, the coexistence of which allows the claims for damages to be satisfied based on the Montreal Convention.

The procedure of the compensation for damages is presented step by step in the book, divided into five phases, treating each provision of the Convention separately.

Phase I concerns the applicability and binding character of the Montreal Convention, the conditions necessary to bring a claim, and other procedural issues (e.g., the establishment of jurisdiction, international carriage, limitation periods).

1. Examination of the *documents of carriage* (air ticket and air waybill).
2. Does the court have *jurisdiction* for the adjudication of the case?
3. Does the given legal relation fall under the *substantive scope* of the Convention?
4. Does the *personal scope* of the Convention cover the parties concerned?
5. Was the claim of action for damages submitted within *the prescribed time limit*?
   Was the complaint filed with the air carrier within *the prescribed time limit*?

In Phase II, the question of whether the air carrier has liability is examined based on the facts of the specific legal case.

6. Is the air carrier liable for the injury suffered by the passenger?
7. Is the air carrier liable for the damage to the baggage of the passenger?
8. Is the air carrier liable for the damage to air cargo?
9. Is the air carrier liable for the damage caused by the delay of passengers, baggage, or air cargo?

In Phase III, the author reveals in which cases the air carrier can adduce circumstances that exonerate it wholly or partly from the obligation of indemnification.

10. Can *the air carrier be exonerated from liability* according to the provisions of the Convention on the possibilities of exoneration?
11. In case the air carrier is wholly exonerated from liability under the provisions of the Convention, can it *be held accountable later* under national or other laws?

Phase IV examines the air carrier's liability in cases where the carrier is unable to exonerate itself and the court obligates it to pay damages. The air carrier has limited liability for the destruction, loss of, or damage to baggage or cargo as well as for delayed carriage, whereas it has unlimited liability for the death or bodily injury of the passengers.

12. In which cases can the air carrier *limit* its liability?
13. When does the air carrier's liability become *unlimited*?

In Phase V, the exact amount of indemnity is ascertained after taking all the circumstances of the case into consideration.

14. Which elements of the damage caused to the claimant can be remedied by the indemnity and how?

This volume invites the reader to think through the arising questions—along with the author—in order to form their own standpoint not only on theoretical questions but also on practical problems. To that effect, the author relies on primary sources—on international treaties, court decisions, and the regulations of international organisations—and guides the reader with a firm hand in the world of international civil aviation regulations and legislation.

This book is a fascinating and expedient analysis, written not merely for legal academics but also for a broader circle of legal practitioners as well as aviation experts. Aviation law is a separate branch of international law, representing a particular specialty, and guidance in it is necessary for those who have to deal with the raised issues. As the old adage goes, 'The jurist must know everything, and a little beyond'.

Bibliography

Documents

ICAO Annual Reports of the Council, 2019–2022.
ICAO Doc 9807 Universal Security Audit Programme Continuous Monitoring Manual. 3rd edn., 2021.
ICAO State letter – AN 1/1–11/28; ICAO Council Working Paper/13954.
ICAO Doc 9809-Cl/1142, Council Min. 166/1–14, 2002.
ICAO Integrated Safety Trend Analysis and Reporting System (iSTARS).
ICAO Safety Partnership Meeting. States' Reports, Montreal, 20 November 2012.
ICAO Report – Appendix H, Interception Procedures Issued by USSR. 1993.
ICAO News Release PIO 10/2005, ICAO Council President calls for increased global transparency in sharing of aviation safety information.
ICAO Eastern and Southern African Office: Workshop on the development of national performance for air navigation systems, 2010, NPF/SIP/2010–WP/22.
ICAO officially transfers control of Somali airspace to Government of Somalia. Hiiraan Online, 10 December 2014.
ICAO Special Meeting on Limits for Passengers under the Warsaw Convention and The Hague Protocol, Montreal, 1–15 February 1966.
ICAO Adrep Summary 4/88 (#11).
ICAO Circular 259–AN/153.
ICAO Secretariat: Status of Montreal Convention 1999 and Declarations.
IATA Annual Review 2020–2022.
IATA Economics' Chart of the Week. A return to industry profitability in 2023. 9 December 2022.
IATA Transferability of Tickets. IATA Position Paper, 2012.
IATA 77th Annual General Meeting. Boston, Press Release No. 66, 4 October 2021.
IATA Safety Report 2015, 52nd edn., April 2016.
IATA Interline Staff Travel Agreement. Version 15. 1 June 2019.

A. Sipos, *International Aviation Law*, https://doi.org/10.1007/978-3-031-39066-1

ATAG Report. Aviation Benefits Beyond Borders. Executive Summary. September 2020.

ATAG Commitment to Fly Net Zero. 5 October 2021.

ECAC Air Passenger Health Issues. WG, 2005.

Authority in Handling Offences and Certain Other Acts Committed on Board Aircraft. International Conference on Air Law (Montreal, 26 March to 4 April 2014) – Presented by Indonesia, DCTC Doc No. 24, 21 March 2014.

International Conference on Air Law, Authority and Protections for In-Flight Security Officers, at 1, DCTC Doc. No. 7, 23 January 2014.

FAA Advisory Circular. Extended Operations (ETOPS and Polar Operations), 120–42, 6 June 1985.

FAA NOTAM – Airspace Special Notice Ukraine, FDC 4/7667 (A0012/14), 23 April 2014.

FAA Final Report: Human Error and Commercial Aviation Accidents: A Comprehensive, Fine-Grained Analysis Using HFACS. DOT/FAA/AM–06/18, Office of Aerospace Medicine, Washington, D. C. 20591. July 2006.

Last Act in the Hainan Incident (HistoricWings.com) Parts 1–3, July 2012.

Report of the ICAO Fact-Finding Investigation, July 2022.

Dutch Safety Board: Crash of Malaysia Airlines (MH) Flight 17. The Hague, 13 October 2015.

FedEx Corporation Annual Report 2006. Semiconductor Industry Association, 2007.

Aviation Benefits Beyond Borders. Executive Summary. ATAG Report, September 2020.

World Population Prospects 2022: Summary of Results. UN Department of Economic and Social Affairs (DESA), Population Division, New York, July 2022.

European Commission: Road safety 2017.

European Commission: European Road Safety Observatory, Annual statistical report on road safety in the EU 2022. 13 March 2023.

Bisignani, Giovanni: IATA Director General Statement. IATA Annual Conference, Vancouver, 3–5 June 2007.

Institute of Air and Space Law, University of Cologne (1925–2015). Hobe, Stephan (Ed.), Cologne, Introduction, May 2015.

Papers relating to the foreign relations of the United States, 1928, Volume I – Office of the Historian. Treaty Series No. 840.

National Museum of US Air Force: RB–47H Stratojet Shot Down (posted 2006).

World Nuclear Weapon Stockpile Report. Ploughshares Fund, 31 August 2023.

ESA Space Debris Office: Space debris by the numbers. 12 September 2023.

CRS Report for Congress: China–US Aircraft Collision Incident of April 2001: Assessments and Policy Implications. Order Code RL30946, 10 October 2001.

China's Military Strategy. Xinhua, 26 May 2015. (www.china.org.cn/china/2015-05/26/content.35661433).

S.1450 – Air Transportation Safety and System Stabilization Act. 107th Congress (2001–2002).
The Interception of EgyptAir 2843, Sierra Hotel Blog, 12 October 2020.
United Nations (2022) World population prospects 2022: summary of results. UN Department of Economic and Social Affairs (DESA), Population Division, New York.
Case Concerning Certain German Interests in Polish Upper Silesia, Merits, PCIJ (1926) Series A. No. 7, 30.
Destruction of Korean Air Lines of Boeing 747–200 on 31 August 1983. Report of the completion of the ICAO fact-finding investigation. June 1993.
Report to the President of the United States titled "The Safety of Air Traffic and Terrorism". Washington, D.C., 10 May 1995.
The White House: Statement by the principal deputy press secretary to the President, 16 September 1983.
Sipos, Attila: Mathias Rust esete (The Case of Mathias Rust), Manuscript. Imre Madách Secondary School, Madách Cup Tournament. Budapest, 1987.
Civil Air Transport Agreements, Open Skies Partners. Released by US Department of Transportation. 9 December 2021.
Global Plan to End TB: 2018–2022. Stop TB Partnership, Geneva, 2019.
Trans-Siberian overflights, written question E-6399/09, 10 December 2009.
Improving Just Culture. CANSO, ICAO Assembly 39. A39–WP/1931 TE/73 25/8/ 2016.
Blueprint for the Single European Sky (SES), Delivering on safety, environment, capacity and cost-effectiveness. IATA, AEA and ERA, 2011.
Australian Government: ICAO Council decision on jurisdiction in MH17 legal proceedings. 18 March 2023.
Pilot and Technician Outlook (2023–2042). Flight Operation Solution, Boeing. 2023.
Annual Report of the Council, Human Resources Management and Gender Equity. 31 December 2021.
Review of Management and Administration in the International Civil Aviation Organization (ICAO), JIU/ REP/2019/1.
Encyclopaedia Britannica. New York, 11th edn., 1910.
Cicero, Marcus Tullius: From His Speech Pro Milone (IV. 10), 52 B.C.
Milde, Michael: From Warsaw 1929 to Montreal 1999. IASL/McGill Symposium. (Dubai, 13–14 December 2003).
Harakas, Andrew J.: Aviation Issues in the US. McGill University, Lecture. October 2014.
Harakas, Andrew J.: Aviation Issues in the US. 2014.
DeMace, Kayleigh: Farman F.60 Goliath – The Plane of the Week. (Theflightblog. com).
Bisignani, Giovanni: IATA Press Release. IATA's Director General and CEO, Istanbul, No. 25, 31 May 2008.
Force Majeure Trumps Delay Claim in Québec Aviation Case. Transportation Notes, 10. (2014) 5.

IMF Review of the Method of Valuation of the SDR. Executive Summary, July 2015.

Official Journal L 285, 17/10/1997.

Revised Limits of Liability Under the Montreal Convention of 1999. In 2009 and 2019.

Random House Webster's Legal Dictionary.

Aviation Benefits Beyond Borders. Executive Summary. ATAG report, October 2018.

Final Report. Secretariat of State for Transport, Accidents Investigation Branch, LTS 2291/75, London, February 1976.

Business Insurance, 29 May 1978.

Ground Carriage – Article 16, General Conditions of Carriage, Air France, March 2022.

Kiss, Kálmán: Report on Unlawful Interference on Board, Selection from a Report. Capt. Kálmán Kiss, Pilot-in-command and instructing pilot. Malév Hungarian Airlines Plc., 2009.

Kiss, Kálmán: Memoirs. Manuscript. November 2015.

Lautner, Erzsébet: Report on Unlawful Interference on Board, Selection from a Report, Erzsébet Lautner, Chief flight-attendant, Malév Hungarian Airlines Plc., 1998.

Pallas Nagylexikon (Pallas Encyclopaedia), Pallas Irodalmi és Nyomdai Rt., Budapest, 1893–1897.

Doctor on Board Program (www.lufthansa.com/us/en/doctoron-board).

MedAire's, MedLink and Stat MD. Medical Emergencies – Guidance for Flight Crew.

Inflation Adjustments to Liability Limits Governed by the Montreal Convention Effective, 30 Dec. 2009., 74 Fed. Register 59017, 16 November 2009. 74 Fed. Register 59017, 16 November 2009; 2019 Revised Limits of Liability Under the Montreal Convention of 1999.

The report of the Latin-American Air Law Association (ALADA), September 2004.

Global Market Insight, 10 October 2022.

Jamestown Foundation, Qatar's Role in the Libyan Conflict: Who's on the Lists of Terrorists and Why?, 2017.

Press Release, (non-official). No. 2018/26, 11 June 2018. International Convention on the Elimination of All Forms of Racial Discrimination (ICERD). UN, New York, 21 December 1965. The Pittsburgh Press: Terrorist raid 2 Europe airports. Vol. 102, No. 184, 27 December 1985.

Lufthansa Flight 181. Updates on 22 November 2022.

Plane Attack Shocks Moscow. Miami News, 10 February 1961.

French Try to Shoot the Red Anger. Miami News, 11 February 1961.

Taiwan hosts own event at the ICAO. The China Post, 1 October 2016.

BRD Zeitung and Lübecker Nachrichten, June 1987.

Legal Cases

Public Air Law

Nicaragua v. United States of America, Military and Paramilitary Activities in and against Nicaragua, Merits, Judgement, ICJ Reports 14, 27 June 1986.

Island of Palmas case – Reports of International Arbitral Awards RSA, 4 April 1928.

Bahrain, Egypt, Saudi Arabia and United Arab Emirates v. Qatar, The Hague, Judgement, General List No. 173, 14 July 2020.

ICJ – Appeal Relating to the Jurisdiction of the ICAO Council under Article 84 of the Convention on International Civil Aviation (*Bahrain, Egypt, Saudi Arabia and United Arab Emirates v. Qatar*). The Hague, 14 July 2020.

In Re *Korean Air Lines Disaster of 1 September 1983*, 597 F. Supp. 619 (D.D.C. 1984), 26 June 1984.

India v. Pakistan, ICJ Appeal Relating to the Jurisdiction of the ICAO Council, Judgment of 18 August, 1972.

Islamic Republic of Iran v. United States of America, ICJ Judgment (Case Concerning the Aerial Incident of 3 July 1988), 2001.

Israel v. Bulgaria, Aerial incident of 27 July 1955. General List No. 35 – Judgement 26 May 1959.

Democratic Republic of Congo v. Uganda case, ICJ Judgement, General List 116, 148, 19 December 2005.

Filártiga v. Pena-Irala, 630 F.2d 876 US Court of Appeals, Second Circuit, No. 191, Docket 79–6090, 30 June 1980.

United States v. Cordova, US District Court E. D. New York, 1950. 89 F. Supp. 298, 1950.

United Kingdom v. Albania (Corfu Channel Case), ICJ 4 Reports 22, Judgement of 9 April 1949.

Armando Alejandre Jr. & Others v. Cuba, Report No. 86/99, OEA/Ser.L/V/II. 106, 1999.

M/V "SAIGA" case, *Saint Vincent and Grenadine v. Guinea,* ITLOS, No. 2, 1 July 1999.

Civil Air Transport Incorporated v. Central Air Transport Corporation, International Law Reports, 1952.

Private Air Law

Air France v. Valerie Hermien Saks, US Supreme Court Reports, 470 U.S. 392, 105 S.Ct. 1338, 84 L. Ed. 2d 289, 1985.

Amtsgericht Erding (Court of Small Claims) Case No. 4 C 309/06, 5 July 2006.

Axel Walz v. Clickair S. A., C 179/15, 26 January 2010.

Aziz v. Air India, 658 F. Supp. 2d 1144, C.D. Cal., 2009.

Aya v. Lan Cargo, S.A. (1:14-cv-22260) District Court, S.D. Florida, 18 September 2014.

Best v. BWIA West Indies Airways Ltd., No. 06 581 F. Supp. 2d 359, 2008.

Birgit Bossen, Anja Bossen and *Gudula Gräßmann v. Brussels Airlines,* SA/NV, C-559/16. case, Court of Justice of the European Union (CJEU), Luxembourg, 7 September 2017.

Borham v. Pan American World Airways, U.S. Dist. Lexis 28554 (S.D.N.Y.), 1986.

Buonocore v. Trans World Airlines, Inc., 900 F. 2d 8, 11 (2d Cir.), 1990.

Chan Elisa v. Korean Air Lines, Supreme Court Reporter, 490 U.S. 122, 104 L. Ed. 2d 113, 1989.

Chendrimada v. Air India, 802 F. Supp. 1089 (S.D.N.Y.), 1992.

Chutter v. KLM Royal Dutch Airlines, US District Court, 132 F. Supp. 611, 1955.

Commercial Union Insurance Co. v. Alitalia Airlines, 347 F. 3rd 448 (2nd Cir.), 2003.

CS and Others v České aerolinie a.s., CJEU, Judgment C–502/18 (ECLI:EU: C:2019:604) 11 July 2019.

Dalton v. Delta Air Lines, U.S. Court Appeals, Fifth Circuit, 7 April 1978. 14. Avi. 18.425.

David v. United Airlines, WL 1573423, C.D. Cal., 18 April, 2016.

Day v. Trans World Airlines, Inc., US Court of Appeals, Second Circuit. 528 F. 2d 31, 1975.

Deere & Co. v. Deutsche Lufthansa Aktiengesellschaft. 621 F. Supp. 721 (N.D. Ill. 1985), US District Court for the Northern District of Illinois, 26 April 1985.

DeMarines v. KLM Royal Dutch Airlines, 580 F.2d 1193 (3 Fed. R. Evid. Serv. 5753), 1978.

Dias v. Transbrazil Airlines Inc. 26. Avi (CCH) 16, 048 (S.D.N.Y.), 1998.

Eastern Airlines v. Floyd Marie, Supreme Court Reporter, 499 U.S. 530, 113 L.Ed. 2d 569, No. 89–1598, 17 April 1991.

Ekufu v. Iberia Airlines, 36 Avi. 15,372 (N.D.Ill.), 2014.

EL AL Israel Airlines Ltd. v. Tsui Yuan Tseng, US Court of Appeals for the Second Circuit, No. 97–475, 122 F. 3d, 1999.

Fangbeng Fuondjing v. American Airlines, Inc., WL 1375606 (D. Md.), 2011.

Fedelich v. American Airlines, 724 F. Supp. 2d 274, 284 (D.P.R.), 2010.

Fishman by Fishman v. Delta Air Lines, Inc., NOS 1818, Dockets 96-9345, 132 F. 3d 138, 1998.

Fuller v. Amerijet International Inc., 273 F. Supp. Ed 902, Civil Action H-03–1128, 22 July 2003.

Fülöp v. Malév Hungarian Airlines, 175 F. Supp. 2d 651 (S.D.N.Y.) 2001; WL 202958, (S.D.N.Y.), 2003.

Gatewhite v. Iberia Lineas Aereas de Espana, 1 All E.r. 944 1 Lloyd's Report 160, 225, 226., 1989.

Herman v. Trans World Airlines, Inc., Court case 40. App. D. 2d 850. 337 N.Y.S. 2d 827, 830 (NY AD 2 Dept.), 1972.

Hornsby v. Lufthansa German Airlines, US District Court, C.D., 593 F. Supp. 2d 1132, 6 January 2009.

Hu v. Air China Ltd., No. 399/2009, Tribunal of Busto Arsizio in Case No. 1118, 2007.

Hunter v. Deutsche Lufthansa AG, 863, F. Supp. 2d 190 (E.D.N.Y.), 2012.

Husain v. Olympic Airways, 316 F. 3d 829 (9th Cir.), 2002.

Husserl v. Swiss Air Transport Co., 388 F. Supp. 1238 (S.D.N.Y.), 1975.

John Lisi v. Alitalia, US Court of Appeals Second Circuit, Nos. 91–95, Dock. 30543–30547, 1966.

Jones v. USA 3000 Airlines, 33Avi. 17,442 (E.D.Mo.), 2009.

Kamanou-Goune v. Swiss International Air lines, WL 874600 (S.D.N.Y.), 2009.; US Supreme Court, NY Slip Op 08100, 2012.

Kathleen Robertson v. American Airlines, US Court of Appeals, District of Columbia Circuit, No. 03–7129, 18 March 2005.

Ko v. EVA Airways Corporation, 42 F. Supp. 3d 1296, February 2012.

Lavergne v. ATIS CORP., Civil No. 09-1421 (SEC). Cite as 767 F. Supp. 2d 301, 2011.

Lukács v. United Airlines, Inc., MBCA 111 (CAN LII), November 2009.

Marjorie Zicherman v. Korean Air Lines, Co. Ltd., US Supreme Court reporter 510, 133 L. Ed. 2d 590, 1996.

Masudi v. Brady Cargo Services Inc., No. 1:2012cv02391 - Document 44 (E.D.N. Y.), 8 September 2014.

Maxwell v. Aer Lingus Ltd., 122 F. Supp. 2d 210, November 2000.

McDonald v. Korean Air (Ontario Superior Court of Justice), Docket 29708, 2003.

Mertens v. Flying Tiger Line, Inc., US Court of Appeals 2nd Circuit, 341 F. 2d 851, 1965.

Mohammed v. Air France, NY Slip Op 50462 [11 Misc. 3d 1071(A)], 28 March 2006.

Morris v. KLM Royal Dutch Airlines, UKHL 7, 2002; Judgement of the British Supreme Court of Judicature, case no. B3/2000/3820, 17 May 2001.

Motorola, Inc. and Fireman's Fund Insurance Company v. Federal Express Corporation and Kuehne & Nagel, Inc., No. 00–17374. US Court of Appeals, Ninth Circuit. Argued and Submitted, 13 February 2002.

Mullaney v. Delta Airlines, Inc., 33 Avi. 12,819 (S.D.N.Y.) 2009.

Nastych v. British Airways Plc., US District Court, S.D. N.Y. 09 Civ. 9082 (AJP) February 2010.

Okeke v. Northwest Airlines, Inc., No. 1:07CV538, WL 780167 (M.D.N.C.), 26 February 2010.

Paradis v. Ghana Airways Ltd. 348F. Supp 2d 106 (S.D.N.Y.) 2004, affirmed 194 Fed. Appx. 5 (2d Cir.) 2006.

Paterson v. Air Link Pty Ltd., NSWDC 241, 1 November 2008.

Philippe Duay v. Continental Airlines, INC., United States District Court Southern District of Texas, Houston Division, Civil Action No. H-10-cv-1454 Doc. 13, 2010.

Railroad Salvage of Connecticut v. Japan Freights Consolidators, 556 F. Supp. 124 (E.D.N.Y. 1983), aff'd mem. 779 F2nd 38 (2nd Cir.), 1985.

Ramos v. American Airlines, Inc., WL 5075674 (W.D.N.C.), October 2011.

Razi v. Qatar Airways, 36 Avi. 15,501 (S.D.Tex.) – US District Court Southern District of Texas Houston Division. Case 4:12-cv-02073 Document 25 Filed in TXSD on 6 February 2014.

Renton Swaminathan v. Swiss Air Transport Company, US Court of Appeals, 5th Circuit No. 91–2897, 962 F. 2d 387 – Federal Reporter, 10 June 1992.
Ricotta v. Iberia Lineas Aereas De Espana, 482 F. Supp. 497 (E.D.N.Y.), 1979.
Rónai v. Delta Airlines, US District Court, Eastern District of N.Y. No. 99 CV 6793 (SJ), 21 December 2000.
Rosman v. Trans World Airlines, Inc., US Court of Appeals Second Circuit 314 N.E. 2d 848, 1977.
Rynne v. Lauda Air Luftfahrt Aktiengelsellschaft, QDC 004 (01/5586) Boulton DCJ, 2003.
Safa v. Deutsche Lufthansa Aktiengesellschaft, Inc., 36 Avi. 16,148 (E.D.N. Y.), 2014.
Sakaria v. Trans World Airlines, 8 F. 3d 164, 170 (4th Cir. 1993), cert. denied 114S. Ct. 1835, 1994.
Sedigh v. Delta Air Lines, Inc., 850 F. Supp. 197 (E.D.N.Y.), 1994.
Sethy v. Malév Hungarian Airlines, US District Court, 2d, 2012.
Sidhu v. British Airways, Lloyd's Law Reports. 76. 2, 1997.
Siemens Ltd. v. Schenker International (Australia) Pty. Ltd., High Court of Australia, S158/2003, HCA 11, 9 March 2004.
Singh v. Caribbean Airlines Ltd., 36 Avi. 16,127 (S.D.Fl.), 2014.
Smith v. American Airlines, Inc., No. 09–02903 WHA, 2009 WL 3072449, 22 September 2009.
Spielberg v. American Airlines, Inc., US District Court, S.D. New York, 105 F. Supp. 2d 280, 2000.
Stefania Klos v. Polskie Linie Lotnicze, No. 379, D. 97-7073, US Court of Appeals, 1997.
Susan Philips v. Air New Zealand Limited, EWHC 800, DMC/SandT/09/2002.
Thibodeau v. Air Canada, SCC 67, 3 S.C.R. 340, 2014.
Tismanariu v. Societe Air France, QCCQ 2847, 2014.
Titona Arini v. Eurofly, Tribunal of Marsala, Judgement of 14 April 2007.
Tsevas v. Delta Airlines, WL 767278 (N.D.III.), December 1997.
Turturo v. Continental Airlines, 128 F. Supp 2d 170 (S.D.N.Y.), 2001.
Ugaz v. American Airlines, Inc., 576 F. Supp. 2d 1354 (S.D. Fla.), 2008.
Uthuppan Jacob v. Korean Air Lines Co. Ltd., Case No. 14–11663, 11th Cir., 20 March 2015.
Van Luin v. KLM (New South Wales), 1 DCLR, (NSW) 25, 2002.
Vanderwall v. United Airlines, Inc., F. Supp. 3d, 2015 WL 309094 (S.D. Fla.), January 2015.
Victoria Sales Corporation v. Emery Air Freight, Inc., 917 F.2d, 705 at 707 2d Circ., 1990.
Vigilant Insurance Company v. World Courier, WL 2332343 (S.D.N.Y.), 4 June 2008.
Wallace v. Korean Air, No. 98 Civ. 1039, 1999 WL 187213 (S.D.N.Y.) 1999.
Wallace v. Korean Air, US Court of Appeals, Second Circuit D. No. 99–7597, 214 F. 3d 293, 2000.

Walsh v. Koninklijke Luchtvaart Maatschappij (KLM) 09-civ-01803 (RKE) N.V. (S.D.N.Y.), 2011.
Warren v. Flying Tiger Line, Inc., US Court of Appeals 9th Circuit, 352 F. 2d 494, 1965.
Wea Frams, Lima Peru v. American Airlines, Inc., 31 Avi 18,739 (S.d. Fla), 2007.
Weiss v. EL AL Israel Airlines, Ltd., US District Court, S.D. New York, 433 F. Supp. 2d 361, 2006.
Western Digital Corp. v. British Airways, 2 Lloyd's L. Report, 380, (266), 1999.
Wipranik v. Air Canada, No. CV 06–3763 AHM, 15 May 2007.
Wright v. American Airlines, Inc., WL 446077, 2010.
Wrobel v. Air France, Tribunal of Rome, 9th Civil Law Section, Decision No. 9153, 28 March 2009.

Webpages

www.icao.int
www.icao.int/secretariat/legal
www.iata.org
www.iata.org/iata-annual-review
www.aci.aero
www.aviationbenefits.org
www.easa.europa.eu
www.ecac-ceac.org
www.eurocontrol.int
www.unidroit.org
www.sita.aero
www.airfrance.us
www.unctadstat.unctad.org
www.caspca.org
www.abisgroup.org
www.nordicao.ca
www.treaties.un.org
www.opiniojuris.org
maliat.govt.nz/home/agreement
www.ats.aq/e/antarctictreaty.html
maliat.govt.nz/home/agreement
www.bbc.com/news/world-middle-east
www.lexology.com/library/detail.aspx
www.applications.icao.int/postalhistory
www.aviationlawmonitor.com
www.unidroit.org/about-unidroit/overview
www.un.org/en/about-us/specialized-agencies
www.clydeco.com/en/insights/2020/02/coronavirus-2019

www.boeing.com/commercial/market/pilot-technician-outlook
www.boeing.com/commercial/market/pilot-technician-outlook
www.skybrary.aero/index.php/Medical_Emergencies_Guidance_for_Flight
www.transportation.gov/policy/aviation-policy/open-skies-agreements-being-applied

Regulatory Sources

ICAO Annexes 1–19 (see, Part I, Chap. 4.7, Figure 4.2).
ICAO related Treaties (Conventions, Agreements, Protocols), [see, Part I, Chap. 1.2.1, the Legal Sources of International Aviation Law].
United Nations Charter (1945).
United Nations General Assembly Resolution 51/33, Proclamation of 7 December as the International Civil Aviation Day. 6 December 1996.
UN Security Council Resolution 748, 3063rd meeting, 31 March 1992.
UN Security Council Resolution 1067, 3683rd meeting, 26 July 1996.
UN Security Council Resolution 1368, 4370th meeting, 12 September 2001.
UN Chronicle, 21 (4), 1984.
UN International Covenant on Civil and Political Rights (ICCPR), General Assembly Resolution 2200A (XXI) of 16 December 1966.
United Nations Convention on Contracts for the International Sale of Goods. Vienna, 1980. the United Nations Commission on International Trade Law (UNCITRAL).
UN General Assembly Resolution, 2758 (XXVI), 25 October 1971.
UN General Assembly Resolution 927, Question of the safety of commercial aircraft flying in the vicinity of, or inadvertently crossing, international frontiers. UN General Assembly Official Records, 10th Sess. Supp. No. 19 on 14 December 1955.
UN General Assembly Resolution 56/83 of 12 December 2001 corrected by document A/56/49 (Vol. I).
UN Convention on the Law of the Sea, UNCLOS (1982).
Vienna Convention on Diplomatic Relations (1961).
Vienna Convention on the Law of Treaties (1969).
Geneva Convention on the Territorial Sea and the Contiguous Zone (1958).
Antarctica Treaty (1959).
Treaty on Principles Governing the Activities of States in the Exploration and Use of Outer Space, including the Moon and Other Celestial Bodies (1967).
ICAO Doc 7600 Standing Rules of Procedure of the Assembly of the International Civil Aviation Organization (ICAO), Published by authority of the Secretary General (SG), 8th edn., 2014.
ICAO Doc 7559 Rules of Procedure for the Council. 11th edn., 2022.
ICAO Doc 7910 Location Indicators.
ICAO Doc 8585 Designators for Aircraft.

ICAO Doc 7970 Agreement between the UN and ICAO. 13 May 1947, UNTS Vol. 8. (Revised in 2002).

Agreement Governing the Activities of States on the Moon and Other Celestial Bodies, UN RES 34/68, 1979.

ICAO Doc 9626 Manual on the Regulation of International Air Transport. 3rd edn., 2018.

Commission Implementing Regulations (CIR) (EU) 2017/373.

ICAO Circular 50–AN/45: Aircraft Accident Digest, No. 7, No. 35.

ICAO Council Working Paper/5764.

ICAO Council Working Paper/5764, Report concerning the Libyan Arab Boeing 727-224, 5A–DAH (Sinai, 21 February 1973), 1 May 1973.

EUROCONTROL Central Route Charges Office (CRCO) Customer Guide to Charges, February 2019.

ICAO Assembly, 39th Session Working Paper, A39–WP/108TE/32, 19/8/2016.

ICAO Doc 8876 International Conference on the Authentic Trilingual Text of the Convention on International Civil Aviation (1944); Protocol on the Authentic Trilingual text of the Convention on International Civil Aviation. Buenos Aires, September 1968.

ICAO Doc 9208 Protocol Relating to an Amendment to the Convention on International Civil Aviation (Final Clause Russian Text).

ICAO Doc 9664 Protocol Relating to an Amendment to the Convention on International Civil Aviation (Final Clause Arabic Text).

ICAO Doc 9722 Protocol Relating to an Amendment to the Convention on International Civil Aviation (Final Clause Chinese Text).

ICAO Legal Committee, 30th Session, LC/30–WP/4 (A-19).

ICAO no. Cir 328–AN/190 on 11 March 2011.

ICAO Manual on Remotely Piloted Aircraft Systems (RPAS), 2015.

ICAO Doc 10019 Manual on Remotely Piloted Aircraft Systems (RPAS), AN/507, 1st edn., 2015.

ICAO Legal Committee/29 Session – WP/2–1, Attachment 1, 1994.

ICAO Doc 9318 Protocol Relating to an Amendment to the Convention on International Civil Aviation (Article 83 bis) signed at Montreal on 6 October 1980, 23rd Session of the Assembly.

ICAO Legal Committee 37th Session, Safety aspect of economic liberalisation and Article 83 bis, LC/37–WP/2–7, September 2018.

The 34th extraordinary Assembly of ICAO – Election of three additional contracting States to be represented on the Council A34–WP/2 P/2, 24 January 2003 and Plenary meetings – Resolutions and Minutes A34, ICAO Doc 9820 Plenary Meetings.

Guidance on the Implementation of Article 83 bis of the Convention on International Civil Aviation. Cir 295 LE/2, February 2003.

ICAO Report by Chief Aviation Medicine Section to the meeting at the WHO on avian (bird) influenza (flu) and human pandemic influenza. ICAO Secretary General, SG 1862/05 AN5/24, 2005.

ICAO Doc 9731 International Aeronautical and Maritime Search and Rescue Manual IAMSAR, Volumes I. (2016), II. (2022), III. (2019).

ICAO Secretariat: Regulatory and Industry Overview, Regulatory Developments, 20 September 2013.

ICAO Council/1139 Attachment to Council Resolution of 13 June 2001, C–Min 163/8.

ICAO Doc 9760 Airworthiness Manual. 4th edn., 2020

ICAO Assembly Resolution A29–1, ICAO's 50th Anniversary Celebrations, 1994.

ICAO Doc 7278 – C/841 Definition of Scheduled International Air Service (1952).

ICAO Doc 9626 Manual on the Regulation of International Air Transport. 2018.

ICAO Doc 9864 Regulations and Procedures for the International Registry. 9th edn., 2022.

ICAO Doc 9756 Manual of Aircraft Accident and Incident Investigation. 3rd edn., 2020.

ICAO Doc 9156 Accident/Incident Data Reporting (ADREP) system.

ICAO Doc 9859 ICAO Safety Management Manual (SMM), AN/474, 4th edn., 2018.

ICAO Circular 98–AT/19, 1970 – Treaty relating to Air Transport in Africa.

ICAO Circular 99-AT/20, 1970 – SAS Consortium Agreement and Related Agreements.

ICAO Doc 7367 Report of the Council to the Assembly on the activities of the Organisation in 1952. A7–P1, 1953.

ICAO Doc 7788, 49, 1956.

ICAO Doc 2222, 14/5/56.

ICAO Doc 7739-C/894.

ICAO Council Working Paper/2661 (1958).

ICAO Council Working Paper/12697.

ICAO Doc 7960 A12–P/1, 1958.

ICAO Doc 8724 A16–P/3, August 1968.

ICAO Doc 4582.

ICAO Doc 9303 Machine Readable Travel Documents (MRTD). 8th edn., 2021.

ICAO Doc 9082 ICAO's Policies on Charges for Airports and Air Navigation Services. 9th edn., 2012.

ICAO Doc 8632 ICAO's Policy's on Taxation in the Field of International Air Transport. 3rd edn., 2000.

ICAO Doc 8126 Aeronautical Information Services Manual, 7th edn., 2021.

ICAO AVSEC Panel, 18th Meeting, AVSECP/18–IP/3, 23 June 2006, ICAO Assembly Resolution A35–1, Doc 10022.

ICAO's North Atlantic Joint Financing Agreements.

ICAO Doc 10075 Assembly Resolutions in Force, Appendix A, 6 October 2016.

ICAO Assembly Resolution A36–13, Consolidated statement of continuing ICAO policies and associated practices related specifically to air navigation. September 2007.

ICAO Doc 9848 Assembly Resolution A29–19.

ICAO Assembly Resolution, A37–5, The USOAP Continuous Monitoring Approach (CMA). October 2010.
ICAO Assembly Resolution A41–4. Appendix C: Ratification of ICAO International Instruments. October 2022.
ICAO Assembly Resolution, A29–13, Improvement of Safety Oversight. September 1992.
ICAO Assembly Resolution A32–11, Establishment of an USOAP. September 1998.
ICAO Assembly Resolution A33–8, Expanded the USOAP to include audits of Annexes 11, 13 and 14. September 2001.
ICAO Assembly Resolution A37–19, Consolidated statement of continuing ICAO policies and practices related to environmental protection – Climate change. October 2010.
ICAO Assembly Resolutions A38–18, A39–2, A40–18, A41–21.
ICAO Assembly Resolution A36/28, Term limits for the Offices of Secretary General and the President of the Council. September 2007.
ICAO Assembly Resolution A35–6 USOAP/CSA.
ICAO Assembly Resolution A35–12, 2004.
ICAO Assembly Resolution A36–1, The comprehensive regional implementation plan for aviation safety in Africa. September 2007.
ICAO Assembly Resolutions A40–10 (2019), A41–WP/64 (2022).
ICAO Assembly Resolution A31–1, 1995.
ICAO Assembly Resolution A8–1, June 1954.
ICAO Assembly Resolution A37–WP/305, A38–WP/18 EX 13, Item 20, 2013.
ICAO Doc 8895 Resolutions adopted by the Assembly (1970): A17–Resolution.
ICAO Doc 9437 Resolutions adopted by the Assembly (1984): A25–Resolution.
ICAO Assembly Resolution A38–18, Consolidated statement of continuing ICAO policies and practices related to environmental protection – Climate change. September 2013.
ICAO Assembly Resolution A39–3, Consolidated statement of continuing ICAO policies and practices related to environmental protection – Global Market-based Measure (MBM) scheme. September 2016.
ICAO Assembly Resolution A4–3, 1950.
ICAO Assembly Resolution A39–4, October 2016.
ICAO Assembly Resolution A39–6, October 2016.
ICAO Assembly Resolution A15–7.
ICAO Assembly Resolution A37–17.
ICAO Doc 10010-C/1172 Council Decision, 197th Session. C.MIN 197/1, Subject No. 52.1. 2013.
ICAO Doc 8970 Protocol Relating to an Amendment to the Convention on International Civil Aviation [Article 50 *a)*]. New York, 12 March 1971.
ICAO Doc 9123 Protocol Relating to an Amendment to the Convention on International Civil Aviation [Article 50 *a)*]. Montreal, 16 October 1974.
ICAO Doc 9561 Protocol Relating to an Amendment to the Convention on International Civil Aviation [Article 50 *a)*]. Montreal, 26 October 1990.

ICAO Doc 9982 (A37–Min. P/6) Increasing the ICAO Council seats to 39, and Proposal to Amend Article 50 *a)* of the Convention on International Civil Aviation so as to increase the membership of the Council to 39 – ICAO Assembly 38th Session WP/17 EX/12, 2013.

ICAO Assembly 39th Session Working Paper, A39–WP/18, EX/6, 31/05/2016.

ICAO Doc 4411 ICAO Assembly Resolution A1–46, Appendix A, 6–27 May 1947.

ICAO Assembly Resolution A36–28, Term limits for the Offices of the Secretary General and the President of the Council. September 2007.

ICAO Council Working Paper/12494, Election of the President of the Council. Presented by Austria and Hungary, 2005.

ICAO Doc 7559 Rules of Procedure for the Council. 11th edn., 2022.

ICAO Doc 7669 Legal Committee (LC/139/5). Ed. 6. Constitution, Procedure for Approval of Draft Conventions, Rules of Procedure. 2018.

PANS: ICAO Doc 8400 ICAO Abbreviations and Codes (ABC).

ICAO Doc 9802 ICAO's Policies on Charges for Airports and Air Navigation Services. 9th edn., 2012.

ICAO Doc 9735 Universal Safety Oversight Audit Programme Continuous Monitoring Manual. 4th edn., 2014.

ICAO Doc 9734 Safety Oversight Manual (Parts A, B) and Oversight Manual (Part C). Parts A, 2nd edn., 2006; Part B, 2nd edn., 2011 and Part C, 1st edn., 2007.

ICAO Doc 4444 Air Traffic Management (ATM).

ICAO Doc 8168 Aircraft Operations (OPS).

ICAO Doc 9868 Training.

ICAO Doc 7030 Regional Supplementary Procedures.

ICAO Doc 9866 ICAO DGCA Conference on a global strategy for aviation safety. Report, 2006.

ICAO Doc 8984, Manual of Civil Aviation Medicine. AN/895, 3rd edn., 2012

Paris Convention on the Minimum Qualifications Necessary for Obtaining Certificates as Pilots and Navigators. The Operating Crew. Annex E, Chapter I, Section III.

ICAO Council Working Paper/12615, Adoption of Amendment 167 to Annex 1, 23 February 2006.

ICAO Doc 10055 Manual on Notification and Publication of Differences. 1st edn., 2019.

ICAO Council Working Paper/11757, Adoption of Amendment 27 to Annex 6 – Operation of Aircraft, Part I. – International Commercial Air Transport – Aeroplanes, 28 February 2002.

ICAO Doc 8876 International Conference on the Authentic Trilingual Text of the Convention on International Civil Aviation (1944); Protocol on the authentic trilingual text of the Convention on International Civil Aviation. Buenos Aires, September 1968.

ICAO Doc 8892 A 17–Min. Ex/1–8, 11, 16–30 June 1970.

US DoT MANPADS: Combating the Threat to Global Aviation.

ICAO Doc 8973 Aviation Security Manual (Restricted).

USA Public Law 113–17, 113th Congress. 12 July 2013 H.R.1151. Taiwan observer status.
Decision of the Council, C–DEC 154/16; C–WP 10864 (Restricted); C–DEC 147/9; C–DEC150/17; C–DEC 152/14; C–DEC 153/14; C–DEC 170/16; C–WP/12075; C–DEC 152/14 and C–DEC 153/14.
Third Package (HL L 240.) (24 August 1992), Council Regulation (EEC) No. 2407/92 on licensing of air carriers; Council Regulation (EEC) No. 2408/92 on access for Community air carriers to intra-Community air routes; Council Regulation (EC) No. 2409/92 on fares and rates for air services. These Council Regulations consolidated into the "Air Services Regulation" (EC) No. 1008/2008 of the European Parliament and of the Council of 24 September 2008 on common rules for the operation of air services in the Community. OJ L 293, 31.10.2008.
The Commission Implementing Regulations (EU) No 923/2012 – laying down the common rules of the air and operational provisions regarding services and procedures in air navigation. L 281/1, 13 October 2012.
Commission Implementing Regulation (EU) 2019/947 of 24 May 2019 on the rules and procedures for the operation of unmanned aircraft. C/2019/3824, OJ L 152, 11.6.2019.
Decree No. 2111/2005 (EC) of 14 December 2005 of the European Parliament and of the Council on the adoption of a Community list of air carriers subject to an operating ban within the Community and on informing air passengers about the identity of the operator, and repealing Article 9 of Directive 2004/36/EC. HL L 344, 27 December 2005.
Regulation (EU) 1139/2018 of 4 July 2018 of the European Parliament and the Council on common rules in the field of civil aviation and the establishment of a European Union Aviation Safety Agency. HL L 212., 22. 08. 2018.
Council Regulation (EC) No. 487/2009 of 25 May 2009 on the application of Article 81 (3) of the Treaty to certain categories of agreements and concerted practices in the air transport sector. OJ L 148, 11.6.2009.
Council Directive 83/416/EEC of 25 July 1983. OJ 1983 L 237.
Council Regulation. (EEC) No. 95/93 of 18 January 1993 on common rules for the allocation of slots at Community airports. OJ L 14, 01.22.1993.
Council Decision 2001/539/ (EC) of 5 April 2001 on the Conclusion by the European Community of the Convention for the Unification of Certain Rules for International Carriage by Air (the Montreal Convention 1999). Official Journal L 194, 18/07/2001.
2007/339/EC Decision of the Council and the Representatives of the Governments of the Member States of the European Union, meeting within the Council on 25 April 2007 on the signature and provisional application of the Air Transport Agreement between the European Community and its Member States, on the one hand, and the United States of America. OJ L 134, 25.05.2007.
Regulation (EC) No. 261/2004 of the European Parliament and of the Council of 11 February 2004 establishing common rules on compensation and assistance to passengers in the event of denied boarding and of cancellation or the long delay of

flights, and repealing Regulation (EEC) No. 295/91 – Commission Statement. Official Journal L 046, 17/02/2004.
Regulation (EC) No 785/2004 of the European Parliament and of the Council of 21 April 2004 on insurance requirements for air carriers and aircraft operators. OJ L 138, 30.4.200.
ICAO News Release: Two New Treaties Adopted by International Conference on Air Law. PIO, 12 May 2009.
Regulation (EC) No. 889/2002 of the European Parliament and of the Council of 13 May 2002 on air carrier liability in the event of accidents amending Council Regulation (EC) No. 2027/97/EC of 17 October 1997 on air carrier liability with regard to the air carriage of passengers and their baggage. Official Journal HL L 140, 30/05/2002.
Council Decision No. 2009/370/EC of 6 April 2009 on the Accession of the European Community to the Convention on International Interests in Mobile Equipment and its Protocol on Matters Specific to Aircraft Equipment adopted jointly in Cape Town on 16 November 2001.
Court of Justice of the European Union, Press Release No. 95/19 Luxembourg, 11 July 2019. Judgment in Case C-502/18.
Final Act of the Civil Aviation Conference held at Bermuda, United States Treaty Series, No. 3. 11 February 1946.
Open Skies international agreement, the MALIAT (Multilateral Agreement on the Liberalisation of International Air Transportation) 2001.
WHO – Ebola virus disease – Democratic Republic of the Congo. Disease outbreak news: 10 February 2020.
Regulation (EU) 2018/1139 of 4 July 2018 of the European Parliament and of the Council on common rules in the field of civil aviation and establishing a European Union Aviation Safety Agency, OJ L 212, 22.08.2018.
Headquarters Agreement Between the Government of Canada and the ICAO, E101905 – CTS 1992 No. 7; supplementary E103232 – CTS 1999 No. 20; Supplementary E 105390.
Civil Air Transport Agreements, Open Skies Partners. Released by US DoT, 9 December 2021.
European Council Decision of 31 March 2011 on the signing, on behalf of the Union, and provisional application of a Memorandum of Cooperation between the EU and ICAO providing a framework for enhanced cooperation; OJ L232 of 09/09/2011.
NTSB AAR–15/02, PB 2015–105454, Notation 8614, Adopted on 28 July 2015.
IATA Worldwide Airport Slot Guidelines (WASG). 1 June 2020.
Australian Space Activities Act (1998), [Amended by the Space (Launches and Returns) Act 2018].
FAI Sporting Code (2022).
Preußisches Eisenbahngesetz (Prussian Railway Law) 1838.
Code Civil des Français 1804.

Bürgerliches Gesetzbuch (BGB), 1900.
Responsibility of States for Internationally Wrongful Acts (ARSIWA), United Nations, 2001.
8 U.S.C. §1401 – U.S. Code – Nationals and citizens of United States at birth.
Hungary's Constitution of 2011. Foundations.
Citizenship Act, R.S.C., 1985, c. C–29 (2) Part I, The Right to Citizenship.
Rules for the Provision of Pertinent Data Concerning Aircraft Registered in a State Pursuant to Article 21 of the Convention on International Civil Aviation. C/1155 C-Min. 179/1–20.
Paris Convention (1919), Convention Relating to the Regulation of Aerial Navigation.
Habana Convention on Private International Law. 20 February 1928. League of Nations Treaty Series Publication of Treaties and International Engagements Registered with the Secretarial of the League of Nations. No. 1950. Vol. LXXXVI 1929.
Death on the High Seas Act (DOHSA). Code of Laws of the United States of America. 46 U.S.C.
Montreal Intercarrier Agreement. Agreement relating to Liability Limitations of the Warsaw Convention and The Hague Protocol. 31 Fed. Reg. 7302, Civil Aeronautics Board Order No. E–28680 approving CAB 18900, 13 May 1966.
Japan Airlines' Conditions of Carriage; "The Japanese Initiative". Lloyd's Aviation Law (11), 1995/22.
The Intercarrier Agreement on Passenger Liability (IIA) and the Agreement on Measures to Implement the IATA Intercarrier Agreement (MIA) adopted at the 51st General Assembly of IATA organised in Kuala Lumpur in October 1995.
IATA Resolution 724: Passenger Ticket. Notices and Conditions of Contract, 2000.
IATA Resolution 763: Airline Coding Directory (ACD). 88th edn., June 2017.
IATA Resolution 672: Multilateral Electronic Air Waybill Agreement.
IATA Recommended Practice 1724: General Conditions of Carriage, Passenger Services Conference Resolutions Manual (PSCRM). 42nd edn., 2022.
IATA Guidance for Cabin Operations During and Post Pandemic. 4th edn., 8 September 2020.
On the Proclamation of the Convention on the Civil Legal Aspects of International Child Abduction dated 25 October 1980, The Hague; Decree no. 14. 1986.
US DoT, Office of the Secretary 14 CFR Part 252, Federal Register / Vol. 65, No. 112 /9 June 2000/, Rules and Regulations, Prohibition of Smoking on Scheduled Passenger Flights; Final Rules.
The Rome I Regulation [Regulation (EC) No 593/2008] (successor of the Rome Convention 1980 on the law applicable to contractual obligations) of the European Parliament and of the Council of 17 June 2008 on the Law Applicable to Contractual Obligations; The Rome II Regulation [Regulation (EC) No 864/2007] of the European Parliament and of the Council of 11 July 2007 on the Law Applicable to Non-Contractual Obligations. OJ C 27, 26.1.1998.; OJ L 177, 4.7.2008; OJ L 199, 31.7.2007.

The Paris Convention (1883) revised at Brussels (1900), Washington D.C. (1911), The Hague (1925), London (1934), Lisbon (1958) and Stockholm (1967), amended in 1979.

The Berne Convention (1886) on the Protection of Literary and Artistic Works.

Geneva Convention for the Amelioration of the Condition of the Wounded and Sick in Armed Forces in the Field (Geneva Convention I of 1949); Geneva Convention for the Amelioration of the Condition of Wounded and Sick and Shipwrecked Members of Armed Forces at Sea (Geneva Convention II of 1949); Geneva Convention Relative to the Protection of Civilian Persons in Time of War (Geneva Convention IV of 1949).

Rome Convention (1933), Unification of Certain Rules Relating to the Precautionary Attachment of Aircraft.

Rome Convention (1933), the International Convention for the Unification of Certain Rules relating to Damage caused by Aircraft to Third Parties on the Surface.

Brussels Protocol (1938), the Additional Protocol to the Convention for the Unification of Certain Rules relating to Damage caused by Aircraft to Third Parties on the Surface.

UNIDROIT Convention on International Financial Leasing (1988).

The Helsinki Accords of 1975 Organisation of Security and Cooperation in Europe (OSCE), Final Act, Declaration on Principles Guiding Relations between Participating States (1975).

MIX
Papier aus verantwortungsvollen Quellen
Paper from responsible sources
FSC® C105338

If you have any concerns about our products,
you can contact us on
ProductSafety@springernature.com

In case Publisher is established outside the EU,
the EU authorized representative is:
Springer Nature Customer Service Center GmbH
Europaplatz 3, 69115 Heidelberg, Germany

Printed by Libri Plureos GmbH
in Hamburg, Germany